Western Histories
William Deverell, series editor
Published for the Huntington-USC Institute on California and the West
by University of California Press and the Huntington Library

1 *The Father of All: The de la Guerra Family, Power, and Patriarchy in Mexican California*, by Louise Pubols

2 *Alta California: Peoples in Motion, Identities in Formation, 1769–1850*, edited by Steven W. Hackel

The Father of All

The Father of All

The de la Guerra Family, Power, and Patriarchy in Mexican California

Louise Pubols

Published for the Huntington-USC Institute on California and the West
by University of California Press, Berkeley, California, and
the Huntington Library, San Marino, California

Series jacket design by Lia Tjandra
Interior design by Doug Davis
Copyediting by Susan Green and Jean Patterson
Index by Jean Patterson

Printed in the United States by McNaughton & Gunn

Library of Congress Cataloging-in-Publication Data

Pubols, Louise.
  The father of all : the de la Guerra family, power, and patriarchy in Mexican
California / Louise Pubols.
      p. cm.
  Includes bibliographical references and index.
  ISBN 978-0-87328-240-6 (alk. paper)
  1. California—History—To 1846. 2. California—History—1846–1850. 3. Guerra family.
4. Patriarchy—California—History—19th century. 5. Elite (Social sciences) —California—
History—19th century. 6. Domestic relations—California—History—19th century.
7. Spaniards—California—History—19th century. I. Title.
  F864.P983 2009
  979.4'01—dc22
                        2009023672

CONTENTS

ACKNOWLEDGMENTS

This book could not have been completed without the help and encouragement of many individuals and institutions. I owe an enormous debt of gratitude to the Santa Barbara Trust for Historic Preservation. Not only did the Trust hire me for the first internship many years ago that led to my discovery of the de la Guerra family, but it also has continued to follow and support my work since then, stepping in with internships when I needed the financial help to complete my research in Santa Barbara. Former research director Cathy Rudolph went beyond the call of duty to assist me and to "gossip" with me about the de la Guerras. I am also indebted to the Santa Barbara Mission Archive-Library for sponsoring my research into the de la Guerra papers with its Geiger Fellowship in the summer of 1994; Father Virgilio Biasiol O.F.M. provided critical assistance in navigating the archives. Kathi and Roger Brewster and Karen and Dana Anderson kindly offered me housing during my many research trips to Santa Barbara.

The staffs of a number of other archives and libraries ably assisted my research. The archivists of The Bancroft Library, the Los Angeles County Museum of Natural History, and the Huntington Library were especially professional and courteous. I would like to thank Michael Redmon at the Gledhill Library of the Santa Barbara Historical Society for his infinite patience and persistence in helping me locate local records. The staff at the Santa Barbara City Clerk's office kindly took time away from their other duties to help me find critical documents in the vault, and the County Clerk's office likewise helped me pull down the huge volumes of nineteenth-century records. Finally, Michael Edmonds of the amazing Wisconsin State Historical Society Library alleviated much of the stress of graduate school with his kindness and personal attention to every graduate student who works there.

I would like to thank both the University of California at Santa Barbara and the University of Wisconsin-Madison for offering me a Humanities Special Fellowship and University Fellowship, respectively, which allowed me to finish my coursework with minimal financial burden. At the end of the process, John Gray, James Nottage, and Michael Duchemin of the Autry National Center generously offered me the time I needed to finish my writing and revising while working a full-time job.

I acknowledge with gratitude a number of advisers, colleagues, and friends who read the manuscript at various phases and helped me work out difficult interpretive questions. This project began as part of a research seminar at UC Santa Barbara; classmates Grace Murakami and Beverly Bastian along with advisers Rebecca Conard and Richard Oglesby initially shaped my understanding of the family and their place in Santa Barbara. Beverly Bastian, in particular, did the hard work of compiling most of the genealogy found in the appendix. I wish to thank Nancy Appelbaum, Lillian Guerra, Joe Hall, and Dedra McDonald for their invaluable help with Spanish translations and so much more. Rose Marie Beebe and Robert Senkewicz gave me the incredible gift of checking every one of my translations. Any remaining errors are entirely my own. The wonderful graduate community in Madison helped to keep me sane through the long process of writing. I was extraordinarily lucky to have not one but two supportive and critical dissertator groups; I thank Lynne Heasley, Jared Orsi, Bill Philpott, Greg Summers, and Marsha Weisiger, and Leo Garofalo, Lillian Guerra, Joe Hall, Bert Kreitlow, and Ileana Rodríguez Silva. Bethel Saler, Cynthia Milton, and Jay Taylor also listened and offered suggestions with good nature and humor. I thank professors Jeanne Boydston for asking the hard questions at the right time, Steve Stern for generously sharing his deep understanding of Latin American history, and Bill Cronon for teaching me how to be a scholar.

Fellowships to the Mellon Seminar on Culture and Politics at the University of Wisconsin-Madison in 1997 and the Charles Redd Center for Western Studies at Brigham Young University in 2001 gave me the opportunity to share and discuss my work with peers at critical periods of its formation. Michelle Jolly, Natalia Molina, Juti Winchester, Erika Bsumek, Matt Despain, Thomas Alexander, Richard Etulain, and Glenda Riley provided insights on turning a dissertation into a book manuscript. I am also grateful to Steven Aron and the Autry National Center's Western History Workshop for a chance to vet some of my ideas before friends and colleagues in Los Angeles. I would like to sincerely thank the Huntington Library for a John Randolph Haynes and Dora Haynes Foundation Fellowship for a wonderful summer of study in 1997 and an autumn of revision in 2005; Roy Ritchie, the Director of Research, made me feel especially welcome and encouraged. Everyone at this institution benefits from the community of scholars who work there; I enjoyed the company and wise advice of William Deverell, Steven Hackel, and Peter Mancall, and especially appreciate the friendship of Carla Bittel, Flannery Haug, Aims McGuinness, and Sam Truett.

I presented parts of this work at conferences held at the William P. Clements Center for Southwest Studies and the Huntington Library, and at annual meetings of the Omohundro Institute of Early American History and Culture, the Western History Association, the Berkshire Conference on the History of Women, and the Women's West Conference. Critical comment from David Weber, Lisbeth Haas, Antonia Casteñeda, and James Ronda, and from fellow panelists Raquél María Casas and Donna Schuele, helped to steer me in the right direction. Portions of the book also appeared in the essay "Fathers of the Pueblo: Patriarchy and Power in Mexican California 1800–1880," published in *Continental Crossroads* (Duke University Press, 2004). I'm grateful to my editors Sam Truett and Elliott Young, and to my fellow contributors Raúl Ramos, Bárbara Reyes, Andrés Reséndez, Grace Peña Delgado, Karl Jacoby, Benjamin Johnson, and Alexandra Minna Stern, all of whom offered valuable insights.

This book is dedicated to my parents, who never doubted that I would finish, eventually. I did so because of their advice, support, and constant encouragement.

Louise Pubols
Oakland, California

> I wish to publish a true history of the country. My prin-
> ciple being that our successors, the Americans, will
> know that all the Californians of those times were not
> indigents nor a band of beasts, that when they took the
> country, here was civilization, and men who belonged
> to that race were illustrious . . . I want my friends to help
> me in every way possible . . . You must see that this is too
> much for me alone, but it is necessary to be done, if not,
> we will disappear, ignored of the whole world.[1]

When Mariano Guadalupe Vallejo wrote these lines to his cousin Anastasio Carrillo, California had belonged to the United States for just twenty years. Yet in that time, Americans had already begun to write their own version of California's Spanish and Mexican past, and of a supposedly inevitable conquest. Vallejo proposed a historical corrective—a narrative of the heroic deeds of the Californios— to refute Yankee claims of racial superiority.[2] In Vallejo's story, great men such as himself had wrested the land from savage Indians and brought civilization and prosperity to the region. This, he reminded his relatives, was the "true history of the country." Without it, the Californios, unremembered, would cease to exist.

This study, in a way, answers Vallejo's call for help. It places Spanish-Mexicans at the center of California's early history, and it sees the world through their eyes. In so doing, it refutes the notion that Mexican California was a backward, tradition-bound place, waiting for American enterprise to bring it into the modern world, and remaining helpless before the inevitable march of progress. And Vallejo would certainly recognize the main characters, his cousins the de la Guerras. But this story is

1

not the one that Vallejo would have told. This book does examine closely the lives of a few of those in the elite class, but it does not simply record their great deeds and individual glory. It explores the nature of conquest on the peripheries of empire, but does not tell the triumphal story of Hispanic civilization brought to a wild frontier outpost. And although it studies the lives of fathers and sons, it does not grant them the only voices of authority. Through the story of one family, this book investigates the ways in which Mexicans on a coastal frontier constructed and negotiated patriarchy from one generation to the next, from the late colonial era through to the U.S. occupation of the 1840s.

In many ways, my own scholarly journey reflects the path that most Americans have taken when it comes to the history of the nation's Southwest—that is, if they start that journey at all. Growing up on the East Coast, I was only dimly aware that six whole states, and parts of four others, had once belonged to the nation of Mexico, or that, for over three centuries before, this land had formed the northern-most reach of the vast Spanish Empire. In my textbooks, the U.S.-Mexico War was presented as a great chasm that could not be bridged. Before that break, places like California existed as static prologue and counterpoint to the dynamic stories of nation building that followed. This was the land of the time "before"—before the market, before democracy, before progress.

When I moved to Santa Barbara to begin my graduate work, I discovered that this earlier history, left unspoken at the national level, resonated strongly at the local level. It took the form of a dreamy past of flirtatious señoritas and caballeros on horseback—images like those from the novel *Ramona* that had drawn so many chilled Easterners there before me. This haze of romance made discerning a real Mexican past, and connecting it to the Mexican present, all the more difficult. Yet, the community's boosterism ultimately brought me to the subject of this book. In my first semester of graduate school, I was introduced to the Casa de la Guerra, now owned by the Santa Barbara Trust for Historic Preservation. This large, single-story house in the center of Santa Barbara, built by the de la Guerra family and renovated in the 1920s, has played a critical role in the city's embrace of its romantic "Spanish" past.

The students in my public history class were charged with working closely with the Trust for Historic Preservation as it sought to transform what had become the centerpiece of a Colonial Revival–style shopping complex back into a house, or rather, a house museum. At this point, I was confronted with the de la Guerra Papers, housed at the Santa Barbara Mission Archive-Library. The de la Guerras, Santa Barbara's leading family for over sixty years, had preserved a rich assortment of over four thousand letters, journals, accounts, and legal papers—more than twelve thousand pages spanning the entire nineteenth century. Though it is the largest collection of Californio family papers in the state, only a fraction of it had been translated, and little of it had been used. I did my best to piece together a narrative of the house, its furnishings, and the daily life of its residents, but the larger picture of the family who had lived there eluded me. I knew there were answers in all that flowing Spanish handwriting, but what were the questions?

My next stop was the history department of the University of Wisconsin, where I immersed myself in the histories of both the western United States and northern Mexico. I learned that many historians had traveled before me, hoping to piece together the history of this forgotten time and place. And yet, like the textbook authors and the boosters of Santa Barbara, many of them had continued to describe an essentially timeless, premodern place, lost to the relentless onslaught of American expansion.

In the early decades of the nineteenth century, the first Americans to visit the Mexican province laid the foundations for this view of California. Informed by both the Black Legend—the view that Spain's colonies had been particularly backward and cruel in their conquest of Native peoples—and their own self-confidence, many early Anglo observers saw Californios as a people at a lower rung on the evolutionary ladder of civilizations, and thought they had woefully underused their land and resources. For these early travelers, conquest seemed natural and justified; only Yankee enterprise and ingenuity could organize such a simple, pastoral economy, kept from reaching its fullest potential by a lazy and corrupt race.[3]

In the late nineteenth century, the "Spanish Fantasy Past" likewise had as its core the narrative of a traditional, pastoral society doomed to conquest at the hands of Yankee capitalists.[4] But in an era in which real Mexican-Americans could no longer pose a serious threat to Anglo domination of the economy or political system of California, the story took on a romantic tinge, as a nostalgic critique of modern commercial society. From the 1880s through the 1930s, on fruit crate labels and in novels, at parades, in pageants and plays, with tourist promotions and postcards, California's boosters projected an image of the state's pre-American past as unhurried, untroubled, and gracious. "Never before or since, was there a spot in America where life was a long happy holiday, where there was less labor, less care or trouble," wrote California historian

Hubert Howe Bancroft in 1888.[5] As I had seen for myself in Santa Barbara, this tale took on great importance for the formation of Southern California's regional identity and for the marketing campaigns of the tourism industry. Yet it, too, made little claim that the Spanish or Mexican past played any continuing part in the national development of the United States.

In the early twentieth century, however, academic historians of the Spanish Borderlands, led by Herbert Bolton and John Francis Bannon, called for the integration of the Spanish colonial past into America's national story, organizing their interpretations around the impact of the Spanish mission, the military, and the civilian government on U.S. development in California, New Mexico, and Texas. Although the acknowledgment of non-English empires in North America certainly broadened the perspectives of U.S. historians, the pro-Spanish bias of the Bolton school led to a conceptualization of the frontier as a theater for the Spanish Empire and its institutions; for them, Mexican Independence made little impact on life at the border. This institutional approach was also largely silent on issues of society, culture, and economic and labor systems. While emphasizing the process of Spanish colonization, it showed a remarkable resistance to looking at this process from an Indian or mestizo perspective. In addition, by avoiding comparison with the rest of northern and central Mexico, a Spanish Borderlands orientation had serious limitations for a unified understanding of New Spain's northern frontier.[6]

In the late 1960s and the 1970s, influenced both by nationalist struggles in Africa, Asia, and Latin America and by the civil rights movement in the United States, a new generation of historians sought to re-envision the history of Mexican-Americans. These scholars asserted the importance of Indian and mestizo culture in the formation of Mexicanness and celebrated resistance to the majority Anglo culture. The moment of U.S. conquest in 1846 was again the central event in this narrative, and those working in the field shed light on the American penetration of Mexico's northern economy, the loss of land and political power, the process of "barrioization," and the eventual segmentation of the region's labor force by race and ethnicity.[7] Later scholars, looking at the dynamics of gender, focused on images of Mexican men and women in American culture, and on intermarriage as a precursor to conquest.[8] Others focused on border identities and the experiences of individuals who held not a single identity, but multiple identities and contradictory positions within categories of culture, ethnicity, region, gender, sexuality, class, and race.[9] Such scholars made great advances in their examination of the complexities of border life, but many continued to tell a familiar story in which "traditional" Mexican society is overwhelmed and defeated by modern, capitalist America.

The U.S.-Mexico War, then, continued to act as the pivot around which all Southwestern history turned. Historians of the Mexican-American experience made enormous strides in recovering the Spanish and Mexican story, yet in many ways the arrival of Americans remained the central story for early California. Scholars of Mexico, on the other hand, might be expected to pay less attention to the United States, and to integrate California, New Mexico, and Texas into their analysis of late colonial and early republican Mexico. But here, too, until recently, the history of Mexico's northern frontier has fallen through the cracks of shifting national borders and identity. As José Cuello argues, "a powerful stereotype has developed which depicts Northern history as a vast wasteland of frontier violence whose exotic themes have very little in common with those of the core Mexican regions."[10] Likewise, there has been a strong tendency in Mexican history to start their national story after the 1840s. Mexicanists have long dismissed the era from Independence to the liberal reforms of the 1850s and 1860s as nothing more than the unbroken continuation of the colonial order, meriting little more than a paragraph in many textbooks.[11]

Despite this strong tendency to dismiss the north and the early republic as outside the bounds of Mexico's main national story, recent Latin American historiography in general does suggest a number of theoretical approaches that can illuminate a study of Mexican California in particular. Studies of gender and the family in Latin America, for example, have provided critical insights, particularly works that explore the intersections of family and mercantile capitalism, such as Susan Socolow's research on the Argentine merchant class as well as several works on elite families in Bourbon Mexico.[12] In addition, a rich body of literature has examined women and gender in late colonial and republican Mexico, and a few historians of early California and New Mexico have joined the discussion. These works explore the dynamics of the honor/shame complex and integrate gender into discussions of social hierarchies based on race, wealth, and culture.[13] A few look specifically at masculinity and the multiple roles of men in a patriarchal culture, such as Steve Stern's study of late colonial peasant society and Ana María Alonso's work on frontier Chihuahua.[14]

Perhaps most promising has been the recent body of work that at last pays significant attention to Latin America's young republics in the decades after Independence. Historians have begun to look past colonial survivals to the creation of national identities in such places as Mexico and Peru, where the king's subjects struggled to become citizens. In these histories, the ideologies of liberals and conservatives are taken seriously, as multifaceted and evolving ways of thinking about the state and the social order. Concerned mostly with nation building at the community level, these historians look at the spread of print culture, popular expressions of political culture, changing attitudes about race and caste, and the continuing articulation of gender norms and concepts of honor within liberal law. Others explore liberalism's impact on free trade and land reforms in these early decades.[15]

California, on the northern periphery of Mexico, offers particular local variations on these themes of gender and nation building. The last territory settled by the Spanish Empire, California became a frontier that turned its back on the interior and looked out to the Pacific. Spaniards in interior borderlands contested dominance with independent Indian societies, such as the Comanche in North America and the Araucanians in South America.[16] But in California, isolated by deserts and mountains, Indian peoples lacked access to horses, guns, or alliances with Spain's European rivals. And unlike other areas of Spain's empire, the Franciscan order and the mission system dominated California well past Independence, holding rights to much of the land near the coast. A Quechán uprising at the Colorado crossing in 1781 cut off access to California by land for fifty years and prevented much further migration. And long after Independence, California continued to be run as a territory with a military system of government. As a result of these factors, California developed two zones: the coast, which had small Hispanic military and civilian settlements and large missions; and the interior, marked by violent clashes with Native peoples. On the coastal frontier, settlers from Sonora and Sinaloa arrived with notions of gender, generational precedence, race, and honor, but the complex *casta* system of the Mexican heartland flattened into two categories: *gente de razón* and Indian. Isolated, but controlled by the central government, attracting little colonization but open to the world of mercantile capitalism, with few schools or printing presses, yet hungry to absorb the intellectual currents of America and Europe, California proved a unique setting for the dynamic changes that were to come.

The impulse to fix Spanish and Mexican California in time has been a strong one, and it has arisen from many sources. Yet, what I eventually discovered was that far from being a land lost to time or a counterpoint to modernism, Alta California was in many ways an experimental ground for liberal reformers, swept up in the dramatic changes and up-heavals that were characteristic of all of Spain's former colonies in this era. Through the analysis of one frontier outpost—where elites grappled with these changes in the new republic, and conversations about patri-archy continued between elite men and women, humble settlers, and Indians—I seek to offer historians of Latin America a new perspective on the early national period, and students of the American West and of the Mexican-American experience what I hope is a nuanced foundation for narratives of continuity and survival across the great divide of the U.S.-Mexico War.

I read evidence of California's transformation and struggles at the levels of community, family, and individual. The de la Guerra family of Santa Barbara is the subject of this study, and what follows is a group por-trait and family saga, set against the backdrop of California society in the early nineteenth century. Historians of one town, person, or family usu-ally take one of two possible approaches: they either claim the "plausible typicality" of their subject, as a way to uncover structures and the way they operate; or, they revel in anomaly, as a way to look more actively for change and agency in the "interstices" of normative systems, whether symbolic or material.[17] In this work, I hope to combine these two ap-proaches, telling the story of an elite family—not to show the workings of a "typical" Californio family—but through the de la Guerras to uncover the operation of power, negotiation, and individual choices within the constraints of a particular patriarchal social and economic order in tran-sition. I have chosen to focus on one family, not necessarily because it was "great" or "illustrious," although contemporaries would certainly have recognized it as such, but because I believe a study on this scale can reveal critical historical dynamics that a study of an entire class, gender, or nationality can overlook.

Close attention to the members of one family leads the researcher outward, through webs of familial relationships that knit Californio soci-ety together from top to bottom. These relationships were the founda-tion of California's political economy. Marriage, parenthood, and the fictive kinship of godparentage, or *compadrazgo*, created relationships of obligation and dependency in Mexican California.[18] These relationships in turn structured the way in which men and women, parents and chil-dren, workers and owners, and subjects, Church, and state all under-stood the hierarchies of society and their options within that structure. This is not to say that all who lived within this society understood the obligations of such relationships the same way, but it does mean that they shared a common language of negotiation—the language of patriarchy.

The term "patriarchy" can be, and has been used to mean many different things. Most often it refers to a system of gender and sexuality that subordinates women to men in society as a whole. In this study, I use "patriarchy" in a more specific sense: to refer to the cultural and political pattern in Mexican California that linked father-elder dominance within families to the understanding of authority generally. One's generation, in this formulation, is at least as important as one's gender in determining relationships of rights, obligation, and dependency. Patriarchy also reflects a particular Mediterranean and Latin American set of values known as the "honor/shame complex," in which male honor ideally rested on a set of positive accomplishments—the ability to show force of will and command over others, the ability to protect and provide for one's dependents, and respect for the rank of other powerful men—whereas female virtue depended on a more passive ability to show submission to husbands, fathers, and elders, strict adherence to sexual propriety, and respect for social decorum. As standards for appearance, rather than action, all of these virtues were much easier for the wealthy to maintain than those of the poorer classes. At every level of society, a person's age and stage in the life cycle further ranked him or her in family and community hierarchies of deference and authority.[19] Thus, a history that tells the story of patriarchy in one elite family also reveals the relationships in both the family and the community that sustained it.

Telling the story of one family also forces the historian to consider the dynamics of change over time: the construction, varied articulation, and development of normative systems like patriarchy in lived experience. As such, this work is necessarily narrative, and the form places certain constraints on the way material can be organized.[20] Narratives are driven by the imperative to tell a meaningful and coherent story with a beginning, middle, and end, yet within a family, individuals have different and intertwining strategies and perspectives. Despite these challenges, narrative offers great power of explanation, revealing agency and choice to put in motion the structures of institutions and ideas.

The story of the de la Guerra family is based primarily on the family's personal and business papers. In some ways, these are really the same thing. Although the account books that have survived are too fragmentary to reveal exactly how large the de la Guerra fortune might have been, or even how much the family earned in a year, the letters and records do give a good sense of how deeply enmeshed the family was in global trade

networks, and of the extent to which personal relationships bled into political and business relationships. Supplementing this vast collection are
governmental and sacramental records; *testimonios*, or oral histories,
collected by American historian Hubert Howe Bancroft in the 1870s; and
other correspondence, newspaper accounts, and narratives, all of which
expand our knowledge of the family and place it in the context of its era.

These records, while extensive, did not answer every question I
brought to them. Particularly difficult to uncover were the voices of
women and of non-elite dependents, most of whom were illiterate. A
major exception, however, was the strong voice of a de la Guerra daughter, Angustias de la Guerra. Born in 1815, she became a sharp and intelligent observer of both her family and the world around it. In March 1878,
Thomas Savage went to her home in Santa Barbara on behalf of Bancroft,
seeking sources for Bancroft's multivolume history of California.[21] As
Rosaura Sánchez argues, the creation of the Bancroft testimonials was
itself a location for struggle between dispossessed Californios and the
Anglo world that had conquered them—a war over how the past would
be represented.[22] Savage asked Angustias particular questions about the
public actions of her male relatives, but more often than not, as she
spoke, her husband, father, and brothers receded into the background,
while women emerged at the center of politics. Angustias also kept a
journal during the U.S.-Mexico War, and in 1880 dictated a memoir to
her youngest daughter. Presumably produced under less constrained circumstances, these accounts were not totally transparent either. "These
are difficult times," she wrote in her journal, "and if I dared to say everything in this diary, but no!"[23] Despite the mediation apparent in all of
these sources, the voice of Angustias de la Guerra remains clear and
vivid. As a woman who commented on, and acted in, the public sphere,
she is easiest to see, and yet she was not alone. Through census documents, court records, and other memoirs, we can uncover the lives of
women and dependents who pushed up against the boundaries of patriarchy, negotiated its terms, and created space for themselves within it.[24]

If we cease to read the history of California in reverse, if we cease to
look before the American conquest and see a timeless land of colonial
charm or of colonial oppression, we can begin to make out a new narrative
for the early decades of the nineteenth century. The significance of the
de la Guerra family read this way is not in how "traditional" elites can be
viewed as counterpoints to their American conquerors, resisting them or
not, but in how, across time, the Mexican patriarchal family reinvented
itself as both a fundamental economic and political institution and a

metaphor for power, during a period of great debate and change. Over the course of the republican era, generational and ideological challenges altered aspects of this system and ideology, but at the dawn of the American era, patriarchy continued in a new form as the foundation of relationships between husbands and wives, parents and children, patrons and dependents, owners and workers, rulers and the governed.

In the first chapter, I introduce José de la Guerra and his wife, María Antonia Carrillo, in the context of the Spanish colonization of California. Through this couple, I look at the creation of California's elite class, weighing the importance of race, patronage, wealth, and military rank; exploring the particular conditions of the frontier and the impact of the liberal Bourbon Reforms on social mobility; and examining the creation of a political economy resting on the connections and obligations of patriarchal families.

The second chapter is a more thematic study, covering patriarchy at the community level in both the late colonial and early national eras in California. Among the men of his generation, de la Guerra was remarkably successful, positioning himself at the head of Santa Barbara's economic and social hierarchy, while being widely accepted as a benevolent patriarch through the first half of the nineteenth century. This chapter explores how he was able to do so, and the ways in which he and the rest of the community defined his role as "town father" over several decades, giving particular attention to elite relationships with Indians, soldiers, and settlers.

The first challenge to this family's economy came with the lifting of trade restrictions in 1821 and the arrival of independent foreign merchants. In the third chapter, I challenge the notion that the intermarriage of Californio daughters with foreign merchants represented the introduction of Yankee capitalism to a pastoral backwater and foreshadowed the eventual triumph of that foreign nation. Rather, such marriages were part of a strategy to capture the potentially hostile traders and integrate them into Californio systems of family obligation and dependence.

In the fourth chapter, I explore the second challenge to California's patriarchal political economy. This time, an internal weakness—the conflict between fathers and their adult sons—emerged when the sons came of age and struggled to become independent patriarchs themselves. I place the contest over mission secularization and the development of Californio nativism into this context of generational rebellion and examine how this conflict shaped the particular forms of political and economic liberalism that emerged in California in the 1820s and 1830s.

This youthful rebellion came to a head in 1836, when native sons in California's legislature overthrew the newly appointed centralist governor and declared California free and sovereign. Within a few years, however, with almost all the mission land firmly in private hands, California was back in the Mexican fold. In the fifth chapter, I look at the ways in which patriarchal family relations served to mitigate civil conflict and continued to structure the society and economy of post-revolutionary, post-secularization California from 1836 to 1845. Women, children, and mission Indians found some openings to claim autonomy and voice in these years, but not as much as liberal ideologies might have promised.

The sixth and final chapter examines the impact of American conquest on California, through 1850. I explore the de la Guerras' roles within the Californio patronage system before and during the war, the impact of gender on national loyalties and political action, and the ways in which the de la Guerras navigated the unstable years of occupation and the transition to representative democracy. I also discuss how the de la Guerra brothers positioned themselves to represent all Californios to American occupiers and emerged as a powerful political force in Santa Barbara by reinventing themselves within local patriarchal understandings of authority.

Together, the de la Guerras traded on world markets, operated vast ranches, ruled Santa Barbara's government, and helped define what it meant to be a Californio. At the center of nineteenth-century Californio life—politics, economic success, and ethnic identity—were the relationships and ideals of the patriarchal family. To confine our view to government actions, landholdings, or military conquest would be to miss the critical obligations and dependencies that family relations demanded, and thus to misunderstand the nature of nation building and of conquest itself. Far from being passive victims or willing collaborators, stuck in timeless tradition, elite families like the de la Guerras used the strategies of their evolving patriarchal society to contain and meet the challenges of liberal reform and of trade and political engagement with the Americans. Across the chasm of the U.S.-Mexico War, they built a bridge, surviving as historical actors in a modern American state.

José de la Guerra y Noriega, ca. 1855. Courtesy of the Santa Barbara Trust for Historic Preservation.

CHAPTER ONE

"A THING OF HONOR AND PROFIT":
THE CREATION OF CALIFORNIA'S ELITE FAMILIES

In May 1804, Santa Bárbara, California, was little more than a remote outpost of the great Spanish Empire. Just over eight hundred Chumash Indians had received baptism the year before at the nearby mission. Formerly traders and hunters of marine life, they now worked the mission's wheat and corn fields and tended its sheep and cattle, and still greatly outnumbered the missionaries and soldiers who held this northern frontier town for Spain. Most of Santa Bárbara's four hundred or so colonists lived in simple adobe huts or in the apartments that made up the eastern wings of the presidio, or military fort. The men were there as members of the Royal Presidial Company of Santa Bárbara: about sixty soldiers and artillerymen, commanded by a handful of officers.[1] On May 16, a special event broke up the tedium of duty: the commander's only daughter married an ensign of the Monterey company. Up at the mission chapel, a whitewashed adobe structure roofed with tile, Father Estevan Tapis performed the ceremony and carefully recorded the couple's names in his marriage registry: José Antonio Julián de la Guerra y Noriega, twenty-six, and María Antonia Carrillo y Lugo, eighteen. With this, he bound an emerging elite class together.

California's colonial society formed in the late eighteenth and early nineteenth centuries. In this late colonial era, the elite class of Mexico (or New Spain, as it was called prior to Independence) found itself in flux, between an old civilization, for which ascriptive categories like race, nobility, and legitimacy determined status; and a new society, for which achievement and wealth outweighed almost any other consideration. This change occurred everywhere in New Spain, but conditions on the frontier were unique. Administrative reforms favored Spanish officers for the frontier military but also encouraged the social mobility of mixed-race soldiers from humble origins. In addition, the near monopoly of arable lands by the Church suppressed the creation of a landed elite, while liberalized trade emerged as the key to economic success. At the end of the colonial era, California's elite eventually blended the old and the new: Spaniards whose birth and connections landed them in the governing class, socially ambitious frontier soldiers, and profit-oriented entrepreneurs. Eventually, the class wove itself together through kinship and the common experience of conquest. Honor and profit were the basis of California's emerging elite class.

Colonial Elites on the Frontier: De la Guerra and the Privileges of Birth

The first strand of the emerging Californian elite originated thousands of miles from the tiny colonial outpost on the Pacific where de la Guerra wed María Antonia Carrillo. This strand was the most invested in the old hierarchies of the Spanish colonial world and the status intrinsic to the highborn. On a spring day in 1779, Doña María Teresa de Noriega y Barreda gave birth to her first son, José Antonio Julián. Doña María and her husband, Don Juan José de la Guerra y Ceballos, were local nobles in Novales, a valley town in the bishopric of Santander, Spain, and could trace their ancestry back to a war hero in the armies of Ferdinand and Isabella.

María Teresa and Juan José, though they lived in a small provincial town, could in fact journey just a few miles to smell the salt air of Santander, a major port of trade with the Americas on Spain's northern Atlantic coast. María herself had a personal connection to Spain's colonial holdings: her brother Pedro González de Noriega had already left this mountainous region to make his fortune in Mexico City as a merchant. At age thirteen, on October 25, 1792, José de la Guerra y Noriega followed his uncle and set sail for New Spain, joining the hundreds of other Spaniards who governed the largest and richest of Spain's colonial holdings in the New World.[2]

Other young men destined for similar posts probably joined José onboard, for it was a common pattern to send Spanish boys aged ten to fourteen to apprentice in an uncle's merchant house in the colonies. This helped the apprentice nephew, who learned a trade and secured an inheritance. But it also served the uncle, who groomed either an heir to take over his enterprises or a partner to extend his empire into the colonial hinterland. Such merchant houses combined the entrepreneurialism of an emerging capitalist economy with the more traditional and personal relationships of patriarch to son, and patron to client. A merchant like Pedro Noriega needed an immigrant nephew in his business because a trusted family member in the top post guaranteed that lines of credit and correspondence would remain unbroken.[3] This system became the model for young de la Guerra's future career as a merchant himself—but this was still years away.

When he arrived in the capital city, de la Guerra exchanged not only the Old World for the New but also a small seaside town for the largest city in North America. Mexico City in the last decade of the eighteenth century had a population of over one hundred thousand and acted as the commercial, manufacturing, and administrative center of a large colonial hinterland. Peering out of the windows of his coach, the young man could glimpse impressive sights as he made his way across the city for the first time: broad tree-shaded avenues, expansive plazas with bubbling fountains and bright flowers, churches glittering with gold and silver, and opulent residences owned by the city's elites: merchants, high-ranking bureaucrats, top military officers, and titled nobility. New Spain had grown rich from silver mining, Indian tributes, and the cheap Indian labor that worked large agricultural estates called *haciendas*. The dynamic economy of the city attracted many immigrants, offering a well-educated and well-connected man opportunities in commerce and in the government bureaucracy; for the skilled, there were jobs in service, the crafts, and bookkeeping. Artisans and professionals arrived daily from provincial cities and even from Spain. But the city's prosperity was not spread evenly: the upper class made up only about four percent of the population, and the middle class about eighteen percent.[4] Don José must also have been assaulted by the sight of a city teeming with poor workers, peasants recently arrived from the countryside, and beggars as the coach swayed along the cobblestones on the way to his uncle's house.

High above the filth of the street, de la Guerra could have been confident that the privileges accorded him by birth ensured him an equally high position near the top of the colonial social order. Over eighty percent of Mexico's population in the 1790s was Indian, African, or "casta" (of mixed racial heritage), but these people did not set colonial policy or live in fancy metropolitan houses. In Spain's colonial holdings, a racial order called the *sistema de castas*, elaborated from the sixteenth century, subordinated nonwhites and fixed legal rights and restrictions accordingly. In theory, at least, occupation, wealth, and social status would follow. Being white was not the only advantage granted José by his ancestry. In Mexico City, the majority of the population claimed to be white, but those who had actually been born in Spain were an even more select group—no more than fifteen thousand in a viceroyalty of six million, most living in the capital city.[5]

Official Spanish policy had done much to create this concentration of *peninsulares*. In the second half of the eighteenth century, the Bourbon kings of Spain had turned to their colonial holdings for desperately needed revenue after a series of costly wars in Europe. Inspired by Enlightenment theories of efficiency and free trade, Charles III (r. 1759–88) and his dynamic Inspector General, José de Gálvez, attempted reforms in New Spain that were designed to secure the borders of the colony while streamlining its administration and increasing the income for the Crown. Colonies such as New Spain had in the previous century become increasingly autonomous, but Bourbon reformers—Spanish intellectuals and bureaucrats—considered creole control inefficient and corrupt, and moved strongly to oust native-born Mexicans from power. Under the Bourbon administration, peninsular Spaniards enjoyed legal privileges in international commerce, government administration, the Church, and the judiciary, and as a result they dominated the occupations in these institutions. In addition, about half of Mexico's military was Spanish-born.[6] In a way, the Bourbon Reforms represented a second conquest of the New World, and José de la Guerra was just one of many who took advantage of the opportunities presented to those born in the Old World.[7]

The Noriegas welcomed their young nephew from Spain and introduced him to the life of a big-city merchant. Each day, for most of his teen years, José followed his uncle to work, learning the basics of accounting and bookkeeping. Though it appeared that his future as a merchant would be secure, at age nineteen he left Pedro Noriega's house and entered the officer corps of the newly created Habilitado General, or military salary and supply administration, for the Californias.

As an officer in the colonial bureaucracy, de la Guerra formally established his position in the colonial social order. As many colonial elites saw it, society, headed by the king, was rigidly hierarchical and corporate. Rights and obligations inhered not in individuals, but in corporate organizations such as the military, the nobility, religious orders, guilds, and Indian towns, each with their own relationship to the king, and with their own function and privileges, or *fueros*. At the same time, the king's authority over colonial society was imagined to be like that of a benevolent father over his family. Society maintained coherence and stability because no one could exist outside this order; individuals would know their place in it and submit willingly. This ideal, in turn, was asserted in laws that shaped the social order. As the Council of the Indies expressed it in 1806, "It is undeniable that the existence of various hierarchies and classes is of the greatest importance to the existence and stability of a monarchical state, since a graduated system of dependence and subordination sustains and ensures the obedience and respect of the last vassal to the authority of the sovereign."[8]

Like whiteness and Spanish birth, the ability to prove membership in the class of nobles smoothed the way for young men like de la Guerra as they entered the military. The first step for an aspiring officer was to secure the title *soldado distinguido,* meaning that a young man like José had the means to outfit himself and a horse, and possessed the rank and wealth to associate with officers on a social basis.[9] Having presented documents "attesting his noble birth" to Viceroy Miguel José de Azanza, de la Guerra was enrolled directly in the officer corps of the royal army of Spain as a cadet, and in October 1798, was assigned to one of the presidial companies of California.[10]

For two years, de la Guerra was officially a cadet in the San Diego presidial company, but he continued to live in Mexico City, working as an assistant in the office of Lieutenant-Colonel Manuel Cárcaba, the first habilitado general of the Californias.[11] It is likely that the California military was a principal client of the Noriega commercial house, and that this was the basis for Cárcaba's patronage of Pedro Noriega's nephew. Patronage was the young cadet's fast track to promotion. Cárcaba petitioned the viceroy on his behalf, and on December 23, 1800, just two years after his appointment as cadet, de la Guerra was made *alférez*, a rank equivalent to ensign or second lieutenant, and was reassigned to the presidial company of Monterey. Cárcaba, in his letter of recommendation, assured the viceroy that his protégé had "discharged his duties with zeal, industry, and ability; his conduct was in every way worthy of his illustrious birth, and he showed himself a thorough accountant."[12] In other words, José de la Guerra combined the ideal attributes of the nobleman and the devoted bureaucrat. Birth had secured him a position of dominance in the colonial hierarchy; submission and loyalty to his superiors would secure his advance.

As alférez, de la Guerra was required to serve a tour of duty in the distant province, and at age twenty-one he followed the route of California's military supplies, out of Mexico City, overland to the outfitting port of San Blas on the Pacific Coast of Mexico. From there, in February 1801, he sailed north on one of the official supply ships, along with crates and barrels of cloth, knives, hats, sugar, chocolate, tobacco, brandy, and nails. These goods were destined for four presidial towns whose populations numbered in the hundreds, a far cry from the busy and dynamic capital city. José de la Guerra arrived in Monterey on August 9, 1801, to find a low adobe and stone compound fallen into disrepair.

His friends back in Mexico City called California "that treacherous peninsula or Siberia," but de la Guerra put up with the low wages and isolation because the path of promotion was clear: a California tour of duty would be a temporary but necessary step on his way up the ladder of Mexico's governmental bureaucracy.[13] Cárcaba wrote to his protégé en route, urging him to do his best to impress California's governor, José Joaquín de Arrillaga, "forgetting idleness and utilizing every minute, because in those distant regions there are no distractions and pastimes."[14] And indeed, de la Guerra's rise seemed quite fast. Cárcaba's recommendation convinced Governor Arrillaga to grant Alférez de la Guerra the *habilitación* of Monterey in November 1801, putting him in charge of the presidio's supplies just three months after his arrival in the province.[15] The salary of an alférez was only four hundred *pesos* a year, but the added duties of the habilitación could net an extra commission of one thousand pesos.[16] On receiving the news, young de la Guerra's father encouraged his progress: "Even though the pay may not be much," he admitted, "a position such as this is of great honor and merit."[17] In addition to his commission as habilitado, Alférez de la Guerra took over as acting commander of the Monterey presidio in October 1802, less than two years after his arrival in the province.

De la Guerra and a very few Spaniards like him chose to use their class precedence and nobility to jump into positions of command on the frontier—most likely intending to return to metropolitan Mexico, or even Spain, and to continue their rapid rise through the ranks there. The Bourbon Reforms, after all, encouraged Spaniards to replace creole elites at the highest levels, in an effort to reassert Spanish control and colonial dependency. But despite Cárcaba's assurances that there were no distractions in the "Siberia" of the north, José de la Guerra apparently did find one, submitting a request to the viceroy in October 1803 to marry the daughter of Tomasa Lugo and José Raymundo Carrillo, his commanding officer.

Carrillos and Lugos: Mobile Soldiers and Settlers

José Raymundo and Tomasa, both children of frontier soldiers, had taken a very different path to California from de la Guerra's, one that was much more typical of Alta California's first colonists. California may have held little to entice a young, well-born Spaniard like José de la Guerra, but it was the land of opportunity for the Lugos and Carrillos. The Bourbon

Reforms, by encouraging migration and economic development, dramatically shook up Mexico's social order, especially on the northern frontier. Whereas a few men of the officer corps, like de la Guerra, used the privilege of noble status, carefully cultivated patronage, and Spanish birth to start at the top, many lower-class and mixed-race men in the military took advantage of frontier conditions to propel themselves into the ranks of the elites, even reinventing their race.

The drive to colonize California, like the effort to replace powerful creoles with peninsular Spaniards, began with the restructuring efforts of the Bourbon Reforms of the late eighteenth century. Spain had held colonial possessions in its far north—New Mexico, Sonora, Sinaloa, and Baja California—centuries before the first colonists were sent to Alta California. The extension up the Pacific Coast was designed as part of a more active Spanish effort in the second half of the eighteenth century to recolonize New Spain in the face of strong challenges to the empire from Britain, France, and Russia. Spain feared in particular that rival empires would discover the mythic Northwest Passage and gain definitive control of world trade routes. This new policy had distinct implications for California and, just as importantly, was shaped by the special conditions of the north.

Rugged, mountainous, and dry, New Spain's vast northern frontier was reorganized into the Interior Provinces after 1776, and administered directly by the Crown.[18] Sparsely settled with colonists, the region had a long history of violent encounters with independent Indians such as the Apache and Yaqui.[19] Towns such as the Villa de San Felipe y Santiago de Sinaloa, also called Villa de Sinaloa, served as administrative centers. Villa de Sinaloa, founded in 1590 in the flat river valley of the Río Sinaloa in Mayo Indian territory, also contained a military garrison and the Jesuit order's regional center serving nearby missions. On a clear day, townsfolk could see the western slope of the Sierra Madre mountains. The soldiers stationed at the presidio were known as *soldados de cuera*—a special breed of frontier cavalry soldiers with their own body of military law, trained to fight with lances, and outfitted in leather jackets designed to repel the arrows of Indian warfare. When the command was issued to find colonists for California, recruiters went again and again to this town of 3,000.

Despite promising beginnings, by the late eighteenth century a series of catastrophes had brought the town to its knees. In 1740, Villa de Sinaloa lost its role as capital of the province. In 1767, royal officials expelled the Jesuit order from the Americas, and its school, granaries, pharmacy, and infirmary in town were abandoned. Finally, in 1770, the

Sinaloa River flooded and brought down much of the town, leaving only the bell tower of the church. One official, sent to survey the region that year, reported that Villa de Sinaloa was "very poorly disposed, and its people have little to wear and no commerce."[20] Conditions were equally bad in other regions across Sonora and Sinaloa, as mines gave out and independent bands of Apache and Seri stepped up raiding. Captain Juan Bautista de Anza, charged in 1774 with recruiting new colonists for California, recommended gathering them from these northwestern provinces. "Submerged in the greatest poverty and misery," he argued, local residents would "eagerly and with great willingness" jump at the chance for a fresh start.[21] Spanish authorities sweetened the deal by offering potential farmers small plots of land, seed, livestock, tools, clothing, rations, and tax exemptions; for soldiers and their families, they promised livestock, supplies, clothing, and pay in advance.

One of the first to go from Villa de Sinaloa was the soldier José Joaquín Cayetano Espinosa, who left with the Fernando Rivera y Moncada expedition of 1769, across the Gulf of California to La Paz, and up to San Diego overland. Espinosa left behind his wife, Serafina Lugo, and their seven children. The initial expedition to California brought only men, but as with most other colonization schemes in the north, viceregal officials soon were deliberately moving entire families from nearby regions to the new settlements.[22] The imperative to hold the frontier with married men and families also came from local experience. Pedro Fages, who arrived with the first soldiers and became an early governor of California, quickly learned that "the Indians were hostile to men without women, believing them to have been outcasts from their own societies who had come to take away the Native women."[23]

Serafina and her children joined her husband in California in 1774, going north with another expedition led by Rivera y Moncada, now appointed California's governor. Serafina had plenty of company on the trek north: her brother Francisco, his wife, Juana, and four children, Rosa, Tomasa, Salvador, and José Antonio, as well as two of Serafina's sisters, Gertrudis and Petra, and their husbands and children. All the men were enrolled as soldados de cuera. Francisco Lugo and his family, including seven-year-old Tomasa, settled in at the Mission San Luis Obispo, where Lugo served as a guard, attached to the Monterey presidio. Only Francisco's sister Pascuala and her family remained in Villa de Sinaloa. Just two years later, Pascuala's husband and eldest son also left for Alta California with Juan Bautista de Anza. Although Spanish officials tried to move entire families, the colonization process could still tear them apart.

In its recruitment of families from nearby frontier provinces, California fit a larger pattern in the colonization of northern New Spain. But this northernmost territory differed from the rest of the northern provinces in the amount of emphasis placed on the mission as colonizing institution. As agents of empire, communal missions were meant from the start to be transitory: they were to be used to acculturate frontier Indians, then secularized or turned into regular Spanish parishes after a period of about ten years. But by the middle of the eighteenth century, many long-settled regions continued to maintain active missions. Aiming to reduce the wealth and power of the Church, Bourbon reformers at last secularized long-standing missions and transferred mission lands to the ownership of Indians and their Hispanic neighbors.[24] Presidios took the place of crumbling missions as the dominant Spanish presence in the far north. But in California, lack of resources forced Bourbon planners to compromise and rely on the Franciscan order to supply cheap "pacification" of the local Native population.[25] In return, these missions held most of the arable land in the colony, as far north as the San Francisco Bay, by right of occupation and use under the Crown.

The missions of California were designed to act in concert with two other colonial institutions: the pueblo, or civilian settlement, and the presidio, or military outpost. Royal officials founded three civilian settlements—San José in 1777, Los Angeles in 1781, and Branciforte in 1797—but despite the officials' best intentions, civilian pueblos never became significant forces in the political economy of Spanish California.[26] In other regions of the north, various colonization schemes could lure civilian settlers with promises of land or cheap Indian labor, but in California the missions blocked that option. Instead, because the Spanish Empire expanded up the Pacific Coast largely to check the expansion of other imperial powers, the colonization plans for California gave special emphasis to the military. Eventually, the Spanish built four presidios: San Diego, Santa Bárbara, Monterey, and San Francisco, with a total military presence of four hundred men. Under Spanish rule, soldiers on the royal payroll made up over half of the non-Indian adult male population of California.[27]

Far from their hometowns on the northern frontier, the new arrivals reinvented themselves in California. Reflecting the population of the northern frontier as a whole, they were a diverse group. A minority of California's first settlers and soldiers were classified as "español"; most others had some mixture of Indian, African, and European ancestry. In New Spain, the term "español" did not indicate European birth—instead, as a racial term, it sat at the top of the *sistema de castas,* with the categories "negro" and "indio" at the bottom, and various mixtures such as "mestizo," "coyote," and "mulato" in between.[28] People of different castas were recognized and ranked by a constellation of criteria that might include not only skin color but also legitimacy of birth, education, occupation, moral conduct, religion, dress, and speech.

Ordinarily, the rights and opportunities of non-españoles were limited, but on the frontier the system was not as strictly applied as in the central regions of New Spain. Reflecting a desperate need for soldiers with frontier experience, for example, the Instrucciones of 1786 specified that frontier officers should be chosen for "justice and competence rather than social standing, and without reference to color or circumstance of birth."[29] In core areas of New Spain, the top rung of society was strictly limited to those with inherited wealth, noble titles, and European birth. But few who lived on the frontier possessed any of these attributes, and as a result, the gap between rich and poor, and high and low status, tended initially to be much narrower. Even the full wardrobes new California military families received—including hats, shoes, stockings, shawls, and petticoats—were designed to eliminate visible differences among the various castas.[30]

Conditions on the frontier made it easier for lower-ranked people to move up in status, and this social mobility in turn was reflected in racial drift.[31] This process had already begun before the first recruits left for California. One Jesuit missionary writing from Sonora in the late eighteenth century reported that "practically all those who wish to be considered Spaniards are people of mixed blood."[32] An even greater percentage of soldiers claimed to be "Spanish" in the official records, perhaps as a result of a 1762 regulation that required frontier garrisons to be at least two-thirds "español" in their ranks. This order proved impossible to implement, and under pressure to meet their quota, some officers whitened soldiers on reports. Further shifting took place once colonists moved to California. Although it began as a majority mestizo, mulato, and indio society, California became increasingly "Spanish" over time. In the 1781 census of the pueblo of Los Angeles, less than five percent of the population claimed to be español, but by 1790, forty-six percent of those same settlers had that designation.[33] Seven of the eight men who appear in both census documents were reclassified to a lighter category in 1790—from indio to coyote, from mulato to mestizo, from mestizo to español.[34] At the presidio of San Francisco, the number of military settlers listed as español jumped from thirty-nine percent in 1776 to fifty-seven percent in 1790.[35]

Certain achievements made it more likely that an individual's español status, and any upward racial drift, would be accepted, and chief among them was military rank. Tomasa Lugo, daughter of common soldier Francisco Lugo, cemented her status in April 1781, when she married Corporal José Raymundo Carrillo.[36] José Raymundo had arrived from Loreto, Baja California, as a young enlisted soldier in 1769 with his uncles Guillermo and Mariano Carrillo. Unlike José de la Guerra, the Carrillos had humble origins and a lack of connections, which meant they could not qualify as soldados distinguidos, and had to serve in the ranks for several years before they could hope to make corporal, and if they were lucky, sergeant, lieutenant, or captain. On the strength of their literacy and service, José Raymundo Carrillo and his uncles steadily moved up into Alta California's officer class.[37] By the 1790 census, Raymundo held the rank of sergeant, and both he and his wife, Tomasa Lugo, and their three children, Carlos, María Antonia, and Anastasio, were classified as "español."[38]

Not all colonists moved up in status and race; disreputable appearance or conduct might push a person down the porous hierarchy of castas. Tomasa's Aunt Pascuala learned this the hard way. Pascuala, left behind in Villa de Sinaloa by her brother and sisters, husband, and son, must have found life very difficult and lonely indeed. After smallpox hit the town in 1780, taking with it ten percent of the population, she made a desperate decision. In 1781, she packed up her children and left with a cousin and his family on what would turn out to be the last great colonizing party to leave Sonora and Sinaloa. An uprising among the Quechán at the Colorado River crossing that year closed the interior trails to California for the next fifty years. Pascuala's husband, José Miguel Silvas, was in for a surprise. He had left her six years earlier with three daughters, but when she arrived in California, Pascuala brought five children, including a two-year-old daughter and a baby son. For unmarried women, the plain evidence that they had had sexual relations outside of marriage was enough to dishonor them and lower their social standing, but married women risked physical punishment, even death.[39] We can't know what went on in the privacy of the Silvas household after this reunion, but there is evidence of Pascuala's loss of status. By the 1790 census, all of her children are recorded as "español," but Pascuala, now a widow, has become a "mestiza."[40]

Interestingly, after the 1790 census, Church and governmental records classified the Carrillos and Lugos, and most other settlers, only as "gente de razón." Gente de razón, a non-casta term, meant "people of reason," and was used to draw a stark line between California Indians, the "people without reason" to understand Catholicism, and the multiracial Hispanicized peoples "with reason," whose religion, dress, manner, speech, and occupations all marked them as culturally Spanish, and in their own minds as superior.[41] "The only two castes we know of here are the gente de razón and Indians," reported the priests at Mission San José in 1814.[42] This is not to say that racial categories within the gente de razón ceased to matter at all.[43] Privately, Californians continued to remark on the physical differences that marked some of them as not-quite-white, even if they would never acknowledge such differences publicly.[44] This duality is reflected in the comments of Father Ramón Olbes of Mission Santa Bárbara, who noted in 1813, "Although it is well known that not all [the inhabitants] are genuine Spaniards, if they were told to the contrary they would consider it an affront."[45]

For the Carrillos and Lugos, rank, status, and respect came from years of service and honorable conduct, not from an accident of birth. Bourbon bureaucrats and planners had hoped for a northern border populated by Spaniards, loyal to the mother country and to Spanish culture. The conditions they met on the frontier thwarted these plans and led eventually to an officer class in California that was made up of two sorts of men: poor soldados de cuera who could cast aside their humble origins and rise through the ranks, and those, much fewer in number, who used their connections and status as a shortcut to the top. These men, from very different backgrounds and with very different expectations, understood their position in colonial society from two contrasting perspectives. Men from Spain believed that their honor was bestowed at birth: a precedent courtesy of nobility and racial purity. Command was their birthright. Men born into the frontier military considered honor a thing to be earned on the battlefield against Indians and foreigners— their reward for defending the borders of empire. In this way, the experience of colonial conquest encouraged and enabled poor, mixed-race soldiers to claim a common identity with elite commanders who had been born in Spain.

The "California Family": Husbands and Wives

María Antonia Carrillo y Lugo, daughter of a frontier officer and granddaughter of a common soldier, married José la Guerra y Noriega, peninsular Spaniard and aspiring colonial official, in 1804, less than three years after de la Guerra's arrival in Alta California. It is tempting to view this wedding as a romantic interlude, incidental to the story of conquest and empire. But marriage was serious business in late colonial Mexico.[46] It represented an indissoluble link between two families, and as such, a wedding was a dangerous moment, when the interests and fortunes of one family joined those of another. The frontier, with its flattened racial categories and ambitious settlers, could be a particularly risky place in this regard. Couples like Raymundo Carrillo and Tomasa Lugo had used California's social fluidity to rise in status, remaking themselves as elites by the time they married in 1781. When their daughter María Antonia married José de la Guerra in 1804, however, status differences within California were widening and hardening, and marriage laws increasingly served to patrol the border of rank and status.

In the early years of California's colonization, Bourbon bureaucrats had no interest in holding up any marriages among the new arrivals. On the contrary, with promises of land, they encouraged soldiers to marry Christianized California Indian women, and they designed colonization schemes to bring marriageable women to California, even those who were not wealthy or "pure" español, with the hope that military men would find wives among them and colonize the area through reproduction.[47] As a result, the initial gender imbalance in the colony was nearly righted by 1804, and the officer class could look to its own for marriage partners.[48] Bourbon policy, aimed at shoring up imperial defense and boosting migration to the north, had created conditions on the frontier that encouraged upward mobility. Yet the Crown also maintained a cross-cutting interest in protecting the elite status of its representatives who governed the colonies. Marriages between unequals might disrupt the social order, creating the potential for dangerous racial mixing, a bleeding of wealth out of the ranks of the elite, and a weakening of noble rank. In response to fears of this social fluidity, expressed by the old elites of New Spain, official policy changed by the end of the eighteenth century to reduce marital choice.[49] These regulations became increasingly important in California after the colony began to produce a second generation.

Because elite status was synonymous with the military officer class in California, it was through the military that the state exercised the greatest control over marriage alliances. These restrictions applied particularly to the few well-born officers like José de la Guerra. The military regulations, or cédulas, of 1760 and 1772 dictated that officers with a rank of captain or above could marry only "daughters of royal officials, or with daughters whose parents are members of the nobility, and themselves of noble birth, or at least daughters of good parentage—honorable, pure of blood, and untainted by ignoble occupation." Failure to comply would result in a loss of rank or of pension funds, an effective way for the state to maintain the social and racial composition of its ruling elite.[50] But in California, even ordinary soldiers were affected by the move to protect the racial composition of the military. In 1791, the Crown reversed its policy of awarding land in California to soldiers who married Christian Native women, and as a result the number of such marriages dropped precipitously.[51]

Beyond incentives and restrictions aimed at the military, the Crown further expressed its desire for social control and a firm social hierarchy by giving all fathers discretion to arrange the marriages of their presumably unpredictable children. The 1776 Royal Pragmatic on Marriage was extended to the colonies in 1778, just as the first settlers were arriving in California. This Bourbon legislation was based on the centuries-old notion of *patria potestas,* which granted fathers the right to control their children's property, required them to give consent for a minor's marriage, and gave them the right to disinherit children who married against their wishes. The Royal Pragmatic explicitly allowed fathers to prevent unequal marriages that would "offend family honor and threaten the good order of the State." In the wording of the law, a potential marriage partner could be rejected on the basis of illegitimacy or lack of *limpieza de sangre*—"purity of blood"—meaning someone with non-Christian Jewish or Moorish ancestry. In the Americas, however, fathers interpreted the law more broadly, screening out the unequal in race and wealth. In 1803, a new law caught up with practice, officially allowing parents to prevent marriages of sons under twenty-five, and daughters under twenty-three, on any grounds.[52]

José de la Guerra was still an ensign, or second lieutenant, when he married María Antonia Carrillo y Lugo, and he was over the age of consent, but as a commissioned military officer, heir to estates in Spain, noble, and a peninsular Spaniard overseas, de la Guerra was obliged to apply for royal permission to marry, "under pain of forfeiting his titles and inheritance."[53] The permit arrived at the end of March, 1804.[54] Watching this greater level of state surveillance, California's aspiring elites began to officially document their own claims to elite status. When Tomasa Lugo and José Raymundo Carrillo had wed in 1781, Father Junípero Serra had noted their legitimacy of birth but did not record "purity of blood" or noble status.[55] But in 1804, when their daughter married into true nobility—from Spain, no less—Raymundo Carrillo submitted proof that María Antonia, too, could claim nobility and limpieza de sangre as "a descendant from the same ancient and noble house as that of

Alfonso Carrillo, the warrior-Archbishop of Toledo and Primate of
Spain in the reigns of Enrique IV of Castile and of Isabela of Spain and
Aragon."[56] Two years later, perhaps out of anxiety that the law might be
invoked to prevent his own daughters' marriages, Ygnacio Vallejo, María
Antonia's uncle, secured for his family an official decree of legitimacy and
purity of blood.[57]

With the arrival of European-born Spaniard José de la Guerra, upwardly mobile frontier soldiers were at last faced with someone who
had real credentials in the upper ranks of Spanish colonial society, and
whose presence threatened their newly minted español status. In California, tightening marriage restrictions encouraged striving families to
identify with all the trappings of the elite, as defined by the state: "clean
blood," racial purity, nobility, and honorable occupation. The Carrillos,
Vallejos, and Lugos, like many families on Mexico's northern frontier,
were headed by men who moved up through the ranks, and probably
"whitened" themselves as they did so. Because of this ability to rise
through the casta system, and then document their qualifications to
marry members of the elite, lower classes with ambitions accepted and
even promoted the inherited hierarchies of the colonial social order. As
a result of José de la Guerra's marriage to María Antonia Carrillo y
Lugo, and many others like it, the California elite grew increasingly
exclusive—"whiter," more "noble," and more firmly connected to military rank.

The "California Family": Cousins and Godparents

From the start, María Antonia's creole father, Raymundo, and her immigrant husband, José, drew upon their family tie to their mutual benefit. No doubt, a young woman like María Antonia understood her vital
role as linchpin, and had been taught to perform it from an early age.
Upon his daughter's marriage, Raymundo Carrillo advised her to submit
to the male authorities in her life, to persevere, "out of fear of God, a rev-
erent love of your husband, [and] respect for the priests who are the ministers of the Almighty."[58] In his next letter, however, he requested her
active help as a go-between with her husband, "my Noriega," asking her
to tell him to send along invoices as soon as the ship might arrive, and
"not to forget to buy forty or fifty arrobas of flour for me as cheap as he
can."[59] Two years later, in 1806, de la Guerra was promoted to senior lieutenant and second-in-command of the Santa Bárbara Company, as a
cousin later remembered, "owing to the good offices of his father-in-
law."[60] With this fortunate union, Carrillo acquired a son-in-law with

good connections and sharp trading abilities, and José de la Guerra acquired a father-in-law with the pull to reward his skills. María Antonia held them together.

José de la Guerra arrived in Santa Bárbara in June 1806, three months after his promotion, but had barely enough time to unpack with his wife and newborn son when orders came through, posting him to San Diego to sort out the accounts there. On November 15, the lieutenant left for the south, to serve in his third presidio as habilitado. His model, fellow Spaniard and Cárcaba protégé Manuel Rodríguez, had just left the command of the San Diego Company and was on his way to the central offices of the Habilitado General in Mexico.

De la Guerra's swift promotions owed as much to his new family ties and accounting skills as they did to his Spanish birth or noble status. Could it be helped if he thought himself a little superior to officers who had risen from humble station? Unlike him, they had no hope of promotion out of the backward frontier to the cosmopolitan hub of the Spanish Empire in the New World. Although de la Guerra's marriage gave him clear advantages and important connections within the emerging military elite, it did not guarantee that the young upstart would be fully accepted by the older officers, who still based their notions of honor and status on military skill, and who might resent a young swell who used the advantages of birth to leapfrog over them in rank. One of these resentful officers was Francisco María Ruiz.

On March 15, 1807, the soldiers and their families in San Diego witnessed an unusual spectacle: two officers yelling and shoving, drawing their swords. The new commander of the presidio, Raymundo Carrillo, had not yet arrived to replace Manuel Rodríguez, and in his place Carrillo had sent Lieutenant Francisco María Ruiz. Lieutenant José de la Guerra y Noriega had also just arrived to sort out the accounts as the new habilitado. Both lieutenants, José de la Guerra and Francisco María Ruiz, demanded recognition as the acting *comandante*. Ruiz pointed to Carrillo's orders, but de la Guerra argued that his promotion had come through first, and that made *him* the superior officer. At twenty-eight, de la Guerra was younger than many of the soldiers he would be commanding, but he was born into privilege and had more education than any of them. His marriage and new family proved him to be a responsible man. Fifty-one-year-old Ruiz was a member of the Santa Bárbara Company, a native of Baja California, and a man who had served a long career in the military, working his way up through the ranks. From November 1806 to March 1807, neither man would budge.

Finally, on March 15, de la Guerra forced the issue, demanding before the troops that Ruiz carry out his order to take five volunteers to San Miguel, Baja California. De la Guerra was acting on a letter from Governor Arrillaga, which suggested that Ruiz go "personally" to deliver the men to the Loreto jurisdiction. Ruiz refused. This was the last straw for Lieutenant de la Guerra, who ordered his troops to load their weapons and place the insubordinate Ruiz under arrest. From that moment, what had been a disagreement over the technicalities of rank escalated into a full-blown shouting match. In a rage, Ruiz hit de la Guerra in the face, knocking him to the ground, whereupon de la Guerra drew his sword. Each demanded that the troops recognize his authority over the other. Unsure of what to do, the men watched as their two highest-ranking officers nearly killed each another. Finally a few men rushed over, and with the help of Father Sánchez, separated the two before blood could be spilled.[61]

This nose-bloodying fracas might seem at first glance the result of an insignificant quibble over rank that had gotten out of hand. Both officers received reprimands from the viceroy and the governor. Raymundo Carrillo arrived at last to take over command, and José de la Guerra stayed on at the presidio, keeping the books as habilitado. When Raymundo Carrillo died in 1809, Ruiz stepped in as acting comandante with no opposition from his fellow officers. But there is more to this story than meets the eye. With closer examination, the fight reveals the tensions within California's developing elite class, and within its understandings of masculine honor. De la Guerra, a noble Spaniard, had begun the argument by insisting on the technicalities of military order. Ruiz, on the other hand, had achieved his status through physical dominance. When confronted by a threat to his position, he was the first to resort to his fists, striking his rival in the face. Yet the eventual resolution of the affair also demonstrates the forces that mitigated this tension and bound the emerging class together. De la Guerra and Ruiz shared not only a project of frontier conquest but also family ties—Ruiz and Raymundo Carrillo were first cousins. Although he could not see it in 1807, de la Guerra's fight with Ruiz and its aftermath revealed the critical importance of family, both real and symbolic, to the development, strength, and survival of Californio elites well into the second half of the century.

California's government officials, military officers, missionaries, and major merchants became a tightly knit group, loyal and exclusive. In writing and in person, they expressed this relationship through the metaphor of family. As Carlos Híjar, a later arrival, remembered, "They all treated one another as cousins, even though there existed no relationship whatsoever . . . They considered themselves as members of a single family."[62] The sense of "family," in turn, structured almost every aspect of California's political economy.

In fact, Híjar underestimated the extent to which relations of blood, marriage, or godparentage connected almost every member of California's elite into a dense web of kinship in the Spanish and Mexican eras. In part, so many were cousins because so many were siblings. Because elite Californio couples had large families, within one generation, almost every child had an abundance of first cousins. The high birthrate was no accident, but was encouraged by government officials as a way to hold the territory for Spain. Father Viñals of Mission San Fernando repeated this message to a young José de la Guerra a few months after the birth of the officer's third child, Teresa, in 1809. "Continue, friend, being useful to the Public," he encouraged, "and providing the native land with children."[63]

The number of children in the de la Guerra family was large for the time but not unusually so. The average number of children per household in California was three or four in 1790, and grew slightly over the next few decades, but among elite families the average was probably closer to eight or nine.[64] Infant mortality rates were low in California compared to the rest of New Spain, as was the number of deaths of women in childbirth.[65] In addition to eight children born under the Spanish flag (José Antonio, Rita de Jesús, Teresa, Juan José, Angustias, Francisco, Pablo, and Anita), José and María Antonia added Joaquín, Miguel, Antonio María, and María Antonia to their family after Independence, in 1822. Each of these children represented potential links to other elites, and the more children who made good matches, the greater the scope and density of the extended kinship network.

Marriages alone would have been enough to connect a large portion of the California elite, but another strategy strengthened group solidarity. Ignacio Sepúlveda, who belonged to one of the oldest families in the province, remembered, "There was one link in the chain of society of those days which contributed to keep in a strong and affectionate unison the social relations of men and women. It was the relation of *compadre* and *comadre*."[66] As in other Catholic cultures, godparent relations, or compadrazgo, were taken very seriously, and when a man or woman sponsored a child, he or she created a fictive kinship with the child and the child's parents. Sir George Simpson, the English merchant, remarked that compadres in Mexican California considered themselves "fellow-fathers or fellow-mothers of one and the same infant, who in turn is bound to regard the adoptive parent and the natural one with equal veneration."[67] In fact, Californios, like other Mexicans, considered co-parenthood a higher and more sacred connection than marriage and parenthood, since parents and compadres shared "spiritual substance," while spouses, parents, and children based their relationships to each other on carnal bonds.[68]

Spiritual kinship could be a way to create a "family" relationship where none existed before, and many historians assume that this was its primary function. But as it turns out, Simpson was closer to the mark when he observed, "Perhaps nothing can give a better idea of the closeness of the connection than that brothers and sisters often sink their natural relation in the conventional titles of compadres and comadres."[69] In fact, careful examination of de la Guerra compadrazgo reveals that godparentage reinforced existing blood or in-law relations more than it created new family ties.[70]

For their own children, the de la Guerras chose godparents almost exclusively from their brothers and sisters-in-law, aunts and uncles, nieces, nephews, and cousins. In fact, "Uncle" Carlos Carrillo—María Antonia's elder brother—his wife, and their daughter considered themselves the spiritual parents of five de la Guerra nieces and nephews born in Santa Bárbara. This was a common pattern: Californio elites often demonstrated particular closeness to one another by sponsoring more than one child of a couple. "Uncle" Carlos was his sister's only older sibling and the next to start a family after her. Throughout his life, he remained a favorite of the de la Guerra children and a close ally of their father.

As parents, the de la Guerras were very selective, repeatedly choosing Carlos Carrillo as a godfather, but as godparents, they cast their net wider. Before Independence, de la Guerra and his wife sponsored eleven gente de razón in the mission church of Santa Bárbara. Over the course of the Mexican era, they would become godparents another twenty-three times at Santa Bárbara, sometimes as a couple, and sometimes separately. Often, José and María Antonia strengthened political kinship with spiritual kinship, as when they stood as godparents to several of their own grandchildren, thereby becoming compadres of their sons- and daughters-in-law. Not surprisingly, they sponsored five children of "Uncle" Carlos, but they also became co-parents with three of *his* sons-in-law by sponsoring four of Carlos's grandchildren. As godparents, they also drew in María Antonia's younger Carrillo brothers, as well as her Lugo, Pico, and Ortega cousins. This group of in-laws, or "political" siblings, linked again through compadrazgo, expected to receive direct announcements of any important family news, like births and marriages, and called upon those relations with good connections to buy them imported goods, loan scarce religious texts, and send domestically made goods.[71] This kin cluster was one of many like it within Californio elite society.

Marriages among officers' families reinforced the elite class not just because marriage restrictions maintained class boundaries, but also because the relationships they created obligated elite men and women to aid each other. Soon after their marriage, José de la Guerra and María Antonia Carrillo began the careful work of strengthening their political bond: they started a large family, and through it created spiritual and fictive bonds to the Carrillos and beyond. By the end of the colonial era, most of the officer class, the joint creation of Spanish and frontier soldiers, considered themselves as not just belonging to the same class, race, or culture but also to the same family. These new relationships of kinship, of obligation and dependence, operated at the same time as critical components of the California economy, as commerce became a primary activity of California's elites.

On March 15, 1807, José de la Guerra was absolutely convinced that he was in the right when he drew his sword on Francisco María Ruiz. He outranked the other lieutenant, if only by a few days, and on the basis of education, nobility, and purity of race, de la Guerra knew himself to be the superior man. That day, and in the weeks that followed, de la Guerra learned an important lesson. His standing as a man who commanded respect would depend not just on his ability to dominate others, but also on his own respect for the wishes of his superiors, and, just as importantly, on his self-mastery and his ability to meet the obligations he owed to his dependents and relatives. By openly fighting, Ruiz and de la Guerra disgraced themselves in front of their underlings, showing themselves to be men who could not control their passions. Government service demanded self-control and deference to institutions such as the military and the family; by publicly and forcefully claiming his superior status, de la Guerra risked further promotion, even his career. In the aftermath of this incident, de la Guerra learned to cultivate virtuous action in every sphere of his life: commanding others, but also fulfilling the duties that such power required. Such were the attributes of a good father.

Commerce and Kinship: The Habilitado and Family Trade

Entrepreneurial wealth was just beginning to become a significant marker for California's elites in March 1807, when José de la Guerra and Francisco María Ruiz drew swords over rank and command. This would soon change. A few weeks later, as things began to settle down, José received a letter from his cousin in Mexico City, now poised to take over his father Pedro Noriega's commercial house. José Antonio Noriega urged his cousin not to fight over rank, even if he might be technically right.[72] Noriega had a personal reason to fear his cousin's possible dismissal from the army: José might one day rise to the position of Habilitado General of the Californias. With such a connection, Noriega was sure to have a lock on the lucrative and steady business of outfitting the presidial companies of California. Already, de la Guerra had opened a private account with him worth over one thousand pesos. As it turns out, a reputation for self-mastery and the ability to meet obligations were essential in the world of commerce as well. But this hotheaded cousin in California could have blown every deal by risking promotion and even dismissal over a silly matter of machismo.

For those with the right connections, a habilitado commission could open doors to trade and profit in a place where mercantile restrictions otherwise made such commerce difficult at best. De la Guerra, trained as a clerk in Mexico City and posted to California straight from the Habilitado General's office, held the position of habilitado in one presidio or another almost from the moment he stepped off the boat in 1801. Next to the position of comandante, the post of habilitado was accorded the most respect, and only those officers with training in account-keeping and financial management rose to the top. In fact, there were so few of these educated men on the frontier that one man frequently served in both positions at once.[73] The rewards for a man who attained such a commission went beyond those of command or respect: a clever habilitado could use his contacts to make himself a tidy income and take a great deal of control over every aspect of the local economy.

The presidial stores, kept under de la Guerra's watchful eye, came from two sources: manufactured goods sent from Mexico and agricultural products—flour, corn, beans, soap, shoes, and blankets—from the missions. In theory, California was a colonial dependent of Spain; the soldiers lived on fixed salaries, payable in credit at the presidial store. This store was to receive goods at fixed prices on official supply ships from San Blas or the missions, and ports were officially closed to all other nations. The job of the habilitado was to maintain the presidial supplies, keep track of each soldier's account, and exchange manufactured goods for mission produce when appropriate. Exchanges were recorded in terms of pesos and reales, but very little currency actually changed hands. For his services the habilitado received a two percent commission on every order.[74]

This regulated system had been designed to maintain a decent standard of living for the military, while keeping the provincial economy firmly within the Spanish orbit. But in practice, the economy of California slipped constantly from official oversight. As much as the governor and the Habilitado General tried to fix fair prices, the forces of the market constantly pulled them up or down, and neither the missions nor the traders at San Blas stuck consistently to the published lists. Frustrated, Governor Arrillaga compared the requisitions with the incoming inventories, and in 1807 wrote to Habilitado de la Guerra in San Diego, "There is a variation of prices on some of the same lines. It is necessary to stop this abuse, and to set them at an equal price."[75]

A look at de la Guerra's account book from these years shows how difficult it was to follow this order. According to his entries, the value of imported goods did indeed fluctuate. In addition, it is almost impossible to separate private accounts with José de la Guerra the individual from official ones with José de la Guerra the habilitado. The salaries of soldiers appear as credits, in exchange for corn, beans, soap, and tobacco, but so do labor and otter pelts for luxuries like silk, ribbons, and chocolate. One individual's account specified that a tithe of thirty-seven head of cattle was "to be satisfied by works of tailoring, at the rate of 10 reales, 8 grs."[76] Several people were given lines of credit "owed to José de la Guerra" running up to 1,500 pesos or more, which were paid off over the course of the year. Debts and credits shifted on the books from one account to another, without cash changing hands.[77]

Throughout this time, de la Guerra was setting himself up as a private trader, building the personal contacts necessary for lines of credit and trust in Mexico and California. One letter to de la Guerra from San Blas trader Juan Martínez y Zayas makes clear how commercial arrangements could be made. On March 31, 1809, Martínez sent a letter to de la Guerra, whose acquaintance he had made as an official working the military supply ships. The Mexican official reminded de la Guerra of this contact, hoping he had "confidence in my friendship and good faith." Martínez expressed the hope that the San Diego habilitado would "send me all the tallow that you can, and if you have a little extra requisition on hand that can be sent without causing an uproar, send it to me in care of the steward of the *Princesa* and we will share it."[78]

Clearly, Martínez was proposing private trade, but sending the goods on the *Princesa*, an official supply ship, seems to have given him pause. It should not have: in 1803 the viceroy had liberalized rules governing trading via the San Blas supply ships. Officers and crews on ships like the *Princesa* could no longer trade privately themselves but were required, if they had room, to carry goods consigned by individuals in California or San Blas.[79] In fact, Martínez was a little late with his proposal. By 1809, Habilitado de la Guerra already had a good business going with his uncle's merchant house in Mexico City.

Two years before Martínez proposed business with de la Guerra, and just a few months after the confrontation with Ruiz, José Antonio Noriega had written an excited letter from Mexico City to his cousin. Along with news of family and friends in Spain, Noriega told de la Guerra, "I would not want you to have doubts about me with regard to the serious business you tell me you have in hand, and maybe in next month's communication you will tell me about it. I will celebrate what may be a thing of honor and profit."[80] Thus began a regular stream of communication between de la Guerra and his cousins José Antonio and Nicolás Noriega, both sons of Pedro Noriega. Over the next three years, with de la Guerra firmly ensconced as habilitado in San Diego, they built a steady and profitable commercial relationship, arranging shipments of goods, sending notes of credit, and exchanging news of commercial regulations and market conditions.[81]

It wasn't all business. In fact, these letters are most remarkable for the way they mix family news with commercial business. But it was just this personal bond of family that glued the trading relationship together so firmly, and that was brought to mind every time José sent a letter to his parents through his cousins, or one of the Noriegas forwarded news of the family in Spain. At first, José Antonio Noriega only sent a few personal items to de la Guerra on order: guitar strings, shoes, a cookbook, and sewing boxes. Tucked in the crates were a few gifts for his cousin's new wife. "Because he who has a family," Noriega told him, "should not give presents but rather accept as many as he is given, so that he will always have enough to support his family."[82]

Soon, de la Guerra was in a position to return the favor, letting the Noriega brothers in on the "serious business" of California trade. The exchange started in the spring of 1807, when de la Guerra collected together 1,126 pesos' worth of outstanding debts owed to him in California and Mexico and converted them into a *libranza*—a sort of bill of exchange that served as a bank draft or personal check in an economy with no banks.[83] Trust was critical: thousands of miles separated these men, and an unscrupulous merchant could easily send a bad libranza, but, as Noriega told his cousin, it was "understood that you are an honest man, and that you are not capable of trickery."[84]

In return, Noriega over the years sent de la Guerra goods like *rebozos* (a type of long scarf or shawl) and chocolate, which fellow officers had ordered specially or which José speculated would find buyers in California.[85] These goods arrived on the only ships sailing from Mexico to California: the supply ships of the California habilitado. At one point in the exchange of letters, Noriega jokingly called Habilitado General Manuel Rodríguez, now one of the most powerful bureaucrats in the California military, a "muleteer" for the role he played in transporting their goods back and forth.[86]

The cousins depended a great deal on the goodwill of their friend Rodríguez, but over the years that friendship became strained. Rodríguez would only take goods when he had enough extra room, and orders often sat on the docks at San Blas for months waiting for the next available ship. At other times, the Noriegas ran into a great deal of difficulty in getting their libranzas honored. On one occasion, Rodríguez refused to pay his for several months; de la Guerra had sent a libranza payable on the account of Manuel Rodríguez, but Rodríguez insisted that the military salaries needed to be credited to his account before he would pay. In frustration, Noriega told his cousin, "Every Libranza is either good or bad. If it is good he should accept it in accordance with the law . . . Rodríguez is my Friend," he went on, "but friendship is one thing, and vested interests another: I am requesting something quite legitimate."[87] Noriega must have been very eager at this point for his cousin to take Rodríguez's job in Mexico City. A family member could be trusted.

This trade and government alliance between cousins reflected a common pattern in late colonial Mexico. In Mexico City, Sonora, and San Diego, the family, more than any other corporate organization at the time, was the institution around which capital and class were organized.[88] Just below the "Great Families" stood families like the Noriegas, whose members were large-scale merchants or owners of estates, mills, factories, and mines. Diversification was a hallmark of these families, who also frequently integrated their varied economic activities. A single extended family might own several types of agricultural and mining enterprises, the means to manufacture raw materials, and the merchant houses to transport and trade on the national and international markets.[89]

Both Mexico's legal system and its social expectations combined the interests and assets of individual family members into one larger family economy, which guaranteed predictable behavior from each family member and sheltered family assets from risk.[90] For example, unlike the coverture laws in effect in the English-speaking world, Mexican marital property law dictated that all property acquired during a marriage belonged jointly to both spouses, and therefore could not be sold without the permission of both. Creditors could not seize the property of minor children, and many parents shielded their assets by assigning property to them.[91] What kept such varied enterprises coordinated, and prevented individual family members from competing against one another, was a strong reliance on the structures of the patriarchal family. One father or brother functioned as manager of the family corporation, enabling the extended kin network to consolidate its holdings and direct management from a single source, and thus to increase its economic power.

This pattern of family-based enterprise, followed by the successful metropolitan elite, was one that de la Guerra knew as a nephew-apprentice in Mexico City, and fell into again easily with his cousins after 1807. But conditions they could not control began to pull apart the de la Guerra–Noriega mercantile connection just a few years later. From July 1809 through February 1810, Noriega repeatedly reminded his cousin that he owed "three hundred seventy-one pesos six and three quarters reales" on his account; by November 1809 Noriega's creditors were calling in their debts, and his debtors were refusing to pay. "I would appreciate it if you could send me more," he begged his cousin in California. "[I need] ten thousand pesos in order to get out of some difficulties."[92] An economic crisis in Mexico was tightening lines of credit, choking off the business. The year of his last pleading letter turned out to be a watershed for all of Mexico, even in faraway California, for it marked the start of ten years of civil war.

Crisis and Retreat

Without the war, things would have turned out much differently for the young officer. De la Guerra's marriage a few years earlier could have been taken as a sign that he was thinking of settling down in California, but in fact the opposite was true; José intended to use his new connection to move up and out of the California military. Even in his marriage announcements, he assured his Mexico City circle that he would be coming home soon. One astute friend wrote back, "I agree with you that those lands are isolated and with your desire to abandon them, but the fact is that there are reasons for delaying and your new [married] state will make leaving more difficult."[93] So, for a few years, de la Guerra settled in and started a family, all the while cultivating his new connections to the Carrillos, and through them, many of the other officers. This patronage paid off in promotions. But the trading obstacles thrown up by

Manuel Rodríguez and the quarrel with Lieutenant Ruiz certainly served as further incentives for José de la Guerra to leave New Spain's frontier "Siberia," where commercial opportunities were limited, and where the status of noble birth didn't seem to count for as much as it should.

Months away from the capital and even further from Europe, de la Guerra must also have been eager to hear reports from his homeland. In the fall of 1808, a letter arrived from his cousin José Antonio Noriega with the news that Napoleon's armies had overrun Iberia, kidnapping the royal family. In New Spain, this caused much uncertainty, as the colonial order was predicated on a Spanish king as the ultimate source of all authority. "This iniquity has no equal in History," proclaimed the cousin, "I only regret not being in Spain in order to . . . seek out the enemy, and be able to die in defense of the King, of the Holy Religion, . . . and for the Homeland."[94] This trinity of loyalties became the rallying call of Spanish royalists all over New Spain, who quickly organized to support Fernando VII as a symbol both of the Spanish nation and as a defender of the Catholic faith against the revolutionary French. José de la Guerra himself sent two hundred pesos, "as a good subject . . . in order to help the defense of the Homeland, of the Religion, and of our most beloved King."[95] He also asked his cousins in Mexico City to subscribe to a newspaper, the *Gaceta del Reyno* (Gazette of the Kingdom), and send it to California so that he could keep up with the fast-changing news.[96]

In the fall of 1810, de la Guerra at last packed his bags and boarded ship for Mexico. He basked in the knowledge that his years on the frontier had finally paid off, and in his pocket he carried the prize he had been waiting for: promotion to the Habilitado General's office in Mexico City, succeeding Manuel Rodríguez. With his wife and daughter by his side, he stood on the deck of the brig *Santísima Virgen* and pondered his new status and responsibilities as one of the most important bureaucrats for Spain's colonial frontier. In the hold of the ship, along with their china and housewares, was a private shipment of tallow to sell upon his arrival in San Blas.

While it was no doubt difficult for María Antonia to leave her birthplace, particularly after the death of her father the year before, she took what advantage she could out of the move. She ordered linens and furniture, to be picked up on their arrival, and perhaps looked forward to the status and luxuries of a bureaucrat's wife in the capital city.[97] Beyond that, she used her husband's promotion to gain advantages for the Carrillos, suggesting that some of her brothers might accompany them south on the government ship. She would not allow her immigrant husband to forget his obligations. Governor Arrillaga remarked wryly to José, "For my part, I have no objection to your bringing all the relatives of Señora María Antonia," but in the end, the families settled on María's youngest brother, fourteen-year-old José Antonio.[98] In the fall of 1810, José and María Antonia also had three children of their own to consider: a five-year-old son, José Antonio, and two daughters, aged three and one. In the end, the de la Guerras took only the middle child, Rita de Jesús.[99] María Antonia must have been distressed at leaving her other children, most likely with her newly widowed mother, Tomasa, but in a way they were her assurance that she and her husband would be back.

On the eve of their departure, in November 1810, the governor wrote to José, "I already imagine that you are . . . in an element that is different than what you are accustomed to, but since you are young and strong, soon you will command respect."[100] De la Guerra knew from his cousins that conditions were difficult in Spain, but he had little idea of how personal the troubles were going to get. After traveling down the coast, the party caught sight of San Blas; for José it was the first time in ten years, and for María Antonia it was the first time ever. They planned to unload crates and boxes, furniture and clothing, and travel by coach to Mexico City. José, María Antonia, her brother José Antonio, and daughter Rita never reached the capital. Revolutionary forces loyal to Miguel Hidalgo captured the ship and took the Spanish government official and his family captive.

The system that upheld status hierarchies based on nobility, race, and Spanish birth was coming to a bloody end. The rebels who captured their ship, under the local leadership of the curate Mercado, were part of a widespread uprising in the autumn of 1810 that called for independence and liberty, broad agrarian reform, and the abolition of Indian tribute and slavery. Seventy percent of Mexico's population in 1810 was identified as Indian, and another ten percent was classified as mulato or negro. This enormous sector of society served the state and the colonial economy as a cheap labor force, whereas whites, particularly European Spaniards like de la Guerra, held nearly every important post in commerce, the government, and the military. A number of factors pushed the system to its breaking point late in the first decade of the century— among them a series of crop failures that caused corn prices to quadruple (the same economic crisis that choked off trade with the Noriega merchant house) and the news that the Spanish monarchy had been forced to abdicate in 1808. On September 16, 1810, Miguel Hidalgo y Costilla, a rural priest in the Bajío town of Dolores, issued the famous "Grito de Dolores," a call to rebellion now interpreted as the spark of Mexico's independence movement.

Over the next few months, Hidalgo's insurgency spread across the country, picking up at least 80,000 followers who pillaged settlements and attacked Mexico's colonial elites. The port of San Blas, the outfitting center for the Californias, was an enticing target, with its warehouses filled with food, clothing, arms, and other supplies. One more ship arriving from California was one more ship to loot. In a way, though, José de la Guerra and his family were among the lucky ones. Many peninsular Spaniards and even some creoles who found themselves in the path of the revolution were simply killed outright. Still, the rebels at San Blas came close to killing María Antonia with a saber cut, separating her and her child Rita from José de la Guerra and José Antonio Carrillo. The latter two they took in chains from San Blas to Ixtlán, where the rebels condemned them to death.[101]

De la Guerra and his brother-in-law languished in jail for several months, until Spanish troops released them on February 2, 1811, shortly before their scheduled execution. Two weeks earlier, Hidalgo's forces had been routed at Mexico City, and they were on the retreat, heading north. The regular and militia forces of central Mexico outnumbered Hidalgo's army, while to the north other royalist forces were coming to the aid of the Spanish government.[102]

On his release, de la Guerra joined the royalist armies under Francisco Valdez, captain of infantry and commander of the battalion of Tepic, near San Blas. Acting as adjutant major, de la Guerra served under Valdez through the spring, while to the north, royalist armies captured and executed Hidalgo and the remnants of his forces. On three occasions, de la Guerra asked Valdez if he might leave Tepic and fight parties of revolutionary guerrillas in the area, but Valdez refused, valuing de la Guerra's managerial service in the town over the young man's desire to see action.[103]

Unfortunately, no records have survived that shed any light on the fate of María Antonia and her daughter Rita during those long months. We know simply that at the end of March, José de la Guerra petitioned the viceroy for permission to return to California with his family, and that little Rita was no longer among them. On May 16, 1811, the viceroy wrote out his return passport, and at the end of August, Valdez provided José with a certification of his service in Tepic.[104] Some time that autumn, José de la Guerra, María Antonia, and José Antonio Carrillo boarded a ship out of San Blas to face an uncertain future. De la Guerra's dream of becoming a high-ranking colonial bureaucrat had come crashing down, and his beloved daughter was dead. As the bedraggled family made their way back north, at least they could take comfort that their destination would provide a safe haven for loyal Spaniards.

Wartime: Liberalization and Smuggling

Prospects looked grim in the autumn of 1811, when de la Guerra and his wife returned home. Because of the disturbances at San Blas, the official supply ships had stopped leaving for California. Although the de la Guerras did not know it at the time, they had sailed south in 1810 on one of the very last ships to make the run between central Mexico and its northernmost province. Now only passengers and letters made their way north, including one missive from Father Guardian Agustín Garijo of San Fernando College, the home base of the California missions. Missionaries and military officials passed it around the province, eager for news. Father Garijo's letter painted a bleak picture. Although loyalists had recaptured San Blas, insurrection was spreading rapidly across Mexico, the government was in dire financial straits, and roads and ports had been cut off. "It has been impossible," he wrote, "to send either the supplies or five or six padres whom I had meant to send this year . . . the supplies for this year have not yet left Mexico [City], nor can the padres be sent while the roads are obstructed."[105]

On the isolated frontier, Californians did not feel the full force of the wars for independence. What they did feel was an economic shock. With most Pacific ports in the hands of rebels, the central government in Mexico City could no longer control California's economy, which it had so carefully designed as a contained and regulated system within the larger economy of New Spain. Over the next ten years, without the yearly supply ships from Mexico, most Californians faced shortages and deprivation. Between 1810 and 1821, only one official supply ship left San Blas for California.

In such a state, the colonial economy of California might have been expected to collapse, and de la Guerra's fragile trading networks to shatter irreparably. Yet, by 1817, records show him taking charge of an inventory of goods from Peru worth over three thousand five hundred pesos, selling it in California for silver and tallow, and pocketing a commission of over five hundred pesos for the deal. What happened? How was de la Guerra able to make such tremendous profits in an era when almost no supplies or subsidies were arriving from Mexico? The answer, quite simply, is that California's ports were finally opened—officially to the Spanish Empire, and unofficially to the rest of the world. The same liberalizing forces that were behind Mexico's independence movements had also begun to dismantle the mercantilist policies that had kept Mexico's markets closed to outsiders. And where trade restrictions were not lifted, local authorities bent them with a wink. During these years, the mission estates, built on Indian labor, produced surpluses of hides and tallow. So, although most soldiers sank into poverty, a clever, well-placed man like de la Guerra could grow rich delivering California's bounty to the world market. During the wars for independence, California's economy reoriented itself away from New Spain, and toward the Pacific.

Although rebellion effectively prevented all military supplies from reaching California, legitimate Spanish trade did not end in 1810. De la Guerra continued to maintain an account with Nicolás Noriega in Mexico City, and his commercial world widened considerably after 1811, as private Spanish ships began to arrive in California waters from Peru, other parts of New Spain, and even the Philippines. Under wartime conditions, California's ports were now officially open to all Spanish vessels, not just the ships from San Blas. In addition, the Crown gave up all pretense of price regulation in California: trade with Spanish nationals from around the Pacific flourished unregulated.[106]

By 1813, de la Guerra had jumped wholeheartedly into this world of commerce, at the urging of men like José de la Yen, who wrote from Compostela, "You will send me whatever you wish, and a list of the prices."[107] This message came north on the ship of Peruvian Nicolás Noé, who was looking to sell goods in exchange for California's produce. California tallow was in high demand in Peru, where it was used to make candles, but merchants also snapped up cattle hides, sea otter pelts, hemp, wool, coarse blankets, wine, dried fish, and other local items.[108] To feed their sailors, the officers of seagoing vessels purchased California wheat, beef, beans, eggs, vegetables, and other foodstuffs.[109]

In return, de la Guerra ordered manufactured goods and accepted consignments, beginning, it seems, with an order for rebozos and capes he placed while still in San Blas in 1811.[110] This, and another order that included chocolate, cinnamon, sugar, and mescal, were all on the shipment that Noé was bringing north in 1813.[111] Governor Arrillaga, hoping to buy sugar, candle wax, and tallow, discovered that Noé "brought some things but not enough to satisfy us." The goods Arrillaga needed were already earmarked for de la Guerra, the governor told his lieutenant, "which has obliged me as *alcalde* of the Pueblo to depend on your bountifulness ... that I have to answer for with the price that you exact and charge to the habilitado of Monterey ... the wax should be for the presidio and mission. The rest is for my personal use."[112]

This order for goods established a common pattern within California. First in San Diego, and after 1815 in Santa Bárbara, de la Guerra developed a reputation as a man with excellent contacts and a full warehouse, and everyone from humble *pobladores* to the governor himself maintained an account with him. As before, de la Guerra ordered items for specific clients, but he also took entire cargoes as the agent of Spanish ship captains if he felt there would be a market for the goods. For example, on arrival from Manila in the autumn of 1814, José María Narváez lamented that he had lost almost all of his merchandise in a storm, but that he was giving de la Guerra what linen and cambric were left. "Friend, here you have all my stock up to this day," he told the Californian, "which amounts to four and a half years."[113] A month later, Narváez was on his way back to San Blas, leaving behind "a lacquered Chinese trunk containing the goods of the attached invoice, . . . for you to handle." If the prices did not seem suitable, he instructed his partner, "hold onto the goods until you receive orders from me regarding to whom they should be delivered."[114] In 1819, de la Guerra took his biggest risk to date: buying over nine hundred pounds of cinnamon on speculation from Gonzalo Gómez de Ulloa and Pedro Rodríguez, traders based in San Blas.[115]

Trust was even more critical in these unsettled times, and over the years, de la Guerra built relationships with these traders and ship captains, most of whom, like him, had been born in Spain. When trader Fermín de Genoa y Aguirre left the business in 1818, he professed, "Now, more than ever, I know the grief that the separation from friends I love truly causes me. You are my best friend."[116] But the trader gave a fellow Spanish-born Peruvian entry into the commercial old-boy network: when Antonio José Cot arrived the next year, he immediately sent de la Guerra a note asking to do business and explaining that he had learned of the Californian through their mutual friend.[117] Cot was destined to become a close friend and major trading partner for the next thirty years.

Although de la Guerra had been blocked from taking his post in Mexico City, the Habilitado General still functioned during the war years, so the young officer continued to pay for imported goods with credit from the military. But he also balanced his accounts by exporting local products such as otter pelts and, increasingly, tallow and hides.[118] In fact, de la Guerra, who owned very little land himself, served a critical role for small producers in these years, acting as middleman between them and the Spanish merchants. "I am not for accounts, or small accounts; I am very, very busy," one of the traders explained, asking de la Guerra to assemble a large shipment of tallow for him.[119] This consolidation meant that even the poorest Californians could participate in the trade, and buy in return manufactured goods like cloth and nails. But a handful of retired soldiers and townsfolk who kept a few cows on communal property cannot possibly account for the large amount of luxury goods and silver coin that flowed into California between 1811 and 1821. Only mission smuggling could have produced activity at this pitch.

As an officer of the Spanish army, de la Guerra was sworn to uphold maritime restrictions on foreign trade, and in the official records it appears that he was a faithful servant of the Crown. The truth of the matter is that he was deeply implicated in the widespread smuggling that was becoming a necessity in California. British, Russian, and American ships had, of course, been showing up along California's shores for decades. Interest in the sea otter trade, after all, had in part led to California's colonization in the first place. The Nootka Sound Conventions of 1794 had established Spain's exclusive right to the coast of California, and Spain's mercantilist policies officially prohibited foreign ships from landing. Nonetheless, smuggling and otter hunting were common practices from the late 1790s.[120] As the independence wars increasingly hampered government support for the military and missions, contraband trade took off. Over the next decade at least twenty American ships, as well as a number of British and Russian vessels, sailed into California's secret coves and cached merchandise on its offshore islands. After 1817, when Governor Pablo Vicente de Solá imposed import and export taxes, even Spanish nationals began to trade undercover.[121]

In the official correspondence, de la Guerra insisted that he checked the papers of every foreign ship and reported any suspicious activity, and in their reports, Governors Arrillaga and Solá also came down hard on contraband trade.[122] But in reality, government officials in California needed this trade to make up for the supply ships that no longer came. An informal system developed: as long as foreigners negotiated terms with the governor or local presidial commanders, they could take on supplies and trade without fear of seizure or imprisonment.[123] Those who refused to go through such channels were subject to seizure by Spanish traders, who were only too eager to put their competition out of business. In return for permission to trade, government officials insisted that the missions donate to the presidios some of the foreign goods they bought for tallow.

Men like Governor Solá and Captain de la Guerra rationalized this arrangement in official correspondence; the poverty of the troops and the sad condition of hungry sailors demanded that the rules be bent a little. What they did not record was how much the trade benefited them personally. Only the foreigners themselves noted exactly what was going on. In his log, dated September 1821, Captain Eliza Grimes of the *Eagle* remarked that the comandante of Santa Bárbara, José de la Guerra, treated him to a lavish supper, after which they got down to business. Grimes unpacked samples of his merchandise, and de la Guerra ran down the prices listed on his invoices. "It would be advisable at this place to always deal with the Comdt. in the first instance," Grimes recorded for those who might follow,

> as in that case he will lay no obstacle in the way of trading with others although he requires a duty of 12 ¹/₂ per cent on all goods not sold to himself. These are free. At this place I sold more goods than I had any reason to calculate on and should no doubt have sold considerable more had I the articles suited for this market, as many were wanted.[124]

Using his official status in the California military, de la Guerra assured himself a commercial advantage.

De la Guerra had one final ace up his sleeve. By maintaining good relationships with his fellow Spaniards the missionaries, he persuaded them that he might act as their purchasing agent, giving himself a share of their ill-gotten silver. In this way, although he did not engage directly in smuggling, de la Guerra did benefit by it enormously. This, then, explains the delivery in 1817 of goods worth over three thousand pesos to Mission San Gabriel. Juan José Mayo, the supercargo, or business agent, of the Lima brig the *San Antonio,* let the padres of the mission know that their order, mostly medicine, medical supplies, and hardware, was coming through de la Guerra, and that he "will try to sell at the best price he can in exchange for silver, and if he cannot get that, then for tallow," at twelve reales per arroba.[125] Anything the missionaries did not want would return to de la Guerra, whom Peruvian merchant Don José Cavenecia had authorized to sell his goods on consignment. This sale to the mission earned de la Guerra a commission of 522 pesos, two reales.[126]

Soon, the missions became de la Guerra's primary clients. Soldiers could pay for their goods only in drafts on the Habilitado General, and after 1810 it became quite clear that these libranzas had little hope of being honored. Trade with the missions, on the other hand, was much more secure. Not only could they still order goods on the safe credit of their stipends from the College of San Fernando, but they also had on hand lard, tallow, and foodstuffs, as well as cash derived from smuggling operations. And because their primary needs for food and simple manufactured goods were met at the mission, missionaries turned to de la Guerra not only for necessary imports like cheap cotton cloth and coarse stockings, paper, hardware, and medicine, but also for luxury goods with a high profit margin for their factor. Inventories of sales include such items as wax candles, chocolate, saffron, silk handkerchiefs, a beaver hat, crystal rosaries, Chinese tortoise-shell combs, and books.[127] Sending tallow and placing an order for cloth in 1818, Father Mariano Payeras of Mission La Purísima Concepción wrote, "If Don Fermin has them at reasonable prices, send some pieces . . . You are a good person, and you understand the art [of negotiation]."

Interestingly, it appears that mission Indians may also have had some control over what the padres bought on their behalf. In that same letter from La Purísima, Payeras told his purchasing agent, de la Guerra, "I am returning the six shaving razors because the Indians say that they are not of any use to them, and the six short necklaces because the same Indians say they are of no value to them."[128] A few Indians even managed to trade sea otter pelts directly with foreign smugglers, putting further pressure on retailers like de la Guerra to meet their demands for ironware and fancy cloth.[129]

Because of the Franciscan vows of poverty, members were forbidden to handle financial transactions (although many obviously did), and they found in the pious de la Guerra a man whom they could trust with their mission's blossoming wealth. In 1820, de la Guerra unofficially took on the role of *síndico*, or banker and accountant. He handled the missions' financial affairs within California and between the missions and the mother college in Mexico. As síndico, de la Guerra arranged for the slaughter and sale of cattle, the payment of debts, and the purchase of goods, further cementing his economic connections. But some missionaries complained that de la Guerra was not always acting from purely disinterested motives. In 1819, Father Payeras claimed that the trader used ships paid for "at the expense of the friars and of the missions" to haul his own private shipments, "so that under the pretext of benefiting [the missions], they will be able to supply the non-Indians."[130]

Between his return to California in 1811 and the end of the independence wars, de la Guerra became the commander of the Santa Bárbara presidio and was promoted to captain. He also became a wealthy man. He built on his trading contacts from before the war and established a reputation as a man who could be trusted, one who knew "the art" of get-

"View of the presidio or town of Santa Bárbara, taken from a hill near the fort,"
ca. 1830, from Alfred Robinson, *Life in California*. Courtesy of California State Parks.

ting things cheaply. Although the military itself was in far worse shape
than it had been before 1810, and common soldiers grew ever more im-
poverished, the mission fields, workshops, and ranches produced great
surpluses of tallow, hides, and other goods. With the first wave of trade
liberalization, and a willingness to bend the rules, a well-placed man like
de la Guerra could connect these goods with the Pacific market, taking
his own cut to do so. As a result, wealth began to overshadow birthright
and military rank as the foundation for the elite class. De la Guerra used
the profits he made from commerce to make his family more comfortable and cultured, buying furniture, carpets, books, musical instruments,
and dolls for his children.[131] His well-furnished quarters must have
seemed quite a contrast to the bare one-room adobes most townsfolk
crowded into. But as the stories of mercantile connections suggest, none
of this wealth would have been possible for an isolated trader; personal
relations of patronage and kinship unlocked the doors of profit.

Creating Patrons in the War Years

By the time the wars of independence drew to a close, de la Guerra had lost
his patrons in Mexico's government, and the connections to his cousins'
merchant house had weakened. Yet, just as de la Guerra turned to new
sources for wealth and trade, so too did he create and strengthen bonds of
patronage and kinship within California. Conditions had changed, but de la

Guerra understood the continuing power of patriarchal relationships. By 1821, for example, he was nurturing working relations with several young men as a mentor and patron, just as he had been helped by Manuel Cárcaba and Raymundo Carrillo. These patron-client bonds could be surprisingly close, with deep emotional commitment on both sides, affection, trust, and loyalty. The men involved modeled their association on that of father and son, with the submission and reciprocal obligations that this implied. In 1818, Santiago Argüello, a twenty-seven-year-old lieutenant at San Francisco and the son of the governor of Lower California, exclaimed to his mentor de la Guerra, "I will not forget your advice, and I would like for you to correct me and advise me, as a Father to a son, when you perceive that I am mistaken, and I will accept it as such."[132]

De la Guerra not only created fictive father-son relationships with useful dependents but also worked hard to find his own patrons. During the late colonial era, the de la Guerras generally selected godparents for their children among local relatives—their social and economic equals. In 1819, they scored a coup when Governor Solá agreed to sponsor baby Pablo.[133] Contemporaries described Solá as a solidly built man whose florid complexion set off a full head and beard of short white hair. Governor Solá, like de la Guerra, had been born in Spain and had made his way through the colonial bureaucracy on the strength of his noble birth, polished manners, and managerial skill. Solá, governor since 1814, lived in Monterey and had no local ties in Santa Bárbara, but he influenced provincial, and even central, government policy.

Before long, de la Guerra was reaping the fruits of this connection. Such patronage was particularly important for those who sought their own lands. Under Spanish law, the Crown held ultimate rights to all land, and this right was delegated to the king's representatives in the colonies. In California, the governor had exclusive rights, with approval of the viceroy, to grant lands not claimed by the missions. Very little of the arable land in California, in fact, was available for private grants in 1822, and fewer than thirty soldiers who petitioned for grants on the basis of their service had received them. In April 1821, José de la Guerra wrote to Governor Solá, reminding him that the Santa Bárbara commander had twice left California in service to the military—once as habilitado general in 1810, and again as representative of the presidios in 1819. In neither case had he been reimbursed for traveling expenses. Captain de la Guerra pointed out that he now had six children to support, including Solá's godchild Pablo, and that one more was on the way.[134] De la Guerra urged Solá to grant him a ranch for their support. Solá agreed in turn that de la Guerra's family was "as large as the descendants of Adam" but complained that the quantities asked for were "great." Nonetheless, he assured de la Guerra that he would look into getting him a ranch and added, "If you believe that my position can influence the outcome, tell me, so that I can put the wheels into motion." Solá signed off by sending his greetings to his "*hayjadito* [*ahijadito*]"—his "little godson"—Pablo.[135]

Only land not claimed by the missions might be granted, and de la Guerra used his own dependents to scout out potential grants to suggest to the governor. José Joaquín de la Torre y Enterría, a Spanish military man who had arrived on the same ship as de la Guerra in 1801, became a crucial ally. In 1821, de la Torre acted as the commander's inside man while de la Guerra negotiated with Father Señán to acquire part of Mission San Buenaventura to the south.[136] Torre copied the missionary's letters and forwarded them to his "beloved jefe," or "boss," leaked confidential information from meetings he attended, and lobbied the governor on de la Guerra's behalf. When missionaries insisted that they were using the land that de la Guerra wanted, de la Torre "assured the Governor that it was a lie." In a later letter, he warned his "always venerated *jefe*, countryman, and Sir" that the missionaries were gossiping about the transaction: "who knows what . . . you divulged at Mass in Santa Bárbara which was about our business."[137] In return for this work, Torre respectfully asked his patron to buy some of his wine and brandy "at double price." "It would be of great use to me," he explained, to take "baby steps" toward stocking his own ranch, "and to buy cattle I would sell pearls."[138]

Alas for de la Guerra, the deal with Señán fell through, as did attempts to obtain the ranches Piru and Sespe from the mission. Solá soon made good on his promise to find de la Guerra a rancho, however, granting his compadre a half interest in Rancho El Conejo in October 1822 (see map on page 209). Having scouted out the surrounding area, de la Guerra learned that, twenty years before, this private ranch had been granted to Ignacio Rodríguez, who was now dead, and the retired soldier José Polanco, who had abandoned his share and moved to the settlement at Los Angeles. The widow Rodríguez and her children now lived there alone, cultivating a field or two of corn and tending a small herd of cattle. In a rather disingenuous letter to compadre Solá, de la Guerra pleaded destitution and petitioned, as someone who "deserved" it, to take over Polanco's half interest.[139]

In less than a week, Solá made the grant. Officially, he recorded, it was in payment for "the merits and services performed by Captain Don José de la Guerra y Noriega . . . and the disinterestedness with which he has executed several important commissions for this province, which have been entrusted to him by this Government."[140] In truth, this act of government was as much a result of Solá's spiritual kinship with the de la Guerra family. Poorer, less well-connected families like the heirs of Ignacio Rodríguez had no way to counter what seemed to them a thinly legalized theft of land they had come to think of as theirs alone. Animosities simmered under the surface, as the wealthy merchant began to send his workers out to Conejo, where they staked off ranch lands and planted thousands of grapevines under the hot valley sun.[141] Soon these laborers brought in mission-made barrels and brandy stills purchased from the Mexican ships. De la Guerra was diversifying his portfolio.

The captain had one final favor to ask of his compadre Solá. This request, most likely, came from his wife. Solá had the power to promote officers in California's military—couldn't he be persuaded to further the careers of her younger brothers? Once again, María Antonia made sure that her husband's connections benefited the Carrillos. A Spanish man's link to a creole family through his wife, like that of an immigrant nephew's connection through a resident uncle, was a well-known configuration in a range of blood, political, and fictive kinship patterns that structured the operation of capital and class across the Spanish colonies.[142] At first, the benefits accrued to just de la Guerra and his father-in-law, Raymundo, but even after Raymundo's death in 1809, José de la Guerra took seriously his obligations to the Carrillo family.

Indeed, personal connections with the Carrillo brothers would advance his own interests in Los Angeles and San Diego, where most of them lived. In the spring of 1821, de la Guerra prevailed upon his compadre Solá to transfer his brother-in-law Domingo Carrillo from the Santa Bárbara presidio to the company of San Diego. In his letter announcing the decision, Solá let de la Guerra know that this appointment was "in view of your insistence." "I will be mindful," Solá went on, "of the opportunity to assist your brothers with their promotions, and you, as a good brother, will give them sound advice so that they will fulfill their duties to the letter."[143]

After Solá made the transfer, thirty-year-old Domingo Carrillo kept his patron de la Guerra in touch with the political situation in San Diego, from the inside.[144] Likewise, José Antonio Carrillo, the young man imprisoned at Ixtlán, and his brother Anastasio Carrillo both took active roles in Los Angeles government, and in addition acted as local business agents for their brother-in-law. De la Guerra had two official roles in the civil life of Los Angeles, even though he did not live there: he had taken the role of *padrino* to the Los Angeles Church, and, as Santa Bárbara presidial commander, he was also the chief government official of Los Angeles. Both offices involved him in tithe and tax collection in

Los Angeles. He came to rely on the Carrillos to help him collect outstanding debts from the townsfolk—usually in the form of tallow. Solá, in turn, relied on de la Guerra to tell him what the Carrillos were up to in the pueblo.[145]

But as time went on, de la Guerra and the Carrillos learned the limits of their economic and political partnership, when personalities clashed and family arguments had significant material consequences. Young José Antonio Carrillo caused de la Guerra the most headaches. From 1818 to 1821, de la Guerra asked his brother-in-law to make up lists of those who owed money, and to travel to the neighborhood ranches, visiting the debtors and collecting tallow for sale to the Peruvian traders in the port of San Pedro.[146] José Antonio seldom did as his brother-in-law demanded. At times, he testily replied that he didn't get the instructions in time to comply; other times he wrote that "these *poblanos* [townsfolk] have tricked me in a vile manner, because most of them told me to go the beach . . . and they did not bring anything."[147]

By July 1822, pretenses of brotherly love had completely crumbled. José Antonio demanded a loan of two hundred pesos; José de la Guerra refused. "Can you send [your account] to me to immediately settle any debts?" replied a wounded José Antonio. "You have a good way for us to preserve the brotherly style that I want and without a doubt you do, too."[148] Less than a year later, Juan Malarín, the merchant from Peru, confirmed de la Guerra's lack of confidence in José Antonio: "I had great difficulty," he complained to de la Guerra, "on account of not being able to collect the account from your brother-in-law, . . . and to cover the debt, the Mission of San Gabriel paid it . . . Never will José Antonio amount to anything, and his anger and pride increase every day."[149] If de la Guerra had meant to teach his brother-in-law a lesson by scolding him and refusing him loans, José Antonio never learned it. He became known as a gambler and political schemer; this was not the last time the two would clash.[150]

Usually, overlapping business and family relationships worked to de la Guerra's advantage, as long as the drive for his own individual profit also brought well-being to the entire family. But the demands of capital accumulation did not always accord with the expectations of proper "brotherly" behavior. De la Guerra was perfectly happy to place relatives in strategic posts, and then call on his young brother-in-law for favors, but he recoiled when José Antonio demanded too much in return. Significantly, the two men were never joined in compadrazgo. Eventually, the weak in-law tie broke under the strain; de la Guerra could not both accumulate wealth and fulfill this family obligation. He chose profit. Though one individual dropped out of the family economy, however, the structure remained solid; the other Carrillos remained under de la Guerra's direction, essential elements in their brother-in-law's hide-and-tallow empire.

From compadres and in-laws to brothers and sisters, aunts, uncles, and cousins, the members of California's elite deliberately wove "family" into almost every relation of their society. Successful patriarchs like de la Guerra, and elite wives like María Antonia, made strategic connections, strengthened important ties, and allowed less significant ones to fade. By 1822, de la Guerra sat at the center of a dense web of relations, with recognized authority over a large, multifamily alliance, held together by blood, marriage, and compadrazgo. This kinship served significant economic functions in a province with few other institutions. It gave de la Guerra extraordinary resources on which to draw and also provided family members with their own investment in his success. Patriarchs like de la Guerra knew when to call in certain favors and when to grant them, and they knew how to use the obligations of kinship to promote their own interests and those of their families. Creole wives, too, drew influence and status from their roles as linchpins, connecting cousins and in-laws in an empire of kin.

Independence

In the autumn of 1818, José de la Guerra commanded the Santa Bárbara presidio and had begun construction on a fine new house. Like other royalists, he had taken heart four years earlier when word arrived that Fernando VII had returned to Spain.[151] Surrounded by Spanish missionaries and loyal soldiers, he must have felt quite secure from further harassment at the hands of revolutionaries. But on October 6 of that year, de la Guerra received an alarming piece of news upon the arrival of an American ship, the *Clarion*: an Argentinean privateer, Hipólito Bouchard, was fitting up two ships in the Sandwich Islands in order to disrupt Spanish trade and spread insurrection. He had already brought the ports of Callao, Peru, and Valparaíso, Chile, to a standstill, and had sunk sixteen Spanish vessels in the Philippines; now he and the forces of rebellion were headed toward Spain's northern frontier on the Pacific Coast.[152]

De la Guerra acted fast: On October 7, he sent a letter to the governor in Monterey and a circular to his friends at the missions, warning them to prepare for attack. Under subsequent orders from the governor, de la Guerra assumed command of both the troops and the mission establishments in his jurisdiction. Father Luis Martínez, stationed at Mission La Purísima, spurred on his friend the commander: "Watch out, and

Long Live Fernando, while we live, long live our Holy Religion and our Homeland, although we all might die. We are in a critical time...so sharpen knives, little Countryman, those two epaulets serve not only to adorn the body but also the homeland and the soul."[153]

By the time Bouchard and his ships the *Argentina* and the *Santa Rosa* sighted land in November, the central and southern coasts were ready: missionaries had moved their valuables to the interior, families had evacuated to the missions farthest from the sea, and troops had gathered at the presidios. The danger from the insurrectionists was quite real: on November 22, their combined crews of over four hundred soldiers and sailors took the presidio of Monterey and sacked the town, and on December 2 they burned the buildings of Rancho Refugio, only a few dozen miles up the coast from Santa Bárbara.

But de la Guerra was determined to hold the territory for the king. On December 6, Bouchard and his insurgents arrived off the coast of Santa Bárbara. With fewer than one hundred and fifty soldiers, and eight barely functional cannons, de la Guerra knew he was outmanned and outgunned. Santa Bárbarans years afterward told the story of how, to trick Bouchard, the wily Captain de la Guerra ordered his men to march in a circle around a small thicket of willows at the water's edge. Fearing an engagement with this apparently formidable force, Bouchard instead proposed a prisoner exchange. De la Guerra expressed his willingness to take on the revolutionaries; in a note to Bouchard, he warned, "If your men are so anxious to fight, let me assure you that mine are desperate to come to blows." But this bluster hid the commander's deeper motivation to avoid confrontation and spare California from attack; in the end the two agreed to exchange captives, and Bouchard departed on December 12.[154] De la Guerra chased him down the coast with reinforcements, but the Argentinean had already determined that California was barren ground for a revolution.

The violent rejection of peninsular Spaniards, part of the creation of a common American identity across Latin America, failed in California to unite a population where so many aspired to a Spanish identity. De la Guerra's nearest friends and neighbors, his trading partners and subordinates all shared his royalist sympathies and distrust of revolutionaries. Through the years of civil unrest and rebellion in Mexico, California's military and religious leaders defended New Spain's frontier as an oasis of Spanish fidelity. When yet another rumor of insurgent attack swept California in the spring of 1820, Father Antonio Ripoll of Mission Santa Bárbara assured de la Guerra, "They are killing themselves to form a company of royalist gente de razón in every presidio."[155] In Captain de la Guerra's own case, his capture and imprisonment in 1810 by revolutionaries in San Blas, and the subsequent death of his infant daughter there, must have seared a hatred of Mexican rebels even more deeply into his consciousness. The dangers of toppling established authorities had been made all too clear.

Still, New Spain's chronic neglect of its frontier led California's elites to hold a complicated and wary attitude toward the Crown's representatives in the viceroyalty. They understood this relationship in familial terms. As one Californio explained, when pay, supplies, or reinforcements failed to arrive on the frontier, soldiers tended to blame the bureaucracy in Mexico, not the Spanish king: "The Mexican government declared itself California's stepfather," Antonio María Osio remembered, "and denied it protection as if it were a bastard child. This attitude was demonstrated by the way it created insurmountable obstacles to carrying out the royal orders which the Mexican government would receive."[156] In other words, just as honorable men owed obedience to higher powers, like a son did to his father, the power of the state and its obligations to its subjects were analogous to those of fathers protecting children. California's military had submitted as good sons to the king, but Mexico proved its unworthiness as a surrogate father by failing to protect and provide for its subjects as the king, their true father, would have wished. This attitude would make it much harder for the newly independent nation of Mexico, the successor to the viceroyalty of New Spain, to win the loyalty of its most distant province.

At last, between 1820 and 1825, Californians made the hesitant and uneven transition from being subjects of the king to being citizens of the republic. Hidalgo's revolt had pushed New Spain toward Independence, but the real revolution in California's social order had actually begun in Spain, with the reforms enacted following Fernando VII's abdication. In his absence, the Spanish Cortes, or parliament, passed the constitution of 1812, turning Spain into a constitutional monarchy and conferring citizenship on all Spanish subjects, including Indians (but excluding Africans and those considered dependent, such as women, domestic servants, debtors, and criminals). Dominated by young liberals, the Cortes also passed a number of laws that would reverberate in the colonies, even if they did not go into effect right away, including the abolition of Indian tribute, the establishment of popularly elected town councils, and the secularization of the California missions. Fernando VII annulled the constitution on his return in 1814, but in early 1820 liberal officers in Spain staged a revolt and forced the king to restore it.

In October 1820, de la Guerra joined the governor and local friars in the presidio chapel, where, out of respect for the king's acquiescence, they all grudgingly took their own oaths of allegiance to this constitution.[157] These men would have preferred to reject the Spanish liberals but knew they had few allies. "If we follow the King in the *old* laws," reasoned Father Luis Martínez, "we have no hope of help, . . . it seems to me that the best thing to do is to be neutral."[158] As late as January 1821, Californians still held out hope that revolutionary changes might end with the new constitution; news from loyalist friends in Mexico certainly suggested this possibility. One high-ranking military bureaucrat wrote to de la Guerra that things remained calm, "in spite of some spirit that always exists, aspiring for revolution and independence, but they are pieces of furniture that attract little attention."[159]

Less than a month later, in the heart of Mexico, Agustín de Iturbide issued the Plan de Iguala, declaring Mexico independent. Unlike Hidalgo, Iturbide was conservative, a landowner and creole officer who had served in the royalist armies. His Plan of February 24, 1821, gave citizenship to people of Indian and African ancestry but preserved the privileges and property of the Church, the military, and the oligarchy. Hoping to gather the support of royalists, Iturbide also called for independent Mexico to continue as a constitutional monarchy. Mexican elites found much to like in this conservative independence, but up in California Father Martínez still worried that taking sides might draw another attack: "If we follow Iturbide with his ideas (which seem favorable) we must remember that help is some distance off. If the insurgents come here and encounter resistance in the province they will destroy it."[160] Governor Solá was less enthusiastic, ridiculing Iturbide's "absurd views" and calling independence "a dream."[161]

Mexico's provisional government was under little illusion that it would be easy to pull every province into the national project, and it sent explicit instructions detailing how to stage spectacular celebrations on the occasion of their leader's triumphant arrival in Mexico City in September 1821.[162] Governor Solá received two sets of the instructions, but did not in fact officially announce Mexico's Independence there until March of the next year. At the governor's house, José de la Guerra met with Solá, representatives of the other five presidios of Alta and Baja California, and Father Mariano Payeras, representing the missions. On April 9, this junta swore their allegiance to the regency, then regrouped in the plaza on April 11 and publicly administered the required oath of loyalty to the troops and a crowd of townsfolk. Father Payeras led prayers, and the soldiers fired their guns into the air, shouting, "Viva!" to the new republic. Music and fireworks rounded out the day.[163] With this act, California became the last province to acknowledge Independence.

Still unsure of California's loyalty, Iturbide sent a representative from the capital, Canónigo Agustín Fernández de San Vicente of Durango. On his arrival in September 1822, the canónigo found no evidence of open rebellion, but neither did he find much enthusiasm. On his orders, the Spanish flag was lowered for the last time over the presidios, to be followed by, "feasts . . . salvos, processions, mock battles, and an oath to support independence, parties, dances, bullfights, and other activities that lasted for three days or more."[164] Despite the festivities, Californians felt mixed emotions at these events. When the Spanish flag dropped in Monterey to grim silence, Governor Solá was forced to explain, "They do not cheer, because they are unused to independence."[165] María Inocenta Pico was struck by "the tremendous emotion expressed by the Spaniards, especially the missionary Fathers, because of that event.[166] José María Amador recalled that the priests refused to participate in the ceremonies, "believing that they would be violating the rights of the Spanish King."[167] José de la Guerra found an excuse not to be present at all for the change of flags in Santa Bárbara, traveling up to "some rancho," according to his daughter.[168]

Raymundo Carrillo rose from humble origins to command as a captain in California. José de la Guerra was a peninsular Spaniard who took advantage of openings in the bureaucracies of the Bourbon Reforms to move in and take plum colonial jobs. Together, their families would help create a new society on the northern frontier of the Spanish Empire, and then the Mexican nation. By 1822, California's elites drew their wealth from mission production, Indian labor, and international trade. These powerful families had crafted an elite network from the officer class of the military, and held their position through successful accumulation of wealth through trade. Binding them together were a shared identity as Spaniards and gente de razón, and a patriarchal kinship system that underlay every political and economic relationship.

In 1822, Mexico stood on the verge of a new society in which liberal reformers imagined a nation of independent citizens and private entrepreneurs, free of fixed colonial categories and equal before the state. Although revolutionary ideas unleashed in 1810 and 1812 did not overturn the social order of Mexico's periphery overnight, they would reverberate in Alta California for the next thirty-five years. But even after the missionaries, soldiers, and government officials swore their loyalty to the republic, the old social order lingered. Patriarchy would blunt the upheavals promised by liberal reform and continue to structure the social, economic, and political orders of Mexican California.

CHAPTER TWO

PADRE DE LA PATRIA, PADRE DE FAMILIAS[1]

> Prostrating ourselves at Your Mercy's feet with the most
> profound respect and submission . . . we turn to you as
> loving father to give us the best consolation.[2]
> —*Luisa Varelas, Demetria Ramírez, Juana Inocencia*
> *Reyes, María Luisa Reyes, and Valeriana Lorenzana to*
> *José de la Guerra, Los Angeles, February 1, 1822*

> With regard to her father, Señor Captain de la Guerra y
> Noriega, . . . this great man who knew how to earn the
> glorious title of "Father of the Pueblo" . . . his many
> virtues are still fresh in the memory of the grateful
> Barbareños.[3]
> —*Teresa de la Guerra, "Narrative of the Distinguished*
> *California Matron," 1875*

From the overwhelming praise and respectful appeals that survive, it would be easy to present José de la Guerra as the ideal patriarch of the Spanish colonial and Mexican eras—benevolent, wise, and powerful. As the wealthiest man in the Santa Bárbara region and the commander of a presidio where half the local Hispanic population resided, he extended his authority over the women and children in his household, a large retinue of servants and laborers, and current and former soldiers, pobladores, and elite dependents. Along with the missionaries, he could even claim some authority over the thousands of Indians who lived in the coastal zone of southern California. In the words of de la Guerra's dependents and in the memories of the elite, such men enjoyed unquestioned authority as husbands and fathers. Wives kept to the house, children did as they were told, and poor folk offered grateful loyalty to their benefactor and protector.[4] In truth, however, the power of California's patriarchs was never so one sided, or so secure.

As noted in the first chapter, patriarchy—the submission of women to men, and of children to their father—formed the underlying logic of the hierarchical colonial social order. The relationship of the king to his subjects was compared to that of a benevolent father to his children. But the patriarchal family was not just a metaphor of power. Actual fathers were considered critical components of the corporate state—governed by the king, and in turn governing their own wives and children as the king's representative. Fathers and households, real and imagined, played a critical role in how Californians understood legitimate authority within their entire community.[5]

For men like de la Guerra—presidial commander, wealthy merchant, husband, and father—patriarchy was a given, part of the natural order of things. As a man of the elites, he expected to command and dominate others, especially the children, Indians, soldiers, and household dependents who fell within the bounds of his authority. It would be wrong, however, to describe patriarchy outside of the human relationships that sustained it. It was not something imposed from without, but a set of relationships and assumptions under continual negotiation. De la Guerra's authority carried with it an understanding that honorable men owed obedience to their superiors, respected their equals, and fulfilled their obligations to their dependents. This cluster of sometimes-conflicting ideas provided elite men the language to express and resolve their conflicts, and dependents the voice and authority to make claims upon patriarchs. As we will see in succeeding chapters, as California experienced the transition from royal colony to republican territory, and as Californians debated the meanings of liberty and egalitarianism, patriarchs like de la Guerra shifted strategies, all the while keeping the patriarchal family a vital foundation of the social order and of their own authority within it. Among the men of his generation, de la Guerra was remarkably successful through the first half of the nineteenth century in positioning himself at the head of Santa Bárbara's social hierarchy as a "benevolent" patriarch. This chapter explores how he was initially able to do this, how the work of his wife and other dependents supported his position, and the ways in which he and the rest of the community understood and shaped his role.

Command: Indian Bodies

The very nature of the colonial enterprise made one attribute of the honorable man, dominance through strength of will, available to every man in the military and mission system. In the early years, such men, even soldiers from the humblest origins, could point to their race, their religion, and their culture as signs that they were gente de razón—people of reason—who enjoyed natural superiority to Indians. This distinction was especially acute on the frontier, where the term "Mecos" was sometimes employed to further distinguish the "wild" Indians of the north from the "civilized" Indians of the Central Valley of Mexico.[6] Soldiers and missionaries demonstrated their dominance through physical control of their Indian subjects: their labor, their sexuality, even their movement across the land. Californio men understood this mastery to be the kind of control that a father would naturally exercise over his children.[7] Many Indian peoples simply refused to recognize this authority, but some, in turn, learned how to manipulate Spanish cultural expectations of proper paternal behavior for their own benefit.

Missionaries justified their authority over Indian movement and labor by using an explicitly paternal metaphor. "Just as a father of a family has charge of his house and of the education and correction of his children, the management, control, and education of the baptized Indians pertains exclusively to the missionary fathers," agreed the viceroy in 1773.[8] From the very start of his career, de la Guerra worked hand in hand with missionaries to subdue and control California's Native population, and in so doing collaborated in the cultural project of making California's Indians "children," subject to their colonial "fathers." On arrival, this military officer was careful to signal his willingness to cooperate fully with the mission program, becoming a lay brother in the Franciscan religious community of the Apostolic College of San Fernando—the home institution for California's missions—on July 6, 1803. Father Guardian Josef Gasol welcomed him as a "brother" and "participant in all our prayers, fasts, disciplines, spiritual exercises, . . . as much in the reduction of the infidels and the catechizing of the neophytes, as in the reform of the Faithful."[9] Just over a year later, de la Guerra further demonstrated his piety in Monterey by becoming a member of the Franciscan confraternity calling itself "the Slaves of the Holy Virgin Mary."[10] Submission and service to one's superiors in the colonial social order brought honor to men.

Often, de la Guerra's gray-robed "brothers" called on him to bring back those neofitos, or baptized Indians, who ran away. While comparatively few Indians fled the missions, some did leave to collect traditional foods, visit their home villages, or find informal work or trade in Spanish settlements. Franciscans feared that their flight could set a bad example if left unpunished, so they requested help from the military. De la Guerra's encounter with Guchapa, an Indian leader of several *rancherías,* or Indian settlements, near Mission San Miguel, is typical. In January 1804, Father Juan Martín went out to convert these Indians and convince any runaways among them to return, but Guchapa refused to allow anyone from his jurisdiction to leave for the mission, threatening the priest with physical harm, should he return. De la Guerra was summoned, and thirteen of his soldiers left promptly to arrest Guchapa, his son, and two runaway neophytes. De la Guerra offered Guchapa beads in return for the runaways but also held on to the Indian leader's son as security. With this show of both generosity and control over another man's dependents, de la Guerra proved that he was a powerful man. Guchapa had little choice but to return all of the fugitive neophytes.[11]

Over the years, de la Guerra was pressed into service several more times to explore the interior of the province and search there for the hiding places of runaways.[12] This he did on the orders of the governors, but with the aid of missionaries from San Miguel, La Purísima Concepción, San Fernando, and Santa Bárbara, who sent their neophytes as interpreters and guides and often went out themselves. Still, this collaboration between "brothers" was not without conflict. In 1816, Father Pedro Muñóz, a veteran of these expeditions, became exasperated and wrote to de la Guerra, "I know that things did not go very well with the campaign . . . Since the troops left four more have run away. So, for God's sake, do not neglect [the runaway Indians] to the point that they all go back to congregate together, unless they have learned their lesson."[13] Generally, de la Guerra's operations met with some success, but the swamps and brush of the central valley remained a safe haven for runaways, and finding the fugitives was a chronic problem. As motivation for one more expedition, Father Luis Martínez tried to shame the captain by suggesting that he was neglecting this duty, and threatened to unmask de la Guerra's front of valor and manly vigor. "You are too much taken up with others," he complained, "and it is necessary for you to be pulled away from your checkerboard . . . P.S. If you don't try to go out and retake the runaways I will write to my friend that you have fooled him and there are many here who will not vacillate and who are not fooled."[14]

De la Guerra, in turn, used the language of masculine honor to call the paternal authority of priests into question. This was never clearer than in February 1824, when the Indians of the Santa Ynez, La Purísima, and Santa Bárbara missions staged a full-scale revolt. Angustias de la Guerra, a girl of eight at the time, no doubt picked up the language of her father when she retold the story fifty years later. One evening, she remembered, after de la Guerra had sent troops to put down the uprising at Santa Ynez and La Purísima, Father Ripoll of Mission Santa Bárbara went to the de la Guerra home to say Mass with the family. "The padre was very sad, and my father asked him what was the matter," she recalled. After some hesitation, the friar at last admitted that the Indians at Santa Bárbara had risen, too. De la Guerra immediately ordered his troops to attack and prevented Ripoll from warning the Indians. "Padre Ripoll stood up," she said, "crying like a woman, and said, 'My God! Do not kill my children.'"[15] "Padre Ripoll loved his neophytes like a loving mother," she explained.[16] In other words, because he had lost command over his "children," Father Ripoll could no longer claim the title of "father." Instead, in the mind of de la Guerra, Ripoll took on the attributes of a woman: concerned with his offspring but emotional and irrational, incapable of discipline.

Runaways, rebels, and other "disobedient" Indians faced corporal punishment, and like a strict father, de la Guerra frequently was the one to mete it out. Generally, it was the missionaries' job to discipline Indians who did not follow their rules, but friars called in the military for repeat offenses and more serious crimes such as theft and murder. One of de la Guerra's cousins, José del Carmen Lugo, captured the cultural understanding underlying this relationship when he commented, "The minor faults which the Indians committed, the kind that would come into the category of faults that the father of a family would punish, these the *padres* were permitted to correct themselves, always knowing that they could call for aid from the soldiers if necessary."[17] For crimes that fell under the jurisdiction of the Spanish judicial system, the cases went to the only courts available: those held under military law. In such cases, presidial commanders such as de la Guerra took over.[18] In the case of the 1824 uprising, for example, Governor Argüello instructed de la Guerra to "act immediately" to find the organizers, noting "the usefulness of quick punishment in these cases as a warning to the rest." In a later message, he stressed the need for public order: "Work judiciously, such that all the republic is satisfied that it was done according to the Law and Justice, and that each one was given a reward or punishment according to what they deserved."[19]

Missionaries in such cases lost direct control over their "children" but could petition the military courts for punishment or clemency. In so doing, they often rhetorically transformed the accused Indians into disobedient children. When several Indians were caught stealing horses at the Mission Santa Ynez in the fall of 1816, for example, Father Francisco

Xavier Uría delivered them to de la Guerra, calling the adult men "boys," and asking him "to punish them well with leather and send them back to me."[20] Valerio, a neophyte from La Purísima, on the other hand, placed himself in this dependent position that same year, in order to appeal to his mission fathers for leniency. Valerio had run away repeatedly, and perhaps fearing capture and the fate that awaited those caught for such offenses, he returned to the mission and presented himself as a penitent son. Touched by this appeal, Father Antonio Ripoll and Father Mariano Payeras both urged de la Guerra to show mercy. "Valerio put himself in my arms, as the prodigal son in those of his Father; I cannot reject him . . . So, my Señor Comandante, and my Don José," Payeras wrote, "when you find Valerio in your power . . . do not look upon him as a malefactor that force and violence has placed in your hands, but as the Prodigal Son whom his own father, by his own hands, has delivered to you."[21] Valerio understood, perhaps, that in the Hispanic social order the ability to protect dependents from domination by others was also considered an attribute of men and fathers. Thus, conceding his subordinate status, he used the language and expectations of patriarchy to avoid the harshest physical punishment.

De la Guerra himself on occasion took up the role of defender and petitioner when accused thieves and murderers went to trial. Such was the case in 1808, when San Diego neophytes Fermín, Francisco, and Fernando brutally murdered Mayordomo Pedro Miguel Alvarez. De la Guerra was appointed the accused men's *defensor*, or defender, and wrote his plea to Governor José Joaquín de Arrillaga. In it, he noted the severity of the provocation: the "severe punishment" Alvarez had given them, the "slavery" he had kept them in, and the "common knowledge" that Alvarez had had repeated sexual encounters with Fermín's wife, María Cecilia, and had intended to do the same with the wives of the other two. But de la Guerra, calling the accused his "godsons," also reconfigured these husbands and workers into simpleminded boys who deserved mercy because they understood so little of what they had done. The courts apparently agreed, sentencing the men to ten years of labor at the San Diego presidio.[22]

In fact, a term of labor at the presidio was the most frequent punishment for Indians considered rebellious or delinquent; it gave commanders like de la Guerra the opportunity to control not just their movement but also their labor.[23] Some of the impressed laborers were neophytes convicted of crimes at the mission, and others were gentiles, or unconverted Indians, captured in military expeditions against those who had raided livestock or Spanish settlements. In 1821, for example, Governor Solá informed de la Guerra that several Indian prisoners would be arriving soon in Santa Bárbara, "leaving the five with you for the work of that Presidio . . . So that they are useful for work, I order you to have [them] in shackles, and also with the trustworthy soldier or soldiers who guard them."[24] When an Indian was convicted in 1818 of accidentally setting fire to the hills while roasting mescal, Father Uría sent him as a "favor" to the captain. "The Indian is good," Uría told the commander, "only a big liar, but a good worker and a mason; he will be all right for you."[25] For these Indian men, impressment for public works was punishment for their crimes; naturally they received no pay.

De la Guerra often used his authority to demand convict and contract Indian labor, not only for the presidio but also for personal service: to cook, perhaps, or garden, or carry wood. De la Guerra even had some say over whether his officers and soldiers might be granted this same privilege, to have neophytes as their own domestic servants. Father Sánchez assented to such an arrangement in 1815, noting, "If you have at your Presidio two Indians, why don't you keep Hermenegildo, and then Tamariz will be for [Alférez José] Maitorena."[27] In 1819, Father Uría told de la Guerra, "I am sending you ten Mecos" from Mission Santa Ynez, presumably so that the commander could distribute them as he saw fit. "I have told them not to get any rations," he added, "supposing that whoever employs them will give them food . . . The Mecos will be changed every six weeks."[28] In the same letter, Uría even tried to tempt de la Guerra to accept a particular Indian who had special skills suitable for domestic service: "Tell [your wife] María Antonia that among them there goes a musician who is a good chocolate maker named Constantino."[29]

Townsfolk and soldiers readily came to depend on this cheap labor, both convict and contract, not only as an escape from physical toil but also as an expression of cultural difference between laboring Indians and leisured gente de razón. As Steven Hackel has shown, California's soldiers developed an attitude about manual labor that paralleled their striving for upward mobility. Elsewhere in the Spanish colonies, their status as poor, mixed-race people would have marked them as just the class of soldiers who would be expected to engage in the hard work of constructing presidial structures, and the presidial regulation of 1772 explicitly assigned them this role. Yet most of them saw service in the frontier military as a way to transcend their humble origins. Manual labor was beneath them now, and they complained, refused to do the work assigned, and in some cases deserted.[30] Officers like de la Guerra, then, found ways to transfer hard labor to the backs of California's Indians, whom the colonizers agreed were socially, culturally, and racially inferior. In arranging for such labor, de la Guerra upheld gente de razón mastery and made this marker of status available to all, including ordinary soldiers. As Father José Francisco Señán observed in 1800, "It is common that the soldiers, and their wives, when they take Indians [as laborers], begin to act like nobles [*Damas y Caballeros*]."[31]

As the war dragged on, and California received no more salaries from the military with which to pay for contract labor, de la Guerra was forced to come up with other tactics for finding workers. In some cases, he turned to individual gentile Indian laborers, or the labor of those who had washed up on California's shores as a result of the rampant, and illegal, otter fur trade.[32] In 1816, a year after receiving Tamariz from Mission San Diego, Alférez Maitorena asked the governor for more servants, and Solá agreed that he might use one of the Kodiak Indians, captured from Russian otter hunters. "You can grant this to him," Solá informed de la Guerra, "as soon as he asks for it."[33] De la Guerra also occasionally negotiated free labor from the missions, invoking the missionaries' supposed paternal obligations, not just to the neophytes, but also to the soldiers engaged in guarding them. In 1818, for example, de la Guerra asked Father Payeras to send him Indians from Mission La Purísima to aid in building new houses for the Santa Bárbara soldiers. "I concede from the present moment that those Indians of La Purísima are at your disposal; [you], as organ of the voice of the greater government of the Province, will know how to employ them," Payeras granted. "In this case, as in whatever other in which a Father ought to give opportune help to his sons, you can count on my consent without consulting me."[34]

Payeras's slightly officious tone suggests that the command of Indian labor could become a point of contention with the missionaries, who either needed the workers themselves or distrusted the influences of the enlisted soldiers. When Father Uría sent his horse thieves for a whipping in 1816, for example, he specifically asked de la Guerra not to detain them at the presidio, "so that they won't get worse."[35] In 1819, Father Marcos Victoria of Mission San Fernando begged de la Guerra to return some of his neophytes so that he could hold a rodeo and repair the Indians' houses. "The roof is almost falling in," he complained, "with only the mercy of God holding it up . . . This Mission demonstrates to you the great need it has for people, since the greater part of them [here] are old and sick."[36] That same year, the disgruntled Father Payeras had had enough. Just a year after sending work crews to build houses for Santa Bárbara's soldiers, Payeras wrote to his superiors, explicitly accusing de la Guerra of oppressing "the poor Indians" by requiring them "to be useful both inside and outside the missions to those de razón," and taking "all the neophytes as far as possible from the jurisdiction of the missionary so that consequently those de razón will be masters of their will, labor, and sweat."[37] Likewise, elite men who contracted this labor did not always believe the missionaries had the best interests of the neophytes at heart. As José del Carmen Lugo noted, Indians under contract "were not paid for the work they did, but the padre received it for the benefit of the community, as he said; but we did not know what part of these receipts reached the community."[38] Many of these elite men convinced themselves that they, in fact, could protect and care for their Indian workers better than the missionaries could.

In a sense, then, an Indian man who left the missions to work under de la Guerra had two patriarchs, and some Indians learned to exploit this overlapping authority and the contention it could provoke. This seems to be the case with Sebastián, a neophyte from San Buenaventura, south of Santa Bárbara, who ran away from the mission in the summer of 1816 and sought refuge as a domestic servant. Father Señán told de la Guerra to be on the lookout and gave him instructions to allow the fugitive to stay at the commander's house. "For some days," he wrote,

> we have been missing the little Indian Sebastián . . . so it always happens when one removes them from the shackles or stocks. Hopefully, the calling to stay in your house might be true, and he might live peacefully, and quietly; and on our part there is no impediment [to that] . . . If he goes on being wicked on all sides, and giving his opinion, send him here.[39]

Sebastián, it seems, succeeded in escaping mission discipline without disrupting the social order by moving from the mission to the household of another patriarchal authority.

Indian men, pressed into hard labor constructing adobe houses or performing domestic chores, had much to complain about. But Indian women faced an even more brutal form of physical control; many soldiers considered them outside civilized society and therefore legitimate objects of sexual dominance. A man's honor derived in part from the power to dishonor other men's women and the ability to protect his own dependent women from shame, and thus to keep them sexually modest and chaste. A woman's honor, by contrast, was considered passive. Depending on her station in life and the circumstances of her birth, a woman was born with a certain store of honor; she could not actively earn it through honorable deeds, but by her actions could preserve or even restore it by consenting to enclosure and protection by men. The exercise of sexual dominance over Indian women thus became an issue between soldiers, who considered them born without honor, and missionaries, who attempted to instill Hispanic notions of sexual shame among the neophytes.[40]

Missionaries attempted to control the sexuality of neophyte girls by cloistering them in locked dormitories, or *monjeríos*, thereby maintaining their chastity in the model of properly shameful Spanish women. Despite this surveillance, sexual encounters at the mission between soldiers and Indian women, forced or otherwise, were not uncommon. There is no evidence one way or the other that de la Guerra himself exercised sexual dominance over Indian women, but judging by the complaints of missionaries, his soldiers at the mission guardhouse, or *escolta*, clearly did. As their commander, de la Guerra was held responsible: his position was to exercise the "virtuous" and protective side of sexual control by containing the aggression of his soldiers. Father Payeras of Mission La Purísima appealed to de la Guerra's power over his soldiers when he complained in 1816, "By the proper government of your predecessors this escolta was maintained with the honor that corresponds to it. Now you maintain it with single men, who, experiencing heterogeneous necessities, look for a way to remedy them."[41]

By the end of the colonial era and into the Mexican period, de la Guerra enjoyed a physical dominance over Indians, asserted as the prerogative of powerful men. Despite the missionaries' exclusive claim to ruling California's Indians as their children, de la Guerra's role gave him great control over the movement, labor, and to some extent, the sexuality of the Native population. But, as Father Payeras, Valerio, and Sebastián reminded de la Guerra, legitimate patriarchal authority rested on more than sheer physical force and the power to dominate others. Men who commanded by fear alone were little more than brutes themselves; true masculine virtue also derived from submission to one's masters, respect for one's equals, and, especially, the protection of one's dependents. Commanding work, deference—even fear—were all critical elements in patriarchal authority, but so was maintaining the perception that subordinates gave their labor and respect freely.

Obligation: Servants, Soldiers, and Pobladores

On his return from San Blas in 1811, de la Guerra told his friends in California the following amazing tale. Insurgents had captured him at San Blas, he said, then marched him to Ixtlán, where the revolutionaries put him and his brother-in-law in shackles and threw them into prison at the fort with four hundred other Spaniards. There, they awaited death. On the day scheduled for their execution, José Antonio Carrillo went to the window to have a last look at the people of Ixtlán, strolling up and down the street. Suddenly, Carrillo cried out, "Look, Don José, there goes your servant Puchinela dressed up as a captain of the insurgents!"[42]

Sure enough, there he was. De la Guerra shouted down to him, "Puchinela, Puchinela!" "Who dares to recall the past to me?" shouted back the former servant.[43] For, de la Guerra explained later to his friends, this man had joined the rebels under the name "Captain de la Guerra." Granted, servants in one's home customarily took the name of the family they served, but this was too much. This man was actually passing himself off as a member of the distinguished de la Guerra family! Hearing the voice of his former master, Puchinela was filled with shame and ordered his troops to halt.

Entering the jail cell of the true de la Guerra, Puchinela removed his hat and saluted the two Spaniards with respect. On learning of their intended fate, he exclaimed that he would order their release instantly. He knew them to be good men and good masters who had treated their servants very well, especially the *chinos*—those of mixed African and Indian ancestry.[44] Rebel Sergeant Ramón Iriarte then arrived and questioned the release: wasn't de la Guerra born in Spain, and didn't he support the Crown? But Puchinela stood up for his old master, and another Californian passing by—Juana Alvarado, a strong supporter of the insurgent cause—attested to the California birth of Carrillo. With this force against him, Iriarte yielded and freed his captives. And so, de la Guerra concluded, he owed his life to the loyalty of his old servant.[45]

There is no way of knowing how much of this story is true, but in a way it does not really matter. In de la Guerra's own mind, this story demonstrated that he had been a good master to his servants. He had not only the power to make them work for him but also the ability to instill loyalty: such loyalty that they would risk opposing revolutionaries to save their master's life. Puchinela, probably a chino himself, was obviously de la Guerra's inferior by birth. When de la Guerra confronted the servant with his social climbing, and thus his clear challenge to natural hierarchies, Puchinela immediately recognized the proper order of things and gave de la Guerra the respect due him. This story gave listeners a lesson about the way the world ought to work: de la Guerra had fulfilled his obligations as master and received faithful service and loyalty as his reward.

Whereas the honor that came from physical domination derived in part from simply being a man, and in part from status as a military commander, wealth was the critical factor that made it possible for de la Guerra to emulate the second element of an ideal patriarch: to take on the responsibilities that came with being the father of a family. The mere fact of having a wife and children gave him the status of an adult man of responsibility and honor. De la Guerra's wealth gave him an increased social standing. The two, combined and used properly, made him worthy of a position as "the father of all in that place"—the father of his household, the presidio, and the pueblo.[46] As he provided for his family, so did he take care of the material needs of his servants, godchildren, and other dependents. As he sheltered his wife and daughters from shame, so did he protect the virtue of other women. As he tended the morality, education, and health of his family, so did he ensure the development of others under his wing. And as he made the rules and settled quarrels in his house, so was he called on to arbitrate local disputes.

Household

When de la Guerra returned from Mexico in 1811, he knew that going back to Mexico City would be impossible, and he began in earnest to acquire the wealth he needed to support not only his own growing family but also a large retinue of domestic workers. "Do not put your cares on me," scolded Father Payeras in 1816, "because you have many servants and I have none."[47] Over the years, as de la Guerra took in more servants, as his wife gave him more children, and as he bought more crates, barrels, and boxes of private goods, the officers' quarters at the Santa Bárbara presidio began to seem cramped. In 1818 de la Guerra ordered construction of a fine new house not far away. This one-story, U-shaped adobe had

Exterior of Casa de la Guerra, ca. 1860–80. Santa Barbara Historical Museum.

one wing for housing merchandise, a central section with large public dining and entertaining rooms and a corner office, and one wing of connecting bedrooms. All of its windows looked out on the central courtyard;
from a bench in the center of the veranda, de la Guerra could look down
a gentle slope to the harbor and watch for ships, loaded with his merchandise, to drop anchor.[48] All around him, his large staff of servants followed orders and kept the household humming. In a town where every
other family made do with one or two cramped rooms, the de la Guerra
house stood out: large, secure, and impressive.

This extensive home did not just convey status; it sustained honor.
As noted above, in a society that assumed female moral fragility, a man's
honor depended in part on his ability to protect the women of his household from any hint of sexual dishonor. De la Guerra expressed mastery of
his household both in the structure of the large house he was building
and in his oversight of the movements and behavior of his wife and
daughters. The door of the house did not sharply separate public from
private space. Instead, the layout enabled a gradual and blurred transition
from the most public spaces, the courtyard and store, through the semi-
public patio, dining room, and sala, on through interior doors to the most
private spaces of de la Guerra's personal office and family bedrooms.
Windows and doors faced only the courtyard, so that de la Guerra could
more easily protect and shelter those who were virtuous but weak: the
women of his house. A flower garden at the back of the house, enclosed
by a high adobe wall, was known as "Doña María Antonia's Garden."[49]
When his wife and daughters left the security of the building, they always
had a servant to accompany them. Just as wealth made it easier for a man
like de la Guerra to demonstrate his own honor, so was it easier for his wife
and daughters to maintain their good reputations as women sheltered

from the offenses of the world. This was particularly important in Mexican frontier regions, where more primitive conditions made it especially difficult for aspiring elites to secure privileged space away from public scrutiny.[50]

At the same time that the de la Guerra household presented a public face of family honor, de la Guerra continued to strive for the ideals expressed by the story of Puchinela. He was a wealthy, powerful man who could command labor, but his relationship to his servants went beyond that of simple force: de la Guerra considered himself the father of his workers. In private, he used subtle (and sometimes overt) coercion to obtain labor. But publicly, he sought to project the image of a man who inspired loyalty and obedience among his servants through fulfillment of his obligations to them. Some domestic workers rejected this permanent state of minority, but many more appealed to that image to claim rights as dependents.

De la Guerra's wife, María Antonia, played a large supporting role in the household, but it is difficult from the records to determine the exact scope of that labor. A few isolated hints, however, offer clues about the way women's input contributed to the public image of a well-ordered house. It is likely that María Antonia modeled her role on a sixteenth-century volume that sat on the family's bookshelf, one that her husband had ordered from Mexico in 1815.[51] *La Perfecta Casada*, or *The Perfect Wife*, by Father Luis de León, was written to León's niece María Varela Osorio on the occasion of her wedding. In it, the author lays out the Catholic ideal of a woman's role in the family, ascribing to her not just motherhood but also an active responsibility for household management. The perfect wife, he argued, oversees the work of servants and dependents and keeps the household supplied with meals, clothing, and linen.

Memoirs collected in the 1870s offer another clue. Most Californio elite men remembered that part of their mastery extended to instructing the women of their families to manage the domestic economy. Salvador Vallejo, for example, claimed that "we taught our girls to be good housewives in every branch of the business; our wives and daughters superintended the cooking and every other operation performed in the house."[52] But women themselves remembered things a little differently. Rather than assigning instruction in management to the men of the household, elite women asserted their own independent and responsible role.[53]

Few spoke of actual labor. As for elite men, the ability to refrain from manual labor served as a marker of status for elite women. While poorer women who lived in town or on small ranches often did agricultural work, tended livestock, and processed goods like candles, soap, and clothing, elite women like María Antonia generally did not appear in public working in the fields or roping cattle, and within the home would have assigned domestic labor to as many servants as the budget would allow. In correspondence, de la Guerra and his male associates wrote of the hiring and oversight of servants as almost exclusively his prerogative, but they did occasionally acknowledge her role in managing servants' work and movement once they entered the house. Father Uría, for example, spoke to her authority to choose workers and assign tasks when he offered de la Guerra ten "Mecos" in 1819 and asked the captain to tell his wife about one who was an especially good chocolate maker.[54] Although María Antonia probably also contributed her own labor, this activity is largely absent from the historical record.

It is safe to say that Indians did the vast majority of domestic labor for the gente de razón of Santa Bárbara. For large projects at the presidio or in town, the missions supplied contract or convict workers, and individual soldiers might likewise have paid the missions occasionally for one or two day laborers.[55] But off the books, an underground economy in labor flourished. Casual laborers, mostly Chumash, came either on their own initiative from the mission or from the dwindling population of unconverted, independent Indians.[56] These individuals worked in settlers' homes and fields in exchange for trade goods such as cloth, knives, and beads or for food such as corn or beans. As disease, warfare, and other pressures of colonization broke apart Native villages and families, the gente de razón increasingly had the upper hand in negotiating such terms of labor.[57] Adding to this largely Native workforce, de la Guerra occasionally hired potentially disruptive outsiders, like convicts or sailors who had jumped ship. Ysidro Molina, for example, was captured at Monterey during Bouchard's attack in 1818 and ransomed by de la Guerra in Santa Bárbara. After serving six years in a chain gang for drunkenness, Molina went to work for de la Guerra as a servant "and died in that role," according to de la Guerra's daughter Angustias.[58]

The de la Guerras employed laborers for a wide range of tasks: tending cattle, planting and harvesting grapes and fruit trees, making soap, threshing wheat, and hauling wood; and within the household, cooking, cleaning, and serving. Cousin Salvador Vallejo captured a common Californio attitude when he recalled many years later that the workers who did such labor, "our friendly Indians . . . [were] considered members of our families."[59] De la Guerra and his wife symbolically transformed their workers into obedient children in several ways. An American trader observed that, as a master, de la Guerra showed an "almost universal distrust in the faithfulness of his menials."[60] Indeed, the relationship of servant to master required a constant reinforcement of control, and de la Guerra was known for achieving discipline through sharp words and perpetual surveillance.

But the family also employed more subtle means of refashioning adult men and women into their "children" and of weakening the workers' connections to their biological families and cultures. De la Guerra's ability to enforce Spanish gender roles, for example, no doubt contributed to his servants' sense of dependency and cultural disruption. When dining at the de la Guerra home in 1841, American ship captain William Dane Phelps noted that the "table [was] waited upon by Indian men servants," while "an Indian girl [was] appointed to the care of each" child.[61] Men, in general, were assigned heavy construction work and outdoor labor, while women did domestic tasks such as cooking and laundry. De la Guerra also reinforced his paternal authority by restricting the movement and clothing of his workers. For example, the Indian girls observed by Phelps were required to sit with the de la Guerra children on mats on the floor.[62] De la Guerra provided imported clothing for his staff, but it was not the same rich fabrics he bought to clothe his own family. Instead, servants wore *manta*, or cheap cotton, and ready-made garments, a sign that they were working people with neither the time nor resources to care for silk and velvet.[63] Those who waited table, remarked Captain Phelps, "have no other *livery but* a cotton shirt and the extremity of which in some cases appear to have been 'curtailed of their fair proportions' to repair breaches elsewhere . . . The scantiness of their clothing," he added, "would doubtless be considered against the notions of propriety entertained at home."[64] Finally, the de la Guerras even took the liberty of renaming their dependent laborers, referring to them by nicknames, like "La Zorilla" (The Fox), "La Bonita" (The Pretty One), "La Fierusca" (The Fierce One), and "La Pelona" (The Bald One).[65] These pet names were similar to the ones family members invented for one another, and the practice served to integrate the servants into the extended "family." But by renaming their servants, the de la Guerras also erased their former identities as members of other families and communities.

All of these examples show how a powerful master might reinforce a sense of dependency among his domestic workers. But de la Guerra did not simply control his servants with force and surveillance. He also hoped to inspire loyalty by offering them the protection and care of a father—

providing food, shelter, clothing, and, in the case of neophytes, relief from mission work. At a time when the resource base of Native peoples had collapsed, such goods could be essential for survival. Each week, for example, he distributed soap; on occasion he handed out "clothing, blankets, sugar, lard, and other essentials."[66] In at least one case, de la Guerra seems to have arranged a servant's marriage: "I am very glad you engaged in marrying off Luis," wrote Santiago Argüello in 1819, "as I think it suits him."[67] As this example suggests, the relationship of master to servant was often intensely personal, and de la Guerra frequently took on the role of mentor and spiritual authority to his workers, both Indian and non-Indian. In some cases, de la Guerra and his wife formalized this relationship by adding the role of godparent to that of master, further increasing their responsibility for the material and spiritual welfare of their charges. In the case of the Indian sent to work for setting a fire while roasting mescal, for example, Father Uría encouraged de la Guerra, "If you want to act as his Padrino and bring him to your house after his public work it would be more agreeable to me."[68] In 1814, de la Guerra was so pleased with the work of a mission Indian named Simón that he asked the head of the missions whether his servant could stay. "If the Indian Simón is willing to remain to serve you," Father Juan Sainz de Lucio wrote back from San Francisco, "we the Father Ministers grant your request, according to the style of the land, and clear our consciences, as long as you take care of said Indian that he may say his prayers and lead a Christian life."[69]

Despite such fatherly attention, some Indian men asserted their right to live with their own families, to come and go as they pleased, and to own their own property: these were the rights of adult men. Vicente Juan, a neophyte of Mission Soledad and a de la Guerra servant, arrived at the Mission La Purísima in 1816, riding a new red horse and declaring his intention, on account of his rheumatism, to leave de la Guerra's employ and live with his family. Father Payeras could not bring himself to believe that an Indian could afford to buy his own horse, as Juan claimed he had done, nor that de la Guerra had permitted such independence. Spaniards thought of horseback riding as the preserve of elite men, and they feared the military advantage it gave Indian peoples. As a result, officials restricted the use of horses by Indians at the missions, and punished soldiers who employed gentiles on horseback.[70] "I have made [Juan] some pressing arguments to return [to you]," explained Payeras to the captain, "and he replied to me that he couldn't, that he is going to his people who have called for him. I hope then that you will instruct me in the matter; and if it is not inconvenient, and the horse is really his, I will dispatch him on it with the Corporal, Antonio Castro."[71] In 1834, an Indian man named Guillermo asserted a similar right to freedom of movement and employment when he left de la Guerra and requested employment from Governor José Figueroa. Figueroa considered hiring the cook, but like Father Payeras, would not take the Indian's word that de la Guerra did not still have claim over his labor. "Have the goodness to tell me if he is free to be able to move into service for another person," he asked the captain.[72]

Gentile Indians, who were independent of mission oversight, asserted even greater freedom from Hispanic cultural and sexual proscriptions. De la Guerra's daughter Angustias, born in 1809, remembered that one morning as a child, she was sent to awaken a servant who was from the island of Santa Cruz. "On my entering the room I found her lying between two men," she later told her own daughter. "'Why are you there between those two men?' [I asked]. Then the husband (who was one of them) answered me, saying:—'This man is my countryman; he came from the Island; he has no wife and I lent him mine.'"[73] This incident clearly made an impression on the young woman, who had been brought up in a culture that carefully controlled the sexuality of women and limited it to monogamy within marriage.

Though Indian men could and did claim some independence for themselves and their wives, unmarried Indian girls had less opportunity to leave the oversight of their gente de razón masters. Missionaries often sent eight- to ten-year-old Indian girls "to homes where the owners enjoyed the finer things of life," as one Californio remembered; "The intent was that the girls would be taught sewing and other domestic chores."[74] No doubt, the missionaries also hoped that they would in turn attract gentile husbands with their skills and recruit the men into the missions when they returned. Like other mission Indians, however, these girls found themselves with two Hispanic patriarchs: their mission fathers, plus their household masters, who sometimes quarreled over questions of authority.

In 1839, for example, de la Guerra arbitrated the case of an Indian girl named Tecla, who apparently refused to leave her biological family at the former Mission Santa Bárbara to work as a servant in town. Although by this time Father Narciso Durán no longer had direct control over the mission, he still worked to advise and defend his former dependents, and on this basis supported Tecla's right to remain.[75] Durán granted the "moral, domestic, and religious gains" these girls made by working for the gente de razón: "in some cases (not all) they learn something more of praying, they make confession, and acquire some ideas of public modesty."[76] But, he went on, they did not tend to retain this education once they returned to the mission. What was more, by leaving the missions, they left the care and protection of their own families and became vulnerable to "offences."[77]

Control of female sexuality constituted a key part of patriarchal authority. This was true of non-elites in town as much as it was of wives sheltered at home and neophyte girls secured in monjeríos at the mission. Within Spanish and Mexican society, women whose sexual conduct and movement took them outside the protection of patriarchs were exposed to disrespect or even rape, and lost the legal right to protect themselves. Moreover, this sexual code placed entire categories of women—Indians, servants, and poor women—in danger of dishonor if they did not appeal to the protection of some powerful patriarch. Many elite men openly engaged in sexual relations with accessible lower-class women like servants or tradeswomen, these encounters ranging from longterm concubinage to rape. This is what Father Durán feared, then, when he complained that Indians girls who worked for the gente de razón were open to "offences." Neophyte girls like Tecla, in turn, learned to demand the paternal protection of their mission "fathers" to avoid being forced to leave the security of their parents' homes.

Masters like de la Guerra pressed for their own paternal authority over girls like Tecla. In his letter explaining Tecla's case, Father Durán complained of the "aversion" such masters often had "to releasing the [female] Indians . . . for matrimony, when they are mature."[78] For gente de razón men, extending the time single girls remained enclosed in their houses would lengthen the term of their total dependency on their male masters, but it would also, according to the missionaries, prevent neophyte men from taking over that role, starting families and becoming responsible patriarchs themselves. Although they often encouraged their male workers to marry and settle down, then, patriarchs of the gente de razón blocked the marriages of their female servants in order to retain unquestioned control over their labor, movement, and sexuality.

In the Spanish and Mexican eras, de la Guerra used his wealth and authority to create a household befitting a man of his standing. He supported a large staff of servants, and with the aid of his wife's management transformed them into his paternal dependents. Native peoples stocked the kitchen with wood and water, prepared meals, cleaned the house, washed and repaired clothing, and cared for the de la Guerra children. Some of these workers appealed to outside authorities to mitigate the patriarch's control; others depended on it when they had exhausted other avenues of protection and relief. A very few, like the gentiles who shared a wife under de la Guerra's very roof, got away with simply ignoring it. But for most servants, like the women and children of the household, de la Guerra was the supreme authority in their lives. He commanded their labor and regulated their movement, appearance, and morality, but he also offered shelter and material security, and demonstrated that he could protect the honor of those under his roof. All of these things made de la Guerra the master of his household and a commanding patriarch. But de la Guerra's paternal authority and obligations extended beyond the women, children, and servants of his household to cover the entire community-wide "family" of soldiers and settlers. This role was rooted in two overlapping places: first, in de la Guerra's position as military commander and habilitado and second, in his role as merchant and retailer.

Presidio

> My father was the commander of the Pueblo of Santa Bárbara for several years. When the command was taken away from him because of Mexico's independence from Spain, he was still considered a figure of authority. Even up until recently, there were people who would refer to him as "my captain" when they would speak about him. For this reason, many poor people would come to my father's home and would receive courteous attention from him.[79]
>
> —*Angustias de la Guerra, 1880*

De la Guerra served as the presidial commander at Santa Bárbara from 1815 on, receiving a promotion to the highest rank of captain in 1817, and counting seventy men under his command in the colonial era. After 1827, other officers periodically replaced him as acting commander, but he retained the rank of captain.[80] As a military officer, de la Guerra expected obedience and respect as a matter of course, but the trust and loyalty of his men outlasted his active career. As with his retinue of servants, the captain achieved this authority because townsfolk in Santa Bárbara remembered a time when their commander used his rank, and the position of habilitado, to fulfill his obligations as a benevolent and community-minded patriarch.

As men of lower rank, de la Guerra's soldiers faced his physical command over their movement, labor, and even sexuality. And like mission Indians, they experienced the tension between rival patriarchs at the presidio and mission. De la Guerra regularly claimed the power of his office to determine when, where, and how his soldiers would work, but at the mission and in town, missionaries inserted themselves into these decisions to negotiate the boundaries of their overlapping authority. Joaquín Villa, for example, was a member of the Santa Bárbara Company who served de la Guerra as a military guard in the escolta at Mission La Purísima. Father Antonio Rodríguez, however, had better use for him as mayordomo, or overseer, of the mission estates. "I need for you to give your permission," Father Antonio told de la Guerra, "he is a boy that the Indians like very much, intelligent in the field, always in a good mood, nothing haughty, and what is more, he knows the language, which for me is the best quality. I have spoken to him, and he tells me that he is dis-posed for it, assuming that he obtains permission from his superiors."[81] De la Guerra even pressed one of his own soldiers into personal service, but suffered qualms that he might have overstepped his bounds. He asked Father Vicente Francisco de Sarría, the prefect of the missions, for advice. "A soldier destined to your assistance does not seem sinful to me," Father Sarría replied, as long as de la Guerra made sure that his servants tended the soldier's own needs, and that he was serving voluntarily, "that is, that he is not doing it for fear that in not doing it he will not be well thought of by you, or in some other similar respect out of fear."[82]

Indeed, it was important to de la Guerra's image as a benevolent patriarch that he not be seen as arbitrary or cruel to those under his command, but that, as a good father, he kept their welfare in mind. In some cases, he offered small loans and credit to soldiers in need. In oth-ers, he made sure to take care of widows and orphans. "It is very good that succor was given to the widow Guadalupe Briones," approved Gov-ernor Solá in 1817, "on account of her sons, and I am keeping it in mind for the future."[83] As habilitado, de la Guerra was particularly responsible for providing his troops with the necessities and luxuries that might make their lives more comfortable. The accounts of common soldiers show them or their wives buying imported sugar, tobacco, ribbon, and shaving razors from his storerooms, along with cheaper cloth like nankeen, chambray, and baize. (Many of these items, like the ribbons, they could then use to purchase informal labor from individual Indians.) Officers might purchase more expensive silks and satins, silver buttons, or braid. As explained in the first chapter, these accounts slid easily between offi-cial exchanges based on a soldier's salary, and unofficial exchanges for labor, otter pelts, tallow, and cattle hides.[84]

De la Guerra's wealth and connections were especially welcome dur-ing the years of civil unrest, which cut the California military off from its yearly delivery of supplies. From 1811 to 1821, soldiers and officers alike experienced widespread destitution. The governor himself told de la Guerra in 1813, "Even I found myself without a single peso, and in order to buy a few chickens it was necessary for the Alférez to lend me 2 pesos in change."[85] Want was particularly sharp in 1815–16, and again in 1818–19, when revolutionaries in Peru attacked port cities, cutting off the tallow trade. "On account of this," Lima trader José Cavenecia explained to de la Guerra in April 1816, "I have not been able to send any of my vessels to your coast."[86] Adding to the strain on California's resources, two hundred new soldiers from San Blas and Mazatlán arrived in 1818.

As habilitado, and later, commander, de la Guerra was responsible for providing for his troops in these lean years, and because of his own success at trade, was able to do a much better job of it than many other officers. De la Guerra's international accounts and lines of credit allowed him to take greater advantage of the legal and semi-legal trade with foreign merchants. José Díaz, for example, arrived in 1814 from Manila, with goods destined for the Russians at Fort Ross. But when bad weather diverted his brig, the *Santa Eulalia*, south, the governor gave Díaz permission to take on water and supplies in exchange for delivering 4,000 pesos' worth of goods to de la Guerra in San Diego.[87] These goods were meant for all the presidios, but it is safe to imagine that the soldiers of San Diego got first choice, thanks to their well-connected habilitado.

De la Guerra also used his authority and accounts with the missions to benefit his soldiers. We have already seen how de la Guerra helped provide his officers and soldiers in Santa Bárbara with the manual and domestic labor that built their houses and enabled them and their wives to feel like "ladies and gentlemen." As the decade wore on, the California government pressed the missions for more direct material contributions, and here, too, de la Guerra was the one who not only collected the cash—in 1818 this amounted to 300 pesos of silver—but also bought supplies made at the missions and distributed the goods to the presidios. The accounts of common soldiers during these years show regular rations of mission corn, beans, lard, chiles, and rice, as well as the occasional mission-made blanket, side of beef, pair of shoes, or bar of soap.[88]

Missionaries frequently complained about the strain this placed on the missions, and this convinced de la Guerra that he could not always rely on good relations if he wanted to ensure the material well-being of his soldiers. A more direct control of production would be necessary. Each presidio had its own "royal ranch" to supply the troops with livestock, but the one for Santa Bárbara was apparently inadequate. In 1817, de la Guerra moved to carve out part of Mission La Purísima for the support of his men.[89] Naturally, any threat to the mission lands provoked alarm among the missionaries. "It would be like stripping an altar of all its precious adornments to dress another," exclaimed Father Payeras in April 1817. Payeras reminded de la Guerra of all the "sacrifices that this Mission makes annually for the welfare of your Comandancia," sending "blankets, coarse cloth, and everything else that can be manufactured out of wool."[90] De la Guerra remained unconvinced, and in the end secured eleven leagues of Purísima land, forming the new ranch, San Julián. This government-owned ranch prospered well into the Mexican era, supplying Santa Bárbara's soldiers with horses, beef, and cash from the sale of hides and tallow.[91]

As the civil unrest in Spain's empire dragged on, however, staving off hard times in California became harder and harder. By 1818, trade with Lima was becoming increasingly difficult: prices were high, and few traders would accept payment in anything but Peruvian or Mexican silver.[92] In the following year, almost no trading ships of any nation dropped anchor in California's waters, and both the missions and the presidios felt the effects of the constriction of trade. On top of this, none of the California officers had received any pay in years. Governor Solá felt the only solution left to him was to send an envoy directly to the viceroy to lobby for more supplies for the struggling province. De la Guerra, of course, was the logical choice.

The forty-year-old must have had very mixed feelings in November 1819, as he stood on the deck of *La Reyna de Los Angeles* and sailed south toward San Blas. The last time he had left California, in 1810, it was to take up a prestigious post in the imperial government and live, he presumed permanently, in Mexico City. He had been lucky to escape with his life. Since then, he had tied his fortunes firmly to a new life in California, and his goal now was simply to get his friends and dependents there as much help as possible from Mexico City before returning home. "Miseries increase every day, more and more," Captain Luis Argüello prodded him in a letter from San Francisco. "Already, the soldiers cannot be distinguished from the Indians as a whole, and the worst of it is that hunger is now being felt."[93] De la Guerra arrived in San Blas with his eldest son, José Antonio (then fourteen), on November 26, and together they traveled to Mexico City for an audience with the viceroy. In the end, de la Guerra succeeded in only a modest way, getting one thousand pesos of his own back pay, and goods invoiced at $41,319—not quite the $150,000 or $200,000 he had sought, but at least something.[94]

By 1821, however, the competing needs of soldiers and neophytes once again brought military and mission into conflict. Hoping to find a new system that would more directly serve his needy soldiers, de la Guerra authorized them to take mission goods directly from the mission, straining the good will of Father González y Ibarra at Mission San Fernando Rey, who had his own "children" to consider. "In the month of March," he complained, "the soldiers took out 52 arrobas of lard," plus some cattle, shoes, and soap. "At this pace will the Mission ever be able to get out of penury?" But the friar's concern, he stressed, was not for himself, but for his dependents: "Really I see myself in the obligation to act in the capacity of Father, and of Pastor [to] . . . my sheep, and children . . . I believe I have a clear obligation to treat them in a way that is impossible if we have to keep going in this fashion, since I see that it is impossible to work for such costs unless they are treated like slaves."[95]

Perhaps in response, de la Guerra told his soldiers to pay for the mission goods, exchanging such things as cattle, metal goods, cloth, and alcohol directly with mission Indians. But this raised the ire of González yet again, whose authority as mission father was being subverted. "I am tired of telling you that there is a law prohibiting any trade and communication with the Indians," he fumed, "and as a consequence going into the ranchería and workshops."[96] De la Guerra replied that, to his understanding, the mission's products were the property of the Indians, and as a consequence they had the legal right to buy and sell them, but González fired back that the missions were communal property. Only the missionary, like a good father, could manage the affairs of his dependents for the good of all. "They propose to the tanner to sell the leather, the shoemaker the shoes, the warehouse keeper the wheat, the blacksmith the bit and spur, and the basket maker her baskets," he argued. "Who doubts that this goes against the common good, since it robs them not only of the materials that all own in equal shares, but also of time?"[97]

In the colonial era, de la Guerra worked hard to provide for the material welfare of his men and their families. This built his reputation as a benevolent leader and ensured his own prosperity as retailer to those same soldiers. During the last years of Spanish rule, however, the frontier military crumbled along with the abandoned presidial walls, and could no longer guarantee de la Guerra either the material base or loyal population of soldiers he needed. Of all the original presidios, however, Santa Bárbara, under Captain de la Guerra, remained strongest into the early national era.

Despite the arrival in Santa Bárbara of forty-five of the two hundred new recruits in 1819, after Independence de la Guerra faced a constant erosion in the number of men under his command.[98] As the military in the new nation of Mexico began to assert dominance in the politics of Mexico City, scheming officers abandoned the presidios across the northern frontier, concentrating their troops in the capital. The number of troops in California, active and retired, fell from a peak of seven hundred and ten in 1821 to about four hundred in 1831.[99] At Santa Bárbara, the number of enlisted men dropped to fifty by 1830.[100] Up and down California, destitution was widespread, and many soldiers simply deserted. Some in Monterey expressed their dissatisfaction with the poor living conditions and lack of pay by staging revolts in 1828 and 1829.[101] In the year of the latter, more serious, uprising, Governor José María de Echeandía complained to the central government, "In Alta California there is no presidio, for the four [places] which bear the name are mere squares of adobe huts, in ruins."[102]

Over this time, acting as commander or simply as one of many officers, de la Guerra continued to try to get his soldiers their salaries and rations through his contacts in Mexico. In 1829, he corresponded with the comisario's office but was not given much hope, "in the current circumstances of want."[103] Again in 1831, de la Guerra asked his brother-in-law Carlos, then serving as California's congressional deputy, to do the same, and to push for the promotion of old-time Californios over recent Mexican arrivals. Carrillo replied that he would do his best for the "miserable troops" and petition the secretary of the treasury. "I will not let them rest," he assured de la Guerra, "I am going to grind away to see then if out of vexation they give me 50,000 *duros* to be free of me."[104]

Until the mid-1830s, de la Guerra's best efforts, and the continuing prosperity of the San Julián ranch, enabled the Santa Bárbara presidio to maintain a nominal roster of thirty to forty rank-and-file soldiers, and half a dozen artillery men. These soldiers, and those retired men who continued to live near the presidio, did not forget the captain's work on their behalf. As one officer from San Francisco remarked in 1829, "Our soldiers are all of one mind. Whoever pays them the arrears due from the Spanish government is their master; he purchases [them] and to him they belong."[105] Despite setbacks in the Mexican era, then, de la Guerra's efforts to provide for his troops did secure him a lasting reputation as a benevolent father in the presidial town. But as Santa Bárbara's material base went from military supply to trade and agricultural production, de la Guerra increasingly relied on his commercial interests to form the base of his role as town "father."

Pueblo

In 1827, Commander de la Guerra was called on to take a census, and he noted a total population of 4,008 in his jurisdiction, including the Indians at the five nearby missions. A few gente de razón were scattered on a handful of ranches, but most—529 souls—lived in town. Of those, more than half were soldiers and their families who lived within the walls of the presidio. The rest, widows and retired soldiers, artisans, and laborers, lived in sixty or eighty small adobes clustered around the presidio walls, each one with a garden plot. "The inhabitants," remarked the captain, meaning the Hispanic settlers, "make their living principally off their farm products of hides and tallow from their cattle, and their scanty crops of wheat, beans, Indian corn, and some other vegetables, which by anxious care they can preserve from disease and pests that plague their crops."[106] The townsfolk who were lucky enough to own a few cows grazed them where they could, but few owned land outside of town. "In my early years," José del Carmen Lugo remembered, "very few ranchos were owned by individuals, and they were the only ones who could live away from the town... [But] many people occupied ranchos provisionally with their stock, and this was allowed because there was not room enough for them in the town or community corral."[107]

What de la Guerra did not note in his census was how these small producers depended on him; just like the soldiers, nearly every one of them ran up debts at de la Guerra's retail store, buying imported and processed goods like cotton cloth, ready-made shoes, chocolate, and *aguardiente,* or brandy. Although the accounts were kept in pesos, the townsfolk, when they could, paid for their small purchases more often with labor, otter fur, a few dozen hides, or a sack or two of tallow.[108] Such economic relations extended beyond the town of Santa Bárbara to Los Angeles, also in the Santa Bárbara presidio's jurisdiction, where de la Guerra employed his Carrillo brothers-in-law, and later Tomás Yorba, to collect hides and deliver goods. "My palate is already dry from collecting so much," protested Anastasio Carrillo, in the summer of 1825.[109]

The relationship of de la Guerra to townsfolk was not simply an economic one, however. De la Guerra moderated any perceived exploitation, strategically using his wealth to act the role of a benevolent patriarch to every member of the community. Indeed, it was paramount in maintaining his position as town father that de la Guerra perpetually demonstrate that he was not a selfish or self-aggrandizing man, but one who was openhanded and had the best interests of the community at heart. In creating the image of her husband's paternal generosity, María Antonia again served a critical supporting role.

This reciprocity with the entire community found formal expression in the Church through compadrazgo, the spiritual kinship that instilled a sense of community responsibility from the very beginning of de la Guerra's life in California. Before he married and had children of his own, and before he became the godfather of any individuals, de la Guerra took on the obligations of padrino, or godfather, to two churches, at the town of San José in 1802 and Mission San Juan Bautista in 1803. Raymundo Carrillo, his future father-in-law and commanding officer, seems to have urged his protégé to take on the responsibility, perhaps as a way to school him in the duties of the elites.

De la Guerra did not do so, at least at first, from any great love of the humbler classes. In fact, on his return in 1803 from visiting the settlements of San José and Branciforte, near Monterey, he reported to the governor, "They are not so bad as other colonists sent to California; yet to take a charitable view of the matter, their absence for a couple of centuries at a distance of a million leagues, would prove most beneficial to the province and redound to the service of God and the King."[110] Still, private contempt for his clients does not seem to have prevented de la Guerra from accepting the public honor and status of patronage, since in 1817 he once again took on the role of godfather for a civilian settlement, this time for the new church of Los Angeles.

As a church patron, José de la Guerra took on certain duties. The residents of Los Angeles were responsible for raising the money to build the church and ornament its interior. Merchant de la Guerra, with his lines of credit and foreign commercial contacts, was just the man to collect the tithes, consolidate them on his accounts, and place orders for building materials and decorations. Comandante de la Guerra, with a company of soldiers under his command and the ability to make contracts with the missions, could also summon the labor necessary to get the job done.[111] As padrino, de la Guerra was ultimately responsible for seeing the church built, and by extension, responsible for the congregation it would serve. The nearby missionaries approved of this oversight; in 1817 Father Payeras told the comandante such, adding, "I also applaud your idea of going to the Pueblo to cast your eyes over that vicinity and the ranches that compose it. Put in perfect tune the string that is disgracefully out of tune."[112]

While de la Guerra acted as padrino to entire congregations, which in a Catholic state amounted to the whole Hispanic population, he and his wife also took on the role of godparents to specific individuals. The de la Guerras used godparentage to reinforce the family's connection to soldiers and neighbors as well as to servants, and to incorporate outsiders. In the colonial era, for example, de la Guerra took in Margarita Gégue or Peque, a Native Hawaiian consort of American ship captain George Washington Ayres, along with their child. Ayres, in June 1813, had been captured aboard the *Mercury* as a smuggler and expelled to San Blas. His companion Margarita and young daughter stayed behind, accepting baptism as Catholics later that year under the sponsorship of de la Guerra's wife, María Antonia. Margarita took the opportunity to rename herself "María Antonia de la Ascensión Stuart," after her *madrina*. Mother and child lived in de la Guerra's house until Margarita/María Antonia's marriage to a soldier four or five years later.[113] In 1818 she called on María Antonia Carrillo de la Guerra again to sponsor their first child, María Luisa.[114] Margarita/María Antonia, in other words, used the wealth and protection of her godparents and co-parent to vouch for her virtue, and to make a successful transition from concubine to respectable wife.

De la Guerra took responsibility for several women like this, particularly when they had no husband or father of their own. Some women were forced into the arrangement. In the colonial era, women who had defied standards of female virtue by living with men to whom they were not married, or by having children out of wedlock, faced public shaming, followed, if possible, by a ritual restoration of honor. Authorities might, as they did for Anastasia Zúñiga in 1818, order that the woman's head and one eyebrow be shaved, and force her to stand outside church on Sundays. Afterward, she would be deposited in seclusion in a respectable household such as the de la Guerras', called a *casa de honor*, for about six months; this arrangement could be particularly useful in frontier areas without convents or other institutional shelters.[115] Other women chose to deposit themselves. Such appears to have been the case with Margarita, and it was also true of Concepción Argüello, a daughter of San Francisco officer José Darío Argüello. In 1806, Count Nicolai Rezanov, a Russian diplomat, proposed marriage to the sixteen-year-old, but when he did not return from Russia with permission from the tsar (he died en route), she took up residence in the de la Guerra house, refusing all other suitors. Over time, she took on the role of a nun, eventually being publicly recognized as "La Beata," or "The Pious One."

De la Guerra cultivated a reputation as a man who protected the virtue of those women who lived within his household, even relatively disreputable ones, teaching them "public modesty." But shameful single women were not the only potentially disruptive outsiders who re-entered the social order in this way. After 1811, when foreign smuggling picked up, Captain Ayres was just one of many merchant captains who ran into trouble and found his ship confiscated and crew broken up. De la Guerra considered it part of his duties not only to prosecute smugglers (when they did not trade with him first, of course) but also to integrate any foreign sailors left behind into the fabric of Spanish California life—ensuring productive citizens loyal to Cross and Crown. A godfather relationship gave de la Guerra the right to keep tabs on the behavior of what might have been a rootless and unruly group of men. In so doing, he brought them into the community, took responsibility for them, and enabled them to make demands on him in return.

For example, in January 1816, the American otter-hunting ships the *Albatross* and the *Lydia* were captured, and part of their crews taken prisoner, including a handful of white sailors and deserters, two "Kanakas," or Hawaiians, and the captain's "Negro" slave, "Bob."[116] Despite the governor's wish that these foreigners be placed on the next American ship to arrive on the coast, de la Guerra permitted anyone to stay who wished to.[117] Many of those who remained in Santa Bárbara converted to Catholicism, received new names, married Californio women, and found work in California's towns. De la Guerra himself, along with his wife, sponsored twenty-two-year-old Anglo-American José Manuel Lisa (born Eleazer), while María Antonia and their eldest son, José Antonio, became padrinos to the ex-slave, twenty-year-old Juan Cristóbal (formerly "Bob").[118] With this act, Juan Cristóbal/Bob transformed himself from a slave into a free man, and Manuel Lisa/Eleazer integrated himself into the community and found work. With the governor's permission, Lisa took over tending the captain's large gardens.[119] "I agree to it," Governor Solá relented, "your having the responsibility that belongs to you of the conduct, moral and civil, of your godchild."[120]

Which member of the de la Guerra family was godparent to which of these men illuminates larger patterns. María Antonia and her children were much more likely than her husband to sponsor servants, soldiers, and racially mixed sailors and pobladores. In the spring of 1830, for example, de la Guerra noted in his journal of local events that his fourteen-year-old daughter, Angustias, and twelve-year-old son, Francisco, had sponsored "a little Indian," the son of two neophytes.[121] De la Guerra children, in other words, became co-parents to non-elites before they became real parents, and thereby were introduced to the world of adult responsibilities.[122] In rare cases, de la Guerra himself sponsored outsider

Anglo adults like Manuel Lisa/Eleazer, but for the most part the patriarch limited his sponsorship to members of the Californio elite.[123] These unusual occasions, when the de la Guerras brought non-relatives into the compadrazgo network, were the exception rather than the rule, but they could have important consequences for the family, and it was important to limit their impact. Godchildren owed their sponsors deference, and as a consequence, having many godchildren conferred honor and prestige. But in return, a wealthy or powerful compadre or padrino might be called on for economic or political favors. Once a padrino made the commitment, he had a spiritual and moral obligation for life.

Although a material responsibility for godchildren was not mandatory, from the perspective of the elite godparent, the relationship had the potential to be abused. In 1818, Father Joaquín Pascual Nuez of Mission San Gabriel grumbled to de la Guerra, "I don't much like the title of godchild, because I see what all the godchildren are, and how this one like any other ... tries to look for me to do some service."[124] The strain of these obligations became starkly clear to de la Guerra himself in 1821, when he accepted responsibility for the wife and daughter of a man identified in the records only as "Jorge." Jorge had apparently entrusted his family to de la Guerra's keeping on leaving town; the last anyone had heard, he was in Guadalajara, calling himself "Doctor." Perhaps de la Guerra took them in on Jorge's promise to send money, but when this was not forthcoming, the commander asked the missions for help. But Father Vicente de Sarría, reminding him of the duties of a patriarch, refused to compensate de la Guerra,

> especially if you, by the title of compadre, or charity on account of the circumstances, Christianize them and [give them the] consequent education, admitted them and had them in your house; since this is an act of your abundant religion, piety, and edifying charity, for which you can expect an inexpressible and eternal judgment of glory.[125]

As Father Sarría explained, once the patriarch became a padrino and took dependents into his house, he committed himself to providing for them. He could not shirk this responsibility or demand aid without losing honor. Perhaps this is why it was his wife or children, rather than de la Guerra himself, who usually formed godparent ties with poorer, less powerful outsiders. María Antonia and the de la Guerra children could not be expected to have direct access to the same resources as the patriarch, and they risked his public face of generosity less by sponsoring nonelites in his place.

Birth was not the only life occasion that required personal sponsorship; weddings, too, were times when de la Guerra inserted himself into the lives of townsfolk. Occasionally, he acted as an official witness and padrino to the union, but less formally, he could also be solicited to provide the material goods necessary for this important ceremony and to help the young couple start a new household. "When a poor woman got married," Angustias remembered, "generally with a soldier or with his son, her parents asked for clothes, to help dress the bride to be, from the people who had more wealth." Such was the case in 1816, when a poor man, "on the eve of his marriage," came to Mission Santo Tomás to ask for materials for a petticoat and a rebozo for his bride. Father Josef Pineda forwarded the request to his "compadre," explaining to de la Guerra, "We will get whatever we can from the Missions and the Pueblo . . . to meet this need."[126]

Together, José de la Guerra and María Antonia used their wealth and connections in many other similar ways over the course of the Spanish colonial and Mexican eras. Understanding the status that came with belonging to a generous household, Raymundo Carrillo advised his daughter María Antonia to show "charity for the poor, and much more with the sick."[127] As a godfather to congregations, married couples, and individuals, and as the protector of the dependents under his roof, de la Guerra accepted the paternal role of master and benefactor. To prove himself worthy of this position, de la Guerra and his wife not only donated clothing to young couples but also could be called on by townsfolk for small loans, holiday gifts, medical aid, education, and help during natural disasters.

De la Guerra's charitable acts were made possible through his connections to suppliers in the missions, and access to goods and coin from his trade. In 1819, as the governor was contemplating sending de la Guerra to Mexico City, Father Mariano Payeras of Mission La Purísima delivered blue cloth, made by his neophytes, "such that you see it goes to the most destitute poor of your company, especially children."[128] Father Uría sent corn, beans, and lard from Santa Ynez, "so that you will succor the needy."[129] María Antonia often appeared as the benevolent face of the de la Guerra household, distributing items from her husband's storerooms to Santa Bárbara's citizens—dried cod for Lent, new clothing at Christmas, and sugar for making preserved pumpkin at Easter. Much like the gifts of bridal clothing, which made the wedding celebrations possible, these holiday gifts allowed poor people to attend to the ritual demands of each festival.[130]

De la Guerra might also use charity to mitigate the impact of dangerous outsiders on the community. In the spring of 1830, for example, the *María Ester* arrived from Acapulco bearing about eighty convicts, most of them held for serious offenses like murder and robbery.[131] Presidial Commander Romualdo Pacheco sent thirty-one of them to Santa Cruz Island with oxen, dairy cows, tools, and seed, and assigned the rest to work as servants and ranch hands among the Californios; de la Guerra took eight or ten himself.[132] But de la Guerra also let all know that his paternal authority extended even to those who did not live in his household. On their arrival, he gave each one of the convicts "shirts, pants, and his own blankets," and in a public speech "assured them that he would be like a father to all who behaved well."[133] For the ragged men who received them, clothing and blankets were material symbols of de la Guerra's power, his wealth and connections. The message was clear: "Behave well," and expect more of the same. Step out of line, and shiver through the desert evening.

In addition to goods and cash, de la Guerra's dependents turned to him for health care and education, in an era when the government could not be expected to provide such services. At first, de la Guerra collaborated with missionaries like Father Luis Martínez of San Luis Obispo to provide health care. Martínez ordered bottles of essence of peppermint, calomel, and other medicines for his hospital, and in return, the patriarch sometimes sent his sick there to recover (although Martínez groused occasionally about not getting paid for his services).[134] In 1817, de la Guerra bought for Mission San Gabriel a copy of Joseph Jacob Plenck's *Farmacopea*—the better, perhaps, for the missionaries to diagnose and treat the devastating illnesses affecting California's Indians. This was not entirely an act of charity, however, as de la Guerra made a profit of twelve pesos on the deal.[135]

By 1823, de la Guerra was attempting to contract with a foreign surgeon, Dr. Burroughs, to care for the presidio community directly, but the doctor apparently did not stay long.[136] Instead, most pobladores, missionaries, and officers relied on home cures, midwives, and *curanderas* throughout the Spanish and Mexican eras.[137] Nonetheless, the de la Guerras continued to supply the local practitioners with essential herbs and compounds from their gardens and storerooms.[138] "There was no tea except at my father's house," one daughter recalled, "and in case of sickness they would come and ask for some there."[139]

Education was always a precious commodity, particularly in a province where basic literacy at the turn of the nineteenth century probably stood at about thirty percent among soldiers, and five to ten percent among townsfolk generally.[140] Education, especially in the colonial era, was seen as an attribute of the elites, and was coveted by the striving gente de razón. As one American later observed, "They are very ambitious of speaking the pure Castilian language, which is spoken in a somewhat corrupted dialect by the lower classes."[141] An intellectual elitism expressed itself in private libraries among the wealthier families.[142] De la Guerra did what he could to bring these advantages to the lower classes. In 1818, for example, he obtained the governor's approval to establish a school for girls with the "Padres," paid for in part by the children's parents. De la Guerra ordered two types of reading books called *cartillas* and *catones*, notebooks, and paper from his cousin Nicolás Noriega, and found a woman willing to teach.[143] Up in Monterey, Isabel Estrada heard about these books and begged her husband, José, a lieutenant in the Monterey company, to ask for "two *Ejercisios Cotidianos* [daily exercises] and other books of devotion . . . useful for a family, since up here you can find absolutely no reading books or catechisms for children."[144] By 1834, this school for girls no longer existed, but Santa Bárbara still boasted one of the three public schools in the territory. The governor described them as "poorly endowed and served by inept teachers," although the school at Santa Bárbara had a distinct advantage: in addition to municipal funds, de la Guerra made sure that the local company donated part of the military funds to subsidize the school's operation.[145]

Finally, de la Guerra established a reputation as town father by opening his house during natural disasters. Southern California is prone to earthquakes, which were often severe enough to knock down the rough adobe houses of townsfolk. One observer remembered that in the aftermath, poor families would camp on the de la Guerra courtyard and grounds, "and there remain until their fears subsided, subsisting the while upon his hospitality and generosity."[146] In 1831, fire swept up the coast from the hills above San Buenaventura, and for days, worried townsfolk watched as billows of smoke blew toward the town. When flames hit the settlement, and burning cinders began landing on village roofs, de la Guerra's home again became a refuge: "The inhabitants fled from their homes to the beach, or sought the house of Señor [de la Guerra y] Noriega."[147]

De la Guerra spent decades acquiring wealth and, through its redistribution, proving himself as an honorable man and a worthy patriarch in the understanding of the gente de razón. As one foreign visitor observed, "All the people of Santa Bárbara looked upon him as patriarch of their little community."[148] With the support of his wife and children, de la Guerra protected women from shame, maintained servants, sheltered lost souls, and provided for the material and spiritual well-being of his community. Dependents pressed their own claims by appealing to the obligations incurred by this role. De la Guerra thus demonstrated in a ceremonial and a material way his willingness to care for an extended circle of dependents, as a father would for his children.

Performance

De la Guerra's relationship with his household and community was much more profound than the transactions recorded in the ledger books of his store. The mapping of a paternal relationship onto a material one found constant symbolic and cultural expression, and these shared performances in turn reinforced the notion of de la Guerra as local patriarch. In a town whose inhabitants numbered in the hundreds, almost everyone had some regular interaction with de la Guerra or his household. And as one visitor remarked, "It is not unusual to see at public assemblages the most perfect familiarity between the two classes."[149] This quotation is somewhat misleading, however, for the constant, familiar contact between the de la Guerra family and their dependents was not one between equal individuals. In word and gesture, the citizens of Santa Bárbara demonstrated their submission and loyalty to their patriarch, while other elites recognized him as "the father of all in that place."[150]

Because their voices are often silent in the written record, it is difficult to capture the daily signs of respect and humility most soldiers and citizens would have shown de la Guerra, but it is clear from descriptions that survive that de la Guerra did not pass up an opportunity to reinforce his paternal relationship to townsfolk, or they to appeal to this relationship for personal advantage. Each week, as de la Guerra distributed free soap to his workers, for example, he made sure to speak directly to each worker "with a joke or pleasant remark."[151] We can only imagine what the workers might have said in return, but no doubt they understood which words would get a bigger bar of soap or an extra ration of corn. The few letters written by townsfolk and soldiers almost always used the language of submission and respect; they addressed the letters to "mi jefe," or "my patron." For example, when one soldier could not come personally to announce his wedding, he made sure to send a letter on behalf of the new couple to "my honorable jefe," proclaiming that he and María Antonia, his "worthy wife . . . may order your most attentive servants as you like."[152]

If he actually attended a settler's wedding, de la Guerra expected and received the gestures of respect due a generous patriarch. Angustias remembered these occasions from her childhood vividly. The parents of the couple, she recalled, would arrive early in the morning to present the patriarch "a gift of small breads and sweets for his breakfast." After the ceremony, the young couple themselves called on de la Guerra to formally declare their new status, "and drink chocolate with him," Angustias recalled. "Then they would invite the family to the wedding banquet."[153] Pobladores further recognized the unique authority of de la Guerra at these receptions. In June 1830, for example, two children of soldiers at the presidio, Arcadia Ruiz and Francisco Javier Alvarado, married in town. At that time, Romualdo Pacheco served as acting commander in Santa Bárbara, and his wife, Ramona Carrillo, officially sponsored the union as the couple's madrina, hosting the reception dinner and ball. Everyone in attendance, however, recognized de la Guerra as the true patriarch. When the guests took their seats at dinner, de la Guerra recalled, "I . . . had the honor of occupying the superior place, with not a little resistance on the part of my humility, which had in the end to cede to the insistence of Señor Pacheco."[154]

Signs of hierarchy and status were taught as much to the de la Guerra children as they were to the soldiers' and settlers' families. Angustias, for example, remembered that, while she attended the government school with her brothers Francisco and Pablo, her family deliberately sent them lunch on a silver serving dish. Angustias made sure the rest of the town's children understood how special this made her by throwing the plate on the floor when she had finished eating, thus demonstrating that the de la Guerras could afford dishes that did not break. The teacher, Bernardina Alvarez, reinforced this sense of difference when Angustias asked one day to try the teacher's meal of beans and *cuajada*, or cheese curd. "Child," replied the woman, "I would give you and your siblings some of our food, but you are not used to it and it might harm you to eat this." In this case, difference was defined by wealth and accessibility to more refined food, but also by the teacher's less culturally European diet. Alvarez, although deferential to someone higher, was slyly refusing the request of a de la Guerra child. Angustias's mother returned her to the school the next day with instructions to tell the teacher that she was "just the same as the other children." "After that," said Angustias, "we always ate some of their food and we would give them some of what was brought to us."[155] María Antonia no doubt understood that even the behavior of the de la Guerra children had to contribute to a family image of status and wealth balanced with accessibility and sympathy for their subordinates.

Food and tableware marked de la Guerra children as elites when they left their father's home, but the building itself, the largest home in Santa Bárbara, was the most visible symbol of de la Guerra's wealth and power. Townsfolk taught their children to demonstrate respect for their patron by revering his house. "As they passed the door of his dwelling," one American trader noted, "they would remove their hats and give the customary obeisance in the same manner as they did when passing the entrance of their religious sanctuaries."[156] This almost-spiritual veneration appeared even more strongly during natural disasters. During the fire of 1831, for example, townsfolk who sought shelter on the de la Guerra grounds prayed and appealed to the saints.[157] The American observer concluded that settlers, with their "simple minds," showed such reverence because "they considered his person endowed with supernatural grace," although pobladores likely also understood the material consequences of showing their deference.[158]

For pobladores, the interior of the house was off-limits, but it was open to other elites at any time; indeed, California's Spanish-Mexican elites prided themselves on their generosity with one another. "In those days," one of them remembered, "nearly all Californians were bound to each other by ties either of blood or of friendship, so that the traveler could go from one end of California to the other without its costing him anything in money."[159] Hospitality demonstrated to other elites a mastery over the household. In 1820, for example, Señor del Castillo Negrete, a traveling scholar, was impressed by the display put on by de la Guerra, then still living at the presidio. "In Santa Bárbara," Castillo Negrete wrote in his diary, "a beautiful little village, I met a Captain De la Guerra, a noble Spaniard of imposing aspect, who entertained me in a royal manner. He is a veritable lord, his hospitality being daily shown by the large number of guests at his table."[160] In this arena as well, of course, María Antonia's management of household labor to stage these dinners contributed to her husband's public image.

When special occasions were celebrated at the house, the social structures and relationships of the town found their fullest display. During Carnival, or Carnes Tolendas, the period just before Lent, Santa Bárbara's elites reinforced their social exclusiveness. Only social equals were permitted to share in the intimate fun of throwing *cascarones,* eggshells filled with confetti, flour, or cologne, at unsuspecting victims.[161] For other special occasions, however, the de la Guerras opened their house to the whole community of friends and neighbors, mission fathers, and visiting traders. Sir George Simpson, who visited Santa Bárbara in the 1840s, noted that "on particular occasions, such as the festival of the saint after one is named, ... those who can afford the expense give a grand ball, generally in the open air, to the whole of the neighboring community."[162] Angustias remembered, "My father would always host a huge feast for the whole pueblo whenever one of his sons or daughters got married."[163] "On these occasions," claimed an American observer, "no invitations are given, but every one is expected to come."[164]

At first glance, these events seem to put de la Guerra and the towns-folk on the same level. Indeed, José de la Guerra intended such gatherings to reinforce cultural solidarity among all classes of the gente de razón, and this was particularly true of religious festivals. For example, the de la Guerra family occasionally invited townsfolk to a community-wide performance of the Christmas play, *Los Pastores,* which relates the story of the poor shepherds' travels to see the infant Jesús.[165] When Alfred Robinson visited in the Christmas season of 1829, "four or five hundred persons" were gathered to watch a version of the play put on in the de la Guerra courtyard by the neophytes of Mission Santa Bárbara. Robinson remarked that the Indians "had been practicing for some time, under the direction of Father Antonio Jimeno, and a great triumph was therefore an-ticipated over the performances of the 'gente de razón.'" In the end, "their performances were pronounced excellent," and a juggler came forward to keep up the merry mood.[166] With this display, the townsfolk of Santa Bár-bara could share an expression of their common culture and congratulate themselves on successfully converting "wild" Indians into carriers of that culture. The performance also marked de la Guerra in particular as a gen-erous host who provided amusement and edification for his dependents.

Finally, with their public dances, music, and food, de la Guerra wed-ding celebrations expressed and defined the family and community in perhaps the most elaborate form in the Mexican era. Full descriptions survive of two de la Guerra weddings in the 1830s. The first, that of An-gustias de la Guerra to Manuel Jimeno in 1833, was described by both Angustias herself and by the visiting American trader, Alfred Robinson. Robinson, in turn, married a sister of Angustias three years later, and his wedding was recorded by another American, Richard Henry Dana.[167] All three observers remarked on the length and complexity of these services and celebrations.

Angustias de la Guerra's fiancé was the brother of Father Antonio Jimeno, the director of Mission Santa Bárbara who had taught the

"Costume de la Haute Californie" and "Dame de Monterey," from Abel du Petit-Thouars, *Voyage autour du monde sur la frégate la Vénus, pendant les années 1836–1839*, 1841. Courtesy of The Bancroft Library, University of California, Berkeley.

Christmas play to his neophytes, and this association ensured a spectacular wedding in January 1833. Father Jimeno, Robinson tells us, "was determined to outdo all that had ever been known in California." After a
dawn ceremony, the missionary hosted breakfast, then organized a procession to lead the new couple to the de la Guerra house. Jimeno "had
made his Indians happy" by giving them gifts to honor the occasion; "well
attired for the occasion," they joined the parade, some of them as a
marching band in uniform. The bride and her family descended the hill
in carriages, followed by men and women of the town on horseback. As
further compliment to the couple, soldiers at the mission and presidio
fired off guns.[168] Every element of this display vividly reminded the participants and observers of the town's hierarchy and of the de la Guerras'
ability to command respect and deference from Church leaders, townsfolk, the military—even lowly neophytes.

As the procession of bride and groom wound its way down from
the mission, the de la Guerra household would be in an uproar of last-
minute preparation. Servants erected tents to cover the courtyard, set
long tables on the veranda and in the sala, and prepared elaborate meals.
Soon the entire pueblo arrived for the lavish wedding reception, scheduled to last several days. Although every class participated in the celebration, differences in movement, activity, and appearance marked the
social hierarchies. For example, guests at the main reception for Angustias, a one o'clock luncheon, were carefully seated according to community status.[169] According to Angustias, "All of the important people of
Santa Bárbara ate in the *sala grande*. The rest of the people ate at tables
that were set in the interior patio of the house."[170] At the main table, de la
Guerra was given special recognition, just as he was at the wedding of
Arcadia Ruiz: "The married couple," Robinson remembered, "were
seated at the head with the father spiritual [Father Antonio Jimeno] on
the right, and the father temporal [José de la Guerra] on the left." Even
those at the bottom level of society were included in some fashion:
Angustias remembered that, after the meal, "Some good food would be
sent to the prisoners."[171]

After eating, guests prepared for a marathon of dancing that could
last three days.[172] Both Robinson and Dana described a "booth" or "tent"
set up in the courtyard for dancing, capable of holding "nearly all the people of the town." Despite this social intermingling, however, the family
was very careful to show their proper place as representatives of the elite.
Demonstrating their command of wealth, José and Father Jimeno, "the
two fathers, from an elevated position, threw at their feet, silver dollars

and doubloons."[173] As with the meal, the interior of the house was reserved for "private entertainment . . . for particular friends."[174] Certain
dances, too, were reserved for the gentry. Dana noted that, "After the
supper, the waltzing began, which was confined to a very few of the 'gente
de razón,' and was considered a high accomplishment, and a mark of aristocracy."[175] Indeed, while pobladores "apparently of the lower classes"
might enjoy the party throughout the day, "the crowd, the spirit, and the
elite, come in at night."[176] Finally, members of de la Guerra's inner circle
displayed their status by wearing their finest luxury goods, particularly
fragile and labor-intensive clothing. Dana described Juan Bandini, for example, a wealthy Peruvian trader from San Diego, as "dressed in white
pantaloons neatly made, a short jacket of dark silk, gaily figured, white
stockings and thin morocco slippers upon his very small feet."[177]

From elaborate rituals like weddings and religious performances to
the smallest acts of everyday deference, the symbolic world of Santa Bárbara continually assured the gente de razón that they shared bonds of religion and culture, while reinforcing a hierarchy of status and class. De la
Guerra repeatedly enacted the role of a "good father," sitting at the head of
the table, tossing coins to the assembled masses. And through word and
deed, these townsfolk acted out their own family roles, as obedient
children removing their hats and proclaiming their gratitude.[178]

Authority

De la Guerra's political role as military commander, his economic role as
habilitado and merchant, and his community role as charitable "benevolent father" all supported his supreme place in Santa Bárbara. Because
he succeeded in answering the demands of the community, de la Guerra
took on the authority of a legitimate patriarch in their eyes and earned
public displays of respect. This moral authority, in turn, secured for de la
Guerra the consent of those he governed, for "good" fathers earned the
right to make the rules and settle disputes within their households. In
the final few years of the colonial era, one visitor praised the commander
in his journal: "The people look upon him as the absolute ruler of the
district, and his counsels and judgments are sought and followed to the
letter, even by those who come from afar to lay their differences before
him. The rare tact with which he arranges everything is remarkable."[179]

A legal structure backed up de la Guerra's authority in the southern
district during the colonial era: as the commander of the Santa Bárbara
presidio, the captain governed not only his own town but also the civilian settlement of Los Angeles and the surrounding ranchos—about

six hundred and fifty residents by 1820. Under Spanish rule, Los Angeles had its own *ayuntamiento*, or town council, a governing body with a long history in the colonization of Mexico. An alcalde performed the duties of a justice of the peace, more or less, and *regidores* were the rough equivalent of councilmen. Traditionally, officials came from the highest levels of society and enjoyed lifetime appointments. But as a frontier province with a military government, California was a little different; the pueblo fell within Santa Bárbara's presidial jurisdiction. So, above the local appointed officials, a sergeant or corporal from the Santa Bárbara Company, responsible to the commander, served as *comisionado*, or commissioner, of the town.[180] For the last few years of the colonial era, the commissioner for Los Angeles was none other than Anastasio Carrillo, de la Guerra's brother-in-law, and the family tie further strengthened de la Guerra's authority over this position.[181] Many of de la Guerra's former soldiers had also retired to Los Angeles, cementing the connection between the two towns and de la Guerra's authority.

At the dawn of the Mexican era, townspeople from Santa Bárbara and Los Angeles appealed to de la Guerra to solve all sorts of legal and judicial problems, and in so doing tested the limits of his moral authority to govern as a "good" patriarch. It is men, in general, who appear in the government documents: giving testimony at trial, prosecuting or defending the accused, and ruling on the fates of criminals. Women seldom appear; the colonial social order stipulated that they be governed by family patriarchs rather than directly by the state. Nonetheless, women did act in this public sphere, particularly if they had no clear patriarch to act on their behalf. In so doing, many appealed to de la Guerra to take on this role for them. The widow María Rufina Hernández, for example, asked de la Guerra in 1821 to try and collect the debt that Señor Ortega owed her deceased husband, Sebastián Alvitre; goods or tallow would be acceptable.[182] Later that year, another "poor widow," María Teresa Cota, "full of sadness," asked de la Guerra, through Father Senán, to intercede in her son's case, "not that her son will not be punished, but that he may suffer what he deserves in this jurisdiction, since this would be some consolation for her." "I think you can do much in this case," Senán urged the commander.[183]

One of the most striking documents generated by women settlers arrived on de la Guerra's desk in February 1822. Five women of Los Angeles, Luisa Varelas, Demetria Ramírez, Juana Inocencia Reyes, María Luisa Reyes, and Valeriana Lorenzana, together had carefully written out a petition to the commander. Their husbands, they admitted, had committed "coarse deeds" (having attempted to kidnap two foreign traders for ransom and stolen trade goods), and as result of the sentence against them, the alcalde had arrived and was beginning to inventory their houses, the "goods of our livelihoods" and vineyards. "Weighed down by reason of very numerous families," the women feared losing their homes and the tools of their trades. "Prostrating ourselves at Your Mercy's feet with the most profound respect and submission," they wrote, "we turn to you as loving father to give us the best consolation, if our numerous families experience this ruin."[184] In the public language of authority and governance, these subordinate women implied through such petitions that, rather than defying the local alcalde's command, they were good subjects, offering "profound respect and submission" to his superior. A negative response would therefore disgrace de la Guerra and reveal him as someone other than a completely "loving father"—as someone unfit to govern loyal dependents. All the men were soon released.[185]

De la Guerra could not, of course, please all of his constituents at once: his response to these women overrode the decisions of their local male authorities. In at least one other case, de la Guerra put the needs of his specific clients above the needs of the pueblo as a whole. In December 1819, while de la Guerra was in Mexico lobbying for more supplies, the regidores and thirty citizens of Los Angeles signed a petition to acting Commander Moraga at Santa Bárbara. In it, they complained that, just before his departure for Mexico, de la Guerra had granted Rancho de los Quintos (also called Rancho Ballones) to two individuals, Felipe Talamantes, a former soldier of the San Diego garrison, and Agustín Machado, the son of a soldier, even though the pueblo was using this land as common pasture. Commander Moraga allowed the pobladores to build corrals on the land and referred the case to the governor, who upheld the grant.[186] It appears that, all things being equal, de la Guerra felt entitled to redistribute communal property in order to benefit personally favored dependents.

These sorts of jurisdictional conflicts intensified after Independence, when the liberal reforms of the Constitution of 1812 finally went into effect, reorganizing the governing structure of towns. In 1822, under Iturbide, the federal government instituted popularly elected ayuntamientos in Santa Bárbara and Los Angeles, keeping a parallel military government in the first town but removing Los Angeles altogether from military supervision.[187] Canónigo Agustín Fernández de San Vicente of Durango, representing the new government of Mexico, arrived in Monterey in late September 1822 to institute the new regime. Under his orders, Governor Solá sent a representative to Los Angeles to explain the new rules: the ayuntamiento was to be transformed from a closed and appointed body to one elected on a regular basis by male property owners of the community.[188] Although incumbent officers kept their seats that November, this change of government enabled the settlers of Los Angeles to openly assert their own counterclaims to self-rule. In so doing, they reframed and publicly expressed their resentments against a patriarch who appeared to use his power to favor Santa Bárbara's soldiers over the pueblo's settlers.

De la Guerra did his best to resist the new civilian regimes in both Santa Bárbara and Los Angeles from the very start. Fellow elites counseled de la Guerra to back down and save his image. "I have heard some anti-constitutional measures attributed to you," wrote José María Narváez in early 1823, "like not having the Regidor or Alcalde of [the Santa Bárbara] presidio restored in their functions; I would prefer it if this were a lie, and that for now you reconcile yourself with fate, without prejudice."[189] Particularly galling to de la Guerra was the loss of the military office of comisionado over Los Angeles, which he had been accustomed to filling with his brothers-in-law and supporters.

This jurisdictional dispute led, in 1823, to a sharp clash with the civilian government. De la Guerra, who distrusted the recent popular elections in Los Angeles, refused to recognize civil authority over the military and invested Sergeant Guillermo Cota with the power to arbitrate criminal matters among the soldiers, much like the former comisionados.[190] When the Los Angeles regidores and the alcalde, Manuel Gutiérrez, did not in turn recognize Cota, the entire matter was sent up to the governor.[191] Governor Argüello, contradicting the spirit of the constitutional reforms, backed up de la Guerra as the "Jefe Político," noting the "bad government" and "abuses" in Los Angeles.[192] Again in 1825, de la Guerra insisted on appointing Cota comisionado, and the sergeant promptly announced his plans to induct some of the "large number of vagrants" in Los Angeles into the military in order to fill recruitment quotas.[193] Stung, representatives from Los Angeles notified de la Guerra "of the defense that we are making for our rights . . . We are angry on account of the outrages against our authority."[194] But again, the governor refused to intervene to support popular sovereignty.

Armed with a new discourse of governance, citizen Angelenos attempted to reframe political legitimacy and authority under Mexican rule. Pío Pico, the son of a presidial soldier from San Diego, remembered his first encounter with the new defiant mood of Los Angeles in 1827. Sent there as a scribe under military commander Captain Pablo de la Portilla, Pico was ready to take down the statement of the Mexican merchant "Señor Bringas" in a pending court case, but the witness refused to recognize the authority of the military to conduct the investigation. "I was even more surprised," Pico remembered, "when I heard Bringas tell Portilla that the civilians [*paisanos*] were the sacred core of the nation, and that the military were nothing more than servants of the nation, which was constituted of the people and not of the military." Ever after, he declared, "it always appeared to me, deep in my soul, that the citizens were the nation."[195] Colonial elites had framed the question of legitimate political authority in paternal terms, and vested that authority in corporate bodies like the military. In this understanding, "good fathers" deserved to rule, while those who committed "abuses" proved themselves incapable of exercising judgment. In the 1820s, civilian Angelenos, spurred on by new migrants from Mexico, offered a new model in which individual citizens were vested with the authority to rule themselves.[196]

After the first few years of Mexican rule, the conflict between Santa Bárbara and Los Angeles cooled off somewhat, although resentments against the military still lingered. These flared up again in 1834, when de la Guerra attempted to collect *diezmos,* or back taxes, from the pueblo. The military taxes, due in livestock and crops, had not been gathered for six years, and Lieutenant Domingo Carrillo warned "that some [citizens] delivered calves in payment of the diezmos, and this is a fraud; because at least half should be small cows."[197] De la Guerra, in turn, wrote to his friend Tomás Yorba, sending him a list of the debtors who had refused to pay up. When Los Angeles Alcalde Francisco Javier Alvarado declined to prosecute the offenders, the military-settler conflict took on overt racial tones, pitting military men who claimed Spanish blood against the mostly mixed-race population of settlers. "I have pledged myself in the collection of your debts," Yorba assured de la Guerra, "but the Judges of the Pueblo are too much Indians since Alvarado has gone so far as to lose the list of debtors."[198] Several months later, after as much foot-dragging as they dared, the citizens of Los Angeles did finally cough up the last of their military taxes.

De la Guerra, it seems, could not always maintain paternal authority when his responsibilities to one set of dependents, the soldiers of Santa Bárbara, conflicted with the jurisdictional and economic claims of another, the civilian settlers of Los Angeles. When de la Guerra did not measure up to the ideal of evenhanded generosity, pobladores resisted and made demands, threatening him with public disgrace for failing to maintain the image of a good patriarch and bringing into play other rival authorities. Women citizens of Los Angeles insisted that de la Guerra live up to his professed role as "Father of All." Their husbands and brothers used the liberal reform of town government to question the basis of his authority altogether. Yet even in this less-favored town, de la Guerra maintained enough paternal ties with his dependents through memories of military service, economic favors, and church sponsorship to sustain a share of loyal dependents. And while de la Guerra's influence over Los Angeles may have weakened as time went on, his hold over Santa Bárbara remained firm, owing to his ongoing role as military leader and town patron. In that place, his acts as a "good father" strongly sustained his moral and political authority.

Californio society imagined itself as a family, ruled by a father, and built on ties of kinship and compadrazgo, the military, and the economy. This society was structured, like a family, on clear lines of authority and submission, but linked as well by chains of obligation and reciprocity. The local community understood de la Guerra's role as their "father" on two levels. First, he demonstrated command and physical dominance, the "natural" attributes of men. He also used his base of power in the military and his resources and skills in the market to punish crimes, command labor, and establish debt relationships with soldiers and pobladores, while he controlled their ability to sell agricultural products on the world market as well as their access to military salaries and manufactured goods. Yet, most Santa Bárbarans did not revile de la Guerra as a petty tyrant, selfish and self-aggrandizing; he gained the respect that arose from the second, more reciprocal, understanding of patriarchy. In the public perception, de la Guerra, with the support of his wife, children, and servants, sheltered those under his roof and protected the virtue of women; he provided spiritual mentoring, charity, education, medicine, and hospitality; and he integrated outsiders into the social order. All of these things were the responsibility of the father of a family, and in fulfilling his obligations, he was accorded the moral authority to arbitrate disputes. When de la Guerra stepped outside his role as provider and protector, or when the needs of his dependents conflicted, then soldiers, townsfolk, and servants contested his authority.

Rising through the ranks of the military, accumulating wealth, and creating dependents: all this was possible for men who cultivated the right family connections. This level of status was expressed in terms that recognized, both materially and symbolically, the successful man as a "father" of his kin and community. This highly personalistic and patriarchal system was also geared toward profit and the market. After Independence, however, liberal reforms, as they had contested the authority of town fathers, also changed the rules of commerce. With the lifting of trade restrictions that came at the end of Spanish rule, men like José de la Guerra needed new strategies to cope with the unusually strong challenge posed by the arrival of foreign traders. As the second generation came of age, patriarchs turned again to a family strategy: the marriage of their daughters to foreign merchants.

Anita de la Guerra. California Historical Society Collection, USC Libraries Special Collections.

CHAPTER THREE

OPEN PORTS AND INTERMARRIAGE

T he bride wore black. At ten o'clock the captain of the *Alert* watched her through a spyglass from the beach as she entered the Santa Bárbara mission church a mile up the hill, on her way to the confessional. Out in the harbor, his Boston ship lay at anchor, and when the captain turned his telescope to it, he could make out a dozen sailors standing ready on deck. Early that morning, they had rolled all four guns of the *Alert* into position and carefully loaded their cartridges. Now they stood by with lighted matches, waiting for the signal from shore. Standing by the ship's masts, other men grasped the ropes above their heads and maintained a steady eye on the captain.

At last the mission doors opened, and the bride reappeared, changed into brilliant white. As the church bells pealed, the captain of the *Alert* gave the signal. Immediately, every colorful flag and banner unfurled, and a small white plume of smoke lifted off the ship's bow. The report of guns echoed off the hills that cupped the small town. Offshore, the American sailors watched the tiny figures of the long wedding procession wind their way down past open fields, vineyards, and one-story adobe houses to the largest home in the place—the one with three sides, facing the harbor below. A large canvas canopy almost completely covered the central courtyard. Quickly, the space filled with what seemed to be every inhabitant of the town, celebrating the marriage of José de la Guerra's daughter Anita to Alfred Robinson, the resident manager of the Boston firm Bryant and Sturgis. When the wind shifted, the sailors on board the company's ship could just make out the faint sounds of guitars and violins.[1]

Between Mexican Independence in 1821 and the start of the Mexican-American war in 1846, about twelve to fifteen percent of Californian women married Euro-American and European men.[2] The famous 1836 wedding of Alfred Robinson and Anita de la Guerra has come for many to represent all such marriages. Richard Henry Dana, a Harvard student and sailor aboard the *Alert*, brought the scene to a wide audience in the United States through his best-selling travel narrative, *Two Years Before the Mast*, first published in 1840. For many Americans, this marriage of a Mexican woman to a blue-eyed Yankee became a potent symbol of bloodless conquest. At the turn of the twentieth century, too, Santa Bárbara's boosters seized on this wedding as the perfect symbol for the town: the aristocratic grace of the old Spanish rancheros, wed to the modern energy of American business. Even today in Santa Bárbara, the Old Spanish Days Fiesta re-creates this splendid occasion with a yearly entry in the big parade: the bride in a lacy white mantilla, the groom in somber black.

In more recent years, historians of California have turned this symbol on its head, seeing not the charm of a bygone era, and the inevitable progress of economic development, but a simple pastoral society betrayed by its elites. Landed rancheros, it is argued, hungered for the manufactured commodities, the business acumen, and the true "whiteness" that only American and British traders possessed. To get these things, elite men like de la Guerra traded their daughters, conceding much of their precious land. Daughters who did not resist these arrangements are often said to be "complicitous" in an arrangement that eventually opened the door to conquest and assimilation.[3] Ironically, both the boosters and the revisionists, by looking backward at Mexican California from American California, have remained on the boat in the Santa Bárbara harbor with the men from Boston, watching the de la Guerra marriage through a haze of gun smoke.

The view is a little different from inside the church, walking the bride down the center aisle, or kneeling at the altar alongside the Yankee groom. Through the eyes of men like de la Guerra, and daughters like Anita, marriage to a foreign merchant fit into a larger strategy—a strategy that used the family to advance economic standing in a context of local merchant capitalism.[4] To truly understand the intent behind Californio intermarriages, it is necessary to go back ten years, to another de la Guerra wedding—the failed marriage that Robinson's union to Anita was meant to replace. Before Anita married the Boston trader, her older sister Teresa had married a foreign trader of her own, Englishman William Hartnell, in the same church.

Independence and the Challenge of Open Ports

Anita de la Guerra, the bride in white, was born on November 6, 1821, joining six brothers and sisters. Her sister Teresa would turn thirteen in a few months, and their eldest brother, José Antonio, at sixteen, had already been serving as a cadet in the Santa Bárbara Company for three years. Anita was the first de la Guerra born in independent Mexico, although her parents did not know it at the time. Captain de la Guerra was forty-two, and his wife, María Antonia, was thirty-five. This growing family anticipated the new year in a state of uncertainty, but they did not face the future in isolation: they joined another 3,200 gente de razón who held the province for Spain. Already, Californios like the de la Guerras considered the whole of this little society as their "family" and shaped their economic and political relationships according to the model of a proper patriarchal household.

In April 1822, de la Guerra swore his allegiance to Mexico, then resumed his duties at the presidio, unsure what Independence might mean for his career. Governor Solá answered his questions in June. This time, the governor sent the Santa Bárbara commander a more personal message, addressed to "my esteemed compadre." Solá and de la Guerra had enjoyed a close working relationship ever since the governor had arrived in 1815, and Solá had sponsored two of de la Guerra's children in compadrazgo. The June letter announced the governor's election as deputy to Iturbide's Imperial Court of Mexico. With Solá's departure, de la Guerra would lose an ally in California but would gain one in Mexico City. "You will consider me useful in anything that I can possibly do for yourself and family," Solá assured his compadre.[5]

In that June 1822 letter, Solá relayed one other piece of news to de la Guerra: a ship under the command of Hugh McCulloch and William Hartnell had recently sailed into Monterey. "Macala y Arnel," Solá told his compadre, had come as agents of an English firm based in Lima, and were looking to buy cattle hides and beef tallow. This trade, Solá felt, would be "very advantageous for this province"; hopefully its inhabitants would overcome their "lazy and profligate" character and embrace it.[6] Solá, a man of "liberal principles," according to one Californio, supported the opening of California's ports to foreign trade.[7] He enclosed a proposed contract between Hartnell and the missions and told de la Guerra to be on the watch for the merchants.

Hartnell's arrival set into motion a critical series of events, both for the de la Guerra family and for the province as a whole. Much more than Independence itself, the liberalization of trade policy and the consequent arrival of foreign merchants posed the greatest challenge, and the greatest opportunity, to well-connected Californios like de la Guerra. On December 13, 1821, newly independent Mexico decreed that the ports of Monterey and San Diego were open to foreign trade; the news reached the territory several months later. The *John Begg*, owned by McCulloch and Hartnell, was the first foreign ship to arrive.[8] Hartnell was a tall man, an Englishman who had been educated in Europe, and who spoke Spanish, French, German, and Latin. But times had been hard in England, and the young man had had trouble finding work. Finally, his uncle Edward Petty dropped by the offices of a school chum to ask for a post for his nephew. That friend was James Brotherston, who headed a huge trading firm with agents around the globe. As a favor, he gave Hartnell a position as bookkeeper and accountant in Santiago, Chile.[9]

After a few years, Hartnell left with John Begg, who was starting up a new subsidiary of Brotherston's empire in Lima, Peru. The agents of John Begg and Company bought South American products like cattle hides, cocoa, corn, cotton, soap, Indian curiosities, and rum, and sold British manufactured goods.[10] In 1821, this firm was only one of many such English companies based in South America. In Lima, Hartnell met a fellow clerk, Hugh McCulloch, who had bigger dreams. The two hatched an ambitious scheme. They would go into partnership as a subsidiary to Begg and work the newly opened California trade in hides and tallow. After the first trip, McCulloch would return to Lima and act as the intermediary between firms, while Hartnell would remain as the resident manager in California.

When Hartnell's ship sailed into Monterey's harbor, he found a population only too eager to get their hands on his cargo of muslin, cambric, canvas, woolens, shawls, buttons, combs, cooking utensils, dishes, tumblers, cocoa, cinnamon, oil, hardware, and window glass. It is easy to imagine Father President Payeras, the head of the long chain of missions, running his eyes down the lists of useful provisions before he sent out a circular, urging his brother missionaries to sign a three-year exclusive contract with the charming Englishman—at a liberal schedule of one peso per hide, one peso per sack of tallow.

Other merchants arrived on the heels of the *John Begg*, sensing profit in the vast herds of cattle that multiplied over the mission lands and in small private herds outside the settlements. The herds had expanded unregulated since the initial introduction of 204 head of cattle in 1769, and by 1822, the missions alone held 149,730 cattle.[11] Five years later, according to one estimate, the missions possessed 210,000 branded cattle, and perhaps more than 100,000 unbranded; they slaughtered over 60,000 every year just to maintain sustainable stock levels.[12] As we have seen, many foreign merchants had already been eyeing the surplus produce of California, even before ports officially opened. For years, American,

English, and Russian ships had been plying California's waters, smuggling otter pelts, and a few Spaniards and Limeños had been shipping tallow to the Peruvian markets. In the first few years of the 1820s, events all over the Pacific Rim conspired to re-orient trade patterns and to create the hide and tallow trade for which California became famous.

Before Independence, foreigners who ventured south from Russian territory had to take their chances smuggling in the Spanish colonies, but the profits made the risk of capture worthwhile. At the turn of the nineteenth century, the biggest commodity in the Pacific by far had been fur—seal fur and sea otter pelts, which sold in China at an enormous return on investment. A triangular trade developed in which firms like Boston's Bryant and Sturgis sent manufactured goods from New England to the Pacific Northwest, traded them for seal and otter fur, and shipped the pelts to China for gold and silver coin and goods, which then returned to Boston. The Sandwich Islands served as an entrepôt and provided a trade in sandalwood.

The independence of Spain's colonies would seem an invitation to even greater fur harvesting, but at the same time that California's ports opened for foreign trade, other conditions discouraged the trade: the otter herd off the coast, never of the same quality as the northern animals, was dwindling. At the same time, increasing competition among the hunters meant lower profits. Meanwhile, the Russians had closed their ports north of San Francisco, creating a risky situation for traders considering a venture into the usual hunting grounds.[13]

Gradually, American and British merchants shifted their attention from the old Northwest fur regions south to the west coast of the Americas. Sea otter fur continued to be a major commodity in California in the Mexican era, but the men who worked the Pacific trade quickly learned that there were markets, too, for the produce of the land. Fur-hunting Russians needed California wheat to last the winter in their northern settlements, the industries of the eastern United States demanded leather, and the mines and markets of Peru provided ready outlet for soap and candles made of California tallow. Englishmen from South America and the Columbia River, New Englanders from Boston and the Hawaiian Islands, Russians from Sitka, Mexicans based in Tepic and San Blas, and South Americans from Lima and Santiago—all came to the Mexican province in search of hides, tallow, horns, soap, otter skins, wheat, and lumber.[14]

Likewise, British and American traders were learning that they might make a great profit selling their own manufactured goods in Spanish

America.[15] The economy of Mexico had been battered during the wars of independence. From 1810 to 1821, Spanish capital had fled, skilled labor had dispersed, and infrastructure had been destroyed. By Independence, mining production was less than a quarter of what it had been ten years before. Without the mines to sustain demand, agricultural output fell by half, and industry to a third of pre-war levels.[16] Mexican industry, textiles in particular, simply could not compete with the quality or price of foreign goods. Likewise, as a result of Independence, Spanish merchant houses closed. When a December 1821 decree opened Mexico to trade with all nations, foreign merchant houses like McCulloch and Hartnell moved in to replace the Spaniards.

In California, the opening of ports and the shifts in Pacific trading patterns fanned the flames of hide and tallow production in the province and brought on a boom in the local economy. The number of ships that dropped anchor off the California coast increased each year, and by the 1830s, the ships were taking on an average of 285,000 hides and 570,000 arrobas (7,125 tons) of tallow annually.[17] Each ship remained up to two years before its holds were fully loaded, and throughout any given year, fleets of vessels plied California's estuaries and bays, picking up whatever produce was available for sale.

During the late-spring and early-summer slaughtering season, ports like San Pedro, San Diego, and Monterey became carnivals of trade. Shortly before the arrival of a ship, Indian and Mexican workers set out on horseback to round up the cattle that roamed across the arid valleys and scrubby hills. If the ship were from Peru or San Blas, seeking only tallow, vaqueros simply killed the animals on the spot, cut out fat from the bellies, and left the carcasses to rot. As one Californio remembered, price depended on speed of delivery, and "it was not worth the effort to carve up the animal, stretch the hide, and take out the rest of the fat."[18] Answering the needs of Boston traders demanded more care. For that, workers began earlier at the slaughtering fields, skinning the cattle, cleaning the hides, and staking them out to dry in the hot sun. They folded the stiff hides lengthwise and stacked them in adobe warehouses alongside the cowhide sacks of rendered tallow, awaiting the call for delivery. Butchering was hot, messy work. Flies swarmed over the congealing pools of blood, and winds blew the stink of rotting meat and boiling fat across the fields. At the missions, neophytes did the work; poor ranchers who were lucky enough to own a few cows of their own hired neophyte or gentile Indians when they could.

As soon as runners announced the arrival of traders in port, *carreteros*, or cart drivers, began their creaky way down from the missions

"View of the presidio or town of Santa Barbara," ca. 1830, from Alfred Robinson, *Life in California*. Courtesy of California State Parks.

and ranchos, loaded with stacks of hides and greasy sacks of tallow. The sturdy carts, with two large, solid wooden wheels, were made by Indians at the missions or by individual townsfolk. Despite their crude appearance, the ox-driven drays could carry fifty hides easily over the rough, dusty tracks, and renting them out could net the owner a small profit. "Each person had one or two more, according to his means and needs. The missions, of course, had a great many," remembered rancher José del Carmen Lugo.[19] Once in port, the carretero met a chaotic scene.

Beginning early in the morning, buyers and sellers haggled on the beach while droughers balanced hides on their heads, one at a time, wading through the surf to load them on small boats and ferry them to the ships. Onshore, "all was confusion," recalled Alfred Robinson, the Boston trader who arrived in 1829; "cattle and cart laden with hides and tallow, gente de razón and Indians busily employed in the delivery of their produce, and receiving in return its value in goods; groups of individuals seated around little bonfires upon the ground, and horsemen racing over the plain in every direction."[20] Foreign traders opened sacks of tallow to check quality and freshness, spread out hides to look for insect damage and rot, and carefully packed their cargoes in barrels and crates for the long voyage around the Cape.

California was not alone in experiencing this frenzy of trade in the early years after Independence. While the economy of Mexico in general stagnated, the northern border boomed. All across the border between the United States and Mexico, local residents welcomed the arrival of foreigners to stimulate neglected economies. At the same moment that Father Payeras and Governor Solá were poring over the invoices of the *John Begg* with William Hartnell, Governor Facundo Melgares of New Mexico was welcoming William Becknell into his office. The two shook hands, opening a steady trade between Santa Fe and the state of Missouri. Meanwhile, in Texas, Stephen Austin inherited his father's empresario grant and began to bring in American colonists.

These new connections, when seen on the regional and national levels, were the first in a series of critical market shifts that eventually reoriented Mexico's northern economy. Before 1821, Mexico as a whole was a colonial dependent of Spain, and the northern provinces themselves were dependent on the markets of Chihuahua, Durango, San Blas, and Mexico City. After Independence, the United States, France, and England replaced Spain in its hold over the entire Mexican economy. The northern provinces, because of their proximity to the United States, developed particularly close ties with their northern neighbors.[21]

It is easy to imagine foreign traders in California dictating its economy. Indeed, English and American traders did try to do just that, and later believed that they had succeeded. William Hartnell was not the only one to propose exclusive contracts: he met fierce competition from American firms wanting to do the same. William Gale, a seal hunter in the employ of Pacific Northwest fur traders Bryant and Sturgis, persuaded his company in 1821 to send a frigate to California and load its holds with fur and hides. Their ship, the *Sachem,* arrived from Boston in July 1822, just after the *John Begg* sailed into Monterey's harbor. Bryant and Sturgis firmly connected New England to California but were too late to corner the market. Another American, James Smith Wilcox, hoped in vain for his own windfall when he wrote to de la Guerra from Mexico City in September of that year. Wilcox knew de la Guerra from his days as a smuggler in the China trade, and with a contract from a New York firm in his pocket, Wilcox now urged de la Guerra to draw up contracts with the missions. "My aim," he explained, is "to gather all amounts of hides and horns the slaughters may produce there, and that no other buy one following."[22] Although no one firm ended up taking all the produce of California, English and Yankee traders like Hartnell, Gale, and Wilcox did serve as the primary consumers of California's hides and tallow. Surveying their success, they congratulated themselves frequently for "having more industry, frugality, and enterprise than the natives."[23]

But a closer look at California's economy from the perspective of the Californios reveals a slightly different story. Foreign merchants did not completely monopolize the California economy as they would have wished. Instead, they relied a great deal on men like de la Guerra, who in his own right continued to control much of the local exchange of goods and produce. In the summer of 1822, as news of the first foreign ships spread across the province, Francisco María Ruiz, captain at San Diego, had exclaimed to his fellow commander at Santa Bárbara that he was "glad to hear of the arrival of that frigate; it comes well for those who have money."[24] As merchant and habilitado, de la Guerra had made *his* money under Spanish rule as a commercial agent for the missions, and as shopkeeper for the soldiers under his command. After 1821, as the hide-and-tallow trade intensified ranching production, de la Guerra's established middleman role expanded.

De la Guerra gave merchants who did not live in California a contact who could organize the purchase and shipping of local produce. Mexican and Peruvian merchants had been cultivating this contact since the colonial era, and continued to do so into the 1830s and 1840s. Tepic trader Manuel Varela, for example, did not drop his connections with de la Guerra, but went on under Mexican rule to settle their cinnamon deal, and receive de la Guerra's otter pelts, tallow, hides, wool, and libranzas, or notes of credit.[25] After the opening of California's ports, Americans and Europeans who became key players in California trade learned that they would do well for themselves if they followed this example.

From the early 1820s, most foreign traders continued to rely on de la Guerra's friendships with the mission fathers, and the missionaries to rely on his personal knowledge of the traders. As Juan Malarín, a Peruvian ship captain, reminded de la Guerra during a tricky business negotiation, "You have friends, especially Padre Luis, who, with your influence will do something and will get us out of these difficulties."[26] Father Luis Antonio Martínez, a stout man whose nose was permanently bent from a fall from a carriage, oversaw the Mission San Luis Obispo, about one hundred miles up the coast from Santa Bárbara. He was an especially close friend of de la Guerra. They were fellow Spaniards, the friar arriving in California just two years before the young officer, and the two corresponded frequently, in an increasingly friendly, joking tone. During the unsettled war years, the two had encouraged each other to remain loyal to King Fernando. Perhaps de la Guerra sensed in his compatriot a kindred spirit with the same knack for business, and respected the friar's sincere interest in improving California's livestock production. Martínez ran a prosperous operation, set a generous table for guests, and sent abundant supplies to the presidios. Clearly, the two enjoyed each other's company and trusted one another implicitly.[27] Friendships like this gave the captain a key to the economy of the province, which no foreigner could survive without.

This was especially true when de la Guerra acted as the missions' explicit agent, as happened in 1824. Juan Malarín was on the coast as the master of the *Apolonia,* sailing out of San Blas. He carried aboard a large lot of goods for the missions, paid for in Tepic with the mission stipends of 1820–24, amounting to $42,680, which the new government had finally paid out.[28] As he did frequently, de la Guerra served as *apoderado,* or agent, for Father Luis, receiving about $3,000 worth of goods and paying for it with about $2,000 in cash and $1,000 in tallow. "You as *apoderado general* [chief agent] set the prices as you wish," Malarín told de la Guerra.[29]

De la Guerra, through his friendships with the missionaries, brought together producer and consumer. But not every missionary appreciated the cut de la Guerra inevitably took from each transaction. Father Blas Ordaz of Mission Santa Ynez, in particular, took offense at the commander's hard bargaining. "You have to know, Señor Don José, that you don't have to twist me around, as you are accustomed to doing with some of the Poor," he sniped in 1830, "I certainly don't have to buy anything from you, when what you give for eight, I give for six."[30]

Indeed, de la Guerra not only continued to turn a profit as agent for the missions; he also bought and sold goods and libranzas from the merchant vessels throughout the Mexican era, maintaining accounts with missionaries, soldiers, and townsfolk alike. On days when a Boston or Lima ship was in port, local consumers examined wares themselves. "Visitors were numerous, both male and female, who came on board to purchase," noted Alfred Robinson, whose traderoom aboard the *Brookline* "had been fitted up with shelves and counters, resembling in appearance a country variety store." But in the long months without access to such floating department stores, California's residents turned to the warehouses of men like de la Guerra, who had considerable buying power in the province and could purchase manufactured goods at a discount because he bought them in bulk.[31]

Thus, de la Guerra had a hand in most trade in goods, big and small, that took place on the coast, and as a consequence he grew in power and wealth. But it is worth asking if de la Guerra was a rich man only in depreciating goods and in credit with the missions. After all, the usual image of the hide-and-tallow trade is of foreign merchants siphoning hard currency out of the region, as Californios paid for manufactured goods in silver and gold. As Father Francisco González y Ibarra noted, "You are not unaware that the purchase of [imported] goods varies greatly, depending on whether they are bought for money or for [export] goods."[32] But in fact, de la Guerra did manage to maintain a ready supply of cash for himself by selling furs and hides for coin whenever possible.[33] As there were no banks in California, men like de la Guerra could use their stores of coin to make more money. De la Guerra frequently loaned money at interest, particularly to foreign merchants caught short by customs duties. As a result, little coin actually left the province. This fact surprised American observers like Richard Henry Dana, who exclaimed, "I certainly never saw so much silver at one time in my life, as during the week that we were at Monterey," the provincial capital.[34] Father Francisco González y Ibarra understood the advantages of cash as well, noting that he always made more profit by loaning his silver than by selling merchandise.[35]

In truth, it was not all Californians, but instead small producers and townsfolk, who were more likely to be stripped of their currency—as much by Californio middlemen as by Americans or Englishmen. Many former soldiers and civilians between Santa Bárbara and Los Angeles owned small herds, and these small producers depended on de la Guerra as much as the foreign traders did. Without a middleman, dozens of small-time cattle owners would have had to travel long distances to make contact with visiting traders, and these merchants in turn would have had to fill their holds with tiny lots of a few hides or a couple of sacks of tallow. As much as they hated the cut de la Guerra inevitably took from such transactions, both producer and consumer relied on him to buy the produce of small-time ranchers and townsfolk, to collect livestock on his ranches and processed goods in his warehouses, and to negotiate their sale in large lots to the merchants of Boston or Liverpool.

Thus, de la Guerra's role in the California economy continued to be a distinct and critical one; nearly every level of trade depended on him, from owners of a handful of cows to missionaries responsible for major ranches, to agents of powerful merchant houses in Boston. As was true before 1821, this was not a job that de la Guerra could do alone. Over time, he had nurtured in-law and compadrazgo relationships, reinforcing economic partnerships with family ties at every level. He needed agents such as his Carrillo brothers-in-law to visit far-flung ranches, oversee warehouse operations, and organize the transport of goods to port in San Pedro and San Diego. He depended on patrons like Governor Solá to smooth the official path of trade and landholding. And he depended on his personal and family connections with the merchants who came to call at California's ports.

Integration

The arrival of traders from outside the Spanish world posed a serious challenge to the family economy after Independence. Although they presented undeniable economic opportunities, the foreigners had no link at all to California's elite "family," which meant that key sectors of the economy were potentially out of the control of local players. De la Guerra, as middleman, merchant, and agent, was essential to the foreign traders' enterprises, but none of the traders felt any overriding obligation or loyalty to the well-being of their Californio business partners. The solution—as clear to men like de la Guerra as it was to the merchants—was to contain the threat by integrating the useful new arrivals into familial webs of reciprocity and dependence.[36]

William Hartnell, by getting to California first, clearly became the most important of the newly arrived merchants. His contract and his unique position as resident manager made him the most dangerous. The contract Hartnell negotiated with Father President Payeras was for an exclusive trade, and for as much mission production as his firm could absorb. The governor made sure to attach a guarantee that Hartnell would also take in the much smaller bundles of hides and tallow that townsfolk and ranchers offered. If delivered at the waterfront, these would be accepted on the same terms as mission produce.[37] McCulloch and Hartnell agreed to send at least one ship a year, and to take at least 25,000 arrobas (or 312 tons) of tallow, and all hides offered. Payment would be accepted in either goods or coin, as the seller wished.

Hartnell's operation was at first the only foreign trading firm to take up residence in California, and this, too, aided the enterprise. By the summer of 1823, he had persuaded the new governor to allow him to construct local warehouses and to open more of California's ports to his trade. Soon, Hartnell was a common sight up and down the coast, negotiating sales with mission fathers, military officers, and civilian ranchers. Hartnell wrote to an old friend in England, "I am now a partner in the most respectable house on this side of Cape Horn, enjoying better health than ever I did in my life, and universally looked upon here as the greatest personage in California."[38] Among the many coastal traders, Hartnell was a man to be reckoned with.

This fact did not escape the notice of de la Guerra, who had first heard of the young man from his compadre Solá, who had forwarded a copy of the contract. Most foreign traders needed de la Guerra to do the local negotiating for them, to assemble hides and tallow in California's ports, and to take on large orders of their goods. Hartnell's year-round residence in California, his warehouses, and his growing personal relationship with the missionaries threatened to cut into de la Guerra's profits as middleman. On the other hand, good relations with Hartnell's Anglo-Peruvian firm could provide de la Guerra with a reliable news source for political conditions in Europe and South America and for fluctuations in the world market. De la Guerra wasted little time in maneuvering the young man into his household.

The first step was to welcome Hartnell into the de la Guerra home in the presidio's officers' quarters and to shower him with the generous hospitality befitting an important client. In the early 1820s, Hartnell was a frequent guest of the captain, joining the family in Santa Bárbara for dinners of beef and beans, chiles, squash, and bread, all washed down with some of the Captain's Conejo wine. Hartnell was so impressed with de la Guerra's wine, in fact, that he bought ten barrels.[39] After dinner, de la Guerra would lead his family in prayer, then the two men would retire to his corner office, and with the candles burning low, discuss business before retiring for the night. De la Guerra bought large quantities of Hartnell's cargo, including bolts of cloth, handkerchiefs and shawls, flannel petticoats, trousers, shoes, cups and saucers, tumblers, and knives. In so doing, de la Guerra also integrated Hartnell into the essential system of credit, exchanged as libranzas among local producers, middlemen like de la Guerra, and Latin American merchants.[40]

As their relationship developed, de la Guerra used his connections to help Hartnell compete against other traders. In the summer of 1823, Juan Ignacio Mancisidor of Lima and his local manager, Antonio José Cot, began to offer twice as much for hides in order to undermine Hartnell's contract. Hartnell's trade began to slip, and several panicky missionaries demanded immediate payment in cash for the balance of their accounts. For the cash-strapped Englishman, this was impossible, and Hartnell complained to de la Guerra, "From all sides rain bills." Although de la Guerra was a friend and business partner of both Mancisidor and Cot, he stepped in to aid his protégé by reassuring the padres. Hartnell's crisis passed.[41]

With hospitality and favors, de la Guerra had begun to create a father-and-son relationship with Hartnell. But this was not enough to make

Hartnell feel completely indebted to patron de la Guerra, nor did he yet consider California "home." This was about to change. Hartnell had been raised an Anglican in England, and, although he tried to remain true to his faith, personal trials and the guiding hand of de la Guerra pushed the young merchant to reconsider. Before leaving England, Hartnell had stolen money from his uncle and benefactor, Edward Petty. In California, he received a letter from his sister Hannah in the summer of 1824, telling him of this kind uncle's financial reversals. Wracked with guilt, Hartnell pickled himself in rot-gut aguardiente and drifted for weeks in San Diego, unable to work. Finally, the remorseful merchant received a friendly letter of concern from his old business rival Antonio José Cot, who was, like him, now a resident manager. In the letter, Cot chided him for his constant "fiestas" and reminded him that they were to have met in Santa Bárbara. Stirred to action, Hartnell left for the north, stopping for a few days at the de la Guerra home, where he had so often been a guest.

While there, he received a business letter from Father Luis Martínez of Mission San Luis Obispo—a letter that included an invitation for him "to spend a holy week." Cot and de la Guerra urged the young man to give up drink and take up the priest's offer. Faced with such an outpouring of generosity and concern, Hartnell accepted the offer. Under the tutelage of Martínez, he confessed the theft and sent all the money he could spare to his family, in order to make amends. On October 13, 1824, he converted to the Catholic faith, taking his uncle's name as his middle name. José de la Guerra stood as his sponsor.[42]

Baptism and conversion into the Catholic faith not only made foreigners more like the Californios culturally but also rendered them "juridic persons" in the eyes of the Church—full members of the religious community.[43] In fact, the de la Guerras were quite aggressive in bringing as many foreign merchants as they could into their familial, cultural, and economic orbit through the compadrazgo system. Once in the fold, Hartnell himself acted as a go-between, standing as the godfather for several of his friends in the English-speaking population. In 1827, he wrote to his godfather, "I have the pleasure to tell you that on Holy Saturday I sponsored your nephew Dn. Juan Cooper who reconciled on that day with our Holy Church and took the name Juan Bautista; and I believe that *Dn. David* [Spence] is going to follow him!!!"[44] The de la Guerras themselves became compadres of Daniel Hill and Nicolás Den and of the foreign sons-in-law of María Antonia's brother Carlos Carrillo.[45] One of her foreign nephews, William Goodwin Dana, frequently stressed his compadre relationship to de la Guerra when the two did business.[46]

Baptism and a well-placed godfather made other, deeper, connections possible, as Hartnell himself knew. In 1819, five years before his conversion, he had written to his sister Hannah from Chile, "If you know any pretty girl that wants a husband, pray send her as I am almost dying for a wife, and should find some difficulty in meeting with one here unless I were to turn Catholic."[47] It is perhaps of little surprise, then, that on April 30, 1825, less than a year after his baptism, William Edward Petty Hartnell was wed in Santa Bárbara to de la Guerra's eldest daughter, Teresa. For good measure, the new couple that same day became godparents to María de Jesús Antonia Ortega, a niece of Teresa's eldest brother, José Antonio.

Teresa and William

Historians can never know exactly how this marriage was arranged; the documents are silent. For those with a romantic nature, it is easy to picture the first meeting in 1822 of shy Teresa, just thirteen, and the serious Englishman, twenty-four. As her mother graciously pours the guest a steaming cup of hot chocolate, Teresa quietly hovers, offering candied pumpkin or sweet bread. Her eyes open wide at the stranger's European dress and odd accent. De la Guerra emerges from the shadows of the interior with a bottle of wine under his arm, excuses himself for his rudeness and introduces the children, from seventeen-year old José Antonio down to two-year-old Pablo; baby Anita is asleep inside. Does Teresa think their guest is handsome, or hope to see him again?

Others, more pragmatic, can imagine a conversation held two or three years later in de la Guerra's office. Perhaps the two men lingered, sipping brandy after dinner. They discuss the political situation in Mexico and the price of tallow in Lima. The warehouse in San Diego needs repairs already, and Father Martínez is looking for a good price on muslin for the neophytes. The men slip into silence, puffing cigars and blowing out blue smoke into the whitewashed room. Then Hartnell clears his throat and brings up a subject they both know is coming. Will de la Guerra grant Teresa's hand in marriage? Beaming, the father stands up to shake the merchant's hand and says, "Welcome to the family."

Each man had much to gain. With this union, Hartnell secured full participation in the family economy. Elite families, he had learned, controlled access to critical resources: connections to Latin American merchants, the credit system, missionary-producers, and customs officials. But one thing that Hartnell did not gain was California land. In Mexico generally, the major objective in most elite marriages was to keep as much property from leaving the family as possible, so marriage to a land-owning cousin became a preferred strategy. And, in fact, this seems to have been the case with the marriage of Teresa's eldest brother, José Antonio, who wed just five months before she did.

In November 1824, nineteen-year-old José Antonio, a cadet in the Santa Bárbara company, married sixteen-year-old María Concepción Manuela Ortega y López. Concepción, or "Chona," was the daughter of the late José María Ortega, who had served as corporal of the Santa Bárbara Company and commander of the guards at Mission La Purísima.[48] Before his death, her father had been the lucky recipient of one of the few grants made to officers in the colonial era: the coastal Rancho Refugio just north of Santa Bárbara (which then developed a persistent reputation as a hot spot for smuggling). Chona would have inherited a small interest in this land, but even without it, she was a good match for an aspiring patriarch; her family had ties to the military, and her sister Soledad was married to Luis Argüello, the provisional governor of California at the time. Soon, José Antonio was posted to a more responsible position with the guards at La Purísima himself.[49]

While elite sons hoped to marry elite daughters like Chona Ortega, who had land and connections, a small but significant number of elite daughters, about fifteen percent, were wed to propertyless foreigners. This has led some historians to see such matches as a failure in the fathers' foresight, leading to a steady erosion of Californio landholding into the hands of the newcomers.[50] Yet, at the time of Teresa's wedding, very little of California's land was held in private hands. In fact, Teresa brought no real property to her marriage, Hartnell received no land as a dowry, and no de la Guerra land ever passed into his hands during their long marriage.

If Hartnell gained access to the commercial networks of Alta California through his marriage, de la Guerra, in turn, gained a dependent who was himself an important player in the hide-and-tallow economy, one who appeared to have the connections, education, and business acumen to continue his rise. Obviously, Hartnell, with his ability to secure exclusive contracts with the missions, and his access to the markets of South America and England, would give de la Guerra an immediate avenue to expand his own business enterprises. But this merchant possessed other qualities that seemed to guarantee a bright future. Hartnell's education and his connections to the world of literature and learning brought high esteem. Hartnell conversed in Latin with the missionaries, further cementing his good relations with these important clients. Each ship from Europe brought him books and newspapers, courtesy of friends in Europe, which he passed on to his patron de la Guerra. With his Continental education, access to current news, connections to the world market, and training in accounting and international trade, Hartnell made a helpful ally for changing times.

Along with political and economic advantages, Hartnell brought to the alliance a clear claim to "whiteness," and a pure European ancestry, so it is worth asking how much this figured into de la Guerra's decision. To hear contemporary Yankee and European observers tell it, race mattered a great deal. Officially, after Independence, the Mexican government banished the caste system and no longer set racial barriers to marriage, but locally, remnants of a racial hierarchy continued to order Californian society. Bostonian Richard Henry Dana explained the importance of biology and appearance: "Each person's caste," he observed, "is decided by the quality of the blood, which shows itself, too plainly to be concealed, at first sight." Merchants from the United States and Europe, obviously white, would further whiten the families of the elites and set them apart from low-class townsfolk and Indians.

And yet, in mixed-race California, where many of the elites had transcended their humble origins, the commonly used terms "gente de razón" and "Spanish" had come to mean something more than "white." Even families like the Picos, who were known to have African ancestry, were accepted as full members of the elite, as long as they dressed and acted Spanish. As Dana later explained, "The least drop of Spanish blood . . . is sufficient to raise them from the rank of slave . . . and to call themselves Españolos [sic], and to hold property, if they can get any."[51] De la Guerra himself rarely mentioned the racial classification of fellow elites, even of his English and American sons-in-law.[52] In the end, Hartnell's ability to take on the full spectrum of attributes associated with the gente de razón was much more important than simple whiteness to his eventual acceptance in the Californio family.

Hartnell was the first of a handful of foreigners who put down roots in California in the 1820s, most of whom moved directly into the Californio social structure at the highest levels. These men were not the shaggy trappers of New Mexico, nor the hardscrabble colonists who eked out a living on the empresario lands of Texas. By 1830, only about 120 foreigners lived in California, the majority of them prominent men of business.[53] That decade, a few American trappers and horse traders began to move through the interior, but they stayed away from the settled regions, and Hubert Howe Bancroft's Pioneer Register recorded no marriages between them and Californio women.[54] As Dana observed, "The people are generally suspicious of foreigners, and they would not be allowed to remain, were it not that they become good Catholics, and by marrying natives, and bringing up their children as Catholics and Mexicans, and not teaching them the English language, they quiet suspicion, and even become popular and leading men."[55] "With regard to Hartnell," remembered the retired soldier José Ramón Sánchez, "his entry into high society was owed, in part, to his fine education, and in part to his marriage to Doña Teresa de la Guerra, daughter of a distinguished Spanish officer."[56]

Clearly, marriage was of material benefit to Californio fathers and foreign sons-in-law, but what power did women like Teresa or her mother have in the choice of a mate? Had the young woman spoken privately with Hartnell before he had broached the subject with her father, or did her mother wake her with the news the next morning? According to the romantic view of post-conquest Americans, Californian women chose their blue-eyed conquerors freely. But the documents tell a different story: in wealthy families like the de la Guerras, fathers did indeed exercise a great deal of legal and customary authority over their daughters.

In part, de la Guerra's role as paternal gatekeeper to his daughter stemmed from the generational precedence granted as a matter of course to all fathers. As one observer later insisted, "These arrangements took place only between the fathers of the children, and they tried to keep them from learning of their plans."[57] And when the suitor arrived without family, like Hartnell, fathers arranged marriages directly with the young man. Over time, as suitors did throughout Mexico, a young man in California would build a relationship of deference to the girl's father, presenting gifts and favors to the young woman and her family, and gradually coming to a formal understanding with the elder man.[58] No doubt Hartnell's process of conversion under de la Guerra's baptismal sponsorship dovetailed nicely into this budding relationship between respected elder and young man.

Fathers claimed a special interest in controlling the marriages and sexuality of girls because, as noted previously, a father's masculine honor, in large part, depended on his ability to protect his wife and daughters from sexual dishonor. Male control over female sexuality was based on the notion that the blood relation of father to child, and therefore a man's ability to pass property on to his rightful heirs, could only be guaranteed if sexual access to women was carefully monitored.[59] The very fact that Teresa and Hartnell met at all, in fact, must have been a deliberate choice by her father.

The legal system backed up these cultural standards. In the 1820s, the new republican government of Mexico had still made few legal changes to the Spanish laws, based on patria potestas. A new national civil code would not be enacted until 1870, in fact, leaving it up to state and local officials in the meantime to adapt the colonial-era laws as best they could. These laws made the father his children's guardian, with control over their education, legal transactions, and property until their own marriages. A father's consent was required for a minor child's marriage—before age twenty-three for girls and before age twenty-five for boys. In California, most elite girls married well below that age, in some cases only a few years over the legal age of twelve—Teresa was almost sixteen when she married, Angustias was seventeen, and little sister Anita was just fourteen.[60] Few children dared oppose a father's choice, in any case, because the law also allowed fathers the right to disinherit children who married against their wishes.[61]

With custom and the law behind them, fathers took the lead in negotiating their daughters' marriages. Still, mothers often worked within the "natural" authority Mexican culture assigned to women—that of higher morality—to appeal directly to men and thus influence the marriages of their children. Although the father was presumed to have the last word in such matters, and legally, mothers did not have to be consulted, in practice mothers could demand discussion and agreement with their husbands over the choice. And mothers took a great deal of interest in protecting the virtue and honor of their daughters, as their shame would reflect on the family as a whole. Likewise, mothers like María Antonia understood the great benefits a man like Hartnell would bring as a son-in-law. Sometime after getting to know the young Englishman, and before her husband consented to give his daughter's hand, María Antonia must have strolled alone with her husband in the nearby garden or spoken with him privately after dinner about their daughter's future. Having assured herself of Hartnell's sincere conversion and of his intentions to remain in California, she would have sent her husband to talk to the merchant with her assent.

Mothers also took an active role in preparing their daughters to become wives, beginning around the time girls turned ten or eleven, just before they reached the age for legal marriage. Prior to that, girls were considered children. When Anita was nine, for example, her mother's good friend María Estevana de Cot (the wife of tallow trader Antonio José Cot) sent the girl "a lovely doll, proper for her age."[62] But at age eleven, Teresa was learning household management and "had become a woman with the help and teaching of her mother."[63] Indeed, de la Guerra family oral tradition holds that all of the de la Guerra daughters learned home management by "each taking a turn about as mistress."[64] Teresa, married at fifteen, no doubt resented being pulled from her studies, particularly when her younger sister Angustias was allowed to go on reading and developing a more cultured polish through her late teens. Angustias, however, was the exception: María Inocenta Pico, a cousin of the de la Guerras, complained that "many girls did not complete even those basic subjects because their mothers would take them out of school, almost always to marry them off. The bad custom existed of marrying off very young girls whenever men asked for their hand."[65]

Did Teresa have any right to refuse the marriage or choose her own mate? Certainly, some young women in Mexican California found ways to subvert the wishes of fathers and prospective husbands, generally by pitting one against the other, or by making an appeal to outside sources of authority. A resourceful daughter might seek an ally in the Church, since in Mexico, the Church also claimed jurisdiction over marriage contracts and mandated free will as a prerequisite of marriage. This latter tactic could not be depended on, however, as the presence of Church and state in the Californian family became even weaker after Independence.[66] In the Mexican era, the shrinking military no longer enforced dowry requirements, and the state no longer forbade marriages on the basis of race.

Daughters with their own ideas needed strength of will and a degree of cleverness to negotiate within a system that favored their fathers so strongly. Two examples from Teresa's family demonstrate, perhaps, alternate paths that Teresa could have explored within the structures of California patriarchy. In 1829, cousin Josefa Carrillo eloped with Henry Delano Fitch, an American ship captain, who she said attracted her with his "refined manners and handsome presence."[67] Fitch had agreed to be baptized Catholic, and the couple had secured the consent of Carrillo's parents and the local priest, but the governor sent a messenger to stop the wedding mid-ceremony, claiming (apparently incorrectly) that marriage to a foreigner was illegal. Josefa believed his motive was simple jealousy. Unwilling to challenge state authority, both the priest and Josefa's father complied with the order. A few days later, Josefa defied her father, the Church, and California's government, and sailed with Fitch by moonlight for Chile, where the two were married in a Catholic ceremony.

On the couple's return a year later with their newborn, Josefa shrewdly overcame her familial dishonor and secured recognition of the marriage by appealing to her father's sense of political honor. Her father considered his family deeply dishonored by her flight and elopement, and as Josefa remembered, "had vowed to kill her the moment he laid

eyes on her again." She went to see him alone in his office and threw herself on her knees and begged forgiveness, telling him, "that if she had
disobeyed him, she did it for the sole purpose of getting away from an
odious tyranny that laws and customs condemned." This reference to
Governor Echeandía, an opponent of her father, worked as she had intended. Joaquín Carrillo put down his gun and rose to embrace his
daughter, exclaiming, "Daughter, I forgive you because it is not your fault
that our leaders are despots." That night, her father sponsored a ball and
invited all his relatives and neighbors as a formal recognition of his head-
strong daughter's marriage.[68]

Teresa's younger sister Angustias apparently used her own strategies
to escape a marriage she did not want. As she later told her daughter, in
1831 the new governor, Manuel Victoria, "wanted to marry me, but I did
not marry him because he was Mexican and was very anti-Spanish.
Ironically, I later ended up marrying a Mexican."[69] At first, she said, she
had been determined to meet Victoria shortly after his arrival in the
province, and took advantage of her father's political position to do so.
She went up to the mission to hear mass with some girlfriends and suggested to them,

> "Let's go see if we can meet the commander general to
> see what he is like"... At that moment we saw a rather
> dark-complected man who was leaning on the railing.
> He was wearing a red flannel shirt with a jacket over it.
> We took him for a soldier but he turned out to be Señor
> Victoria... My father came out shortly after and called
> me into the room and introduced me to Señor Victoria.
> I noticed that he had very beautiful eyes... it was said
> that he had been a fine soldier in the Mexican War of
> Independence.[70]

Clearly, Angustias's father, by presenting his daughter to someone he
hoped would become a political ally, was signaling his assent to a possible
match. After all, Angustias was already fifteen and eligible for marriage.
And yet, the union did not take place, despite the initial moment of intrigue at Victoria's "beautiful eyes." Soon after his arrival, Angustias became convinced of Victoria's "despotism," and it is likely that she played up
her father's distrust of Victoria's anti-Spanish leanings and of his race (Victoria was also known as "the Negro of Acapulco") to secure de la Guerra's
rejection of the marriage. Despite the attempt in her memoirs to obscure

the actors in this decision, the choice not to marry Victoria was clearly the result of a negotiation between Angustias, her proudly Spanish father, and the dark-skinned Mexican governor—a negotiation over the boundaries of race, class, and political ideology in the Californio family economy. For her part, Angustias tells us, she was not in theory averse to marrying a Mexican and proved it by marrying one in 1833.

These two examples illustrate the ways in which a daughter might exploit tensions within Californio patriarchy to influence the selection of her future husband, but in practice such situations were rare. In truth, most young women submitted willingly because they identified strongly with their fathers' families.[71] Daughters like Teresa understood quite well that accepting a valuable match would aid the family at large and secure their own long-term prosperity and status. And because foreign men like Hartnell had no established kin network of their own, they would presumably be absorbed entirely into their wives' families, much the same as immigrant José de la Guerra had joined his fortunes to the creole Carrillos. Tellingly, in a testimonio given in 1875, fifty years after leaving her father's household, Teresa identified herself first as a de la Guerra and spoke with pride of her father's wealth and influence; in comparison, she mentioned her husband rather briefly.[72]

Thus, in the first decades of Mexican rule, patriarchs like José de la Guerra, with the aid of their wives and the presumed consent of their daughters, were the primary force behind the selection of sons-in-law among the foreign population of California. Prior to 1848, de la Guerra's daughters married an Englishman, a Mexican, an American, and a Spanish national born in France. All arrived as international merchants or customs officials. These choices were made with specific economic and political goals in mind—goals shaped by the family economy of California's hide-and-tallow market. As in core areas of Mexico, fathers used marital alliances to increase and consolidate their families' holdings and absorb potential threats. The singular conditions of California's frontier economy made marriages to foreign merchants particularly appealing. The patriarch ensured the dependence and full integration of men like William Hartnell by insisting that he demonstrate his Catholicism, knowledge of Spanish culture, residence in California, and personal deference to his elders. De la Guerra made no sacrifice by marrying off Teresa; he entered into a mutually beneficial arrangement with another businessman. He had no way of knowing that failure loomed on the horizon.

Intermarriages at the Santa Bárbara Presidio

Time Period	Total Marriages	Percent of Marriages between Californios and Foreigners	Groom's Country of Origin
1821–29	48	8.3%	3 United States, 1 England
1831–39	68	14.7%	5 United States, 1 Scotland, 2 England, 1 France, and 1 without country of attribution (Juan Davis)
1840–46	72	6.9%	3 United States, 1 France, and 1 Netherlands

Reversals of Fortune

At first, the future looked quite sunny for the young family and their patriarch. In June 1825, Hartnell returned to Monterey with his new bride, Teresa, to encounter the news that a recent sale of his hides in London had netted him considerable profits.[73] Hartnell's new assistant, David Spence, had just completed work on a splendid new house for the couple. Hartnell settled into California society as a wealthy and powerful man. Back in Santa Bárbara, de la Guerra had faith that his daughter would be well taken care of, and that his new *yerno* would bring him great benefit as well.

Perhaps the most significant and immediate advantage that this marriage brought to de la Guerra came in an indirect form: Hartnell provided de la Guerra the means to secure a European education for one of his sons. Following the lead of many businessmen in the early national period, de la Guerra invested enormous resources into the education of his sons, and he used his contacts with foreign traders to secure

schooling abroad for them.[74] Juan José de la Guerra, the next eldest son
after José Antonio, had left home for Tepic at the end of 1823, at age ten.
De la Guerra's well-cultivated partners in that town arranged Juan's
situation there; in April 1824, Manuel Varela sent a letter assuring the
Californian, "Your son Juan . . . was placed in a school which a man by the
name of Lavin has here, who admits pupils, giving them meals, lessons,
and washing their clothes; all for 20 pesos a month."[75] The bill of
172 pesos, credited in full from the cinnamon account, paid for Juan's
passage, two suits of clothes and shoes, and tuition from January 1824.[76]
José Cardoso, another merchant acquaintance, offered that March to
take any of de la Guerra's sons as students in a naval academy where he
had just been appointed teacher and director.[77]

But an even better foreign contact, Hartnell, brought de la Guerra
the chance for a truly stellar education for Juan. At the very time his
daughter was marrying the Englishman, de la Guerra's partners in Tepic
were booking his son passage on a ship to England, where Juan arrived in
October 1825. From Liverpool, James Brotherston announced to his old
protégé, Hartnell, "You will please tell his Father I assume the charge with
much pleasure, and shall pay every attention to his son's improvement in
his education by placing him under those who are capable to instruct
him. He is a fine boy and clever, and I expect he will do credit to his
teachers."[78] In all, Juan remained in England for six and a half years. No
less than his sister Teresa, Juan sacrificed his childhood freedom and
the security of family life in Santa Bárbara for the larger good of the
de la Guerra family's economy.

On the basis of such favors, the relationship between Hartnell and
de la Guerra deepened significantly in the mid-1820s. The two continued
to depend on each other to connect their local markets, north and south,
and they traded in hides and tallow, different sorts of imported cloth, and
aguardiente.[79] Hartnell maintained both a "general" account and a "private" account with de la Guerra, and used them to pay de la Guerra's duties in Monterey, and to exchange other sorts of libranzas, debits, and
credits with him.[80] Hartnell, living in the well-forested Monterey area,
also arranged for the cutting and shipping of lumber and boards to the
more arid Santa Bárbara, probably for de la Guerra's new house, still
under construction in 1825.[81]

But no sooner had Hartnell settled down in Monterey with his new
bride than a series of troubling reversals threatened to unravel every one
of his California ventures, and with them the hopes of his new father-in-
law. The first sign of trouble came with the change of governor in Novem-

ber 1825. The former provisional governor, Luis Argüello, had been a local man and was generally willing to bend the rules to encourage trade—not so his replacement, José María Echeandía, a former engineer and architect who was republican Mexico's first gubernatorial appointment for California.[82] Tall and thin, Echeandía was thirty-seven when he arrived from his hometown of Mexico City, leaving a wife and four daughters behind. Declining the governor's quarters in Monterey, Echeandía set up his new residence in San Diego. The liberals who came to power after Independence at first promoted free trade along with political liberty, and it was this thinking that led to the original opening of California's ports in 1821. But within liberal circles, debates quickly arose between those who favored stimulating commerce with open ports and low tariffs, and those who wanted greater protections for the home industry, particularly textile production, that had been so damaged by the war years. A political tug-of-war ensued and played out in California as a series of unpredictable decrees—now opening ports, now closing them; now raising tariffs, now lowering them; and sporadically banning foreigners from trading or fur-hunting altogether.[83]

The first salvo came from Echeandía, who, on his arrival from Mexico, imposed heavy import duties and gave immediate orders that every port but Monterey and San Diego be closed to foreign vessels. This was a severe inconvenience for resident manager Hartnell because, as he told Begg and Company that December, "The priests will sooner let their produce rot in the missions than attempt to carry it by land to the two above mentioned ports." At the same time, Echeandía limited fur-hunting to Mexican nationals.[84] Hartnell turned to his new family to get around the law, suggesting that the "license could be asked for in the name of José Antonio [de la Guerra]," his brother-in-law.[85] But when Echeandía discovered the subterfuge, he canceled the license.[86]

Hartnell had reason to try diversification: his exclusive contract with the missions had come to an end on January 1, 1826. Rival traders—American, Mexican, and Peruvian—circled the missions eagerly, eyeing their chance to capture a piece of Hartnell's trade. From Hartnell's perspective, Juan Ignacio Mancisidor was perhaps the most devious. In late 1825, he slipped quietly from mission to mission, telling the padres that, with the expiration of Hartnell's contract, the Englishman was planning on closing his accounts and leaving California altogether. Luckily for them, Mancisidor explained, he could offer competitive prices with no interruption in trade. By April 1826, Hartnell was forced to concede to de la Guerra "that according to appearances Mancisidor will get all the production of San Gabriel and San Juan Capistrano. This is a blow that I was not expecting, and proof that the Padres are very ungrateful."[87] That September, two new ships, the *Yuca* and the *Fulham*, under Enrique Virmond, arrived, looking for hides and tallow. Never again would Hartnell enjoy a total monopoly over California's mission produce. "Long live Commerce!" he wrote ruefully to his father-in-law.[88]

In England, markets seized up in the summer of 1826. Captain Lincoln, the commander of the *John Begg*, lamented, "the present state of Commerce was in a most deplorable situation, the failures being so great in the Money Market that all Confidence is lost."[89] To make matters worse, Hartnell's partner Hugh McCulloch began that summer to charge a commission for selling cargoes of California goods in Lima. In August, an exasperated Hartnell fumed at him:

> Instead of devoting all your time and attention to this concern as you bound yourself to do, I am informed that you never bother your head at all about it . . . it appears you wish that I who am toiling from years' end to years' end and getting bald and blind in the concern should pay you for doing what is no more than your bounded duty.[90]

Yet another blow struck in November 1826, when Hartnell received word that his company's schooner, the *Young Tartar*, had run aground during a storm at San Diego.[91] Hartnell employed this ship to transport goods up and down California's coast, and when it sank it took down a hold full of cargo—including more than three hundred botas of tallow and fifty-two boxes of candles.[92] Finally, Hartnell received word that the articles of copartnership between his company, McCulloch and Hartnell, and its parent company, Begg and Company, were about to expire, and John Begg told Hartnell that, with Hartnell's recent losses and the deepening depression in England, he had no interest in continuing the California enterprise.[93]

In a few short years, reversals of fortune turned Hartnell from "the greatest personage in California" to a struggling merchant, "getting bald and blind" in the process. More and more, Hartnell leaned on his father-in-law as a trading partner, business advisor, and potential investor in his now-solo commercial enterprise. By July 1827, the *John Begg* again sailed south from Monterey to fill its holds in the slaughtering season and sell its goods. Hartnell asked de la Guerra for "the favor of writing to Padre

Altimira" to persuade him to sell Hartnell his mission produce. In return, the Englishman offered his father-in-law first choice of his supplies of white percale, canvas, and scarlet cloth.[94] Two days after offering de la Guerra the pick of his current cargo, Hartnell told his father-in-law that he would be leaving for Lima to settle company accounts in September and suggested that he start "making [his] list of orders in advance."[95]

Hartnell was gone a full year, from September 1827 to September 1828, leaving Teresa and their two children in her father's household. In Lima, away from the scrutiny of Californio society, he briefly renewed a relationship with an Englishwoman and dissolved his partnership with McCulloch, and McCulloch and Hartnell's with John Begg.[96] Striking up acquaintances in the Lima taverns that served the merchant community, he took every opportunity to make new deals, including a joint venture with an American, Daniel Coit. Coming back in the summer of 1828, Hartnell brought goods consigned to him and contracts for a collection of return cargo.[97] As his ship sailed toward California, he could imagine Coit on the docks of New York, outfitting his ship the *Danube* with an assorted cargo of printed cottons, hardware, shaving razors, hats, and crystal vases. Next year, Hartnell would be waiting in Monterey to receive the boxes, barrels and crates. Hartnell would receive one-third of the profits, which he had assured the American would be significant. Hartnell had reason to believe things would be looking up; he had wound up his Lima business successfully, and his status as first son-in-law to the powerful de la Guerras guaranteed the connections so essential to trade in California. Meanwhile, José de la Guerra was reconsidering this trade himself.

Rethinking the Patriarch's Role

In 1827, an impressed visitor described de la Guerra as a man of "large fortune."[98] Indeed, de la Guerra's trade had brought his family considerable profits, based on the enormous productivity of California's missions and the labor of their Indians. But, as workers were putting the finishing touches on his fine new home, de la Guerra reflected on his position in California's economy. His attempt to capture the most powerful foreign merchant had had mixed results; Hartnell still promised some benefit to the family, but at times de la Guerra surely felt saddled with a son-in-law who, instead of buoying his finances, dragged them down. Meanwhile, new merchants and their resident managers arrived daily, increasing competition. It was all de la Guerra and the Carrillos could do to pull them into family networks as sons-in-law and compadres. To top it off, the new governor, Echeandía, seemed perverse in his regulation of trade and customs. Over the next year, de la Guerra devised new tactics to maintain his grasp over the local economy.

In July 1827, as commander of the Santa Bárbara presidio, de la Guerra compiled a census of his jurisdiction, including the nearby missions and ranchos. This was done at the request of the Mexican government, which had at last turned its attention to its northern possessions and formed a new planning council entitled the "Junta de Fomento de California," or the Board of California Development. De la Guerra explained that the majority of the region's gente de razón farmed and raised livestock, but (no doubt thinking of himself) also reported that "there are also a few individuals dedicated to commercial pursuits, who probably will soon have to take up another line of endeavor and leave these to the foreigners who speculate in every way and against whom they cannot compete." De la Guerra did all he could to encourage the Junta to support his enterprises, appealing for help with commercial competition and relief from the capricious taxation that threatened to undermine sales of his wines and aguardiente. "One becomes discouraged in an undertaking that promises no advancement," he pleaded, "and his efforts cease altogether when his industry finds no support from the government."[99]

As Hartnell himself had discovered, mastery of the deal was not enough. Because the Mexican government and its local representatives enforced some of the terms of trade—opening and closing ports, raising and lowering tariffs—a merchant's influence with the governor and customs house could be critical to the success or failure of any venture.[100] Obviously, being able to limit tariffs on one's own goods, while hindering competing imports, would be essential strategies for promoting one's enterprises. Until Echeandía's arrival, de la Guerra had been able to rely on his personal connections with government officials in Monterey to bend rules and obtain waivers for himself and for his partners.[101] But now, with California not yet a full-fledged state, the governorship was in the hands of appointees from Mexico City, who thought less of local needs, and more of the needs of the nation as a whole. By closing ports and raising tariffs, Governor Echeandía aided the textile mills of Puebla and Oaxaca at the expense of California's retail merchants. Tariffs were also the primary source of California's provincial revenue, adding to the pressure to keep them high. Likewise, while the Mexican government periodically blocked the entry of foreign ships, it could offer little shipping alternative to local merchants like de la Guerra, who needed some means of transporting their goods.

Perhaps this struggle for local control over commerce explains why, despite his previous experiences in Mexico, and against the advice of his friends, de la Guerra accepted the post of California's deputy to congress in February 1827.[102] De la Guerra, then forty-eight, waited to see his wife safely through the delivery of their twelfth and final child, also called María Antonia, born at the end of September. Teresa, in Hartnell's absence, settled into the Santa Bárbara household with her own newborn, Nathaniel, in October. Finally, in January 1828, the commander started for Mexico on the *María Ester* with sons Pablo and Francisco, to serve what remained of his two-year term. But on arrival, de la Guerra discovered his alternate, Gervasio Argüello, already in his seat, and the entire Congress convinced that de la Guerra harbored lingering loyalties to Spain. De la Guerra, sensing that a battle against such nationalism would be a losing proposition, declined even to present his credentials, and instead petitioned for a passport to return home. After a great deal of delay, a final avowal of national loyalty to the president secured his passport on December 16.[103]

De la Guerra lost his opportunity for a political career, but the trip was not a total loss for his family or for his commercial business. Hoping to ease his dependence on foreign merchants for shipping and transportation, de la Guerra further delayed his return, arranging for the purchase of a coastal schooner, the *Santa Apolonia*.[104] Through his agent in Mazatlán, Juan Machado, de la Guerra paid $3,500 in cash and agreed to send $3,000 in tallow.[105] De la Guerra acted quickly once the ship arrived, loading up and leaving in May 1829. He sailed on his own schooner, renamed the *Dorotea*, into Monterey harbor in July 1829, after being away for almost two years. De la Guerra, acting as his own supercargo, carried a large order from Juan Bautista Martiarena, the syndic of the California missions, to be sold on consignment, plus several boxes of goods and barrels of mescal that Martiarena hoped to have sold privately. "Send, in return, some good tallow, not lard," Martiarena instructed.[106]

As the ship eased into the harbor, word spread quickly that the captain had returned, and on his own ship, no less. It is easy to picture the servants at the Hartnell household bustling to put out the best imported china, tap barrels of the finest wine, and roast a young calf. De la Guerra stayed in Monterey for several days, renewing acquaintances and spinning stories of the cosmopolitan capital city. He then gave his ship's crew orders to sail on to San Francisco, where he would meet them in a week or two. De la Guerra spent the interim traveling at a leisurely pace from mission to mission; the sounds of bells and gunshots welcomed him at each arrival. By the time he arrived in San Francisco, he was ready to unload the entire cargo, for he had sold everything, and at very advantageous prices.

He loaded up with another consignment from Juan Malarín and headed south. Unfortunately, the final journey to Santa Bárbara proved the *Dorotea*'s last; it ran aground in a narrow inlet near the town.[107] Despite this setback, de la Guerra otherwise came out rather favorably from his latest business venture. His political career might have been a flop, but his friends in Mexico were certainly glad to see him back at his desk in Santa Bárbara, "since," as Tepic merchant Manuel Varela put it, "it interests all of us to have someone to send us tallow."[108]

Quite a bit had changed in de la Guerra's absence. His new house in Santa Bárbara was finally finished, and his family rushed to prepare for his arrival, carefully dusting the family *santos*, plumping mountains of bed cushions, and sweeping the shaded veranda.[109] Up in Monterey, William Hartnell and Teresa had greeted their *amado padre* with their third child, Jorge, born just two weeks before de la Guerra's return. Counting José Antonio's children, de la Guerra was now the proud grandfather of six.

But these were not the only new arrivals swelling California's population. New immigrants from Mexico and the United States landed daily, and signaled more immediate challenges and opportunities for California's hide-and-tallow traders. In the coming years, two of these men would secure key sectors of California's economy—one by holding the reins of government power, the other by controlling access to critical markets in the United States. Hartnell, on the other hand, would slip out of the commercial world almost entirely, trying one career after another in an attempt to remain a player in California's elite network. In each case, de la Guerra would be there, pulling the men into his household, demanding dependence, and meeting his obligations in return. A flexible patriarch found ways to prosper under changing circumstances.

De la Guerra, as he stepped off the *Dorotea* that July, had quickly discovered that the staff of the customs house had been shaken up again, and a young Mexican named Manuel Jimeno y Casarín now served as administrator of revenues in Monterey. Jimeno was born and educated in Mexico City, and had followed his two brothers to California; Antonio and José Joaquín had both arrived as missionaries in late 1827. Witty and intelligent, Manuel Jimeno was also a Mexican nationalist, but one who did his best to promote legitimate trade with foreigners, while ensuring that the customs house got its fair share of the revenues.

In February 1829, Jimeno struck up a friendly acquaintance with another new face on California's shores, the shipping clerk for the Boston ship the *Brookline*, Alfred Robinson. This Bryant and Sturgis venture carried one of the largest and most varied cargoes of manufactured goods yet to arrive in California, plus $70,000 in cash. Its twenty-one-year-old clerk, on his first trip to California, remembered that the customs officers of Monterey

> appeared much pleased when informed that we wished to trade on the coast, and particularly so, when made acquainted with the nature and amount of the ship's cargo. The conversation soon became general, and the more intelligent of the two (Don Manuel Jimeno) gave us an account of the country, its government, missions, and its political condition at that time.[110]

Jimeno might prove an ally for coastal traders, and Robinson's firm in turn promised huge revenues for the customs house: $31,000 on this trip alone.[111]

Alas, Jimeno told the *Brookline*'s officers, a recent smuggling incident had caused the governor once again to tighten trade and close all ports save San Diego and Monterey to foreigners. This being unacceptable, William Gale, the *Brookline*'s master, determined to sail to San Diego for an audience with Echeandía and ordered the sailors to ready the ship for the journey. "Whilst these preparations were going on," Robinson recalled, he took the opportunity to see something of the country around Monterey, and introduce himself to the local English-speaking residents "married to pretty Californian women." "I became acquainted particularly," he wrote, "with Mr. H[artnell] and Mr. S[pence], the former from England, and connected in business with a mercantile house in Lima, having an extensive trade on the coast, and making large contracts with the missions."[112]

Hartnell may have seemed the model of commercial success to the young American, but in truth, Hartnell was barely hanging on in 1829. On returning from Lima the previous year, Hartnell had found many of his personal contacts at the missions gone. Over the next year, he managed to sell his consignment from the *Huascar* and send a respectable cargo back to Lima, but he had no profits to pay off his debts to Begg and Company.[113] Meanwhile, Hartnell awaited the *Danube* and kept up appearances for visitors like Robinson. But as the days lengthened, and the

Alfred Robinson. Courtesy of The Bancroft Library, University of California, Berkeley.

fog of May and June gave way to the heat of summer, William Gale and Alfred Robinson busily made their way from mission to mission, buying up the year's production of hides and tallow. José de la Guerra returned from Mexico, sold his cargo, and moved into his new home, and still they heard no word of the *Danube*. In August, baby Jorge died, casting a deeper shadow over the entire household. The *Danube* and its precious cargo was Hartnell's last hope to keep from sinking into bankruptcy.

Finally the ship sailed into Monterey Bay in September, having missed the peak season of trade for hides and tallow. Hartnell made sure to pay Jimeno's steep customs duties—9,000 pesos.[114] Some small fraction of the imports were sold on the ship's way down the coast, but little was left for Hartnell to buy. His father-in-law did what he could. Their account of September amounted to $10,361 for deals going back to 1827: de la Guerra owed Hartnell for Juan's tuition, a series of local libranzas, and goods, including dimity, canvas, and scarlet cloth, house wares, forty-eight chairs, hats, and a clock. De la Guerra settled up with $3,766 in cash and credit, 569 pounds of tallow, 515 hides, $416 worth of panocha, a kind of raw sugar, and twelve barrels of mescal.[115]

Hartnell might have been able to eke out another year as a trader, with de la Guerra's help, but on December 31, disaster struck. The *Danube*, still loaded with most of its original American merchandise, was lying at anchor in San Pedro when a winter storm blew up out of the southwest. At this point along the California coast, the shoreline tucks in and faces south, but even in this relatively protected harbor, sailors doubtless hurried to pull in sails and secure their precious cargoes in the face of such a storm's fury. All the experience of Sam Cook, the *Danube*'s seasoned captain from New York, was still no match for the force of wind and waves. Helpless before the gale, the *Danube* tore free, crashed into the rocks, and began to sink.

Hearing of this misfortune, Hartnell must have felt utterly crushed with debt, now beyond his ability to repay. His wife, Teresa, at age twenty, was pregnant again, and Hartnell must have felt, too, the burden of her expectations. Helplessly, he sat down at his desk in Monterey to compose a letter to John Begg in Lima. "Everything which I undertake appears to miscarry," he wrote:

> The flattering hope I had conceived of the advantages which would accrue to me from my connexion with Coit have been dashed to the ground. I am now reduced to the necessity of informing you that I have no longer any prospect of being able to fulfill my engagements to you, and to request that you will appoint someone to wind up our affairs and make a bankrupt of me at once. I am perfectly willing to give up everything I possess to satisfy my creditors.[116]

A few weeks later, on February 5, the salvaged goods from the *Danube*, plus its hardware and tackle and still-submerged hull, went on the auction block at San Pedro. De la Guerra, in partnership with his nephew and compadre William Goodwin Dana, bought it all for $5,076.[117] On the day of the auction, William Gale, still loading hides and tallow with Alfred Robinson for Bryant and Sturgis, remarked, "Capitalists such as [de la Guerra y] Noriega will have a fine chance for a speculation today."[118] De la Guerra did what he could to help his hapless son-in-law, but his own accounts did not suffer for the experience.

For the next several years, Hartnell lived a tentative existence, trying every means he could to recover old debts owed to him. At every step, he called on his wife's father.[119] De la Guerra, as commander of the Santa Bárbara district, did what he could to facilitate collection, and as trader, to maintain active accounts with his son-in-law.[120] Late in 1830, for example, de la Guerra sold Hartnell an assortment of goods to resell in Monterey, including cloth, buttons, hats, paper, cigars, hardware, and fifteen "kaleidoscopios."[121] But eventually, both Hartnell and de la Guerra were forced to confront the end of Hartnell's career as a merchant. As luck would have it, Hartnell was soon relieved of all his debts; a Scottish trader based in Lima, Stephen Anderson, bought Hartnell's obligations to John Begg in 1831, and over the next two years, assumed the whole of Hartnell's debts as well as his trading contacts with the missions.[122]

Unsure of what to do next, Hartnell realized that his only remaining asset was his marriage to Teresa de la Guerra, and his consequent high status as a dependent of her father. Hartnell chose to begin again as a rancher, having becoming a naturalized citizen in 1830 to start the process. All Mexican territory was open to foreign colonization by the laws of 1824 and 1828, but foreigners who lived in Mexico for more than two years were required to become citizens. In practice, until the mid-1830s, California's governors issued no grants to foreigners.[123] In May 1831, Hartnell worked out a deal with the Soberanes family to an equal right in their Alisal rancho near Monterey, in exchange for his labor at sowing time. "We will see," he told his father-in-law, "if as a Rancher I have the same chance, or better said, mischance, as a Merchant."[124]

De la Guerra again stepped in to prevent whatever mischance he could. At Hartnell's request, he defended Feliciano Soberanes in a case of cattle rustling in June, and thereby built goodwill with his son-in-law's landlords. De la Guerra also sent more immediate help in the form of his eldest son, José Antonio, who pitched in at slaughtering time that summer.[125] Hartnell even suggested that his father-in-law sponsor a lottery in Santa Bárbara to help him pay for a new house at the ranch. "I need your advice," he wrote in April 1832. "I was thinking of making 100 chances at 60 pesos each . . . I don't see another way of making myself some money and without money I cannot leave behind the little trade that I have in Monterey and live as I want, entirely on the ranch, and if I am not there I will never advance. So tell me what I ought to do to succeed."[126]

De la Guerra gave what advice he could, but his confidence in the Englishman's business abilities was wearing thin. Hartnell had been a drag on the family finances for quite some time. Their relationship was strained nearly to the breaking point in the autumn of 1832, when Juan de la Guerra arrived home from his studies in England. In his pocket, Juan carried a letter to his father, dated February 1831, from James Brotherston. After a joyful reunion of parents and child in Santa Bárbara, José de la Guerra retired to read over the long message. Its contents truly alarmed a man who depended on his good name to trade abroad. Apparently, Hartnell had not repaid his benefactor for the last three years of Juan's education in England. Brotherston had been forced to send Juan back because he was no longer certain he could count on sufficient funds to keep the young man in school.[127] In his letter, Brotherston warned de la Guerra to "inform yourself well and write to me on the details" of Hartnell's financial situation.[128]

De la Guerra immediately forwarded the letter to Hartnell and demanded an explanation; after all, he had given Hartnell the money—what had happened to it? Where was Hartnell's honor? Hartnell replied to his "beloved father" that he suffered under the debts he had taken on as his partnership dissolved, "because then I flattered myself with the hope of being able to cover [them] . . . but the time has undeceived me miserably as it is well evident to you." Still, Hartnell insisted that he had indeed repaid many of his outstanding debts, starting with those owed in California. "You will make for your part the reflections that you may judge convenient to said Señor with respect to my conduct," Hartnell wrote stiffly, "since I have been in California long enough for you to know me."[129] Juan's education, it was turning out, may have been Hartnell's chief contribution to the de la Guerra economic empire, and now Hartnell's mismanagement and debts meant that this, too, was coming to a premature end.

Juan's return meant that certain decisions had to be made. The young man could no longer hope to receive the training in medicine his father had requested, but after six and a half years of education abroad, Juan did possess the skills for any number of careers. De la Guerra needed to choose what role his second-oldest son would play, and whether he could be incorporated into his commercial empire. The de la Guerras had been warned of their son's imminent return the previous year, when the seventeen-year-old had arrived in Mexico City from the port town of Veracruz. Running low on funds, he had the good luck to meet up with his uncle Carlos Carrillo, now serving as California's deputy in congress. Soon, Juan was accompanying his uncle on his official rounds as deputy, paying calls on the vice president and the ministers of state. Juan made such a good impression, in fact, that Don Rafael Mangino, the minister of the treasury, offered him a position. "I want to enter the Ministry," Juan told his father in June 1831, "because it seems to me that something can be learned there."[130]

But the elder de la Guerra had other plans. In that same letter from Juan, he read with interest the young man's comments on California: "I was extremely happy to hear the improvements of Santa Bárbara"; Juan had written, "and much more when they told me that three boats had been at the Presidio; May God wish it to continue progressing; because within a little time New California may not be the poorest Province that the Republic has."[131] De la Guerra quickly sent his brother-in-law Carlos a list of questions to ask Juan, in order to test the young man's business acumen. A few months later came the reply: "Little Juan knows a lot... do not doubt that [he] has the talent for being thrown into the purse, to the extent that there is such in California." As for the career in Mexico City, Carrillo told de la Guerra he had forbidden it outright: "If I did not put him in the Secretariat of the Minister of Treasury (although Sor. Mangino demonstrated to me that he would receive him with great pleasure) it was because here in Mexico the youth are in danger of their ruin, and as Juanillo is so quick, it seemed much better to me to send him to Tepic."[132]

Word spread of Juan's arrival in the Pacific town, and de la Guerra's business partners in turn began to imagine new opportunities and stronger connections through him to the powerful California merchant. Antonio José Cot from Lima told de la Guerra of an important deal there and suggested that if Juan made the trip to Peru, "You might for convenience have had him put at the front of the negotiation."[133] But de la Guerra's plans and Juan's own homesickness meant that any role as his father's agent abroad would have to wait. On May 12, 1832, exactly a year after his arrival in Veracruz, Juan de la Guerra boarded a ship heading north.

Juan's early return from England brought the unwelcome news of Hartnell's failure to pay his debts. As patriarch, de la Guerra would never shirk his duties toward Hartnell, but neither would he encourage Hartnell to continue as a businessman. Juan's return, however, suggested a new arena for Hartnell's skills, for the young man came accompanied by a chest full of books. One of the more attractive qualities of the Englishman was his fine education; perhaps that could serve him in a new capacity. The decision was made: Hartnell would open his own school in Monterey with Juan.

Juan, after a brief stay in Santa Bárbara, moved in with the Hartnells and continued his training with Father Patrick Short at nearby Mission San Carlos, learning the skill of surveying.[134] While in Monterey, he met another frequent guest of the Hartnells, Scottish botanist David Douglas. Douglas loaned the young Californio books from his traveling library and fired Juan with the notion of bringing modern agricultural techniques to California.[135] No doubt Juan hoped the new school would give him an opportunity to share what he had learned and to make his mark on California's economic development.

Tragically, we can never know what Juan would have accomplished in his brother-in-law's school because he contracted a fever and died suddenly, just as plans for the school were coming to fruition in the fall of 1833.[136] José de la Guerra seems to have lost the heart to continue with the project, for over the next months, Hartnell was forced to write to his father-in-law often, begging to borrow books, for a little more time to pay off debts, and for de la Guerra to make good on his promise to send a son or two as paying students.[137]

Hartnell's own son Nathaniel died in December, but the Englishman soldiered on. "There is nothing like poverty to make one lose all shame," he begged de la Guerra in January of the new year. "After so many favors that I owe to you and that I will never be able to pay as meriting, I see myself in the need of asking you another of good size . . . In order to assure to my children a piece of Land of their own." Could de la Guerra help him to purchase his section of the ranch outright? For this, he needed another two hundred head of cattle to pay the Soberanes family. "Maybe you would . . . give them on the account of the pension of the boys you are thinking of sending to the new college."[138] Once again, de la Guerra came through with the needed loan, but he did not send fourteen-year-old Pablo and eleven-year-old Joaquín for another few months.[139]

When they finally arrived in the spring of 1834, they moved into a crowded house. Not only did their sister Teresa live in Monterey with her husband and five surviving children, but now sister Angustias lived there, too, with her new husband, Manuel Jimeno, and their daughter, Manuela. Angustias had met Jimeno on one of her many visits to her elder sister, for Jimeno was a close friend of the Hartnells in the small circle of the Monterey elite. Pablo and Joaquín, transplanted from the rigid discipline of their father's house in Santa Bárbara, must have opened their eyes wide at the society that gathered in the Monterey house of the Hartnells and Jimenos. At dinner parties and balls, their sisters played hostess to the most important visitors and highest-ranking government officials while their brothers-in-law traded stories of life abroad and discussed the political issues of the day.

From his position in Santa Bárbara, José de la Guerra had probably not been able to control the marriage arrangement of Angustias to Jimeno as closely as he had that of Teresa to Hartnell. Angustias, at age seventeen, was older than Teresa at the time of her marriage. Still, de la Guerra must have been pleased to welcome an important customs official into the family, especially one whose brother was de la Guerra's priest at Santa Bárbara; their wedding was as grand an affair as Santa Bárbara had seen in many years.[140] With Jimeno as his son-in-law, de la Guerra might finally have the influence in the customs house that had eluded him as California's deputy to Mexico City. In the early 1830s, it was as important as ever to control the cut of tariffs, but de la Guerra had as yet little personal connection to this critical aspect of his trade. Every year now, de la Guerra imported thousands of pesos' worth of manufactured goods: cloth, paper, sugar, rice, and house wares—even luxuries like playing cards, silk, combs, hand mirrors, furniture, candlesticks, and musical instruments.[141] He also continued to produce wines and brandies at Conejo. Tariffs still made up almost the entire budget of provincial California's government, and their cut could be steep for merchants who bought and sold in such large quantities. Troublesome Governor Echeandía was gone after 1831, but his replacements were not much better: centrally appointed, they, like their predecessor, had little sympathy for bending the custom-house rules to suit California's merchant elite. But with the *contador* married to his daughter, de la Guerra might expect the duties of the customs house to be subsumed by the duties of son to father. No letters between the two survive from that period, but it is telling that, in an era when cash was becoming more and more scarce, de la Guerra somehow managed to retain quite a large store of his own—enough to lend out to other merchants to pay their own tariffs.[142] On the other hand, Jimeno, as contador, knew of Santa Bárbara's reputation as a hotbed of smuggling. Marriage to Angustias de la Guerra brought her father's honor into the tariff equation and ensured that the trader would hesitate before deceiving his own son-in-law.

The Rise of the Yankee Trade

Over the course of the 1830s, de la Guerra continued his tallow commerce with Peru and Mexico, but new economic pressures gradually shifted the bulk of his lucrative trade to the United States. Naturally, the loss of Hartnell's business connections in Lima took a toll on de la Guerra's trade there, but the captain was prepared to be flexible and lean more heavily on his other contacts like Antonio José Cot. But in 1830, Cot sent disturbing news to de la Guerra from Peru. Political unrest and population decline were creating economic chaos in the Lima tallow markets and casting doubt on the longterm stability of this enterprise. "Commerce is paralyzed, the harbor without ships," he told de la Guerra, "and many of the foreign merchant houses leaving the country." Tallow, he said, was piling up in the warehouses; "no buyers come now for what we have brought. Consequently we have to anticipate losing the work of three years in California."[143] This, then, may be why, by the mid-1830s, most of de la Guerra's letters to his agent in Los Angeles, Tomás Yorba, refer not to the collection of tallow, but to the collection and sale of hides.[144]

The Lima markets eventually recovered, but from 1830 on, de la Guerra depended more and more on his trade with Americans.[145] Between 1826 and 1848, as some historians estimate, Boston traders alone carried off more than six million hides and seven thousand tons of tallow from California.[146] The biggest firm of all, by far, was Bryant and Sturgis. From 1822 to 1827, William Gale worked the trade alone for this company, doggedly trying to build up his firm's business in California, but Hartnell's mission contract made for slow going. "Gale will find it very difficult to meet with a cargo," Hartnell had told his partner McCulloch in 1825. To their employers they explained, "The greater part will always fall to our share."[147] "Four-Eyes," as the bespectacled Gale was known on the coast, was able to pull together only two cargoes before 1828.

But after the dissolution of McCulloch and Hartnell and the collapse of the Lima tallow markets, Bryant and Sturgis moved in for the kill. From 1828 to 1840, Bryant and Sturgis was the single-biggest hide-buying operation in California, sending sixteen vessels, each capable of holding 40,000 hides. In five years, McCulloch and Hartnell had sent the same number of ships, but the American vessels stayed for two slaughtering seasons, not sixty days, and they held four or five times the number of hides.[148] Just as José de la Guerra knew of the power of William Hartnell, and moved to contain it within the family economy, so, too, did he move to contain the threat that Bryant and Sturgis posed to his coastal trade. De la Guerra had gambled that Hartnell would have great future worth, and had lost the gamble, but he did not walk away from the table. Changing circumstances meant simply that it was time to play another hand, this time with Alfred Robinson.

The paths of Robinson and de la Guerra first crossed in the summer of 1829. De la Guerra was just returning on the *Dorotea* from his final ill-fated trip to Mexico City. Robinson, on his first trip to California as clerk for the Bryant and Sturgis ship the *Brookline,* was in Monterey doing business and visiting with Hartnell, Jimeno, and the rest of the small political and commercial circle of elite Monterey.[149] At that point, neither de la Guerra nor Robinson noticed each other. In his journal, Robinson paid more attention to de la Guerra's ship than to its master: "A Mexican Schooner and the Brig *Colly* from the Sandwich Isles were lying here & trading," he wrote on August 15, 1829.

When, in late summer, de la Guerra at last sold his merchandise and returned to his family in Santa Bárbara, he discovered that Robinson and the *Brookline* had been there already, in May. No doubt the de la Guerra family had stories to tell their patriarch of the largest merchant ship they had ever seen, of sailors carrying hundreds of hides through the surf on their heads, and of visits to the ship's overflowing stockrooms. "Our decks were crowded with men and women of all classes," Robinson remembered of this visit, "many coming to purchase, some to see the vessel, and others to accompany their friends, so that it was not unusual for us to have a party of twenty or thirty at dinner."[150] Robinson and Gale had already loaded up at least 5,400 hides, plus horns and tallow, and sold $13,000 worth of goods.[151]

Gale was a man with a reputation for "integrity and honor"; seven hard years on the coast had also taught him the necessity of California manners.[152] Training his protégé Robinson meant that the first order of business in Santa Bárbara would be a visit to present gifts to the inhabitants of "the most stately house in the place"—the Casa de la Guerra. In May 1829, de la Guerra was still in San Blas, preparing to leave, so his wife received the visitors with chocolate on the veranda. Robinson noticed her daughters Angustias, almost fourteen, and Anita, seven, who made their appearance and "eagerly distributed the several gifts."[153]

Robinson stayed in San Diego during the autumn of 1829 while the *Brookline* continued to buy and sell up and down the coast. Then, in the spring of 1830, Gale ordered Robinson to Santa Bárbara to find a building for a permanent Bryant and Sturgis store in town. Robinson and Daniel Hill (Teresa's compadre) chose Santiago Burke's one-story house, which they fitted up as stockroom, showroom, and living quarters.[154] De la Guerra, chief retailer of the region, reacted to a rival store with alarm. On June 7, he remarked in his journal, "God knows the good or evil that will result from such a neighbor to the [Santa] Bárbaran land."[155] Robinson, on the other hand, seems not to have made much of an impression on de la Guerra, who referred to the newcomer simply as "a subordinate."[156]

Quickly, though, Robinson elicited de la Guerra's curiosity. The young American perhaps lacked his predecessor's charm, but his business dealings were done in good faith.[157] When Gale returned a year later, Robinson had sold $44,000 worth of the *Brookline's* goods up and down the coast and collected 7,000 hides, 354 bags of tallow, 10,000 horns, and a few otter skins.[158] Only $9,000 worth of merchandise still filled the shelves of the Santa Bárbara store in November 1831. That year, Robinson and de la Guerra struck up a friendly, if wary, relationship. But as neither one spoke the other's language with fluency, de la Guerra turned to Hartnell for a measure of the man. In May 1831, Hartnell told his "amado padre," "Robinson is in truth a good fellow, I have good hopes for him, I have loaned him good books and given brotherly advice."[159]

Over the next few years, the relationship between Robinson and de la Guerra developed from uneasy tolerance to mutual regard. Robinson, unlike Hartnell, proved to be an excellent businessman; the sale of the *Brookline's* produce in Boston brought Bryant and Sturgis such good profits that they sent Gale back with three more ships, the *California*, the *Plant*, and the *Roxana.* These arrived in late 1831 and 1832. Robinson spent the year sailing up and down the coast with Gale, collecting hides and selling merchandise.[160] It was becoming obvious to the residents of California that Bryant and Sturgis was emerging as the leading firm on the coast; de la Guerra opened his accounts with them in April 1832, selling among other things, 163 hides, a ream of paper, 320 horns, and eight otter pelts.[161]

At first, neither man expected Robinson would become a permanent resident of California, but in 1833 he made a decision to remain as resident manager and take up the life of a Californio. In January, he was detained in Santa Bárbara while his brig sailed off for two weeks to wait out a storm, and so by chance the Yankee attended the lavish wedding of Angustias de la Guerra and Manuel Jimeno.[162] Maybe it was the sight of José de la Guerra casually tossing "silver dollars and doubloons" at dancers from the veranda, or perhaps it was a discussion with de la Guerra's sons-in-law, Jimeno and Hartnell, that made the American decide to stay in California and try his luck at securing the patronage of such a powerful man. Whatever the cause, when the *California* at last set sail for Boston in March 1833, Robinson chose to stand on shore and watch the sails disappear over the horizon. On May 4, Robinson was baptized a Catholic in Monterey, sponsored by none other than Hartnell.[163]

Now thoroughly vetted, Robinson moved quickly into de la Guerra's networks of obligation and reciprocity. By early the next year, he was de la Guerra's agent in Monterey, delivering money and supplies for Hartnell's new school.[164] Soon, Robinson's gifts became more personal, and more pointed. "I am sending . . . a silk reboso for Anita," he told her mother in May 1834, "I hope that you will receive it as an expression of my esteem."[165] Two months later, Alfred and Anita became the godparents of Daniel Hill's son José María.[166]

Anita, the elder of de la Guerra's remaining unmarried daughters, turned thirteen in November. At the end of the year, her father sold Robinson 300 hides; shortly after that, he received a letter in which Robinson asked for Anita's hand, "the favor which only you have the power to grant."[167] Robinson pointed out to de la Guerra that he had been seen courting Anita in Santa Bárbara for some time, at "the many gatherings which were graced by her presence." He coyly reminded the captain of his own wealth, saying, "my circumstances are well known." But lest all this seem too much of a business arrangement, Robinson hastened to add, "Her attractions have persuaded me that without her I cannot live or be happy in this world." "It is not necessary to say," he concluded, "that my principal object will be to grant all her desires and to become worthy of her esteem."[168] De la Guerra consented. This agreement reached, the two men resumed their business, and in March 1835, Robinson began to reap the benefits of the connection, when he borrowed $5,000 of those "silver dollars and doubloons" from de la Guerra to cover new customs duties.[169] Meanwhile, Anita spent the next year learning to become a wife. The same month that her father paid Robinson's customs duties, Antonio María Ercilla at Mission Santa Bárbara sent "a little lamb" to the Casa de la Guerra, "so that Doña Anita might take charge of ordering it to be dressed for tomorrow, Sunday."[170] ("You can count on my worn-out molars to help you in the devouring," he added, hopefully.) In June, María Antonia took it upon herself to reunite her daughters in Monterey, no doubt so that Teresa and Angustias might share with their little sisters the secrets of motherhood.[171]

Alfred and Anita

The bride wore white. As she and her Yankee husband left the coolness of the mission church and walked out into the bright day, perhaps de la Guerra lingered a moment at the top of the steps. At the report of gunfire echoing from the hills, his gaze lifted from his daughter, past his house and gardens, and out into the harbor. The bridegroom's 342-ton ship, the *Alert*, bobbed in the channel like a prize. Eleven years before, the captain's daughter Teresa had married the most significant trader on the coast. Angustias had been more willful, but she was a lively child, and through her marriage to Manuel Jimeno, she had brought control of the tariff into the household. With active use of compadrazgo networks, de la Guerra had extended his reach to minor American traders, a number of whom had married daughters of his brother-in-law Carlos Carrillo. In the meantime, with the triumph of Bryant and Sturgis, Alfred Robinson had replaced William Hartnell as the resident manager of the most powerful foreign trading house in California. Teresa's husband had not brought the family the benefits they had hoped for, but her father did not consider abandoning the tactic of intermarriage as a result. Today's celebration, January 24, 1836, was like a second chance at the promises of the first wedding. De la Guerra could be forgiven if he sank back into the cushions of his coach with satisfaction. He was wealthy, well connected, and secure, and his household encompassed local retailers, international merchants, and custom-house officials.

Over the next few months, Robinson sailed up and down the coast of California, loading up the *Alert*, and unloading goods from the *California*. In early May, the *Alert* was ready to head back for Boston, and Robinson wrote to his employers, "I can have the flattery to say that I have dispatched the largest Cargo ever collected on the Coast of California": 39,000 hides, 31,000 horns, 709 pounds of beaver furs, and nine barrels of olives.[172] Meanwhile, up in Monterey, a census taken at Alisal showed forty-four people attached in some way to Hartnell's school, including his wife and six children, Pablo, Joaquín, five other gente de razón, and six Indian students, "Professor" Patrick Short, four artisans, and twelve servants and their families.[173] At last, the Englishman had found a respectable career and a use to his protector, de la Guerra.

This moment of triumph was short lived. At the height of his success, Robinson sounded a note of caution to his employers. "I have had a hard time of it, I assure you," he wrote to Bryant and Sturgis in May 1836, "I cannot promise that I will continue receiving consignments after the completing of the cargo of the *California*."[174] A few days later, Robinson confided to his old mentor Gale, "I sometimes think that . . . I shall retire & rest awhile probably take a trip to the United States."[175] That summer, Hartnell announced that his college would be closing.[176] These two distressing events had a single source: the civil unrest that had been building for ten years, revealing the hidden flaw in the family economy.

Angustias de la Guerra. Courtesy of The Bancroft Library, University of California, Berkeley.

CHAPTER FOUR

NATIVE SONS:
LAND HUNGER, LIBERALISM, AND REBELLION

In December 1831, William Hartnell had just given up his career as a merchant and was starting over on a ranch near Monterey. His brother-in-law Juan de la Guerra had just left the Mexico City home of his uncle Carlos Carrillo, California's deputy in the capital, to meet up with his father's trading partners in Tepic. Alfred Robinson, who hailed from Boston, was celebrating a year and a half's residency in Santa Bár-bara as a retail merchant for Bryant and Sturgis. And that month, young Californio rebels took over the presidio of San Diego and the pueblo of Los Angeles, eventually forcing Governor Manuel Victoria to surrender his command. A bewildered Victoria found himself on a ship bound for Mazatlán, watching the coastline of California slip over the horizon.

The connection between the Californio patriarchal family and California's political revolution is not obvious on the surface. Indeed, as it has been portrayed until recently, the history of civil unrest in the territory can seem both petty and faintly ridiculous. In the Mexican era, Californians engaged in minor rebellions and uprisings every few years, none of which provoked significant bloodshed or prolonged warfare. Some of the narratives of these incidents even take on a comic-opera tone: Californios meet on the field of battle, a few people fire shots into the air, someone hits a horse, the governor gets on a boat, and then everyone goes home. Many historians downplay the Californios' own ideological justifications for their actions and instead interpret such unrest as self-interested factionalism: Would the customs house stay in Monterey or move to San Diego? Should not Los Angeles, with its greater population, be the rightful capital of the territory? Who would distribute the spoils of secularization and grant former mission estates to their friends?[1] In this view, California resembles many Latin American nations in the decades after Independence: controlled by one elite group or another, and fractured by political instability, civil wars, and military coups.[2]

But if the family economy is taken into account, it becomes clear that something more significant was going on in Mexican California than simple factional disputes. Only the family economy of California can explain why such rebellions took the form they did, and why they were settled with so little bloodshed. The true fissure was not just between federalist and centralist, or California and Mexico, or north and south, but also between father and son. If we take seriously the political rhetoric employed by the young men of Monterey, we can see that they were attempting a true revolution after all: a generational revolution.

This rebellion of native sons threatened to bring down the economic empires their fathers had so carefully constructed, but it was a crisis destined to happen, because it sprang from a flaw inherent in a system in which the family functioned as an economic institution. Reliance on the family could provide great strength to an elite patriarch who wished to increase trading profits and expand his empire. But the family economy in California was dangerously vulnerable at the moment of transition when a son came of age and struggled to become an independent patriarch. A family could split apart at that moment, and the careful webs of alliances and obligations unravel.

At no time was this danger more apparent than in the 1830s, when political pressures added to generational conflict. By this time, young men like de la Guerra's eldest son, José Antonio, were reaching adulthood and discovering that foreign merchants had locked up the profits of trade while the missions controlled most of the ranching and agricultural land. A few Californios, like José de la Guerra, had established footholds in these economic realms, but such elder men made little room for their sons to become autonomous. Neither could elite sons be sure that the government would be sympathetic to their predicament: as a territory, California was assigned its military governor directly by the central Mexican government. However well intentioned, such men were outsiders, never native sons with Californio interests at heart. But the governors, and the other Mexicans who followed them, did bring a very useful ideology—liberalism—that questioned traditional sources of authority like the Church, elder men, and the military. With this analysis to guide them, second-generation Californians channeled their personal frustrations into political action. At their base, the revolutions of the 1830s were rebellions of the second generation against the first over land and over the economic and political autonomy that owning land would bring.

The Spread of Liberal Ideology

In the years after Independence, Mexican liberals who led the nation sought to build a unified republican state, replacing colonial institutions such as the military and the Church. California, remote and sparsely settled, served as a space for liberal experimentation.[3] In the 1820s and early 1830s, representatives from Mexico arrived to reform the government and economic system, preaching their philosophies to the native-born sons of California. In small study groups and by late-night candlelight, young men read philosophical works by Voltaire and Rousseau, purchased off ships from Europe and Mexico. Many of California's second-generation elite drank up these ideas, and this liberal education formed a critical stage in their political development.

Liberalism as an ideology arrived in Mexico from Europe during the Bourbon Reforms of the late colonial era, and was upheld in independent Mexico by Agustín Iturbide's Plan de Iguala. But it was primarily after the passage of the constitution of 1824 until its abrogation in 1835 that liberals held the reins of power in Mexico. In theory, liberal policy was a coherent one—rationalist and secular—that called for a constitutional government, free trade, and individual liberty. In practice, liberalism often fractured into clusters of ideas, some of them contradictory; any given "liberal" might adhere to various sets of these ideas, which might be further mixed with more conservative beliefs. Nonetheless, certain common notions emerged. For liberals, corporate entities like the nobility, the Church, and the military posed obstacles to state building and economic development because these institutions retained independent governing privileges called *fueros*, and in the case of the Church, a great deal of land and property. Liberals responded by attempting to abolish corporate privileges and seeking to tax, control, or secularize Church property. They also called for the division and distribution of communally held village and Indian lands.[4] Although most Mexican liberals favored this platform of economic liberalism—free trade and private property—and a political liberalism that advocated federalism over a centralized state, a smaller number extended their platform to include more radical elements: popular suffrage, public education, and abolition of the caste system.[5]

Liberal ideals had particular implications for California. We have already seen, for example, the citizens of Los Angeles asserting their authority over military rule, and liberalized trade policies transforming the economic structure and family strategies of the territory. Likewise, liberal notions of private property and individual liberty would have profound consequences for California's missions. Already, the presence of communal missions in California made the territory something of an anomaly. Bourbon officials in California like Governor Felipe de Neve had attempted to weaken the missions in the late eighteenth century, but practical needs overruled desires to abolish them. After the fall of the Bourbons in 1808, however, liberals moved decisively. In Spain, the liberal Cortes of 1810–14 passed legislation that freed Indians from paying tribute, permitted them to engage in any employment they wished, and prohibited whipping as a punishment. The constitution of 1812, reinstated in 1820, granted full Spanish citizenship rights to Indians. And on September 13, 1813, the Cortes ordered the immediate secularization of all of Spain's New World missions.[6]

After Independence, liberals took the reins of power in Mexico, declaring Indians equally entitled to the rights of man, and secularization the law of the land.[7] Ideally, secularization would transform mission fathers into parish priests, mission lands into civil pueblos, and neophytes into full-fledged Mexican citizens. Since mission lands and goods were considered to be held "in trust" for the Indians who lived at the mission, the property would be divided up among the former neophytes; any excess would revert to the nation and be made available for granting to any citizen.[8] For Mexican liberals, secularization was a tool in the project of nation building. It would not only release Indians from oppression and make them full participants in the market economy but also break the power of the Church in secular affairs, make huge tracts of developed land available to private ranchers and farmers, and give the national economy a needed shot in the arm.[9]

Liberals in Mexico, and those who brought their political theories to California, had an institutional base that might seem at first unlikely: Freemasonry. During the chaotic years of the early republic, Masonic lodges rather than political parties offered Mexican political elites the space to develop political consensus and discuss legislative agendas. The "Scottish Rite" lodge, brought to Mexico by Spaniards in the waning years of the empire, tended to be conservative, centralist, and pro-Church. The "York Rite" lodge, founded in 1825, on the other hand, was generally composed of federalist liberals. Two of these Mexican *yorkinos*, Governor José María Echeandía and Lieutenant José María Padrés, would be instrumental in introducing liberalism to California's second generation, while a third, Governor José Figueroa, would set the terms of the debate as the mission lands were finally secularized in the 1830s.[10]

Echeandía replaced native-born interim ruler Luis Argüello as the first governor of the new order. "When he arrived in California in 1825 he talked about republican and liberal principles that were stirring in the minds of Mexicans at the time," remembered Angustias de la Guerra, "He was a man of advanced ideas and an enthusiast and lover of republican liberty. He was sent to California to introduce the new regime and he certainly put these ideas into practice."[11] So that the new liberal regime might take root in California, the governor organized study groups modeled on Masonic lodges, where he taught young Californios the importance of popular education and the emancipation of Indians. "If I resolved to give liberty to the Indians," Juan Alvarado recalled later, "I did it impelled by humanitarian sentiments; I did it because my republican education did not permit me to continue to be . . . insensible to the cry of anguish from the breast of thirty thousand Indians who, deprived of their liberty, were nothing more than puppets in the hands of the priests."[12]

But other factors, perhaps, added to the humanitarian motives. Echeandía also preached to young men like Juan Alvarado and his friends Mariano Guadalupe Vallejo and José Castro that the missions in California unfairly locked up all the arable coastal lands, forcing California's gente de razón to beg for scraps. These lands more than any others were developed with wheat fields, vineyards, orchards of olive and fruit trees, and blacksmith, carpentry, and weaving shops. With over 21,000 neophytes at Independence, the missions also controlled most of California's agricultural and artisanal work force.[13] The scales dropped from their eyes, these young men later remembered, and they began to question a system that would forever leave them propertyless.[14]

Alongside Echeandía worked José María Padrés, another member of the York Rite Masons. Lieutenant Padrés was an officer in the Corps of Engineers, selected by Echeandía to accompany him to California. A militant Mexican nationalist, Padrés remained in Baja California in the 1820s, where he actively promoted the expulsion of Spaniards from Mexico, particularly Spanish missionaries, whom he considered conservative agitators.[15] In July 1830, at age thirty-three, he arrived at last at Echeandía's San Diego headquarters as assistant military inspector and immediately began to promote his anti-mission agenda. More radical than Echeandía, Padrés stressed the universal rights of man and the tyranny of missionaries, whom he said treated their subjects as little more than slaves.[16] José de la Guerra noted in November 1830 that several young men of San Diego's better families took "lessons in Arithmetic and politics," from Padrés, a man de la Guerra dismissed as "the geometrician."

Joaquín Ortega, twenty-nine, and Santiago Argüello Jr., seventeen, followed Padrés north "in order to continue their apprenticeship in Monterey" with the young men there.[17] One of those Monterey students,
Vallejo, later justified their conversion: "[O]f course the young men made
common cause with the bold preacher of doctrines that were in harmony
with our own progressive and philanthropic outlook."[18]

Young men of the Californio elite also turned to imported books for
lessons in the new liberal ideologies, although the conservative forces of
California worked hard to contain their spread. Vallejo recorded bitterly
in his memoirs:

> The missionary fathers were adamantly opposed to the
> circulation of books among us that might inspire lib-
> eral ideas and knowledge of the rights of free men in
> young people; they knew that books were the most
> fearsome emissaries of the goddess of liberty and con-
> sequently were relentless in trying to stop their circula-
> tion among us.[19]

Within Mexico, French schools of thought influenced liberals more than
British or American philosophers, and works by Baron de Montesquieu,
Jean-Jacques Rousseau, Benjamin Constant, and Voltaire circulated there
well before Independence.[20] Indeed, even before the liberal Echeandía
arrived, William Hartnell had brought a stash of books to California that
included works by Voltaire as well as Jean-Baptiste Blanchard's *L'école des
moeurs*, a Catholic adaptation and critique of Rousseau's *Émile*.[21] In the
first few years after his arrival, Hartnell was already using this library to
tutor the elite sons of Monterey in English, French, Latin, and history;
among others, he taught Alvarado and Vallejo.[22] In 1823, these "young
men of education" formed a secret "Historical Society," to "compile the
history of our homeland," as Alvarado later remembered. But only one
session was held, at which, Alvarado remarked, "the object of the meeting forgotten, [we] talked about the best means to improve the condition of the territory... and in the end things got quite heated."[23] Such
discussions must have come to the attention of Governor Argüello, because a year later he ordered de la Guerra and the other commanders to
confiscate "seditious papers and books, particularly against the Faith and
Roman Catholic religion and against the Governor," in the possession of
"certain individuals of this Province, being natives of it or foreigners."[24]
Even under Echeandía's reign the scrutiny of literature entering the ter-

ritory did not stop; when José Antonio Carrillo purchased prohibited books from an American ship, missionaries burned them on arrival.[25]

Foreign merchants continued to bring "seditious" books into the territory, however, and in 1831 the conservative Victoria regime threatened to confiscate the floating library of German trader Enrique Virmond, which contained works by Voltaire and Rousseau. Vallejo bought the entire collection by cover of night for 400 hides and 10 botas of tallow, and he shared books like François Fénelon's *Telemachus*, a critique of the French monarchy, with his friends Alvarado and Castro. When the ruse was detected, Father President Durán of the missions excommunicated the three, aged just twenty-four, twenty-two, and twenty-one respectively. Later, they were granted absolution on the condition that they would not loan the books to anyone else, but from that point on, José de la Guerra referred to Vallejo as "the heretic."[26]

In the late 1820s and early 1830s, then, liberals from Mexico, some of them quite radical, created study groups to introduce liberal ideologies to the young native-born sons of California. Banned books by French philosophers passed from hand to hand. In this heady era, the young men of the territory earnestly debated how a liberal society might overcome the entrenched corporate privilege of the colonial order and create a new nation of free citizens. They began to see missions not as necessary for the paternal guidance of Native peoples but as oppressive institutions that discouraged economic growth and denied Indians their rights as free men. De la Guerra, in relatively sheltered Santa Bárbara, succeeded for a time in keeping these dangerous ideas out of the hands of his children, but he could not keep them in the dark forever. The seeds of liberal political theory had been planted in California, and the young men of Monterey and San Diego had quickly taken up the cause. Mexican liberals seemed to have every reason to believe that their plans would soon bear fruit.

Hijos del País: Learning to be Californios

Unfortunately for the national project in California, however, Mexican representatives did just as much to push native sons away as they did to pull them into the nation. From the first public acknowledgment of Independence in 1822 to the celebrations over the republican constitution of 1824, the residents of California had been treated to new flags, fireworks, bell ringing, and solemn oaths of loyalty. Mexican officials deployed image and ritual to transform Spanish subjects into Mexican citizens. But as more and more actual Mexicans arrived to reshape the territory, native-born Californians felt themselves increasingly at the mercy of a central authority that looked upon their homeland as a dumping ground for undesirables, or as a prize awarded to sycophantic politicians, and that looked upon its citizenry as nothing but disloyal Gachupines and uneducated rubes.[27] As a result, the older generation of Californians still clung to their identity as Spaniards, and their sons struggled to form a new identity: not quite Spanish, but not completely Mexican, either. Eventually, young men like Juan Alvarado, José Castro, and José Antonio de la Guerra began to express a different sense of themselves, inspired by Mexican ideals of self-rule, but able to incorporate Spaniards and rooted in the territory of California. In a series of pranks, insults, and proto-rebellions, they would defy both Mexico and their Spanish parents to become true *hijos del país*—sons of the country.

Most of California's older gente de razón had watched the Spanish flag lowered one last time with serious misgivings, which they continued to voice privately throughout the Mexican era. As one Californio put it thirty years later, "[W]hen the government changed in 1821, if the Californios had been offered the opportunity to serve the republic or to serve the King in the labors of the conquest, in spite of their advanced age there is no doubt that they would have chosen the King."[28] Officials in Mexico, convinced that sending instructions for Independence Day celebrations would not be enough, attempted to replace this older generation of Spanish loyalists. They were able to do so, ironically, by subverting their own republican principles.

Ideally, the old governing structures were to be swept away. Canónigo Fernández put into place popularly elected town councils in 1822, inspiring the settlers "that the citizens were the nation."[29] José María Padrés, remembered Angustias de la Guerra, "was the first to instruct our young Californios ... in the principles of the federal system that prevailed in Mexico."[30] But the central government continued to treat California as an immature territory and to appoint military men as California's chief executives. With them, the incoming governors brought artillery and infantry units, many of whom were not trained soldiers but conscripts sent north as punishment for criminal offenses or vagrancy. Californians called these men *cholos*: mixed-race degenerates with no sense of discipline or order—"lost men," one said, "full of vice."[31] "The majority of these cholos were very depraved and corrupt soldiers," Alvarado concluded, and their short hair made them easy to pick out from the "meritorious veterans" who still "wore long hair down their backs."[32]

The new military officers who arrived with them seemed little better. During the wars for Independence, many lower-class and mixed-race men had risen through the ranks of the insurgent military, and their service had earned them high ranks after the war. Echeandía, governor from 1825 to 1831, brought a number of new officers on his arrival, and immediately began to force out the old military men in the presidial companies and "to assign the posts there to the officers who had accompanied him."[33] Artillery Captain Miguel González was one such officer, and as soon as he arrived in California, he began to complain that Californian officers and soldiers refused to obey his orders. They dismissed his authority with insults to his character, calling him ignorant, brutal, and despotic, and they publicly called him by the racial slur El Macaco, or "The Monkey."[34] Using such language, Californians drew a distinction between themselves— white, cultured, civilized—and other Mexicans—dark-skinned, uncivilized, and criminal.

Spanish-identified missionaries and military officers like de la Guerra did try to forge alliances with the newcomers from Mexico based on a shared allegiance to Church and state. In Santa Bárbara, Romualdo Pacheco, who arrived as an aide to Echeandía in 1825, took over as presidial commander in 1829, but de la Guerra continued to serve as captain in the company, and periodically took over as acting commander throughout the Mexican era. One foreign visitor described meeting de la Guerra and Pacheco at the priest's quarters of Mission Santa Bárbara in 1830, having breakfast together and engaging in "familiar conversation."[35]

Despite these efforts to work with the new administration, de la Guerra and other European-born Spaniards found their loyalties consistently doubted by those in the capital city. Although the Plan de Iguala had guaranteed the rights of European Spaniards who continued to live in Mexico, creoles in most regions continued to distrust and fear them. Local politicians across the nation, hoping to unite supporters against a common enemy, labeled Iberian Spaniards as economic exploiters, tyrants, and slave masters who were planning to rise up at any moment and reconquer Mexico in the name of the king.[36] This perception would dog the commander for the rest of his life. In 1828, de la Guerra was prevented from taking his seat in the national congress because of his alleged loyalty to Spain—a suspicion that was not misplaced.[37] To persuade the president to grant him a visa to return home, de la Guerra was forced again to avow loyalty to Mexico, but he did it in a rather backhanded way. "After having found out in this province that Mexico had pronounced for independence," de la Guerra told President Victoria,

> wasn't I the first of my brothers (and it is sufficiently public) that said: California must follow the lead of the

Capital?!! Thus I believed and I believe now; and however much I may be at heart a royalist, I shall never assent to the contrary, because Spain is not capable of giving immediate assistance to California, nor has the latter sufficient resources to subsist without assistance.[38]

The threat to California's Spanish-born population became even more intense after the passage of two national expulsion laws in 1827 and 1829. The first spared those who had creole wives and children, but the second expelled all Iberian Spaniards, regardless of circumstance. In California, popular sentiment ran against these laws; Angustias de la Guerra remembered that, despite her father's misadventures in Mexico City, he "was sure that as soon as he returned, nobody would touch him, because the Californios at that time were a people who were very Spanish, except for a few who were supporters of independence."[39] Governor Echeandía recognized that carrying out these orders would threaten the social order, so he simply asked European-born Spaniards to sign oaths of loyalty to the republic. Even then, he looked the other way when a handful refused.

Ironically, in the very year that Captain de la Guerra again found himself forced to swear loyalty to the republic of Mexico, choosing obedience and military discipline over royalism, his son back in Santa Bárbara was testing the limits of his own submission—to Mexico, and to his father. José Antonio, de la Guerra's eldest son, was twenty-three years old in 1828, already married and the father of two children. But ten years after his initial enlistment in the military, at an age when his father had been a lieutenant and the acting commander at Monterey, José Antonio still held the rank of cadet in the Santa Bárbara company, and was still his father's subordinate in the presidio's chain of command.

In June 1828, with his father away in Mexico, José Antonio and his two cousins, Raymundo and Joaquín Carrillo, staged a prank at the presidio. After rummaging in their fathers' wardrobes, the three cousins dressed up as Spanish officers and marched into the central square of the fort, pretending to have just come off a Spanish ship. The charade was so successful that the sentries saluted the three cadets, and when these "Spanish officers" rang the bell summoning the troops, several of the more recently arrived Mexicans hastened to load the cannons, for fear of a counter-revolution. In central Mexico, newspapers reported that the garrison was in fact very nearly captured in the name of the kings of Spain, before the cadets revealed their joke.[40] Artillery Captain Don

Miguel González wasn't laughing. In a letter to a Mexican newspaper, he warned, "[I]f they call it a joke today, tomorrow it will be for real."[41]

The next year, the incident was officially investigated and dismissed as a silly joke perpetrated by boys. Indeed, under Mexican law, Joaquín and Raymundo had not yet reached the age of majority and could not be prosecuted as adults. Still, the stunt marked the end of José Antonio de la Guerra's stalled career as a military man. After this date, he no longer appeared in the rolls of presidial troops and instead left his father's command to find another way to support his family. In so doing, José Antonio started down a path that would lead to independence from his father, and to a new identity as a Californio. With this prank, three young men of California's second generation expressed contempt for the intelligence and martial abilities of the Mexican newcomers and at the same time defied their fathers' insistence on discipline and military honor. Yet, by pretending to be Spanish, these cadets were beginning to create a Californian identity that, unlike the national identity of Mexico, managed to incorporate Spaniards.

The next rebellion in California was, as González warned, "for real," but ironically, it was led by one of the soldiers who had arrived with him in 1825. Its outcome brought to light the fractured nature of the emerging Californio political consciousness. On the evening of November 12, 1829, destitute soldiers of the Monterey presidio rose up, took possession of the garrison, and imprisoned their officers, demanding back pay and rations. This revolt soon spread to the presidio of San Francisco, and in December, rebels marched south to Santa Bárbara. Their leader was Joaquín Solís, a convict soldier who had committed brutal crimes in Mexico, but because of his service during the wars of independence, had his sentence reduced to banishment to California.[42] It is perhaps surprising, then, that Solís encouraged the troops to overthrow the Mexican governor and all other Mexicans on behalf of native Californians, but he soon undermined his attempt when he imprisoned most of the leading young Californios in Monterey.[43] By the time the rebellious troops arrived in Santa Bárbara in January 1830, Solís had abandoned his demand for home rule, and now claimed to be acting to restore Spanish dominion in California. Perhaps he switched tactics to gain the support of the San Luis Obispo, Santa Ynez, and La Purísima missionaries, or perhaps to win the backing of royalists like de la Guerra, but no one in Santa Bárbara was fooled; after two days outside the fortified presidio, Solís and his men retreated.[44] In groups of three or four, the defeated men made their way back to Monterey, where most were pardoned.

Solís's appeals to home rule and to Spanish sympathies failed to win Californians to his supposedly anti-Mexican cause, but he had struck a nerve with alarmed Mexican officials. In 1829, actual Spanish forces had in fact assembled in Cuba, and over the summer invaded Mexico at Tampico; Echeandía declared Solís an accomplice to this plot to reconquer the republic.[45] The Solís rebellion also awakened Governor Echeandía's suspicions that the missionaries, particularly Father Luis Martínez of San Luis Obispo, were plotting a similar counter-revolution to restore California to Spain. After all, it was widely known that many missionaries had refused outright to swear loyalty to the new republic. And Echeandía took seriously the rumors that Solís had obtained the support of mission fathers along the central coast; perhaps he thought Martínez had been behind the entire rebellion from the start.[46] Father Martínez, for his part, said simply that if he had not treated the rebels well as they marched south, they might have sacked his mission.[47]

Fearful of losing the territory, Governor Echeandía ordered the arrest of Martínez and had him brought to Santa Bárbara "without any respect or consideration," it seemed to his friends there.[48] Angustias de la Guerra, at fifteen the oldest child still living in her father's household, recalled many years later how Father Martínez, one of her father's closest friends, was detained in a room of the commander's quarters and forbidden to talk with outsiders—particularly other Spaniards like de la Guerra. She was able to slip the padre a note from her father, but in the end they were helpless to stop the expulsion.[49] On that same ship in March 1830, Echeandía forced the departure of Juan Ignacio Mancisidor and Antonio José Cot, Spanish-born tallow traders, friends, and frequent business partners of de la Guerra, along with Cot's wife, three children, and their servant, "a quite decrepit Negress named Juana."[50]

This incident was not quickly forgotten. Expulsions like these removed key producers of California's hides and tallow and severed ties to Pacific commercial networks. Father Martínez would be missed for spiritual reasons as well: California had no parish priests before 1840, so the entire non-Indian population of California relied on missionaries to provide them with the sacraments essential to their religion. In his absence, babies could not be baptized, young couples could not marry, and the dying could not receive last rites. So, while politicians in other parts of Mexico whipped up support with anti-Spanish proclamations, in California such tactics had the opposite effect. Purging Spaniards there felt less like an attack on foreign oppressors than on the community itself.

As if this weren't enough, the same month that Martínez, Mancisidor, and Cot were taken to a waiting ship and sent south, the *María*

Ester arrived from Mexico, bringing about eighty convicts. As noted in chapter two, de la Guerra did his best to turn the prisoners into grateful dependents, sending them clothing and blankets and taking a handful into his personal employ. The guards, however, were another story. Shortly after most of the convicts had been sent to Santa Cruz Island, a Mexican guard, described as a "Negro from Havana," attacked an English sailor from the same ship, shouting, "I am *criollo*, and I have made my purpose to kill all the Foreigners or Gachupines that I can!" Even more shockingly, Commander Pacheco set this guard free the next day on the basis of his "patriotic" and nationalistic motives. "I don't know if with thanks," the Spanish-born de la Guerra commented sardonically.[51] Later, rumors circulated that the soldiers and convicts were plotting together to rob and kill foreign residents, like newly arrived hide-and-tallow trader Alfred Robinson. Robinson was further alarmed on Independence Day that year, September 16, 1830, when convicts and Mexican soldiers gathered in the presidio square to burn the figure of a Gachupín in effigy, "and as the valiant 'Mazatecas' let off their rockets they cried 'Death to the Spaniard and foreigners.'"[52] These Mexican newcomers, whether soldier, convict, or guard, again provoked local hostility by asserting a national identity that excluded some of the oldest and most essential elements of California's society and economy: the Spanish-born, and Spanish-identified, missionaries and presidial officers. And while Californio elites worked hard to integrate foreign traders into the Californio "family," the Mexican soldiers and convicts drew firm boundaries around "Mexican-ness" that seemed to exclude them.

In the fall of 1830, as Mexicans burned a Spaniard in effigy in Santa Bárbara, the younger generation in Monterey reached their breaking point. Many of the young Californios had already sent petitions to Governor Echeandía protesting the arrival of the convict ship, so support was eroding for the Mexican government and its representatives in Monterey. The trouble started when Lieutenant Rodrigo del Pliego, who had arrived with fellow officer Miguel González in 1825, insulted Californios at a dance held to celebrate Independence Day. Native son Juan Alvarado was just twenty-one that year but had already held the post of secretary to the California *diputación*, or territorial legislature, for three years; he responded with his own toast to those "who may know how to appreciate the frank hospitality with which the Californians are accustomed to treat them . . . I loathe every man who, forgetting his education and good taste, might insult them, as just happened in this room," he added pointedly. According to Alvarado's account, Pliego answered the challenge by throwing his drink at Alvarado, who in turn knocked the Mexican to the ground.[53] Other versions of the event held that Pliego had simply refused to raise his glass to this toast and received a slap in the face in return.[54] Perhaps significantly, all these attacks were to the face and head, making the affront to masculine honor especially grave.

Alvarado's friend José Castro had his own run-in with Pliego, slapping him for an insult about the stupidity and poor education of the Californio native sons.[55] That same year, Castro was arrested for posting *pasquinades*, or satirical broadsides, and otherwise publicly expressing his contempt for Mexicans. Unfortunately, Castro's pasquinade doesn't seem to have survived, but the form had a long history in Mexico for oppositional speech. Many were written to counter official edicts, or *bandos*, with what purported to be the voice of the people. Sometimes the content appeared in verse, or with illustration, and frequently contained insults and violent threats.[56] If Castro's broadside attacked Pliego in particular, we can imagine what it might have said, based on other assessments of Pliego's character left by Castro's contemporaries. Angustias de la Guerra, for example, called Pliego a "sycophant" and "blind instrument of despotism . . . one of the most cowardly men known in this country."[57]

By the beginning of 1831, then, young, native-born Californians had developed strong nativist feelings at the same time that they were beginning to enter public service as military officers and elected officials. In this remote territorial capital, young men had been working hard to catch up with the liberal and republican theorists in far-off Europe and Mexico City, but they continued to be acutely sensitive about their isolation from these centers of thinking and debate. "Given the great distance separating California from the capital of the Republic," noted Juan Alvarado, "the sons of that department were considered foreigners."[58] In this, they seemed to have the sympathies of their Spanish-identified fathers, whose loyalty to the new nation was also a tenuous one, and who were subject to suspicion and threats of expulsion. In 1831, this anti-Mexican, nativist sentiment culminated in the ouster of the new Mexican governor, Manuel Victoria. The success of the venture convinced native sons that together they could be a potent political force against Mexicans in California.[59]

The actual armed uprising was a fairly short affair. On November 29, 1831, Pío Pico, at age thirty the senior member of the territorial diputación; his thirty-five-year-old brother-in-law José Antonio Carrillo (also José de la Guerra's brother-in-law); and Juan Bandini, the alternate congressman from California, issued a *pronunciamiento*, or declaration, against newly arrived Governor Manuel Victoria, and then took the presidio of San

Diego with little opposition. The rebels then marched north to Los Angeles, where local citizens gladly accepted their plan and joined them in the effort to carry it out. Meantime, Governor Victoria, hearing rumors of discontent to the south, set out from Monterey with a handful of soldiers to restore order. At the Santa Bárbara presidio, they met with Victoria supporter Captain de la Guerra, who persuaded the governor to take Mexican nationalist Commander Pacheco and another dozen of the soldiers from the San Blas and Mazatlán companies as reinforcements.

On December 5, the opposing forces met a few miles from Los Angeles. One man died in the skirmish on each side: José María Avila from Los Angeles and Captain Pacheco from Santa Bárbara. Even these deaths could have been avoided, Angustias later argued, had it not been for Victoria's overweening machismo. "When they arrived in Los Angeles," she reported,

> Pacheco saw that the enemy forces were far superior in number, and he reported this to Commander General Victoria. With an insulting tone, Victoria responded that if Pacheco was somebody who allowed himself to be ordered around by women, then he should retreat, because he [Victoria] did not allow women to control him, or words to that effect. Pacheco, who was not cowardly at all, spurred his horse and headed straight for the rebels. He was killed immediately.[60]

Governor Victoria himself was wounded and taken to Mission San Gabriel, where he surrendered his command. On December 27, healing from his wounds, Victoria boarded a ship for Mazatlán, accompanied by the hated Rodrigo Pliego.

According to the rebels, the uprising had everything to do with home rule. Chief among the accusations contained in their pronunciamiento was the claim that Victoria, appointed by the central government and imposed on California, had suspended the territorial diputación, tried to restore military rule, and attempted to abolish locally elected city governments. In addition, as Angustias de la Guerra put it, "in the administration of justice, he demonstrated an unusual inflexibility that scandalized the inhabitants."[61] According to the rebels, Victoria had harshly and arbitrarily executed thieves, expelled citizens without trial for political reasons, and prosecuted a civil alcalde by military court-martial.[62] Attempting to explain his brother José Antonio Carrillo's actions to the vice president of

Mexico, and pleading for leniency, Carlos Carrillo insisted that "the governors consider themselves crowned heads in that place, to work as they please, and not as they ought."[63]

All of these accusations were true, but they do not explain why men of the Spanish-identified older generation, like Captain de la Guerra, chose to side with a Mexican nationalist, or why young Californios who had accepted Mexican governors readily enough before, now turned against one. Californio native sons did not exile this governor only because he was Mexican, or for his usurpation of local power, but also for the agenda for which his power was employed: halting the secularization of mission lands. As de la Guerra cousin Julio Carrillo remarked later, "[F]rom the year 1829 to 1846 . . . the desire to dispose of the lands and cattle belonging to the ex-missions was undoubtedly the incentive of every revolution."[64] Secularization threatened to split the Californio elites by generation, and set them at each other's throats.

"A Harmful Effect": Resisting Secularization

As Mexico's new republic struggled to establish itself, the remote territory of California became a deeply contested space. Liberal nationalists saw open ground to remake the social order. Native-born Californians sympathized with their nation-building projects and Enlightenment theory, but balked at a new national identity that excluded the many Spaniards among them. And conservative Spaniards, mission fathers and merchants like de la Guerra, maintained a strong interest in upholding the traditional authority of patriarchs and the Church and in retaining the economic status quo. Through the 1820s, these California conservatives, along with many of the foreign merchants who depended on the mission economy for their profits, pushed to delay the implementation of secularization laws. By 1831, many conservatives began to hope that the tide had finally turned in their favor, and that the process might even be reversed.

In the minds of conservative men, secularization would completely overturn the economy of California, which had come to rely on the missions for most of its agricultural production and Indians for its labor force. If mission lands were distributed as private property, with Indians having priority for these grants, the economic role of men like de la Guerra would be in peril; acting as a middleman between mission and merchant gave him his main source of income. Further, insistence on the citizenship rights of Indians would deeply undermine not only the main source of labor but also the very identity of the gente de razón in California, who posed themselves in contrast to laboring Indians, "sin razón."

Indians, to the minds of conservatives, were uncivilized: either savage and brutish, or like docile children, easily misled and incapable of self-government. Under secularization, conservative Californios imagined a world turned upside down, in which Indians refused work, commanded Spaniards, and bowed down to neither king nor God.

On January 20, 1821, the 1813 secularization decree was at last published in the northern territory.[65] As a territory, California was subject to direct national enforcement of such laws; instead of being swift and final, however, this enforcement stretched out over years, was endlessly argued, and was unevenly carried out. Part of the hesitation came from the Episcopal agency itself, which did not have enough priests to fill the parishes that would be created.[66] But beyond this lack of priests, the constantly changing regimes in Mexico and local pressures within the territory created an opening for contestation and debate.

At first, California's missionaries were quite successful at stonewalling in face of the new orders. After the decree first arrived in California in 1821, Governor Solá began a tentative implementation by demanding a full accounting of mission resources and releasing select Indians to found their own towns, but Father President Payeras refused to abandon control over either.[67] A year later, Iturbide's representative, Canónigo Fernández, arrived. He was successful in ordering the Spanish flag lowered for the last time, and in creating popularly elected ayuntamientos in California's towns, but he had no more luck than Solá did in reorganizing the missions. On October 8, 1822, in the face of demands for compromise, he issued the new regulations: the missions would be reformed but only partially.[68] Select Indians, with the permission of the governor and the padres, might leave the missions with their share of the property and could support themselves. All Indians had the right to move from one mission to another and receive pay for their work, but could only do certain types of labor. Missionaries still had the right to assign work but the use of the lash was now forbidden.

These reforms stopped far short of secularization but were enough to spur several missionaries to write to a sympathetic de la Guerra with complaints. "It can be seen that the Señor Comisionado does not know what Indians are, or he would not have produced such regulations," groused Father Josef Pineda, who feared "a huge, huge chaos in the Missions."[69] Father Martínez was even more blunt: "The Indians are free now and the Missionaries slaves . . . There are no whippings &c. and to go on horseback you don't put spurs on, and all because it is the style."[70] But Father Payeras was more sanguine. "The Indian populace is somewhat agitated by the ideas of liberty and equality," he wrote to his superiors, "but I believe that these ideas will quiet down as soon as the gentlemen have gone."[71] At least for the moment, fears of disorder were unfounded. In 1822, the governorship was handed off to the mission-friendly Luis Argüello, who, in any case, had few resources to devote to the enforcement of secularization. A new mission was even established at Sonoma in 1823.

It was left, then, to the next national administration to hammer out regulations that would work for the obstinate territory, and for another governor to carry them out. After Iturbide's fall, federalists passed a new liberal constitution in 1824, and in 1825 President Guadalupe Victoria appointed the Junta de Fomento de Californias to make recommendations for California's development. This commission functioned for several years, and though none of its suggestions were enacted as submitted, they formed the basis for much of the later legislation.[72] In published reports and instructions to federalist Governor Echeandía, the Junta recommended that secularization be closely based on the original decree of 1813, tempered with careful study and a gradual approach. Under this plan, mission lands would gradually be distributed to individual Indians, while they were given tutelage in the responsibilities of citizenship.[73] Echeandía, recognizing the power of the missionaries but also wishing to implement the liberal agenda, issued an experimental decree on July 25, 1826, which permitted select neophytes to petition for their emancipation, provided they had been Christians for fifteen years and could earn their living outside the mission estate.[74]

Even this very tentative step, however, provoked strong reactions from the missionaries and from conservatives like de la Guerra, who argued that the neophytes were not ready for freedom. "My father and Echeandía were on very friendly terms," Angustias de la Guerra remembered:

> A number of times they spoke about the effects of having instilled the ideas of citizenship and liberty in the neophytes. My father advised Echeandía to temper his enthusiasm and try to keep the Indians in check, because many of them were traitors. He said that on any given day the Indians could revolt and kill the white people, including Echeandía himself, the man who was giving them so much encouragement.[75]

De la Guerra had very personal reasons for fearing Indian liberty. In 1810, he had experienced firsthand the terror of the Indian insurgency led by Father Hidalgo, and was very nearly its victim in Ixtlán; perhaps he still blamed this rebellion for the death of his daughter Rita de Jesús.

More recently, only two years before Echeandía's decree, in February 1824, the Chumash Indians of de la Guerra's jurisdiction had staged one of the largest and most sustained revolts in memory, and de la Guerra himself, as presidial commander, had been charged with suppressing it. Contemporaries and historians have pointed to multiple causes of this revolt. It was sparked by the flogging of a neophyte at Santa Ynez, but beneath this, many argue, lay Indian discontent with work conditions, resistance to cultural suppression, and opposition to the abusive behavior of the missions' military guard.

De la Guerra, however, interpreted Indian motives for rebellion as liberal ideology in action, as a rejection of the hierarchies of class and caste that rightfully governed society, and of the paternal relations that promised social harmony under benevolent rule. As the rebellion spread to Mission La Purísima and then Santa Bárbara, neophytes not only attempted to take over the missions but also threatened to kill the mission guards and their families living nearby. As with the Bouchard attack of 1818, de la Guerra showed less interest in engaging the enemy in bloody battle than he did in quickly restoring order and economic production.[76] An undated letter in the de la Guerra family papers appears to be from the captain to a leader of the revolt, whom he addresses as Patricio. In it, he admonishes the Indian leader, "you should fear God whom you brazenly offend because sooner or later you will appear in his court and then you and your people will fruitlessly repent for the injustices which you now commit; you kill, rob, and burn the houses made with the sweat of the poor."[77] Young liberals might argue that the missions "treated [Indians] as slaves," but to conservatives like de la Guerra, Indian freedom posed a direct threat to the lives and property of those whom de la Guerra, as town "father," was responsible for protecting.[78]

It was in this role as community protector that the captain negotiated with the Indian leaders. In his letter to Patricio, de la Guerra attested to his own Catholic faith and to his loyalty to "the Monarch to whom [I have] sworn obedience." He demanded that the rebels surrender, claiming, "the pious Spanish King, from whose dominion you so wickedly withdraw, loves his subjects with the tenderness of a father; and interpreting his paternal sentiments, I offer in his name to you and all others that you repent your actions."[79] This assertion of the king's paternal rule occurred a full two years after de la Guerra himself had sworn allegiance to the new republic of Mexico, but to de la Guerra and the mission neophytes, it would have been understood as an offer to restore the balance and reciprocal obligations of colonial society. Eventually, de la Guerra succeeded in enforcing order, but a number of neophytes escaped to the interior, where they joined with independent Indian communities and, several hundred strong, posed a constant threat of further attack in the minds of the gente de razón.[80]

Even after this flight, mission Indians in California outnumbered the gente de razón by at least six to one, and talk of secularization continued to encourage Indians to resist and rebel throughout the mission estates under the new governor.[81] "Echeandía," remarked Angustias, "led the Indians to believe that they too were free men and citizens. This produced a harmful effect on the Indians' minds, for they began to demand that those rights be put into practice."[82] Liberals might make a case for human perfectibility and the rights of man, but conservatives like de la Guerra argued that Indians were not capable of self-government now, and their behavior showed that they never would be. Mexico's new leaders, he thought, showed little concern for the real dangers of their social experimentation. In his mind, Indians were treacherous, and only the missions and the military provided the coercive force necessary to maintain public tranquility, law, and order.

Neophytes, in the opinion of de la Guerra, foreign merchants, and the mission overseers, also needed the paternal oversight of mission life because without it, Californians were in danger of losing their labor force. Under Echeandía's decree, an unknown number of Indians petitioned for their freedom, and beginning in this period, thousands more simply walked away from the missions. Father Francisco González y Ibarra of Mission San Fernando Rey complained, "with the apparent liberty that is given to some in the Presidio, and complete satisfaction with which others find themselves in the mountains, they go off as often and whenever they feel like, to the point that we don't have anyone to work on what is needed, and necessary in the Mission."[83]

The degree to which neophyte Indians truly absorbed Mexican liberal ideologies is not clear, although the new regime certainly provided openings for greater personal freedom. In 1822, neophyte Paulina Joseph Soletasay of Mission San Carlos rejoiced as the Spanish flag was lowered for the last time: "Nowadays you think [the] same as we," he told young Mariano Guadalupe Vallejo, "now anybody [may] dance when [he] want[s] to."[84] And if Native peoples did not demand the right to be citizen-farmers, they did use this moment to demand more individual control over their spiritual lives, movement, and labor, and used the new means at their disposal to get it. Pacífico, a neophyte of San Buenaventura, for example, sent three letters to Governor Echeandía in October and November 1826 on behalf of a list of Indians who petitioned for their freedom.[85] When a personal visit to Echeandía in San Diego failed to sway the governor, it appears that the neophytes of San Buenaventura, just a few months later, came up with another way to claim their liberty. In February 1827, Father Francisco Suñer of that mission griped to de la Guerra that neophytes with trade skills were leaving the mission, some under the pretext of attending religious festivals in town, and others "with the motive of the dreamed-about liberty, that so many crow about in our day." Worse, Suñer claimed that de la Guerra was employing some of them himself. "I reclaim José Aurelio, your celebrated soap maker," he asserted, "and his son, faithful excellent chocolate maker." Of course, it had long been standard practice for many of the gente de razón to negotiate with missionaries for Indian labor, but it seems that at this point neophytes were taking it upon themselves to set the terms of their own work and compensation. The Indian Bruno, said Suñer, was known to be working for Alférez Maitorena, "and according to what they have told me, for wages, at so much per month, and who has given the authority either to the Indian, to hire himself out for wages, or to the other to retain him in his House?"[86]

Within the mission system, those Indians who did remain often refused to obey orders as they had in the past, and resisted the authority of the priests.[87] Alfred Robinson, who arrived in 1829, two and a half years after the decree, became alarmed at what this might mean for his new business.[88] "In some of the Missions," he claimed, "the Indians abandoned their labor, and, when chastened, insulted the priests. These flourishing institutions, as they had been, were in danger of immediate subversion and ruin." He, too, believed the Indians incapable of self-government, arguing that "through the encouragement of Echeandía, vice of all kinds had become prevalent, and the poor misguided Indians saw in the terms *libre* and *independente* a sort of license for the indulgence of every passion."[89]

Thus, the emancipation of neophytes, according to the conservatives, indirectly threatened society and economy in California because it released Indians from the parental discipline they needed at the missions and encouraged them to abandon their work, fall into lives of vice, and even kill whites. But worse was yet to come: liberals next threatened the property of the missions themselves. On July 20, 1830, as José María Padrés joined him in San Diego, Governor Echeandía proposed the next step in secularization to the provincial assembly of California: a plan that would transform every mission, "one by one," into pueblos for Indians and any Mexicans who chose to live there. The former mission land, now pueblo land, would be divided into house and farm lots of eight acres for ex-neophyte families, who would also receive livestock and tools, and all of this would be inalienable for five years. Communal pueblo property left over after the partition would be in the care of a Californio administrator. In a time marked by the Solís revolt and increasing California-Mexican tensions over the recent arrival of convict settlers, the diputación, composed almost entirely of men born in California, took less than two weeks to pass the decree and forward it to Mexico for approval.[90] Clearly, for the younger generation, "humanitarian sentiments" and economic interest took precedence over resistance to Mexican rule.

For men like de la Guerra, and his business partners in the missions and on the foreign hide-and-tallow ships, this proposal represented a naked grab for the spoils of secularization on the part of young Californios who would serve as "administrators" of mission lands and, no doubt, take their own cut of the rich profits. "What all believe," Father President Durán complained, "is that, under the specious pretext of this Plan, there was a secret project of a general plunder of mission property."[91] José de la Guerra himself had little respect for the high-flown ideals of Padrés, who was promising the mission administrations to his young followers. In November 1830, de la Guerra remarked in his journal, "Padrés . . . passed by here with his little twittering wife days ago, just as extreme in his old ideas about the missions, in which he intends to put secular Administrators, and two of those will have to be . . . Joaquín Ortega and his nephew Santiago, the son of Don Argüello."[92] De la Guerra dismissed Padrés as a crank who dangled prizes before impressionable youth, and the secularization plan as a dangerous threat to his own livelihood, and he set about doing what he could to contain the damage. "Fortunately for the country," his future son-in-law Robinson declared, "at this crisis the new General, Don Manuel Victoria, arrived at Santa Bárbara."[93]

For, while Echeandía had been formulating his plan, the government of Mexico had changed hands and had entered a phase in which it would be much less sympathetic to liberal schemes. In January 1830, conservative Anastasio Bustamante had taken the government of Mexico in an armed revolt, and he had no intention of turning Church lands over to Indians or of keeping a liberal like Echeandía in office in California. Bustamante's choice to be California's new governor was Lieutenant-Colonel

Manuel Victoria, the principal commander of Lower California, whose motto was "love of order, respect for authority, and constant consecration to duty."[94] Victoria was a military man, a conservative, and a friend of the mission system. His conservative position allied California's older generation with the new Mexican government. As Juan Alvarado later recalled, Victoria "counted on the aid of the soldiers, the friars, and the Mexicans."[95]

Angustias de la Guerra remembered that, on hearing of this appointment, "it was believed that the missionary padres would be benefited by Victoria," no doubt because her father had already heard this from his trading partner (and liberal) Enrique Virmond.[96] Indeed, de la Guerra seemed pleased that the new governor would apparently leave his economic empire untouched. Victoria, who arrived in San Diego in December 1830 to find Echeandía off touring the missions, then traveled up to Santa Bárbara. While the new governor lodged at the mission, de la Guerra and the other presidial officers met with him; Victoria "received them warmly," although de la Guerra was naturally wary about any new agent of Mexico.[97] In the end, the captain was won over, wryly noting in his journal, "the new Mandarin is manifesting judicious ideas about the missions."[98]

What were these "judicious ideas"? Echeandía, faced with the arrival of his replacement, and hearing of no official approval of his secularization scheme, had issued a preemptory decree on January 6, which the territorial diputación was eager to put into practice.[99] Later, Echeandía defended this decision to proceed without national approval,

> knowing well that to insure the integrity of the nation and tranquility and prosperity at home, it was best to abolish once and for all the oppression of the neophytes by establishing a secular government, since once converted from slaves to proprietors they would become enthusiastic supporters of the federal system, a means of defense against foreign schemes, and of support of the territorial government and troops.[100]

Victoria, needless to say, did not agree, and on arrival in Monterey at the end of January, the new governor repealed this last-minute secularization decree and refused to convene the territorial assembly that had wanted it so badly. Not long afterward, Victoria expelled the radical José María Padrés, who promised his young acolytes that he would soon return to give them management over the mission estates.[101]

It was in this context of political flux and conservative resurgence, then, that José de la Guerra pushed for a repeal of secularization plans and took his case to the national assembly. In the spring of 1831, "uncle" Carlos Carrillo, de la Guerra's brother-in-law and closest supporter, arrived in Mexico as the new territorial deputy. "I have the satisfaction of communicating to you," he wrote de la Guerra in April 1831,

> that ever since I put foot on these Republican lands, I have merited the appreciation of the principal gentlemen and ladies, as much on account of your recommendations as by you having been my brother-in-law, and finally on account of my well-adorned presence . . . not giving anyone a reason to say, "Ah, what a Barbarian California ranchero!" not that, this did not happen, with my good trousers, frock coat, bald head . . . chest out, and ornamented, I inspire admiration.

The family connection between the two men was firm enough that Carrillo acted much like de la Guerra's proxy in Mexico, having the chance to speak as a deputy that de la Guerra had been denied in 1828. "You know how much I esteem you," Carrillo assured his compadre, "and will esteem you till the end of my life."[102]

In that same letter, Carrillo reported on what he had learned about the progress of California's secularization in the national assembly. Echeandía's proposal to turn the missions into pueblos, he said, was still under debate, but "the greater number of Diputados were of the opinion not to do so." As things stood, the Camera awaited California's representative for further advice; friends assured him, "don't worry, that all is good with my being well instructed and well prepared."[103]

Once in Mexico City, Carrillo swiftly made his opinion known, culminating in a major speech on September 15, 1831.[104] Ostensibly, the speech was designed to persuade the deputies to preserve the Pious Fund, a trust made up of private donations intended to support the missions of Baja and Alta California. In the 1830s, several proposals were put forth to seize the properties of this fund for the national treasury. Although Carrillo was not directly addressing the question of mission lands themselves, this speech, no doubt strongly influenced by de la Guerra, laid out in the most complete way yet the conservatives' opposition to secularization and their support of the mission system. In clearly paternalistic rhetoric, Carrillo countered point by point those who argued that the missions blocked colonization and economic development of the frontier, and oppressed their Indian subjects.

As for colonization, Carrillo, perhaps thinking of his nephew William Hartnell, or his eldest daughter's marriage to the American William Goodwin Dana, pointed out that the missions had "attracted many foreigners not only to trade but also to establish themselves and contract family relationships to the notorious advantage of the progress of that territory." Likewise, the mission had encouraged "indirect" colonization by converting the Indians "from savage wandering vagabonds into established families and useful workers in agriculture and the arts, and into men capable of social relationships."[105] Thus, the missions helped to incorporate potentially hostile outsiders, and held California for Mexico against foreign encroachment and Indian attack. Mission Indians, the "embryo of a population," were responsible for this security. Far from oppressing Indians, the missions were raising them to a state of civilization. "To take several hundred men like those Indians, completely in a state of nature and overcome the obstacles which their crudity and stupidity necessarily present in order to make them useful to themselves and to . . . society . . . is a meritorious task," he insisted.[106]

Not only were the missions no hindrance to California's economic and social development, he claimed, they were in fact the very foundation for any prosperity in the territory. Certainly, the military had been no help; the Mexican government had practically cut off supplies and salaries, and the families of soldiers, forming "a separate class" now, depended on the missions for food and other aid. The missions gave them "protection in their undertakings, succor in their necessities, remedy for the infirmities which afflict them, consolation in their troubles, and counsel in their doubts and anxieties."[107] Destruction of the missions, he warned, "may drive the inhabitants to a despair so deep that it is not easy to calculate."[108] On the strength of this speech, Carrillo saved the Pious Fund properties from being nationalized, in a law passed May 25, 1832.[109]

In the meantime, Carrillo had been pressing to have the military command of California separated from the civilian governorship, and was successful enough in his politicking that the vice president offered the job to Carrillo himself, or anyone Carrillo recommended. "You as a good Brother tell me what I ought to do," Carrillo pleaded with his brother-in-law in October 1831.[110] Before de la Guerra could reply, however, events in California overtook his plans. Native sons, including Carlos's younger brother, José Antonio Carrillo, issued a pronunciamiento against Governor Victoria on November 29, 1831, and by the end of December, Victoria was on a ship headed back to Mexico. This is the same rebellion we've seen before, usually explained as the culmination of growing Californio nativism and increasing demands for local political control; but in the context of the battle over secularization, the underlying cause becomes clear. Victoria had repealed Echeandía's secularization decree, expelled José María Padrés, and refused to convene the native son diputación for the rest of the year. An emerging nativist identity allowed young Californios to frame their dissatisfaction with Victoria in terms of home rule and nationalism, and gave them the confidence that they could act as an independent political force to push for what they had wanted ever since they joined Echeandía's and Padrés's study groups: the transfer of mission estates from the Church to private hands.

This rebellion divided the Californio elite by generation: conservatives like de la Guerra and his foreign sons-in-law supported Victoria's choice for a successor, Captain Agustín Zamorano, a conservative member of the Scottish Rite Masons.[111] For a year, Echeandía, who had never left the territory, took over at the call of the revolutionaries. Horrified, Alfred Robinson observed Echeandía seeking support from mission Indians, and in typically melodramatic fashion wrote: "his promises of liberty and land were sufficient to entice all from their labors, and caused the subsequent abandonment of their former pursuits. Rapine, murder and drunkenness were the result; and, in the midst, reveled the Mexican chieftain."[112] William Hartnell organized about fifty foreign residents into "La Compañía Extranjera," a sort of ad hoc police force to support Zamorano in the north.[113] From Mexico, Carlos Carrillo complained that the rebellion had "raised the Devil," and upset their careful plans with the national government.[114]

By the end of the 1831 rebellion, the lines of political contention were sharp and clear. On one side, many Indians, California's native sons, and liberal reformers from Mexico allied to argue that the mission system in California hoarded California's wealth and made slaves of its Indian subjects. On the other, older, conservative men like de la Guerra insisted that it was in everyone's interest for the missions to flourish unmolested, for they were the basis of the territory's prosperity. Secularizing the missions would not spread this wealth around, but destroy it. This position rested on a strongly paternalist outlook: to this way of thinking, neophytes were not born with the rights of free citizens but were essentially children who must be disciplined and monitored to prevent them from falling into vice and to make them "useful" workers instead. The mass of poor settlers, too, depended on the missions like a child did on his father, for succor

and protection. "And just as a son detests and curses the hand which ruined his father," Carlos Carrillo had told the national congress, "depriving
him of his well-being and his inheritance," so would Californians "make
the supreme powers of the Federation the object of their hatred," should
the missions be destroyed.[115]

To patriarchs like Carrillo and de la Guerra, the misguided young
men of California seemed determined to destroy the source of their families' wealth by breaking up the productive mission estates and letting
loose their workforce. Elite sons, of anyone, ought to feel allegiance to the
economic institutions so carefully built and nurtured by their fathers; as
their fathers' dependents, they would be taken care of; and as his heirs,
the family fortunes, trading networks, and other enterprises would one
day fall to them. Until then, sons should be justly subject to the authority
of older, wiser men. De la Guerra could feel fortunate that his own sons
understood this.

Hijos de Familia:
Patriarchal Authority and the Limits of Submission

Even a "good" patriarch like de la Guerra, however, would eventually face
the tensions inherent in patriarchal authority. Young men, struggling to
become adults, faced a contradictory situation. They owed their fathers
customary deference and obedience (as long as their fathers continued to
provide for and protect them), yet to be dominated by another was to be
a man without honor. De la Guerra could expect unquestioning loyalty
from his minor children, even marriageable daughters, but José Antonio, his eldest son, was no longer a child. During the late 1820s and early
1830s, José Antonio, at first an obedient son, grew more and more frustrated with his position in the family as he searched for a way to become
an independent patriarch himself, free of his father's household.

In part, José Antonio's frustration stemmed from what he saw as his
father's inability to fulfill his duties to provide for his eldest child. Dating
back to the Siete Partidas of the medieval era, Spanish and then early
Mexican law gave primary responsibility for raising children to fathers,
not mothers.[116] Custom followed law, and in Mexican California, as elsewhere in the Hispanic world, fathers had the obligation to provide for the
basic necessities of their children's lives—food, clothing, and a home—as
well as to plan for the educations and careers of their sons and the honorable marriages of their daughters. By rights, José Antonio should have
gotten the most attention as eldest son, but events conspired against his
father's hopes.[117]

Born in 1805, José Antonio had spent his childhood stranded in California during the wars for independence. Along with the children of other local officers, he was probably taught basic reading and arithmetic by the local padres. But beyond this, Santa Bárbara in the colonial era could offer the children of such men only a minimal education; nowhere in California could they hope to find secondary education, an advanced college, or professional training.[118] In 1818, de la Guerra therefore chose the only profession for his eldest son that seemed to offer status and advancement: he pulled the thirteen-year-old from his studies and enrolled him as a cadet in the Santa Bárbara Company. One final chance for a better education came the next year, when de la Guerra took his eldest son along to Mexico City, while he petitioned the government for more aid for California's starving military.[119] But if de la Guerra's intention had been to place José Antonio in school, he did not carry out the plan, returning in less than a year. José Antonio resumed his duties as a cadet. In the end, a posting in the officer class was the best de la Guerra could offer his firstborn.

Even though José Antonio's 1824 marriage to Concepción Ortega promised the connections for a rapid rise in the ranks, it quickly became apparent after Independence that a military career could no longer guarantee elite status in California. The future seemed to belong to those with access to education. In the Mexican era, liberal reformers in Mexico placed a special emphasis on universal public education and literacy as a foundation of republican government. As a result, primary schools initially proliferated in California, offering new opportunities to José Antonio's younger siblings.[120] Angustias de la Guerra remembered attending class at two government schools in the 1820s with her younger brothers Pablo and Francisco. The first was taught by a woman, Bernardina Alvarez, and the second by Diego Fernández, who received fifteen dollars per month. At school, Angustias recalled, young students "learned our first letters and we would read from primers or from the catechism." But like many other frontier schools in both the United States and Mexico, Santa Bárbara's government school struggled to find pupils, and by 1828 it had none. Liberal Governor Echeandía ordered Santa Bárbara's commander to compel parents to send their children but eventually declared the teacher's salary a "useless expense."[121]

Although the de la Guerra family had stopped sending their children to the government school, José de la Guerra had no intention of giving up on his sons' educations.[122] In 1828, as Santa Bárbara's school stood empty, de la Guerra was already on his way to take his seat in congress, accompanied by sons Francisco and Pablo, eleven and nine, who were to be edu-cated in Mexico City.[123] The boys spent only a year in Señor Miguel Calderón's private boys' school, but they picked up a cosmopolitan polish, excellent handwriting, and a working knowledge of foreign languages, all of which would serve them well in the years to come.[124] That year, their elder brother Juan studied English, French, Latin, algebra, geography, and the classics at Stonyhurst College, in England.[125] To twenty-three-year-old José Antonio, any discussion of his younger brothers' intelligence and success echoed with the sound of slamming doors—doors to higher edu-cation, to commercial wealth, to California's elite. From José Antonio's perspective, it must have seemed that his father had failed him.

If de la Guerra could be said to have failed in his duty to launch his eldest son into the highest levels of California's society, he certainly did not avoid exercising his right to demand obedience from his son, an au-thority derived from the legal notion of *patria potestas*. As noted in pre-vious chapters, under Spanish law, carried into the republican period, children of both sexes reached adulthood at age twenty-five. Simply reaching the age of majority, however, did not release a son or daughter from paternal authority. Unless specifically emancipated by marriage or legal decree, children were still *hijos de familia,* and were not independ-ent during their father's lifetime. Only after emancipation could children freely choose where to live, administer their property, enter into con-tracts, or be tried as adults.[126]

Californians not only enforced the laws of patria potestas, but also, as with marriage practices, accepted and extended their legitimacy in everyday, customary ways. As Angustias de la Guerra, a younger sister, later remembered, "[P]aternal authority had no limits, and it continued even after children married and had children of their own."[127] The cus-toms of California, for example, allowed fathers close monitoring of their sons' courting and sexual behavior—surprisingly, almost as much as that of their daughters. Cousin José del Carmen Lugo remembered that "the respect in which our parents and elderly persons generally were held was so great that no young man ventured to dance in their presence without first having received permission."[128] Others described the de la Guerra household as unusually rigid. "Long after the sons had grown to be men, and some of them married," one observer noted of this family, "obedience to the father did not lessen. It was an established rule with the old man that every one of his sons should be at home by 9 o'clock at night, or give a satisfactory account of where they had been, and this rule applied as strictly to married as to the single sons."[129]

More extreme liberal ideas, learned from smuggled books and at the feet of California's Mexican officials, challenged native sons to see things from a different perspective. "Young men full of liberal ideas," Mariano Guadalupe Vallejo remembered, "were, under no circumstances, willing to pay homage to individuals who based their rights on rancid parchments or on the glorious deeds of their ancestors; we were disposed to consider the merits of the individual."[130] Liberal ideology questioned privilege based on birthright and blood, and some reformers proclaimed that all men were free citizens, capable of self-government and economic independence, who owed no one allegiance out of mere custom. Such ideals challenged not only the caste system, and the subjugation of Native peoples to the authority of missionaries, but the absolute power of elder men as well. Works circulating in California by such authors as Rousseau and Fénelon argued for a new sort of relationship between fathers and sons—one based not on blood, coercion, and duty to obey, but on the obligation of fathers to gently guide children into moral, independent adulthoods.[131]

All over Mexico in the federalist period, liberals debated the idea of limiting the father's authority over his household. States such as Zacatecas, Oaxaca, and Sierra lowered the age of majority and the age at which minors needed paternal consent to marry. These states took the even more extreme measure of automatically releasing single adults from patria potestas.[132] As a territory, California did not have the legal standing to make such legislative changes for itself, but liberal ideas did have an impact on the customary practice of paternal authority. This was especially true after liberal young men overthrew Victoria; José del Carmen Lugo, a cousin of the de la Guerras, recalled that in the early days, parents could keep a tight reign over young men's behavior at public dances, but "from 1831–1832 on, customs became less strict."[133] The soldier José María Amador confirmed that "[u]ntil 1830, . . . respect for parents and authority went unquestioned . . . [but]from 1830 on, society became more lenient due to the greater contact with outsiders."[134] With this new philosophy, California's native sons found a voice to claim personal freedoms and to question blind obedience to their own fathers.

On the other hand, liberal theory as it developed in Mexico did not destroy older notions of patriarchal authority completely. Although Mexico's laws allowed for almost universal male suffrage in the 1820s, for example, many states restricted suffrage to property owners, and barred women, minors, domestic servants, debtors, and imprisoned criminals from voting or holding public office.[135] Real and metaphorical fathers, as enlightened republicans, would continue to guide and represent the weak and dependent, who were themselves considered incapable of exercising the rights of citizenship. Paternal authority as practiced in California went further, giving fathers the power to dictate the political activities of any dependent living under the patriarch's roof, no matter the child's age or marital status. Describing a pattern that must have been widespread among certain elite Californios, Lugo claimed that, as an eighteen-year-old living at home, he was only an observer of the Victoria ouster in 1831. "I had no part in any of the revolutionary movements," he explained, "since my father did not permit his sons to do so. The only one who had any part was my brother, Felipe, who was married, and consequently lived in his own home and managed his own affairs."[136] In California, only heads of household—married men, preferably with children—were considered to have shown enough responsibility to enter the world of public decision-making as independent citizens.

In 1824, José Antonio de la Guerra's marriage released him by law from patria potestas, and in 1830 he reached the age of majority. Yet into the early 1830s, he still lived in his father's household and was subject to his rules. His father had failed to launch his son to independence; José Antonio had no clear career path, little education, and no property of his own. His dependence prevented him from becoming a free citizen. His 1828 prank, taking the presidio in the name of the Spanish kings, clearly shows how much the young man chafed at his father's discipline. While Echeandía and Padrés spread the gospel of liberalism, and while his peers in the diputación promoted secularization and overthrew the governor, José Antonio held his tongue. Instead, the young man quietly promoted his father's interests and submitted to paternal authority, neither claiming a position as an independent patriarch nor questioning all such customary authority, as his cousins were beginning to do.

José Antonio's rudimentary education and geographic isolation prevented him from immersing himself in the ideological debates raging in the capital and in the cities to the south, and because he lived at home he was subject to his father's social and political dictates. But José Antonio had more positive reasons to place his first loyalties with his father's fortunes. Already, the young man was deeply enmeshed in local godparent networks, giving him motive to promote family interests.[137] And after he left the military in 1828, governmental reforms of the 1820s gave José Antonio an opening to develop a civil career for himself that would provide him an essential role in the family empire and that promised rewards for himself and his own small family. This brief interlude of family solidarity would be short lived, however.

As we have seen, Captain de la Guerra resisted the establishment of popularly elected ayuntamientos, or town councils, as much as possible, disputing the authority of the defiant ayuntamiento of Los Angeles, and delaying elections in Santa Bárbara until December 1826. De la Guerra need not have worried that Santa Bárbara would challenge him as much as Los Angeles. Under the new regulations, de la Guerra's military position disqualified him from holding civil office. But he had someone to take his place: his eldest son. José Antonio began his career as síndico, or treasurer and public attorney, elected in 1829, then moved up to alcalde by 1832, presiding over the ayuntamiento.[138] Here, in his own town, José de la Guerra had been careful to enact the role of the "good father" to the settlers and soldiers, and as such in their eyes possessed the moral weight necessary for judicial reconciliation and compromise, the hallmark of the ideal alcalde, a position that roughly combined the roles of justice of the peace and administrator. José Antonio was able to take on this reputation for himself by acting as a good hijo de familia, and obeying his father's wishes in office. The substitution was so explicit that the younger de la Guerra occasionally took to using his father's full name, "de la Guerra y Noriega," instead of the proper "de la Guerra y Carrillo," and to calling himself "Capitán."

Such an arrangement could prove quite useful to the family, particularly when de la Guerra confronted local challenges to his rule. One case, brought in the summer of 1833, perfectly illustrates the power of a family that could coordinate its economic and political ventures, but also hints at the cracks that were starting to develop in de la Guerra family solidarity.[139] On July 5, 1833, María del Carmen Rodríguez petitioned the new governor, José Figueroa, taking advantage of his presence on a tour through the south. She and her husband, she stated, had begun to build a corral for their "few cows" at Rancho El Conejo, but work soon halted when one of her brothers ordered them to stop in the name of the captain. "Said rancho is possessed by Don José [de la Guerra y] Noriega," she explained, "without my knowing how he possesses it." She demanded to know "on what ground he is enjoying it without our consent, we being the legitimate owners."[140]

Such disputes over property ownership and ranch boundaries were not uncommon in California, but María del Carmen faced an almost impossible hurdle in getting her case heard. Not only had Alcalde José Antonio de la Guerra thrown out her complaint, she said, but he "has threatened me." The elder de la Guerra, meanwhile, reaped the benefits of having an alcalde who lived under his roof and owed him the deference

of a son to his father. But, as the case played out, this coordination of interests between father and son began to unravel. As far as the facts of the
matter were concerned, de la Guerra had indeed owned a half-interest in
El Conejo since 1822, along with María del Carmen's now deceased father, Ignacio Rodríguez. This information should have settled the matter,
but as it turns out, more was at stake here than a simple misunderstand-
ing over grants and ownership rights. For in stating his side of the matter,
Alcalde José Antonio de la Guerra expressed to the governor his own understanding of local inheritance practices, and what rewards a dutiful
son had the right to expect. These expectations soon ran up against the
governor's more egalitarian interpretation of the new inheritance laws.

In his explanation, dated July 8, José Antonio told Governor Figueroa
plainly that in stopping María del Carmen Rodríguez from building her
corral, he had acted to "eject the unjust intruder" and prevented her from
construction that would have falsely indicated ownership. "Neither María
del Carmen Rodríguez nor her husband have ever been reputed owners of
the land of El Conejo," he argued. The only legitimate owner of the ranch,
he stated, apart from his own father, was José de Jesús Rodríguez, María
del Carmen's older brother. For the last fourteen years, José Antonio
stated, José de Jesús had taken responsibility as executor for paying the
debts of his father's estate, and for providing for his widowed mother and
his brothers and sisters, allowing them use of the ranch for their livestock.
In exchange, José de Jesús had been recognized by everyone in the community as the sole inheritor of the grant, and "no one except María del
Carmen has disputed his exclusive ownership." Indeed, the de la Guerras
had dealt only with this brother and his wife, Bernarda Ruiz, over the
years, allowing their cattle to mix in one herd, and sponsoring two of their
children in baptism to cement the business relationship.[141] Such arrangements, Alcalde de la Guerra argued, while not strictly speaking covered
under the law of inheritance, were widely understood in practice. "It has
been observed," he told the Mexican governor, "that here only that child or
those children, who have charged themselves principally with the estates
of their parents, have entered upon the enjoyment of possession in such
lands, and this with the knowledge of the government."[142]

Governor Figueroa, however, did not see things this way. Under liberal reforms, entail had been abolished in Mexico in 1823, and according
to the new inheritance laws, a man could dispose of only one-fifth of his
property freely; the rest was automatically split between the widow, who
received two-fifths, and the children, who divided the other two-fifths
evenly. In his ruling of July 16, 1833, Figueroa stated clearly that, whatever

the custom had been, no child could be deprived of the right of inheriting from his or her parents, "especially lands distributed to the settlers of Californias, which their descendants only can enjoy, and can never be entailed, encumbered, or alienated."[143]

This ruling no doubt came as a shock to twenty-eight-year-old José Antonio, who probably expected to be recognized as the sole inheritor of his father's lands one day. The year before, his hopes had no doubt soared when his father had dramatically increased the family land holdings. Alcalde José Antonio de la Guerra himself had filled out the paperwork, deeding over the Rancho Simi—over 113,000 acres of prime ranch lands—from the Pico family to his father for 819 pesos in silver coin and 200 pesos in goods.[144] Along with El Conejo and Refugio, the ranch owned by his wife's family, Simi was the only Spanish grant made to private citizens in the Santa Bárbara area.[145] Before the Figueroa ruling, José Antonio might have expected as eldest son and executor to have all of Simi and half of Conejo one day; afterward, with eleven brothers and sisters inheriting two-fifths of the estate equally, he could hope for just a fraction. José Antonio had done everything expected of a dutiful son, suppressing his own claims to autonomy for the good of the family. But in 1833, with little education or opportunity for land ownership, he would have had difficulty seeing any payoff for his sacrifices, and no possibility that he would eventually have the economic and political independence of a substantial patriarch and householder.

Land and Labor: The California Compromise

To make matters even more galling, while José Antonio's dreams of becoming a wealthy ranchero faded in 1833, those of his cousins were finally being fulfilled under the new governor, General José Figueroa. Before Figueroa's administration, California's governors had doled out a handful of small private grants each year, usually small lots of pasturage or marginal or frontier lands unclaimed by the missions. Land hunger only increased as California's population grew, blocking young men's abilities to establish their own households and thus claim political independence and full citizenship. By 1831 one foreign visitor remarked, "The clamor for land is greater than ever. Many soldiers…do not know how they are going to settle with their growing families."[146]

After Figueroa's arrival in January 1833, however, the number of grants skyrocketed to twenty-one, then thirty-nine, then forty a year.[147] For the first time, young Californios had found a governor who addressed their demand for land and autonomy. Yet Figueroa, the former

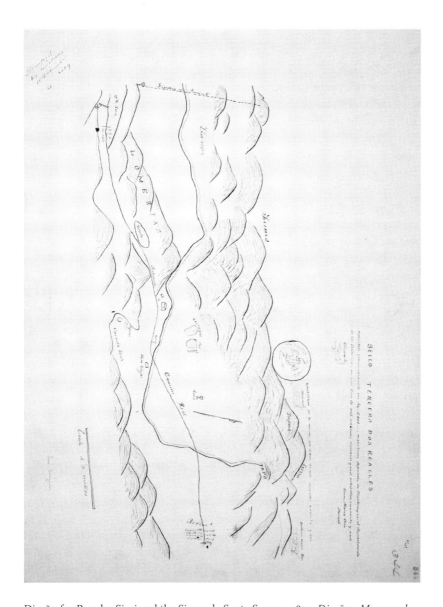

Diseño for Rancho Simi and the Sierra de Santa Susana, 1852. *Diseños: Maps and Plans of Ranchos of Southern California* (Bound Manuscripts Collection). Department of Special Collections, Charles E. Young Research Library, UCLA.

governor of the state of Sonora-Sinaloa, was able to accomplish the feat without implementing the secularization act of 1813, and with a paternalist Indian policy that pleased the older generation. Figueroa's administration was characterized by compromise, yet it rendered significant material benefit for the native sons, and for this he became the most popular governor in Mexican California's history.

It would have been difficult to predict such a record on the new governor's arrival. Carlos Carrillo, still in Mexico, warned his brother-in-law in April 1832 that he had heard from Sonora's deputy, Gómez de la Madrid, that Figueroa was "a great despot, ... that he went to Sonora poor, and came back rich, and I believe ultimately he became poor [again] in Mexico City, and he wants to go look for something in California ... Is a governor never to go there ... who is not out for his own interests?"[148] "Make friends of Figueroa," he instructed his brother-in-law cynically, "give him a gift of a pair of horses, and a good pair of mules, which is what is done these days with Governors, in order to be able to get what one wants."[149] Although suspicious of any Mexican governor, California's well-connected conservatives could at least feel some security that he was appointed by the same administration that had sent Victoria.[150]

Unlike the former governor, however, Figueroa was a moderate "yorkino" federalist, instructed by the central government to calm the rebellious sentiment kicked up by his predecessor.[151] Liberals in California quickly found a new ally in the governor, whose first act was to grant amnesty to all concerned in Victoria's overthrow. Reconciled with the new administration, and with Mexico's authority in the territory, young rebels like Vallejo and Alvarado returned to Monterey and began to reassemble the diputación, while Figueroa exchanged friendly letters with Echeandía on matters of policy.[152] Among conservatives, such liberal resurgence ignited fears of a return to disorder and repression of the Spanish-born. Juan José de la Guerra, back from his studies in England and living in Monterey, wrote to his father that "the enlightened" men of the town were living so scandalously, except for his uncle Anastasio Carrillo, that "even the English" were shocked.[153] "As to what you say about the inhabitants," he reassured his mother, "I will take good care not to give them the slightest reason to talk, which until this date they have not done since I have seen them several times and they have not said a word of Gachupines."[154]

But Juan and his father need not have worried, for Figueroa had determined to proceed with caution. The liberal territorial assembly, in fact, did not meet for the whole of 1833, and in the meantime Governor

Figueroa busied himself with settling local disputes and carrying out the instructions he brought with him from Mexico. Figueroa was himself mestizo, and widely known to be proud of his Indian heritage, so it is not surprising, perhaps, that his first order of business was to begin emancipating California's neophytes. These poor subjects, an official in the Ministry of Relations had told him, were in a "state of abasement"; Figueroa was thus charged with causing "to be distributed, to such as are fitted for it, such fields of the mission lands as they may be capable of cultivating, in order that they may thus become fond of labor and may go on acquiring property."[155] Figueroa also, however, was told to "act with prudence and tact," on this issue, and did just that, visiting the southern missions in the summer of 1833 and consulting extensively with the missionaries about the state of the neophytes.[156] California's missionaries convinced Figueroa on this trip that most Indians still needed paternal oversight, so when he issued his Provisional Regulations for the Emancipation of Mission Indians in July, they looked much like those of Echeandía, emancipating select neophytes who might be ready and giving them plots of land in new pueblos, but maintaining commissioners to regulate their labor. The state, under this decree, maintained the ability to force Indians back to the missions if they abandoned their new lands and work. At base, these new regulations did little to undermine the mission system or to redistribute its estates, and in the end most qualified neophytes refused to leave the missions under the conditions established by these decrees.[157]

In fact, after Figueroa had spent just a few months in California, conservatives had persuaded him not only that most neophytes were not ready to be free but also that intact missions were the sole source of prosperity in California. Only a gradual approach to secularization, he decided, would extinguish the missions' hold over the territory. In October 1833, Figueroa had sent his recommendation to the national government opposing any sudden and radical change, but by then, word of a new secularization law, passed August 17, 1833, had already reached California.[158] For the rest of the year, and well into the next, Figueroa's own reticence to make changes, and the delay in receiving the new instructions, conspired against any radical redistribution of mission lands. Oddly, however, according to the territorial records, the young men of California were still getting the land grants they had long been clamoring for.

Figueroa, it turns out, had found a way to circumvent the sticky issue of secularization: he granted lands under a different set of national laws, the colonization acts of 1824 and 1828. This tactic was no independent stroke of creativity, but was suggested by a second national imperative:

settlement of the northern territories. When he arrived in January 1833, the new governor also carried in his pocket explicit instructions designed to strengthen Mexico's hold over its wayward northern territory, still threatened by encroachment from Russians, Americans, and independent Indians. In particular, Minister of Relations Lucas Alamán had ordered Figueroa to proceed with colonization by all possible methods, taking care that Mexican citizens would be given preference over foreigners in obtaining land.[159]

Alamán might have been encouraged to give these instructions to Figueroa by a petition he had received directly from California's deputy, Carlos Carrillo, on May 9, 1832. "The distribution of land, I understand, is now about to be carried into effect," Carrillo ventured, and he asked the minister for a share of it for his eldest son, José Gertrudis. In his petition, Carrillo spelled out the difficulties that such young men in California faced when they reached adulthood and had no means to establish their independence. José, he explained, was married, and "forming a family separate from mine, and finds himself consequently under the obligation of providing for its sustenance."[160] Agriculture and ranching were "the only profession in that country, and that which he best understands, as he has been occupied in the practice of it since he was very small." But, Carlos explained, his son had no land of his own on which to pasture the livestock Carlos had given him when he married. In the name of this son, a Mexican citizen and native of California, Carrillo petitioned the minister to order the governor "to give him in fee some one of the many vacant lands which there are in that Territory, and to put him in possession of it." On May 16, the day before Alamán sent his formal instructions on colonization to Figueroa, the minister officially forwarded this petition to the new governor to carry out its request.[161]

Figueroa, then, was well aware of native son land hunger even before his ship sailed north from San Blas. Of course, when Figueroa attempted to carry out his orders, he ran up against the same difficulties that Californios had always faced: there were no truly "vacant lands" in the territory. Despite numerous attempts at secularization, the missions still held most of the arable lands in California, making it difficult for anyone else to establish farms or ranches. In 1833, Figueroa was not yet ready to implement full-scale secularization, but the Carrillos, among others, suggested a legal loophole. No legal document granted the mission fathers title to their land or specified the boundaries of any mission; friars held the land by occupation. In other words: no use, no ownership. Two and a half months after Figueroa's ruling on inheritance dashed José Antonio de la Guerra's hopes to someday acquire all of his father's ranch, his first cousin José Gertrudis Carrillo petitioned the governor for Las Posas, 26,623 "vacant" acres of Mission San Buenaventura lands.

In a letter of September 30, 1833, José Gertrudis Carrillo reiterated his father's petition, claiming that he ought to be given land, "being separated from the paternal authority, by reason of having set up for myself, (married) and being at present under the obligations consequent upon it" —in other words, because he was now a patriarch of his own. With "sufficient personal property to keep said place continually occupied," "Citizen José Carrillo" argued, he would be "of notable benefit to myself and to the public in this Territory."[162]

The land, "between" Missions San Buenaventura and San Fernando, was not claimed, José Gertrudis Carrillo said, but "is a vacant place in which only some wild horses are met with." This, however, turns out to have been not quite true. Before he would grant the land, Figueroa ordered an investigation; witnesses testified that Carrillo himself met all the prerequisites, being a citizen, married, and the father of three.[163] Las Posas, however, "belongs to the Mission of San Buenaventura," according to Juan Ibarra, the Santa Bárbara commander, who added, "as to whether said mission needs it or not, it belongs to its father minister to say."[164] Other witnesses, however, testified that the mission had indeed abandoned the land, and that it was being used instead as "the watering place of the cattle of some individuals who have ranches near."[165] Perhaps hoping to forestall a full-scale attack on his estates, Father Blas Ordaz of the mission finally agreed to give up the "unused" land. By February 1834 the permission probably seemed like a formality anyway, as Carrillo had already put five hundred cattle to pasture at Las Posas. Ordaz grumbled that the new owner would have to build a fence to keep his cattle from straying onto what remained of the mission land.[166]

José Gertrudis Carrillo had to wait several months for the new diputación to convene, but on May 15, 1834, Figueroa finally granted him Las Posas. The diputación, which included his father, Carlos, and uncle José Antonio, confirmed the grant on May 21.[167] Perhaps aware that this grant might appear irregular, the diputación issued a new law the next day that not only allowed, but ordered, "vacant" mission lands to be granted according to the Mexican colonization laws.[168] With this law, the floodgates opened, and scores of new grants, carved from mission estates, transferred to the hands of the native sons each year thereafter. Grants like Las Posas solved many problems facing the Mexican government: they chipped away at the Church's hold on the land and encouraged economic development without risking Indian disorder, and they offered a way to colonize the northern frontier without opening the doors to foreign occupation.

By the early 1830s, Carlos Carrillo, de la Guerra's stalwart compadre, had little scruple left about claiming "vacant" mission land for his son, or for that matter, himself.[169] Under Figueroa's administration, young men like José Gertrudis and fathers like Carlos Carrillo finally began to address one of the problems inherent in the transition from child to independent patriarch in that territory. And in the end, they did so without implementing the full liberal program. Working out a compromise with the governor, the young men of Monterey took mission lands but did not yet destroy the heart of the mission system or make free citizens of California's Indians. José Antonio de la Guerra, the dutiful son, could only grind his teeth in frustration as he contemplated the success of his younger first cousin, busy setting up his wife and children on ranch lands right next to Simi and El Conejo. The fact that José Gertrudis Carrillo and José Antonio de la Guerra were married to sisters no doubt made the comparisons all the more irritating to the landless young man.

José de la Guerra managed to add ranch lands to his empire as well but refused to take even "unused" mission lands—El Conejo and Simi had been originally granted to individuals under the Spanish flag—and he gave none of these to his son. Once again, the Spaniard began to look like an active threat to the new regime. In May 1834, five days after the territorial diputación granted Las Posas to José Gertrudis Carrillo, a special messenger arrived in Monterey from the south, breathless with the intelligence that José de la Guerra and his friend, Father President Narciso Durán of Mission Santa Bárbara, were plotting a counter-revolution with Father Tomás Esténega and Sergeant José Antonio Pico. A guard at San Gabriel, it seems, had heard Durán and de la Guerra ridicule the federal system, watched them sign mysterious papers, and then transfer money from San Gabriel to Santa Bárbara.[170] After that, Pico made the guard sign a paper; being illiterate, the soldier could only assume its purpose to be part of the conspiracy.

On hearing of the plot, Figueroa reconvened the diputación at once in secret session, and all agreed that the story sounded all too plausible. California's government took quick and decisive action, authorizing the use of military force and the arrest of the accused for immediate trial. José Antonio and Carlos Carrillo left for the south immediately to try and stop any popular uprising. Five days later, the whole thing blew over when the Carrillos discovered that the guard had merely witnessed de la Guerra going over mission accounts with the friars and settling the transfer of cattle on Rancho Simi with its former owner, Pico.[171] Nonetheless, suspicions remained high that José de la Guerra would continue to oppose the administration's plans for distributing mission lands to aspiring young patriarchs.

No Haven for Liberals

It may have seemed that missionaries and their allies were the biggest threat to the ongoing transfer of mission lands to young Californios, but in the end the biggest challenge came not from local conservatives but from the very Mexican liberals who had inspired the plan in the first place. Through the 1820s and 1830s, as they grew to adulthood, the native sons and daughters of California had become eager disciples of the liberal cause, and they enthusiastically championed many elements of liberal nation building, such as civilian government and the secularization of the missions. Liberals from the capital quickly discovered, however, that frontier California was hardly the blank page they were expecting. Young Californios felt pushed away from an emerging national identity as they struggled to shape national initiatives to their own desires. As a result, nation building in California parted ways from national identity. The struggle to control these projects would pit the territory against the nation for the next five years.

The first inkling that trouble might be brewing came in the form of somewhat-garbled reports from Mexico that a new secularization plan had passed the Mexican congress, and that a colony of new settlers was assembling in Mexico City to take possession of mission lands. In September 1832, the conservative government of Anastasio Bustamante, four months after appointing Figueroa, had fallen to the kind of provincial pronunciamientos that had ousted Governor Victoria in California. In early 1833, a coalition led by civilian reformer Valentín Gómez-Farías and military dissident Antonio López de Santa Anna took power. New president Santa Anna promptly "retired" to his stronghold in Veracruz, leaving Vice-President Gómez-Farías in charge for the next year. Gómez-Farías, a radical liberal and strong nationalist, quickly moved to break the power of the Church and instituted policies to develop and colonize Mexico's northern frontiers.[172] Gómez-Farías took a particular interest in the far north as a space for liberal experimentation, buying property in Texas and telling friends he hoped to retire to California.[173] From his government's initiatives came several pieces of legislation and presidential orders specific to California that threw the territory into turmoil.

The first order of business for Mexico's new regime was to lay the groundwork for colonization by instituting immediate secularization of California's missions and requiring the prompt replacement of the Franciscan missionaries with secular clergy. This bill, which was silent on the dispersal of mission lands and properties, passed on August 17, 1833.[174] Meanwhile, Gómez-Farías began to organize a colonization project, and, finally splitting the governorship of California into military and civilian posts, made the civilian governor also the director of the colony. For this position, replacing Figueroa, he chose José María Híjar, a federalist from Guadalajara, and for the position of comandante general of the troops, and sub-director of colonization, none other than the radical José María Padrés, who had been expelled from the territory in 1831 as a danger to Governor Victoria's conservative regime.[175] Finally, the national congress addressed the material basis for the new colony: on November 26, 1833, it passed a vaguely worded law authorizing the government "to use every means to assure the colonization, and make effective the secularization of the missions of Upper and Lower California" and allowing use of the Pious Funds to do so.[176]

While Híjar and Padrés began to advertise for colonists and stockpile supplies, word of the new initiatives made its way up to California. Acting on the advice of California's missionaries and on his own investigation of mission conditions, Figueroa sent a warning to the national government in October 1833 to proceed with caution, but it was little heeded in the capital. Eventually the new secularization law arrived in California, but with no formal orders to implement it, Figueroa told the diputación when it finally assembled on May 1, 1834, that they would all have to wait for the new governor, Híjar, to bring further instructions.[177] The diputación, however, in the midst of distributing "vacant" mission land, was growing impatient. Some claimed that missionaries had begun to slaughter their herds, and rumors were arriving from Mexico that the new colonists, who left Mexico City in April, intended to take the rest of the mission estates, and that Padrés was bringing his own handpicked administrators to oversee the remaining mission lands.[178]

Assemblymen Carlos and José Antonio Carrillo, now fully converted to the cause of land distribution, submitted a preemptive secularization program to the governor on July 19, 1834, and on August 9, after a little mild protest, Figueroa officially proclaimed it the law of the land.[179] This plan immediately secularized ten of the twenty-one missions, with the rest to follow as soon as possible. The regulation permitted the Franciscans to stay until their secular replacements arrived but gave authority over the mission lands and estates to the territorial government. Government-appointed commissioners would choose small plots of land, livestock, tools, and seed for each ex-neophyte head of household; these Indians would also be expected to elect local government for their new pueblos. The remaining mission lands, however, would come under the administration of government-appointed mayordomos, or administrators, who could require the ex-neophytes to labor on the surplus lands. Indians were forbidden to sell their properties, and the missionaries from preemptively slaughtering cattle and giving the proceeds to them.[180] Taken as a whole, these regulations promoted the interests of California's emerging ranchero elite. Although elites did not secure direct transfer of the main estates into their hands, they had the next best thing in being able to appoint themselves commissioners and administrators of the prime mission ranches, orchards, and farms. Mexican colonists, foreigners, and poor Californios with no connections would find themselves blocked from access to these plum appointments. Indians, in theory now freeholders and voting citizens, continued to be subject to forced labor on the "surplus" lands. The mission economy changed legal status, but it would function practically uninterrupted under its new directors.[181]

In September and October 1834, the colonists finally arrived. At their farewell ball five months before, Vice-President Gómez-Farías had toasted them with the prediction that California would become "a haven for liberals when they could no longer remain in Mexico."[182] That day had come all too soon. By the time the 239 families, mostly teachers, farmers, and artisans, set foot on the shores of California, Santa Anna had expelled his liberal vice president and declared a centralist dictatorship.[183] Figueroa, informed that Santa Anna had revoked the new governor's appointment, refused to hand over California's administration to Híjar and Padrés. Despite carrying instructions that they occupy "all the property belonging to the missions," the colony directors ran into another brick wall when they demanded that the governor and diputación turn over to them control of the missions, ten of which were already under the command of native son commissioners.[184]

Híjar and Padrés's conflict with Figueroa and the diputación—many of whom had been Padrés's ardent supporters just a few years before—led to a heated exchange of proclamations and letters, culminating in an abortive uprising in March 1835 and the subsequent expulsion of the colony directors on suspicion of conspiracy against the government.[185] Figueroa defended his actions toward the colonists in a lengthy "Manifesto to the

Mexican Republic," published in September 1835.[186] In it, he expressed paternalist sentiments widely held in California, claiming that California's territorial government had passed its own secularization decree to protect Indian rights to mission lands in the face of a colonization project that threatened to uproot the Indians.[187] While Híjar had promised that Indians, like any free citizens, could petition to receive grants of mission lands, and would have the freedom to live where they chose and wages for their work, Figueroa argued that such tactics would only result in ex-neophytes being swindled out of what little property they had left. Indians, he argued, were like children, "ignorant, still beggarly and half wild." If California followed Híjar's principles and treated them as citizens and absolute equals, then this would be like being forced "to forego all laws from our codes regulating *patria potestad*, those guaranteeing a man's authority as head of the family and all those stipulating the care and tutelage of minors, retarded, insane, and other individuals ... Equality before the law," he explained, "taken to such extremes, would throw society into upheaval."[188]

Eventually, many of the colonists scattered throughout the territory, where they continued to preach liberal ideals and generally found welcome use for their skills and educations. But the fact that California's emerging ranchero class rejected the plan to give the colonists the mission estates shows just how far California's native sons had come from their idealistic days, when they had studied at the feet of Governor Echeandía and Lieutenant Padrés. By 1835, the "enlightened" saw themselves as potential patriarchs, wealthy and independent. Liberal projects to weaken paternal authority, give Indians the rights of free men, or colonize California with enlightened settlers were what they had been demanding all along, but now these same projects looked more like a threat to snatch a different, glittering future from their grasp.

By the end of 1834, Californio commissioners, mainly drawn from California's elite native sons and the officers who had arrived with Echeandía, had already introduced the new system to ten missions, taking inventories, distributing property, and assigning land. By the end of the next year, another six missions were in some stage of this transformation. Neither California's conservatives nor Mexico's liberals could halt the native sons' land grab. But one more group claimed an interest in the disposal of the mission estates and shaped its course. Many of the ex-neophytes who had worked this land for so long resisted their classification as laborers in need of paternal oversight, and they acted to claim mission property as their own, even if in small allotments or grants. At some of these missions, the ex-neophytes remained and apparently accepted the new regime, but at others many Indians refused to work for the administrators, stole horses, and killed cattle from the "surplus" herds to sell for cash.[189] Many others simply left their former homes altogether, migrating to the new private ranchos and to towns like Los Angeles, picking up whatever work they could find as farmhands and servants. Despite an epidemic of malaria that hit the central valley in 1833, some joined with the independent Indian villages of the territory's interior, returning periodically to raid livestock.[190]

Of those who remained on mission land, a few managed to manipulate the new system for gain. Some petitioned for, and received, ranchos of hundreds of acres with title and the right to sell. Others took advantage of paternalistic protections in the allotment process. In the summer of 1835, for example, seventeen-year-old Francisco de la Guerra bought a sorrel horse from Sacarías, an ex-neophyte at Los Berros, the new Indian pueblo at the former Mission La Purísima. Domingo Carrillo, Francisco's uncle and the administrator of the mission, was forced to write to José de la Guerra when Sacarías demanded the horse back for its original owner, with no compensation for young Francisco. "Now you know very well," Domingo explained, "that the regulation says that they can't be sold, the things that were given to [the ex-neophytes] are inalienable, and that all buyers lose that which had been given for that which was bought."[191] De la Guerra, apparently, would have none of this, and protested that his son had entered into the transaction legally. But under the law, a father was still held responsible for a minor son's purchase; unemancipated children could not enter into contracts or administer property independently. "I have nothing to do with Cuchichito [Francisco] for being hijo de familia," Domingo reminded the elder de la Guerra, "and for being under the *patria potestad*."[192]

But lest de la Guerra think his brother-in-law too scrupulous in the enforcement of the law, he added, "if [Sacarías] hadn't demanded it from me, I would have said nothing."[193] Some ex-neophytes, in other words, understood the new regulations quite well. Men like Sacarías rejected aspects of the law that compelled their labor but demanded enforcement of those parts of the law that sheltered their property. By these actions, Sacarías pitted elite men against each other, and as a result, elites struggled to keep the family economy on an even keel while fulfilling their self-proclaimed responsibilities as fatherly protectors of the Indians. An exasperated Domingo Carrillo blamed the spread of empowering information to the Indians for getting him into trouble with his brother-in-law. "If the regulation which governs this pueblo had not been made known here," he complained to de la Guerra, "I would not be at fault [with you]."[194]

By 1835, then, California's second generation finally reaped the benefits of their rebellion against the first. Seeing themselves as more "Californio" than "Mexican," they had taken control of the territory's diputación and now cooperated with a sympathetic Mexican governor whom their political action had helped put into place. With this power, they employed their own "liberal" programs to redistribute the mission land as private property and secure the remainder as government-owned estates under their administration. Nevertheless, this new order did not represent a complete rejection of the past: older caste and paternal relationships remained, governing both California's elite families and its labor system. Native sons, after all, wanted not a rejection of all patriarchal authority, just the authority that governed them.

While Mexican liberals might have seen the native sons as their converts, and California as a blank page for their nation-building projects, Californios themselves molded the ideology to their own problems. Californio native sons, swayed by the conservative agenda of the older generation, Indian acts of rebellion, and their own desire for a compliant and cheap work force, claimed to be acting to protect Indians while they rejected the full political agenda of more radical liberals like Padrés. In the hands of California's native sons, liberalism in California eventually took a form that stressed economic liberty and rejected facets of the discourse that challenged patriarchy or argued for the rights of Indians as citizens.[195] Individual Indians could and did learn to manipulate this new regime, rejecting its coercive aspects and negotiating for what protection the law would allow, depending on circumstance, but the new rancheros continued to rely on Indian labor, as the missions before them had done.

By the end of 1835, as Anita de la Guerra trained to be a good wife to her Yankee fiancé, almost one hundred new ranches had come into the hands of California's native sons, and sixteen estates of "surplus" mission lands were under the supervision of Californio administrators. Not one of them, however, had made it into the hands of a de la Guerra son. José Antonio, the eldest, would soon commit himself to getting his own piece of the pie. In October 1834, the same month that Híjar arrived in Monterey to take the governorship from Figueroa, José Antonio had moved to the capital town and begun his belated education in liberalism and rebellion. That month, he took his position as Santa Bárbara's elector, charged with appointing California's new deputy to the national congress. On October 16, he met with the young activists of the diputación, who chose him and Juan Bautista Alvarado to be their secretaries, and together they elected his uncle José Antonio Carrillo to the post of deputy.[196] From then on, José Antonio lived in Monterey, most likely with his sister Angustias and her new husband, Manuel Jimeno, the customs official and alcalde, and with sister Teresa and her husband, William Hartnell.[197] In the capital town, José Antonio was at last free of his father's supervision, and he plunged into the heart of Monterey politics, helping the Californio diputación defeat the Híjar-Padrés colonization project. Finally, it seemed, the last obstacle to native son wealth and independence was gone, and José Antonio could begin to imagine again a glorious future as a patriarch when the rest of the missions would be broken up and he would finally get his share. Two years later, he found himself taking desperate measures to keep that shining dream from slipping through his fingers.

CHAPTER FIVE

HOME RULE:
FAMILY HONOR IN FREE CALIFORNIA

O n September 29, 1835, Governor José Figueroa died of a heart attack. Although Figueroa had been complaining of illness for
months and had repeatedly asked his superiors if he could retire,
José Antonio de la Guerra and the rest of the diputación in Monterey had
not met for the past year, certain that they had plenty of time to distribute
more grants of mission lands to themselves and to their relatives. Legisla-
tors quickly ordered a state funeral with full military honors for their
beloved leader, and deputy Juan Alvarado declared in session, "All is
bitterness—all is grief! The Californians weep for a beneficent father."[1]
For reform-minded Californios, Figueroa's paternal authority derived
from his success in offering his subjects well-being, protection, and the
means to become adult patriarchs—allowing them to increase their
landed wealth through secularization and grants of ex-mission lands,
while sheltering them from Mexico's "despotic" rule.[2] The next centrally
appointed governor would have a difficult job convincing California's
native sons that he could be such a good father to the local elites and still
serve Mexico's national interests.

They were right to be suspicious. In November 1835, Antonio López
de Santa Anna, Mexico's president and now an avowed centralist, repealed the national secularization law of August 17, 1833, and sent conservative Mariano Chico to replace Figueroa.[3] Over the next few months,
Santa Anna and a conservative congress abolished the federal constitution of 1824, and opposition to this move inspired resistance in several
departments, including Zacatecas, Yucatán, New Mexico, and Texas.[4]
By the time Chico landed at Santa Bárbara in April 1836, native sons in
California had a good idea of what was to come, and nearly eighty of
them met the new governor dressed in black, wearing "in the buttonhole
of the frock coats a small red rosette which was the distinguishing badge
of the federalists," according to one of them.[5] No doubt, José Antonio

de la Guerra was somewhere in this welcoming party, and no wonder, too, that this young man joined his peers a few months later to oust Chico and his successor and to sign the pronunciamiento that declared California "free and sovereign." In the face of a centralist and pro-Church government, young Californios moved to protect what gains they had made.

While José Antonio celebrated the revolution, American trader Alfred Robinson took a gloomier view. That summer in San Diego, Robinson had listened carefully for news while he loaded up his ship with hides, tallow, and horns. With reports of rebellion in Texas still fresh, the whole American community of traders grew alarmed at the prospect of an armed invasion from Mexico. "My fears are such that I do not consider our property as safe," he told a business associate.[6] By December 1836, his unease had become full-blown alarm. "A month or little more has now elapsed," he wrote his employers, "that we have been disturbed by the anarchy and confusion of a Country whose inhabitants are desirous of becoming an independent nation."[7] That same day, Robinson wrote to his friend and partner William Gale, "California for the present is not in a situation to encourage speculation . . . it is my intention to give up the business."[8] The young American, who had seemed like such a good catch for José Antonio's sister Anita, remained in the unsettled territory only long enough to settle up accounts, and then sailed for Boston with his wife in October 1837.

For Anita's father, José de la Guerra, her marriage to the foreign merchant, as we have seen, was part of a common and deliberate strategy to advance the family's fortunes. With this union, de la Guerra had placed the foreign trader in a paternal relationship of obligation and dependence, and thereby had joined Robinson's economic power to the family's own commercial empire. Now, in 1836, the actions of de la Guerra's eldest son in Monterey threatened to undo these plans and unravel the new trade alliance, jeopardizing the family's wealth and the elder man's political authority based upon that wealth. "My father was not at all pleased to see my brother mixed up in revolts," Angustias remembered, "but there was nothing he could do about it."[9] In the 1820s and early 1830s, as we saw in the previous chapter, Mexican liberalism and native son land hunger combined to produce a generational conflict and a political rebellion that were now threatening to pull apart California's elites, setting father against child, brother against brother-in-law.

California did not, however, become a bloodbath of fratricidal warfare. Instead, by 1845, it was a relatively prosperous province of Mexico, for the revolution in California, political and generational, was only a partial one. In the late 1830s and early 1840s, California's rebels abandoned much of the liberal platform and rejoined centralist Mexico under a native-born governor, while families like the de la Guerras successfully negotiated their children's transition to independence without seriously disrupting their father's empires or the system of patriarchy on which they were based. Even Robinson returned a few years after his panicky departure.

Patriarchal family relations, as it turns out, served to mitigate civil conflict and to structure the society and economy of post-revolutionary California, just as they had before. Because he was so good at meeting his obligations as a community patriarch and compadre, and because his wife was so skillful at supporting family honor and his position, Captain José de la Guerra had great influence in Santa Bárbara. His son needed that power to spread territorial rebellion, and in return offered influence in the new government and the spoils of patronage and land that such influence would bring. The liberal ideology of the young rebels did challenge social and legal hierarchies of status, and some women, Indians, townsfolk, and young men found an opening to claim public voice and education and to control their own property and sexuality. But by 1845, Indians, townsfolk, children, and wives, although they had more room to negotiate, still did so within a strongly patriarchal system. Despite the challenge of Mexican liberalism and the rebellion of the second generation, the last ten years of Mexican rule in California proved to be a period of increasing consolidation of elite wealth and land holdings, and of the patriarchal family.

Unnatural Men and Obedient Sons

The summer and fall of 1836 proved to be a dangerous and unstable moment for all Californians. Provoked by an open declaration of secession from Mexico, the people of the territory at all levels argued over the legitimacy and consequences of this action. In so doing, they framed the debate within the language of patriarchy and masculine honor. In their written pronunciamientos and public speeches, the young men of Monterey declared their position as the true and loyal sons of Mexico and of the federalist constitution, and they described the centralists in power as despots, usurpers, and "unnatural sons." The towns to the south had a different take on the matter. Through rumor, riot, and declaration, women and men debated the rebels' own legitimacy as honorable men: were they obedient to Nation, to God, and to the Church? Did they protect, or threaten, female virtue and family honor? The answers to these questions would determine whether California's young men could finally control their own destinies.

By the time California's citizens met their new governor while sporting federalist badges in their buttonholes, de la Guerras of the second generation had become fixtures in the territory's political world; in May, a month after Chico's arrival, José Antonio was once again elected to the diputación. The eldest de la Guerra son now most likely lived with his sister Angustias and her husband, the alcalde and sometime deputy, Manuel Jimeno. Younger brothers Pablo and Joaquín shared the Monterey home when they were not at school with sister Teresa and William Hartnell. Conversation at the de la Guerra dinner table was no doubt lively after the May election, as the native son deputies sorted out committees and anticipated the first words from their new jefe político. José Antonio had particular reason to worry: he had been appointed to the powerful "colonization and vacant lands" committee and was charged with granting former mission lands—a function that would be crippled if Chico carried out his orders from Santa Anna.

The deputies did not have long to wait. On May 28, 1836, three days after the election, Chico delivered a flowery inaugural address that, although expected, shocked the Californio native sons with its blatant support of Santa Anna's centralist program. Under the new regime, laid out in the Siete Leyes, or Seven Laws, of 1835, all territories and states in Mexico were transformed into "departments," their governors appointed by the Mexican president and their popularly elected state diputacións replaced by indirectly elected *juntas departamentales,* their power stripped down to a mere advisory role. These constitutional amendments also abolished most popularly elected town councils; instead, municipalities fell under the authority of prefects and sub-prefects who reported directly to the governor. Income requirements limited those who could vote and hold office.[10] Pablo de la Guerra, just sixteen but already immersed in liberal and federalist circles, sat in on the sessions that day and remarked to his cousin Mariano Guadalupe Vallejo: "Chico promises us honor, glory, and grandeur if we <u>meekly</u> follow his politics, which amount to telling us to renounce our rights as free men and simply accept his centralist plan."[11] In other words, the "Monterey clique"—young, liberal, federalist, and elite—found themselves facing a familiar villain. Like the ill-fated Manuel Victoria, Governor Chico had revealed himself to be no "beneficent father" but a tyrant who threatened to reverse land distribution and wrest governing power away from the local elites. Like Pablo de la Guerra, Vallejo considered the speech a turning point, when Chico "threw off the mask" of legitimate authority and exposed himself as a "despot."[12] To make things worse, Chico scandalized Monterey society by openly flaunting his mistress.

Once Californios declared their ruler's power illegitimate, there could only be one solution: rebellion and expulsion. But the young men of Monterey, despite their liberal rhetoric, could only challenge a ruler's legitimacy within the traditional understanding of paternal authority; they could not afford to defy patriarchy itself if they were to succeed.[13] Expulsion could only be achieved if all of California, especially the conservative stronghold of Santa Bárbara, could be persuaded to back up the young federalists. And to sway Santa Bárbara, one had to sway its patriarch, fifty-seven-year-old José de la Guerra. "Although to all appearances he was removed from public life," remembered Vallejo, "*sub rosa* he took an active part in politics," guiding all the public officials in Santa Bárbara. Monterey's deputies, Vallejo assures us, "were aware of the *modus operandi*."[14] For this rebellion to triumph, it had to appear not as a liberal defiance of authority, but as a conservative effort to restore the status quo.

Such a transformation might prove tricky; after all, the elder de la Guerra had little sympathy for the secularization plans of the young deputies. But the de la Guerra children in Monterey provided their friends with a model for persuasion. These siblings had lived through the 1829 expulsion of Father Luis Martínez, which had galvanized the entire town of Santa Bárbara and brought their father to oppose the governor, his commanding officer. So in the summer of 1836, Monterey's deputies engineered the expulsion of another popular priest, Father Narciso Durán, then living at ex-Mission Santa Bárbara. Governor Chico provided the opening himself in July when he returned from a tour of the southern districts and denounced the padre before the diputación. Durán, he complained, had refused to give him the full honors due his station, had declined to say mass at certain state functions, and had expressed anti-Mexican political sentiments from the pulpit. The chief offense, as everyone knew, was that Durán had also been denouncing Chico in his sermons for abandoning his wife in Mexico and living in California with a married woman, Doña Cruz.[15] The deputies gave Chico their full sympathies and, apparently outraged at Father Durán, ordered his expulsion on July 25. But "the members of the diputación," Angustias recalled, "which included my brother, . . . had had an ulterior motive for doing this. It was well known that Father Durán was loved by the Barbareños without exception. And since the people of Santa Bárbara had never rebelled against the government before, they wanted to goad them into rebelling against Chico."[16]

Once Chico's regime threatened the conservative junta of Santa Bárbara, José de la Guerra and the rest of Santa Bárbara's leaders carefully orchestrated the course of their district's rebellion, hiding their own defiance behind a drama of children's gossip, female riot, and apparent capitulation to popular will. News first reached de la Guerra through his brothers-in-law. Governor Chico, with expulsion notice in hand, had sent José Antonio Carrillo to capture Durán at Mission Santa Bárbara, but the family grapevine spoiled the surprise. On arrival, José Antonio first paid a visit to his brother Domingo Carrillo, and Domingo in turn slipped out in the middle of the night to whisper the news to his sister María Antonia Carrillo and her husband, José de la Guerra. Angustias de la Guerra, staying in the house to recover from typhoid fever, heard the commotion and rose to demand the cause. Knowing her father would be turned back well before he could get near the mission and warn Father Durán, she again took the role of go-between, as a young woman on her way to breakfast at the church would elicit little comment. "Tell the patriarch . . . he should not worry," Durán told her with a laugh, but his friend de la Guerra had already launched his plan.[17]

Unable to openly organize resistance, de la Guerra devised a clever way to spread the news and encourage popular indignation. He called one of his younger sons aside and gave him a handful of coins to buy as many eggs as he could, for poor Father Durán was going to be sent away and needed provisions.[18] This was a great secret, he warned the boy, and he mustn't tell anyone. Of course, he knew his son "wasn't capable of keeping a secret for five minutes," remembered Juan Alvarado. From house to house, the boy told shocked women that Durán was ordered to be put in "heavy chains" to be sent to China "so that he would be eaten by savages."[19] Grateful for the information, the women gave him the eggs for free. Gossip was currency and a form of political action. The news spread quickly among the women of the town—in backyards, in the market, and at the public *lavandería*. When the order came a few days later to take Father Durán to the waiting ship, "all of the women from the pueblo" were waiting at the beach to surround his cart, "except for the women from the more important families . . . It was a well-orchestrated plan," remembered Angustias.[20]

Although Santa Bárbara's women did not have a formal voice in government, non-elite women did have recourse to riot and public demonstration to express their opinions. In fact, in late colonial and early republican Mexico, women often took active roles at the front of these local displays of community will. Usually in the face of a threat from the outside, women took to the streets, putting their voices and bodies in action to defend their families and using their moral authority to dare officials to attack or seize them in reprisal. If authorities took the bait, the men of the community would then be forced to step in to defend their womenfolk and their own masculine honor.[21] In this case, the threat was the removal of not only a beloved community leader but also his ability as a priest to meet the sacramental needs of the community, to legitimate births and marriages and to provide last rites.[22]

The outrage Santa Bárbara's women felt was real—Chico was a threat to family honor and community cohesion—yet the form of their protest, and the apparent resistance and inevitable capitulation of Santa Bárbara's male leaders, turns out to have been less a spontaneous riot, and more a tableau put on for the benefit of Chico's troops. The ship's captain, José Aguirre, for example, was known to Santa Bárbarans as a close friend of Durán and de la Guerra, but he appeared angry at the hindrance and ordered the women to disperse; as he did so, one woman raised a stick as if to hit him.[23] Other women "commenced to moan and cry." After a certain amount of this female demonstration, some of the male town leaders ran down to the beach, and Fathers Antonio and José Jimeno emerged from behind trees to declare their support for the will of the women. Together, the men threatened to take Aguirre prisoner if he continued to resist them; outnumbered, Aguirre and the provincial troops allowed "the people" to return Durán to the mission. During all the excitement, José de la Guerra could have watched quietly, and apparently innocently, from his front porch—yet he had set all of it in motion when he sent his son to buy eggs. "Well, we finally see the pueblo of Santa Bárbara openly rebelling against Chico's authority," declared Angustias.[24] Soon, Chico received a letter from the captain: "Californio soldiers . . . prefer death to fighting against the people of Santa Bárbara, who unanimously defend their idol."[25] Faced with such an ungovernable population, Chico resigned his post less than a week later, vowing to return someday with reinforcements, and leaving a subordinate, Nicolás Gutiérrez, in charge.[26]

For the Californio diputación, Lieutenant Colonel Gutiérrez was hardly an improvement, and in October 1836, after he tried to dissolve the legislature, they demanded that he, too, resign the civil command.[27] When he refused, the young men of Monterey again deployed the language of masculine honor to voice their complaints. Four deputies, including

José Antonio de la Guerra, recruited a somewhat-hesitant Mariano Guadalupe Vallejo and set out to seize Monterey. On the night of November 3, the rebels reached the capital and surrounded the presidio, but Gutiérrez refused to surrender. The next day, José Antonio de la Guerra entered the presidio under a flag of truce and was taken blindfolded to negotiate with Gutiérrez. Again, the lieutenant colonel refused to give up command. Juan Alvarado at last took the fort, forcing the surrender of yet another governor.[28] On November 6, 1836, José Antonio de la Guerra and the other revolutionaries sharpened their pens and signed a pronunciamiento that declared the territory of California "free and sovereign," severing all ties with Mexico.[29] Even with this apparently radical step, however, California's natives defended themselves as "obedient sons of the Madre Patria" who would return to the fold as soon as Mexico "ceases to be oppressed by the present dominant faction called central government"—a group they renounced as Mexico's "unnatural sons."[30] A month later, Alvarado took command as interim civil governor, and Vallejo, now commandant general, as head of the military. Alvarado was twenty-seven; his uncle and friend Vallejo was twenty-nine.[31]

Juan Alvarado, José Antonio de la Guerra, and the rest of the Monterey rebels expressed their actions in terms of respect for legitimate paternal authority, yet they continued to inspire the fear that they did indeed threaten the old understandings of patriarchy and masculine honor. This was particularly true in southern California, where news of the latest uprising arrived from Monterey later in November with Judge Luis del Castillo Negrete.[32] As legal adviser to the ousted governors, Castillo Negrete certainly was no fan of the new native son regime, and he spent every moment of his southern sojourn, including a stay at the de la Guerra home, undermining the rebellious deputies and alarming local residents and foreign traders. The revolutionary leaders, Castillo Negrete told southerners, intended to plunder the missions and the treasury, attack private fortunes, and encourage Protestant heresy. Echoing the rebels' own words, he condemned them as "unnatural men, without God, law, or country, and headed by four hallucinated deputies."[33]

In the waning months of 1836, Antonio María Osio tried a similar argument. A member of the Los Angeles ayuntamiento, Osio feared that independence would make California vulnerable to attack, and he desperately wanted to persuade Angelenos to send a force north to put down the rebels. So he took Castillo Negrete's abstract argument about "unnatural men" and turned it into the one specific complaint he knew would trigger outrage. The Monterey secessionists, he told "the mothers" of the town, were scheming to grant Protestants the authority to perform marriages between Californio daughters and American men. "Moreover," Osio said, the Protestant ministers "would personally seek out the brides and take them to their homes for safekeeping, so that the girls' parents would not interfere with the marriages." Osio later recalled the effect his words produced: "A snake which is seized by a falcon and dropped for the first time is not as angry as those women were at that moment. They were asking one another if men of character existed, men who would permit such a thing to happen to their daughters." Using their moral authority as defenders of their families, the women of Los Angeles provoked their men into action. "Each woman pledged to ensure that her husband, children and grandchildren, from seventeen to sixty years of age, would take up arms for the sake of family honor," Osio recalled with satisfaction. "They would rather cry for them because they had died on the battlefield," the women told their husbands and sons, "than experience the sorrow of reprimanding them for a disgraceful escape."[34]

Fears of sexual disorder were particularly acute in Los Angeles, perhaps, because of a shocking event that had taken place there the previous spring. A married woman, María del Rosario Villa, and her lover, the vaquero Gervasio Alipás, had killed María's husband, ranch owner Domingo Félix, and hidden his body in a ditch. Convictions for capital crimes required review in Mexico City, a process that could take more than a year. Recalling "the frequency of similar crimes" and "believing that immorality has reached such an extreme that public security is menaced," a group of fifty men formed a vigilance committee, broke into the jail, and shot the lovers in the street.[35] Family honor depended on the sexual purity and good marriages of wives and daughters. María del Rosario Villa had clearly left the oversight of her respectable husband's household, and this shameless woman and her lover had brought violence and chaos to the town. This incident no doubt left the town feeling on edge, ready to link sexual transgressions with civil anarchy.

Castillo Negrete and Osio, in other words, incited regional resistance to the members of the Monterey faction by challenging their honor as men—as obedient sons and benevolent patriarchs, and as defenders of female virtue and family honor. Castillo Negrete had little luck with this approach in Santa Bárbara; the population there had already agreed that the young rebels of Monterey were the true defenders of family honor against a Mexican governor who flaunted a married mistress and tried to remove a trusted priest. But Osio's words hit home in Los Angeles. By apparently threatening to take marriage choice out of the hands of parents, and specifically of fathers, the young liberals of Monterey seemed to be endangering the most basic social, political, and economic institution of their society: the patriarchal family. It was not long before Angelenos declared their city the new territorial capital and began to assemble a military force to resist the dishonorable and unnatural men from Monterey.

"Here We Are All Related to One Another"

In the end, the older generation of southern California did not need to fear for the established social and political order, or for family honor in particular. Despite a flirtation with liberalism and its challenge to patriarchal authority, the young men of Monterey maintained an understanding of political authority in paternal terms and continued to defend notions of masculine honor. Over the next two years, this understanding, and the real family obligations and dependencies that linked every member of the ruling class, served to mitigate regional conflict and prevent the fratricidal war that constantly threatened to erupt between north and south. José de la Guerra and his wife, María Antonia Carrillo, proved the critical link. As conservatives, they discouraged the young liberals from abandoning the old relations of deference and obligation. More importantly, through his role as family patriarch, and her continuing influence as the connection between political kin, they held the elites together as a family.

Over the years, historians have pointed to several possible causes for the rivalry between California's *arribeños* and *abajeños*—northerners and southerners. Ideologically, Los Angeles and San Diego appear in 1836 to have been particularly receptive to Castillo Negrete and Osio and their denunciations of Monterey liberalism. But the spread of federalist and liberal ideologies was fairly even in California, and at other times the southern towns seemed much more to be the strongholds of liberal sentiment. Other observers have noted differences in national identity. Southerners tended to feel a greater sense of Mexican nationalism and maintained closer contact with other regions of northern Mexico like Sonora, Sinaloa, and the Pacific port towns of Acapulco and Loreto.[36] Residents of Monterey, on the other hand, had developed a stronger nativism, and with it, support of federalism.[37] Yet, even after Monterey rebels abandoned their demand for Californian independence, southern leaders continued to resist their rule.

In fact, the true basis of this regional rivalry may not have been ideological, but material and patriarchal. Two-thirds of California's people lived in the south, but with the capital at Monterey, customs house revenues, government salaries, and mission administration went disproportionately to their northern cousins.[38] Abajeños wanted their share and the ability such resources would provide them for creating local relations of patronage and dependence. Twenty-six-year-old Juan Alvarado and the young men who supported him would have to show that they could provide for the southern elites and their families as much as they would their own friends and dependents in Monterey.

On Christmas Day in 1836, native son Juan Alvarado and his supporters started south with fifty mounted soldiers, both to display their ability to command and to calm southern fears of the revolutionaries' liberal agenda. On this trip, Alvarado deliberately set out to bring the conservative leaders of the south to his side by showing respect for his elders and promising support to the most powerful families. José de la Guerra, in particular, enjoyed influence over a large region of dependent pobladores, and along with Bernarda Ruiz, his wife's widowed first cousin, convinced the interlinked elite families of the region to back Alvarado. At Mission Santa Bárbara, Father Durán welcomed the new governor, and soon Santa Bárbara's leaders met to swear their loyalty to independent California.[39] On the strength of this support, representatives from the major towns met in Los Angeles and agreed to an election of new deputies. These representatives, among them José Antonio de la Guerra and his brother-in-law Manuel Jimeno, in turn gathered at Santa Bárbara in April to recognize the new government.[40] From January until the end of May 1837, Alvarado remained in Santa Bárbara, conferring with José de la Guerra and his sons.

The elder de la Guerra could just as easily have sided with Alvarado's opponents. After all, he was a military man. Discipline and respect for one's superiors was ingrained in the captain, and open declarations of independence an anathema. Beyond this, the revolutionary philosophy of Monterey's young men and their blunt desire to distribute mission lands flew in the face of de la Guerra's own interests. Far more logical would have been to support Santa Anna's repeal of secularization. "Some people have assumed that my father and Father Durán were supporters of Alvarado and his followers in the revolt," Angustias de la Guerra later argued. "That assertion is groundless. Neither man could be a supporter of an array of issues that were destroying the missions."[41] And yet, when Alvarado arrived in Santa Bárbara in 1837, José de la Guerra received him warmly and swore his allegiance—why?

Teresa de la Guerra offers us one explanation. Her father, she asserted, "yielded to Governor Alvarado because he was tired of seeing the Mexicans send governors and officials to this country who were men of very bad principles."[42] In particular, she singled out Governor Chico as "crazy and lecherous." If local control presented Monterey's liberals with the opportunity to continue breaking up the mission estates, it gave Spanish-born men like de la Guerra and Durán freedom from the threat of harassment or expulsion by governors who had no family or godparent ties in California to call into play. This was the lesson learned in July 1836, when Durán so nearly lost his position at Santa Bárbara on Chico's orders. Alvarado, on the other hand, offered public recognition of Father Durán and open support of Spanish-born citizens.[43]

In fact, stability and peace themselves were great advantages for de la Guerra, no matter who promised to preserve them. "I have sought constantly to avoid as far as it has been possible the disastrous evils of fratricidal warfare," de la Guerra claimed later, "all will testify that I have always exercised my influence in favor of order, of peace, and of the union."[44] Son-in-law Robinson agreed: "Generally, all the political disturbances and differences between the north and south were referred to him, and his inclination was usually to appease parties and keep them quiet."[45] Both Robinson and de la Guerra knew the alternative: any unrest meant disruption of trade. Anarchy was the greatest fear, as the trader from Boston explained to his employers shortly after news of the rebellion reached him in San Diego: "We are relying not upon the laws of a government to secure us our property, but upon the mere will of a revolted & ignorant population."[46] He was not the only foreign trader to get spooked and leave California's shores that year.[47] Quick support of the strongest leader and suppression of dissent offered the best hope to de la Guerra for a stable market and continued profits.

Finally, Juan Alvarado, a cousin by marriage, promised de la Guerra more advantages for his family empire in the form of land and patronage. Only days after arriving in Santa Bárbara, for example, Alvarado distributed the cattle of the state-owned Rancho San Julián among the needy soldiers of de la Guerra's presidio and gave the property itself to the former commander.[48] Alvarado also hoped to demonstrate his good faith by announcing that he had already sworn in William Hartnell, de la Guerra's needy son-in-law, as provincial *recaudador*, or tax collector, in Monterey, with a salary of five percent of collections. The rebel leader pledged more patronage after de la Guerra had promised his support; later that year, Pablo de la Guerra received an appointment to serve as apprentice to Hartnell at the customs house, supplementing his formal education under the Englishman.[49]

So, despite Alvarado's support for continued secularization, and despite the affront his liberal ideals seemed to present to the authority of

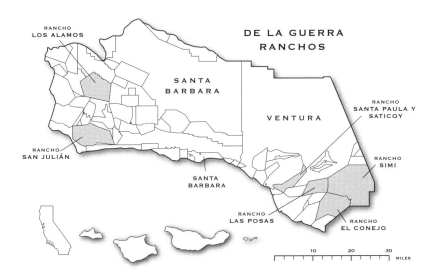

the Church and the older generation, in the end de la Guerra threw his support behind a regime that promised to provide patronage and provision for his children and dependents, the stability needed for commerce, and more landed resources for his diversifying empire. In exchange, de la Guerra maintained his loyalty to the young men of Monterey through the toughest test yet—one that could have torn his family apart.

While Alvarado remained with the de la Guerras in Santa Bárbara, through the spring of 1837, all seemed settled between north and south. Yet tension lay barely concealed under the placid surface. Los Angelenos Pío Pico and Antonio María Osio had refused altogether to attend the April session of the new diputación, and when Alvarado returned to Monterey at the end of May, the disgruntled Los Angeles deputies joined the malcontents of San Diego and pledged their support to Mexico's central authority.[50] By mid-June, an army of local residents had gathered at Los Angeles, prepared to confront the arribeños. With them was Captain Andrés Castillero, a commissioner of the Mexican government who had arrived to proclaim the new constitutional laws of 1836 and exact an oath of allegiance to the centralist administration.

It seemed that the two sides—southern versus northern, loyalist versus revolutionary, centralist versus federalist—would at last clash head-on. Yet Alvarado, the rebel leader, chose not to fight the southerners for California's independence. Instead, he met quietly with Commissioner Castillero in Santa Bárbara. Perhaps under the influence of de la Guerra, the two men found a compromise. On July 9, 1837, Alvarado swore loyalty to the centralist constitution and acquiesced to departmental status for California. In exchange, Alvarado demanded a legal requirement that the governor would be native-born and exacted a promise that Castillero would secure official recognition that Alvarado would be that governor. "What more do you wish?" he asked the citizens of California. A week later, the diputación reassembled at Santa Bárbara.[51]

The southerners had won a political battle, but without the provincial capital, patronage jobs, and political influence, they remained unsatisfied. That autumn, they played a final desperate hand, calculated to pry the crucial support of José de la Guerra away from the new governor. On October 20, news reached Los Angeles that Carlos Carrillo, not Juan Alvarado, had been named the governor of California. As it turns out, José Antonio Carrillo, the youngest brother of Carlos, and now California's deputy in congress, had also persuaded the central government to settle California's rebellion by appointing a native-born ruler—and had suggested his brother, the former deputy. Distracted by events in Texas and unaware of Alvarado's oath of loyalty, the Mexican congress agreed, and José Antonio set off with the appointment.[52] When he brought the news to Los Angeles along with the declaration that this town would serve henceforth as California's capital city, southern Californians eagerly hailed Carrillo as their champion. Although he had initially backed Alvarado, Carlos took the oath of office on December 6, 1837.[53]

Here was a genuine dilemma for de la Guerra and a particularly agonizing turn of events for his wife, Carlos Carrillo's sister. Although María Antonia had done her best to bind together her husband and brothers, her youngest brother, José Antonio Carrillo, had been an irritant to her husband since the early 1820s, chafing at his brother-in-law's requests to transact his business in Los Angeles and getting involved in one political scheme or another. But Carlos Carrillo had been one of de la Guerra's closest friends and allies, despite his recent support for granting "vacant" mission lands. Years later, Angustias de la Guerra still could not believe that her father would side against her uncle, "a man he had been very fond of ever since childhood . . . he could not be hostile to his brother-in-law's aspirations, nor could he favor his rival."[54] Yet when José Antonio Carrillo traveled from Los Angeles to Santa Bárbara, sure that this family tie would override de la Guerra's support of Alvarado, he found instead a population already swayed by Alvarado's ability to provide for them and unwilling to trade peace and security to support a local man who could promise only to support them equally well. Alvarado, too, refused to recognize the appointment before he heard anything more from the central government.[55]

Over the next few months, forces from the north and south, armed with rifles and cannon, met at Mission San Buenaventura and at Las Flores, south of Los Angeles—yet barely fired a shot. Only one man was killed. In the end, Carlos Carrillo surrendered peacefully in March 1838. For this, Carrillo earned a reputation as a "coward" in the south, but it was respect for family, not timidity, that prompted the would-be governor to hold his fire, and José de la Guerra to urge reconciliation.[56] Family ties did trump politics, but not as José Antonio Carrillo would have wished. Almost any two members of California's ruling class could point to some tie of kinship, and this was no less true of Carlos Carrillo and Juan Alvarado: these political rivals also considered themselves uncle and nephew.[57] Initial negotiations for surrender had to be broken off when Carrillo addressed the Monterey governor and revolutionary as "Juanito"—it was not Alvarado who objected to the diminutive but his officers, who had to remind him of his position.[58] Perhaps to reassert his authority over the older generation or to diffuse the conflict with a familial joke, Alvarado later returned Carrillo to his home in Santa Bárbara, saying to Carrillo's wife, Josefa Castro, "Here, Aunt, I bring Uncle to you for safekeeping. Try to make him understand that he is too old now for schoolboy pranks."[59] De la Guerra joined in this teasing, telling his brother-in-law that he was "the governor of the island," referring to the fictional government of Sancho Panza in Barataria.[60]

Not everyone appreciated the humor. "My mother did not like these jokes at the expense of her brother," remembered Angustias. For María Antonia, the battle between north and south pitted her husband against her eldest brother and threatened her role as the linchpin between these two families. As a consequence, she worked consistently to counter the political antagonism, repair the damage, and restore proper relations of respect and order within her extended family.

Her first cousin Mariano Guadalupe Vallejo gave her a new challenge in January 1839. During the upheavals and negotiations of the previous three years, Vallejo had remained in the north and continued to press for major changes in the old order, particularly the notoriously underfunded and neglected military. Vallejo was less willing than Alvarado to compromise with Santa Bárbara's conservative leaders, and he set out to undermine their strength as local patriarchs. In January 1839, Vallejo finally received permission to institute what he considered a new, more rigorous discipline "along European lines," and he began with Santa Bárbara. But the soldiers and officers of the Santa Bárbara presidio, who placed their loyalties with de la Guerra, the "father" who had provided for them, refused the new regime. Within a week, the guardhouse was full of re-calcitrant soldiers, and most of the officers were under arrest.[61]

Vallejo, realizing his error, asked for de la Guerra's public support. Would he lead local efforts at reform? The captain, however, was almost sixty years old and was finally enjoying a well-earned retirement from political intrigue. He was not about to start taking orders from a man nearly thirty years his junior, especially one whose liberal philosophy he considered "heretical" and whose "new discipline" would undermine his own local authority. So when Vallejo ordered him to take command, de la Guerra pleaded ill health and refused.

The young "general" from Sonoma considered this breach of disci-pline "immoderate and disrespectful."[62] Looking to show the local popu-lation that the new system applied equally to all, he immediately placed the elder de la Guerra under house arrest, despite fellow officer José Cas-tro's argument "that the arrest of the venerable retired captain might cause a revolt."[63] At this point, although de la Guerra was forbidden to leave his house, he and his wife coordinated efforts to soothe the over-zealous Vallejo, secure de la Guerra's release, and avoid open rebellion.

The first tack was an appeal from a fellow officer, Captain Andrés Castillero, the Mexican commissioner. But Vallejo dismissed him, saying he could "in no way allow his subordinates to give him advice."[64] Clearly a new approach was needed, and the de la Guerras next tried an appeal from the most powerful religious "father" in the area, Father Durán. Durán appealed as both supplicant and chastising father to Vallejo, "whose youth perhaps does not allow him to realize the whirlwind that will en-gulf him unless he uses more prudence in his treatment of a person whom the people love and the clergy respect."[65]

This attempt met with less success than that of Captain Castillero, however: in Vallejo's mind, the younger generation had already rebelled against their elders' entrenched powers to get control of state power, and he had no intention of submitting now. In this case, there were personal motives at play as well, since Vallejo was still smarting over Durán's order to burn his library years before. "I was never able to forget that attack upon enlightenment," he explained.[66] Vallejo dismissed the padre, telling Durán that he, too, was out of his jurisdiction.

At this point tensions in the town were close to the breaking point. But even so, "under no conditions," declared Vallejo, "would I have con-sented to free Señor de la Guerra y Noriega, because at that time the slightest show of weakness would have been fatal to me."[67] At last, María Antonia intervened directly. Her status as an elder woman—she was

fifty-two and the mother of ten adult children—gave her some precedence of generation over the younger Vallejo. "You know well enough,
brother Guadalupe," she told him, "You have treated my husband
harshly."[68] Vallejo explained to her that the arrest was not an act of personal revenge, however justified, against her husband, but was forced by
strict adherence to military authority. María Antonia, however, insisted
that any interaction between the two relatives was, of necessity, personal.
Vallejo finally softened once his cousin "begged me to forget the past
and establish harmony between our two families."[69] All agreed that de la
Guerra would accept the post of arms commander in exchange for his
release.[70] As part of the negotiation, his brother-in-law Carlos Carrillo,
appeased with land grants, also formally recognized Alvarado on January 19, 1839, and was released from his own house arrest.

Political order returned to the town, but the family had one more
task: healing the dangerous strains within itself. A few days later, María
Antonia extended cousin Vallejo a friendly invitation to dinner, and he
accepted. This party was designed to smooth ruffled feathers but also to
remind the young commander that although de la Guerra had compro-
mised to restore harmony, he was still the most powerful man in Santa
Bárbara and could command the attendance of important local supporters. Vallejo, the last to arrive, found the rest of the company waiting for
him to begin the feast. "There at the home of that estimable matron," he
recalled, "I found all together many of those who had made common
cause with the southerners, but all had accepted the situation and with a
show of affection came forward to greet me."[71] Later, the general discussed the entire incident with Father Durán, and when asked to explain
his change of heart, replied that he had intended to instill a new order,

> to be severe with all and unjust to no one. Two days' ex-
> perience, however, had been enough to convince me
> that, so long as a Californian is in control in California, a
> strict application of the military regulations is some-
> thing which cannot be put into practice, for here we are
> all related to one another and if one has the strength to
> resist the entreaties of the men, he must perforce suc-
> cumb to the tears and sighs of the women.[72]

With "tears and sighs," moans and cries, raised sticks and angry out-
bursts, the political expressions of California's women appear with increasing frequency in the historical records of their male kinsmen. Elite

women like María Antonia de la Guerra and Bernarda Ruiz worked behind the scenes, re-establishing harmony between factions of extended kin. Lower-class women in Santa Bárbara staged riots to retain Church sanction for their families' births, marriages, and deaths. The women of Los Angeles were just as eager to incite their husbands and sons to warfare against their in-laws, in order to prevent their daughters' dishonor. What all these women shared was a notion of family honor and an understanding of their role, as women, to enforce children's and men's loyalties to these families. The revolutionary years from 1836 to 1839 were a time of great strain on California's elite kinship networks—both liberalism and regional rivalries brought Californians to the field of battle, guns loaded and swords drawn. Yet, as Vallejo discovered, the bonds of kinship were strong enough to turn the soldiers back and release the prisoners of war. As Californios looked toward a new era as citizens of Mexico, led by a native-born governor, the patriarchal family still structured the political, social, and economic order.

"Viva California Libre—Mete la Mano [D]onde Quiera": Consolidation of the Ranching Elite

Later in her life, Angustias de la Guerra recounted a story of California's revolution. Cristóval Manojo, she said, an Indian who worked as a servant and lived in the village of Tecolate, was passed on the road by Juan Alvarado and Juan Castro shortly after they had overthrown the last Mexican governor, Nicolás Gutiérrez, at the end of 1836. "Long live free California!" shouted Manojo, "Grab what you want." No doubt pleased by the first sentiment but startled by the second, the young rebels asked what he meant. "Well, you steal everything from it anyway," was the reply.[73] Alvarado and Castro laughed uneasily and rode off.

Manojo's brazen declaration accurately predicted the material impact of self-rule in California. Once the native-born elite families had navigated the dangerous waters of secession and secured their dominance over the department's government, they used its structures to consolidate their hold over local offices and grant land among their friends and dependents. This distribution and co-operation also served to heal wounds in extended family networks. Governor Alvarado and the native deputies immediately pressed for the completion of mission secularization and the distribution of mission lands; almost seventy-five percent of Mexican California's private ranches were granted between 1835 and 1845. This program originated in a liberal ideology imported from Mexico, as noted in the prior chapter, and a handful of Indians did receive very small grants, yet the majority of the rancheros who shaped the new economy quickly abandoned their liberal commitment to Indians as free citizens with the right to become independent freeholders. Instead, most Native peoples would be "free" to work for the new landowning class as servants and ranch hands.[74] Even within the gente de razón, the bulk of the Mexican population remained landless, still employed as artisans and agricultural workers. By 1845, only seven or eight percent of the gente de razón population owned ranchos, totaling about ten million acres.[75] In the Santa Bárbara area, landed wealth was even more greatly polarized; of a population of about one thousand gente de razón and one thousand ex-neophytes, fifty-six individuals were ranch owners in the 1840s. Of those, seven or eight were foreigners, and two were ex-neophytes. The ultimate result of secularization and its control by the elite native sons was a society with extremes of wealth and poverty, and the consolidation of California's elites as a ranchero class.

In fact, this small percentage of landowners does not tell the entire story, for the new ranchero class did not consist simply of striving individuals, any more than did the officer class or the merchant elites before them: California's elite, made up of a handful of families, continued to be bound by ties of kinship and compadrazgo, and continued to call on these connections for economic and social stability. Even de la Guerra, who remained philosophically opposed to this transformation, was deeply engaged in the new economy through his family. Among those who received land grants were his eldest son, José Antonio, and his son-in-law Manuel Jimeno, who with brothers-in-law and nephews also administered the three closest missions. De la Guerra may have refused any grants of mission land for himself or his sons, but he did amass profits from the restructured economy, as a trader with the new landowners, and increasingly as a rancher in his own right. In addition, de la Guerra renegotiated a new paternalism with the ex-neophytes who came under his employ, and he encouraged his sons and sons-in-law to do the same.

In part, the concentration of California's lands into very few hands was a consequence of the rebellions that were fought to obtain local power. Native sons had defied Mexico and their own relatives, mustered armies, and emerged victorious. Although they had ultimately accomplished no true independence—California eventually recognized the centralist constitution—the rebels nonetheless controlled the governorship and junta departamental and cultivated a sense of entitlement to the spoils of secularization. Once the new government deemed mission lands to be state owned, it became easy enough to answer the petitions of one's supporters and relatives first.[76] Teresa and Angustias de la Guerra took a jaundiced view of the process, the elder sister remarking, "In those days, there were many individuals who believed they had every right to dispose of the Indians' property . . . These people were bolstered in this belief by the fact that they had contributed in some fashion to the ousting of Governors Chico and Gutiérrez."[77]

At first, Governor Alvarado did attempt to regulate this land grab and give some attention to the rights of Indians. On January 17, 1839, Alvarado issued a series of regulations for mission management, including the creation of the post Visitador General de las Misiones, and named William Hartnell to it, probably as another favor to the de la Guerras.[78] His duties would involve making inventories of the mission properties, judging the complaints of the padres and Indians against the administrators, and reporting any mismanagement to the government. Hartnell would even have the power to remove especially incompetent administrators from office.[79] With a salary of $2,000 a year, the position of Visitador offered Hartnell less than the custom-house post he had lost to southerner Antonio María Osio, but it did provide some support for Hartnell's wife, de la Guerra's eldest daughter, and assurances to de la Guerra himself that the new governor was serious about controlling the transition from mission to private economy.

The way things turned out, however, Hartnell seemed to be the only one doing the favor. Teresa complained that the job "brought him many troubles and few benefits," took her husband away from home, and as long as he served Alvarado, "he no longer belonged to himself or to his family, but rather to his job."[80] From May 1839 to late that autumn, Hartnell made the long trek from mission to mission, seldom welcomed by the administrators, who feared losing their jobs. That winter, Hartnell drew up his reports, noting the frequent complaints that administrators and their dependents lived comfortably off of the land, labor, and goods of the increasingly destitute Indians. After receiving Hartnell's assessments in the spring of 1840, Alvarado issued a new regulation, replacing administrators with overseers, or mayordomos, and sharply restricting their authority. In March, Hartnell left again to take possession of the missions, but within a week ran up against the resistance of the administrators and their families, who had come to think of the missions as their own property. When Hartnell arrived at San Rafael, Mariano Guadalupe Vallejo not only refused to leave but also personally put the visitador on a boat headed back across San Francisco Bay. In the south, members of the Pico and Argüello families also rejected the new orders. "Soon he was

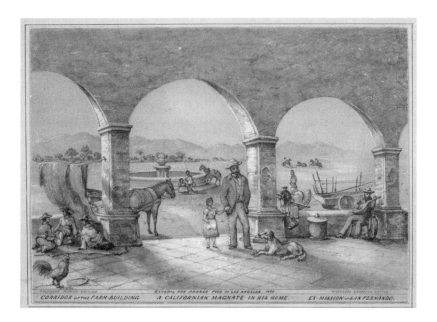

Edward Vischer, "A California Magnate in His Home" [Andrés Pico at the former Mission San Fernando], 1865. Courtesy of The Bancroft Library, University of California, Berkeley.

convinced that all his work was in vain," his sister-in-law Angustias remembered. "He had had enough and resigned."[81] Alvarado could find no one to take his place, and after the fall of 1840, secularization continued with little governmental oversight.[82]

Administrators like the Vallejos, Picos, and Argüellos were willing to defy the governor's representative because the stakes were so high. Mission managing paid about $1,000 a year, but more importantly it offered the resources and labor new landowners needed to establish their own estates and retinue of dependents. Most administrators considered the posts as just compensation from their cousins in government; critics complained that this amounted to the destruction of the mission estates. "Of course," commented Angustias, "many of the mission administrators took advantage of the opportunity at hand to get rich and would steal at will. It reached such a point that they even stole dishes, pots, doors, roof tiles, and other things from various missions . . . Alvarado could not stop the excesses and the squandering because he had to keep his supporters happy."[83]

One of these lucky mission administrators was Angustias's eldest brother, José Antonio. By 1838, no one could question his support for

Alvarado's cause; he had been one of the four who had signed the original pronunciamiento against Gutiérrez, and he had negotiated for the last governor's surrender. On December 21, 1838, José Antonio petitioned the diputación, soon renamed junta departamental, for a ranch, and then as a member of the committee on colonization and vacant lands, he replied to the request by granting himself Rancho Los Alamos on March 9, 1839.[84] Shortly thereafter, he was off the junta, building a house, and stocking the property with "cattle, horses, and sowing grounds."[85] Two years later, José Antonio also took over the administration of Mission La Purísima, from which Los Alamos had been taken. Soon, the administrator of neighboring Mission Santa Ynez, who had been promised what was left of the Purísima property, accused the young man of stripping Purísima of its goods, killing and dispersing the herds. According to Father José Joaquín Jimeno of Santa Ynez, this amounted to "cattle, horses, mules, iron pots, hides, [and] tallow." "If they ask me," he warned José Antonio's father, "I will introduce many witnesses, not Indians but white people."[86]

Father Jimeno was forced to look for whites to testify, not because Indians could not give evidence in court—they could—but because the ex-neophytes of Purísima feared reprisals from José Antonio de la Guerra. Many of them continued to live at Los Alamos at his pleasure; when the grant was first considered, the previous administrator of Purísima had testified that ten Indian families, about forty-seven ex-neophytes, lived on the property, "as it has been set apart for the purpose of designating a piece of land to each individual who may be separated from the community."[87] José Antonio had promised in writing not to remove them, but if he changed his mind, they would have little legal recourse against the recognized grantee of the ranch.[88] As a consequence, when Father Jimeno denounced de la Guerra, he could find no Indians willing to testify against their landlord. In a letter to his father, José Antonio defended his actions and asked him to help restore his "inheritance"—his reputation.[89] When José Antonio de la Guerra finally agreed to turn over the property of Purísima to the administrator of Santa Ynez, only a few broken pieces of furniture remained; the young de la Guerra meanwhile retired quietly to his well-stocked ranch.[90]

If her eldest brother, José Antonio, had made out well, Angustias and her husband, Manuel Jimeno, did even better, even without a mission to administer. Jimeno was first *vocal*, or representative, of the junta departamental, and he was also secretary of government under Alvarado, a position that helped him acquire land and livestock. In 1840, he was granted Salsipuedes—eight square leagues in Santa Cruz County. That same year, he petitioned for land closer to his wife's family: four leagues of San Buenaventura land along the Santa Clara River called Santa Paula y Saticoy.[91] To stock this land, Jimeno turned to the former mission herds, borrowing two hundred heifers from Santa Ynez with the promise to pay this back with increase in five years. In addition, he bought outright "45 mares and 2 jackasses" from La Purísima.

For labor, Jimeno looked to his wife's family for help. In a letter of May 1840, Jimeno assured his father-in-law that he would never disturb the ex-neophytes of San Buenaventura who had settled on his property. This land, he told de la Guerra, was "much in demand" among his peers, but unlike the others who applied for it, "I will assist and protect [the Indians] well in so far as my means permit."[92] "What is necessary," he went on, "is that you do me the favor, if you can, . . . of making the Indians know that it is better for them to have me as a neighbor, than someone who wants to see them burned out."[93] In other words, Jimeno assured de la Guerra that, although taking San Buenaventura land went against his father-in-law's principles, Jimeno would not abuse the Indians or force them out. De la Guerra could do him the favor in return of calming the resident Indians, who might form a compliant workforce.

Jimeno next asked his wife's father to find him the skilled labor needed to construct infrastructure and start up ranch production. His brother-in-law, Francisco de la Guerra, he suggested, could build a temporary "little house of timber walls…and a corral for the livestock."[94] Would his father-in-law order his sons José Antonio or Francisco de la Guerra to move the herds to Santa Paula y Saticoy, and to loan him more paid laborers to get things started? Jimeno had already arranged to pay some workers but counted on his father-in-law's knowledge to find him a "half-mayordomo, honest man" and an "Indian vaquero," and to determine "the salary you know to be sufficient."[95] Jimeno asked de la Guerra to send him the bill, and as a down payment, he sent along with the letter twenty-five ounces of gold. Thus, young men of California's ruling elite, like José Antonio de la Guerra and Manuel Jimeno, either drawing on their own "administration" of mission estates, or with the help of more wealthy and well-connected relatives, established their landed fortunes in the late 1830s and early 1840s.

Despite his own opposition to secularization, after 1838 the elder de la Guerra also found ways to profit by it. De la Guerra showed no qualms, for example, about hiring ex-neophytes to work his ranches and run his household. In terms of who owned the land of California and who profited from it, things changed drastically after secularization. But, in terms of labor, the same cannot be said of the Indians released from the missions.

A few ex-neophytes held small plots of ex-mission lands and lived independently, but most were forced off the land by the new owners, moving to the interior of the province or looking for work in the towns and on ranchos. In Los Angeles, ex-neophytes replaced gentiles as the town's Indian majority in the years after secularization, as the total number of Indians in the city tripled to over 500 in 1836.[96] Los Angeles had its own separate Indian village, but Santa Bárbara looked more like Monterey, where Indian workers blended into the town, and most lived in Californio households. The number of ex-neophytes who moved into Santa Bárbara probably topped out at 100 to 150 during the post-secularization period.[97]

As they had before secularization, many mission Indians continued to do domestic and day labor in town, and agricultural work on the estates of the gente de razón.[98] "As there was no other labor," one observer noted of Santa Bárbara, "the words Indian and laborer came to be almost synonymous, and the condition of the two was expressed in the single term, Indian."[99] Indian labor was critical to rancho production, and it was a major factor in the development of a ranching economy in the south. One foreign observer noted in 1842, "The number of half-civilized Indian laborers is much larger here than in the North. Hence it is much easier to get agricultural workers and make farming more remunerative."[100] Indians also accounted for most domestic labor. Sir George Simpson, visiting California in the early 1840s, remarked, "Such a thing as a white servant is absolutely unknown."[101]

Although workers nominally earned wages after secularization, cash rarely changed hands. Instead, workers generally received rations of food and took advances in goods, obligating them to work off the balance. In 1842, William Heath Davis calculated that de la Guerra "paid his vaqueros in goods, as they had not much use for money, and on these he made more or less profit." Profit, since de la Guerra charged his workers retail prices for goods he had bought at wholesale.[102] In one case, de la Guerra was not above enticing indebted workers away from a neighbor. In December 1842, José María Ramírez complained that his servant Vidal had run away, "owing me 24 pesos that he put down on his note"; Ramírez suspected that de la Guerra was using Vidal to work the vineyards at the Simi ranch, an area called Tapo. "Don't ignore my demand," he insisted testily, "as you did last year with the one I reclaimed; the one who was at Tapo for as long as you wanted."[103]

De la Guerra continued to oversee these household and agricultural workers as he had done in the early years, demanding adherence to Catholicism and to strict rules of conduct, while providing shelter, food, and medicine. It was becoming painfully clear that he could no longer count on the missions as similar sites of discipline. In 1841, for example, Santiago Argüello, the prefect for southern California, complained to de la Guerra that the mayordomos and administrators of the southern missions were encouraging a total breakdown of morality and order. "The unfortunate missions of San Gabriel and San Juan," wrote Argüello, "have been converted into brothels by the three mayordomos."[104] With the missions and Indian villages now open sites where Indians and Californios met to drink, gamble, and generally flout the rules of orderly society, it seemed all the more important to de la Guerra that he reinforce control over his own household.

Unlike the young men in charge of these missions, the elder de la Guerra continued to take his duties as patrón seriously. He continued, for example, to ensure that all under his roof joined the religious community of the Church. The baptismal registry of 1843 lists a four-year-old "Indian child," Antonio María, whose parents, ex-neophytes from San Gabriel, worked as "jaboneros," or soap-makers, in the de la Guerra household. The child's godmother was another ex-neophyte from San Luis Obispo named Quiteria, who also worked for de la Guerra. In those years, de la Guerras of the second generation also stood as godparents to the children of their father's servants in Santa Bárbara.[105] The patriarch also continued to provide for his workers' upkeep and health. In 1844, for example, he contracted with William Streeter to vaccinate the Indians in his employ for smallpox.[106] De la Guerra's objections to placing the missions under secular administrators, in other words, had little to do with a failure to live up to the liberal program of turning Indians into freehold farmers. Instead, he criticized the young administrators for failing to act in appropriately paternal ways—for taking advantage of their dependents, rather than protecting their morality and well-being.

Although de la Guerra apparently opposed secularization, then, he did profit from the new arrangements. Not only did he facilitate the establishment of his sons and sons-in-law on ex-mission land, but he also hired from the large pool of ex-neophyte labor to develop his own ranching interests, reinforcing paternal modes of control. His adaptation did not stop there. De la Guerra also participated directly in the restructured economy as a merchant, continuing to act as middleman with foreign merchants while adjusting to a new client base of shopkeepers, ranchers, and administrators in California.

De la Guerra did act as síndico and trade once again with the former missions after 1833, but this trade was very limited and not very profitable.[107] In 1838, for example, Father Abella of San Luis Obispo thanked de la Guerra for sending twenty-one pieces of calico print for the administrator to distribute "according to the needs of each one" of the Indians, but the missionary could only promise that "God will repay you." "When I go to see how the Indians are getting along with the crops," he explained, "I find that others are taking away the products, and when the time comes to give them something, there is nothing there."[108] Nonetheless, in 1840 José Aguirre, de la Guerra's old friend and trader, was still able to secure a large account with the missions' Mexican supplier, the Pious Fund, and suggested that de la Guerra join him in the venture. "I think it is not a bad thing to do to charge the amount," he told de la Guerra, "and to divide it among the Indians."[109] In addition to payment from the Pious Fund (if in fact, it ever arrived), missionaries paid off old trading debts in cattle and horses for de la Guerra's own ranches at Conejo, Simi, and San Julián.[110]

Because their role in managing the mission temporalities had ceased with secularization, however, missionaries were no longer such steady clients. De la Guerra found greater advantage in dealing both with the private ranchers who now owned parts of the mission lands and with the civilian administrators and mayordomos of the mission estates and Indian pueblos. Much of the literature on California's economy in this period notes how quickly Californio ranchers ran up debts buying manufactured goods at inflated prices.[111] Although this dynamic undoubtedly occurred, it is worth noting that Californio traders with cash, like de la Guerra, also benefited from such credit sales by advancing their cousins loans (at interest) to pay off the debts with traders.[112] These internal arrangements with de la Guerra, noted one Boston trader, "were made on promises to repay in beef cattle at the killing season . . . or in hides and tallow after the cattle had been killed."[113] In the winter of 1838, for example, Antonio José Cot, de la Guerra's old commercial partner from Lima, persuaded rancher Antonio María Lugo, de la Guerra's uncle by marriage, to borrow 550 pesos in silver from de la Guerra, even though Lugo still owed shopkeepers in Los Angeles 150 pesos from the year before. Cot assured de la Guerra that he had received "a good advantage out of this . . . it is my opinion that you ought to be content."[114]

De la Guerra and Cot were also able to work out profitable deals with mission administrators, who bought large assortments of goods to re-sell to the Indians under their charge.[115] These deals, too, were worked out through family connections. Domingo Carrillo, for example, administered the mission of La Purísima in the mid-1830s, and along with it the

new Indian village of ex-neophytes, Los Berros. In 1835, he wrote to his
uncle José de la Guerra to explain, "the deal is that I conceded to [Cot] on
behalf of this Town 200 pesos worth of whichever goods he wanted to
sell, to be paid for in silver . . . that is to say, that Cot is the principal one
who profits."[116]

Through the early 1840s, de la Guerra continued to trade with Mexican and foreign merchants as well as with the increasing numbers of
small shopkeepers in Los Angeles. William Heath Davis, supercargo of
the *Don Quixote*, made "four or five sales," to de la Guerra, "ranging from
$2,000 to $4,000 each" in the 1842–43 season, and a couple of years later
Juan Machado was writing de la Guerra from Mexico to explain that as
soon as the price of cotton goods in the market dropped a little, he would
be sending the Californian "a shipment of a thousand to two thousand
pesos" in cloth.[117] In return, de la Guerra sold California wines, aguardiente, hides, and tallow. In these years, contrary to the impression given in
their own accounts, American vessels accounted for just over a third of
the total coming to trade. Mexicans and South Americans sent almost a
quarter of the commercial ships, and de la Guerra, according to his account books, disproportionately favored these older connections over
the new arrivals from Boston and Liverpool.[118]

De la Guerra sold local retailers large lots of imported goods such
as panocha and cloth, as well as a few items that he manufactured or
processed himself. De la Guerra bought wheat from his cousins the
Vallejos, for example, and ground it to flour in his horse-powered grist
mill.[119] Cart drivers negotiated with de la Guerra's sons over deliveries of
ash that the captain's workers made into soap in his back yards.[120] And
de la Guerra continued to make wine and distill aguardiente throughout
the Mexican era. Such manufactures were, of necessity, small scale, but
they did account for a portion of de la Guerra's local profits. Through
local shopkeepers, de la Guerra collected small debts and arranged the
collection of larger amounts of hides and tallow for shipment.[121] With
Tomás Yorba as middleman, for example, de la Guerra sold the mayordomo of Los Alamitos, a private rancho in Los Angeles, various goods for
the Indian workers there.[122]

From 1834 to 1845, the economy of California underwent a drastic
restructuring, as young Californios broke up the large mission estates
and distributed their lands and management. Family relationships, more
than any other factor, determined who would grab a share of this vast fortune, for Californios depended on their connections to receive grants,
stock the ranchos, and find labor to work them. Mission Indians became

nominal wage earners in the new system, but paternal work relations continued; employers still connected to their household workers through compadrazgo, and ranch workers and farmers still became debtors to the gente de razón for manufactured goods. Even conservatives like de la Guerra, who refused direct participation in the land distribution and mission administration, became wholehearted participants in the new economy, setting up dependent sons on new ranches, employing ex-neophytes, and trading with the new ranchero class.

Patriarchy and Patronage

Patriarchal relations not only structured the economy of the new ranchero class but also guided the function of the government, now firmly in the hands of native Californios. Politics after 1837 was still the business of the elite families, who jockeyed for the spoils of patronage and influence, and in this regard, the de la Guerra family was not exceptional. José de la Guerra, although at the end of a military career, nevertheless commanded the loyalties and deference of the second generation, and he used his connections in the local and departmental levels of government to advance his ranching and mercantile interests. Likewise, the second generation of de la Guerras began in these years the political careers that they would pursue for the rest of their lives.

Thanks to their support of Alvarado's revolutionary government, the de la Guerra family was quickly able to take advantage of strong connections to the California departmental government. Eldest son José Antonio, who had the closest connection to Alvarado's rebellion, quit government service after securing Rancho Los Alamos in 1839. Likewise, after his stint as mission visitador in 1839 and 1840, William Hartnell had a government career that consisted mainly of low-level positions without much pull. Nevertheless, the de la Guerra family retained its influence within the provincial government through Pablo de la Guerra and Manuel Jimeno, the husband of Angustias de la Guerra, who became key players in Monterey politics after 1838. Through them, José de la Guerra learned of the inner workings of the government, influenced the outcomes of local conflicts, and obtained patronage posts for himself and his own dependents.

Jimeno's career reached its peak after February 1839, when he was elected first vocal of the junta departamental, and simultaneously accepted a position as secretary to Governor Alvarado.[123] The junta met infrequently over the next few years, but Jimeno stayed in the capital, at the center of political influence.[124] On several occasions, Alvarado left the government in Jimeno's hands for months at a time; Alvarado claimed illness, but others complained that the cause was an addiction to aguardiente.[125] While in Monterey, Angustias and Manuel remained in constant contact with her family, showing deference and affection to the patriarch with letters and gifts, and depending on him, in return, to help them set up and stock their new rancho, Santa Paula y Saticoy.[126]

De la Guerra took full advantage of this powerful dependent in Monterey, particularly to help him settle the jurisdictional conflicts in Santa Bárbara that threatened his nearly exclusive hold on power. In February 1839, as the last challenge from the Carrillos died down, Alvarado issued orders to restructure the internal government under the terms of the new constitution. This meant dividing California into two districts governed by prefects, each with two sub-sections governed by sub-prefects, and dissolving Santa Bárbara's elected town council, or ayuntamiento. The town of Santa Bárbara was henceforth governed by alcaldes or justices of the peace. For the most part, the new posts in the Santa Bárbara jurisdiction went to relatives and fictive kin of the de la Guerras.[127] Nonetheless, the first year of the new system was marked by squabbles and challenges to the old ruling families from the upwardly mobile gente de razón.

Santa Bárbara never fully adopted the political ideals of liberalism. Los Angeles, a town that retained its popularly elected ayuntamiento, provides an instructive contrast. There, a new gauge of political authority had taken root: the willingness of middling and lower-class men to support themselves with hard work. Inspired by liberal ideals of a virtuous and disciplined citizenship, the artisans, shopkeepers, and small farmers of that town, many of whom had arrived with the Híjar-Padrés colony, adopted a new work ethic as a measure of masculine honor and worthiness for the rights of citizenship. As a result, a large number of those elected in Los Angeles were merchants, tradesmen, and farmers, rather than wealthy landowners. Even in Los Angeles, however, some kinds of labor failed to bring honor. No matter how hard they worked, women and Indians remained subject to the patriarch's rule, and thus ineligible for the rights of citizens.[128]

In Santa Bárbara, less influenced by liberal reform, it was de la Guerra's reputation as an openhanded and generous patriarch, rather than as a hard worker, that maintained his political authority. One American recalled meeting de la Guerra in the 1840s. "Every day when I went to see him," William Streeter remembered,

> his first question was, well who is sick. The next invariably was, have they food or can they afford to get what

they need. If they were needy he at once told me to take
the key to the storeroom and take them whatever they
were in need of . . . When money was need(ed) that too
was always forthcoming.[129]

Such displays were intended to secure de la Guerra the moral authority
to govern, and, as Mariano Guadalupe Vallejo had discovered, they en-
gendered enough loyalty that in January 1839, soldiers were willing to be
imprisoned en masse for their former commander.

But there were times when de la Guerra was not so considerate of all
his dependents in town, and local citizens might publicly challenge his
authority. At these moments of conflict, de la Guerra needed his family
connections to reassert dominance. In the spring of 1839, for example,
citizens of the pueblo complained to the new justice of the peace, José
María Rojo, that de la Guerra's slaughtering pen at the Arroyo de la Viña
was creating a smelly, messy nuisance and polluting drinking water in a
populated area. Rojo ordered de la Guerra to move it to the beach or
north of the town, but de la Guerra protested to the governor, calling the
accusation "insubstantial and chimerical."[130] Manuel Jimeno responded
in May, informing his father-in-law that the departmental government
would overrule Rojo and allow the pen to stay.[131] Likewise, in July of that
year, the arrest of citizen José Andrade for debt prompted another clash
between Rojo and de la Guerra. Claiming that Andrade was his servant,
de la Guerra invoked his right to try the case under the military fuero;
when Rojo refused to surrender his prisoner, de la Guerra took Andrade
by force. The matter was referred to the departmental government,
where acting Governor Jimeno decided in favor of his father-in-law and
dismissed the hapless Rojo.[132]

De la Guerra got similar support from the departmental government
when aspiring rancheros challenged his property rights. In the summer
of 1840, for example, de la Guerra clashed with José Antonio Domínguez,
ordering him off land he believed to be within the bounds of Rancho San
Julián, the "National Ranch" that Alvarado had granted to de la Guerra
in 1837. Domínguez countered that his parcel had been granted in 1836,
predating de la Guerra's claim, and that this powerful neighbor was forcing him to abandon his fruit trees and vines and move his five hundred
cattle and two hundred horses.[133] At first, Prefect Santiago Argüello
and Governor Alvarado supported the claim of Domínguez. But after
de la Guerra complained to his son-in-law, Jimeno, Domínguez was forced
to abandon claim to the property.[134] After the rebellion, then, the new

government might appear to promise a new order, but well-entrenched patriarchs like de la Guerra still used their family connections to suppress local dissent.

Well-placed dependents in government gave de la Guerra the edge in local legal and property disputes, and they also offered him advantages as a merchant. Jimeno, for example, used his influence to give a competitive edge to Mexican and Californian merchants and kept his father-in-law apprised of the latest regulations that might affect him. No doubt the quick arrival of such news was an advantage to de la Guerra. In January 1841, for example, Jimeno informed de la Guerra that Alvarado had prohibited foreign vessels from trading because their shipboard stores had been driving local land-based retailers out of business. Jimeno admitted that this measure might have an adverse effect on the public treasury, but in the absence of aid from Mexico, the departmental officials had to do what they could "to see good warehouses on land, and many other things that they say we will see."[135]

Balancing the needs of local merchants with the demands of the treasury department was a constant struggle in California, for the departmental budget depended almost exclusively on import and export duties. As a consequence, California rarely enforced prohibitions against foreign trade, instead hitting the merchants with duties that often exceeded one hundred percent.[136] "Because the territory was in need of foreign goods whose importation was technically prohibited," Administrator Osio noted, "everyone accepted a fairly high duty's being placed on them."[137] Customs revenue increased to about 80,000 pesos a year after 1838, he remembered.[138] From this total, California's government workers secured a steady income and attempted small improvements in education and infrastructure. Such high tariffs, of course, also encouraged a great deal of smuggling. Indeed, one distant Carrillo cousin later claimed that the customs house after 1838, "if truth must be told, was the focus of corruptions with very few exceptions. The parties in charge of it always aided and abetted our wealthy foreign merchants, who day and night made a study of the art of smuggling."[139] Some historians estimate that traders paid duties on as little as a quarter of the goods actually sold in California.[140]

Under such conditions, it was particularly important for mercantile families like the de la Guerras to have a well-placed agent within the customs department. This agent was the young Pablo de la Guerra, who in January 1839 was sworn in as first official at the Monterey Customs House under Administrator Antonio María Osio.[141] Pablo was just nineteen, but in addition to his two years as an apprentice, he boasted knowledge of

French and English—essential skills for the job. Still, it was his wealthy family that enabled him to pay the $2,000 bond required of officeholders under the new constitution.[142] By the spring of 1842, Pablo frequently filled in as the acting administrator of customs, and in December 1843 was officially promoted to contador, or chief inspector.[143]

Over the years, Pablo used his post in a number of ways to benefit the de la Guerras. It was Alvarado's obligations to his father that first got Pablo his post, and as he took on greater responsibilities, the young de la Guerra was able to return the favor to his family. In May 1844, for example, Pablo named his father to the post of administrator of the recently opened port of Santa Bárbara.[144] As his job took him aboard nearly every ship that stopped in Monterey, Pablo was able to inform his father of the incoming cargoes, conduct business for him with local sellers, retailers, and foreign merchants, and ship cargoes south. José de la Guerra was an exacting businessman, however, and Pablo often apologized for his choices, fearing that the quality of goods he selected would not meet his father's high standards. "Still," he explained in 1839, "I had to take them, based on the principle better something than nothing."[145] With his increasing power to set customs duties and enforce compliance, it is also possible that Pablo de la Guerra could have used his position to secure lower duties on imported goods destined for his father. Certainly, José de la Guerra had done much the same for himself as habilitado in the late colonial era.

Under Santa Anna's constitutional reforms, a restructuring of the California and Santa Bárbara governments took power away from citizens to elect their leaders and put greater emphasis on appointments, patronage, and family connections. José de la Guerra used his patriarchal relations to godsons, sons, and sons-in-law in government to attain a wide variety of favors and bolster his local power. Dependents in Monterey sent the captain important news, settled local disputes in his favor, and bestowed patronage. But his son Pablo, it appears, never actually broke the law and smuggled in foreign goods. It was his sister Angustias who admitted to this crime.

"Now Is the Time to Take Advantage": Women after the Rebellion

Late in her life, Angustias sat down with her youngest daughter to tell her side of the story. In August 1845, she said, her younger brother Pablo lived with her in Monterey while he held the post of administrator of customs. One day, a cousin and friend, Gaspar Oreña, returned from a voyage to Lima, bringing with him a few trunks of fine goods to sell. The exorbitant duties, however, would wipe out any profits, so Oreña turned to his cousin, and together they hatched a plan. Angustias and Gaspar returned to the beach together, where the would-be merchant announced loudly, "Señora, I am sorry to leave you here, but I have to board ship." "It does not matter," Angustias replied with a wink, and turned to the customs house guards stationed on the beach. As a decent woman, Angustias could not walk the streets home alone, so she demanded an escort, and then invited all four guards to come in for a little tea and fresh tortillas. "They were afraid that the Administrador would come," she remembered, and reprimand them for leaving their posts, "and I told them that they were cowards. I said this to see if I could hurt their self-respect." Carefully stationing her own servants to keep guard, Angustias served tea and chattered away at the customs house guards, so "that they did not have a chance to say 'let's go.'" As soon as she got the signal that Oreña's trunks were safely off the ship, she recalled, "I was no longer interested" in the conversation and let the four young men leave. "I thought it best to put the trunks under my bed," she concluded, "Oreña sold everything for a good price and even Pablo, the customs administrator, bought some goods."[146] Cousin Gaspar netted a nice profit of $5,000.

Angustias, as a woman, should not have played an active role in trade or government, according to the expectations of her culture. Yet, in her remembrances, she gave herself a central place in this drama of smuggling and political intrigue, showing that she had the intelligence to outwit four customs guards and the independence to thwart her brother's official interests. It may seem, then, that strong-willed women were beginning in these years to resist their subordination to men in the family, the economy, and the government. Examined more closely, however, this story demonstrates that, rather than challenging the fundamentals of her social order, the privileges of class, or the expectations of patriarchy, Angustias manipulated these same hierarchies and expectations to create a public space and role for herself. In this case, she cleverly called upon both the cultural demand to protect elite women from sexual shame and the connection of "bravery" to honorable masculinity in order to convince four customs guards to leave their posts. Angustias knew that these men would be forced to follow her if she demanded an escort, and be called cowards if they did not.

Cases of criminal behavior may be at the extreme of what a particularly willful woman might accomplish, but they do fit within the range of options available to some women in the late 1830s and early 1840s. In this post-rebellion era, women and children of the de la Guerra family found some room to maneuver within what was still a strongly patriarchal culture. As the stories of Santa Bárbara's female riot to defend Father Durán and of María Antonia Guerra's tearful audience with her cousin Vallejo attest, women had a certain leverage in the public sphere if they were seen to be protecting the honor of their families and communities. But in the years after 1836, second-generation elite women, like the de la Guerra daughters, also began to claim a degree of personal independence and power. In part, this increased status was grounded for elite women in the same land distribution and political power that their husbands and brothers grabbed in the 1830s. But young women also began to listen to the language of liberalism and its call for companionate marriage and the civic role of well-educated mothers.

Angustias, like many elite wives and daughters, became just as invested in the ranching economy in these years as her husband, brothers, and father were. Under Mexican law, women retained title to their own property brought into a marriage, the right to half the communal property on the death of their husbands, and an equal right to inherit with their brothers on the death of their parents. This was the right that María del Carmen Rodríguez had successfully defended in 1833 against José Antonio de la Guerra.[147] A few single women and widows also applied separately for their own land grants during the Mexican era. By 1845, over sixty-six women had been granted their own ranchos, and many more shared title with a husband or with siblings.[148] In later documents, Angustias referred to Pájaro, part of a grant made in Manuel Jimeno's name, as "my ranch," and she was probably not alone in thinking of her husband's land grants as equally her own to manage and take profit from.[149] Angustias went so far as to learn the skills of a ranch hand herself: one American was amazed to discover in 1850 that Angustias "was a splendid horsewoman, and had even considerable skill in throwing the lariat."[150] Likewise, the wives of merchants, like Teresa de la Guerra, also later claimed to have had intimate knowledge of their husbands' business dealings and accounts.[151]

As her tale of deceit and smuggling attests, Angustias was also particularly well placed to observe and influence the political world of Monterey. She shared her house with her brother, the customs inspector, and her husband, the first vocal, governor's secretary, and frequent acting governor. As a consequence, the very structure of her private residence became an arena of politics. "Before the government headquarters were built," she told her daughter, "a room in my house served as an office . . . All important papers that needed to be saved were kept at my house."[152] Angustias expanded her political role beyond that of passive witness to

Monterey, California rancho scene [Manuel Jimeno and Angustias de la Guerra Rancho], ca. 1849, Alfred Sully. Courtesy of the Oakland Museum of California, Kahn Collection.

active social organizer and hostess. Observers frequently noted that she seemed to be at the center of Monterey society. According to her sister Teresa, for example, a Frenchman named Duflot de Mofras came to the Hartnell ranch in the early 1840s, abused Teresa's hospitality, drank up all the sacramental wine, and left without saying goodbye; the next she heard of him he had been seen "in Monterey, dancing with her sister Doña Angustias."[153] It may appear, of course, that giving parties and dancing with foreign dignitaries were simply the frivolous pastimes of privileged women, but Angustias used her position to patrol the boundaries of elite society and pass judgment on the workings of departmental politics—a role that would become increasingly important as war broke out with the United States, and American officers flooded Monterey.[154] For well-connected women like Angustias, high position and a prominent family made government and politics her natural domain and tricking the customs administrator an easy game.

Thus, a clever woman of the elites might use her family's increased wealth and power to gain a measure of her own influence and independence. The impact of liberal thought in California also shifted definitions of female honor, giving a "virtuous" woman a potentially larger role in the public sphere of the republic. As previously noted, liberals challenged colonial concepts of authority based on birthright and replaced them with notions of the rights of citizens. In theory, this challenge extended to the absolute power of elder men, and on this foundation many of California's second-generation men found the justification for rebellion against their fathers. Compared to men, however, women still did not fit the definition of "citizen" and continued to be judged by their sexual purity and their ability to fulfill domestic roles within a patriarch's household. Even so, women who met the high standards of morality could expect a public recognition of their social value to the republic.[155]

It is difficult to trace the spread of liberal ideas among the young women of California. Prior to the 1840s, it appears to have been quite limited. Women did not attend the study groups of the 1820s and 1830s that Mexican theorists set up for their brothers. Nor were many of them even literate enough to take advantage of books by such authors as Fénelon and Rousseau, brought by foreign traders. Yet some may still have discussed the new ideas with their brothers and boyfriends. José Castro's *querida*, or sweetheart, confessed to Father Tomás Esténaga that Castro owned banned books, and that "every night he reads them [to me] with great pleasure."[156] Young women in these circles heard stories that held up a family ideal, not of fathers who demanded perpetual duty and obedience, but of parents who lovingly prepared sons and daughters for independent adulthood. These books also promoted the ideal of companionate marriage over arranged marriage. Changes to the law in other parts of Mexico reinforced this notion, freeing children, including daughters, from many restrictions of the patria potestas. The extent to which this new thinking affected Californio daughters can be gauged in Antonio María Osio's memoirs. When this conservative spoke to the people of Los Angeles in 1836, warning that the new regime would break down the authority of parents to arrange marriages, he noticed that "the girls who were present reacted very favorably, but their mothers did not."[157]

Despite young women's eagerness for free choice of marriage partners, in practice Mexican liberals shied away from undermining patriarchal social control within families. Daughters may have had a bit more freedom from their fathers, but the legal status of married women changed very little. Women did not become citizens; they could not vote or hold office. Within households, men still guarded and controlled women's labor, property, and sexual propriety, and the legal system backed them up. If anything, standards for modesty, domestic virtue, and decorum actually became stricter. Nonetheless, some married women found a small opening in the liberal glorification of motherhood. Teresa de la Guerra, who had grown up in an earlier time, explained her role as a mother in passive terms: "My husband gives me everything that I want. I give him myself and his children. There is an Indian girl for every baby as soon as it is born; I have only to bear and love them."[158] But in the 1840s, that view of motherhood and women's roles was changing.

In that decade, a new literature emerged in Mexico that targeted women and elevated their roles as wives and mothers within the republic. Yearly calendars included romantic poems, stories, and advice, while women's magazines coached women on their appearance, morality, and domestic roles.[159] Two issues of *Panorama de las Señoritas*, published by Vicente García Torres, made their way to Los Angeles in 1842. They contained articles on family hygiene and health care, the quick wit of historical women like Delilah, and the way to properly educate strong sons for the republic.[160] The de la Guerras also stocked their bookshelves with prescriptive books, aimed at young wives. After her marriage, Angustias turned to *Instructions for Young Women at the Age of Entering Society and Getting Married: A Wise Governess Instructs Her Noble Disciples in all the Obligations Pertaining to the State of Matrimony and the Education of Their Children*. Written by the French governess Jeanne-Marie le Prince de Beaumont, a promoter of women's education, and translated into Spanish in 1780, the work contained advice on negotiating marriage proposals, educating children, and performing acts of charity. Echoing the story of *Telemachus*, de Beaumont urged her young charges to turn to her, a "wise person," "without (personal) interest" for guidance, lest their passions overrule their reason, the true source of liberty.[161] Virtuous women, this literature proclaimed, learned self-discipline, maintained proper standards of morality, and actively nurtured republican values in their families.

For this, liberals agreed, they needed better educations. In fact, it is in the realm of female education that liberals may have had the greatest impact on the lives of Mexican women. But on the frontier, where schools struggled to stay open, finding an appropriate education for "republican mothers" could be a challenge.[162] Ironically, it was mercantile connections to New England that offered a chance for at least one young woman to fulfill the new ideal of educated motherhood. In the 1820s and 1830s, the de la Guerra daughters had married young, effectively ending time spent in the classroom. Teresa attempted only a handful of laboriously written letters in her adult life.[163] Her younger sister Anita married an

American at age fourteen in 1836, and when she gave birth to her first child in California a year later, she seemed to be headed for a life like that of her oldest sister: married to a foreign trader, raising children, and managing a household. But when civil unrest in California persuaded her husband to return to Boston, Anita went with him and discovered that New England society had very different expectations for sixteen-year-olds. It was here, and not California, that Anita discovered the means, and the justification, to demand her own belated schooling.

Alfred Robinson and Anita left California in October 1837 and arrived in Boston the next March, settling initially in Lowell, Massachusetts.[164] The young "Spanish" bride created a sensation in New England society. Elizabeth Fairly, a neighbor of Alfred's brother, later explained, "the surprise that one so young should be a wife and mother—she was about my age and I was still in school—can never be forgotten."[165] No doubt, the educated New England girls made an impression on Anita as well, for just months after her arrival, her husband wrote to the de la Guerras, "Anita says she is going to study how to write letters."[166] Still, with the arrival of a second child in November, and the job of running a household, Anita found little time for herself, and her education progressed at a frustrating pace.[167] Anita held on to the dream, and the following February 1839, she explained to her parents that "for me it would be shameful to return again without my having first advanced somewhat in my studies . . . Also I know that it would be pleasing for you to have an educated daughter like the girls that I see here every day."[168] In other words, although Anita had grown up believing that educated daughters were not in fact necessary to the family economy of California, she now justified her personal claim to education as a way to avoid dishonor and serve her parents.

At last, Anita found her opportunity for serious study in 1840. The unrest in California finally over, Alfred determined to outfit another merchant ship and make his way back to the coast for more hide-and-tallow trade. He left in January 1840, but Anita remained behind, staying with "the Misses Porter" in Bridgeport, Connecticut. Although this meant an even longer separation from her family and homeland, Anita had the support of a society that also encouraged young women to attend school. And just before Alfred left in January, she added a new argument: "My girl some day will have need of the good instruction of her mother, and now is the time to take advantage when such a good occasion has been presented to me."[169] In 1840, elite and middle-class New England society, like that of reformers in Mexico, subscribed to the notion that women needed to be educated because raising children and overseeing their moral values fell within their domain. By attaching herself to this strain of thinking, Anita may have had the best chance of convincing Californians of her right to an education.

Still, the story of the youngest de la Guerra daughter, María Antonia, shows perhaps the limits of this new liberal role for wives and mothers in California. In 1839, Anita asked her father if he might also send eleven-year-old sister María Antonia to join her at a New England academy, perhaps delaying the younger sister's transition to adulthood and marriage. De la Guerra refused. Unlike Mexico's liberal reformers, he did not see the use in educating a woman. For him, only sons were worth the expense, and Miguel and Antonio María were next in line. And as the only remaining unmarried daughter, María Antonia was needed at home to take care of Anita's first child, Elena, and to assist her own mother in running the house. "How I regret that María Antonia is not coming," Alfred Robinson told his mother-in-law, and to his sister said, "I am sure you would have learned more here than in your whole life in California."[170]

The voices of de la Guerra women, almost silent before 1837, burst forth in the documents after that date. After the rebellion, elite women like Angustias and Anita remained firmly within a patriarchal system that maintained strong standards of female submission, virtue, and decorum. The elements of liberalism that advanced equality and individualism did not have a significant impact among California's elite women, any more than they did among the mission Indians. Yet, like some ex-neophytes, a few women found ways to call upon the obligations of patriarchs to find a measure of protection. And some women drew on the increasing material resources and political influence of their male relatives to carve out independence. Armed with books, magazines, and talk of their new role in society, younger women dreamed of choosing their own husbands and demanded the education they needed as mothers of virtuous children.

Familiar Patterns

By the end of the Mexican era, de la Guerra sons and daughters had established their independence as adults. José Antonio lived on his own ranch and conducted his affairs almost entirely apart from his father. Teresa struggled to run a decent household on a small ranch, supplemented by her husband's sporadic income. Angustias and Pablo worked in the heart of Monterey politics, and Anita studied English in a New England academy. Yet in the early 1840s, José de la Guerra continued to operate a ranching and trading empire that depended on his children and extended kin. The family economy, established in the first decades of the century, had bent with the challenge of liberalism and secularization, but it did not break. De la Guerra turned to the same strategies in the last years of Mexican rule that he had used at the beginning.

Francisco de la Guerra cost his father perhaps more sleepless nights and pulled hair than his siblings did. During the heady days of the rebellion, nineteen-year-old Francisco began an affair with twenty-year-old María del Rosario Lorenzana. Marriage of his son to Lorenzana would have been unthinkable for de la Guerra; her last name identified her with the abandoned infants who took the name of Archbishop Lorenzana of Mexico City and were sent north as children from his asylum in 1800.[171] Not only could she offer no connections to other elites, but her status as the child of an *expósito*, or foundling, cast doubt on her legitimacy and racial status.[172] No doubt de la Guerra fumed at Francisco's display of independence, but the two lovers continued to see each other, in the end having two illegitimate children: Felipe Santiago, born May 5, 1837, and Clotilde Inez Soledad, born May 9, 1839. Francisco and María del Rosario were not alone in their transgression. In the colonial era through the 1820s, eight percent of Californio children were born out of wedlock. But in the 1830s and 1840s, when liberal ideologies were the most widely debated and influential, and paternal oversight the most relaxed, that figure rose to thirteen percent.[173] Santiago was baptized an *hijo natural*, and both parents came forward to claim him as their own. This suggests that Francisco and María probably intended to marry in the future and thereby automatically legitimate their children.[174]

In February 1839, however, almost three months before the birth of Clotilde, Francisco wed Ascención Sepúlveda, the daughter of a wealthy landowning family from Los Angeles. It is probably no coincidence that soon after, José de la Guerra stood before the justice of the peace in Santa Bárbara to give Francisco his agency to receive juridical possession of Rancho San Julián.[175] Francisco also took juridical possession of Simi, living there part of the year with his family.[176] Over the next few years, Francisco was transformed: the troublesome young man became his father's trusted agent, overseeing his large ranching operations and helping his brother-in-law move cattle to his new ranches nearby.[177] In June 1846, when de la Guerra purchased yet another ranch, the 26,623-acre Las Posas, Francisco was again the one who represented his father and managed ranch production.[178] As he reached adulthood, Francisco took over the sorts of roles once filled by his uncles, and it may not be too much of a

Sala of Casa de la Guerra: Francisco de la Guerra, one of his daughters, and Josefa Moreno, ca. 1876. Santa Barbara Historical Museum.

stretch to suppose that he was induced to marry into the Sepúlveda family in exchange for such an important role in his father's empire.

The youngest de la Guerra daughter, denied an education with her sister Anita, discovered the demands of filial obedience in these years as well. On Christmas Day, 1843, her mother, María Antonia Carrillo y Lugo de la Guerra, died at age fifty-seven. Francisco's wife, Ascención, followed unexpectedly the next summer, the victim of a tainted smallpox vaccination.[179] With no other adult women in the family who lived nearby, seventeen-year-old María Antonia managed her father's household on her own, supervising servants, caring for Francisco's legitimate orphaned son and daughter, and entertaining her father's many business associates.[180] Sensing the burden this placed on her little sister, Angustias made sure to visit frequently in these years.

But María Antonia did not remain alone for long. In June 1845, she married Cesareo Lataillade, a Mexican trader. Just like her sisters Teresa and Anita, María Antonia wed a man whose commercial connections could bring advantages to her father. Lataillade had first arrived in

California in July 1842 as supercargo of the *Trinidad*. Soon after, he and de la Guerra shook hands on a deal totaling $1,429—the Mexican acquiring hides and tallow, and the Santa Bárbaran filling his warehouse with panocha, refined sugar, and challis cloth.[181] Lataillade made one trip to Mexico and back, and on June 23, 1845, he married the last of de la Guerra's daughters, not quite eighteen. As with the earlier marriages, no evidence survives that would reveal how much the decision was María Antonia's and how much was her father's. By this time, several Mexican states had limited fathers' legal authority and lowered the age of consent; popular ideals at the same time endorsed love matches over arranged marriages.[182] Nonetheless, marriage to a foreign merchant continued a well-established strategy within the California family economy, and should have pleased de la Guerra.

Younger sons Antonio María and Miguel, too, followed in the footsteps of older siblings, in their case, elder brother Juan, and received educations abroad, thanks to their father's trading contacts. While Miguel studied in Hawaii with other Californio boys, Antonio María spent four years in Chile.[183] Arranged through merchants Antonio José Cot and José Aguirre, Antonio María's education began in 1840 when he was fourteen, and lasted until the young man's declining eyesight forced him to return home four years later.[184] Antonio María had a few familiar faces to accompany him in Chile; Patrick Short had relocated to Valparaíso after Hartnell's school failed, and some of Mariano Guadalupe Vallejo's children joined the young de la Guerra's college in 1843.[185] When Antonio María sailed home in the summer of 1844, 889 pesos, 6 reales for "the latest expenses in Chile, passage to Callao, and Acapulco, and equipment to embark your son" were already charged to Aguirre's account.[186]

The merchant Aguirre served de la Guerra one more time, as the captain turned to an old family tactic, placing a nephew in the mercantile profession. In 1841, Gaspar Oreña, the seventeen-year-old son of de la Guerra's niece, left Cádiz, Spain, to begin life in the New World. "He was going to follow the career of medicine," explained his father, Lorenzo, "and now he has broken my head, wanting to go off there and follow the career of a merchant for which I hope for your goodness. Look after him as a son."[187] Originally, Gaspar hoped to land a position with Alfred Robinson's trading firm, but finding Robinson already gone for California, Oreña spent a brief time with cousin Anita, then followed her husband around the Horn.[188] On his arrival in December 1842, Oreña found a welcome home with the de la Guerras and a position in Mazatlán, then a post as clerk with Aguirre.[189] In February 1843, on his way back to New

England, Robinson stopped to visit Gaspar in Mexico and gave de la Guerra the encouraging news, "It appears to me that he is in good standing with his employers."[190]

Oreña traveled back and forth along the Pacific Coast with Aguirre for a few years, and de la Guerra maintained a steady eye on his protégé. "I have warned him that in the business in which he intends to get involved, he should receive your counsel and proceed accordingly," de la Guerra told Antonio José Cot.[191] In another instance, when Aguirre became too ill to pay Gaspar his wages, de la Guerra reimbursed other traders in his network for the advances they had given Oreña to keep him going.[192] The Spanish nephew, apprenticed to a New World uncle's merchant house, repeated the same pattern that de la Guerra himself had experienced at the turn of the century. It is not clear whether de la Guerra intended to complete the arrangement, grooming Oreña to take over his mercantile business on retirement; events of the next ten years made this ultimately impossible. But in the early 1840s, de la Guerra certainly was invoking another strategy of the family economy, calling on his network of trading partners and relatives to set up a dependent relative in the family business. Ironically, though, it was his daughter Angustias who provided the means, by smuggling, to set up her cousin with his own commercial fortune.

By the mid-1840s, then, the patriarchal family remained firmly entrenched: a crucial institution in the economy and government of Mexican California and a foundation of social hierarchy based on honor, paternalism, and patronage. For this reason, despite sporadic civil unrest, declarations of independence, and the successful secularization of mission lands, California experienced no true family revolution. During the rebellion, California's elite native sons never abandoned a paternal model of authority; they hoped instead to become "legitimate" patriarchs themselves. Even those, like Mariano Guadalupe Vallejo, who attempted more radical reform of the government and military, eventually gave up in the face of continuing popular adherence to the regime of paternalism and family obligation. At the same time, women of the older generation played a major conservative role themselves, enforcing familial honor and loyalty.

After the unrest, California began to experience a major shift in property-holding, but chiefly from the missions to elite men. The new rancheros, guided by old understandings of patriarchal authority resting on both command and fulfillment of obligations, retained resources and political influence within a relatively small and inter-related elite class.

Although liberal-influenced native sons had initially championed the rights of Indians to live as free citizens, once the neophytes were freed from mission oversight, they became not small proprietors or political actors but dependent labor to these same elite men, on ranches and in town. Conservatives like José de la Guerra, who opposed the end of mission oversight, continued to enforce the old paternal system at home but also took advantage of the new economy and profited from it. Finally, second-generation women of the elite, like their brothers, achieved some political voice, economic independence, and education after 1837 but remained subject to the codes of female virtue and patriarchal authority. In the end, California's liberal revolution had taken Mexico's nation-building projects—secularization and home rule—and placed them firmly in the hands of local patriarchs. Although California's elite families had, in a generation, converted themselves from military officers and merchants into rancheros, social stability continued to be based on shared understandings of family and patriarchy.

CHAPTER SIX

REINVENTING PATRIARCHY IN TIME OF WAR

On a quiet Sunday in June 1846, General Mariano Guadalupe Vallejo awoke at dawn to the sound of hammering blows on the front door of his home in Sonoma. Vallejo and his wife, Francisca, peered through the curtains of their *casa grande* to see a motley collection of American trappers, horse thieves, and runaway sailors dressed in torn buckskin, many of them barefoot, milling about the plaza. Each one carried a gun, and a few brandished tomahawks notched to mark the owner's kills. Taking the time to dress in his military uniform, Vallejo at last ordered his servants to unlatch the heavy wood door and admit the men—a party from John Frémont's camp at the Sutter Buttes, above the Sacramento Valley. Through an interpreter, a representative declared their intent to arrest Vallejo and seize Mexican army weapons and supplies for the cause of Californian independence. Vallejo assured the Americans that he sympathized with American plans to make California a protectorate, then gave them the keys to his arsenal and ordered wine and brandy to refresh the men waiting in the plaza. While he wrote out the terms of surrender, Vallejo ordered breakfast and tea to be prepared for the hungry rebels.

Despite this hospitality, the men in the plaza grew increasingly drunk and impatient, finally insisting that Vallejo, his brother Salvador, and son-in-law Jacob Leese be sent as prisoners to Frémont's camp. Vallejo, the friend of American settlers in the north, found himself in jail at Sutter's Fort without charges or trial until August. Meanwhile, those left to guard Sonoma raised a handsewn flag bearing a single star, the likeness of a bear, and the phrase, "California Republic." These "Bear Flaggers," though they acted without official sanction, were quickly incorporated into the U.S. Army after July 7, 1846, when Commodore John Drake Sloat of the Pacific Squadron took Monterey and announced the war between the United States and Mexico.[1] Soon forces of the U.S. Navy under Commodore Robert F. Stockton and those of the U.S. Army under Stephen Kearny joined them. Overpowered, Californians finally capitulated on January 13, 1847. For the next three years, an American military government ruled California, until it was accepted as a state in 1850.

The story of Mariano Guadalupe Vallejo—an accommodationist eventually betrayed by the Americans he befriended—often serves as the classic example of elite Californio attitudes and experiences during the Mexican-American War.[2] In this interpretation, elites like Vallejo saw their true interests to rest not with the greater Mexican or Californio population, but with their class, and they welcomed their conquerors to advance their own economic standing. In a variation of the story, elite women who had married Americans are seen as especially prone to wartime disloyalty to Mexico. For these accommodationists, goes this line of reasoning, only Americans could end the civil conflicts that marked California's government, put an end to Indian raiding and unrest, and bring the entrepreneurial spirit and skills needed to develop California's latent resources. Promises of wealth and stability, in other words, outweighed any tenuous concern that elites might have felt for the welfare of lower-class Mexicans.

An examination of Vallejo's cousins in the de la Guerra and Carrillo families demonstrates, however, that the general's story was only one of many that played out for Californios in these years. "I admit," Julio Carrillo later wrote, "that the general government of Mexico was like a very mean step-mother to us . . . but in my estimation this was no reason why we should have renounced our birthrights."[3] Despite later charges of disloyalty, nativism still ran strong in California, and elite Californios constantly negotiated between accommodation and resistance in their attempts to preserve power, wealth, and autonomy amid rapidly changing circumstances. The path an individual chose depended on gender, family connections, political ideology, and personal calculations of risk. Members of the de la Guerra family could, and did, temper their action to fit immediate circumstances, taking up arms at one moment, and dancing at an American officers' ball the next.

Vallejo's story is misleading in another way, too, for elite Californios like the de la Guerras, Vallejos, Carrillos, and Lugos did not act as individuals when they calculated their reaction to American conquest. Elites during the war, just as much as before it, continued to depend on patriarchal relations of power, both within extended family networks and with their non-elite dependents in the local community. Over the course of the war, the military occupation that followed, and the boom and massive migration of the concurrent Gold Rush, members of these families and communities reinvented older hierarchies and dynamics within a restructured state, population, and economy. Second-generation de la Guerras emerged as local and statewide leaders, and they assured that the Mexican population would continue to have a voice in the newly constituted electorate. At the same time, they moved to protect family assets and adapt to changing markets. The war years saw a transformation of Mexican-era patterns and determined the ultimate ability of Californios to survive in the second half of the century under American rule.

Prelude to War

Of course, Californios had had plenty of experience with Americans before the summer of 1846, when Vallejo found his house surrounded and citizens of Monterey awoke to the sight of the Stars and Stripes being raised over the harbor town. Californio ranchers and merchants had been dealing with Boston traders for years, and many of these foreign men had settled in the province, converted to Catholicism, married into local families, and sworn allegiance to Mexico. But, beginning in the late 1830s, a new kind of immigrant began to arrive in California from the United States. Trappers and farmers, arriving overland from New Mexico and the Mississippi Valley, began to settle in groups near Los Angeles and San Bernardino, in the Central Valley, and on the Sacramento River.[4] These new migrants sought the cheap land and large Indian workforce coveted by Californios in the same period, and they learned of these enticements through American boosters. Their interests were not so easily integrated into Californio family empires. In these last few years of Mexican rule, California's native sons and daughters began to understand the true nature of the threat from their expansive neighbor.

In the early 1840s, the central government of Mexico was not unaware of the trouble posed by increased migration to its northern provinces. Mexico City sent frequent orders to provincial governments on the frontier to stop illegal immigration and expel those who arrived without proper documentation, but these orders went largely unenforced in California. Most Californios greeted these newcomers with deep ambivalence, alarmed at the stream of foreigners but unwilling to send families back over mountain passes in the wintertime, and hopeful that the new migrants would settle the inland frontiers. Rebel governor Juan Alvarado reversed his predecessors' anti-immigration policies, but only foreigners who had taken Mexican citizenship were eligible for land grants. Those who had married into local families, like William Hartnell, tended to receive grants near the coast and already populated areas, but those without family ties were encouraged to look farther afield; one of the first ranchos in the Central Valley, considered an uncivilized haven of "wild Indians," went to "Dr." John Marsh, late of Minnesota, in 1837. Perhaps the most famous foreign outpost belonged to Johann Sutter, a Swiss migrant who arrived two years later and immediately petitioned for a Texas-style empresario grant to settle Swiss families in California. The experience of Texas appears to have been also in Alvarado's mind, for the Californio governor urged Sutter to petition instead for a private rancho and to select the property from the interior. Sutter began to develop a site on the Sacramento River and was formally granted eleven leagues there in 1841.

Californios made such grants in part to secure a buffer against raiding parties of Indians from the interior, and further secure the frontier, but in Sutter's case, Alvarado and his secretary Manuel Jimeno may have also been motivated by rivalries with Mariano Guadalupe Vallejo. Under Governor Figueroa, Vallejo had not only been granted a sizable area in the Sonoma region and lucrative administration of Mission San Francisco de Solano but also had become "director of colonization" of the northern frontier, with special powers to grant land. Alvarado and Jimeno, hoping to create a counterbalance to Vallejo's unique fiefdom, made their concession to Sutter without consulting the general. By the end of August 1840, they also gave the Swiss, now a naturalized Mexican, similar ability to sell land as "representative of the government" in the Sacramento Valley.[5] In 1841, Sutter stocked his grant at New Helvetia with livestock and building materials from Fort Ross, purchased from the Russians when they abandoned their colony.

If Alvarado and Jimeno hoped that Sutter's grant would block further Anglo-American migration to the coast, they were disappointed. Soon, Sutter and Marsh both began to write letters back East, encouraging settlement in California. Many of the overland parties who arrived carried with them the newspaper articles that had encouraged their immigration and that predicted the eventual acquisition of California by the United States. Sutter also overstepped the bounds of his official powers to issue illegal passports to new arrivals and to sell land to unnaturalized citizens. When he had arrived in 1839, only three hundred or so foreigners lived in California, but over the next six years the stream of overland migration increased steadily. Most came through Sutter's Fort.[6] In November 1845, the Mexican government at last tried to buy the fort back, but Sutter refused to sell. By then, foreigners, mostly Americans, made up about nine percent of California's total gente de razón population, with over five hundred more starting out on the overland trails the next year.

The steady increase in settlers, most of whom had no intention of becoming Mexicans, set many Californios on edge and brought to mind the example of Texas. There, Mexico's empresario system had brought in over 35,000 Americans and their slaves, outnumbering Tejanos by ten to one shortly before the state declared independence in 1836. In California, the non-Indian population had grown more slowly, by natural increase and immigration, to about 7,300 in 1845; of those, 680 were foreigners.[7] Attempts at encouraging the migration of Mexicans had met with limited success, largely because the population of Mexico as a whole was not growing fast enough to exhaust the supply of vacant land in Mexico's heartland.[8]

In the early 1840s, Californios still made up an overwhelming majority of the gente de razón, but two clashes with Americans, the Graham Affair of 1840 and the capture of Monterey harbor by Commodore Jones in 1842, crystallized for many the imminent danger of American conquest. In particular, second-generation members of the de la Guerra family, just establishing themselves in the provincial government, found themselves swept up in the conflicts and retained a lasting impression of American hostility and Mexican weakness.

The Graham Affair, a planned uprising by Americans, came to light in late March or early April 1840 when one of the conspirators revealed it in a deathbed confession to Father Suárez del Real of Mission San Carlos. Suárez del Real then warned Manuel Jimeno and Governor Alvarado.[9] The mastermind behind the plot, Isaac Graham, was a Kentucky hunter and frontiersman who first migrated to New Mexico and then moved to California in the mid-1830s, operating a distillery near present-day Salinas. He and his supporters were well known to Alvarado; in 1836 twenty-five or thirty of them had helped him overthrow Gutiérrez. But by 1840, they had become arrogant and rude: "I was insulted at every turn," Alvarado later told Alfred Robinson, "by the drunken followers of Graham; and when walking in the garden they would come to its wall, and call upon me in terms of the greatest familiarity: 'Ho! Bautista, come here, I want to speak to you.'—'Bautista, here.'—'Bautista, there'—and Bautista everywhere."[10]

News of the confession traveled fast in the elite circles of Monterey; Angustias de la Guerra, as wife of the governor's secretary, "found out about the planned takeover from my husband."[11] On April 4, the California legislature debated its response to the threat, and the next day Alvarado gave the order to arrest all foreigners who had entered the country unlawfully, in both north and south. Three days later, Manuel Jimeno sent word to his father-in-law, José de la Guerra, of the thwarted "plan in the Texas method," and of the arrests that day, enclosing the governor's decrees.[12] In this and a follow-up letter, Jimeno assured de la Guerra that only foreigners "introduced illegally into this country" would be arrested, "leaving here those married and those known to be honorable, &c."[13] In other words, the order would not affect foreigners like William Hartnell and Alfred Robinson, already enmeshed in Californio family networks. All told, sixty rootless men in the Monterey area, Englishmen and Americans, found themselves in prison, to be deported aboard merchant José Antonio Aguirre's ship later that month.

A week after the Monterey arrests, José de la Guerra wrote his official report, having rounded up the undocumented foreign residents of Santa Bárbara and Los Angeles.[14] Although de la Guerra and his officers followed Alvarado's instructions, reactions in Southern California tended to be less alarmist. Only twenty or so found themselves in Santa Bárbara's lockup, and most of these were later released.[15] Far fewer foreigners of the "dangerous" sort lived in the area, and even those Californios who had direct knowledge of Graham tended to shrug off the threat. As a customs official, Pablo de la Guerra had encountered Graham in Monterey, but visiting sheltered Santa Bárbara that month, he took a moderate tone toward the threat of foreign invasion. Writing to his cousin Vallejo shortly after the arrests in Santa Bárbara, he observed that foreigners were "about to overrun us, of which I am very glad, for the country needs immigration in order to make progress."[16] Pablo would not hold this opinion much longer.

As Aguirre's ship left Santa Bárbara with nearly fifty prisoners on May 8, 1840, Californios could breathe a sigh of relief. They had rid themselves of a dangerous pack of unassimilated foreigners and decreased the threat of a Texas-style "independence" movement in their province. They might fully have expected congratulations from the Mexican government, but were shocked to discover that, thanks to vigorous protests from the British consul in Tepic, most of the prisoners were found not guilty. They were released and given new passports, and even made claims against the California government for financial compensation. José Castro, head of the guard aboard ship, on the other hand, found himself tried by court martial in Mexico City before his own eventual release. Nineteen of the expelled, including Graham himself, returned to Monterey in July 1841, and according to Robinson, "came on shore, dressed neatly, armed with rifles and swords, and looking in infinitely better condition than when

Pablo de la Guerra. Courtesy of The Bancroft Library, University of California, Berkeley.

they departed."[17] Meanwhile, warships from France, Britain, and the United States anchored in Monterey, demanding reparations for the arrests. In the aftermath of the Graham Affair, Californios learned an important lesson: the Mexican central government seemed less interested in protecting its northern provinces than in maintaining good international relations with its creditors and neighbors.[18]

The second incident that clarified the American threat for the de la Guerras came just a year later. By the early 1840s, Mexico owed the British government fifty million pesos, and rumors circulated that Mexico would cede California to pay the debt. Meanwhile, Mexico had never officially recognized Texas's independence, and attempts by that territory to join the union strained relations between Mexico and the United States. On October 19, 1842, acting on reports of war and the imminent arrival of the British fleet to take possession, Commodore Thomas Ap Catesby Jones sailed two vessels of the U.S. Pacific Squadron into Monterey's harbor and demanded immediate surrender, giving the Californios one day to respond. Government officials and other leading citizens of Monterey quickly assembled in the governor's house, and after determining that the warships drastically outgunned the presidio, agreed to negotiate. The next morning, Alvarado and the junta departamental signed terms of surrender, and Jones raised the Stars and Stripes over Monterey. A day later, however, Jones was given more recent newspapers and documents and, realizing his mistake, restored Monterey to Mexico with apologies.[19]

According to the Americans, the leading Californios had been embarrassingly quick to surrender their territory in exchange for stability and the promise of American rule. But the de la Guerras showed more determined resistance to Commodore Jones's demands. As interim head of the customs house in Monterey, Pablo de la Guerra participated in the all-night negotiation with the Americans, and as soon as Alvarado signed his surrender, he slipped out to lock up the treasury. With several of his subordinates, he then escaped to Santa Bárbara to spread the news of war. His sister Angustias remembered her own role in protecting the assets of the province from plunder. Later that day, she recalled, the commodore's secretary came to the house she shared with her brother and husband to demand the key to the customs house. "But I did not hand it over," she claimed. "He threatened to break down the customs house door, and I told him to do whatever he pleased."[20]

Meanwhile, unaware of the retractions and apologies, Pablo de la Guerra sped down to Santa Bárbara. His American brother-in-law awoke the night of October 24 to hear Pablo urgently waking his father in the next room with news of the hostilities and surrender. "'Wheugh! here's a go!' said I," Alfred Robinson remembered, "What is the matter? What is all this you are talking about?" Family relations apparently made no difference to the agitated young Californio, who exclaimed, according to Robinson, "Talking about? . . . why, we are going to cut the throats of all you Yankees!"[21] By the next morning, news of the surrender had spread across town, and Robinson found himself surrounded by worried Californios demanding to know if the United States would respect their property and religion. The next day, however, a courier arrived to announce the mistake.

No permanent harm seems to have been done by the one-day occupation of Monterey. Yet, this apparent revelation of official American designs on California, combined with increasing overland migration and the threat of rebellion made manifest in the Graham Affair, pushed many members of the de la Guerra family toward a more hardened stance against the United States. Pablo de la Guerra, who only a few years before had been "glad" at the prospect of increased American colonization, became openly hostile to many Americans by 1843. In February of that year, the American Congress took up the Jones affair, and that spring, American newspapers filtered back to California filled with news of the debates and editorials condemning or praising the action. Preserved in the de la Guerra archives is one such letter "to the Editors" of an unidentified American newspaper, carefully copied out and translated by Pablo de la Guerra. In it, the author denounced the taking of Monterey as a "rash absurdity," and with irony declared American intentions

> to take this delicious region of the globe, from men so barbarous, that do not want to keep the Africans in slavery, nor eradicate the Indians from their native soil, and colonize it with our noble lineage of champions of Liberty . . . we want the territory of our neighbor to scatter it among a population of slaveowners and slaves.[22]

The young customs inspector was no doubt impressed with Americans who favorably compared Mexico's liberal reforms with their own nation's laws permitting slavery and enforcing wholesale Indian removal east of the Mississippi.

While Pablo de la Guerra was studying and debating the meaning of American liberty with his peers, as customs administrator he also began to clamp down on American importers, demanding unexpected duties, for example, on machinery imported on the *George and Henry* in March 1843. William Streeter, aboard the ship, recalled hearing Pablo de la Guerra remark "that he had yet to see the American who was a gentleman." On being challenged by the American clerk, Pablo de la Guerra amended his statement with "an air of pompous dignity" to say that he meant simply that Americans were not men of leisure. According to Streeter, however, "the incident was not forgotten, although nothing more was said on the subject."[23]

In the late 1830s, Californios began uneasily to welcome American overland colonists, hoping that they would both secure the frontier against Indian raids and contribute to the local economy, as their predecessors by sea had done. But the new arrivals quickly convinced California's elite families that they would not be so easily integrated and controlled through compadrazgo or intermarriage. Nor did the overland migrants' goals of independent farming or trapping so easily mesh with Californio ranching and trading interests. By 1842, aggressive threats of uprisings and conquest prompted California's native sons to abandon their hard-won autonomy and send for help from Mexico City. That help arrived in the autumn of 1842 in the form of Governor Manuel Micheltorena and his army of three hundred convict soldiers and their families. The last few years of Mexican California would be marked by increased civil unrest, yet this upheaval provided the de la Guerra siblings with an indispensable education in negotiation and conciliation.

Men of Note:
De la Guerras under Micheltorena, Pico, and Castro

Both Juan Alvarado and Mariano Guadalupe Vallejo sent vigorous warnings about the threat from the United States in 1840 and 1841, but uncle and nephew also worked at cross-purposes to request the removal of the other from office. President Santa Anna responded to the squabbling by appointing a new governor, Manuel Micheltorena.[24] Micheltorena arrived in southern California just before Commodore Jones hoisted the Stars and Stripes, and according to Angustias de la Guerra, Alvarado "did not show any signs of surrendering the command to him at first ... [but] After Jones seized Monterey, he no longer objected to having the weight of responsibility lifted from him. He was actually rather happy about it."[25] Micheltorena ruled for another two years before Californios staged yet another overthrow of the government and attempted to split California's rule among increasingly hostile factions. Such factionalism had always been a danger, but this time the family relations, reciprocal obligations, and displays of paternalism that had held the Californio elites together showed serious signs of strain. But through these unstable final years of Mexican rule, the men of the de la Guerra family, father and sons, took on the role of wise elders in the territorial government, negotiating intra-family rivalries and civil conflicts to emerge as figures of Californio unity.

Despite their earlier consistent support for Alvarado, members of the de la Guerra family were quick to throw their loyalty behind centrally appointed Governor Micheltorena. Their calculation no doubt rested more on hopes for stability and order under Mexico than it did on disloyalty to native son rule. Micheltorena also laid claim to legitimate authority by distributing proper patronage to members of the family. In a flattering letter, he explained to the elder de la Guerra that he had requested Pablo, with his "fine education," to serve on his receiving committee when Jones arrived that winter, "in order to have a person of absolute confidence in my interview with the Commodore."[26] A year later, in December 1843, Pablo was promoted to chief customs inspector.[27] In a letter to the president of Mexico, informing him of the appointment, Governor Micheltorena explained Pablo's qualifications as "a young man of excellent education and integrity . . . who gives guarantees of being of a well-to-do family, and remits the necessary bonds to enjoy the salary."[28] Pablo used his authority to place his brother-in-law William Hartnell in a minor custom-house job and got his father an inspectorship in Santa Bárbara.

Pablo was not the only de la Guerra to hold a position of responsibility during the Micheltorena administration. Francisco de la Guerra was elected to the junta departamental in November 1843, and thus began his own political career.[29] And although Manuel Jimeno lost his position as vocal in that same election, Micheltorena appointed him secretary of state.[30] Soon, the governor and his wife were frequent guests at the Jimeno home in Monterey. Jimeno's wife, Angustias de la Guerra, remembered the governor as "a very handsome man," whose "manners were excellent," but as a jaded political observer she also recalled a fundamental weakness: "he was ill-suited for the position of jefe because of that generosity of spirit which guided him."[31] Despite a return to centrally appointed leadership under Micheltorena, then, members of the de la Guerra family were gratified to retain critical positions in California's governance.

Though they held a generally favorable opinion of the new governor, the de la Guerras felt increasingly threatened by the soldiers sent to support his rule. Angustias called them "unbearable," and their officers "vicious" and "corrupt"; she agreed with the general opinion that such men were nothing better than "cholos"—a racial slur encompassing their mixed-race heritage, Mexican origin, and low character. "The soldiers were consummate thieves," she said, "who committed all sorts of crimes every day." Soldiers snatched jars of food right out of her kitchen, and a Mexican captain stole her brother Pablo's writing desk, thinking it contained money.[32] Old nativist resentments against Mexican officials, dormant since 1836, flared up again after 1842. But Micheltorena believed himself too dependent on these convict soldiers to dismiss them.

Californios reached the breaking point in November 1844, when Manuel Castro and Juan Alvarado issued a pronunciamiento demanding the expulsion of the disruptive soldiers. Once again, they phrased their relationship to the governor in paternal terms: on meeting with the native-born rebels, Micheltorena reported, "they begged that I, like a father, would hear their complaints."[33] Micheltorena succeeded in placating the Californios for a few months, promising to send away the soldiers, but instead broke his agreement and turned to Sutter for armed support. What had once been a grievance against the convict soldiers became a personal campaign against the governor. "The sons of California will do us justice," wrote Alvarado and José Castro to Micheltorena, as they marched south to collect supporters that January.[34]

As the conflict shifted to the south, the de la Guerras took up a determining role as conciliators—a role José de la Guerra had earned as a respected elder and patriarch, and one that his younger sons began to emulate.[35] At Alvarado's urging, Pío Pico convoked the junta departamental in Los Angeles on January 28, 1845, and on February 1 it recommended the formation of a committee to meet with Micheltorena and put forth their demands.[36] On February 3, Pico appointed José de la Guerra as head of the commission. De la Guerra duly reported back a few days later that, motivated by "the ardent desire . . . for the reestablishment of the peace and avoidance of the evils which are the consequence of Civil War," he had met with the governor, but that Micheltorena had refused to recognize either the junta departamental or the commission.[37] Meanwhile, Pablo de la Guerra mediated in a similar manner in Monterey to prevent clashes between Micheltorena's garrison and a force of native Californians determined to take the town.[38] On February 15, the Los Angeles junta departamental gave up its negotiation, and Pico was declared, as first vocal, the interim governor. José de la Guerra's official role was over; he and his son both stepped out of the action after acting as agents for peace. After some maneuvers and a show battle at Cahuenga, Micheltorena surrendered his command on February 21, leaving José Castro the military head, and Pío Pico the civil governor of California.[39]

Both José de la Guerra and his son Pablo walked a carefully neutral but deeply engaged path during the overthrow of the last Mexican governor. It would have been easy for Castro and Pico to fault them for a lack of commitment to the rebellion; indeed, shortly before departing California, Micheltorena wrote a letter of appreciation to Pablo and his subordinates at the customs house, counting them as his "commendable friends."[40] Pablo wrote back that Micheltorena's resignation came at "the greatest regret to us, for it deprives us of the company of your Excellency."[41] And yet, Pablo and his brothers found welcome homes in the Pico and Castro regime, continuing their family's now-established function as conciliators.

As under the Alvarado regime, displays of protection and patronage would hold the key to the unity of the new native son government. Indeed, Alvarado himself probably harbored a desire to take over again as governor, but stepped aside for Pico and agreed to move the capital to Los Angeles in order to please his southern supporters. Pico rewarded Alvarado with Pablo's old job as chief customs inspector (with apologies to Pablo).[42] The customs house, treasury, and seat of military government remained in Monterey. Soon, Pico and Castro tumbled over each other in their eagerness to hand out government jobs and patronage to their followers, and the de la Guerra family benefited as much as any from the munificence. In July 1845, Pablo was restored to his old post at the head of customs, whereupon he immediately promoted his brother-in-law William Hartnell to the position of first official.[43] That month, Pico suggested twenty-two-year-old Joaquín for the position of governor's secretary. "I desire," he told José de la Guerra, "that it should be occupied by a person of capacity and good circumstances."[44]

Such correspondence with the elder de la Guerra suggests that the second generation of de la Guerras did not have complete independence from their father but were expected to serve in a coordinated way, with his permission and oversight. Perhaps this is why the aura of neutral mediation and wise counsel extended from father to sons. The same was apparently true of de la Guerra's godchildren in the new government, who also deferred to their padrino. José María Covarrubias, for example, took over as secretary of state in July, and after placing himself at de la Guerra's disposition, asked his godfather for influence in getting certain mutually beneficial appointments made, "as it is necessary for men of note to occupy the positions of the hierarchy to see if order can be preserved."[45] José de la Guerra had no official position of his own, but worked to maintain his standing as a local "father," loaning money to pay the salaries of soldiers in Los Angeles, and consulting with Pico to form a new military company.[46] The young men of California's last Mexican government continued to respect him as a commanding paternal force in the province.

Under the short reign of Pío Pico in the south and that of José Castro in the north, elite Californios continued to understand leadership as they had before: like a good father, a legitimate ruler would build moral and political authority not just through favors to specific clients but also by creating the appearance that he was willing to give generously to all members of the community. In practice, however, the young rulers of California in these years did not distribute patronage evenly, and the mask of the "good father" began to slip as the ruling class split into factions. Angustias de la Guerra lost her central place in political circles when the governorship moved south, and her husband, Manuel Jimeno, found himself without either a seat on the junta or a post as secretary of state.[47] From her perspective on the outside, the spoils system took on a radically different cast, and the leaders of Monterey seemed petty tyrants who only served themselves, not all Californians. "The worst cancer of all," she remembered bitterly,

> was the widespread thievery. There was such squandering of government resources that the funds in the treasury office had bottomed out. Commander General Castro kept a roster of officers that was large enough to staff an army of three thousand men. Somehow they all received a salary. These officers had no other use for the money than to grease the palms of their supporters who would help them achieve their personal goals.[48]

Soon after the Californios had taken over, some Americans had been predicting that just such partisanship would overcome hopes for tranquil home rule. "There will be a flare-up no doubt before many months between the Californians themselves," John Coffin Jones remarked to the U.S. Consul Thomas Larkin in March 1845.[49]

The sort of resentments expressed by Angustias de la Guerra found an echo in the south, where southern elites, granted the capital at last, imagined northern factions to be scheming to take back governance of the province and its spoils. Indeed, many northerners refused to take part in the new civil government, choosing instead the protection and patronage of the local military government under Castro. When the junta departamental met in Los Angeles from March to July 1846, not a single elected official from the north took his seat. And when Castro warned Pico of rootless Americans once again threatening rebellion on the northern frontier, southerners suspected a ruse to declare military rule and thwart the civil government.

In the tense months of spring 1846, the de la Guerras refused to choose sides, and when the rivalry threatened to blow up into open warfare, both Pío Pico and José Castro turned to members of the Santa Bárbara family to work out their differences. On March 9, the junta departamental in Los Angeles gave representative Francisco de la Guerra instructions to go north in order to suggest a conference between the two governors, Castro and Pico, on the neutral ground of Santa Bárbara. But Francisco's mission was doomed to failure; instead of persuading Castro to travel south and work with the civil authorities, he found an alarmed Castro convinced of the need to act immediately to thwart American invasion, with or without Pico's permission. Castro sent Customs Administrator Pablo de la Guerra south to explain the situation and urge a meeting between the two governors at San Luis Obispo. "Make known to the Governor of the Department," he wrote Pablo de la Guerra, "the imminent danger in which we find ourselves of an invasion by sea and land."[50] Pablo left with his brother Francisco on April 28, and the two appeared before the Los Angeles junta departamental on May 11, 1846. By then, however, the conflict had gone too far for reconciliation.[51] Pablo returned north with the news that the southerners rejected the proposed meeting, and suggested another at Santa Bárbara among leading men. The northerners refused to attend. Taking this as a declaration of war, Pico marched out of Los Angeles to meet Castro's supporters on the field of battle.[52] But this battle, caused by a breakdown of the patronage system, was preempted by other events. On June 23, 1846, just after he arrived in Santa Bárbara, Pío Pico received the urgent news that John Frémont had taken the town of Sonoma and was holding Mariano Guadalupe Vallejo his prisoner.

War: Resistance and Loyalty

Castro, it turns out, was right to have been suspicious of the Americans earlier that spring. The American government had begun sending expeditions to map the area, confident that Mexico's northern territory, from California through Texas, would soon belong to the United States. Frémont arrived at Sutter's Fort with his armed "Topographical Corps" of sixty men in January 1846, a month after the United States had voted to annex Texas. Refusing Castro's orders that they stay away from towns and ranches near the coast, Frémont and his men camped near settlements at San José, Santa Cruz, and the Salinas Valley, including the Hartnell ranch at Alisal. While there in early March, Frémont received orders from Castro to leave the province altogether, but the American responded instead by retreating to Gavilán Peak, on the road between Monterey and San Juan Bautista, where he hoisted the Stars and Stripes. On news that Castro had raised an army of two hundred to oust his men, Frémont fled for Oregon.[53]

In April, another suspicious-looking American arrived in Monterey: Archibald Gillespie, who claimed to be a merchant in search of a better climate to ease his chronic illness. In fact, he was an agent for the United States, and he carried instructions from President Buchanan to American merchant and consul Thomas Larkin. Larkin, thus appointed a "confidential agent" of the United States, was to assure Californians that Americans would not interfere in the province unless Mexico began hostilities, but also to encourage them to turn to their "sister republic," should they declare independence from Mexico.[54] The clear implication was that California would be occupied once war was declared, and Larkin was to persuade Californians to accept this inevitability. Gillespie then headed north with similar instructions for Frémont.

Larkin devised a course of action designed to bring California under the American flag without bloodshed. On April 20, 1846, he sent an official report to the U.S. national government in which he noted that "it would be sound policy to pension some of those high in Office, and influence, or give them a sinecure. They would thus gently and quietly carry many of their countrymen into their new circumstances."[55] Later interpretations of elite Californio attitudes and behavior during the war suggest that this plan was successful, and that elites were quick to surrender at the promise of favor and security. But during the war, Pablo, Francisco, and other members of the de la Guerra family acted as agents for resistance and California independence. At the same time, they began to present themselves to the American conquerors as representatives and mediators for all Californios.

Resistance began in Monterey on July 2, 1846, as Commodore Sloat of the Pacific Squadron sailed into the harbor. That day, military governor José Castro, as "quartermaster general," dashed off an urgent letter to Pablo de la Guerra, the customs administrator, requesting him to use his influence over family friend José Antonio Aguirre in order to get a loan of cash to carry on the war, "on the account of the duties that his ship will have to pay."[56] Citizens of Monterey waited four nervous days before Sloat finally raised the American flag over Monterey and made the official announcement of war, which had been declared between the United States and Mexico on May 13. "There were many armed boats filled with people who came ashore. They took possession without any resistance," remembered Angustias de la Guerra, who explained, "there was no garrison whatsoever."[57] Castro and the remaining military had already fled south to join Pico's forces and organize a joint resistance. And, as he had when Commodore Jones seized the port, Pablo de la Guerra refused to hand over the customs house and treasury. On July 13, he met with four other customs officers, and at Pablo's urging they resolved to resist and join Castro and Pico. Faced with an occupying army, he refused to give up the customs house flags and boats and escaped to the south.[58] Two days later, Commodore Stockton arrived in San Francisco to take over the Pacific Squadron and California's military command from an ailing Sloat.

By the time Pablo arrived in the south, Californians had been pulling their forces together for a few weeks, and Francisco de la Guerra had abandoned his role as mediator for that of resistance organizer. As soon as news of the Bear Flag Revolt hit Santa Bárbara on June 23, governor Pío Pico issued a proclamation of resistance and appointed Francisco to call men to arms, "Satisfied as I am, of the good reputation of which, with justice, you are considered among the inhabitants, as well as your credited enthusiasm for the well-being of the homeland."[59] The elder de la Guerra, a few days later, dipped into his personal treasury to loan the war effort four hundred pesos.[60] In other words, where the de la Guerra family had been using their local reputation and wealth to reconcile opposing factions within the ruling class, they now turned them into assets for a province-wide resistance to the invasion.

Even as they actively opposed the American conquest, the de la Guerra men attempted to project a public image of themselves to the Americans as moderates and mediators between the American forces and the more radical or militant Californios of all classes. This was an image that would become the hallmark of de la Guerra politics well into the American era, but it was not a role that came easily at first. Pablo de la Guerra, who would become the most adept of his generation in this later negotiation, found his first attempt at it a miserable failure. In part, this had to do with his reputation for hostility to Yankees, and his flight in July to aid the resistance, a confrontational stance known to the American forces who sailed south at the end of that month. But perhaps more importantly, the newcomers' sense of cultural superiority left them little understanding or respect for local patriarchal rule.[61] It was not until occupying forces understood this source of power that the de la Guerras could begin to reconstruct a space for themselves as elites within the new order.

So, when Stockton arrived at San Pedro on August 6, 1846, and found Pablo de la Guerra to be Castro's official representative, he treated the administrator of the customs house, the son of Santa Bárbara's patriarch, with contempt. Although Pablo swallowed his pride and suggested very conciliatory terms—cessation of hostilities, interim recognition of the American occupation, and the resignation of Castro and Pico—Stockton declined, with an insult, to suspend his operations and insisted that the Californios themselves raise the American flag. Pablo de la Guerra refused. Bancroft suggests that this was just what Stockton had been hoping for—a rejection, rather than negotiation—in order to avoid recognizing the local authorities and leaving them in power. If this is the case, he was successful, for Castro and Pico fled to Mexico the next day, leaving the de la Guerras, among others, to pick up the pieces. Stockton marched into an empty Los Angeles, stripped of government documents and furniture, and a few days later declared himself interim governor. "My word is at present the law of the land," he boasted to the president, "My person is more than regal."[62] His troops then rounded up the Californio officers who had retreated into the hills around the city; Pablo and Francisco along with their cousins in the ruling class gave their *parole*, or word of submission, and were released.[63] Soon after, Pablo left for Monterey on horseback.[64]

Up in Santa Bárbara, the de la Guerras faced similar contempt from the occupying Americans. On his way to take Los Angeles, Stockton had landed at Santa Bárbara on August 3, raised the American flag, and departed with all but a handful of men to hold the garrison, but this incursion into de la Guerra authority was a pinprick compared to the insults to come.[65] As Stockton was landing his troops at San Pedro, Frémont and his battalion were arriving by sea in San Diego, and after that town's surrender, a detachment of the California Battalion marched north to capture remaining Californio officers. Along the way, they stopped in Santa Bárbara and "requested" fresh horses; de la Guerra complied by sending his sons Francisco and Miguel to San Julián with an order for ten or twelve. Such a display of generosity, even under duress, should have been a commonly understood sign of the patriarch's command over resources, and the dependence of Americans upon him, but the following events revealed again how little the invaders respected these older hierarchies.

In court testimony later that month, José de la Guerra explained that although he had sent the order for horses, Frémont's men did not wait.

The mayordomo of Rancho San Julián, Gregorio López, testified that when the Second Division arrived at his house on the ranch, they read him orders in English, which he did not understand, and when he did not comply they forced him to his knees at gunpoint. López told the Americans defiantly "that he would die to protect the property in his charge," but under threat, delivered the horses up. Antonio Leiva, who had brought the order, testified that the soldiers took more than was offered, including the patriarch's own horse and saddle, and when he protested and asked for a receipt, one of the soldiers told Leiva that his boss was a "damned fool," addressed the ranch workers "as if they were hogs or bears," and explained that "they were enemies of the government and the troop could take anything and everything."[66] At this, they took Leiva at gunpoint to round up the horses. According to the American commander, de la Guerra had "deceived" them in the delivery of the horses, and as a consequence they felt entitled to take two for each man—forty-three in all, at their own count.[67] In the uncertainty of war, de la Guerra responded in the only way he knew would work to his advantage: an appeal to a Californio judge, who not coincidentally was also his relative by marriage. No records survive that record the outcome, but it is safe to assume that de la Guerra never received the "$6.00 per head" the Americans had promised him.

The tide soon turned in southern California, however, as Californios regrouped and mounted one of the most effective campaigns of the war against the United States. At the beginning of September 1846, Stockton left Los Angeles and Santa Bárbara in the hands of Archibald Gillespie and Theodore Talbot respectively.[68] Stockton had declared that Mexican institutions and laws should continue under the military occupation, but he also instituted a curfew, forbade the assembly of potential rebels, and ordered the search of private homes.[69] The conquest seemed to be well in hand; how shocking, then, to read dispatches from the south announcing that Gillespie had been forced to surrender Los Angeles on September 29. Soon, the entire southland from San Diego to San Luis Obispo was back under Californio control under Captain José Flores. De la Guerras in the south quickly joined forces with the rebels; when the junta departamental reconvened on October 26, Francisco de la Guerra took his accustomed seat, and in late November, Flores requested more monetary aid from the elder de la Guerra.[70] Cesareo Lataillade, the husband of youngest daughter María Antonia, came forward with the remarkable sum of $27,000.[71]

The Californios sustained their resistance in the autumn of 1846 with a combination of guerrilla warfare and the cooperation of local rancheros, who moved their livestock away from the coast and out of reach of the marching American armies.[72] And as Stockton moved his armies south to quell the uprising, prominent Californios escaped from Monterey to aid their southern relatives. Fearing such an action, the American occupying forces imprisoned Pablo and Miguel de la Guerra in early November without trial or charges and held them for several months.[73] Of course, this simply hardened the stance of the de la Guerras against the conquerors. The same American who had heard Pablo's anti-Yankee remarks before the war was present in Santa Bárbara to hear those of his father and brother during Pablo's imprisonment. "The Capt.," Streeter remembered, "complained bitterly of the injustices of the U.S. making war upon a much weaker nation than herself, and the seizure of Mexican territory." Francisco then joined the conversation to declare "that he had been born a Mexican and would remain one, regardless of the flag he might live under; that as long as he lived he would never cease to oppose the Americans in every manner possible."[74]

It is quite likely that post-war politics motivated William Streeter to discredit the de la Guerra political machine, which still held power in the 1870s, when he gave his account; nonetheless, this evidence seems accurate, and certainly Streeter was perceptive when he commented, "the old man had other reasons for disliking American occupation: he realized that it would deprive him of the authority and power he had long enjoyed . . . Nevertheless," he observed, "he never allowed his feelings to show themselves and always enjoined moderation and prudence upon his sons."[75] This public stance of "moderation and prudence," however it masked true feelings, eventually secured the de la Guerras a place in the new regime.

As the rainy season continued and the holidays approached, Frémont's forces marched back down the coast of California. The de la Guerras, fully aware of the threat drawing near, maintained a watchful eye on recent American arrivals and searched their houses for arms.[76] Americans who had not joined Californio compadrazgo and kin networks, or whose low-level occupations meant weaker ties to the local economy, came under special scrutiny. One such immigrant was George Nidever, an otter hunter from Tennessee, who, although married to a local woman of lower class, found himself arrested by the de la Guerras on suspicion of involvement with Frémont; they ordered him to pay an extra $200 duty on his freshly caught otter pelts. Nidever remembered that this demand gave rise to a curious situation: "Capt. de la Guerra was the only person in the place who had money and from him I obtained the $200, but he compelled me to leave him as security 15 otter skins."[77] On the promise that he would leave for Los Angeles, the de la Guerras then allowed the trapper to go home, but Francisco de la Guerra and his Carrillo cousin Raymundo returned that night with a party of men to take Nidever again.

Escaping to meet Frémont, the backwoodsman at last took his revenge on the family, whose father "was even at that time like a king in authority here." On arrival at Frémont's camp, Nidever complained of his treatment, and in response Frémont ordered his men to take the trapper along and identify those Californio homes he suspected of containing arms. "As a matter of course," Nidever recalled, "I led them first to the de la Guerra house." As they entered the town on December 27, 1846, Frémont's troops found deserted streets and boarded-up houses, the only exception being the de la Guerra home, which remained open to receive the opposition.[78] On the porch stood José de la Guerra, his youngest son, twenty-one-year-old Antonio María, and Cesareo Lataillade, his youngest daughter's husband. Behind them, other members of the extended family and their servants presented a solid front. At last, invading Americans began to understand and recognize the nature of the local power of the de la Guerras.

Nidever stepped forward, and with the American soldiers at his back, told de la Guerra that he had come to return the favor and search the captain's house. De la Guerra stood his ground and refused. The American lieutenant had this declaration translated for him, and then told the de la Guerras that if every door, box, and trunk were not opened for him voluntarily, he would break them down. No doubt seething at the affront, de la Guerra allowed the soldiers to search the house, but even in this capitulation the patriarch refused to humble himself personally, handing his large chain of keys to son Antonio María. The Americans found no arms, no ammunition, not even saddles and tack for the de la Guerra horses—nothing that could be considered war materiel, but "a large quantity of gold and silver coin." "The de la Guerras never forgave me for thus humiliating them," Nidever said later.[79] The humiliation for José de la Guerra came from his inability to prevent the invasion of his very household, which as patriarch he had the responsibility to protect and defend. Yet the incident did help the family eventually earn recognition among both the Californio community and American occupying forces as the leaders and representatives of the town, proud even in defeat.

During the fall of 1846, the battles that were fought on California soil cost the local population only a few deaths, and brought them victory over General Kearny's forces, recently arrived from New Mexico, at San Pascual near San Diego on December 6. But by the time Frémont marched into Santa Bárbara, it was clear that the war effort would be too difficult to sustain without reinforcements from Mexico. Knowing this, perhaps, and wishing to avoid further bloodshed, the widow Bernarda Ruiz paid Frémont a visit. A first cousin of José de la Guerra's late wife, Bernarda had been a strong partisan of Juan Alvarado's in the 1830s. She now did what she could to sway the American to make peace on terms favorable to the Californios. "Naturally," remembered Frémont, "her character and sound reasoning had its influence with me."[80] A few days later, on January 3, 1847, Frémont and his men pulled up stakes to join Kearny and Stockton for the last hostilities of the war.

At last, the Californios were forced to sue for peace. On January 11, 1847, Francisco de la Guerra and Francisco Rico met with John Frémont outside of Los Angeles. The Treaty of Cahuenga, signed on January 13 and influenced by Bernarda Ruiz's appeal, generously assured Californios of the rights of American citizens: life, property, and movement. In exchange, the men pledged to lay down their arms for the duration of the war.[81] Santa Bárbarans enjoyed a brief period of self-rule before three companies of Colonel Jonathan Stevenson's 1st New York Volunteers landed on April 8, 1847, for seventeen months of military rule.

"With All This Dancing We Are Anxious": California Women, American Men, and National Loyalties

At the beginning of 1847, as the American forces were finally subduing the southern insurrection, First Lieutenant William Tecumseh Sherman sailed into Monterey harbor with Company F, Third Artillery. Accompanied by First Lieutenant Edward Ord and his brother Dr. James Ord, Sherman was greeted with news "that war was then going on at Los Angeles, that the whole country was full of guerrillas." "We imagined," he later recalled, "that we should have to debark and begin fighting at once."[82] Instead, the twenty-six-year-old Sherman found a local population apparently reconciled to their fate—indeed, happy to greet it. "The girls," he noticed, seemed especially eager to get to know the smartly dressed American officers; they "were very fond of dancing, and they did dance gracefully and well. Every Sunday, regularly, we had a *baile*, or dance, and sometimes interspersed through the week."[83] Some wags composed a song to commemorate the accommodating women of California:

> Already the señoritas
> Speak English with finesse.

"Kiss me!" say the Yankees,
The girls all answer "Yes!"[84]

The image of compliant and welcoming señoritas played a key role
in the American justifications of conquest. "Spanish ladies" who welcomed their conquerors began their cultural existence in the Mexican
era, embedded in the accounts of American men who married Californio women. Writing for an American audience, these men hoped to
make their wives respectable, yet distance themselves from what other
Americans perceived as the "degenerate" mixed-race population of Mexico. In published memoirs and travel reports, these men cultivated a notion of the flirtatious yet virtuous and industrious Spanish beauty. Alfred
Robinson, married to Anita de la Guerra, distinguished in his 1846 account between Californio men, "generally indolent and addicted to many
vices," and the women, like his wife, marked by "chastity, industrious
habits, and correct deportment."[85] American men described the daughters of elite, landowning families as eagerly awaiting the blue-eyed men
(such as themselves) who would save them from a life of drudgery, shack-
led to lazy and dark-skinned Mexican men—men who lacked the intelligence and moral strength to develop California properly.[86]

Anita sat out the war in New York, but her sister Angustias, rich and
well placed, surely attended the balls described by Sherman and seems to
embody the stereotype perfectly. On the eve of her homeland's conquest
by the United States in 1846, Angustias was thirty-one, a mother of
seven, and still lived in Monterey with her husband, Manuel Jimeno.
During the war and occupation, Angustias gained a reputation among
the Americans stationed at Monterey as a generous and welcoming lady.
Sherman not only danced with her, but he and the Ord brothers boarded
in her house as the war drew to a close, all four becoming close friends.
She even nursed an ailing officer, Colville Minor, in her home in the summer of 1847. Lieutenant Edward Ord comforted the young officer's family
after his death in August, assuring them that he had been tended by "the
best and kindest lady in Monterey . . . day and night, like a Mother, she
was by his side."[87] Three years after Jimeno's death in the early 1850s, Angustias married the lieutenant's brother, Dr. James Ord. From all appearances, Angustias seems to have been willing to abandon loyalties to her
homeland in exchange for handsome dancing partners in uniform and
the promise of greater wealth and security under the United States.

Yet if we read her own accounts—a journal kept during the war, a narrative given to an American historian in 1878, and memoirs dictated to her
daughter in 1880, Angustias presents herself not as a willing accomplice to

American conquest but as an intelligent and self-aware woman attempting to negotiate her place under rapidly changing circumstances.[88] Her actions during the war years built upon her earlier experiences as the wife of a political insider—someone who was clever enough to manipulate the expectations and constraints of patriarchy while using the resources of her class to push the boundaries of respectable female behavior. This woman of the elites, it turns out, was no stereotype, but she expressed instead a complicated mixture of resistance to conquest and to Mexican men, an enjoyment of her racial and class privileges within California's patriarchal society, and an ambivalence about Americans. She claimed the right to speak, to act, and to tell her own story.

The most striking aspect of Angustias's accounts of her own life is how much she emerges as a key actor in a wartime struggle presumed to be taking place among men. Bancroft discovered this when he sent Thomas Savage to interview her in 1878 for information about the public action of her male relatives. Instead, Angustias told Savage stories like this one: during the height of the southern resistance, she bravely hid a wounded Californian soldier from the American military. At that time, she was living in Monterey, tending to a newborn while her husband was away from home. Her brothers Pablo and Miguel were political prisoners in the Monterey jail. According to Angustias's testimony, when she got word that the wounded soldier, José Antonio Chávez, was hiding nearby, she visited the jail to ask her brother Pablo for advice. "I was so angry with the Americans," she remembered, "for mistreating my brothers and keeping them imprisoned for no rhyme or reason." But when Pablo doubted her ability to pull off a deception, she remembered, "I angrily asked my brother if he really believed the Yankees could find someone I had hidden."[89]

Angry at the Americans, and angry at her brother, Angustias devised a scheme that, like her successful smuggling ruse of the previous year, exploited cultural assumptions about male honor and female propriety. "I did not tell anybody about my plan," she said, "and nobody suspected a thing." Assisted by the other women in the house, Angustias hid Chávez in rolled-up blankets and placed her new baby on this makeshift couch in her room. American soldiers surrounded the house, then forced their way into this very private space. The lieutenant in command held a pistol to her head, but she feigned innocence. When the officer apologized for frightening her and asked for a chair, she coolly replied "that nothing frightened me and he could go rest in his own home, because only family and friends were allowed to rest in my room." After the danger had passed, Chávez made his break "dressed as a woman."[90] In the telling of this one incident, Angustias pointed to the inability of Californio men like her brothers to act, the disrespectful behavior of the American military, and her own cleverness and courage in the face of crisis.

When she spoke to Bancroft's representative in 1878, Angustias noted that the incompetence of Californio men had been visible in the early 1840s, when she and her husband found themselves frozen out of patronage under Castro's regime. Californio officials, she remarked, constantly fought each other instead of uniting to fight the Americans, and they weakened the state by plundering the treasury. In particular, she linked General Castro's strategy of putting large numbers of his supporters and dependents on the military payroll to California's ultimate inability to protect itself from conquest. "Few of those officers," she bitterly recalled to Bancroft, "served their country when the time came to defend it against foreign invasion. The majority of them did about as much work as a figurehead on a ship."[91]

Clearly, by the 1870s, Angustias was ready to blame the conquest on weaknesses in a Californio political system based on patronage and a paternal understanding of power. But in her private journal, written during the war, and in the memoirs given to her daughter in 1880, de la Guerra did not blame the conquest on Californio men. In her journal, she instead put "all the blame" on California's long distance from the central government in Mexico City, and concluded that the loss of the territory was "Destiny!"[92] Only her dictation to Bancroft reinforced American notions of incompetent Californio leadership; either she had reconsidered, or she had altered her message to fit her audience. But in no account, even to Bancroft, did Angustias claim that she or any other "Spanish lady" preferred American to Mexican rule, however weak and corrupt. "The taking of the country did not please the Californios at all," she declared, "and least of all the women."[93]

During the war, Angustias struggled to imagine what the conquest would mean for her and for her family. In her journal, she staked out a private place to record public events, jotting down her personal hopes and fears, moments of vanity, and small triumphs. The journal begins on January 6, 1846, when Californians were still hotly debating their territory's possible prospects under England, France, or the United States. The last entry is dated August 21, 1847, six months after the Californio resistance surrendered at Cahuenga. She made it clear that she had the right to an opinion in an entry of May 1846. Just before the Bear Flag Revolt, Angustias wrote of her role in a debate among leading citizens that took place in her home. Some argued for independence, others for

British protection. Her English brother-in-law "Guillermo" Hartnell argued that California should become part of the United States because only that nation could guarantee equal rights to all its citizens and unlimited opportunities to their children. Angustias watched the debate, then jumped in herself: "'Don Guillermo is right,' I said, because I was listening to everything."[94]

At first, Angustias devoted much of her journal to musings on the qualities of Americans and the American style of government. In July 1846, after Frémont's men had taken Sonoma, she fumed, "If the Americans are going to come, let them come, just as long as they send decent people who know how to treat us more reasonably than Frémont did. He arrived wanting to give us orders."[95] A few days later she was more hopeful: "We should judge them based on those who came in the past and married native Californio women. When one thinks about everything that has been done by the Americans who came here before, who knows—with time, California may be the envy of the world."[96]

Only a month later, though, Stockton raised the American flag over Santa Bárbara, and Angustias began to consider what might be lost. In her journal, she carefully catalogued all the ranches in her family, their extent and ownership. On receiving a new plaid dress from Britain at the beginning of September, she reveled in California's ideal circumstance: free of the population density and factories of Boston and Liverpool, but enjoying the manufactured goods sent from their ports. She wondered "how the people who come from those big cities feel when they see us scattered about and each person in the possession of leagues of land?"[97] In other words, Angustias had no special interest in transforming her homeland into an American-style industrial landscape; indeed, she feared the threat such a transformation would pose to her family's commanding economic position in the ranching and trading economy and to her own identity as a ranching woman. Considering this upheaval and the imminent birth of her daughter, she remarked, "There is something tragic about the sadness that I have been feeling. It seems like the sorrowful death of an era!"[98] At first ambivalent about the tumultuous changes of these years, Angustias grew increasingly convinced that they would usher in loss and dislocation.

By the beginning of 1847, as the southern resistance came to an end and Frémont captured Santa Bárbara, Angustias began to accept California's fate. In her journal, she recorded her delight in the balls sponsored by the American military officers, although a current of uneasiness continued to undercut her enjoyment. "With all this laughing and dancing," she remarked, "we are all anxious because we do not know how we, the owners of all this, will end up!"[99] As Angustias described it, dancing itself was no escape from the war. The world of dances and balls had been, in the American version of the story, the occasion for dashing American men to make personal conquests over the hearts of flirtatious Spanish maidens. But in Angustias's accounts, spaces that these men marked as private or domestic emerged as important political arenas where women astutely defined and commented on the boundaries of elite society, particularly at the unstable moment of conquest.

In her version of international relations, Angustias began by noting in her journal the significance of Monterey's elite dancing parties for the events of 1842. That October, Commodore Jones had forced Monterey to surrender to the United States before realizing his mistake a day later. After the restoration of the capital, Jones and his officers were eager to make amends and pay courtesies to the Californios, and Angustias remembered herself as judge and receiver of such protocol. An official reception for the Pacific Squadron came next, but Angustias insisted that this event occurred after Jones himself had left the harbor. "Some people have said that a dance was held in Monterey for Commodore Jones and his officers after he returned the plaza," she remarked. "If such a dance was given, I did not know about it, which would have been impossible because of my standing in Monterey."[100]

As the war between Mexico and the United States drew nearer, the interactions between Americans and Mexicans at local balls took on even greater significance. On April 19, 1846, as Pablo and Francisco de la Guerra consulted with José Castro in Monterey, American consul Thomas Larkin hosted a dance. "All the families attended," Angustias recalled, "because we had been told that a refined and well-bred young man would be at the dance."[101] But Angustias soon suspected that Archibald Gillespie, supposedly visiting California for his health, was instead "an emissary who was up to no good," and she brought her suspicions to the attention of General Castro, suggesting that Gillespie "should be arrested and sent off to Mexico. But Castro told us that we were thinking badly of a man who was ill. He accused us, and all women in general, of thinking badly of others . . . Our response to Castro was that women almost always hit the nail on the head—more often than men do."[102] As it turned out, Gillespie was indeed an agent from Secretary of State Buchanan, and in relating this incident, Angustias was able to show her own abilities in detecting an impostor, and to point out how less socially skillful Californio men made mistakes that could play into the hands of their conquerors.[103]

The post-conquest world of Monterey society, after the failure of Californio armed resistance, appears to have been a space where Californio women could have an even greater impact on the course of conquest than their male relatives did. It was again at public dances and parties, in homes that took in American boarders, and at the bedsides of dying American officers that women like Angustias could take the initiative to integrate American officers into Californio elite society, and in return assure their own continuing visibility in the post-conquest world. Grateful for the comparative lack of bloodshed in the Monterey conquest, Angustias herself remarked in her journal on the key role of Californio women in integrating American officers into the ruling class, and the resentment this created among their brothers and husbands:

> The Americans did not come here with cannons blazing. The first people they conquered were the women, and that is why it worked out so beautifully for them. There were lots of unhappy people, including many of my relatives. But they have always wanted to give orders, and it is going poorly for them.[104]

Alienated from her brothers, she confided, "It is hard to believe that such envy and jealousy can exist in people who were brought forth into this world from the same mother's womb."[105]

Yet, two days after confessing that Americans had "conquered" the women of Monterey, Angustias had another encounter with American officers at a dance. In both her journal and in the memoirs given to her daughter, Angustias told with great relish a story of that night, showing how even flirtation could be a political act of resistance. In February 1847, just after the fall of the southern resistance and the arrival of Sherman and the Ord brothers, she attended an officer's ball. Since it was held during Carnival, she armed herself with blown eggs filled with tinsel and glitter, called cascarones. As she told her daughter, "A certain colonel [Richard Barnes Mason] . . . had distinguished himself by his skill in removing arrows from his body from fighting the Indians. I found out about this from the American officers and I set out to see if I could break an eggshell on him." Drawing his attention to her right hand, she outsmarted him by planting the cascarón on his forehead with her left. "I told him, 'You were able to escape from the Indians but not from a clever woman!'" she remembered. "While we were engaged in this 'conflict,' everyone drew closer to see who would triumph. There was much applause. My pride had been satisfied."[106] In her journal she added, "ay! ay! what fun!"[107]

On one level, this incident can be dismissed as an act of superficial conceit, the lighthearted prank of a very privileged woman, flirting with the American soldiers who had just overrun her country. But it can also be read as a sharp comment on the power relationships between her and the American officers, made in the acceptable space of Carnival role reversals. The American officer may have defeated her people on the battlefield, but in her world, she still had the upper hand, literally. Although she could effect no lasting change, she did get her point across to the embarrassed officer, who was forced to spend the rest of the evening covered in glitter. Deftly using the feminine spaces of bedroom, sala, and ballroom, Angustias hid soldiers, jumped into political debates, and exposed spies during the war. After the war, she employed those same spaces to integrate the new elites into her Monterey society, reminding them of her status and independence.

What are we to make of these contradictions? At some moments, Angustias seemed to be open to the takeover, dancing with American officers. At other times, she said she risked her life to oppose it. She criticized Californio men and then relieved them of blame for the conquest. Neither mindlessly accommodating for herself or for her class, Angustias showed political awareness and action, even in contexts that seemed private and apolitical. Chafing at the limitations Californio society placed on women, she used her hard-won public voice to defend the aspects of the old Californio society she considered worth saving: a ranching economy unscarred by factories or overcrowding, marked by generosity, by loyalty to family, and by personal relationships based on respect. Smart, sarcastic, and proud, she claimed for herself a central role in the new American regime. In the end, she may have criticized Californios and befriended Americans, but she stayed rooted in a stable self-identity as an elite Californiana.

During the war, Anita and her husband, Alfred, lived thousands of miles away from Monterey; their sister Angustias could not imagine such a life of isolation from California's politics and high society. After attending a ball with the American officers in Monterey, Angustias reflected, "I have always been so fond of dancing, that I don't know what I would do were I transported like my sister Anita to Boston, where one has to say prayers and sing hymns all day Sunday."[108] Yet Anita's marriage to Yankee Alfred Robinson, as it had given her the chance for an education, also put her in a unique position to influence her family's destiny under the conquering armies of the United States. Was the strategy of intermarriage finally about to backfire?

In April 1847, Captain Francis J. Lippitt of the 1st New York Volunteers, Company F, caught his first glimpse of the conquered Mexican town of Santa Bárbara as his ship sailed between the Channel Islands and the south-facing harbor. Unlike William Tecumseh Sherman, Lippitt had every hope of being received cordially by the most prominent local families, for, "having become acquainted with a Mrs. Robinson" in New York, he carried in his pocket her letters of introduction to her father and to her brother Pablo.[109] Anita, through her husband, had made the acquaintance of this American military officer on his way to occupy her homeland, and had offered him a personal recommendation, the proper entry to local society. But as we have seen with Angustias, Californian women rarely fit the stereotype of meek compliance, or even eager welcome. These letters are the only indication of Anita's feelings; apart from them, it is difficult to know to what extent she supported or disapproved of the American occupation.[110] Anita wrote no letters directly to her brothers or father to sway them on political issues. Her sister Teresa, married to Englishman William Hartnell, did not record any opinions in the 1840s, although her husband is on record as supporting an American takeover. By the 1870s, however, Teresa consistently referred to Americans as "foreigners," and asserted that "my grandparents and other relatives" were the "true founders of this country."[111]

Although Anita and Teresa appear to have done little to facilitate the conquest of their homeland, their husbands made a more concerted effort. At first, Robinson and Hartnell showed no signs of infidelity to the family or to Mexico, and over the many years of their marriages, they had gained the trust of the de la Guerra family. In the early 1840s, as the pressure from the United States built and war loomed on the horizon, both men reassured the de la Guerras of their loyalty. In 1842, for example, when Commodore Jones mistakenly took the harbor of Monterey, Hartnell served as official interpreter to demand an explanation and apology on behalf of the Californian government.[112] Robinson, in letters to his father-in-law from New York, worked even harder to maintain a face of allegiance to his adopted homeland on the opposite coast. In January 1845, for example, he wrote to de la Guerra of his opposition to the annexation of Texas, recounted his and Anita's acquaintance with "many Spaniards from Spain, Havana, and South America," and assured him that "we are still members of the Catholic Church and all our children are members of the same faith."[113] Apparently, Robinson's political views were sincere, and rested on his allegiance to the Whig party, which opposed annexation of either Texas or Oregon. A few months later he wrote to California's American consul Thomas Larkin that thousands were preparing to head west, and commented ironically, "our *democratic* disposition is getting to be rather *aristocratic,* and the *people* require an extension of freedom e'en to the acquisition of the whole northern continent."[114]

Yet at this very moment, Robinson was preparing his memoirs of California for publication—memoirs that carried a very different message. *Life in California*, which first appeared for sale in New York in 1846, is an unmistakable call to fellow Americans for colonization of the Mexican province. "In this age of 'Annexation,'" he concluded, "why not extend the 'area of freedom' by the annexation of California? . . . Everything would improve; population would increase; consumption would be greater, and industry would follow."[115] As war appeared imminent, many foreign husbands like Robinson and Hartnell began to take active roles to persuade their relatives of the same, as Californios up and down the coast engaged in deep discussion of their fate. In May 1846, for example, prior to the Bear Flag Revolt, Angustias recorded in her journal that Hartnell had strongly advised "all our important friends" to support an American protectorate.[116] After American warships occupied Monterey harbor that summer, and while the southern resistance was coming together, Angustias noted that many Americans married to native women, including her brother-in-law Robinson, "all good Yankees, tell us on the sly that we are not going to regret it if we belong to the U.S. government."[117]

Once the war was underway, Robinson became more vocal and insistent, hoping to head off any Californio resistance through his connections to the de la Guerras. By the time Lippitt arrived in Santa Bárbara in April 1847, Anita's letter of introduction in his pocket, the de la Guerras had been expecting the captain for some time. On September 20, 1846, Robinson had written to Pablo that four frigates were about to set sail from New York, with munitions, food, and troops to occupy California. "The officers of the greater part are persons of good families," he assured Pablo, "and graduates of the military institution, 'West Point.' Two or three of them bear letters of introduction to our father."[118] In this and later wartime correspondence, Robinson tried to gain Californio sympathies by admitting regret at the bloodshed of war, and expressing chagrin on hearing news of Frémont's outrages at his father-in-law's house and ranch, but nevertheless he counseled his brother-in-law to think of the bottom line. "Never have motives of sorrow," he wrote a few months after the start of the war, "for the great change in the administration from the

Mexicans to that of the Yankees, for all will be for the better and everyone's property will increase threefold in value."[119] American husbands like
Robinson may not have fully convinced their wives, but they had every
hope that their male relatives could be swayed to support conquest. Yet
Robinson, like the colonel with glitter on his head, would find his California in-laws a hard sell.

Never Reconciled: Reinventing Patriarchy under Occupation

When Companies A, B, and F of the 1st New York Volunteers landed to
begin military occupation of Santa Bárbara that April, Captain Lippitt of
Company F could expect that his New York acquaintances Alfred and
Anita Robinson would be his ticket to collaboration with the town's elite.
Unfortunately for Lippitt, as one of his men recalled, "the de la Guerras,
who were the leading family, never got reconciled to us."[120] Despite the
apparent efforts of Alfred to make Yankees of the de la Guerras, and to
ally them with conquering Americans, the de la Guerra brothers resisted
collaboration. Over the course of the seventeen-month occupation, the
de la Guerras did resume their leading position by taking up posts in the
American government, but in so doing they walked a careful line to retain a separate political identity. Lingering undercurrents of Californio
resistance ultimately culminated in the Cañón Perdido, or Lost Cannon
Affair, a year after Lippitt's arrival, serving to underscore their entrenched
authority and the tenuous hold of the American military. In these critical months, the de la Guerras learned to reconstitute Mexican patterns
of paternal authority both within the Californio community and under
the American system of government.

From the start, things did not go well for Captain Lippitt. On the day
his troops made their way ashore that April, Lippitt took a dunking in the
surf and badly injured his leg. Looking "somewhat like a drowned rat," according to one of his men, the captain was overseeing landing operations
when Pablo de la Guerra approached from the shore, "dressed in full uniform," and lodged a formal complaint against the occupation on behalf of
the town.[121] Lippitt replied that he was obeying orders and intended to
remain, but hoped that he could do so on friendly terms with the people
of Santa Bárbara. Lippitt soon set up his headquarters opposite the de la
Guerra house, perhaps to display his understanding of the family's significance, and as soon as he could walk again, tried once more to make a
good impression on them. Bringing the letters of introduction he believed would open the door to amicable conquest, Lippitt called on his
new neighbors but again met with rebuff. "Don José," he remembered,

"received the letters very stiffly at the front door without asking me in." A week later, the de la Guerras fulfilled their social obligations by inviting Lippitt to a formal supper at the house, treating him, he remembered, with "the most punctilious politeness . . . This was the only time I was ever in the house," he later recalled, still smarting from the rebuff. "Although, as in duty bound, I called and left my card, I was never invited to any of their weekly soirées musicales."[122] Isolated from the town patriarch, Captain Lippitt remained a critical representative of the American regime, particularly after July 4, 1847, when Companies A and B departed and Lippitt's Company F took over military rule alone.

The de la Guerras, of course, had their own reasons for disregarding Alfred and Anita's encouragements and for holding the military government at a polite but firm distance. Over the last five years, newly arriving Americans had shown plainly how they coveted Californian lands, and how little they respected Californio traditions of authority. During the war, the family had suffered personal insults—stolen horses, a house search at gunpoint, and the imprisonment of two sons without charges or trial. Pablo in particular had reason to hold a grudge: his five months in jail had interrupted plans for his wedding to Josefa Moreno, the niece of José Castro.[123] Nor had the de la Guerra sons-in-law been very persuasive. Indeed, Robinson himself had undermined his own position with his wife's family with the publication of *Life in California.* Intended for an American audience, it not only baldly called for California's annexation to the United States but also sharply criticized the ability of Californio men to govern their own homeland. Teresa recalled heated discussion of the work when it hit the province and her brother Pablo's own opinion that "Señor Robinson's narrative was quite biased."[124]

It is within this context of distrust and resentment that the de la Guerra family carefully tread a path between cooperation and resistance during military occupation, participating in the American government without fully recognizing its right to govern them. They first did so by securing a leading role in Santa Bárbara's civil government. On May 9, 1847, shortly after the New York Volunteers landed to establish American military rule, Pablo de la Guerra and his cousin Luis Carrillo were elected first and second alcaldes, respectively, of the Santa Bárbara district.[125] According to a proclamation issued by military governor General Stephen Kearny on March 1, Mexican laws that did not conflict with the U.S. constitution were to remain in effect until the war's end and the establishment of legal government in California. The position of the alcalde, then, carried over into the American era as the only judicial post in the territory under the governor, with broad authority over criminal and civil cases, plus its usual executive and legislative roles.[126] The position carried over, that is—not the men serving. The governor reserved the right to appoint new alcaldes, and even those elected required his approval. Every American military governor took full advantage of this power. Throughout the conquered province, while some Californios were allowed to continue in office, many found themselves displaced by American naval officers under the arrogant Stockton, and then by civilians under his rival, Kearny.[127] The American governors thus had the power to keep close watch over local government.

Despite this apparent stranglehold of civil government by the American military, powerful Californios with strong ties to the local community, like the de la Guerras, could assert authority. Governor Kearny, a thirty-five-year veteran frontier officer, gave official approval to Pablo de la Guerra and Luis Carrillo's election, the only other requirement for holding office being an oath to uphold the U.S. constitution.[128] They refused.[129] Yet so strong was their perceived power over Santa Bárbara's Californio community, and so great the American fear of local resistance, that de la Guerra and Carrillo were permitted, even encouraged, to serve as alcaldes for the rest of the year.[130] The most important concession came a month after their election, at the change of military governor from Kearny to Virginia-born Richard Barnes Mason, another longtime frontier officer and the unfortunate victim of a cascarón attack from Pablo's sister Angustias in Monterey the previous February. "In the present state of affairs in California," the new governor conceded in June 1847, the alcaldes served neither the United States nor Mexico, but only California. Would Pablo, a "good man," he pleaded, "continue to California those good services which I know you are so capable of performing"?[131]

During their term, through the end of 1847, alcaldes Pablo de la Guerra and Luis Carrillo decided criminal cases and settled disputes over business contracts and land titles. In most cases, it appears that they continued to enforce pre-conquest law and community standards of behavior. Significantly, Pablo upheld the "paternal authority" of Don Miguel Cordero over the movement and labor of his fourteen-year-old son Juan, ordering the runaway to return from Los Angeles.[132] They also challenged the right of the American military courts to try locals, protesting that Captain Lippitt had overstepped his authority in charging two Californio civilian men with using "seductive words" on American camp women. Governor Mason agreed. Attempted seduction, Mason argued

Josefa Moreno. Santa Barbara Historical Museum.

that August, amounted to "civil resistance" to the occupation but posed no military threat.[133] Perhaps Pablo de la Guerra and his father were aware of this irony: José de la Guerra, the highest military authority in the region, had been accustomed in his day to defend the military fuero against civilian challenges, but his son now fought for civil government against an occupying military. What they had in common was an understanding that they shared with their subjects: "town fathers" had the right to settle local disputes.

As the Americans consolidated power state-wide heading into 1848, however, they clamped down on such compromises.[134] Governor Mason, despite his desire for local elites to manage and control local resistance, now insisted that the Santa Bárbara alcaldes swear loyalty to the United States and recognize the governor's authority. The de la Guerras, in turn, would not accept a post under these conditions. Throughout the year, two new local elections were called, and failed, as de la Guerras refused to run or serve, and other citizens protested the legality of the process.[135] By this point, only a handful of Californios continued to serve as alcaldes throughout the territory. In this moment of instability, their cousin Pedro Carrillo moved in to break the domination of the de la Guerra family over Santa Bárbara politics. In February 1848, Pedro accepted Governor Mason's appointment as alcalde and swore loyalty to the United States. The de la Guerras had preserved their perceived autonomy, but for the first time their principles cost them official roles in territorial and local governance.[136]

The new Santa Bárbara alcalde, Pedro Catarino Carrillo, was a nephew and godson of José de la Guerra's late wife, María Antonia Carrillo.[137] From his blood and spiritual kinship with the de la Guerras, Pedro Carrillo might have been expected to support their efforts to preserve Californio property and political autonomy in Santa Bárbara. But Carrillo, who had been educated in Hawaii and Boston, chose to risk losing de la Guerra protection to achieve his own alliance with the American authorities and the independent power that might give him. Santa Bárbara's crisis of authority came to a head in April 1848 with what has come to be known as the Lost Cannon Affair, a sequence of events that exposed the ragged edges of de la Guerra dominance while providing the family with the opportunity to reclaim public and American recognition of that authority.

By the spring of 1848, Captain Lippitt had given up all hope of an invitation to soirees at the de la Guerra house. In fact, he was something of a nervous wreck, constantly on the alert for signs of resistance and hints of war.[138] Taking advantage of the skittish Captain Lippitt, Alcalde Pedro Carrillo began his campaign to curry American favor and damage the position of his cousins. De la Guerra men and their associates, Carrillo quietly told the Americans, had been overheard in a local tavern hatching a counter-revolt. When questioned, Francisco de la Guerra of Santa Bárbara and Andrés Pico of Los Angeles protested that they had simply been planning an expedition against suspected cattle and horse thieves, authorized on April 3 by Colonel Jonathan Drake Stevenson in Los Angeles.[139]

On April 5, 1848, the stakes grew dramatically higher. A six-pound cannon belonging to the wrecked brig *Elizabeth* disappeared from the beach at Santa Bárbara. At last, American authorities were convinced that the rumors of conspiracy might have substance. On April 12, Lieutenant William Tecumseh Sherman, now performing administrative duties in between dances in Monterey, wrote on behalf of the governor to revoke Pico and de la Guerra's authority to enroll and arm men "for any purpose."[140] Sherman wrote to Captain Lippitt the same day, explaining, "but one use can be made of that gun, and that a hostile one towards us." The ranchero expedition against the horse thieves came to an abrupt end, an indirect casualty of Pedro Carrillo's whispered campaign against his cousins. "You must already know about the steps taken here in the last days in order to organize a regular expedition," Francisco wrote to Pico, "and the ridiculous and flimsy reason that ruined it." Captain Lippitt, he reported, "together with Don Pedro Carrillo," had written to the governor, "making us appear suspects and instilling him with suspicion that the campaign under consideration could take on the object of a revolution...It will be very distressing if the Indians go on enjoying their liberty to steal, and we remain passive spectators to the destruction of our ranchos, just because of calumny."[141]

With the mysterious disappearance of a cannon, however, what started as Pedro Carrillo's potentially effective attempt to weaken the reputations of the de la Guerras backfired. Over the next month, Lippitt's investigations into the suspected conspiracy brought the tactics of rumor and scandal into the harsh light of public scrutiny. In so doing, those who employed such tactics were exposed to the consequences, the retribution of the de la Guerras, who ultimately emerged even more powerful than before.

Captain Lippitt held his first hearing on the issue on April 18. "About three or four weeks ago," he reported to his superiors, "Don Pedro, First Alcalde of Santa Bárbara, informed me that at a meeting which took place in the commercial house of one Camarillo in Santa Bárbara, certain individuals spoke about a plan." According to the "plan," Lippitt said, the Californios would surprise and disarm American soldiers who accompanied the supposed expedition to capture horse thieves. Meanwhile, other Californios would take the relatively undefended garrison. Lippitt named the conspirators: Francisco de la Guerra, his brother Pablo, Antonio Rodríguez, Juan Ayala, and José "Chato" Lugo.[142]

When Lippitt interviewed his informants for the record, however, he found them suddenly vague and reluctant to confirm this story. José Genaro Alvarez, for example, the clerk at the tavern, swore he only heard the accused men talking about a horse race and attempts to foil horse rustlers.[143] Pedro Carrillo insisted in his testimony that he had not even believed this rumor and that he had "told Captain Lippitt to pay no attention to these conversations." He also described a much longer chain of rumor, and at each step a relative and rival to the de la Guerra family. The original source, Juan Rodríguez, had informed his mother Bernarda Ruiz, who had told cousin José Carrillo, who passed along the information to his brother Pedro.[144] Juan Rodríguez and Bernarda Ruiz, however, denied having heard or said anything.[145] José Carrillo told the court that Bernarda had begged him to keep quiet as well, since "the hijos del país would want to kill" her son Juan for informing on them.[146] By forcing him to testify, Pedro Carrillo objected, Lippitt was betraying his promises "that the whole matter would remain between us, and that he would communicate it to no one."[147] No doubt, Carrillo's family network of allies and informants expected to use gossip to loosen the hold the de la Guerras appeared to have on American authorities. Instead, Lippitt's investigations uncovered the backstage strategy and exposed disenfranchised townsfolk and cousins to reprisals. Such individuals, rival gente de razón enmeshed in de la Guerra godparent and family networks, had little choice but to deny the gossip and presumably return to the protection of de la Guerra authority.[148]

Meanwhile, the investigation into the lost cannon and into the limits of de la Guerra leadership continued at another level. In a series of letters, William Tecumseh Sherman and Francisco de la Guerra sparred over responsibility for the investigation—Sherman singling out the de la Guerras and blackmailing them for information, and Francisco de la Guerra strategically arguing ignorance and his lack of official authority in the matter. The first shot came from Sherman. In a letter of April 12, he informed Captain Lippitt that Governor Mason was "strongly disposed to seize some of the Chief men of Santa Bárbara and hold them as hostages until the gun is returned."[149] Enclosed was a letter of the same date addressed to Francisco de la Guerra, his chosen representative of these "Chief men," warning him to find out who stole the gun and why, or "some influential men in your midst will have to suffer a penalty."[150]

In reply, Francisco de la Guerra expressed surprise that he should serve as the source of information, "because I am as ignorant and perhaps more so than you about its whereabouts." He went on to challenge

Sherman for holding a private citizen responsible for the behavior of others. "I am convinced," he argued, "that this commitment will be carried out more thoroughly by the authorities here whose obligation it is."[151] In other words, by refusing to accept official posts within the American occupation government, the de la Guerras had placed themselves out of the reach of legal obligation to cooperate, while they retained their unofficial but universally understood role as town fathers. Even blackmail would not force them to investigate or testify for the Americans. "I see that many influential persons in these environs will have to suffer a penalty," wrote Francisco, "but this, Sir, is not in my power to remedy."[152]

Various accounts circulated of what might have happened to the cannon—perhaps it had been taken aboard a passing ship, or the *Elizabeth*'s crew had accidentally dropped it in the surf, or it had been taken by oxcart to Los Angeles.[153] Most were proved wrong when it was discovered ten years later, buried in the sand on the beach in Santa Bárbara. Although its story remains a mystery, José E. García gave perhaps the most convincing explanation to Bancroft in 1878.[154] "The plan to steal the cannon," he revealed, "was conceived by Don José Antonio de la Guerra, son of Captain de la Guerra, and José Lugo." The two picked up co-conspirators, including García, and buried the cannon at the beach with the intent to use it "in case of an opportunity for a revolt against the Americans." In other words, if García is to be believed, Captain Lippitt had been quite right to suspect a plan against his forces. And, as it turns out, Sherman had also been right to pinpoint Francisco de la Guerra as someone with knowledge of Californio resistance. The day after the heist, García claimed, he and the others attended mass, and "while we were there, Don Francisco de la Guerra called us aside and took us to a room and very seriously told us that the Americans were very angry about the cannon and we should be very careful not to tell anyone about it."[155] As much as Francisco opposed collaboration, he may also have acted within Californio society to contain those oppositional elements (even his eldest brother) that he knew would trigger strong reprisals from the nervous American occupiers.

The de la Guerras could not maintain their authority in the community simply by squelching rivals, however; during the military occupation their power continued to derive from the "good" patriarch's moral authority to govern. In the end, one final negotiation sealed this status in the eyes of both the Americans and the town. Unable to identify the culprits or force town leaders to give up the cannon, Governor Mason ordered a general fine of $500, levied on townsfolk according to their relative wealth. The de la Guerras stepped forward to accept this punishment on behalf of the town. Colonel Jonathan Drake Stevenson, headquartered in Los Angeles, arrived in Santa Bárbara in June 1848; a private meeting with Pablo de la Guerra was the first item on his agenda. Pablo warned the colonel that the people of Santa Bárbara resented this tax but would pay out of respect for the family. He then suggested a way to resolve the issue.

Stevenson delayed the immediate call for the assessment, and on July 3, he relocated his headquarters to Santa Bárbara, bringing his regimental band. The musicians entered town that evening playing "Spanish" music and marched immediately to the de la Guerra house, attracting a crowd along the way. While the band serenaded the family, Stevenson called on Pablo to pay his official respects. The next morning the band took up its concert again at the house, and the townsfolk who attended the day-long fiesta turned in their portion of the fine. That evening, the family held a ball for Santa Bárbara's high society in honor of Stevenson, and the next morning on the officer's departure the elder José de la Guerra gave a speech.[156] All of this—the music, open fiesta, elite ball, and public speeches—served to give Californio residents reason to feel that they were not paying a fine out of coercion but in honor of the leading Californio household. Likewise, the de la Guerras, with this ability to negotiate such a display from the Americans, reconfirmed their own status among both elite and non-elite Californios. That month, Alcalde Pedro Carrillo submitted his resignation, refused to pay the fine, and was punished by the seizure of some of his property.[157]

In the unstable moment of occupation, some elements within the Californio community, like Pedro Carrillo, had attempted to improve their position through cooperation with the Americans. Others, like José Antonio de la Guerra and José "Chato" Lugo, opted for another chance at armed resistance. Pablo and Francisco de la Guerra, by continuing to engage the Californio community in the publicly acknowledged role of "Town Father," skillfully negotiated a middle way to emerge as celebrated representatives of that community. By the end of the occupation, they had reestablished positions of political authority on their own terms, as civil patriarchs within the Californio community, and as mediators between that community and the Americans.

The Sovereign Pueblo

While Lugo, Carrillo, and de la Guerra cousins sparred in Santa Bárbara over local authority, a discovery far to the north was putting events into motion that would soon transform California even more profoundly than the war itself. On January 24, 1848, James W. Marshall picked a few flecks of gold from the tailrace of a lumber mill he was constructing for Johann Sutter on the American River. Sutter tried to keep news of the discovery from leaking out, but by the time Captain Lippitt had begun his investigation into the mission cannon, inhabitants of San Francisco were shutting up homes and shops to head into the Sierras. By May 1848, the town of a thousand had been reduced to fewer than a hundred inhabitants. The newspaper *The Californian* put out its last issue on May 29; the *Star* on June 14. Sailors from naval and commercial vessels, volunteer troops, and regular forces from the occupying armies all deserted and rushed for the mines. Outgoing ships left port with the news, bound for Hawaii, South America, the East Coast, and Europe.

As the Lost Cannon Affair drew to a close in Santa Bárbara and gold fever hit San Francisco, news of the war's end reached California. In June 1848, Californians learned of the cessation of hostilities, but Californios remained confused about their status under U.S. rule. "It seems that we belong to our beloved Native Republic of Mexico," Andrés Pico wrote to his friend Francisco de la Guerra on June 11.[158] The Treaty of Guadalupe Hidalgo, signed in February and ratified on May 30, arrived in early August to clear up the misunderstandings. Treaty in hand, Governor Mason proclaimed on August 7, 1848, that a new territorial government would arrive soon by act of Congress, but that in the meantime the existing laws would remain in force, and civil officers should continue their functions. Any vacancies that opened in the future would be filled not by his appointment but by general election, and Mexicans living in the conquered territory would be automatically granted citizenship and the right to participate in these elections. Mason concluded by proclaiming Americans and Californios "one . . . a band of brothers."[159]

The decision to continue with California's de facto civil government, and to remove the military government, resulted in worsening instability in Santa Bárbara's governing authority, as the Lost Cannon Affair had severely undermined the ability of the chosen alcalde, Pedro Carrillo, to govern the local population. At the conclusion of the affair, Carrillo had tried to resign, but the military government would not accept this resignation. Nevertheless, he apparently refused to serve, and in July Captain Lippitt complained that there were no civil magistrates in Santa Bárbara.[160] So, when the hapless Lippitt's Company F finally mustered out on September 8, 1848, there was no local government left at all in Santa Bárbara. Perhaps townsfolk could have coped for a time in this condition; certainly they had suffered through stretches of instability in the Mexican era. But in December 1848, a crisis struck the community and catalyzed the formation of the "sovereign pueblo" under de la Guerra leadership.

In the first days of December, William Reed and his pregnant wife, María Antonia Vallejo, entertained a group of five men, sailors and soldiers, who had recently come from the gold mines. The Reeds, their son, Indian workers, and a young man of African descent who worked as their cook lived at the former Mission San Miguel, north of San Luis Obispo. That night, they were joined by Josefa Olivera, a midwife who had come to attend María Antonia, and her daughter and nephew. The Reeds had recently made a good profit themselves from the sale of sheep in the gold fields. They told their visitors of this good fortune: more gold than their little boy could lift. Sadly, the Reed family would never live to spend the bags of gold dust they were so proudly showing off. On December 7, the alcalde of San Luis Obispo dashed off urgent notes to points south: "There has been committed one of the most atrocious of murders," he told William Goodwin Dana and Cesareo Lataillade, and commanded them to organize a posse to find the perpetrators.[161] Famed mountain man James Beckwourth, employed as a mail carrier, had found the bodies of the entire family and dependents in a pile—variously shot, stabbed, and struck repeatedly with an axe.[162]

Lataillade, the Spanish vice consul and husband of the youngest de la Guerra daughter, María Antonia, immediately gathered fifteen residents, who set out to apprehend the murderers. "The very next day," their son later remembered, Indian sentries reported the men passing by the town on a little-used road, "and my father immediately gathered his men and started in pursuit. They were overtaken at the present site of Summerland," a few miles south of Santa Bárbara. Ramón Rodríguez seized one of the men by the collar and pulled him off his horse, but the American pulled a gun and killed the Californio. In the battle that followed, the suspect was shot, and a second jumped in the ocean and drowned. The posse subdued the remaining three and brought them to town, imprisoning them in an abandoned house.[163] The men were Joseph Lynch, a German formerly of the New York Volunteers, and Peter Remer and Peter Quin, both born in Ireland and deserters from the U.S. warship *Warren*.[164]

Under ordinary circumstances, the alcalde would have taken over to call a trial, preside, and pass sentence. This, however, was not an ordinary time, and in the absence of an acting alcalde, the Spanish vice consul was the only official of any kind in the jurisdiction. Technically, townsfolk could have waited until an election could fill their judicial vacuum, but shocked by the brutality of the crime, they acted quickly to call a civil trial. On their return from apprehending the criminals, Lataillade sent a list of citizens to José Antonio de la Guerra and summoned them all for a meeting.[165]

These men, forty-nine in all, signed the meeting notes as an "Acta" on December 12, 1848, to justify their action. In this extraordinary document, "the better part of the residents of all types that today represented the *Sovereignty of the Pueblo*," as they declared themselves, ratified the actions of Lataillade and elected a commission to investigate the crime, "*believing* ourselves with the right, lacking civil and military authority, to investigate the deeds in order that public vengeance be left satisfied." What is immediately noticeable in the list of the "Pueblo," apart from the fact that all were men, are the twenty-three X marks—almost half were illiterate. In addition, seven who signed were Carrillos, and one was a de la Guerra: twenty-three-year-old Antonio María. Many of the rest had marriage or godparent ties to this family, though a number did not.

The English-speaking investigative commission they elected, two of them Yankees married to daughters of Carlos Carrillo, and one a discharged officer of Company F, were instructed to give account of their actions "to the aforementioned *Pueblo* in order that *It, in representation of its Sovereignty* pronounces its irrevocable sentence."[166] From December 11 through December 13, the committee recorded inventories of the items seized from the prisoners and took testimony from the suspects Lynch, Quin, and Remer.

As the investigation continued and took on a more official tone, most of the "residents of all types" who had signed the Acta began to lose their voice, as the patriarchs of the pueblo spoke more and more for them. Among those who watched the English testimony and signed the confessions as witnesses were Pablo and Francisco de la Guerra, and when it came time to choose a jury at the end of the month, Pablo's role expanded from witness to president of that jury. Thus, as the prosecution of the crime developed from informal posse, through a collection of the "sovereign" pueblo, to a carefully selected jury, the role of the de la Guerra brothers became increasingly dominant. On December 26, 1848, the day after Christmas, Pablo recorded the judgment of the jury: guilty of murder "in cold blood." A firing squad executed the three culprits on Thursday, December 28, 1848.[167]

Along the side of this sentence, in a different hand, appears the notation, "The foregoing findings and sentences . . . are approved by authority of Col. R. B. Mason, Govr. of Calia., E. O. C. Ord, 1st. Lt. U.S. Artillery." Governor Mason had sent Lieutenant Edward Ord to Santa Bárbara, and on the day after the execution Ord gave the American's regime's approval to the town's actions. In addition, the lieutenant asked Mason for an account to compensate the posse for the weapons and ammunition used; the jailkeepers for food, candles, and salary; the court for paper and tea consumed; and the family of Ramón Rodríguez for their loss.[168] The governor approved this expense but soon began to doubt the legality of the town's action.[169] Ord, more practically, reminded his commander that "I knew the people had just as much right to execute justice without as with that approval, . . . but as you expect to exercise any command in California; amongst Californians, 'tis well to say as little on that subject as possible."[170] Mason at last was forced to concede the point.[171] Thus, the "people" of Santa Bárbara, represented in large part by the Carrillo and de la Guerra families, were able to seize a moment of crisis and reconstitute themselves as a "sovereign" unit, with the authority to govern themselves—a power that transcended the authority of the American occupying government.[172] The alliance of extended kin and family supporters that made up the "pueblo" in December 1848 became the basis, once voting rights were secured, of a de la Guerra political machine that would last for another twenty-five years.

Statehood: Race, Language, and Citizenship

Californians lived under a chaotic and unstable state authority after the official declaration of the end of the war in August 1848. As soon as news of gold reached Mexico, Peru, and Chile that autumn, and the United States, China, and Europe soon after, hordes of immigrants rushed in, further destabilizing the territory. In April 1849, Brigadier General Bennet Riley arrived to take over from Governor Mason and continued to claim that, absent a lawfully appointed civil governor, the commanding officer of the U.S. military was still ex-officio governor of California. Finally, in June, President Taylor's agent Thomas Butler King arrived in California with instructions to Californians to apply for statehood as soon as possible. Elections were called for August, and a state constitutional convention in September.

Once California had been officially annexed to the United States, the de la Guerra brothers quickly determined that if they were to stay in power, they would need to integrate the old system of paternalism and reciprocity with the new one of American-style electoral politics. Working behind the scenes or acting outside the authority of the American government would no longer work once California's state government was established. If their continuing power under American rule was to be determined by election, the first order of business, then, was to ensure that de la Guerra supporters and dependents would continue to have the power to keep de la Guerras on top. This power came in the form of voting rights, and the most active and respected son, Pablo, became the voice for Californio citizenship rights when he was chosen to represent Santa Bárbara in the state constitutional convention. This initial confirmation of political rights became the bedrock of future de la Guerra political dominance in American Santa Bárbara.

During the military occupation, Pablo and Francisco had made the strategic decision not to recognize the authority of the American forces to govern them, but by late 1849, they had come to believe that their best interests, and those of the community, would be served by active participation in state government. Two things had changed: the Treaty of Guadalupe Hidalgo had guaranteed full rights of religion, property, and citizenship to conquered Mexicans, and in Santa Bárbara, the informal declaration of sovereignty by the Californios under de la Guerra leadership had been fully accepted and approved by the American governor, showing their ability to retain local power under American government sanction. In June, as the call for a state constitutional convention went out, Manuel Jimeno in Monterey passed along to Pablo and Francisco the request of the secretary of state, "that you will be pledged to come as delegates or Deputies on behalf of Santa Bárbara in order to help at the enterprise, better than others."[173] Dr. James Ord, who had become friendly with the family through Jimeno's wife, Angustias, welcomed Pablo to the United States in a mix of Spanish and English: "I am very pleased to receive you in the list of those called <u>Yankees</u>, and as you have been a good Mexican, you will be a better Yankee." He went on to encourage the new Yankee to promote statehood in the south, "as it is the duty of all good Paisano's."[174]

After his election as delegate in August, Pablo arrived for the convention in Monterey to find his sister's house a favorite meeting place of most of the leading delegates, Californio and American. No doubt she had a great deal to add to the informal discussions there during the convention, and her participation was remarked upon by one traveler. Unfortunately, she did not leave a record of her input; only the official meeting at Colton Hall has been recorded.[175] Of the forty-eight delegates who began meeting on September 1, eight were Californio, and another six were foreigners who had lived in California for ten years or more.[176] Among the rest were Thomas O. Larkin, Johann Sutter, Captain Francis Lippitt, and in the observers' gallery, John C. Frémont and William Tecumseh Sherman.[177] Hartnell also served, as translator.

Of the Californios, only Mariano Guadalupe Vallejo and Pablo de la Guerra had any facility in English, and although the other delegates had

Spanish translators, it was de la Guerra who took the lead in speaking for Californio interests. One subject in particular drew his attention. "I should be doing a very great injustice to my constituents," de la Guerra proclaimed, "did I not speak upon the subject." Early in the proceedings, Charles Botts of Virginia proposed limiting suffrage to only the "white" Mexicans who had become citizens by the terms of the Treaty of Guadalupe Hidalgo. Unwittingly, Botts had opened a Pandora's box of racial and status differentiation, which had never been strictly based on appearance or bloodlines in Mexican California. Pablo de la Guerra rose to encourage the delegates to understand clearly

> the true significance of the word 'White.' Many citizens of California have received from nature a very dark skin; nevertheless, there are among them men who have heretofore been allowed to vote, and not only that, but to fill the highest public offices. It would be very unjust to deprive them of the privilege of citizens merely because nature had not made them White. But if, by the word 'white,' it was intended to exclude the African race, then it was correct and satisfactory.[178]

Unlike the Americans, Californios considered one's public racial identity as somewhat fluid, and only one part of a calculation that allowed those of darker skin or non-European ancestry—the majority of the state's native-born population—to be recognized as something other than Indian or African, and to exercise political rights. When pressed about racial restrictions on suffrage in Mexico, de la Guerra admitted that there were none—people of Indian and African descent could vote—and that with regard to Indians in Mexico, he argued, "so far were they considered citizens, that some of the first men of the Republic were of the Indian race."[179] And, while it may appear that de la Guerra was willing to exclude anyone of African descent, he knew quite well that, strictly interpreted, this would prevent members of the Pico family from suffrage; but because of their wealth, power, and relation to elite families, they were among those Californios who had a "very dark skin" but were nonetheless "white." As one Anglo was forced to admit, in California, "men who have Indian blood in the veins are not for that reason Indians."[180] Bott's language eventually passed, but the category of Mexican "whites" remained a slippery one in practice.

Meanwhile, de la Guerra laid the groundwork for full Californio participation in American government by insisting that all laws, decrees, regulations, and provisions of the state be published in both English and Spanish. "They cannot obey laws unless they understand them," he argued.[181] This guarantee of bilingual government passed the convention unanimously and provided the foundation not only for compliance to the law but also for full participation in Santa Bárbara's local government by non-English-speaking Californios. The delegates sent California's first constitution to the voters on October 11, 1849, and threw themselves a grand ball. After the festivities, Pablo returned home, and a little over a month later learned of more good news: he had been elected Santa Bárbara's only state senator.[182]

Conclusion

By 1850, the de la Guerras were beginning to look like assimilated Yankees, swiftly entering the commercial and political world of American California. Pablo de la Guerra served in the state senate, and that May he sold Rancho Nicasio, granted him in 1843, to Henry Wager Halleck for $30,000.[183] Francisco de la Guerra and Cesareo Lataillade tried their hand at mining, but the venture came to an abrupt end with Lataillade's accidental death in April 1849. Still, the family overall did quite well by the Gold Rush, selling livestock from their ranches to the gold fields, and luxury goods to other newly rich Californios in the south. Manuel Jimeno contemplated breaking up his own ranches and selling them to farmers, while his wife, Angustias, arranged for an education at Georgetown College in Washington, D.C. for two of their sons, through one of her boarders, William Tecumseh Sherman. Her eldest daughter, Manuela, married American officer Alfred Sully later that year. It might seem that elite families like the de la Guerras had listened to their Anglo in-laws and betrayed Mexican interests out of greed and personal ambition. In fact, their reaction to American conquest was more complex and ambiguous, and remained firmly grounded in sustained patriarchal relations of power in family and community.

Of course, there was no single Californio response to conquest. Others within the network of elites chose different paths, from armed resistance or flight to Mexico, to cooperation with American occupiers. Dissension and rivalries strained the Californio elite "family," as relatively weak younger men and some women sought advantage through alliance with the Americans. Those who chose this path against the de la Guerra family, however, faced sanction from its core. Angustias provoked censure from her brothers when she opened her Monterey house to American officers. Pedro Carrillo suffered even harsher consequences when he attempted to use gossip to unseat his powerful cousins in Santa Bárbara; Carrillo lost his political career and some of his property.

What separated the de la Guerras from those who could not retain power was their ability to reinvent themselves within Californio patriarchal understandings of authority. De la Guerra sons took over local leadership as "the father of all" from José de la Guerra—the commander who looked out for the best interests of the entire community and protected his dependents. The years before the war set the stage: the de la Guerras learned both of American designs on their homeland and of Mexico's weakness in protecting it. Drawing on their father's reputation, and committed to California's independence, the brothers developed a role for themselves as wise mediators and conciliators in a Californio political system entangled in patronage rivalries, becoming figures of Californio unity. Through the war and occupation, the family in Santa Bárbara recast their position as town "father," refusing to recognize American authority but serving as representatives of the conquered to that government. In the early years of the conflict, Americans failed to understand de la Guerra leadership and the paternal system of politics at its base, but by the eve of the constitutional convention, conquering officials had no choice but to concede de la Guerra authority. With these local efforts, and the guarantee of voting rights and a bilingual government at the constitutional convention, the de la Guerras helped to embody the local community and its paternal understanding of power in American structures of electoral government. By protecting their wealth and property through the war years, too, the de la Guerras ensured that they would have the material resources to continue as publicly accepted "generous patriarchs."

At the dawn of the American era, the de la Guerra family exercised a dominant role in Southern California, with over 200,000 acres of prime ranchland and secure positions in local and state government. Even with voting rights and a newly politicized pueblo, however, population dynamics in California gave the de la Guerra men reason to question their ability to maintain power. From 1848 to 1850, in the heat of the Gold Rush, California's non-Indian population rose from 15,000 to nearly 93,000, and the vast majority of the newcomers were young men of voting age.[184] Even more of a threat was the fact that this rush of new immigrants had no ties to the ranching economy or to ranching families, and the de la Guerras feared that they would feel no loyalty or dependence on the Californio patriarchs. Pablo de la Guerra, watching hordes of immigrants overwhelm his northern cousins, worried, "What will become of us in a republican state whose majority of inhabitants are a rabble? God save us."[185]

Epilogue

In the summer of 1893, thirty-two-year-old Delfina de la Guerra, a daughter of Pablo de la Guerra, took a sightseeing trip across the United States that would have been typical for an American woman of the middle class at that time. With Niagara Falls as their destination, she and her companion chose a northerly route that led through Chicago, and they remained long enough in the booming industrial city to visit the crowded exhibit halls and stroll the midway at the Columbian Exposition.

Delfina's letters from this trip to her married sister Francisca reveal a woman who lived in the present, but for whom the memory of her family's history was still very much alive, a heritage to be nurtured and celebrated. At the fair, she made a beeline for the California display, and she wrote Francisca in Spanish of her gratification to find California's agricultural progress so well represented by pyramids of giant fruit and "an immense horse with a man mounted with chaparreras, etc etc. all done of dried plums . . . I will tell you," she said, "that Spain has shone brightly in everything from California."[1] Delfina was especially intrigued to find the exhibit from Mexico, and she came up with a novel way to get herself in before it opened. *"Yo quiero ver el departamento de Mexico,"* she remarked loudly while passing the entrance. Startled to hear their native tongue, the two Mexican women standing there replied, "Would you like to enter, señorita? Please come in; we are very pleased to allow you to do so because you are Spaniards." The workers setting up the exhibit seated the Californian woman in one of the chairs brought for the display and showed her an embroidered cushion and handkerchief belonging to the wife of President Porfirio Díaz. "When we were speaking Spanish," Delfina told her sister, "their pleasure was so great, that they were blushing and getting bewildered in such a way, that for some minutes they didn't know what to say; in truth it brought tears to my eyes because I put myself in their place."[2] Forty-five years after California passed from Mexican to

American hands, descendants of the old Californio families, like Delfina, easily combined identities as Californians, Americans, and "Spaniards," while contemporary Mexico captured their imaginations as a kindred culture. A year later, in fact, Delfina was traveling across Mexico and sending letters to her mother recounting the sights of the capital city.[3]

Delfina may have identified with her Mexican and Spanish roots, but her life and adventures must have struck her mother, Josefa, as quite a contrast to the lives of the women of her generation. Born in 1829 in Mexican California, Josefa had married late at age eighteen, and by age thirty-two, she had five children and was in charge of the Santa Barbara household of her husband, Pablo, who served as lieutenant governor, and of his brothers who ran the political machine of Santa Barbara. In 1893, Delfina at thirty-two was still unmarried and traveling across the continent. Her father, Pablo, had been dead almost twenty years; about her grandfather, who had died in 1858, three years before she was born, she had only stories. Only her mother and sisters remained in the house on De la Guerra Street, increasingly isolated from the centers of Santa Barbara power and influence. The last traces of her grandfather's empire were fading from memory, and Delfina no doubt felt herself to be a modern, independent woman. The era of Californio patriarchy was finally over.

A form of the patriarchal family had served as a foundation of California's political economy from the colonial era. At the levels of nuclear family, extended kin, and local community, Californian society had been based on an idea of patriarchy in which men, and especially fathers, gained respect by both commanding others and providing for and protecting their dependents. Certainly, conflicts arose between Indians and colonizers; military officers, settlers, and missionaries; traders and producers; husbands, wives, and children. But they were negotiated within an established cultural system of expectations and arguments about precedence and obligation. The roots of this society extended back almost a hundred years, from the arrival of Delfina's grandfather and the men and women of his generation.

Although it may appear that the Spanish-Mexican social order based on patriarchal relations belonged to the dying world of "tradition" and the colonial order, destined to fall before the forces of modernity, this cultural understanding of power was surprisingly flexible, and combined relatively smoothly with an economy of merchant capitalism, economic and political liberalism, and later with American forms of democracy. Fathers controlled daughters' marriage choices to connect the family to global trade networks. Aspiring rancheros appealed both to their paternal obligations to the Indians and to liberal notions of private property and federalism as they pressed for mission secularization. Political reformers extended the rights of citizenship, but only to male heads of households. This is not to argue that California's patriarchy was a seamless system. Children, women, and dependents most often accepted patriarchy as long as they benefited, and exploited weaknesses and contradictions when they did not. Sons, influenced by liberalism, rebelled against their fathers to secure property and political power, and daughters did the same to escape arranged marriages. "Republican mothers" claimed their right to education by appealing to their "traditional" roles as family nurturers, and expanded their accepted roles as "virtuous" hostesses and keepers of the household to enter the political fray. Indians appealed to multiple "fathers" for protection and advantage, while using the uneven process of mission secularization to claim a measure of autonomy.

This work ends in 1850, following a tumultuous decade in the story of the de la Guerra family, but in many ways the continuities after the war were as significant as the ruptures it inflicted. American historians usually represent the first thirty years of California statehood as the era of the "decline" of the Californios and their transformation into a segregated working class.[4] The case of the de la Guerras, however, shows how active these "victims" could be in shaping and resisting the post-war conquest. Santa Barbara was the stronghold of Californio power after 1846, and the de la Guerra family played a pivotal role in responding successfully to Anglo challenges to Californio society for the next twenty years.[5]

Throughout the war and the Gold Rush, the family moved to protect family assets and adapt to changing markets, preserving the resources necessary to act as benevolent patriarchs. Because they continued to play this role so well, and because they skillfully organized extended family networks, the de la Guerras could command an organized bloc of Californio voters. At any given time in the 1850s, 1860s, and even 1870s, José Antonio, Francisco, Pablo, Antonio María, or their allies could be found holding office as sheriff, justice of the peace, mayor, city council member, county supervisor, district judge, state assemblyman, or state senator.[6] They ran election tables, held the majority on the grand jury, and dominated the Democratic Party's county committee. Once in office, the de la Guerras used their roles to defend the interests of Californios.

In particular, the de la Guerras did what they could to protect Californio landholding. Although the 1848 Treaty of Guadalupe Hidalgo had promised the Californios citizenship and "the free enjoyment of their liberty and property," a Land Claims Court was set up in 1851 to confirm the legality of Mexican deeds. Most Californios lost their ranch lands, so hard won in the 1830s, as their cases dragged out and lawyers, translators, and surveyors demanded payment. The de la Guerras were able to prove title to their ranches, but lost most of their land in the 1860s when a drought pushed over the first domino of debt and foreclosure. They had long since given up the trading business.

While powerful patriarchal families strengthened the Californio community in the face of the American conquest, they also limited the range of responses to it, while opening the door to challenges from Californio women, children, and non-elites. After the war, new constraints and opportunities shaped the lives of Californio women. Many women took the brunt of their families' declining fortunes and were forced to find wage work outside the home to support their families. Others took advantage of a new legal system and chose to exercise their new right to divorce.[7] The sisters of the de la Guerra family struggled to maintain their fortunes in the decades after the war. After William Hartnell's death in 1854, Teresa found herself in court on a regular basis for payment of back taxes on their ranchos. In 1859, she married again, to Manuel Maturano, but their situation did not improve, and she was forced to sell much of her land.[8] Her sister Angustias separated from Manuel Jimeno in 1852 after he sold their ranchos Pájaro and Santa Paula without her consent.[9] He moved to Mexico City and died there in 1853. She spent more than a year in the capital city attempting to claim her share of his estate from his siblings, but returned empty-handed in early 1856.[10] That fall, she married her former boarder James L. Ord.

Two years later, in July 1858, Angustias broke the seal on a letter from Santa Barbara, sent by four of her brothers—Pablo, Francisco, Antonio María, and Joaquín. "We the undersigned," she read,

> have just acquainted ourselves with the disrespectful, antifilial and denigrating language used by you, against the venerated ashes of our beloved Father in a document that we just received. This, together with the calumnious imputations that you spill in it against our character, demands of us the most imperious obligation to cut all fraternal and any other relation with you forever.[11]

What insult could possibly have provoked such an outburst? Angustias, it seems, had challenged her father's will. The captain had died at home on February 22, 1858. In his will, de la Guerra left all of his ranches, undivided, to his sons, and just 800 cows to her. She demanded that her brothers break up the family estates and give her a fair share, a total of $88,000. But within a few years, Angustias and her brothers settled their suit out of court, granting her a large amount of livestock and a parcel of land in town, but preserving the ranch lands under one owner.[12] Angustias divorced her second husband in January 1875 for adultery, receiving a settlement of $100 a month and more plots of land in Santa Barbara.[13] Acting on her own behalf, she continued to buy and sell property in Santa Barbara. She died in San Francisco in 1890.[14] Anita de la Guerra died a few days after her thirty-fourth birthday and the birth of her tenth child in 1855. The youngest de la Guerra daughter, María Antonia, married her father's protégé Gaspar Oreña in 1854 after the death of her first husband. During the war, she had purchased properties from the original Indian grantees, and she and her first husband had also received grants totaling over 88,000 acres; half were rejected by the Land Claims courts. Nonetheless, Gaspar Oreña, a shrewd businessman, was wealthy enough in 1861 to loan his brothers-in-law $150,000. Ruined by the drought and unable to pay back the loan, the brothers sold ranchos San Julián, Simi, and Las Posas in 1864, and their half-interest in El Conejo in 1872.[15]

By the middle of the 1860s, the family had lost most of the material base they had depended on to enact the public role of generous patriarch. Yet, for a decade after the de la Guerra family had passed out of the core of Santa Barbara's economy, the solid bloc of the de la Guerra Democracy held firm because, as elected officials, the brothers could still deliver patronage and advocate for the interests of their constituency. In the end, the de la Guerras lost their dominance with the erosion of their voting base. The "rabble" Pablo had feared arrived at last when a real estate and tourist boom in the early 1870s pulled in a massive influx of Anglo citizens and tipped the balance of the voter rolls.[16] By 1870, for the first time, census takers recorded a majority of non-Spanish surnames in the county. The new voters had no memory of the family's role as town patriarch, and no interest in learning it. That decade, José Antonio, Francisco, Pablo, Joaquín, Miguel, and Antonio María all passed away. After that, only their widows and daughters lived in the house on Plaza de la Guerra. It was not Californio greed, ignorance, or betrayal that brought their rule to an end, but the dwindling numbers of those who spoke the language of Mexican patriarchy.

As the California tourist trade boomed in the last two decades of the nineteenth century, travel writers began selling stories of a proud but reclusive family who refused the entreaties of the curious for a quick peek at the inside of their crumbling Santa Barbara adobe. But soon, the family began to embrace a new role for their house, as a showpiece of the city's "Spanish" heritage. In the spring of 1891, President Benjamin Harrison visited the aspiring tourist town of Santa Barbara. As part of the festivities, residents held a parade in his honor, featuring a "Spanish cavalcade" of men in snappy uniforms and women of the pioneer families waving from flower-decorated floats. Thirty-year-old Delfina de la Guerra, the daughter of the town's most illustrious native son, was chosen to represent "Saint Barbara" in the procession. A scrapbook later presented to the president's wife featured photographs of the de la Guerra mansion.

For the next thirty years, boosters and businessmen worked hard to capitalize on their town's setting and history, and they created the "Spanish"-themed festivals and architecture for which the city is famous today. "The romance and aroma of the past are to be revived," one editorial asserted, "in order that the picturesque period of this locality's history may not . . . [be] trampled under the onrushing feet of modernity."[17] Delfina and her sister Herminia, who still lived in the de la Guerra house, took active roles in the re-creation of their own past. In 1919, Delfina served as chair of the Spanish pageant committee, and Herminia as organizer of the Spanish parade. A year later Herminia trained dancers for the historic pageant "El Barbareño."[18] Through architect Francis Underhill, married to Francisca's daughter Carmen, and promoters Bernhard and Irene Hoffman, Delfina, Herminia, and Francisca helped transform even the structure of their house into the centerpiece of the town's "Spanish Colonial" revival in the early 1920s.[19]

Their vision received a huge boost after the devastating earthquake of 1925. With the restored house and shopping complex as its inspiration, a newly christened Architectural Board of Review met in the casa and approved over two thousand designs for new construction, mandating a unified look for the town that stands to this day. Soon after its renovation, the Casa de la Guerra became a community center for the annual Old Spanish Days Fiesta, four days in August of parades, rodeos, and concerts that still take place every year. The de la Guerras hosted a reception for the Fiesta Queen there, and over the years the structure provided the backdrop for potluck suppers attended by descendants of the "Old Spanish" families, community dances, and today, a festive beer garden.[20] In 1924, addressing descendants of the old families assembled at the de la Guerra house to receive the queen of the first Old Spanish Days Fiesta, writer and booster Charles Fletcher Lummis proclaimed, "As the blood of Castile represented the highest culture of Old Spain, so the blood of

Delfina de la Guerra as the first Saint Bárbara, 1891. Santa Barbara Historical Museum.

the early Santa Barbara and Ventura families represents the highest aristocracy of California."[21] No doubt the de la Guerra sisters were gratified to bask in such compliments.

Participation in the Spanish Fantasy Past could be a way for Californio descendants to assert cultural relevance in an era in which economic and political power had eroded for the community.[22] But behind the fancy backdrop of moonlight and bougainvillea, the de la Guerra granddaughters focused on the conditions of Mexican migrants. In the same years that they worked to provide Spanish costumes, dances, and "aroma" for the town's fiesta, Pablo's daughters Delfina and Herminia also worked with the immigrants in the barrios on the east side of town, volunteering at the East Side Social Center as translators. Herminia was a charter member of the first social service agency in Santa Barbara, the St. Cecilia Club, and served on a number of other advisory boards.[23] As she lay dying of pneumonia in 1927, the old Casa de la Guerra courtyard filled, as it had on the deaths of her father and grandfather, with those townsfolk who felt obligation to the family for aid and protection. Echoes of the Mexican past sounded in the twentieth century.

Herminia de la Guerra at the East Side Social Center, acting as an interpreter,
ca. 1920. Santa Barbara Historical Museum.

APPENDIX

THE FAMILY OF
JOSÉ ANTONIO JULIÁN DE LA GUERRA
AND MARÍA ANTONIO CARRILLO

Don José Antonio Julián de la Guerra y Noriega b.3/6/1779; d.2/22/1858
   m. María Antonia Carrillo y Lugo b.3/15/1786; d.12/25/1843; md.5/16/1804

FIRST CHILD
José Antonio Bonifacio b.5/14/1805; d. ca. 1878

    m. María Concepción Manuela Ortega y López (Chona)
       b.9/12/1808; d.7/28/1885; md.11/23/1824
      José Antonio Lugardo b.9/23/1825; d.?
      María Dolores de Alta Gracia (Dolores) b.4/8/1827; d.?
      Juan de Dios de Alta Gracia b.2/22/1829; d.3/5/1829
      María Soledad de Alta Gracia (Sola) b.4/25/1830; d.2/2/1838
      Catarina Feliciana Ramona b.4/1/1832; d.5/16/1887
      Juana de Dios b. 10/14/1833; d.1/4/1885
      José Antonio b.10/16/1834; d.1/13/1885
      José Ramón Dolores (Ramón) b.3/24/1836; d.?
      Guillermo Eduardo b.11/26/1837; d.1874
      José Joaquín Gaspar b.9/5/1841; d.2/24/1842
      José Joaquín de Alta Gracia b.2/20/1843; d.6/26/1844
      José Federico de Alta Gracia (Federico) b.4/9/1844; d.?
      Alejandro b.7/4/1846; d.1/29/1895
      Cristina Francisca b.5/14/1848; d.?
      María Antonia Zoila b.12/8/1849; d.?

This family chart was originally compiled by Beverly Bastian from Hubert Howe Bancroft, *California Pioneer Register and Index 1542–1848: Including Inhabitants of California, 1769–1800 and List of Pioneers,* Extracted from *The History of California* (Baltimore: Regional Publishing Co., 1964); Marie E. Northrop, *Spanish-Mexican Families of Early California: 1769–1850,* 2 vols. (Burbank, Calif.: Southern California Genealogical Society, 1984); the de la Guerra Geneaology Files in the Gledhill Library of the Santa Barbara Historical Museum; and the Joseph Thompson Papers and de la Guerra Papers, in the Santa Barbara Mission Archive-Library. It was corrected using the ECPP.

SECOND CHILD
Rita de Jesús b.4/25/1807; d.1810 or 1811 [in Mexico]

THIRD CHILD
María Teresa Isidora (or Ysidra) de Jesús (Teresa) b.5/18/1809; d.1885

    m1.William Edward Petty Hartnell b.4/24/1798 (in Backbarrow, England);
        d.2/2/1854; md.4/30/1825
        Guillermo Antonio (El Consul) b.3/31/1826; d.?
        Nathaniel Mariano de la Natividad b.9/8/1827; d.12/?/1833
        Jorge Albano Manuel b.6/16/1829; d.8/9/1829
        Juan Eadbert (Everto) b.5/6/1830; d.?
        Adelberto (Alberto) Pedro b.6/25/1831; d.?
        María Teresa Gregoria (Teresa) b.11/17/1832; d.?
        José Gonzalo b.4/15/1834; d.12/28/1902
        María Matilde (Matilde) b.4/25/1835; d.?
        Urbano (Ubaldo) Pablo b.5/16/1836; d.8/18/1836
        María Ysabel Ana Prudenciana (Anita) b.5/19/1837; d.?
        María Magdalena del Refugio b.7/22/1838; d.?
        Nataniel (Nathaniel) Finiano b.9/10/1840; d.11/20/1847
        Pablo Eduardo b.2/8/1842; d.?
        Ulrico (Uldarico) b.2/19/1843; d.?
        Francisco Gumesindo b.1/13/1845; d.11/17/1845
        Silvestre Albano b.12/31/1845; d.?
        Margarita Amelia b.2/22/1847; d.?
        Arnulfo Benjamin b.7/18/1849; d.5/17/1852
        María b.11/1851; d.?

    m2. Manuel Maturano md.8/?/1859 div.1873

FOURTH CHILD
Juan José Antonio María b.3/8/1813; d.9/5/1833

FIFTH CHILD
María de las Angustias Josefa Antonia Bernabe (Angustias) b.6/11/1815; d.6/21/1890

    m1.Manuel Jimeno y Casarín b.?; d.12/23/1853; md.1/12/1833
        María Manuela Antonia (Manuela) b.12/12/1833; d.3/28/1851
        Juana Ufega (María Angustias) b.4/19/1835; d.?
        María Antonia Josefa Narcisa Barnaba b.6/12/1837; d.?
        José Antonio Sebastián (Antonio) b.2/25/1839; d. ca. 1/1866
        Porfirio Juan de Dios b.8/14/1840; d.11/9/1870
        María Carolina b.2/4/1842; d.?
        Ricardo Belisario b.3/30/1844; d.?
        Carolina de la Trinidad b.12/25/1846; d. post 1924
        Santiago b.1848; d.?
        Juan b.1850; d.1852?
        Alfredo Justo and Enrique Pastor b. ca. 1/1853; d.?

m2.Dr. James L. Ord md.10/31/1856; div. 1875
   Rebecca María b.1857 or 1858; d.?

SIXTH CHILD
Francisco Antonio María de Alta Gracia (Cuchichito) b.6/25/1817; d.1/8/1878

   ms. María del Rosario Lorenzana b.5/13/1816; d. ca.1857–58
      Felipe Santiago (Santiago) b.5/1/1837; d.5/31/1918
      Clotilda Inez Soledad b.5/9/1839; d.?

   m1.María Ascención Sepúlveda y Serrano (Ascención) b. ca.1821; d.8/2/1844;
         md.2/16/1839
      José Francisco Guadalupe b.4/9/1840
      María Antonia Adelaida (La Tuna) b.10/31/1841

   m2.Concepción Sepúlveda y Serrano (La Guila) (sister of 1st wife)
         b. ca.1823; d.?; md.1/5/1846
      Juan José (El Guilo) b.5/23/1847; d. ca.1940
      María Concepción Ramona b.12/16/1849; d. pre 1860
      Anita b. ca.1850; d. post 1878
      Osbaldo b. ca.1853; d. post 1878
      José (Peregrino) b. ca.1854; d. pre 1878
      Erlinda (Herlinda) b. ca.1858; d. post 1878
      Rosa b. ca.1861; d. post 1878
      Hercules b. ca.1863; d. post 1878
      Victoria Adriana Elvira b. ca.3/1867; d. pre 1878
      Pablo Eduardo Ramón b. ca.9/2/1868; d. post 1878
      Diana b. ca.1868; d. post 1878
      Anibal Absalom b.10/16/1869; d. post 1878
      Victor Alfredo b.10/24/1870; d.?
      Joaquín Cipio Genardo b.2/27/1872; d.?

SEVENTH CHILD
Pablo Andrés Antonio María Saturnino b.11/29/1819; d.2/5/1874

   m.Josefa Moreno y Castro b.2/27/1829; d.3/9(?)/1904; md.3/7/1847
      Cristina Francisca b.3/12/1848; d.5/2/1848
      María Francisca Antonia (Francisca) b.9/21/1849; d.8/17/1931
      Carlos Pablo b.7/10/1852; d.6/18/1912
      María Paulina (Paulina) b.3/25/1855; d.8/23/1861
      Ana María Elena (Elena) b.5/6/1857; d. post 4/1866
      Delfina b.3/21/1861; d. 4/25/1953
      Delfina's twin brother, stillborn
      Herminia Andrea (Herminia) b.11/30/1862; d.5/12/1927
      Ynez b.? d.?

EIGHTH CHILD
Ana María de Alta Gracia Leonarda Severa (Anita) b.11/6/1821; d.11/24/1855

    m.Alfred Robinson b.1806; d.1895; md. 1/24/1836
        Ana María Elena (Elena) b. ca.1837; d.2/10/1860
        James Alexander (Santiago Alejandro) b. ca.11/1838; d. ca.1855
        Angustias b.184(?); d. pre 1855
        Alfredo b.184(?); d. pre 1855
        Francisco Miguel (Miguel) b.2/29/1853; d. pre 1855
        María Antonia b.?; d. post 1882
        Antonia b.?; d. pre 1855
        Paulina b.?; d. pre 1855
        James Alexander b.11/3/1855; d. post 1882

NINTH CHILD
José Joaquín Francisco María de Alta Gracia (Joaquín) b.10/16/1822; d.3/5/1870

    m1.Ramona Lisaldi b.?; d.?
        José Timateu b. ca.1/25/1853; d.?

    m2.Rafaela Olivera b. ca.1832; d.?
        María Olimpia b.9/21/1862; d.?
        José de los Santos b.2/30/1864; d.?
        Paulina b.6/25/1866; d.?
        Amalfo [Arnulfo?] b.7/15/1868; d.?

TENTH CHILD
Miguel Carlos Francisco María de Alta Gracia b.11/3/1823; d.4/25/1878

    m.María de la Trinidad Serafina Ortega y Pico (Trinidad) (niece of Pío Pico
        and Gen. Andrés Pico) b.8/28/1832; d.9/19/1903; md.?
        Andrés b.10/?/1854; d.9/12/1855
        Gaspar b. ca.1856; d.1906
        María b.12/19/1858; d.4/30/1942
        Josefa b. ca.1860; d.12/27/1946
        Ydelviges[?] Carolina Olimpia (Olimpia) b.10/18/1862; d.1937
        Gloria Joaquina (Joaquina) b.1/16/1866; d.1929
        Ulpiano b. ca.1867; d.?
        Leon b. ca.1869; d.12/21/1954
        Paulina (Polly) b.7/2/1872; d.10/9/1941

ELEVENTH CHILD
Antonio María de Alta Gracia Francisco Remigio b.10/1/1825; d.11/28/1881

TWELFTH CHILD
María Antonia de Alta Gracia Geronima (María Antonia) b.9/30/1827; d.11/25/1916

m1.Cesario Armand Lataillade b.?; d.4/12/1849; md.6/23/1845
    María Antonia b.7/5/1846; d.?
    Carlos María Alberto b.11/4/1847; d. 4/12/1849
    Cesario Eugene (Eugene) b.12/2/1849; d.?
    a fourth child?

m2.Gaspar Oreña b.5/10/1824; d.?; md.1/5/1854(?)
    Acasia Teresa b.?; d.2/24/1958
    Orestes b.1857; d.1930
    Darío b.?; d.?
    Leopoldo b.?; d.?
    Ana Juana (Anita) b. ca.5/29/1864; d.?
    Arturo Gaspar b.8/21/1865; d.9/10/1908
    Serena Rosa b.11/11/1867; d.?
    Teresa Acasia María b.7/28/1872; d.?
    Rosa b.?; d.?

Notes

INTRODUCTION

1   Mariano Guadalupe Vallejo to Anastasio Carrillo, Sonoma, December 19, 1866, translated by Mary Bowman, vol. 1, letter 795, p. 551. Bowman's two volumes of translations of the de la Guerra papers were done for the California Historical Survey Commission prior to the deposit of the collection in the Santa Barbara Mission Archive-Library. In some cases, only the translation has survived. Copies of these translations are available at the archive. References to Bowman's translations are given henceforward by volume, letter number, and page number.

2   "Californio" is a regional term that native-born Spanish-Mexicans in California, and sometimes Spanish-speaking migrants, used in the nineteenth century to refer to themselves.

3   See, for example, Richard Henry Dana, *Two Years Before the Mast and Twenty-Four Years After*, ed. Charles W. Eliot, The Harvard Classics (New York: P. F. Collier & Son, 1969); and Alfred Robinson, *Life in California: During a Residence of Several Years in That Territory, Including a Narrative of Events Which Have Transpired Since That Period When California Was an Independent Government*, introduction by Andrew Rolle (Santa Barbara, Calif., and Salt Lake City, Utah: Peregrine Smith, 1970), 26–27.

4   The great California historian Carey McWilliams first coined the term "Spanish Fantasy Past" to describe the phenomenon. Carey McWilliams, *Southern California: An Island on the Land* (1946; reprint, Santa Barbara, Calif.: Peregrine Smith, 1973). The deconstruction of this "Fantasy Past" has been a fruitful field in California history recently. See William Deverell, *Whitewashed Adobe: The Rise of Los Angeles and the Remaking of Its Mexican Past* (Berkeley: University of California Press, 2004); Richard Griswold del Castillo, "The del Valle Family and the Fantasy Heritage," *California History* 59, no. 1 (Spring 1980): 3–15; Phoebe Kropp, *California Vieja: Culture and Memory in a Modern American Place* (Berkeley: University of California Press, 2006); and Genaro M. Padilla, *My History, Not Yours: The Formation of Mexican-American Autobiography* (Madison: University of Wisconsin Press, 1993).

5   Hubert Howe Bancroft, *California Pastoral, 1769–1848* (San Francisco: The History Company, 1888), 179.

6   Herbert Eugene Bolton, "The Mission as a Frontier Institution in the Spanish American Colonies," *American Historical Review* 23, no. 1 (October 1917): 42–61; David J. Weber, "John Francis Bannon and the Historiography of the Spanish Borderlands: Retrospect and Prospect," *Journal of the Southwest* 29 (Winter 1987): 348; Susan M. Deeds, "New Spain's Far North: A Changing Historiographical Frontier?" *Latin American Research Review* 25, no. 2 (1990): 227; James Sandos, "From 'Boltonlands' to 'Weberlands,'" *American Quarterly* 46, no. 4 (1994): 595–604. For a Latin Americanist perspective, see José Cuello, "Beyond the 'Borderlands' Is the North of Colonial Mexico: A Latin-Americanist Perspective to the Study of the Mexican North and the United States Southwest," *Proceedings of the Pacific Council on Latin American Studies*, vol. 9, ed. Kristyna P. Demaree (San Diego, Calif.: San Diego State University Press, 1982), 2. The nation now known as "Mexico" was known as "New Spain" prior to Independence; "Mexico" referred only to the capital city.

7   Rodolfo Acuña, *Occupied America: A History of Chicanos* (New York: Longman, 1972). For California, see Albert Camarillo, *Chicanos in a Changing Society: From Mexican Pueblos to American Barrios in Santa Barbara and Southern California, 1848–1930* (Cambridge, Mass.: Harvard University Press, 1979); Juan Gómez-Quiñones, *Roots of Chicano Politics, 1600–1940* (Albuquerque: University of New Mexico Press, 1994); Richard Griswold del Castillo, *The Los Angeles Barrio, 1850–1890: A Social History* (Berkeley: University of California Press, 1979); Robert F. Heizer and Alan F. Almquist, *The Other Californians: Prejudice and Discrimination under Spain, Mexico, and the United States to 1920* (Berkeley and Los Angeles: University of California Press, 1971); and Leonard Pitt, *The Decline of the Californios: A Social History of the Spanish-Speaking Californians, 1846–1890* (Berkeley and Los Angeles: University of California Press, 1966).

8   On intermarriage, see María Raquél Casas, *Married to a Daughter of the Land: Spanish-Mexican Women and Interethnic Marriage in California, 1820–1880* (Reno: University of Nevada Press, 2007); Albert L. Hurtado, *Intimate Frontiers: Sex, Gender, and Culture in Old California* (Albuquerque: University of New Mexico Press, 1999); Douglas Monroy, *Thrown Among Strangers: The Making of Mexican Culture in Frontier California* (Berkeley: University of California Press, 1990); and Rosaura Sánchez, *Telling Identities: The Californio "Testimonios"* (Minneapolis: University of Minnesota Press, 1995). Among the works that deal specifically with nineteenth-century images of Californianas are: Antonia I. Castañeda, "Gender, Race, and Culture: Spanish-Mexican Women in the Historiography of Frontier California," *Frontiers* 11, no. 1 (1990): 8–20; Antonia I. Castañeda, "The Political Economy of Nineteenth Century Stereotypes of Californianas," in *Between Borders: Essays on Mexican/Chicana History*, ed. Adelaida R. Del Castillo (Encino, Calif.: Floricanto Press, 1990), 213–36; Harry Clark, "Their Pride, Their Manners, and Their Voices: Sources of the Traditional Portrait of Early Californians," *California Historical Review* 52 (Spring 1974): 71–82; and David Langum, "California Women and the Image of Virtue," *Southern California Quarterly* 59 (Fall 1977): 245–50.

9   See, in particular, Gloria Anzaldúa, *Borderlands/La Frontera: The New Mestiza* (San Francisco: Spinsters/Aunt Lute, 1987). For nineteenth-century California, see Lisbeth Haas, *Conquests and Historical Identities in California, 1769–1936* (Berkeley, Los Angeles, and London: University of California Press, 1995); Padilla; *My History, Not Yours*; and Rosaura Sánchez, *Telling Identities*.

10   Cuello, "Beyond the 'Borderlands,'" 1.

11   For a discussion of the shaping of this historiography, see Peter Guardino, *The Time of Liberty: Popular Political Culture in Oaxaca, 1750–1850* (Durham, N.C.: Duke University Press, 2005), 159.

12   John E. Kicza, *Colonial Entrepreneurs: Families and Business in Bourbon Mexico City* (Albuquerque: University of New Mexico Press, 1983); Susan Migden Socolow, *The Merchants of Buenos Aires, 1778–1810* (Cambridge: Cambridge University Press, 1978); John Tutino, "Power, Class, and Family: Men and Women in the Mexican Elite 1750–1810," *The Americas* 39, no. 3 (January 1983): 359–81; and David W. Walker, *Kinship, Business, and Politics: The Martínez del Rio Family in Mexico, 1824–1867* (Austin: University of Texas Press, 1986).

13   See, for example, Silvia Marina Arrom, *The Women of Mexico City, 1790–1857* (Stanford, Calif.: Stanford University Press, 1985); Richard Boyer, *Lives of the Bigamists: Marriage, Family, and Community in Colonial Mexico* (Albuquerque: University of New Mexico Press, 1995); Asuncion Lavrin, editor, *Sexuality and Marriage in Colonial Latin America* (Lincoln: University of Nebraska Press, 1989); Steve J. Stern, *The Secret History of Gender: Women, Men, and Power in Late Colonial Mexico* (Chapel Hill: University of North Carolina Press, 1995); Ann Twinam, *Public Lives, Private Secrets: Gender, Honor, Sexuality, and Illegitimacy in Colonial Spanish America* (Stanford, Calif.: Stanford University Press, 1999); and Patricia Seed, *To Love, Honour, Obey in Colonial Mexico: Conflicts over Marriage Choice 1574–1821* (Stanford, Calif.: Stanford University Press, 1988). For the border regions, see Virginia Bouvier, *Women and the Conquest of California: Codes of Silence* (Tucson: University of Arizona Press, 2001); James Brooks, *Captives and Cousins: Slavery, Kinship, and Community in the Southwest Borderlands* (Chapel Hill: University of North Carolina Press, 2002); Antonia Castañeda, "Presidarias y Pobladoras: Spanish-Mexican Women in Frontier Monterey, Alta California, 1770–1821," (PhD diss., Stanford University, 1990); Miroslava Chávez-García, *Negotiating Conquest: Gender and Power in California, 1770s to 1880s* (Tucson: University of Arizona Press, 2004); Deena González, *Resisting the Favor: The Spanish-Mexican Women of Santa Fe, 1820–1880* (New York: Oxford University Press, 1999); and Ramón A. Gutiérrez, *When Jesus Came, the Corn Mothers Went Away: Marriage, Sexuality, and Power in New Mexico, 1500–1846* (Stanford, Calif.: Stanford University Press, 1991).

14   Ana María Alonso, *Thread of Blood: Colonialism, Revolution, and Gender on Mexico's Northern Frontier* (Tucson: University of Arizona Press, 1995); and Stern, *The Secret History of Gender*.

15   See, for example, Benedict Anderson, *Imagined Communities: Reflections on the Origin and Spread of Nationalism* (New York: Verso, 1983); Sarah Chambers,

From Subjects to Citizens: Honor, Gender, and Politics in Arequipa, Peru, 1780–1854 (University Park: University of Pennsylvania Press, 1999); Sueann Caulfield, Sarah C. Chambers, and Lara Putnam, eds., *Honor, Status, and Law in Modern Latin America* (Durham, N.C.: Duke University Press, 2005); Arlene J. Díaz, *Female Citizens, Patriarchs, and the Law in Venezuela, 1786–1904* (Lincoln: University of Nebraska Press, 2004); Guardino, *The Time of Liberty*; Christine Hunefeldt, *Liberalism in the Bedroom: Quarreling Spouses in Nineteenth-Century Lima* (University Park: University of Pennsylvania Press, 2000); Florencia Mallon, *Peasant and Nation: The Making of Postcolonial Mexico and Peru* (Berkeley: University of California Press, 1995); and Andrés Reséndez, *Changing National Identities at the Frontier: Texas and New Mexico, 1800–1850* (Cambridge: Cambridge University Press, 2005).

16   For recent work on Spanish-Indian relations in these zones, see, for example, David J. Weber, *Bárbaros: Spaniards and Their Savages in the Age of Enlightenment* (New Haven, Conn.: Yale University Press, 2005); Ned Blackhawk, *Violence over the Land: Indians and Empires in the Early American West* (Cambridge, Mass.: Harvard University Press, 2006); Juliana Barr, *Peace Came in the Form of a Woman: Indians and Spaniards in the Texas Borderlands* (Chapel Hill: University of North Carolina Press, 2007); and Pekka Hämäläinen, *Comanche Empire* (New Haven, Conn.: Yale University Press, 2008).

17   On microhistory as a technique, see James F. Brooks, Christopher R. N. DeCorse, and John Walton, eds., *Small Worlds: Method, Meaning, and Narrative in Microhistory* (Santa Fe, N.M.: School for Advanced Research, 2008); Carlo Ginzburg, "Microhistory: Two or Three Things That I Know about It," *Critical Inquiry* 20, no. 1 (Autumn 1993): 10–35; Jill Lepore, "Historians Who Love Too Much: Reflections on Microhistory and Biography," *Journal of American History* 88 (June 2001): 129–44; and Giovanni Levi, "On Microhistory," in *New Perspectives on Historical Writing*, ed. Peter Burke (University Park: Pennsylvania State University Press, 1992), 93–113.

18   Spanish terms appear in italic type on first mention, and thereafter in roman type. Spanish words in quotation marks are spelled as the writer put them down; in an era before Spanish spelling was regularized, there were frequent variants and irregularities in local spelling.

19   This understanding of patriarchy in late colonial and early republican Mexico owes a great deal to the work of Steve Stern as well as that of Ana María Alonso and Ramón Gutiérrez: Stern, *The Secret History of Gender*; Alonso, *Thread of Blood*; Gutiérrez, *When Jesus Came.*

20   For early evaluations of the revitalization of historic narrative, see, for example, Nancy Partner, "Making up Lost Time: Writing on the Writing of History," *Speculum* 61 (1986): 90–117; William Cronon, "A Place for Stories: Nature, History, and Narrative," *Journal of American History* 78, no. 4 (March 1992): 1347–76.

21   Bancroft was a book and stationery dealer, document collector, and professional historian whose collection forms the core of The Bancroft Library's holdings at University of California, Berkeley. The original transcripts of the memoirs can be found there. Hubert Howe Bancroft, *History of California,*

7 vols. (San Francisco: The History Company, 1884–89). Many of the testimonios have been translated and published, including those of all the women interviewed: Rose Marie Beebe and Robert M. Senkewicz, *Testimonios: Early California through the Eyes of Women, 1815–1848* (Berkeley, Calif.: Heyday Books, 2006).

22   Rosaura Sánchez, *Telling Identities*, 13.

23   "*Son tiempos difíciles, y si me atreviera a decir todo en este Diario, pero no!*" Angustias de la Guerra de Jimeno, Journal, February 14, 1847, DLG 725; see also the translation in Beebe and Senkewicz, *Testimonios*, 278. This entry is dated two months after she hid a Mexican soldier in her home and recorded nothing about it in the journal. See chapter six.

24   For more on women writing about the public sphere in this era, see Sarah Chambers, "Letters and Salons: Women Reading and Writing the Nation in the Nineteenth Century," in *Beyond Imagined Communities: Reading and Writing the Nation in Nineteenth-Century Latin America*, ed. John C. Chasteen and Sara Castro-Klarén (Baltimore, Md.: Johns Hopkins Press, 2003), 54–83.

CHAPTER ONE

1   Bancroft, *History of California*, 2:101–2.

2   Joseph A. Thompson, *El Gran Capitán: José de la Guerra* (Los Angeles: Cabrera and Sons, 1961), 2.

3   See John E. Kicza, "The Great Families of Mexico: Elite Maintenance and Business Practices in Late Colonial Mexico," *Hispanic American Historical Review* 62, no. 3 (1982): 439. On the traditional age of transition from childhood to adulthood in late colonial Latin America, see Twinam, *Public Lives, Private Secrets*, 181–83.

4   Arrom, *Women of Mexico City*, 5–8. Arrom defines class by occupation and by the number of servants employed, as recorded by the census. According to her classification, the upper class who could afford three or more servants tended to be "people of independent wealth, prosperous merchants and miners, top-level bureaucrats and clergy, ranking military officers, and the titled nobility." Just below, and aspiring to top ranking, were "the intellectuals, professionals, merchants and businessmen of modest means, government and private clerks, middle-ranked militia officers, and lower clergy" who might employ one or two servants.

5   John Lynch, *The Spanish American Revolutions 1808–1826*, 2nd ed. (New York: W. W. Norton & Co., 1986) 299–300; Arrom, *Women of Mexico City*, 5–7.

6   Lynch, *The Spanish American Revolutions*, 299.

7   The Bourbon Reforms in Mexico have received a great deal of attention. See, for example, David A. Brading, *Miners and Merchants in Bourbon Mexico, 1763–1810* (Cambridge: Cambridge University Press, 1971); Peggy Liss, "Creoles, the North American Example, and the Spanish American Economy, 1760–1810," in *The North American Role in the Spanish Imperial Economy*

1760–1819, ed. Jacques A. Barbier and Allan J. Kuethe (Manchester, U.K.: Manchester University Press, 1984).

8   Lyle N. McAlister, "Social Structure and Social Change in New Spain," *Hispanic American Historical Review* 43, no. 3 (August 1963): 364.

9   Leon G. Campbell, "The First Californios: Presidial Society in Spanish California, 1769–1822," *Journal of the West* 11 (October 1972): 590.

10   Manuel Cárcaba to José de la Guerra, Mexico City, October 14, 1798, folder 126, de la Guerra Papers, Santa Barbara Mission Archive-Library, Santa Barbara, California. Henceforward, references to the archive are abbreviated as SBMAL, except for further references to the DLG collection, which are listed by folder number.

11   William Henry Phillips, "Don José Antonio Julián de la Guerra y de Noriega, of California" (master's thesis, University of Southern California, 1950), 8.

12   The original of this letter has been lost; quoted in Phillips, "Don José Antonio Julián," 10.

13   Manuel Cárcaba to José de la Guerra, Mexico City, 1801, DLG 126; translation in Thompson, *El Gran Capitán*, 7.

14   Manuel Cárcaba to José de la Guerra, April 29, 1801, DLG Box 9, folder 18; translation in Thompson, *El Gran Capitán*, 5.

15   Thompson, *El Gran Capitán*, 7.

16   The peso through the Mexican era was worth roughly the same as a U.S. dollar.

17   "[A]unque el sueldo no levante mucho, es de mucho ônor y merito semejante empleo," Juan Josef de la Guerra to José de la Guerra, August 16, 1802, DLG Box 9, folder 3.

18   The Interior Provinces included both Californias, Sonora, Sinaloa, Nueva Vizcaya, New Mexico, Texas, and Coahuila.

19   Steven Hackel, *Children of Coyote, Missionaries of Saint Francis: Indian-Spanish Relations in Colonial California, 1769–1850* (Chapel Hill: University of North Carolina Press, 2005), 39–40.

20   M. Arroyo, "[M]uy mal ordenada y de jente muy pobre de Ropa y sin ningun Comercio." La descripción de las provincias de Culiacán, Sinaloa y Sonora del ingeniero Francisco de Fersen (1770), Biblio 3W, *Revista Bibliográfica de Geografía y Ciencias Sociales*, Universidad de Barcelona, Vol. VII, n° 430, 25 de febrero de 2003, http://www.ub.es/geocrit/b3w-430.htm [ISSN 1138-9796].

21   Quoted in Bouvier, *Women and the Conquest of California*, 59.

22   Ibid., 52. For a similar scheme of resettling families, applied to the northeastern frontier, see Patricia Osante, "Colonization and Control: The Case of Nuevo Santander," in Ross Frank, *Choice, Persuasion, and Coercion: Social Control on Spain's North American Frontiers* (Albuquerque: University of New Mexico Press, 2005), 227–51 at 230.

23   Quoted in Campbell, "The First Californios," 586. For a similar gendered experience of contact in Texas, see Juliana Barr, "A Diplomacy of Gender: Rituals of First Contact in the 'Land of the Tejas,'" *William and Mary Quarterly* 61 no. 3 (2004): 393–434.

24   Weber, *Bárbaros*, 107–9.

25   They were aided in this effort by the ecological invasion they inadvertently brought along. As European plants and animals pushed out native flora and fauna, local Indian populations lost their subsistence base. The produce of mission estates offered Native peoples a way to survive. Missionaries, aided by the military, gathered virtually the entire coastal population of California Indians into the missions. On the "Columbian exchange" in California, see Hackel, *Children of Coyote*, 65–90; and William Preston, "Serpent in the Garden: Environmental Change in Colonial California," in Ramón A. Gutiérrez and Richard J. Orsi, ed. *Contested Eden: California Before the Gold Rush* (Berkeley: University of California Press, 1998), 260–98.

26   David J. Weber, *The Spanish Frontier in North America* (New Haven, Conn.: Yale University Press, 1992), 253; Salomé Hernández, "No Settlement Without Women: Three Spanish California Settlement Schemes, 1790–1800," *Southern California Quarterly* 72 (September 1990): 205.

27   Weber, *Spanish Frontier*, 205, 328–29.

28   The term "mestizo" meant a combination of European and Indian ancestry, "mulato" signified African and European, "negro," African, and "indio," Indian. Other casta terms in use in California included "coyote," for a combination of Indian and mestizo, and "chino," which literally meant "Chinese" and usually referred to a combination of African and Indian, but was used on New Spain's west coast for Filipinos.

29   As a result of these regulations, by the first census of 1790, only one officer (later governor)—José Joaquín de Arrillaga—could truly claim to be European-born Spanish and of noble birth. Campbell, "The First Californios," 589–90; Max L. Moorhead, *The Presidio: Bastion of the Spanish Borderlands* (Norman: University of Oklahoma Press, 1975), 104.

30   Barbara L. Voss, *The Archaeology of Ethnogenesis: Race and Sexuality in Colonial San Francisco* (Berkeley: University of California Press, 2008), 265.

31   On this phenomenon in the U.S. Southwest, see Gloria E. Miranda, "Racial and Cultural Dimensions of *Gente de Razón* Status in Mexican California," *Southern California Quarterly* 70 (September 1988): 265–78; Weber, *Spanish Frontier*, 326–28; and Ramón A. Gutiérrez, "Ethnic and Class Boundaries in America's Hispanic Past," in *Social and Gender Boundaries in the United States*, ed. Sucheng Chan (Lewiston, N.Y.: The Edwin Mellon Press, 1989), 37–53. On the purchase of legitimacy or whiteness in other regions of Spanish America, see Twinam, *Public Lives, Private Secrets*, 18, 289, 310. On this phenomenon in California, see William Mason, *The Census of 1790: A Demographic History of Colonial California*, Ballena Press Anthropological Papers 45 (Menlo Park, Calif.: Ballena Press, 1998), 53–54. See also Quintard Taylor, *In Search of the Racial Frontier: African Americans in the American West, 1528–1990* (New York: W. W. Norton and Co., 1998), 32; Jack D. Forbes, "Black Pioneers: The Spanish-Speaking Afroamericans of the Southwest," *Phylon* 27, no. 3 (Fall 1966): 235–42; and Miranda, "Racial and Cultural Dimensions," 270–71.

32   Ignaz Pfefferkorn, quoted in Miranda, "Racial and Cultural Dimensions," 269.

33 Mason, *The Census of 1790*, 53–54.

34 Ibid.

35 Voss, *The Archaeology of Ethnogenesis*, 89.

36 Mission San Carlos Borromeo marriage registry, entry 168 [SC00168], Huntington Library, Early California Population Project (henceforth, ECPP), http://missions.huntington.org; Thompson, *El Gran Capitán*, 12; Bancroft, *History of California*, 2:100; 4:719.

37 Literacy rates at the presidios of Monterey and San Francisco stood at thirty percent in 1782. Real Presidio de Monterey, Lista de la Compania del Referido Presidio, 31 Julio de 1782, Prov. St. Pa. B. Mil iv 663–94 and R[eal] Presidio de San Francisco, Lista de La Compania, 31 Agosto de 1782, Prov. St. Pa. B. M. iv 601, The Bancroft Library.

38 Mason, *The Census of 1790*, 86. Tomasa, and probably also José Raymundo, likely had both European and Indian ancestry. Skeletal remains of their granddaughters indicate a mix of European and Native American traits. Julia Costello and Phillip Walker, "Burials from the Santa Barbara Presidio Chapel," *Historical Archaeology* 21 (1987): 3–17.

39 Twinam, *Public Lives, Private Secrets*, 86.

40 The drop was even more profound in the next generation. Whereas her brother's daughters married officers, Pascuala's legitimate daughter Bernarda married a Yaqui Indian *vaquero* of Los Angeles. Implicated in his murder in 1792, she was sentenced to serve as a house servant in Monterey. William Mason, *Los Angeles Under the Spanish Flag: Spain's New World* (Burbank, Calif.: Southern California Genealogical Society, 2004), 28.

41 Miranda, "Racial and Cultural Dimensions," 268; Voss, *The Archaeology of Ethnogenesis*, 101–2.

42 Narciso Durán and Buenaventura Fortuny, quoted in Weber, *Spanish Frontier*, 328.

43 José Cuello makes a similar point in his study of Saltillo. José Cuello, "Racialized Hierarchies of Power in Colonial Mexican Society: The Sistema de Castas as a Form of Social Control in Saltillo," in Jesús F. de la Teja and Ross Frank, *Choice, Persuasion, and Coercion*, 201–26.

44 José de la Guerra, for example, referred to his wife's first cousin Bernarda Ruiz as giving birth to "a little Negro," in April 1830. *"El 7 de Abr . . . dio a Luz la Sarnosa Bernarda un Nigrito."* José de la Guerra, "Occurrencias curiosas, 1830–31," Documentos para la historia de California, 1799–1845, The Bancroft Library, BANC MSS C-B 73, p. 24. See also the baptismal record BP00866, ECPP.

45 Quoted in Weber, *Spanish Frontier*, 328.

46 There is a large literature on marriage in the late Spanish Empire. Among these works are Arrom, *Women of Mexico City*; Ramón Gutiérrez, "Honor Ideology, Marriage Negotiation, and Class-Gender Domination in New Mexico, 1690–1846," *Latin American Perspectives* 12, no. 1, issue 44 (December 1985): 81–104; Stern, *The Secret History of Gender*; Verena Martinez-Alier, *Marriage, Class, and Color in Nineteenth-Century Cuba: A Study of Racial Attitudes and*

Sexual Values in a Slave Society, 2nd ed. (Ann Arbor: University of Michigan Press, 1989); Seed, *To Love, Honour, Obey*; and Boyer, *Lives of the Bigamists.*

47   The pressure to find wives led to very young brides; Tomasa and her sisters ranged in age from thirteen to fifteen when they wed in the 1780s and 1790s. Bouvier, *Women and the Conquest of California,* 114–16; Chávez-García, *Negotiating Conquest,* 16–17.

48   The territory was still full of single men when the first census was taken in 1790: sixty-two percent of the adult Hispanic population of California was male, and fewer than two soldiers of three were married, but the number of boys and girls under ten years of age was equal. Campbell, "The First Californios," 586; Hackel, *Children of Coyote,* 61; Gloria Miranda, "Gente de Razón Marriage Patterns in Spanish and Mexican California: A Case Study of Santa Barbara and Los Angeles," *Southern California Quarterly* 63, no. 1 (Spring 1981): 3–4.

49   Gutiérrez, *When Jesus Came,* 328, 336.

50   Susan Migden Socolow, *The Women of Colonial Latin America* (Cambridge: Cambridge University Press, 2000), 172–73; Castañeda, "Presidarias y Pobladoras," 232–37.

51   Bouvier, *Women and the Conquest of California,* 16–17; Chávez-García, *Negotiating Conquest,* 116.

52   Socolow, *Women of Colonial Latin America,* 173–74; Seed, *To Love, Honour, Obey,* 207, 223; Twinam, *Public Lives, Private Secrets,* 18, 307–11.

53   Thompson, *El Gran Capitán,* 11.

54   Gov. José Joaquín Arrillaga to José de la Guerra, Monterey, March 23, 1804, DLG 62.

55   Thompson, *El Gran Capitán,* 12.

56   Quoted in Thompson, *El Gran Capitán,* 11. The connection to Isabela of Spain would have carried a special connotation of honor and limpieza de sangre, or purity of blood, as it signals Carrillo's participation in the reconquest of Spain and the expulsion of Moors and Jews in 1492.

57   In 1806, his eldest daughter was fourteen, a marriageable age in California. On the strength of his certificate of limpieza de sangre, Vallejo was also able to secure a commission as soldado distinguido. "Año de 1806 Ynformacion de legitimidad y limpieza de sangre de Don Ygnacio Vicente Ferrer Vallejo," SBMAL; Bancroft, *History of California,* 5:756; Antonio I. Castañeda, "Engendering the History of Alta California: 1769–1848: Gender, Sexuality and the Family," in Gutiérrez and Orsi, *Contested Eden,* 241–42.

58   "[P]erseberando tu (como lo espero) en el Sto. temor de Dios, un amor reberente á tu Marido, respecto á los Sacerdotes Ministros del Altissimo." José Raymundo Carrillo to María Antonia Carrillo de la Guerra, May 21, 1804, DLG 154.

59   "Diele ami Noriega, que luego que llegue el Barco me mande mis Facturas, y demas corresponda. de mi Jurisdiccion con un extraordinario; y que no deje de comprarme quarenta, o cinquenta arrobas de Arina lo mas barata que pueda." José Raymundo Carrillo to María Antonia Carrillo de la Guerra, Santa Barbara, July 22, 1804, DLG 154.

60   *"[D]ebido á los buenos oficios del suegro,"* Mariano Guadalupe Vallejo, "Recuerdos históricos y personales tocante a la Alta California, 1769–1849," 5 volumes, The Bancroft Library, BANC MSS C-D 19, vol. 3 (1835–39), p. 93.

61   This account was taken from the report sent by Secretary of War Galles to Viceroy Iturrigaray, Mexico City, February 28, 1808; cited in Phillips, "Don José Antonio Julián," 26–27.

62   Carlos N. Híjar, "California en 1834, recuerdos de Carlos N. Híjar," The Bancroft Library, BANC MSS C-D 102, p. 21; translation in Monroy, *Thrown Among Strangers*, 146. Híjar arrived in 1834 with the Híjar-Padrés colony and was the nephew of its leader.

63   *"[C]ontinuad amigo siendo util al Publico, y dando hijos á la Patria."* Father José Viñals to José de la Guerra, Mission San Fernando, October 23, 1809, DLG 1010.

64   Gloria E. Miranda, "Hispano-Mexican Childrearing Practices in Pre-American Santa Barbara," *Southern California Quarterly* 64, no. 4 (December 1983): 308; Gloria Ricci Lothrup, "Rancheras and the Land: Women and Property Rights in Hispanic California," *Southern California Quarterly* 86 (March 1994): 61.

65   Robert Wayne Eversole, "Towns in Mexican Alta California: A Social History of Monterey, San José, Santa Bárbara, and Los Angeles, 1822–1846" (PhD diss., University of California, San Diego, 1986), 169–78, quoted in Osio, *The History of Alta California*, 274; Lothrup, "Rancheras," 61. See also David J. Weber, *The Mexican Frontier, 1821–1846: The American Southwest under Mexico* (Albuquerque: University of New Mexico Press, 1982), 206.

66   Ygnacio Sepúlveda to Hubert H. Bancroft, "Historical Memoranda," July 9, 1874, The Bancroft Library, BANC MSS C-E 65:14, p. 6.

67   Sir George Simpson, *Narrative of a Voyage to California Ports in 1841–42* (San Francisco: T. C. Russell, 1930), 124–25.

68   Alonso, *Thread of Blood*, 181. See also Stephen Gudeman, "The *Compadrazgo* as a Reflection of the Natural and Spiritual Person," *Proceedings of the Royal Anthropological Institute of Great Britain and Ireland for 1971*, 50–51.

69   Simpson, *Narrative of a Voyage*, 124–25.

70   The godparent relationships of the de la Guerras were derived from the baptismal registries housed at the Santa Barbara Mission Archive-Library. Since this research was completed, these registries, and those of the other missions in California, have been made available online at ECPP.

71   See, for example, Domingo Carrillo to José de la Guerra, San Diego, February 18, 1823, DLG 141.

72   José Antonio Noriega to José de la Guerra, Mexico City, August 6, 1808, DLG 712.

73   Campbell, "The First Californios," 591.

74   Robert Archibald, *The Economic Aspects of the California Missions* (Washington, D.C.: Academy of American Franciscan History, 1978), 64; Phillips, "Don José Antonio Julián," 33.

75   *"[S]e encuentra variedad de precios en unos mismos renglones, es preciso quitar este abuso, y ponerlos a un mismo precio."* Gov. José Joaquín Arrillaga to José de la Guerra, San Diego, January 7, 1807, DLG 62.

76   *"Por 37 caseras de ganado bacuno del diezmo perteneze. al ppdo. año de 1803 que resibio en el Pueblo de San José, a satisfacer en obras de sastreria que a razon de 10r. 8 grs. cavera importar."* José de la Guerra, Business papers and accounts, 1804–8, DLG 1047.

77   Ibid.

78   *"Espero que V me mande todo el cebo que pueda, y si tuviere con equidad alguna Memorita que pueda venir sin escandalo á cargo del Despensero de la Princesa me la manda V. é iremos á medias . . . espero se fie de mi amistad y buena fee."* Juan Martínez y Zayas to José de la Guerra, San Blas, March 31, 1809, DLG 657.

79   Archibald, *The Economic Aspects*, 118; Thompson, *El Gran Capitán*, 16.

80   *"No quisiera me tuvieras en dudas con el asunto gordo, que me dices tienes entre manos, y que acaso en el proximo Mensal me lo comunicarias; lo que celbrare es que sea cosa de honra y provecho."* José Antonio Noriega to José de la Guerra, Mexico City, September 2, 1807, DLG 712.

81   Thompson, *El Gran Capitán*, 16.

82   *"[P]orque él que tiene Familia no debe hacer regalos sino admitir quantos le hagan, para que tengan en todo tiempo conque sostenerla."* José Antonio Noriega to José de la Guerra, Mexico City, April 22, 1807, DLG 712.

83   José Antonio Noriega to José de la Guerra, Mexico City, April 22, 1807, DLG 712.

84   *"[E]stando entendido de que eres hombre de bien y que no eres capaz de hacer droga."* José Antonio Noriega to José de la Guerra, Mexico City, November 1, 1809, DLG 712.

85   Archibald, *The Economic Aspects*, 128–29.

86   *"Capitan Rodríguez, Arriero."* José Antonio Noriega to José de la Guerra, Mexico City, December 16, 1807, DLG 712.

87   *"Amas de que toda Libranza, ó es buena ó es mala, si buena debe aceptarla conforme á Ley . . . Rodríguez es mi Amigo, . . . pero una cosa es la amistad, y otra los Yntereses: yo pido una cosa mui justa."* José Antonio Noriega to José de la Guerra, Mexico City, June 15, 1808, DLG 712.

88   On this phenomenon in late colonial New Spain, see Diana Balmori, Stuart Voss, and Miles Wortman, eds. *Notable Family Networks in Latin America* (Chicago: University of Chicago Press, 1984); Edith Couturier, "Women in a Noble Family: The Mexican Counts of Regla, 1750–1830," in *Latin American Women: Historical Perspectives,* ed. Ascuncion Lavrin (Westport, Conn.: Greenwood Press, 1978); Kicza, "The Great Families of Mexico," 429–57; Kicza, *Colonial Entrepreneurs*; Tutino, "Power, Class, and Family"; and Walker, *Kinship, Business, and Politics.*

89   Kicza, "The Great Families of Mexico," 434, 447.

90   Walker, *Kinship, Business, and Politics*, 54.

91 Ibid., 63.

92 *"[Y]o apreciara me embiaras mas que fueran diez mil pesos para salir de algunos ahogos."* José Antonio Noriega to José de la Guerra, Mexico City, November 1, 1809, DLG 712. See also their letters in DLG 712 of July 1,1809; December 13, 1809; and February 17, 1810.

93 *"Convengo en la soledad de esos Payses y el deseo de Vms. de desamparanlos, para ello ofrece dilaciones, y Vm. con el nuebo estado dificuta mas la salida."* Antonio Morán to José de la Guerra, Mexico City, January 21, 1804, DLG 688.

94 *"Esta iniquidad no tiene igual en al Historia; . . . solo siento no estar en España para ir como uno de tantos á buscar al enemigo, y poder morir en defensa del Rey, de la Religion Santa, en que por la gracia de Dios fuimos educados, y nutridos, y por la Patria."* José Antonio Noriega to José de la Guerra, Mexico City, August 6, 1808, DLG 712.

95 *[Q]ue como buen basallo contribuyer a nuestro Antigua España para ayuda de defensa de la Patria, de la Religion, y de nuestro muy amado el Rey el Señor D. Fernando 70."* José Antonio Noriega to José de la Guerra, Mexico City, April 19, 1809, DLG 712.

96 José Antonio Noriega to José de la Guerra, Mexico City, July 1, 1809, DLG 712.

97 On the family's preparations to leave, see Francisco María Ruiz to José de la Guerra, Mission San Diego, July 12, 1810, DLG 852; Governor José Joaquín Arrillaga to José de la Guerra, San Diego, September 6, 1810 [Bowman, vol. 1, letter 43, p. 28]; Governor José Joaquín Arrillaga to José de la Guerra, San Juan Capistrano, September 10, 1810 [Bowman, vol. 1, letter 44, p. 28]; Governor José Joaquín Arrillaga to José de la Guerra, Monterey, October 2, 1810, DLG 62.

98 Governor José Joaquín Arrillaga to José de la Guerra, San Juan Capistrano, September 10, 1810 [Bowman, vol. 1, letter 44, p. 28].

99 Francisco María Ruiz, Comandante, and Father José Barón, Certified copy of baptismal record of Rita de Jesús de la Guerra, San Diego, October 26, 1810 [Bowman, vol. 1, letter 77, p. 56].

100 *"Ya supongo á V. emborucado [involucrado] y en elemento diferente al que esta acostumbrado pero como Joben y robusto breve se impondra . . ."* Governor José Joaquín Arrillaga to José de la Guerra, Monterey, November 4, 1810, DLG 62.

101 Thompson, *El Gran Capitán*, 17.

102 Lynch, *The Spanish American Revolutions*, 312.

103 Official document of Francisco Valdez, Captain of Infantry, Comandante of the Battalion of Armes, of Tepic, testifying to the character and services of Don José de la Guerra, August 31, 1811, DLG 989.

104 Viceroy Francisco Xavier Venegas to José de la Guerra, Mexico, May 16, 1811, DLG 1005; Thompson, *El Gran Capitán*, 17.

105 Archibald, *The Economic Aspects*, 61–62.

106 Archibald, *The Economic Aspects*, 11.

107 José de la Yen to José de la Guerra, Compostela, February 15, 1813 [Bowman, vol. 1, letter 90, p. 65].

108   There are many examples of these Spanish merchants requesting such specific produce from José de la Guerra from 1813 to 1821. See, for example: José Cardoso to José de la Guerra, San Blas, March 6, 1813, DLG 127; Antonio Marcial to José de la Guerra, Tepic, October 27, 1813, DLG 899; Father Pedro Gonzales to José de la Guerra, San Ygnacio, Baja California, February 8, 1816, DLG 334; and Joaquín Astiazarán to José de la Guerra, Tepic, May 4, 1819, DLG 66.

109   Captain William Heath Davis, "The Logbook of the Mercury, 1806–1807," DLG 1047c.

110   Joaquín de Astiazarán to José de la Guerra, Tepic, January 29, 1812, DLG 66.

111   Joaquín de Astiazarán to José de la Guerra, Tepic, January 31, 1813, DLG 66.

112   Governor José Joaquín Arrillaga to José de la Guerra, Monterey, April 3, 1813 [Bowman, vol. 1, letter 92, p. 66].

113   *"Aqui tiene V. amigo mi todo mi caudal en el dia mas 4 1/2 años."* José María Narváez to José de la Guerra, Monterey, September 18, 1814, DLG 701.

114   *"Mañana si dios quiere, daremos la vela para San Blas dejando en poder de D. Mariano Estrada un Baul de china maquedo que contiene los efectos de la adjunta facturita para que en primera ocacion lo mande á Sn Diego a la disposicion de V ...Los precios son los ultimos a que los tomara v. si le acomodare, y de no los conservara V. en no poder asta mi orden de aquien se los devera entregar."* José María Narváez to José de la Guerra, Monterey, November 11, 1814, DLG 701. There are scores of these business letters in the de la Guerra collection. Others are very similar, like those of Joaquín Astiazarán in May 1815, who discussed sending Guadalajara rebozos, chocolate, shrimp, and a brandy still from Tepic. Joaquín Astiazarán to José de la Guerra, Tepic, May 17, 1815, and May 30, 1815, DLG 66. Upon the arrival of this shipment, on the boat of Pedro Negrete, de la Guerra also took possession of 69 packages of cigars, 4 pesos per package; 5 *metas* of cotton, 8 pesos per meta; 1 basketful of gourds; 5,187 boxes of cigarettes; 17 baskets of crockery; 3 baskets of *panocha*; and *cigaritos*, 12 pkgs for 1 peso. Pedro Negrete to José de la Guerra, Invoice, San Diego, December 24, 1815, DLG 1048.

115   The correspondence among Ulloa, Rodríguez, and a third partner, Manuel Varela, provides an excellent window onto trading contracts and relations. See Gonzalo Ulloa and Pedro Rodríguez, a contract, 1819, DLG 981; Manuel Varela to José de la Guerra, Tepic, October 4, 1820; April 26, 1821; and April 19, 1824, DLG 1001.

116   *"[A]hora conozco mas que nunca el Sentimiento que me causa la separacion de unos amingos á quienes amo deveras. Vd. es el primero amigo mio."* Fermín de Genoa y Aguirre to José de la Guerra, San Gabriel, November 20, 1818, DLG 322.

117   Antonio José Cot to José de la Guerra, Monterey, September 16, 1820, DLG 203.

118   Archibald, *The Economic Aspects*, 95; Francisco Párraga to José de la Guerra, San Blas, March 10, 1807, DLG 768. See José de la Guerra, accounts and business papers, 1810–19, DLG 1048.

119   *"No estoy para cuentas, ni cuentecitas; estoy muy ocupado; mucho, mucho."* Fermín de Genoa y Aguirre to José de la Guerra, Monterey, July 20, 1818, DLG 322.

120 Archibald, *The Economic Aspects*, 130, 132. The de la Guerra collection contains one example of this trade: Captain William Heath Davis, "The Logbook of the Mercury, 1806–1807," DLG 1047c.

121 Archibald, *The Economic Aspects*, 124, 129–30.

122 See letters from Governor Pablo Vicente de Solá to José de la Guerra, DLG 923.

123 Archibald, *The Economic Aspects*, 137. Governor Pablo Vicente de Solá to José de la Guerra, Monterey, July 27, 1816, DLG 923; Bancroft, *The History of California*, 2:202, 268–70.

124 Archibald, *The Economic Aspects*, 139.

125 "[T]ratar el venderla al mejor precio que pueda á Plata; y si esto no se consiguiere la enajenará á cebos." Juan José Mayo to the Padres of Mission San Gabriel, Santa Barbara, November 14, 1817, DLG 661.

126 Archibald, *The Economic Aspects*, 127–28.

127 Ibid., 121. See also the accounts and inventories in DLG 1047 and 1048, such as Juan José de Zestaje to José de la Guerra, Account, Tepic, 1812–15; and Juan José Mayo to José de la Guerra, invoice, Santa Bárbara, November 13, 1819, DLG 661.

128 "Si Dn. Fermin las tiene, y da a precio comodo mande unas piezas ... V. es buen sujeto, entiende el arte, haga pues en servicio de estos pobres lo que pueda." "devuelvo las 6 navajas de barba [shaving razors] por que dicen los Indios que ni aun para ellos sirven, y las 6 gargantillas [short necklaces] por que dicen los mismos no tienen valor entre ellos." Father Payeras to José de la Guerra, Mission La Purísima Concepción, April 9, 1818, DLG 769.

129 Captain William Heath Davis, "Logbook of the Mercury, 1806–1807," DLG 1047.

130 Father Mariano Payeras to Rev. Father Guardian Fray Baldomero López, San Gabriel, November 6, 1819. *Historia de México,* Primera Serie, Tomo 3, AGN; translation in Donald Cutter, ed., *Writings of Mariano Payeras* (Santa Barbara, Calif.: Bellerophon Books, 1995), 218.

131 For an example of personal goods ordered by de la Guerra, see Father José Sánchez to José de la Guerra, February 19, 1815, DLG 874. In 1818, de la Guerra splurged on "One sala clock, with second and daily hands, and half hour and hour bells, with cedar or mahogany face," for 225 pesos. *Invoice of the Hermosa Mexicana*, July 13, 1818, DLG 1048.

132 "Adios Señor, no me olbido a sus consejos y quisiera que qdo. V. sepa voy errado me corrigiera y aconsejara, como un Padre aun hijo que asi los recivo." Santiago Argüello to José de la Guerra, Mission San Gabriel, May 4, 1818, DLG 56.

133 This was despite the fact that the governor wasn't present at Pablo's baptism in 1819. In the case of the physical absence of a godparent, Californians often designated proxies, but in Pablo's case, the man Solá had designated, Lieutenant Moraga, was also unable to be there. As a result, María Antonia's brother Anastasio stood in for Solá, but Father Suñer, the Reverend Pastor of Mission Santa Bárbara (who had his own grudges against Solá), refused to recognize the proxy. Bancroft, *The History of California*, 2:737; Pablo Vicente de Solá to José de la Guerra, Monterey, September 7, 1819, DLG 923. When Solá learned that Suñer

would not recognize him as Pablo's godfather, he assured José, "But in my opinion, I will always be the padrino, and I will do all I can for the benefit of my godson, brothers and parents." *"[P]ero yo en mi concepto lo soy spre. y haré aveneficio de mi haijado, hermanos y padres, quanto bien pueda."* Pablo Vicente de Solá to José de la Guerra; February 5, 1820, DLG 923.

134   The de la Guerras were so eager to cement this tie with Solá that they asked him to sponsor this next child, Anita, as well. See Bancroft, *History of California*, 2:470–72.

135   *[U]n Padre de familias que estas son tan largas como la descendencia de Adan; . . . y si conociese V. que mi destino pueda influir para su logro avíseme pa. poder lo poner en practica."* Pablo Vicente de Solá to José de la Guerra, April 26, 1821, DLG 924.

136   See Bancroft, *History of California*, 2:566, 569.

137   José Joaquín Torre to *"Mi Amado Jefe"* de la Guerra, no date ("Somos 22"), DLG 978; José Joaquín Torre to *"Mi Siempre venerado Jefe Paysano y Sr."* de la Guerra, Monterey, May 8, 1821, DLG 978.

138   José Joaquín Torre to *"Mi venerado Gefe, Paysano y Sor"* de la Guerra, Monterey, February 22, 1822, DLG 978.

139   José de la Guerra to Governor Solá, October 4, 1822; transcription and translation in Proceedings of California Land Cases, Southern District, Case 107, Conejo. José de la Guerra y Noriega and María del Carmen Rodríguez, claimants, [1852], Huntington Library, MS Film 543:14, p. 54.

140   Pablo Vicente de Solá to José de la Guerra, October 10, 1822; transcription and translation in ibid.

141   José Antonio Carrillo, "Testimony," in ibid., p. 10.

142   Socolow, *Merchants of Buenos Aires*; Brading, *Miners and Merchants*.

143   *"[E]n atencion al empeño de V. . . . y tanto este individuo como a sus hermanos les atendere con oportunidad para sus ascensos, dandoles V. los consejos saludables como buen hermano para el mas exacto cumplimto. de sus deveres."* Pablo Vicente de Solá to José de la Guerra, Monterey, March 8, 1821, DLG 924. For more on Domingo Carrillo's military career, see Bancroft, *History of California*, 2:744.

144   Domingo Carrillo to José de la Guerra, San Diego, July 1, 1821, DLG 141.

145   See, especially, Pablo Vicente de Solá to José de la Guerra, Monterey, June 25, 1821, DLG 924. Solá asks de la Guerra to collect the taxes of Los Angeles and to appoint Anastasio Carrillo to do so. Anastasio Carrillo to José de la Guerra, Los Angeles, August 27, 1821, and January 25, 1822, DLG 133. Carrillo reports on his progress collecting taxes in tallow.

146   José Antonio Carrillo to José de la Guerra, Los Angeles, February 3, 1821; February 26, 1822; DLG 149.

147   *"Estos Poblanos me han engañado vilmte por que los mas de ellos me digeron que me fuese para la Playa, . . . y no llevaron nada."* José Antonio Carrillo to José de la Guerra, Los Angeles, June 18, 1821, DLG 149.

148   *"[P]oniendo por motivo que ya le devia como mas de mil pesos . . . pude V si no le fiarese mal fortuna su cuenta y mandar mela para al instante satisfacer el devito que resulteise, hay tiene V. un buen modo de que conservimos el estilo hermanable que yo deseo y sin duda V tambien."* José Antonio Carrillo to José de la Guerra, Los Angeles, July 16, 1822, DLG 149.

149   *"[H]oy ha tenido el mayor []g[]ijo, por que crei no haber podido cobrarle, a su cuñado . . . ha cubrir lo devida pagó la mision de S. Gabriel . . . nunca José Antonio sera jente, y su soberbia y organyo, cada dia mas."* Juan Malarín to José de la Guerra, Los Angeles, November 5, 1823, DLG 622. This was not the last time a foreign trader asked de la Guerra to clean up his brother-in-law's messes. See also José Cardoso to José de la Guerra, Tepic, March 2, 1824, DLG 127.

150   Bancroft, *History of California*, 2:745.

151   Joaquín de Astiazarán to José de la Guerra, Tepic, October 5, 1814, DLG 66.

152   For accounts of Bouchard and his raid of the California coast, see Patrick O'Dowd, "Pirates and Patriots," *La Campana* (Winter 1997–98): 2–16; Peter Uhrowczik, *The Burning of Monterey: The 1818 Attack on California by the Privateer Bouchard* (Los Gatos, Calif.: Cyril Books, 2001); Thompson, *El Gran Capitán*, 35–51, and María de las Angustias de la Guerra de Ord, "Ocurrencias en California," 1878, The Bancroft Library, BANC MSS C-D 134; translation in Beebe and Senkewicz, *Testimonios*, 202–5.

153   *"Alerta, Alerta, y Viva Fernando mientras nosotros vivimos, viva ntra Sta. Religion. y ntra Patria, aun que moramos todos. Estamos en tpo critico . . . con que amolar cuchillos(?) Paysanito, y que esas dos charreteras no sirban solo para iluminar el cuerpo sino tambien la patria y el alma."* Father Luis Martínez to José de la Guerra, Mission la Purísima, n.d., DLG 649.

154   José de la Guerra to Hipólito Bouchard, Santa Bárbara, December 8, 1818, quoted in Thompson, *El Gran Capitán*, 47.

155   *"Se mata de formar una compa. de realistas de razon en cada Presidio."* Father Antonio Ripoll to José de la Guerra, Mission Santa Bárbara, April 26, 1820, DLG 826.

156   Osio, *The History of Alta California*, 80.

157   Thompson, *El Gran Capitán*, 60–61.

158   *"[S]i seguimos a el rey en la legislacion antigua no tenemos esperanza de socorro, . . . y asi yo soy de parecer que el mejor partido es, estar neutrales."* Father Luis Martínez to José de la Guerra, n.d., after 1819, DLG 649.

159   *"[A]lgunos espiritus que hay siempre haspirando la Rebolucion y la independencia, pero son unos muebles que poco yaman la Atension."* Habilitado General Gervasio Argüello to José de la Guerra, Guadalajara, January 25, 1821, DLG 41.

160   *"Si bienen los insurgentes y encuentran resistencia en la provincia la destruyen. Si seguimos a Iturvide con sus Ideas (que parecen favorables,) debemos de pensar que tendremos el socorro algo destante."* Father Luis Martínez to José de la Guerra, n.d., DLG 649.

161   Pablo Vicente de Solá to Gov. José Argüello, January 10, 1822. See Weber, *Mexican Frontier*, 8.

162   Reséndez, *Changing National Identities at the Frontier*, 84–85.

163   Bancroft, *History of California*, 2:451; and Herbert Bolton, "The Iturbide Revolution in the Californias," *Hispanic American Historical Review* 2 (May 1919), 188–242.

164   María Inocenta Pico de Avila, "Cosas de California," 1878, The Bancroft Library, BANC MSS C-D 34; translation in Beebe and Senkewicz, *Testimonios*, 313.

165   Quoted in Weber, *Mexican Frontier*, 8.

166   María Inocenta Pico, "Cosas," The Bancroft Library, BANC MSS C-D 34; translation in Beebe and Senkewicz, *Testimonios*, 312.

167   Gregorio Mora-Torres, *Californio Voices: The Oral Memoirs of José María Amador and Lorenzo Asisara* (Denton, Texas: University of North Texas Press, 2005), 113.

168   Angustias de la Guerra, "Ocurrencias," The Bancroft Library, BANC MSS C-D 134; translation in Beebe and Senkewicz, *Testimonios*, 209.

CHAPTER TWO

1   This title is taken from Father José Viñals to José de la Guerra, Mission San Fernando, October 23, 1809, DLG 1010.

2   *"Postrandonos a los Pies de Vmd. con el mas profundo respecto y sumicion ... ocurrimos á Vmd. como apadre amoso nos de el mayor consuelo."* Luisa Barelas, Demetria Ramires, Juana Ygnocencia Reyes, Ma. Luisa Reyes, and Baleriana Lorensana to José de la Guerra, Los Angeles, February 1, 1822, DLG 1000.

3   *"Con respeto á su señor padre el captain de la Guerra y Noriega ... el gran hombre que habia sabido merecer el glorioso titulo de 'Padre de Pueblo': ... la memoria de sus muchas virtudes vive aun fresca entre los agradecidos barbareños."* Teresa de la Guerra de Hartnell, "Narrativa de la distinguida matrona Californiana," 1875, The Bancroft Library, BANC MSS C-E 67:2, p. 27; translation in Beebe and Senkewicz, *Testimonios*, 63.

4   Padilla, *My History, Not Yours*, 113.

5   On the patriarchal family as a metaphor for power in late colonial Spanish America, see among other works, Arrom, *Women of Mexico City*, 76–77; Bianca Premo, *Children of the Father King: Youth, Authority, and Legal Minority in Colonial Lima* (Chapel Hill: North Carolina Press, 2005); and Stern, *The Secret History of Gender*.

6   The term derives from the Náhuatl word "Chichimeca," a general and pejorative term for nomadic peoples living north of the Valley of Mexico. For examples of the use of the term "Mecos" to designate California Indians, see Father Mariano Payeras to José de la Guerra, Mission La Purísima, April 9, 1818, DLG 769; and Father Francisco Uría to José de la Guerra, Mission Santa Ynez, May 21, 1819, DLG 982.

7   On this issue, see Castañeda, "Presidarias y Pobladoras"; Monroy, *Thrown Among Strangers*; Padilla, *My History, Not Yours*; and Rosaura Sánchez, *Telling Identities*.

8   "Decision of His Excellency and the Royal Council in Regard to the Petitions of the Reverend Father President (Serra)," May 6, 1773, quoted in Hackel, *Children of Coyote*, 324.

9   *"[D]e admitir á Vm. en el numero de nros. Hermanos, haciendole participante de todas las oraciones, ayunos, disciplinas* [this word could mean rules of conduct but also could refer to self-flagellation], *exercicios espirituales, y demas obras satisfactorias y meritorias que practican los Religiosos de este Colegio, asi en la reduccion de los infieles y catequismo de Neofitos, como en la reforma de la Fieles."* Father Josef Gasol to José de la Guerra, Mexico City, July 6, 1803, DLG 319.

10   The "Slaves of the Holy Virgin," also called the "Slaves of the Mother of God," or the "Holy Slavery to Mary," was founded at the Franciscan monastery of Alcalá, Spain, around 1595. Confraternities such as this one were made up of lay Catholics and some clergy who came together to promote the religious life of their members. The "slaves" demanded a particularly high level of commitment. Thompson, *El Gran Capitán*, 14; Christopher Black and Pamela Gravestock, eds., *Early Modern Confraternities in Europe and the Americas* (Burlington, Vt.: Ashgate, 2006).

11   Thompson, *El Gran Capitán*, 8–9.

12   For example, Father Payeras of Mission La Purísima sent de la Guerra a list of a family of six Indians to bring back who had gone to the wife's Indian village of Tulami and were being sheltered by the unconverted Indian Faciats. Father Mariano Payeras to José de la Guerra, La Purísima, n.d., DLG 769. For more on the use of soldiers to reclaim and punish fugitives, see Hackel, *Children of Coyote*, 332–35; and James Sandos, *Converting California: Indians and Franciscans in the Missions* (New Haven, Conn.: Yale University Press, 2004), 160–63.

13   *"Ya se que no fue muy bien con la campaña ... Desde que salio la tropa ya se han huido 4 mas. Con que por Dios, no los degeis hasta que todos se vuelvan a congregar, pero bien escarmentados."* Father Pedro Muñóz to Comandante José de la Guerra, Mission San Fernando, April 8, 1816, DLG 695.

14   Father Luis Martínez to Captain José de la Guerra, n.d. [Bowman, vol. 2, letter 25, p. 19].

15   Angustias de la Guerra, "Ocurrencias," The Bancroft Library, BANC MSS C-D 134; translation in Beebe and Senkewicz, *Testimonios*, 205.

16   Ibid., 207.

17   José del Carmen Lugo, "Vida de un ranchero," The Bancroft Library, BANC MSS C-D 118; translation in *Historical Society of Southern California Quarterly* 32, no. 3 (September 1950): 227.

18   For more on the legal system as it applied to Indians, see Hackel, *Children of Coyote*, 344–51.

19   *"[O]brara inmediatamente segn Justicia y arreglado a la ley con ellos, no ignorando V. lo util que es el pronto castigo en estos casos para escarmiento de los demas."* Gov. Arguello to José de la Guerra, Presidio of San Francisco, February 24, 1824, DLG 51. *"V. pues obre en justicias, de modo que toda le republica quede satisfecha de que se obró segn. Ley y Justicia, y que se á dado a cada uno*

el premio ó castigo segun sus meritos." Gov. Argüello to José de la Guerra, Monterey, March 31, 1824, DLG 51.

20   *"[L]os muchachos…lo que le pido es los castigue bien con cuero y me los mande."* Father Francisco Xavier Uría to José de la Guerra, Mission Santa Ynez, November 8, 1816, DLG 982.

21   *"[P]uesto Valerio en mis brazos, como el hijo prodigo en los de su Padres, no puedo desecharlo…Asi mi Sor. Comandante, y mi Dn. José, quando veais en vuestro poder á Valerio…no mirais en él á un malechor que la fuerza, y violencia puso en vuestras manos; sino al Hijo prodigo, que su mismo Padre por serlo, por sus manos propias os entregó."* Father Mariano Payeras to Comandante José de la Guerra, Mission La Purísima, December 22, 1816, DLG 769. See also Father Antonio Ripoll to José de la Guerra, Mission La Purísima, n.d., DLG 826.

22   José de la Guerra to Gov. José Joaquín Arrillaga, San Diego, December 22, 1808, DLG 444. See also Hackel, *Children of Coyote*, 179, 222–23, 357, 360.

23   For more on Indian labor in presidios and towns, see Hackel, *Children of Coyote*, 296–320; and Voss, *The Archaeology of Ethnogenesis*, 77–83.

24   *"[Q]uedandose Vd. para las obras de ese Presidio con los 5…aquienes para que sean utiles en los trabajos les mandara Vd. poner su correspondiente grillete y tambien el soldado o soldados de confianza que los custodien."* Governor Pablo Vicente de Solá to José de la Guerra, June 25, 1821, Monterey, DLG 924. These Indians were Pomponio and Lázaro from Mission San Francisco, Valerio from Mission San Juan Bautista, and Juan Antonio and Egidio from Mission Soledad.

25   *"[V]oy a acerle un favor, para que Vm. me aga a mi si ay amistad entre nosotros…el Yndio es bueno, solamente muy en buesttero[?] pero de mucho trabajo y albañil que le vendra bien a Vm."* Francisco Xavier Uría to José de la Guerra, Mission Santa Ynez, August 7, 1818, DLG 982.

26   For more on this, see Steven W. Hackel, "Land, Labor, and Production: The Colonial Economy of Spanish and Mexican California," in Gutiérrez and Orsi, *Contested Eden*, 125; for the Santa Bárbara presidio in particular, see Hackel, *Children of Coyote*, 305–6.

27   *"Si teneis en Vro. Presidio dos Indios por que no copeis a Hermenegildo, y entonces Tamariz será para Maitorena."* Father José Sánchez to José de la Guerra, February 18, 1815, DLG 874.

28   *"[V]an 10 mecos…les digo que no han de sacar racion suponiendo que qn. les ocupe les dara de comer…se mudaran cada 6 semanas los mecos."* Father Francisco Uría to José de la Guerra, Mission Santa Ynez, May 21, 1819, DLG 982.

29   *[D]igale a Ma Antonia ay va un musico buen chocolater llamado Constantino."* Ibid.

30   Hackel, *Children of Coyote*, 287–96.

31   Quoted in Hackel, *Children of Coyote*, 320.

32   Barbara Voss and others note that in the earlier years of settlement, gangs of gentile laborers were often derived from local villages through negotiation with Native leaders, but by the time de la Guerra arrived in Santa Bárbara, that does not seem to have been an option. Voss, *Archaeology of Ethnogenesis*, 77–79.

33   *"El Alfz. Dn José Joaquínaitorena, me escribe solicitando para su servicio al Yndio Coriak que esta ay, puede Vm. franquearselo a luego que lo pida."* Pablo Vicente de Solá to José de la Guerra, Monterey, April 29, 1816, DLG 923. De la Guerra apparently demanded two Kodiaks for himself, having remarked to Solá that he thought they would make good servants. Bancroft, *History of California*, 2:416.

34   *"Asiento desde luego que esos Yndios de la Purísima estan á la disposicion de V. que como organo de la voz del gobierno mayor sabra en que y como ocuparlos ... asi en ese caso, como en qualquier otro en que un Padre deviera con sus hijo dar el oportuno auxilio, puede V contar con mi aprovacion sin consultarme."* Father Mariano Payeras to José de la Guerra, Mission La Purísima, October 24, 1818, DLG 769.

35   *"[S]in tenerlos presidarios, para que no se vuelvan peores."* Father Francisco Xavier Uría to José de la Guerra, Mission Santa Ynez, November 8, 1816, DLG 982.

36   *"[E]sta la azotea casi cayindose que solamente la misericordia del Señor la mantiene ... esta mision manifesta a Vmd la suma necesidad que tiene de gente, pues mucha parte de ellas se compone de viejos y enfermos."* Father Marcos Victoria to José de la Guerra, Mission San Fernando, February 25, 1819, DLG 1016.

37   Father Mariano Payeras to Rev. Father Guardian Fray Baldomero López, San Gabriel, November 6, 1819, Historia de México, Primera Serie, Tomo 3, AGN; translation in Cutter, *Writings*, 218.

38   Lugo, "Vida de un ranchero," The Bancroft Library, BANC MSS C-D 118; translation in *Historical Society of Southern California Quarterly* 32, no. 3 (September 1950): 226.

39   *"Hace unos qtos. dias que echamos menos al Indito Sebastián, unico neofo. que falta, en la mision; y asi sucede siempre en qto se le quitan los grillos, ó corma. Ojala fuese verdadera la vocacion de estarse en casa de vm., y viviese tranquilo, y sosegado; y por nra parte no hai embarazo ... Si anda tunanteando por todas partes, y dando consejo, mandelo vm. para aca."* Father José Señán to José de la Guerra, Mission San Buenaventura, June 19, 1816, DLG 904.

40   There is a large body of literature in Latin American history that explores this honor/shame ideal of patriarchy. See Stern, *The Secret History of Gender*; see also: Alonso, *Thread of Blood*; Arrom, *Women of Mexico City*; Martinez-Alier, *Marriage, Class, and Color in Nineteenth-Century Cuba*; Twinam, *Public Lives, Private Secrets*; Gutiérrez, *When Jesus Came*; and for California, see Bouvier, *Women and the Conquest of California*; and Hackel, *Children of Coyote*.

41   *"Por el acertado govierno de vuestros Predecesores, se ha mantenido esta escolta con la honradez que la corresponde; vos ahora la teneis de solteros, que experimentando necesidades heterogeneas, buscaran por donde remediarlas."* Father Mariano Payeras to Lt. José de la Guerra, Mission La Purísima, May 6, 1816, DLG 769.

42   *"Mira Dn. José, allí va vestido de capitán insurjente su criado Puchinela."* Mariano Guadalupe Vallejo, "Recuerdos históricos," The Bancroft Library, BANC MSS C-D 19, p. 94.

43   *"¿Quien se atreve á recordame el pasado?"* Ibid., p. 95.

44   On the Pacific Coast of Mexico, the term *chino* was also used to identify natives of the Philippines, many of whom had arrived with the Manila galleon trade. Vallejo specifies that he means *"los descendientes de negros y de indias,"* "the descendants of Negroes and Indians." Ibid.

45   This entire story appears in the memoirs of Mariano Guadalupe Vallejo, written in the 1870s for Bancroft's history of California. Vallejo claimed that the story was "not public knowledge," and the circumstances of the story suggest that de la Guerra himself was the source. Ibid., pp. 94–96.

46   *"[E]l Padre de todos en esa."* R. de Yrurreta Goyena to José de la Guerra, Tepic, June 13, 1831, DLG 533.

47   *"No me pondereis vuestros cuidados, por que teneis muchos sirvientes, y yo ninguno."* Father Mariano Payeras to José de la Guerra, Mission La Purísima, January 25, 1816, DLG 769.

48   This description is taken from archaeological investigations of the structure. Michael Imwalle, "Comprehensive Archaeological and Architectural Investigation of the Casa de la Guerra," ed. Michael Imwalle and Louise Pubols, Santa Barbara Trust for Historic Preservation, 1994.

49   Father Joseph Thompson, "Casa De La Guerra—Santa Barbara," ed. Maynard Gieger, *Noticias* 17, no. 1 (Spring 1972): 2. This published article is an edited version of a much larger manuscript housed at the SBMAL, also entitled "Casa de la Guerra—Santa Barbara." The published version is cited as "Casa," and the unpublished as "Casa de la Guerra," SBMAL.

50   For a similar frontier situation, see Cheryl English Martin, *Governance and Society in Colonial Mexico: Chihuahua in the Eighteenth Century,* (Stanford, Calif.: Stanford University Press, 1996), 139–42.

51   Bernardo Crespo to José de la Guerra, Mexico, June 30, 1815, DLG 218. There are no documents that have survived in María Antonia's hand, and it is possible that she could not have read this book herself, but her husband could certainly have read it to her and their daughters.

52   Salvador Vallejo, "Notas históricas sobre California," 1874, The Bancroft Library, BANC MSS C-D 22, quoted in Padilla, *My History, Not Yours,* 109.

53   See the accounts in Beebe and Senkewicz, *Testimonios.*

54   Father Francisco Uría to José de la Guerra, Mission Santa Ynez, May 21, 1819, DLG 982.

55   Hackel, *Children of Coyote,* 306.

56   Census figures for gentile Indians for the Santa Bárbara district are hard to come by, but the 1830 census of Los Angeles recorded that among Indians, gentiles outnumbered neophytes 127 to 71 in that pueblo, and 157 to 104 in the entire district, excluding the missions.

57   George Harwood Phillips, "Indians in Los Angeles, 1781–1875: Economic Integration, Social Disintegration," *Pacific Historical Review* 49, no. 3 (August 1980): 27–51. Los Angeles residents also seem to have been employing Indian captives sold by merchants coming west from New Mexico, although it is difficult to tell if any of them made it as far north as Santa Bárbara. Michael J. González, *This Small City Will Be a Mexican Paradise: Exploring the Origins of Mexican*

Culture in Los Angeles, 1821–1846 (Albuquerque, University of New Mexico Press, 2005), 127–34, 224–29.

58   Angustias de la Guerra, "Ocurrencias," The Bancroft Library, BANC MSS C-D 134; translation in Beebe and Senkewicz, *Testimonios*, 204. See also Thompson, *El Gran Capitán*, 48–49; Bancroft, *History of California*, 2:233, 239–40.

59   Salvador Vallejo, "Notas históricas sobre California," The Bancroft Library, BANC MSS C-D 22; quoted in Rosaura Sánchez, *Telling Identities*, 172.

60   Robinson, *Life in California*, 173.

61   William Dane Phelps, *Alta California 1840–1842: The Journal and Observances of William Dane Phelps, Master of the Ship "Alert,"* intro. and ed. Briton Cooper Busch (Glendale, Calif.: The Arthur H. Clark Co., 1983), 178.

62   Ibid.

63   Haas, *Conquests and Historical Identities*, 52.

64   Phelps, *Alta California*, 178.

65   This list was provided in 1921 by a daughter of Angustias de la Guerra, María Antonia Josefa Narcisa Barnaba, who was born in June 1837. Thompson, "Casa," 5.

66   J. M. Guinn, *Historical and Biographical Record of Southern California: Containing a History of Southern California from Its Earliest Settlement to the Opening Year of the Twentieth Century* (Chicago: Chapman Publishing Co., 1902), 220–21.

67   *"Mucho me alegro esta V. empeñado en casar a Luis pues me parece que le conviene."* Santiago Argüello to José de la Guerra, San Diego, April 22, 1819, DLG 56.

68   *"[S]i Vm. quisiera acerle amo de Padrino, y recojerlo a su casa despues del trabajo publico seria de mas agrado mio."* Francisco Xavier Uría to José de la Guerra, Mission Santa Ynez, August 7, 1818, DLG 982.

69   *"[D]igo que si es gustoso el Yndio Simon de quedarse a servir a Vd. acedemos los P.P. Ministros de esta á la suplica, segun estilo de la tierra; y que exoneramos ntras conciencias con que Vd. cuide que dho. Yndio rece y viva christianamente."* Father Juan Saenz de Lucio to José de la Guerra, Mission San Francisco, April 30, 1814, DLG 861. The next year, Simón married and apparently returned to live at one of the missions, but the missionaries continued to refer to him as "your Indian Simón," and he went on to work for de la Guerra as a courier and messenger to the missions. Father Juan Saenz de Lucio to José de la Guerra, Mission San Francisco, July 31, 1815, DLG 861; and Father Josef Pineda to José de la Guerra, Mission Santo Tomás, October 7 and October 27, 1815, DLG 792.

70   Hackel, *Children of Coyote*, 338–39.

71   *"Le he hecho alguna instancia para que regrese aí, y me replico que no puede, que se va con los suios que lo han llamado. Espero pues que Vos me instruireis en el particular; y si no hay inconveniente, y el cavallo es realmente suio, lo despachare en el con el cab. Antonio Castro."* Father Mariano Payeras to José de la Guerra, Mission La Purísima, no month, 1816, DLG 76.

72   *Tenga V. la vondad de decirme si es libre para poderse trasladar al servicio de otra persona."* Gov. José Figueroa to José de la Guerra, April 3, 1834, DLG 290.

73   Angustias de la Guerra, "Recuerdos," December 31, 1880, DLG 727.

74   Osio, *The History of Alta California*, 134.

75   In 1839, this mission had been secularized, and in theory the missionaries had no authority, and its neophytes were free to leave. The civil administrator, Manuel Cota, however, had been removed from his job for mismanagement and mistreatment of Indians. In the interim, Father Durán took over to advise and protect the Indians, although he refused management of the temporalities. Bancroft, *History of California*, 3:657–58.

76   *"Desde luego concedo las ganancias de las indias en este caso en lo moral, domestico y religioso, y mas si despues se casasen con hombres honrados de razón . . . Yo confieso que en algunos casos (no en todos) aprenden algo mas de rezar, se confiesan y adquieren algunas ideas de honestidad publica."* Father Narciso Durán to José de la Guerra, Santa Bárbara, August 20, 1839, DLG 250.

77   *"Y si á esto juntamos el desconsuelo de sus parientes al verse privados de la compañia de sus hijos ó hermanos (los quales no tienen á su arbitrio el visitarse y consolarse mutuamente todos los dias) suben de punto los agravios que padecan en el peso de la balanza respecto de sus ventajas en los motivos de educacion."* Ibid.

78   *"¿Y la repugnacia que por punto general se experimenta en Soltar á las indias sus amos quando ya estan maduras, para el matrimonio, no merece tambien alguna consideracion . . . ? En las misiones hay notable escasez de mugeres para los casamientos y un sobrante de solteros."* Ibid.

79   Angustias de la Guerra, "Recuerdos," December 31, 1880, DLG 727, 15; translation in Beebe and Senkewicz, *Testimonios*, 287.

80   De la Guerra stepped down as acting commander in 1827 to serve as congressional deputy in the federal government, but was unable to take his seat and returned to California. The chronology of "acting" commanders at Santa Bárbara is not entirely clear, but it appears that José Joaquín Maitorena served in 1828, Romualdo Pacheco in 1829–30, de la Guerra in 1831–32, Juan M. Ibarra in 1833–36, and de la Guerra again from 1837 on. Bancroft, *History of California*, 2:570–73, 3:650–51; President Guadalupe Victoria, December 23, 1826, official order promoting José de la Guerra to the rank of Captain of Cavalry for the Company in the Presidio of Santa Bárbara, a revalidation of his Spanish colonial promotion of October 30, 1817, DLG 1007.

81   *"Necesito que V. de su licencia al soldado Joaquín Villa para que sea el Mayor-Domo de esta Mision . . . Es un muchacho que los Yndios lo quieren mucho, inteligente en el campo, siempre de un humor, nada altibo, y lo que es mas, que sabo el Ydeoma, que para mi es la mayor qualidad. Yo le he ablado, y me dice que está dispuesto para ello, simpre que obtengo la licencia de sus superiores."* Fray Antonio Rodríguez to José de la Guerra, Mission La Purísima, n.d.

82   *"Soldado destinado á su asistencia no me parece pecaminoso ni cosa de grave escrupulo atenta tambien la practica comun el que dicho soldado ocupe V. en cuidar a veces sus cosas ó algun otro servicio semejante haciendo en lo demas*

sus criados o familiares el servicio de el soldado y haciendo este la ocupacion que V. le encarga del todo voluntariamente, esto es que no lo haga pr. temor de que no haciendolo no sera bien mirado de V., ó pr. otro repeto semejante demiedo." Father Vicente Francisco de Sarría to José de la Guerra, July 29, 1819, DLG 902.

83   *"[E]sta mui bien el socorro dado ala viuda Guadalupe Briones pr. cuenta a sus hijos, y que la tengo presente para lo futuro."* Gov. Pablo Vicente de Solá to José de la Guerra, April 15, 1817, DLG 923.

84   José de la Guerra, Accounts and Business Papers, 1810–19, DLG 1048.

85   *"[A]un yo mismo me hallo sin un peso siquiera para comprar unos Pollos fue menester que el Alfz me prestara dos pesos en menudo."* José Joaquín Arrillaga to José de la Guerra, Monterey, June 2, 1813, DLG 62.

86   *"[P]or lo qual no puedo por haora despachar ninguno de mis Buques á esa su Costa."* José Cavenecia to José de la Guerra, Lima, Peru, April 20, 1816, DLG 180.

87   José Argüello to José Díaz, Santa Bárbara, November 9, 1814, DLG 47.

88   José de la Guerra, Accounts and Business Papers, 1810–19, DLG 1048.

89   Thompson, *El Gran Capitán*, 57.

90   *"[S]eria desnudar un altar de sus preciosos adornos para vestar á otro . . . tenga en consideracion los sacrificios que esta Mision hace annualmente en bien de toda su Comanda. de frasadas, y jerga, y quanto puede a la manufacturas de lana."* Father Payeras to José de la Guerra, Mission La Purísima, April 22, 1817, DLG 769.

91   In 1826, for example, the ranch not only supplied meat and livestock, but also cash profits that bought a $350 organ for the presidial chapel, with $940 left over. Of course, after 1821, the property became a "national," not "royal" ranch. Bancroft, *History of California*, 2:574.

92   Archibald, *Economic Aspects*, 129.

93   *"Las miserias cada dia cresen mas y mas . . . los soldados ya no se diferencian de los Yndios en masa y lo peor es que ya se siente el hambre."* Luis Argüello to José de la Guerra, San Francisco, April 21, 1820, DLG 51.

94   Thompson, *El Gran Capitán*, 58–59.

95   *"[E]n el mes de Marzo sacaron los soldados 52 arobas de manteca . . . A este paso podra la Mission salir jamas de penuria? . . . realme. me veo en la obligacion de hacer el oficio de Padre, y de Pastor, . . . mis obejas, e hijos . . . me veo en la precisa obligacion de tratar los como á tales lo qual es inposible si hemos de ir siguiendo de esta manera, pues veo que ni aun tratandoles como esclavos es inposible trabajen para tantos gastos."* Father Francisco González y Ibarra to José de la Guerra, Mission San Fernando Rey, April 14, 1821, DLG 338. An arroba measured 25 pounds.

96   *"Estoy cansado de decirles que hay ley que les prohive el trato y comunicacion con los Yndios; por consiguiente al entrada en la rancheria, y oficinas."* Ibarra added, "In fact on the 5th of the present month I was told there was a soldier in the blacksmith shop. I called the blacksmith to know the motive of his going there. He said the soldier had come to ask him to make a bit for a little piece of cloth." *"En efecto, el cinco del corriente me avisaron estaba un soldado en la*

fragua, llame al herrero para saber el motivo de su ida, y me dijo havia ido solicitando le hiciese un freno por un pañito." Father Francisco González y Ibarra to José de la Guerra, Mission San Fernando Rey, July 11, 1821, DLG 338.

97   *"[E]l propasarsen á vender el curtidor la baguetas el zapatero los zapatos, el llavero el trigo, el herrero el freno, la espuela y la corera las coras. Este quien duda que se opone al vien comun quanto no solo roban los materiales a que todos tienen y qual parte, sino tanbien el tiempo?"* Father Francisco González y Ibarra to José de la Guerra, July 26, 1821, DLG 338. The records do not reveal how de la Guerra and González eventually settled the dispute.

98   Bancroft, *History of California,* 2:254–55.

99   Weber, *Mexican Frontier,* 109.

100   This is from a peak of about 70. Bancroft, *History of California,* 2:572–73, 672–73.

101   Chapter four discusses this incident in more depth. See Bancroft, *History of California,* 3:66–86.

102   Weber, *Mexican Frontier,* 109; quoting Echeandía to the Minister of War, September 18, 1829.

103   *"[E]n las actuales circunstancias de escases."* Ygancio Fletes to José de la Guerra, Tepic, January 13, 1829, DLG 297. At this time, de la Guerra was in Mexico himself, having unsuccessfully attempted to take his seat as California's deputy. This is discussed further in the next chapter.

104   *"[E]sas miserables tropas . . . no lo e de dejar descanzar los e de moler a ber si de enfadados me sueltar siquiera 50000 duros."* Carlos Carrillo to José de la Guerra, Mexico City, November 16, 1831, DLG 137. The *duro,* or dollar, was a silver coin worth ten silver reales.

105   Unidentified San Francisco officer, ca. 1829, quoted in Robert E. Kells Jr., "The Spanish Inheritance: The Mexican Forces of Alta California, 1822–1846," *Journal of the West* 20 no. 4 (1981): 12–19 at 15.

106   José de la Guerra, Padrón, Santa Bárbara Presidio, July 20, 1827, DLG 1095; this is a translation by Joseph Thompson of Departmental State Papers, 7 volumes, The Bancroft Library, BANC MSS C-A 30, pp. 2–7. Description of houses from Auguste Duhaut-Cilly, "Duhaut-Cilly's Account of California in the Years 1827–28," Charles Franklin Carter, trans., *California Historical Society Quarterly* 8 (1929): 131–66, 214–50, 306–36. De la Guerra recorded 249 settlers in town: 27 married couples, 28 single men, 20 single women, 132 minor children, and 15 widows. There were 280 in the presidio: 51 married couples, 26 single men and 12 single women, 138 minor children, and 2 widowers. It is likely that the presidial soldiers and their wives were younger, had smaller families (so far) and younger children, and that townsfolk, many of them retired soldiers, tended to be older, with larger families and older children.

107   Lugo, "Vida de un ranchero," The Bancroft Library, BANC MSS 118; translation in *Historical Society of Southern California Quarterly* 32, no. 3 (September 1950): 216, 230. Lugo was referring here to Los Angeles, but the situation was similar in most parts of California.

108   See also DLG 1049 for small accounts, and Guillermo Cota to José de la Guerra, Los Angeles, n.d. [ca. 1825], DLG 210, for documentation of de la Guerra buying lots of thirty to seventy-five hides from citizens and soldiers of Los Angeles and selling them to William Logan. Lisbeth Haas has examined similar accounts kept by Tomás Yorba in Los Angeles in the 1840s and notes that his documents "indicate a large degree of indebted labor among workers, primarily Californios, whose debts far surpassed a year's wage." Haas, *Conquests and Historical Identities*, 53.

109   *"[Y]a se me seca el paladar de tanto cobrar."* Anastasio Carrillo to José de la Guerra, Los Angeles, July 17, 1825, DLG 133. For a later period, see Tomás Antonio Yorba to José de la Guerra, Los Angeles, 1834–35, DLG 1037.

110   Thompson, *El Gran Capitán*, 10. See also the governor's response: Juan José Arrillaga to José de la Guerra, Loreto, July 1803, DLG 62.

111   See: Gov. Pablo Vicente de Solá to José de la Guerra, Monterey, January 2, 1818, DLG 923; Anastasio Carrillo to José de la Guerra, Los Angeles, August 27, 1821, DLG 133; Father Mariano Payeras to José de la Guerra, May 26, 1822, DLG 769; Manuel Gutiérrez to José de la Guerra, Los Angeles, October 19, 1822; and April 19, 1823; DLG 484.

112   *"Ygualmente aplaudo la ida de V al Pueblo pqe dando una ojeada á todo aquel vecindario, y Ranchos que lo componen, pondra V en su perfecto tono la cuerda que que por desgracia vaia discorde."* Father Payeras to José de la Guerra, Mission La Purísima, April 22, 1817, DLG 769.

113   Bancroft reports that she was "spoken of" as Gégue. Bancroft, *History of California*, 2:269–70. Margarita's baptism was not registered until 1815, probably to correct a clerical error, as it refers back to entry 04068. She is listed as "Margarita Peque" for her first daughter's baptismal record, November 7, 1813, SD04069, and as "María Antonia de la Ascensión," on her own, May 4, 1815, SD04198, ECPP.

114   Baptism of María Luisa Olivera, with mother listed as "María Antonia Stuard," August 25, 1818, BP00541, ECPP.

115   Chávez-García, *Negotiating Conquest*, 47; Martin, *Governance and Society*, 173.

116   Bancroft, *History of California*, 2:277. José de la Guerra to Gov. Pablo Vicente de Solá, letterbook, January 16, 1816, DLG 446. "Bob" was also sometimes referred to as "Francisco" prior to his conversion.

117   Bancroft, *History of California*, 2:277; Pablo Vicente de Solá to José de la Guerra, Monterey, April 29, 1816, DLG 923.

118   José Manuel Lisa/Eleazer was, according to Ripoll, "An Anglo-American, 22 years old, native of Boston." October 7, 1816, BP00497, ECPP. Father Ripoll commented that Juan Cristóbal (Bob) was "Negro," native to Africa, about twenty years old, and "a slave of Captain Smith of an Anglo American ship which arrived within this jurisdiction . . . [Smith] left him under the care of Captain José de la Guerra y Noriega." August 16, 1819, BP00552, ECPP.

119   A similar situation occurred in the aftermath of Hipólito Bouchard's 1818 raid and attempt to incite revolution in California. At least two of his men, "Juan de la Rios" and "Juan Miguel," stayed in California, and de la Guerra as their godfather took on the responsibility of finding them work and making sure that

they followed Christian doctrine and adhered to their oath of allegiance to the nation. See Pablo Vicente de Solá to José de la Guerra, Monterey, April 26, 1821; and June 8, 1821, DLG 924.

120 *"[M]e conformo en ello, teniendo vm. el cuidado que le pertenece de la conducta civil y moral de su hayjado."* Pablo Vicente de Solá to José de la Guerra, August 8, 1817, DLG 923.

121 *"El 14 de Mayo pario la Sra. de Juan Lima una Yndito que no anrico[?] en le Misn. de S. Buenaventure y Bautizado pr. Poder de Angs. y Cuchichito se le puso por nombre Juan Ygno. quizas en mema. del Califo. Limeño."* José de la Guerra, "Occurrencias curiosas, 1830–31," The Bancroft Library, BANC MSS C-B 73, p. 24. See also the baptismal record of May 13, 1830, SB04505, ECPP.

122 José Antonio, the eldest child, sponsored Juan Cristóbal, aka "Bob," when he was thirteen or fourteen years old, and Angustias was only ten when she stood padrina for José Guadalupe Valdez, the first child of a presidial soldier. Francisco was fifteen when he sponsored a child of soldier Francisco Leyba and María Carmen Valencia; Pablo was thirteen when he became co-parents to Vicente Valencia and Margarita Valenzuela one month later; Anita was twelve when she and her future husband both became godparents to the child of Daniel Hill and Rafaela Ortega, a first cousin of Anita's eldest brother's wife.

123 These godparent relations with Anglo and European immigrants are discussed in the next chapter.

124 *"[Y] no me acomoda mucho el titulo de ahijado, porque veo lo que son todos los ahijados, y asi este, como qualquier . . . trate de buscarme para hacer tal oficio."* Fray Joaquín Pascual Nuez to José de la Guerra, Mission San Gabriel, October 23, 1818, DLG 715.

125 *"No le dare reunidad[?] para que pueda V. recompensarse pr. los alimentos dados á la mujer que fue de Jorge e hija, maxime si V. por titulo de Compadre ó caridad por la circunstancia de Cristianizarlas y consiguiente educacion las admitio y tuvo en su casa; pues esto es un acto de su mucha religion piedad y Caridad edificante, por el que puede V. esperar un indecible y eterno peso de gloria."* Father Vicente de Sarría to José de la Guerra, August 25, 1821, DLG 902.

126 *"[U]n pobre, que se halla en visperes de casarse para que le busque un corte de enaguas [petticoat] y un rebozo; no tengo de quien valerme mas que de mi compadre, . . . ; ya salemos que en las Misiones, que en el Pueblo, . . . hai, para socorrer esta necessidad."* Father Josef Pineda to José de la Guerra, Mission Santo Tomás, August 6, 1816, DLG 792.

127 *"Amada hijita mia Ma. Antonia Carrillo: . . . éste será mayor perseberando tu (como lo espero) en el Sto. temor de Dios, un amor reberente á tu Marido, respecto á los Sacerdotes Ministros del Altissimo, Caridad con los Pobres, y mucho mas con los enfermos, y sobre todo la frequencia de Sacramentos pa. ser feliz en esta Vida, y despues en la otra."* José Raymundo Carrillo to María Antonia Carrillo de la Guerra, May 21, 1804, DLG 154.

128 *"[D]e manera que V. viste con el á los mas pobre desvalidos de su copañia especialmente criaturas."* Father Mariano Payeras, to José de la Guerra, La Purísima, January 26, 1819, DLG 769.

129   *"[P]ara que socorra a las necesitadas."* Father Francisco Xavier Uría to Comandante José de la Guerra, Santa Ynez, n.d., DLG 982.

130   Elizabeth Style Madison, "Hacienda De La Guerra: Yesterday and Today in a Spanish *Casa* Built by Three Thousand Indians," *Sunset* 26 (January 1911): 42.

131   The *María Ester* was a Mexican brig used by trading partner Enrique Virmond to carry goods and passengers back and forth from California to Mexico and Peru. See Bancroft, *History of California*, 3:48–49, 147.

132   José de la Guerra, April 23, 1830, "Ocurrencias curiosas, 1830–31," The Bancroft Library, BANC MSS C-B 73, p. 22. See also Thompson, *El Gran Capitán*, 48–49; Bancroft, *History of California*, 2:233, 239–40.

133   Angustias de la Guerra, "Ocurrencias," The Bancroft Library, BANC MSS C-D 134; translation in Beebe and Senkewicz, *Testimonios*, 213.

134   Two letters; Father Luis Martínez to Comandante José de la Guerra, Mission San Luis Obispo, no date, DLG 649. Other missionaries asked de la Guerra to send medicinal herbs and compounds. See Father Pedro Muñóz to de la Guerra, Mission San Fernando, March 19, 1817, DLG 695, stating that he has received medicinal powders but does not trust them.

135   José de la Guerra, account with José Cavenecia, Santa Bárbara, November 13, 1817, DLG 1048b. Joseph Jacob Plenck (1735–1807) first published a pharmacopeia listing over eight hundred medicinal plants in 1788.

136   José de la Guerra to Dr. Burroughs/Boris, Santa Bárbara, 1823, DLG 460.

137   For mention of curanderas, see Francisco María Ruiz to de la Guerra, escolta of Mission San Luis Rey, December 22, 1820, DLG 852; and Father Francisco González y Ibarra to de la Guerra, Mission San Fernando Rey, February 23, 1821, DLG 338. Although González y Ibarra does not use the term "curandera," he does mention that "María Ygnacia" from Mission San Gabriel is treating his companion Father Ramon. And in 1835, Antonio María Ercilla noted on his account that he owed José de la Guerra "8 pesos that he loaned me to pay for my curandera Doña Ysabel, for 16 visits." Account between José de la Guerra and Antonio María de Ercilla, March 14, 1835, DLG 1050. The lack of conventionally trained doctors may be one reason de la Guerra sent his son Juan José to England to receive a degree in medicine. This story is covered in a later chapter.

138   For example, José Cresencio Valdez wrote to de la Guerra from Los Angeles in March 1837, telling him that his wife would soon be arriving there "to recover her health," and asking de la Guerra "who may be favored with what she needs," to supply her with medicines. *"Mi respetado Sor: hallandome con la necesidad de que mi esposa pase á este punto para que recobre la salud, he benido en suplicar á Vmd. el que sea favoresida con lo que pida para sus medecinas."* José Crecensio Valdez to José de la Guerra, Los Angeles, March 15, 1837, DLG 990. An invoice to de la Guerra of 1833 shows what de la Guerra might have had on hand: yellow, mallow, *alabastro*, and white unguents; and essences of anise, orange, cinnamon, lemon balm, cider (*sidra*), and clove, packed in small crystal bottles. José de la Guerra, "vecino," account with Martiarena, on the Alta California in the charge of Thomas Robbins, Tepic, March 9, 1833, DLG 1050.

139   Angustias de la Guerra, "Recuerdos," December 31, 1880, DLG 727.

140   It is difficult to get a precise sense of literacy rates in California in the late eighteenth and early nineteenth centuries. All missionaries were trained to read and write, while literacy rates among soldiers stood at about thirty percent, according to the presidial rolls of 1782. But among women and civilian settlers, the rates were likely closer to five or ten percent, the rate historians estimate for rural parts of Mexico in the early nineteenth century. *Real Presidio de Monterey, Lista de la Compania del Referido Presidio, 31 Julio de 1782,* Prov. St. Pa. B. Mil iv 663–94 and *R[eal] Presidio de San Francisco, Lista de La Compania, 31 Agosto de 1782* Prov. St. P. B. M. iv 601, The Bancroft Library. Mark Burkholder and Lyman Johnson, *Colonial Latin America,* fifth ed. (New York: Oxford University Press, 2004); Eric Van Young, *The Other Rebellion: Popular Violence, Ideology, and the Mexican Struggle for Independence, 1810–1821"* (Stanford, Calif.: Stanford University Press, 2001), 311.

141   Dana, *Two Years Before the Mast,* 79.

142   Miranda, "Racial and Cultural Dimensions," 274. The de la Guerra library, for example, contained histories of Spain, religious and philosophical works, classics of fiction and poetry, and proscriptive literature for women and children. Alan Renga, "The Books of José de la Guerra" (unpublished paper, University of California at Santa Barbara, 1995).

143   Gov. Pablo Vicente de Solá to José de la Guerra, Monterey, February 10, 1818, DLG 923. A cartilla was a simple reading book that showed how the letters of the alphabet formed words, and the more advanced catón was written in dialogue form like a catechism, referring to the wisdom of the Gospel, and counseling obedience to God and his authorities on earth. Peter Guardino, *The Time of Liberty,* 110–11.

144   "[D]os Exercicios Quotidianos y otros libros de Devocion, que Vd. mejor que Yo save son utiles para una familia pues absolutamente no encontramos aqui ni caton ni catesismo para los muchachos." José Estrada to José de la Guerra, Monterey, April 24, 1820, DLG 277.

145   The other schools were in Monterey and Los Angeles. Governor Figueroa al Srio. de Estado sobre Escuelas Públicas, Monterey, May 23, 1834, Departmental State Papers, Vol. 3, The Bancroft Library, BANC MSS C-A 28, pp. 148–49.

146   Alfred Robinson, quoted in Thompson, *El Gran Capitán,* 166.

147   Robinson, *Life in California,* 70.

148   Alfred Robinson, quoted in Thompson, *El Gran Capitán,* 166.

149   Robinson, *Life in California,* 51.

150   This phrase appears, underlined, in a letter from a Tepic trader to de la Guerra: *"me parese imposible que un hombre como V. que es el Padre de todos en esa no se bueno para lo que yo quiera."* R. de Yrureta Goyena to José de la Guerra, Tepic, April 13, 1831, DLG 533.

151   Guinn, *Historical and Biographical Record of Southern California,* 220–21.

152   "[M]i Venerado Gefe...su digna espoza...manden lo que gusten a sus mas atentos servidores." Simeón Castro to José de la Guerra, Monterey, August 18, 1819, DLG 179. José Simeón Juan Nepomuceno Castro, born at Santa Bárbara,

was the son of Macario Castro, a soldier from Sinaloa who rose through the ranks to become a sergeant at San Diego and San José. In the letter, he acknowledges the great love de la Guerra had shown his deceased parents.

153   Angustias de la Guerra, "Recuerdos," December 31, 1880, DLG 727; translation in Beebe and Senkewicz, *Testimonios*, 287.

154   "[T]ube el honor de ocupar el lugr. supr. con no poca resista. por parte de mi humildad[?] que hubo a el fin de ceder a les inst. del Sr. Pacheco." José de la Guerra, June 7, 1830, "Occurrencias curiosas, 1830–31," The Bancroft Library, BANC MSS C-B 73, p. 25.

155   Angustias de la Guerra, "Recuerdos," December 31, 1880, DLG 727; translation in Beebe and Senkewicz, *Testimonios*, 284.

156   Alfred Robinson, quoted in Thompson, *El Gran Capitán*, 166.

157   Robinson, *Life in California*, 70.

158   Robinson, quoted in Thompson, *El Gran Capitán*, 166.

159   Lugo, "Vida de un ranchero," BANC MSS C-D 118; translation in *Historical Society of Southern California Quarterly* 32, no. 3 (September 1950): 224.

160   Thompson, *El Gran Capitán*, 162.

161   Robinson, *Life in California*, 95–96.

162   Simpson, *Narrative of a Voyage*, 122.

163   Angustias de la Guerra, "Recuerdos," December 31, 1880, DLG 727; translation in Beebe and Senkewicz, *Testimonios*, 286.

164   Dana, *Two Years Before the Mast*, 236.

165   For more on the significance of this play in the evangelizing approach of the Franciscans, see James Sandos, *Converting California: Indians and Franciscans in the Missions* (New Haven, Conn.: Yale University Press, 2004), 37, 141.

166   Robinson, *Life in California*, 135.

167   This marriage is discussed more fully in the next chapter.

168   Robinson, *Life in California*, 94.

169   Ibid., 94–95.

170   Angustias de la Guerra, "Recuerdos," December 31, 1880, DLG 727; translation in Beebe and Senkewicz, *Testimonios*, 286.

171   Robinson, *Life in California*, 134. Angustias de la Guerra, "Recuerdos," December 31, 1880, DLG 727; translation in Beebe and Senkewicz, *Testimonios*, 286.

172   Dana, *Two Years Before the Mast*, 239.

173   Robinson, *Life in California*, 134.

174   Dana, *Two Years Before the Mast*, 236.

175   Ibid., 237.

176   Ibid., 239.

177   Ibid., 237.

178   Julio César, a Luiseño Indian, suggested later such courtesies were not necessarily free expressions of respect. Pío Pico, the administrator at Mission San Luis Rey, he said, "required us to carry our hat in our hand as long as we were

within his range of vision." Julio César, "Cosas de indios de California," 1878, The Bancroft Library, BANC MSS C-D 109; translation in Rose Marie Beebe and Robert M. Senkewicz, eds. *Lands of Promise and Despair: Chronicles of Early California, 1535–1846* (Berkeley, Calif.: Heyday Books, 2001), 471.

179   Castillo Negrete, Journal of 1820, quoted in Thompson, *El Gran Capitán*, 162.

180   Bancroft, *History of California*, 2:349; Mason, *Los Angeles*, 19. According to the regulations of 1787, "the power of comisionado [commissioner] for Los Angeles," had the "duties to direct the work, tasks, and other labor. He will pass on the orders and see they are obeyed as they come from the commander of Santa Bárbara . . . The alcalde shall defer to the comisionado in order to assure good judgment and to work in conformity with good government and the policing of the pueblo."

181   In private letters to de la Guerra, Carrillo explained the cases that he could not resolve, and asked for his brother-in-law's advice. In 1821, for example, he asked for help with the Morenas, a husband and wife who created a scandal by bringing their domestic disputes into the open. Anastasio Carrillo to José de la Guerra, Los Angeles, July 9, 1821, DLG 133.

182   María Rufina Hernández to José de la Guerra, Santa Bárbara, February 14, 1821, DLG 29.

183   "[L]leva de lastimas . . . no parage. su hijo no sea castigado, sino parage. sufir el merecido en esta jurisdon. pues le servira de algun consuelo. Creo que Vm. puede hacer en el particular mucho." Father José Señán to José de la Guerra, Mission San Buenaventura, September 26, 1821, DLG 904.

184   "Postrandonos a los Pies de Vmd. con el mas profundo respecto y sumicion . . . nos bemos pesisadas por razon de las mui numerosas familias, de que temerosas á los mayores estragos que se nos muestra en nuestras familias a causa de las cutidianas inpertinencias ocasionados de los Groseros echos de nuestros Esposos, nos destraigan de nuestras casas i bienes de nuestras mantenciones . . . ocurrimos á Vmd. como apadre amoso nos de el mayor consuelo, si se berificará este estrago en nuestras numerosas familias." Luisa Barelas [de Valencia], Demetria Ramires [de Briones], Juana Ygnocencia Reyes [de Alanís], Ma. Luisa Reyes [de Olivera], and Baleriana Lorensana [de Ibarra] to José de la Guerra, Los Angeles, February 1, 1822, DLG 1000.

185   Mason, *Los Angeles*, 61–62.

186   Bancroft, *History of California*, 2:354; Mason, *Los Angeles*, 57. Pobladores protested the grant again in 1821.

187   Bancroft, 2:661. Thompson, *El Gran Capitán*, 79.

188   Unfortunately, the election records for the Los Angeles ayuntamiento are fragmentary, and surviving records contain little before 1834. Originals and English translations of the ayuntamiento records are in the City of Los Angeles Clerk's Office; copies can be found at The Bancroft Library at Berkeley. Originals of the Los Angeles Prefecture records are at the Huntington Library in San Marino; copies with English translations can be found at the City Clerk's Office in Los Angeles and the Seaver Center at the Los Angeles County Museum of Natural History.

189   *"He oydo se le atribuyen á V. algunas providencias anticonstitutionales, como el no haver repuesto en sus funsiones al Regidor ó Alcalde de ese presidio; desearia mucho el que fuese mentira, como igualmente el que se conformarse por ahora con la suerte sin perjuicio."* José María Narváez to José de la Guerra, January 2, 1823, DLG 701.

190   José de la Guerra to Manuel Gutiérrez of Los Angeles, March 3, 1823, DLG 459.

191   Thompson, *El Gran Capitán*, 79–80.

192   *"[E]l mal Govierno en aquel Ayuntamiento . . . me beo en la precision en cortar todas e estos abusos y poner en el mejor orn.(orden) aqa. Justicia."* Gov. Luis Argüello to José de la Guerra, Monterey, December 4, 1823, DLG 51.

193   Antonio Ríos-Bustamante, *Mexican Los Angeles: A Narrative and Pictorial History* (Encino, Calif.: Floricanto Press, 1992), 86. Bancroft, *History of California*, 2:563.

194   *"[D]e la defensa que hacemos de nros derechos . . . nos hallmos resentidos(?) de los ultrajes que experimentan ntras disposiciones."* José Palomares and José Antonio Carrillo to José de la Guerra, Los Angeles, March 10, 1825, DLG 766. See also Thompson, *El Gran Capitán*, 80. Argüello left this decision up to his successor, and the ultimate outcome is not known.

195   Pío Pico, "Narración histórica," 1877, The Bancroft Library, BANC MSS C-D 13; translation in Beebe and Senkewicz, eds., *Lands of Promise and Despair*, 346–48.

196   On the ability of non-elites to absorb and exercise liberal notions of popular sovereignty in Mexico and other Latin American nations in this era, see Mallon, *Peasant and Nation*; Chambers, *From Subjects to Citizens*; and Guardino, *The Time of Liberty*.

197   *"Devo de adbertir que algunos entregaron vecerros en pago de diesmos, y ese es una fraude; pues cuando menos debe ser la mitan baquillas."* Domingo Carrillo to José de la Guerra, Santa Bárbara, April 9, 1834, DLG 141.

198   *"Por esta bera V. que me he empeñado en sus cobros; pero los Jueses del Pueblo son demasiados de indinos pues Albarado asta la lista de deudas a perdido."* Tomás Antonio Yorba to José de la Guerra, August 22, 1834, DLG 1037.

CHAPTER   THREE

1   Dana, *Two Years Before the Mast*, 235–36.

2   At the Santa Bárbara presidio, 8.3 percent of marriages recorded in the 1820s were between American or European men and Californianas. In the 1830s, that figure rose to 14.7 percent and dropped back to 6.9 percent for the period 1840–46. These figures were compiled from the ECPP. For Monterey, the figure was 15 percent for the whole era, and at the missions of San Carlos Borromeo, Santa Clara, and San Juan Bautista in northern California, the figure was about 12 to 15 percent. Of the foreign husbands listed in Bancroft's Pioneer Register, about half were American, and 40 percent were from the British Isles. Castañeda, "Engendering the History," 244; Hurtado, *Intimate Frontiers*, 26, 37.

3   Monroy, *Thrown Among Strangers*, 155–56; and Rosaura Sánchez, *Telling Identities*, 216–17.

4   See Kicza and Walker for similar patterns in the core regions of Mexico. Kicza, "The Great Families of Mexico," 447; Walker, *Kinship, Business, and Politics*, 218.

5   Solá did not serve, as Iturbide dissolved the congress before he arrived.

6   "[E]l contrato hecho con los Yngleses … el cual es muy ventajoso para esta Prova … su caracter flojo y avandonado." Pablo Vicente de Solá to José de la Guerra, Monterey, June 20, 1822, DLG 924.

7   "[P]rincipios liberales," Mariano Guadalupe Vallejo, "Recuerdos históricos," The Bancroft Library, BANC MSS C-D 17, p. 140.

8   Adele Ogden, "Hides and Tallow—McCulloch, Hartnell and Company, 1822, 1828," *California Historical Society Quarterly* 6, no. 3 (1927): 254–64.

9   Susanna Bryant Dakin, *The Lives of William Hartnell* (Stanford, Calif.: Stanford University Press, 1949), 5.

10 Ibid., 27.

11 Hackel, *Children of Coyote*, 80. For figures on individual missions, see: Robert H. Jackson and Edward Castillo, *Indians, Franciscans, and Spanish Colonization: The Impact of the Mission System on California Indians* (Albuquerque: University of New Mexico Press, 1995), 123–31.

12 Thomas Coulter, "Notes on Upper California," *Journal of the Royal Geographical Society*, vol. 5, pt. 1 (1835), 66.

13 Weber, *Mexican Frontier*, 135; Adele Ogden, *The California Sea Otter Trade, 1748–1848* (Berkeley: University of California Press, 1941), 86.

14 Adele Ogden, "Boston Hide Droughers Along California Shores," *California Historical Society Quarterly* 8, no. 4 (December 1929): 305.

15 Many of these goods have already been mentioned: textiles (from prints, ticking, and calico, muslin, cambrics, canvas, and woolens, to silks and velvets), stockings, boots, shoes, trousers; silk ribbon, silk cravats, silk-embroidered shawls and scarves, fancy aprons, handkerchiefs; spoons, forks, knives, plates, tumblers, crockery, earthenware, kettles and other pots and pans; needles, buttons, thread; coffee, sugar, pepper; spades, trowels, rope, varnish, paint, linseed oil, hardware (saws, iron hoops, nails), window glass, buckshot, gunpowder, and spirits of all kinds.

16 Lynch, *The Spanish American Revolutions*, 326–28.

17 Jessie Davies Francis, *An Economic and Social History of Mexican California* (PhD diss., University of California at Berkeley, 1935; reprint, New York: Arno Press, 1976), 521–38.

18 Osio, *The History of Alta California*, 69.

19 Lugo, "Vida de un ranchero," The Bancroft Library, BANC MSS C-D 118; translation in *Historical Society of Southern California Quarterly* 32, no. 3 (September 1950): 230–32.

20 Robinson, *Life in California*, 26–27.

21   Weber, *Mexican Frontier*, 122–46. For New Mexico and Texas, see also Reséndez, *Changing National Identities*, 93–123.

22   James Smith Wilcox to José de la Guerra, Mexico City, September 18, 1822, DLG 1029. For more on Wilcox's (or Wilcock's) career as a smuggler, see Ogden, *Sea Otter*, 77–78.

23   Dana, *Two Years Before the Mast*, 82.

24   "[M]e alegro de la vendia [venida] de esa fragata viene viene vien para los que tienen Dinero." Francisco María Ruiz to José de la Guerra, San Diego, July 6, 1822, DLG 852.

25   See, for example, Manuel Varela to José de la Guerra, Tepic, February 10, 1822, DLG 1001. The cinnamon deal is discussed in the first chapter.

26   "V. tiene amigos y particularmente el P. Luis quien con el influjo de V ara algo y nos sacara de este apuras." Juan Malarín to José de la Guerra, Monterey, July 14, 1822, DLG 622.

27   See 115 letters from Martínez to de la Guerra in DLG 649, and the biography of Martínez in Bancroft, *History of California*, 2:618.

28   Ibid., 2:518.

29   "V. como apoderado general ponga los precios que guste." Juan Malarín to José de la Guerra, Monterey, November 20, 1824, DLG 622.

30   "[H]a de saber el Señor Don José que á mi no me hade traer al retortero, como suele hacerlo con alguos Pobretes ... yo certainemente no necesitabe de comprarle cosa alguna, quando lo que da Vd. por ocho, lo doy yo por seis." Father Blas Ordaz to José de la Guerra, Mission Santa Ynez, July 23, 1830, DLG 731.

31   See, for example, Anastasio Carrillo to José de la Guerra, Los Angeles, November 18, 1822, DLG 133.

32   "Amas Vd. no ygnora que la compra de los efectos varian vastante de tomado a dinero a toms. en efectos." Father Francisco González y Ibarra to José de la Guerra, Mission San Fernando Rey, June 11, 1823, DLG 338.

33   William Heath Davis, *Seventy-Five Years in California: Recollections and Remarks by One Who Visited These Shores in 1831, and Again in 1833, and Except When Absent on Business Was a Resident from 1838 until the End of His Long Life in 1909*, ed. Harold A. Small (San Francisco: John Howell Books, 1967), 185; Francisco Gayetano to José de la Guerra, Mission San Miguel, October 1, 1824, [Bowman, vol. 1, letter 283, p. 184]; and Joaquín de Astiazarán to José de la Guerra, Tepic, May 3, 1822, DLG 66.

34   Dana, *Two Years Before the Mast*, 80.

35   Father Francisco González y Ibarra to José de la Guerra, Mission San Fernando Rey, June 11, 1823, DLG 338.

36   In this era of mercantile capitalism, Anglo-American merchants were similarly concerned with maintaining trust and credit through personal relationships, and also relied on extended family networks. See Alfred D. Chandler, *The Visible Hand: The Managerial Revolution in American Business* (Cambridge, Mass.: Harvard University Press, 1977), 36–38; Lisa Norling, *Captain Ahab Had*

a Wife: New England Women and the Whalefishery, 1720–1870 (Chapel Hill: University of North Carolina Press, 2000), 47, 131–33; Peter Dobkin Hall, "Family Structure and Economic Organization: Massachusetts Merchants, 1700–1850," in *Family and Kin in Urban Communities, 1700–1930*, ed. Tamara K. Hareven (New York: New Viewpoints, 1977), 38–61.

37   Francis, *An Economic and Social History*, 518.

38   William Hartnell to William Dobson, July 10, 1823, quoted in Dakin, *The Lives of William Hartnell*, 54.

39   William Hartnell to José de la Guerra, Monterey, February 3, 1823, DLG 492.

40   Accounts and Business Papers of José de la Guerra, 1820–29, DLG 1049.

41   William Hartnell to José de la Guerra, quoted in Dakin, *The Lives of William Hartnell*, 70.

42   Hartnell had been baptized originally in the Anglican Church so was not rebaptized. Dakin, *The Lives of William Hartnell*, 59–62. Hartnell is described as being "reconciled" with the Church in the baptismal records of his children, such as that of his son Guillermo: April 2, 1826, SC03424, ECPP.

43   Gudeman, "The Compadrazgo," 49.

44   *"Tengo el gusto de participar á V. que el sabado Santo apadriné á su sobrino Dn. Juan Cooper quien se reconcilió en ese dia con ntra Santa Iglesia y tomó el nombre de Juan Bautista; y creo que Dn. David [Spence] le va á seguir!!!"* William Hartnell to José de la Guerra, Monterey, April 22, 1827, DLG 492.

45   José de la Guerra stood as compadre to William Goodwin Dana (married to María Josefa Carrillo), and John Coffin Jones (married to Manuela Carrillo); his wife María Antonia did the same. Their son Francisco de la Guerra was the compadre of Thomas Robbins (married to María de la Encarnación Carrillo). José was the godfather of Alphaeus B. Thompson's wife, Francisca Carrillo. María Antonia was the godmother of her niece María Antonia Carrillo, Luis T. Burton's first wife. Baptismal registry, BP0486; BP0616; BP00840; BP00967; BP00989; BP01383; BP01619; BP01630, ECPP.

46   See, for example, William Goodwin Dana to José de la Guerra, Nipomo, March 11, 1850, DLG 232.

47   William Hartnell to Hannah, Santiago, Chile, October 22, 1819, in William Hartnell Letterbook, The Bancroft Library, BANC MSS C-B 665. Susanna Bryant Dakin and María Raquél Casas both report that Hartnell did in fact become engaged to a Miss Lynch in Lima but did not marry her. Casas, *Married to a Daughter of the Land*, 56; Dakin, *The Lives of William Hartnell*, 28.

48   José María Ortega, Concepción's father, was himself the son of José Francisco Ortega, the commander at San Diego, Santa Bárbara, and Monterey in turn. Concepción's mother was María Francisca López; little is known of her family, which came from Baja California. Concepción's sister Catarina married José Gertrudis Carrillo, José Antonio de la Guerra's first cousin, further cementing ties between the families.

49   "Olindo Fatal" [Father Antonio Rodríguez] to José de la Guerra, Santa Bárbara, November 17, 1825, [Bowman, vol. 1, letter 313, p. 207].

50   Castañeda, "Engendering the History," 242.

51   Dana, *Two Years Before the Mast*, 79.

52   As noted in chapter one, de la Guerra likely did acknowledge racial differences privately, even if he did not do so in public.

53   Weber, *Mexican Frontier*, 180–82.

54   Hurtado, *Intimate Frontiers*, 38.

55   Dana, *Two Years Before the Mast*, 83.

56   "*[E]n cuanto á Hartnell ... su entrada en la alta sociedad fué debida en parte á su fina educacion y en parte á su enlace con Doña Teresa de la Guerra, hija de un distinguido militar español.*" José Ramón Sánchez, "Notas dictadas por José Ramón Sánchez," 1875, The Bancroft Library, BANC MSS C-E 67, p. 181.

57   Carlos Híjar, "California en 1834," p. 22, quoted in Monroy, *Thrown Among Strangers*, 140.

58   In Mexico, historian Steve Stern notes, at this stage, fathers and potential sons-in-law understood and shared a "ritual etiquette," in a pattern of marriage arrangement he terms "masculine transaction and alliance." Stern, *The Secret History of Gender*, 94–95.

59   Alonso, *Thread of Blood*, 86–88.

60   Girls over twelve and boys over fourteen could marry legally. Arrom, *Women of Mexico City*, 57, 69–70.

61   Arrom, *Women of Mexico City*, 57–58; Castañeda, "Presidarias y Pobladoras," 233.

62   María Estevana de Cot to María Antonia de la Guerra, Lima, Peru, June 6, 1831, DLG 206. See also María Estevana de Cot to María Antonia de la Guerra, Lima, June 15, 1830, DLG 206.

63   José M. Estudillo to José de la Guerra, Mission San Antonio, July 28, 1820, DLG 279, [translated by Ruth C. Adams].

64   Thompson, "Casa," 4.

65   "*Muchas niñas no concluían ni esos pocas estudios, porque las quitaban sus madres de la escuela casi siempre para casarlas, porque había la mala costumbre de casar las niñas muy jovencitas, cuando la pedían.*" María Inocenta Pico de Avila, "Cosas," The Bancroft Library, BANC MSS C-D 34, p. 14; translation in Beebe and Senkewicz, *Testimonios*, 312.

66   The Church may have gained somewhat in its authority after a bishop was finally assigned to the Californias in 1841. For an example of an annulment granted by the bishop on the grounds of paternal coercion, see Chávez-García, *Negotiating Conquest*, 32–34.

67   Josefa Carrillo de Fitch, "Dictation of Mrs. Capt. Henry D. Fitch/ Narración de la Sra viuda del Capitán Enrique D. Fitch," 1875, The Bancroft Library, BANC MSS C-E 67:10; translation in Beebe and Senkewicz, *Testimonios*, 78.

68   Josefa Carrillo, "Dictation," The Bancroft Library, BANC MSS C-E 67:10; translation in Beebe and Senkowicz, *Testimonios*, 76–84. Many historians have described this famous marriage, among them: Casas, *Married to a Daughter of the Land*, 91–107; Griswold del Castillo, "Neither Activists Nor Victims: Mexican

Women's Historical Discourse: The Case of San Diego, 1820–1850," *California History* 74, no. 3 (Fall 1995): 233–34; and Rosaura Sánchez, *Telling Identities*, 211–17.

69 "*Dn. Manuel Victoria . . . se quizo casar con migo, pero no me casé por que era mejicano y era muy contra los españoles,—y despues me vine casando con un mejicano al fin.*" Angustias de la Guerra, "Recuerdos," December 31, 1880, DLG 727; translation in Beebe and Senkewicz, *Testimonios*, 285.

70 Angustias de la Guerra, "Ocurrencias," The Bancroft Library, BANC MSS C-D 134; translation in Beebe and Senkewicz, *Testimonios*, 219–20.

71 Kicza, "The Great Families of Mexico," 448, 454, discusses this phenomenon for late colonial Mexico.

72 Teresa de la Guerra, "Narrativa," The Bancroft Library, BANC MSS C-E 67:2; translation in Beebe and Senkewicz, *Testimonios*, 49–67.

73 Dakin, *The Lives of William Hartnell*, 80.

74 Walker, *Kinship, Business, and Politics*, 56.

75 "*Su hijo Juan . . . sepuso en una escuela que tiene aqui, un tal Lavin, el que admite pupilos, dandoles de comer, enseña, y leavidan*[?] *la ropa; todo pagdo. 20 p. mensales.*" Manuel Varela to José de la Guerra, Tepic, April 19, 1824, DLG 1001.

76 Account, April 17, 1824, DLG 1049.

77 "You have here a house and that which goes with it at your disposal," he added. "[*T*]*iene V. aqui una casa y demas cosas anexas de que disponer.*" De la Guerra apparently did not take Cardoso up on this offer. José Cardoso to José de la Guerra, Tepic, March 2, 1824, DLG 127.

78 James Brotherston to William Hartnell, ca. 1825, quoted in Dakin, *The Lives of William Hartnell,* 142.

79 See William Hartnell to José de la Guerra, Monterey, January 22, 1826, February 28, 1826, November 28, 1826, and February 7, 1827, DLG 492. Judging by the tariffs paid, de la Guerra purchased large orders of British goods from the *Junius,* an English (likely McCulloch and Hartnell) brig in California in 1825–26 (which paid $3,663 in total duties); and the *Pizarro,* also an English ship, owned by McCulloch and Hartnell, at Monterey in 1825–26 (which paid $4,712 and $523 in total duties).

80 See for example, William Hartnell to José de la Guerra, Monterey, December 7, 1826, DLG 492; and William Hartnell to José de la Guerra, Monterey, January 7, 1827, DLG 492.

81 William Hartnell to José de la Guerra, Monterey, April 6, 1826, DLG 492.

82 C. Alan Hutchinson, *Frontier Settlement in Mexican California: The Híjar-Padrés Colony and Its Origins 1769–1835* (New Haven, Conn.: Yale University Press, 1969), 124–25.

83 For similar struggles in New Mexico and Texas, see Reséndez, *Changing National Identities*, 117–23. For more on the regional inconsistencies over trade policy and protectionism within Mexican liberal thinking, see David Brading, *The Origins of Mexican Nationalism* (Cambridge: The Centre of Latin American Studies, 1985).

84   William Hartnell to Begg and Co., December 3, 1825, quoted in Dakin, *The Lives of William Hartnell*, 86.

85   "*Esta licencia se podia pedir en nombre de José Antonio.*" William Hartnell to José de la Guerra Monterey, February 28, 1826, DLG 492. For American trappers who hoped that marriages to Mexicans would gain them access to restricted hunting licenses in New Mexico, see Rebecca McDowell Craver, *The Impact of Intimacy: Mexican-Anglo Intermarriage in New Mexico, 1821–1846* (El Paso: Texas-Western Press, 1982), 27.

86   William Hartnell to José de la Guerra, Monterey, April 6, 1826, DLG 492. See also Dakin, *The Lives of William Hartnell*, 130.

87   "*Segun las apariencias Mancisidor conseguirá todos los esquilmos de San Gabriel y de San Juan Capistrano, este es un golpe que no aguardaba, y preuba que los Padres son muy mal agradecidos.*" William Hartnell to José de la Guerra, Monterey, April 6, 1826, DLG 492.

88   Dakin, *The Lives of William Hartnell*, 93. "¡*Viva el Comercio!*" William Hartnell to José de la Guerra, Monterey, September 22, 1826, DLG 492.

89   John Lincoln to William Hartnell, Lima, Peru, ca. March 26, 1826, quoted in Dakin, *The Lives of William Hartnell*, 83–84.

90   William Hartnell to Hugh McCulloch, Monterey, August 19, 1826, quoted in Dakin, *The Lives of William Hartnell*, 109–10.

91   Dakin, *The Lives of William Hartnell*, 85.

92   William Hartnell to José de la Guerra, Monterey, January 7, 1827, DLG 492.

93   Begg & Co. to Hartnell, May 1826, quoted in Dakin, *The Lives of William Hartnell*, 110.

94   William Hartnell to José de la Guerra, Monterey, July 22, 1827, DLG 492.

95   "*Yo he determinado irme á Lima en el barco que espero en Septiembre, con que puede V. con anticipacion ir haciendo su lista de encargos.*" William Hartnell to José de la Guerra, Monterey, July 24, 1827, DLG 492.

96   Dakin, *The Lives of William Hartnell*, 116. Hartnell personally owed $4,087, and in addition agreed to take on outstanding debts owned to his company in California; his ultimate obligation amounted to some $18,885. Presumably, Hartnell bought the libranzas at a discount and hoped to make a small profit in this way.

97   Casas, *Married to a Daughter of the Land*, 56; Dakin, *The Lives of William Hartnell*, 113–18.

98   Duhaut-Cilly, "Duhaut-Cilly's Account of California," 157.

99   José de la Guerra, Padrón, Santa Bárbara Presidio, July 20, 1827, DLG 1095; this is a translation by Joseph Thompson of Departmental State Papers, vol. 5, The Bancroft Library, BANC MSS C-A 30, pp. 2–7. Out of a total population of 4,008, 529 lived at the presidio and in town, and 48 at ranchos San Julián, Simi, Refugio, and Conejo. The rest lived at the nearby missions. As de la Guerra did not record race, it is difficult to know how many of this total number were gente de razón, how many were neophytes, and how many were gentiles.

100   The political advantages that would come with local control of customs revenue are discussed more fully in the next chapter.

101   For example, Juan Malarín informed de la Guerra that he had bought him twelve Chinese chairs tax-free. Juan Malarín to José de la Guerra; Monterey, November 2, 1824, DLG 622.

102   The election took place in San Diego on February 18, 1827. Five electors met to choose the deputy and reorganize the territorial government. Pablo Vicente de Solá, the former governor, was chosen on the first vote. But since he had been living in Mexico City, first as deputy, then as a member of the Junta de Fomento, it was thought he would not be accepted by the congress as a genuine resident of California. De la Guerra was chosen unanimously on the second ballot, with Gervasio Argüello, brother of the former governor, as alternate. Bancroft, *History of California*, 2:33–34.

103   Phillips, "Don José Antonio Julián," 135–36; Bancroft, *History of California*, 2:33–34; Thompson, *El Gran Capitán*, 97; Echeandía's letter of recommendation for José de la Guerra to take to Mexico, January 30, 1828, DLG 255. José de la Guerra's avowal of loyalty to Mexico, December 10, 1828, DLG 465.

104   Mexico left the construction of a California merchant marine up to individuals, who generally lacked the funds or expertise to build their own ships. See Francis, *An Economic and Social History*, 664–713. De la Guerra was quite familiar with this particular ship; it had been sailing in and out of Santa Bárbara in various guises for the previous ten years. At first, it arrived in 1821 as the *Eagle*, under command of Captain Grimes, and was seized for smuggling at the port of Santa Bárbara a year later, on September 14, 1822, and the ship and its goods put up for public auction. Father Antonio Ripoll of Mission San Luis Obispo purchased the ship, and renamed it the *Santa Apolonia*. Then, in 1825, Ripoll sold the ship to Urbano Sánchez of Mazatlán, Mexico, who possibly renamed it *Santa Magdalena*, although most continued to refer to it as the *Santa Apolonia*. He then sold it to Don Francisco Javier de Espeleta in Mazatlán in 1828, who turned around and sold it to de la Guerra in Mexico City.

105   Irco Peña, San Blas, Mexico, May 16, 1829, DLG 880. Bill for repairs of the *Santa Apolonia*. Juan Machado to José de la Guerra, Mazatlán, March 25, 1829, April 27, 1829, April 29, 1829, DLG 613.

106   "[M]e los remita en su citada Goleta invertidoen buen sebo, y no manteca." Juan Martiarena to José de la Guerra, Tepic, May 16, 1829, DLG 641. See also Juan Bautista Martiarena to José de la Guerra, Tepic, May 11, 1829, DLG 641.

107   Alfred Robinson, "Sketches," cited in Bancroft's "De la Guerra Notes," quoted in Thompson, *El Gran Capitán*, 100. It is likely that this is the same ship that de la Guerra renamed the *Joven Angustias*, after his daughter. Juan Malarín to José de la Guerra, Monterey, September 14, 1829, DLG 626; contains a declaration of goods consigned to José de la Guerra on the *Joven Angustias* under Captain José Narváez, from Monterey to Santa Bárbara. The cargo consisted of fifty pounds of agave thread, five "poblano" shawls, and twenty small covered saucepans.

108   "[P]ues atodos nos interesa para tener hay quien nos mande sebo." Manuel Varela to José de la Guerra, Tepic, August 1, 1829. Varela also sent the welcome news that de la Guerra was not to be expelled from Mexico as a Spaniard.

344   Notes to pages 134–138

109   Santos, or "saints," are paintings or sculptures used for home devotion in the Catholic tradition in Mexico.

110   Robinson, *Life in California*, 5.

111   Ogden, "Boston Hide Droughers," 292.

112   Robinson, *Life in California*, 8.

113   Dakin, *The Lives of William Hartnell*, 118.

114   Osio, *The History of Alta California*, 94.

115   An account between José de la Guerra and William Hartnell, Monterey, September 28, 1829, DLG 1049. Total value exchanged: $10,361.

116   William Hartnell to John Begg, quoted in Dakin, *The Lives of William Hartnell*, 145.

117   Inventories of the sales from Hartnell to de la Guerra and W. G. Dana, February 24, 1830, DLG 1050. Total cost of items bought of *Danube* cargo was $3,315, including various types of cloth, four boxes of crystal vases, hats, and shaving razors. The ship and its hardware and tackle were $1,761. De la Guerra hoped to refloat the *Danube*, to replace the grounded *Dorotea*, but attempts to raise the ship proved futile. See José de la Guerra, "Occurrencias curiosas," April 18–September 26, 1830, The Bancroft Library, BANC MSS C-B 73, pp. 21–27.

118   William Gale to John Cooper, February 4, 1830, quoted in Dakin, *The Lives of William Hartnell*, 146. Cooper was a ship captain who worked the Pacific trade. His permanent residence was Monterey, where he lived with his wife, Encarnación Vallejo, the sister of Mariano Guadalupe Vallejo. William Goodwin Dana was married to Petra Carrillo, a daughter of Carlos Carrillo, and was a compadre of José de la Guerra.

119   See Dakin, *The Lives of William Hartnell*, 143. William Hartnell to José de la Guerra, April 7, 1831, DLG 492; José de la Guerra to Miguel Valencia, Justice of the Peace for Santa Bárbara, April 15, 1831, DLG 467; William Hartnell to José de la Guerra, May 22, 1831, DLG 492; Rafael Gómez, *asesor* [legal counsel to the government] to William Hartnell, May 27, 1831, DLG 329; and William Hartnell to José de la Guerra, Monterey, May 30, 1831, DLG 492.

120   See, for example, William Hartnell to José de la Guerra, Monterey, January 22, 1831, DLG 492; William Hartnell to José de la Guerra, Monterey, April 7, 1831, DLG 492; William Hartnell to José de la Guerra, Monterey, May 4, 1831, DLG 492.

121   William Hartnell to José de la Guerra, Monterey, November 22, 1830, DLG 492.

122   Dakin, *The Lives of William Hartnell*, 150–53.

123   Weber, *Mexican Frontier*, 162,181; Francis, *An Economic and Social History*, 125–40. Hartnell's naturalization papers are in the William E. P. Hartnell papers. A letter of November 22, 1830, also suggests that Hartnell was thinking of acquiring land at this date. William Hartnell to José de la Guerra, Monterey, November 22, 1830, DLG 492.

124   "*Vamos á ver si de Ranchero tengo el mismo acierto ó por mejor decir desacierto que de Comerciante.*" William Hartnell to José de la Guerra, Monterey, May 4, 1831, DLG 492, quoted in Dakin, *The Lives of William Hartnell*, 149.

125 William Hartnell to José de la Guerra, Monterey, May 30, 1831, DLG 492; and William Hartnell to José de la Guerra, Monterey, June 7, 1831, quoted in Dakin, *The Lives of William Hartnell,* 150.

126 "[N]*ecesito del consejo de V.; pensaba hacer 100 suertes de á 6op ... Yo no discurro otro modo de hacerme de algun dinero y sin dinero no puedo dejar el poco comercio que tengo en Monterey y vivir como deseo enteramente en el rancho y si no estoy alla no adelanteré nunca, conque V. me dirá lo que debo hacer para acertar.*" William Hartnell to José de la Guerra, Monterey, April 3, 1832, DLG 492.

127 Juan's tuition came to fifty pounds a year (or 750 pesos), and his clothing and other annual expenses were about seventy pounds (or 1,050 pesos). James Brotherston to William Hartnell, ca. 1825, quoted in Dakin, *The Lives of William Hartnell,* 163.

128 James Brotherston to José de la Guerra, Liverpool, February 15, 1831, DLG 106.

129 William Hartnell to José de la Guerra, Santa Bárbara, November 19, 1832, DLG 492. De la Guerra seems to have paid off the balance in a libranza of 259 pounds, 8 shillings, and 1/2 pence in 1833. José de la Guerra to James Brotherston, through James Scott and Stephen Anderson, June 1, 1833, DLG 1050.

130 Juan José de la Guerra to José de la Guerra, Mexico City, June 15, 1831, DLG 387.

131 Ibid.

132 "*Jaunillo sabe mucho ... V. no dude de que Juanillo tiene talente pa. echarse en la bolsa a cuanto Californio hay. Sino lo puse en la Cecretaria de ministerio de Relasiones (aunque el Sor. Mangino se me manifeste de que lo resibiria con mucho gusto) fue pr. que aqui en Mejico estan los jobenes espuesto a su perdision, y como Juanillo es tan bibo, me paresio mucho mejor remitirlo a Tepic.*" Carlos Antonio Carrillo to José de la Guerra, Mexico City, January 22, 1832, DLG 137.

133 "[S]*i llegado a esa su hijo Juan ... hubiese V. tenido pr. conveniente colocarlo al frente de la negociacion.*" Antonio José Cot to José de la Guerra, Lima, Peru, June 3, 1832, DLG 203.

134 Patrick Short, a Catholic missionary, had served in Hawaii from 1827 to 1831, when he was banished by King Kamehameha III (also called Kauikeaouli) and his mother, the regent Ka'ahumanu, at the behest of Protestant missionaries there.

135 Douglas arrived in Monterey from the Columbia River aboard the Hudson's Bay Company ship, the *Dryad,* in December 1830, and carried a letter of introduction to Hartnell from Captain Beechey. He stayed in Monterey collecting samples and getting to know the Hartnells until August 1832. Juan copied out selections of Douglas's book *El Curso Completo, un Diccionario Universal de Agricultura* into a small parchment book. Dakin, *The Lives of William Hartnell,* 169–70.

136 Juan died in the first week of September 1833 and was buried at Mission San Carlos on September 6, 1833. A month earlier, Hartnell had decided to open the school in Monterey itself and not at the ranch; it eventually moved there in May 1836. See: William Hartnell to José de la Guerra, Monterey, August 3, 1833, DLG 492.

137   William Hartnell to José de la Guerra, Monterey, October 1, 1833, DLG 492.

138   "*No hay como la pobreza para hacer á uno perder de á tiro la vergüenza. Despues de tantos favores, que debo á V. y que jamas podré pagar como merecer, me veo en la precision de pedirle otro de buen tamaño…para asegurar á mis hijos un pedazo de Terreno suyo propio sin gravamen alguno,…puede que V. quisiera mas bien buscarlas…á cuenta de la pension de los muchachos que piensa mandar al nuevo colegio.*" William Hartnell to José de la Guerra, Monterey, January 7, 1834, DLG 492.

139   William Hartnell to José de la Guerra, April 27, 1834, DLG 492.

140   This wedding is described in chapter two. Jimeno had arrived at the end of 1828 as acting administrator of revenues, or comisario. In 1829 he received the official title, and more responsible post, of *contador*. Francis, *An Economic and Social History*, 220; See also Enrique Virmond to José de la Guerra, Mexico City, October 12, 1829, DLG 1011: "*A Dn. Manl. Ximeno Casarin, va el despacho de contador.*"

141   Various accounts, 1830–40, DLG 1050.

142   For example, in 1830, Juan Bandini, another local trader, complained from San Diego, "the lack of money in circulation is notorious." "*es notoria la ninguna circulación de dinero.*" Juan Bandini to José de la Guerra, Pueblo of San Diego, March 6, 1830, DLG 79. By 1842, when William Heath Davis paid a visit, he was shown "twelve or fifteen" Indian baskets, "the largest holding, perhaps, half a bushel—all of which contained gold, some nearly full." "Being the wealthiest man in that part of California," wrote Davis, "and having so much ready money, at least $250,000, he was applied to by the rancheros for loans when they were in need of funds. The loans were made on promises to repay in beef cattle at the killing season, or in heifers, or in hides and tallow after the cattle had been killed, the lender taking the borrower's word as security, as was the custom. He also supplied the supercargoes of vessels with coin to pay duties on invoices." Davis, *Seventy-Five Years in California*, 185–86.

143   "*[E]l comercio paralizado, el Pto. sin buques…y muchas casa de Como. extrangs. dejando el Pais…no se ha presentado comprador pr. el que hemos traido ahora. De consiguiente debemos reputar pr. perdido el trabajo de 3 años en California.*" Antonio José Cot to José de la Guerra, Lima, Peru, June 14, 1830, DLG 203. Cot eventually returned to California in 1834 with a cargo of goods. Antonio José Cot to José de la Guerra, Monterey, October 9, 1834, DLG 203.

144   See DLG 1037 for the extensive correspondence from Tomás Antonio Yorba in Los Angeles to José de la Guerra, 1834–36. This offers an excellent example of the patron/agent relationship.

145   Various accounts, 1830–40, DLG 1050. See also the business letters of William Sturgis Hinckley to José de la Guerra, DLG 515.

146   Weber, *Mexican Frontier*, 139. See also Ogden, "Boston Hide Droughers," 301.

147   William Hartnell to Hugh McCulloch, Santa Bárbara, May 6, 1825, and McCulloch, Hartnell and Company to John Begg and Company, Monterey, December 3, 1825. Both in "Hartnell Letterbook," pp. 107–10, 156–60, quoted in Ogden, "Boston Hide Droughers," 290.

148 Ogden, "Boston Hide Droughers," 294–96.

149 Adele Ogden, "Alfred Robinson, New England Merchant in Mexican California," *California Historical Society Quarterly* 23 (September 1944): 211.

150 Robinson, *Life in California*, 32.

151 Ogden, "Boston Hide Droughers," 292; and Ogden, "Alfred Robinson," 195.

152 Osio, *The History of Alta California*, 70.

153 Robinson, *Life in California*, 30.

154 Ogden, "Alfred Robinson," 196; and Ogden, "Boston Hide Droughers," 293.

155 "*Dios sabe el bien o el mal que resultara con tal vecino a el Barbareño suelo*." José de la Guerra, "Occurrencias curiosas," The Bancroft Library, BANC MSS C-B 73, p. 26.

156 "*D. 4 Ojos [Gale] dio la vela . . . dejendo aqui un dependte*." Ibid. See also Robinson, *Life in California*, 61; and Ogden, "Alfred Robinson," 196.

157 Osio, *The History of Alta California*, 70, 198; José Fernández, "Cosas de California," The Bancroft Library, BANC MSS C-D 10, p. 59, quoted in Osio, *The History of Alta California*, 275.

158 Ogden, "Alfred Robinson," 196.

159 "*Robinson es á la verdad buen muchacho, tengo buenas esperanzas de él, le he facilitado buenos libros y dado consijos de hermano*." William Hartnell to José de la Guerra, Monterey, May 4, 1831, DLG 492.

160 Ogden, "Boston Hide Droughers," 293; Ogden, "Alfred Robinson," 197.

161 José de la Guerra, Account with Alfred Robinson, April 6, 1832, DLG 1050. Total value of account: $1,284.

162 Robinson, *Life in California*, 93–96.

163 Maynard Geiger, ed. and trans., *The Letters of Alfred Robinson to the De La Guerra Family of Santa Barbara: 1834–1873* (Los Angeles: The Zamorano Club, 1972), 51n. Robinson took the Spanish name "José María," but he never used it.

164 William Hartnell to José de la Guerra, February 6, 1834, and March 23, 1834, DLG 492. At this point, Robinson was traveling frequently, clearing up the *Brookline*'s remaining accounts and assisting Gale to load up tallow for Lima on the *Roxana*. He was so successful that Bryant and Sturgis gave him an interest in the 1834 voyage of the *California*, in addition to his usual commission. In 1834, Gale left again for Boston, and from then on Robinson managed all of the Bryant and Sturgis ventures on the coast.

165 "*Remito . . . un Reboso de seda para Anita . . . Espero que lo recibira V. como una expresion de mi estimacion*." Alfred Robinson to María Antonia Carrillo de la Guerra, Pueblo [Los Angeles], May 16, 1834, DLG 831.

166 July 9, 1834, BP01064, ECPP.

167 Antonio María de Ercilla to José de la Guerra, San Buenaventura, December 24, 1834, DLG 262; Alfred Robinson to José de la Guerra, Santa Bárbara, December 28, 1834, Santa Bárbara Historical Society, Geraldine V. Sahyun, trans., quoted in Geiger, *The Letters of Alfred Robinson*, 3.

168   Alfred Robinson to José de la Guerra, Santa Bárbara, December 28, 1834, Santa Bárbara Historical Society, Geraldine V. Sahyun, trans., quoted in Geiger, *The Letters of Alfred Robinson*, 3.

169   In early 1834, Robinson was managing both the *Pilgrim* and the *Alert*, which, despite Robinson's instructions, had arrived with insufficient cash to cover their customs duties. Ogden, "Alfred Robinson," 198. "Figure to yourselves Gentlemen my embarrassment, not having one Dollar on board," he told Bryant and Sturgis. Robinson managed to sell enough to scrape together $9,000, but "my friends in Sta. Barbara and elsewhere have assisted me gathering sufficient to satisfy the remainder." Alfred Robinson to Messrs. Bryant, Sturgis & Co., March 14–27, 1835; reprinted in Adele Ogden, ed., "The Business Letters of Alfred Robinson," *California Historical Society Quarterly* 23, no. 3 (September 1944): 315–16.

170   "[R]emito un Borreguito para que Da. Anita se encargue su mandar condimentar para mañana Domingo...pueden contar con mis <u>Gastadas Muelas</u> para aliviarlos en el <u>Devoramiento</u>." Antonio María Ercilla to José de la Guerra, Mission Santa Bárbara, March 14, 1835, DLG 262.

171   Antonio María Ercilla to José de la Guerra, Mission San Gabriel, June 9, 1835, DLG 262; William Hartnell to José de la Guerra, Monterey, June 6, 1835, DLG 492.

172   Alfred Robinson to Messrs Bryant, Sturgis & Co. San Diego, May 1, 1836. Reprinted in Ogden, "Business Letters," 319.

173   Dakin, *The Lives of William Hartnell*, 182–83.

174   Alfred Robinson to Messrs Bryant, Sturgis & Co., San Diego, May 1, 1836. Reprinted in Ogden, "Business Letters," 318.

175   Alfred Robinson to William Gale, San Diego, May 5, 1836. Reprinted in Ogden, "Business Letters," 323.

176   Dakin, *The Lives of William Hartnell*, 186.

CHAPTER FOUR

1   See Bancroft, *History of California*, 3:478; Gómez-Quiñones, *Roots of Chicano Politics*; Woodrow J. Hansen, *The Search for Authority in California* (Oakland, Calif.: Biobooks, 1960); Monroy, *Thrown Among Strangers*, 104–9, 126; Rosaura Sánchez, *Telling Identities*, 237; George Tays, "Revolutionary California: The Political History of California from 1820 to 1848," (PhD diss., University of California, Berkeley, 1934); Weber, *Mexican Frontier*, 255.

2   See the works of François-Xavier Guerra for the argument that this instability was caused by holdovers from the corporate colonial order, leading to clientalist politics, or *caciquismo*. Marie-Danielle Demélas and François-Xavier Guerra, "The Hispanic Revolutions," in *Elections Before Democracy* (New York: St. Martin's Press, 1996). For another perspective on party politics in the early republic, see Guardino, *The Time of Liberty*, 156–222.

3   Rosaura Sánchez, *Telling Identities*, 99. For a discussion of Texas as another haven for Mexican liberalism and liberals, see Reséndez, *Changing National Identities*, 61–74.

4   For more on liberalism in Mexico's early national era, see Brading, *Origins of Mexican Nationalism*; Charles A. Hale, *Mexican Liberalism in the Age of Mora, 1821–1853* (New Haven, Conn.: Yale University Press, 1968); Peter Guardino, *Peasants, Politics, and the Formation of Mexico's National State: Guerrero, 1800–1857* (Stanford, Calif.: Stanford University Press, 1996), and *The Time of Liberty*; Lynch, *The Spanish American Revolutions*; and Jaime Rodríguez, *The Independence of Spanish America* (New York: Cambridge University Press, 1998).

5   Hale, *Mexican Liberalism*, 123–24; Rosaura Sánchez, *Telling Identities*, 97–106.

6   Hutchinson, *Frontier Settlement*, 79–85; Weber, *Bárbaros*, 263–67.

7   This law was, in fact, nullified in 1814, but the Iturbide regime declared it in effect after Independence. Weber, *Mexican Frontier*, 47.

8   Gómez-Quiñones, *Roots of Chicano Politics*, 111; and Carlos Carrillo, *Exposition Addressed to the Chamber of Deputies of the Congress of the Union by Señor Don Carlos Antonio Carrillo, Deputy for Alta California Concerning the Regulation and Administration of the Pious Fund*, Herbert Ingram Priestly, ed. and trans. (San Francisco: John Henry Nash, 1938), x.

9   Weber, *Mexican Frontier*, 47–50.

10   Although there is little evidence that California hosted its own lodges, Californios certainly seem to have been aware of the nature of the Masons. Juan Alvarado, Salvador Vallejo, José Fernández, José de Jesús Vallejo, and Mariano Guadalupe Vallejo all referred to the Masonic affiliations of the incoming Mexican officials in their testimonios. Rosaura Sánchez, *Telling Identities*, 110, 177.

11   Angustias de la Guerra, "Ocurrencias," The Bancroft Library, BANC MSS C-D 134; translation in Beebe and Senkewicz, *Testimonios*, 225.

12   *"Si yo me resolví á dar libertad á los indios, lo hice, impulsado por sentimientos de humanidad, lo hice porque mi educacion republicana no me podia permitir que continuase á ser ... insensible al grito de angustia que salia del pecho de treinta mil indios que privados de su libertad no eran mas que muñecos en manos de los adustos sacerdotes."* Juan Bautista Alvarado, "Historia de California," 1876, The Bancroft Library, BANC MSS C-D 1, pp. 208–9.

13   This was of a total Indian population of about 200,000. Weber, *Mexican Frontier*, 60.

14   Rosaura Sánchez, *Telling Identities*, 111–13.

15   Padrés is often cited as a major force behind the national law of 1829 that called for the expulsion of Spaniards.

16   Bancroft, *History of California*, 3:184; Rosaura Sánchez, *Telling Identities*, 116. Angustias de la Guerra remembered that "this Padrés was a man whose ideas were so liberal that they could be termed extreme." Angustias de la Guerra, "Ocurrencias," The Bancroft Library, BANC MSS C-D 134; translation in Beebe and Senkewicz, *Testimonios*, 222.

17   José de la Guerra, "Ocurrencias curiosas," The Bancroft Library, BANC MSS C-B 73, p. 31. Ortega and Argüello were taking *"sus lecciones de Aritmetica y politica por el Geometra Padres, y han pasado por aqui en su seguimto. para continuar en Monterey su apredizage."*

18   *"Por supuesto, la juventud hizo causa comun con el audaz predicador de doctrinas que consonaban con nuestas miras de progreso y de filantropia."* Mariano Guadalupe Vallejo, "Recuerdos históricos," The Bancroft Library, BANC MSS C-D 18, p. 261. Vallejo also named Juan Alvarado, Joaquín Ortega, and Antonio María Osio as students of Padrés.

19   *"[L]os reverendos padres misioneros eran en sumo grado opuestos á que circulasen entre nosotros libros que tuviesen tendencia á inspirar en la joventud ideas liberales y conocimiento de los derechos del hombre libre; sabian ellos que los libros eran los emisarios mas temidos de la diosa que llamamos libertad, y con el fin de impedir que circulasen entre nosotros, ellos no perdonaban esfuerzos."* Mariano Guadalupe Vallejo, "Recuerdos históricos," The Bancroft Library, BANC MSS C-D 19, pp. 109–10, translation in Rosaura Sánchez, *Telling Identities,* 119.

20   On the impact of French philosophers in Los Angeles, see González, *This Small City,* 149–52. On liberal works circulating in Mexico, see Hale, *Mexican Liberalism.*

21   Dakin, *The Lives of William Hartnell,* 48.

22   Alan Rosenus, *General M. G. Vallejo and the Advent of the Americans: A Biography* (Albuquerque: University of New Mexico Press, 1995), 9.

23   *"[S]e organizó una sociedad secreta en que no debian tener parte sino los jovenes de educacion y cuyo objeto debia ser ... la compilacion de la historia de nuestra patria [California.] ... relegado al olbido el objeto de la convocatoria, se pusieron á discutir acerca de los medios mas á proposito para mejorar la suerte del territorio ... y al fin ... las cosas se puso bien coloradas."* Alvarado, "Historia de California," The Bancroft Library, BANC MSS C-D 2, pp. 42–43. Alvarado claims that the historical society was the inspiration of Joaquín de la Torre, while Dakin credits Hartnell. Dakin, *The Lives of William Hartnell,* 97. See also Rosenus, *General M. G. Vallejo,* 9.

24   *"Habiendo llegado ami noticia que algunos individuos de esta Provincia, sean nativos de ella ó estrangeros, tienen alguos papeles y libros sediciosos, particularmte. Contro la Fee y Religion C.A.R. y contra el Govno."* Gov. Luis Antonio Argüello to José de la Guerra, Monterey, January 31, 1824, DLG 53.

25   Rosaura Sánchez, *Telling Identities,* 119; Mariano Guadalupe Vallejo, "Recuerdos históricos," The Bancroft Library, BANC MSS C-D 19, p. 110.

26   Rosaura Sánchez, *Telling Identities,* 119; Mariano Guadalupe Vallejo, "Recuerdos históricos," The Bancroft Library, BANC MSS C-D 19, pp. 111–18.

27   Gachupín was a derogatory term for a European-born Spaniard.

28   Osio, *The History of Alta California,* 81.

29   Pío Pico, "Narración histórica," The Bancroft Library, BANC MSS C-D 13; translation in Beebe and Senkewicz, *Lands of Promise and Despair,* 346–48.

30   Angustias de la Guerra, "Ocurrencias," The Bancroft Library, BANC MSS C-D 134; translation in Beebe and Senkewicz, *Testimonios,* 222.

31   Osio, *The History of Alta California,* 87.

32 *"La mayor parte de esos cholos eran soldados muy viciosos y muy corrumpidos ... los beneméritos veteranos que todavia ... usaban cabello largo que les daba hasta la espalda."* Juan Alvarado, "Historia de California," The Bancroft Library, BANC MSS C-D 3, pp. 11–12.

33 Osio, *The History of Alta California*, 86.

34 Bancroft, *History of California*, 3:39–40.

35 Robinson, *Life in California*, 65–66.

36 For more on anti-Spanish discourse in Mexico, see Guardino, *The Time of Liberty*, 134–37, 184–86.

37 This incident is also discussed in chapter three. Bancroft, *History of California*, 2:570–71.

38 José de la Guerra to [President Victoria], October 12, 1828, DLG 465; translated by Nancy Appelbaum and in Thompson, *El Gran Capitán*, 95.

39 Angustias de la Guerra, "Ocurrencias," The Bancroft Library, BANC MSS C-D 134; translation in Beebe and Senkewicz, *Testimonios*, 210.

40 Bancroft, *History of California*, 2:576. The November 1828 newspaper reports were based on a communication from Captain Miguel González.

41 *"Ahora si apellidan chasco, mañana lo harán deveras,"* Miguel González, June 24, 1828, quoted by José María de Echeandía, April 25, 1829, San Diego, in "Case against José Antonio Noriega, Joaquín Carrillo, and Raymundo Carrillo," Provincial State Papers, vol. 70, Military, 1829, The Bancroft Library, BANC MSS C-A 19, pp. 35–38. See also Bancroft, *History of California*, 2:576.

42 Bancroft describes him as a "companion" of Vicente Gómez, a notoriously violent criminal nicknamed "El Capador," or The Castrator. Bancroft, *History of California*, 3:68.

43 Among those imprisoned were Juan Alvarado, then secretary of the territorial legislation; Alférez Mariano Guadalupe Vallejo, acting commander of the presidio; and José Castro, their friend. Alvarado, "Historia de California," The Bancroft Library, BANC MSS C-D 2, pp. 148–49.

44 Although de la Guerra was no longer the acting commander, having been removed from active duty for being Spanish-born, he also played a role in resisting the rebels, especially those who threatened his main trading partners; his daughter later remembered, "[T]he few foreigners (men) who lived here in Santa Bárbara created a makeshift barracks at my father's home where they stored their valuables. They themselves kept watch at night." Angustias de la Guerra, "Ocurrencias," The Bancroft Library, BANC MSS C-D 134; translation in Beebe and Senkewicz, *Testimonios*, 215.

45 Bancroft, *History of California*, 3:77.

46 Angustias de la Guerra fingers "Mexican artillerymen, Joaquín and Lázaro Piña" as the source for these claims. Angustias de la Guerra, "Ocurrencias," The Bancroft Library, BANC MSS C-D 134; translation in Beebe and Senkewicz, *Testimonios*, 216.

47   Despite Martínez's political sympathies, this is more likely the case. Martínez was justly proud of his ranchos and farms, and "was not some uncultured man who would get involved in conspiracies of that sort," according to Angustias de la Guerra, "that only a child would participate in, not a friar as intelligent as he was. Father Martínez was a staunch royalist, but he was no fool," she added. Ibid.

48   Ibid.

49   Ibid., 217.

50   Ibid., 218; *"una nega. bien cadosa llamada Juana,"* José de la Guerra, March 20, 1830, "Ocurrencias curiosas," The Bancroft Library, BANC MSS C-B 73, p. 21.

51   *"Un soldado Acapulqueño nego.[?] de la Havana de las que llegn. aqui en el Ma. Ester custodiando los Presos hirio de baste. gravedad entria[?] camino de la Playa a un marino del mismo Buque de nacion Yng., . . . el tal buen hombre decia en voz lavantado 'Yo soy criollo y tengo echo proposito de matar a todo Extrangro. o Gachupín que se me proporcione.'. . . y le fue tan favorable este prenda de patriotismo que el Sr. Pacheco lo dia por libre y absuelto no se si con g."* José de la Guerra, May 1830, "Ocurrencias curiosas," The Bancroft Library, BANC MSS C-B 73, p. 22.

52   Robinson, *Life in California*, 68; Bancroft, *History of California*, 3:576. Both sources also note that the Mexican soldiers shouted *"Viva Pacheco,"* and that the commander took part in the September 16 festivities.

53   Robert Ryal Miller, *Juan Alvarado, Governor of California, 1836–1842* (Norman: University of Oklahoma Press, 1998), 27–28.

54   José de la Guerra, "Ocurrencias curiosas," The Bancroft Library, BANC MSS C-B 73, pp. 30–31.

55   Alvarado claimed that "Castro replied to [Pliego], 'Son of a bitch; since you seized all the good for yourself and left nothing for my countrymen except the bad, take this,' and on saying 'take this' gave him a slap to the face." *"Castro le dijó 'hijo de un cingado; ya que agarrastes todo lo bueno para ti y no dejastes para mis paysanos sino lo malo toma esto' y al decir 'toma esto' le dió una bofetada en la cara."* Alvarado, "Historia de California," The Bancroft Library, BANC MSS C-D 2, pp. 44-45. Bancroft, *History of California*, 2:49–50.

56   François-Xavier Guerra, "Forms of Communication, Political Spaces, and Cultural Identities in the Creation of Spanish American Nations," in Chasteen and Castro-Klarén, eds., *Beyond Imagined Communities,*" 28.

57   Angustias de la Guerra, "Ocurrencias," The Bancroft Library, BANC MSS C-D 134; translation in Beebe and Senkewicz, *Testimonios,* 220.

58   *"[D]ebido á la gran distancia que separaba á California de la capital de la Republica, los hijos de ese departamento eran considerados como estrajeros."* Alvarado, "Historia de California," The Bancroft Library, BANC MSS C-D 5, p. 82.

59   Rosaura Sánchez, *Telling Identities*, 236–37.

60   Angustias de la Guerra, "Ocurrencias," The Bancroft Library, BANC MSS C-D 134; translation in Beebe and Senkewicz, *Testimonios,* 223.

61   Ibid., 221.

62   Bancroft, *History of California*, 3:187–200. Angustias de la Guerra, "Ocurrencias," The Bancroft Library, BANC MSS C-D 134; translation in Beebe and Senkewicz, *Testimonios*, 221.

63   "[S]e consideran dhos governantes en aquello suelo unas festas coronadas, para obrar como quieren, y no como deben." Carlos Carrillo to José de la Guerra, Mexico City, January 28, 1832.

64   Julio Carrillo, "Statement," [before 1918], The Bancroft Library, BANC MSS C-E 67:8, pp. 5–6.

65   Gerald J. Geary, *Secularization of the California Missions, 1810–1846* (Washington, D.C.: Catholic University of America, 1934).

66   Carrillo, *Exposition*, xii.

67   Hutchinson, *Frontier Settlement*, 92–95.

68   Ibid., 106–10.

69   "[U]n trastorno grande grandisimo en este Misciones . . . el Sr. Comisionado, no sabe lo que son Indios, de lo contrario hubiera dejado semejante reglamento." Father Josef Pineda to José de la Guerra, Mission Santo Tomás, October 3, 1822, DLG 792.

70   "Ya los Indios son libres, y los Misionaros escalvos . . . No hay azotes &c. y para andar a caballo no se ponen espuelas, y todo porque es moda." Father Luis Martínez to José de la Guerra, Mission San Luis Obispo, 1822, DLG 649.

71   Father Mariano Payeras to Rev. Father Guardian José Gasol, San Carlos, November 24, 1822. *Historia de México*, Primera Serie, Tomo 2, AGN; translation in Cutter, *Writings*, 340.

72   Francis, *An Economic and Social History*, 23–31; Rosaura Sánchez, *Telling Identities*, 111.

73   Rosaura Sánchez, *Telling Identities*, 122–23.

74   The petitions were to be made to the commanding officers of the presidios and approved by the missionaries and governor. Hutchinson, *Frontier Settlement*, 128. See also Hackel, *Children of Coyote*, 376–84.

75   Angustias de la Guerra, "Ocurrencias," The Bancroft Library, BANC MSS C-D 134; translation in Beebe and Senkewicz, *Testimonios*, 226.

76   Osio, in particular, claims that de la Guerra did not engage in battle with any zeal: "[I]t was the general opinion that Captain Don José de la Guerra y Noriega possessed, professionally, no more than his second last name." Osio, *The History of Alta California*, 63.

77   José de la Guerra to "Señor Patricio," February 22, 1824, DLG 462; translated by Nancy Appelbaum and by Thompson, *El Gran Capitán*, 171. The testimonios gathered by historian H. H. Bancroft in the 1870s are somewhat unclear about the names of the revolt's leaders. This letter seems to support the account of Rafael González, a soldier who took part in putting down the revolt, and who was the only informant to call the leader "Patricio" instead of "Pacomio." González also refers to Patricio as "un hijo de uno de razón llamado Cota," or "a son of one of the gente de razón named Cota." Rafael González, "Experiencias de un soldado de California," 1877, The Bancroft Library, BANC MSS C-D 92, p. 20. See also Bancroft, *History of California*, 2:527.

78   Mariano Guadalupe Vallejo, "Recuerdos históricos," The Bancroft Library, BANC MSS C-D 17, p. 368.

79   José de la Guerra to "Señor Patricio," February 22, 1824; DLG 462, translated by Nancy Appelbaum and by Thompson, *El Gran Capitán*, 171.

80   Several conflicting accounts exist about the causes and course of the uprising. See, for example: Bancroft, *History of California*, 2:527–32; Albert L. Hurtado, *Indian Survival on the California Frontier* (New Haven, Conn.: Yale University Press, 1988), 37–39; and James Sandos, "Levantamiento!: The 1824 Chumash Uprising Reconsidered," *Southern California Quarterly* 67, no. 2 (1985): 109–33. Antonio María Osio, a liberal who arrived after 1824, used the revolt to argue that the mission system had failed, and cast doubt on de la Guerra's ability to keep order. Osio, *The History of Alta California*, 63, 68. Some of the de la Guerra sources related to the uprising include: Angustias de la Guerra, "Ocurrencias," The Bancroft Library, BANC MSS C-D 134; translation in Beebe and Senkewicz, *Testimonios*, 205–9; Gov. Argüello to José de la Guerra, Presidio of San Francisco, February 24, 1824, DLG 51; Gov. Argüello to José de la Guerra, March 31, 1824, Monterey, DLG 51; José Joaquín de la Torre y Enterría to José de la Guerra, April 22, 1824, Monterey, DLG 978; and José Estrada to José de la Guerra, May 22, 1824, Monterey, DLG 277.

81   Weber, *Mexican Frontier*, 62–63.

82   Angustias de la Guerra, "Ocurrencias," The Bancroft Library, BANC MSS C-D 134; translation in Beebe and Senkewicz, *Testimonios*, 225.

83   "[C]*on la aparente libertad que se la da en el Presidio a unos, y conpleta satisfaccion conque se hallan en el monte otros, se van marchando quantos y quando les de la gana, llegando ya a tal miria que no tenemos quien tabaje lo precisio, y necesario en la Mission.*" Father Francisco González y Ibarra to José de la Guerra, Mission San Fernando Rey, May 2, 1825, DLG 338.

84   Quoted in Hackel, *Children of Coyote*, 374.

85   Hackel, *Children of Coyote*, 377–81.

86   "[C]*on el motivo de la soñada libertad, que tanto se cacarea en nuestros dias … Reclamo á José Aurelio, el celebre Jabonero de V. y a su hijo, á Fidel excelente chocolatero … Reclamo á Bruno que esta con el Alfz. Maitorena, y segun me han dicho a sueldo, a tanto por mes, y quien ha dado facultad ni al Yndio para alquilarse, ni al otro para detenerle en su Casa?*" Father Francisco Suñer to José de la Guerra, Mission San Buenaventura, February 12, 1827, DLG 950.

87   Angustias de la Guerra, for example, remarked that after Echeandía's emancipation decree, "an easing of discipline was noticed. The Indians were no longer passively obeying their missionaries. Before that, the Indians would obey their minister like a child obeys his father." Angustias de la Guerra, "Ocurrencias," The Bancroft Library, BANC MSS C-D 134; translation in Beebe and Senkewicz, *Testimonios*, 225.

88   Robinson was well known as a supporter of the mission system. According to one Californio, "Mr. Robinson was, since his arrival in our country, very supportive of the clergy's interests and they in turn on more than one occasion showed him their gratitude." *"El Señor Robinson fué, desde su ingreso al pais*

nuestro, mui adicto á los intereses del clero que en mas de una occasion le probaron su agradecimiento.” José de Jesús Vallejo, “Reminiscencias históricos de California,” 1875, The Bancroft Library, BANC MSS C-D 16, p. 22; translation in Rosaura Sánchez, *Telling Identities,* 216.

89   Robinson, *Life in California,* 69.

90   See the copy of this secularization decree, September 7, 1830, DLG 256. Another subsidiary plan would have created schools at Mission Santa Clara and Mission San Gabriel; see DLG 257. See also the discussion in Hutchinson, *Frontier Settlement,* 131–34. The diputación’s makeup is not completely clear for this session, but the decree was signed by five members in addition to the governor: Antonio Buelna, José Castro, Salvio Pacheco, Carlos Castro, and Juan Alvarado as secretary. Pío Pico, M. G. Vallejo, Anastasio Carrillo, and Juan Bandini also served around this time and may have been present. The assembly approved the entire plan on August 3, then forwarded it to the national government, with a few changes, on September 7, 1830.

91   Durán, report of December 31, 1831, quoted in Hutchinson, *Frontier Settlement,* 134.

92   *“Padres . . . paso por aqui con su trinadita Sra. hace dias sin que se le note menos cabo en sus ideas antigs. sobre misiones en las que intenta poner Administre. seculares y de ellas habran de ser dos . . . Joaquín Ortega y su sobrino el hijo de D. Argo. Santiago.”* José de la Guerra, “Ocurrencias curiosas,” The Bancroft Library, BANC MSS C-B 73, p. 31. In 1830, Joaquín Ortega was twenty-nine, and Santiago Argüello the younger was seventeen.

93   Robinson, *Life in California,* 69.

94   Quoted in Tays, “Revolutionary California,” 147.

95   Victoria *“contaba con el apoyo de los soldados, de los frayles y de los mexicanos.”* Alvarado, “Historia de California,” The Bancroft Library, BANC MSS C-D 2, p. 172.

96   Enrique Virmond to José de la Guerra, June 25, 1829, Acapulco, DLG 1011.

97   Angustias de la Guerra, “Ocurrencias,” The Bancroft Library, BANC MSS C-D 134; translation in Beebe and Senkewicz, *Testimonios,* 219.

98   *“Sobre Misions. manifiesta juiciosas ideas el nuevo mandarin.”* José de la Guerra, January, 1831, “Ocurrencias curiosas,” The Bancroft Library, BANC MSS C-B 73, p. 33.

99   Bancroft, *History of California,* 3:181–86.

100   Bancroft, *History of California,* 3:304, quoting Echeandía, *Carta que dirige á Don José Figueroa,* 1833, MS, pp. 44–50.

101   Rosaura Sánchez, *Telling Identities,* 115; Hutchinson, *Frontier Settlement,* 145.

102   *“Tengo la satisfasion de comunicar a V. que desde que pise estos suelos Republicanos me e meresido el apresio de los señores y señoras mas prinsipales, tanto por las recomendasiones de V. Como por aber sabido ser V. mi Ermano político, y por ultimo por mi gayarda . . . y no dar ningun(?) a que digar ¡a! que Barbaro Californio ranchero, no, eso, sigue no, con mi buen Pantalon, fraque Pelon . . . Pecho al frente, y ornada ago admirasion . . . Sabes que te estimo, y te estmare asta el fin de mi vida.”* Carlos Carrillo to José de la Guerra, Tepic, April 2, 1831, DLG 137.

103   *"[Q]ue la mayor parte de los Diputados eran de la opinion que no . . . no abia cuidado que todo esta bueno, y que con mi (continuation?) bien instruida y en buena disponsicion."* Ibid.

104   Carrillo, *Exposition,* vi–ix.

105   Ibid., 4.

106   Ibid., 10.

107   Ibid., 5.

108   Ibid., 7.

109   Carlos Carrillo to José de la Guerra, Mexico City, October 14, 1831, DLG 137. See also Carrillo, *Exposition,* xii.

110   *"V. como buen Ermano digame que debo aser."* Carlos Carrillo to José de la Guerra, Mexico City, October 14, 1831, DLG 137.

111   Angustias de la Guerra, "Ocurrencias," The Bancroft Library, BANC MSS C-D 134; translation in Beebe and Senkewicz, *Testimonios,* 225. Manuel Victoria to José de la Guerra, December 31, 1831, and July 10, 1832, DLG 1009.

112   Robinson, *Life in California,* 85. Later, Robinson wrote, "What a scourge he had been to California! What an instigator of vice! . . . The seeds of dishonor sown by him will never be extirpated so long as there remains a Mission to rob, or a treasury to plunder!" Robinson, *Life in California,* 99. Even Echeandía decided that he had crossed a dangerous line in freeing and arming Indians to fight civil battles in California. He revoked his emancipation decree and ordered the neophytes back to the missions; after this experience, California's gente de razón never again turned to Indians as factional allies. Michael J. González, "'The Child of the Wilderness Weeps for the Father of Our Country': The Indian and the Politics of Church and State in Provincial California," in Gutiérrez and Orsi, eds., *Contested Eden,* 162.

113   Dakin, *The Lives of William Hartnell,* 202–4. This company disbanded when the new governor arrived.

114   *"[T]odo se lo llebo el demonio con el Horroroso atentado que an echo los Californios."* Carlos Carrillo to José de la Guerra, Mexico City, January 22, 1832, DLG 137.

115   Carrillo, *Exposition,* 7.

116   Twinam, *Public Lives, Private Secrets,* 118.

117   For similar notions of a father's "duty" to his children in colonial Virginia, see Kathy Brown, *Good Wives, Nasty Wenches, & Anxious Patriarchs: Gender, Race, and Power in Colonial Virginia* (Chapel Hill: University of North Carolina Press, 1996), 342–43.

118   In at least one case, in 1816, his father tried and failed to get his son a personal missionary tutor. Father Vicente de Sarria to José de la Guerra, Mission San Fernando, July 17, 1816, DLG 902.

119   Phillips, "Don José Antonio Julián," 50–57. See also DLG 856 and 923.

120   For more on education on Mexico's frontier, see Weber, *Mexican Frontier,* 232–34.

121   With the demise of the public schools, elite families like the de la Guerras could at least turn to their private libraries; Angustias was thirteen when the school closed, but she eagerly drank in the Spanish classics and would drop frequent references to Cervantes into her own writing. Angustias de la Guerra, "Recuerdos," December 31, 1880, DLG 727; translation in Beebe and Senkewicz, *Testimonios,* 284; Bancroft, *History of California,* 2:574. Mexico struggled to increase school attendance, but as late as 1844, only five percent of eligible children went to school. Weber, *Mexican Frontier,* 234.

122   In 1832, the Peruvian trader Juan Mancisidor proposed sending one of de la Guerra's remaining sons—Joaquín, ten, Miguel, nine, or Antonio María, seven —to school in Spain. "I well see the number of your sons," he wrote on Juan's return from England in 1832, "and know also how much you want to furnish each one of them a similar education." *"Veo bien el numero de sus hijos, y conosas tambien cuanto desea el proporcionarles una educacion tal cual."* Juan Ygnacio Mancisidor to José de la Guerra, Los Angeles, June 4, 1832, DLG 63. See also: Juan Ygnacio Mancisidor to José de la Guerra, Lima, Peru, November 1, 1832, DLG 634.

123   José María Echeandía to José de la Guerra, Santa Bárbara, January 7, 1828, DLG 254. A passport to travel to Mexico, accompanied by his two sons, Francisco and Pablo.

124   Joseph E. Cassidy, "Life and Times of Pablo de la Guerra," (PhD diss., University of California, Santa Bárbara, 1977), 30–31. Later, Pablo would boast that "bishops, canons, ambassadors, ministers and attorneys general" had graduated from his school. Pablo de la Guerra to Francisco de la Guerra, Mexico City, January 10, 1855, DLG 409.

125   Juan José de la Guerra to William Hartnell, 1826–28, DLG 386.

126   Arrom, *Women of Mexico City,* 57–58. Single sons over twenty and daughters over eighteen were eligible for a dispensation allowing them to administer their own property.

127   Angustias de la Guerra, "Ocurrencias," The Bancroft Library, BANC MSS C-D 134; translation in Beebe and Senkewicz, *Testimonios,* 225.

128   Lugo, "Vida de un ranchero," BANC MSS C-D 118; translation in *Historical Society of Southern California Quarterly* 32, no. 3 (September 1950): 235.

129   William A. Streeter, "'Recollections of Historical Events in California, 1843–1878' of William A. Streeter," ed. William H. Ellison, *California Historical Society Quarterly* 18 (March, June, and September 1939): 170.

130   *"[L]a juventud llena de ideas liberales, bajo ningun pretexto podia prestarse á tributar homenaje á personas que fundaban su derechos en rancios pergaminos ó bien en los antecedentes gloriosos de sus antepasados; estabamos dispuestos á reconocer el mérito de cada uno."* Mariano Guadalupe Vallejo, "Recuerdos históricos," The Bancroft Library, BANC MSS C-D 18, p. 176.

131   For more on this strain within liberal philosophy, see Jay Fliegelman, *Prodigals & Pilgrims: The American Revolution against Patriarchal Authority, 1750–1800* (Cambridge: Cambridge University Press, 1982).

132   Arrom, *Women of Mexico City,* 92; Guardino, *The Time of Liberty,* 170–71.

133   Lugo, "Vida de un ranchero," BANC MSS C-D 118; translation in *Historical Society of Southern California Quarterly* 32, no. 3 (September 1950): 235.

134   Mora-Torres, *Californio Voices,* 219.

135   In the 1820s, the right to set suffrage regulations in Mexico belonged to the states (territories like California were excepted); after the conservative resurgence of the 1830s, the central government took over this role. Peter Guardino discusses the political nature of expanding and contracting suffrage restrictions in the state of Oaxaca in *The Time of Liberty,* 170–75. Sarah Chambers, in *From Subjects to Citizens,* 189–90, 197, 214, discusses the restriction of "dependents" from citizenship rights in Peru in the same period, as does Arlene J. Díaz for Venezuela in *Female Citizens, Patriarchs, and the Law in Venezuela, 1786–1904* (Lincoln: University of Nebraska Press, 2004), 107–16.

136   Lugo, "Vida de un ranchero," BANC MSS C-D 118; translation in *Historical Society of Southern California Quarterly* 32, no. 3 (September 1950): 193.

137   See baptismal entries April 3, 1822 BP00614; January 14, 1824 BP00656; November 22, 1824 BP00678; April 2, 1826 SC 03424; June 29, 1831 SC 03740; November 13, 1832 BP00960; August 8, 1833 BP01004, ECPP; and for godparent links to Teresa and William Hartnell, William Hartnell to José de la Guerra, Monterey, April 6, 1826, DLG 492.

138   For José Antonio's career, see Bancroft, *History of California,* 2:572, 3:654. For local government organization and alcalde justice, see David J. Langum, *Law and Community on the Mexican California Frontier: Anglo-American Expatriates and the Clash of Legal Traditions, 1821–1846* (Norman, Okla., and London: University of Oklahoma Press, 1987); Gómez-Quiñones, *Roots of Chicano Politics,* 108; and Theodore Grivas, "Alcalde Rule: The Nature of Local Government in Spanish and Mexican California," *California Historical Society Quarterly* 40, no. 1 (March 1961): 11–32.

139   Copies of the documents pertaining to Conejo can be found in Proceedings of California Land Cases, Southern District, Case 107, Conejo. José de la Guerra y Noriega and María del Carmen Rodríguez, claimants. Huntington Library, MS Film 543:14. Petition filed March 13, 1852.

140   María del Carmen Rodríguez to Commandant General, July 5, 1833; translation of Expediente, Proceedings of California Land Cases, Southern District, Case 107, Conejo. pp. 23–24.

141   The wife of José de Jesús, Bernarda Ruiz, was also the first cousin of José de la Guerra's wife, María Antonia Carrillo. Baptism of Juan José Antonio Felipe Rodríguez, May 2, 1828, BP00798, and Mariano Vicente Rodríguez, April 9, 1830, BP00866, ECPP.

142   Alcalde José Antonio de la Guerra to Governor Figueroa, July 8, 1833. Proceedings of California Land Cases, Southern District, Case 107, Conejo. Huntington Library, MS Film 543:14, pp. 24–26.

143   Figueroa's decision. July 16, 1833. Ibid., p. 27. Arrom, *Women of Mexico City,* 63, 84.

144   The Rancho Simi (its full name was San José de Nuestra Señora de Alta Gracia
      y Simi) was originally granted in 1795 to Santiago Pico, a soldier who came with
      the Anza expedition, then reaffirmed to his sons Patricio, Miguel, and Javier in
      1821. De la Guerra bought the ranch from Rafael, Patricio's son (acting for him-
      self, his sister Simona, and uncles Miguel and Javier), on October 6, 1832, and
      by November 20, 1832, the paperwork was finally complete. For more infor-
      mation on the ranch, see DLG 1079; and Proceedings of California Land Cases,
      Southern District, Case 103, Simi. José de la Guerra y Noriega, claimant, in-
      cluding the "Transcript of the Proceedings in Case No. 38 José de la Guerra y
      Noriega Claimant vs. the United States, Defendant, for the place named San
      José de Gracia, alias Simi." Huntington Library, MS Film 543:13.

145   Robert G. Cowan, *Ranchos of California: A List of Spanish Concessions
      1775–1822 and Mexican Grants 1822–1846* (Fresno, Calif.: Academy Library
      Guild, 1956).

146   Enrique Virmond to Lucas Alamán, Mazatlán, February 1, 1831, quoted in
      Weber, *Mexican Frontier*, 62.

147   Cowan, *Ranchos of California*.

148   "[D]ise que es muy despota, . . . que fue pobre a Sonora, y de haya vino rico, y yo
      creo que aora ya pobresio en Megico, y quiere ir a buscar algo a Califor-
      nia . . . ¿que nunca a de ir un governante . . . que no sea por el interes de su bien
      particular?" Carlos Antonio Carrillo to José de la Guerra y Noriega, Mexico
      City, April 21, 1832, DLG 137.

149   "No hay mas remedio que aserle amigo de Figueroa, regalarle un buen par de
      caballos, y un buen par de mulas, que es lo que se usa en el dia con los
      Goviernos, para poder conseguir lo que uno quiere." Carlos Antonio Carrillo to
      José de la Guerra y Noriega, Mexico City, April 21, 1832, DLG 137. A month
      later, Carrillo had met with the new governor, and, more favorably impressed,
      written him a letter of introduction to de la Guerra. Carlos Antonio Carrillo to
      José de la Guerra y Noriega, Mexico City, May 11, 1832, DLG 137.

150   Carlos Carrillo's plan to separate the civil and military command of California
      was quashed in Mexico after the overthrow of Victoria. "Sr. Bustamante is com-
      pletely against the division of the commands," he reported, "telling me, 'No, Sir,
      now there is no way that it could be thus, because your Countrymen are guilty
      of starting a Revolution.'" "El Sor. Bustamante enteramte. es contrario aquese
      dibidan los mandos . . . disiendome: no Señor, ya no hay llegar que seaga eso,
      pues sus Paysanos tienen la culpa de aberse puesto en Rebolusion." Carlos An-
      tonio Carrillo to José de la Guerra y Noriega, Mexico City, April 21, 1832,
      DLG 137.

151   Gómez-Quiñones, *Roots of Chicano Politics*, 114.

152   Figueroa gave orders on arrival for the election of a new diputación, according
      to Osio, and on March 24, 1833, the electors met at Monterey, choosing Juan
      Bandini as the new deputy to congress, and José Antonio Carrillo, Manuel
      Crespo, J. J. Vallejo, M. G. Vallejo, Joaquín Ortega, and Antonio María Osio
      elected to the diputación. Bandini left for Mexico with Echeandía on May 14,
      1833. For some unknown reason, this election was declared illegal, and a new

one was held December 1 and 2, 1833. Bandini was again elected to congress, and Carlos Carrillo (back from Mexico), Pío Pico, Francisco de Haro, Joaquín Ortega, José Antonio Carrillo, José Antonio Estudillo, and José Castro were elected as deputies. Bancroft, *History of California*, 3:245. Osio, *The History of Alta California*, 125.

153   Bancroft, *History of California*, 3:246.

154   *"De lo que V. dice tocante á los cuidadanos—yo tendré buen cuidado de no darles el mas leve motivo para que hablen, lo que hasta la fha no han hecho pues los he visto varias veces y no han dicho una palabra de Gachupines."* Juan José to María Antonia Carrillo de la Guerra, Monterey, March 5, 1833, DLG 388.

155   Bancroft, *History of California*, 3:325–26, quoting Minister Ortiz Monasterio to José Figueroa, Mexico City, May 17, 1832.

156   Father Durán, for example, told Figueroa that Indians, like children, had little ambition and could not look beyond the present. Their freedom in the end was only the "freedom to lead vicious and irrational lives." Durán to Figueroa, July 3, 1833, Los Angeles, quoted in Hutchinson, *Frontier Settlement*, 222.

157   For more on these regulations and Indian refusal to comply, see Bancroft, *History of California*, 3:329–31; Hackel, *Children of Coyote*, 385–86; Hutchinson, *Frontier Settlement*, 222–25, 229; and Weber, *Mexican Frontier*, 64.

158   In August, Figueroa asked for reports from the diputación (which still had not met) and the mission fathers to suggest which missions were ready to be secularized. The missions responded by October 3, and on October 5, Figueroa made his recommendation against radical changes.

159   Alamán to Figueroa, May 17, 1832, summarized in Hutchinson, *Frontier Settlement*, 156–57. For more on the colonization laws of 1824 and 1828, see Weber, *Mexican Frontier*, 162, 182. Alamán reversed earlier instructions making foreigners ineligible for grants, but with the huge American settlement of Texas in mind, Alamán also warned the new governor not to allow Russians or Americans to make up more than a third of the population of California.

160   In May 1832, José Gertrudis Carrillo was twenty-one years old, and had been married to Manuela Ortega for two and a half years. Manuela was the younger sister of Concepción, José Antonio de la Guerra's wife.

161   Carlos Antonio Carrillo to Lucas Alamán, Expediente, Mexico City, May 9, 1832; with marginal notation by Alamán, May 16, 1832. Transcript in Proceedings of California Land Cases, Southern District Case 117 (Las Posas). José de la Guerra claimant. Including "Transcript of the Proceedings in Case 296: José de la Guerra y Noriega, Claimant, vs. The United States, Defendant, for the place named 'Las Pozas.'" Huntington Library, MS Film 543:15, p. 24.

162   José Gertrudis Carrillo to Governor Figueroa, Santa Bárbara, September 30, 1833; Las Posas Land Case, 25–28.

163   Figueroa, marginal notation to Carrillo petition, Santa Bárbara, October 1, 1833; Las Posas Land Case, 25–27, 30. Also Gov. Figueroa, Monterey, November 21, 1833.

164   Juan M. Ibarra (commander at Santa Bárbara) to Figueroa, October 21, 1833; Las Posas Land Case, 29. Later Ignacio del Valle testified that San Buenaventura

had pastured its cattle there as late as 1828. Del Valle testimony, September 3, 1852; Las Posas Land Case, 2.

165 Testimony of Fernando Tico, February 4, 1834; Las Posas Land Case, 31–35. José de Jesús Rodríguez and Antonio Rodríguez also gave testimony.

166 Father Blas Ordaz to Figueroa, October 31, 1833, and February 6, 1834. Las Posas Land Case, 29–30, 36. The fact that, by February, Carrillo had already taken possession of the land without a grant, Ordaz complained, was an "abuse," which "shows the many injuries which may accrue to the *colindantes* [neighbors]".

167 Las Posas Land Case, 38–39. The diputación had not, in fact, met at all in 1833, and did not assemble until May 1, 1834. This new assembly consisted of Carlos Carrillo, Pío Pico, Francisco de Haro, Joaquín Ortega, José Antonio Carrillo, J. A. Estudillo, and José Castro. Bancroft, *History of California*, 3:246.

168 Bancroft, *History of California*, 3:339–40. The title to Las Posas was then issued on July 28, 1834. Las Posas Land Case, 4.

169 In 1833, Rancho Sespe was granted to Carlos Carrillo, a total of two leagues or 8,881 acres "between" Missions San Buenaventura and San Fernando.

170 The conspirators were described as "irreconcilable foes of our country," in letters by Angel Ramírez, a newly arrived liberal from Mexico, Antonio M. Lugo, and Father Blas Ordaz. Bancroft, *History of California*, 3:257. It might seem strange that another friar would want to bring up the Father President on charges, but Ordaz was well known for his ill temper, and had many personal grudges, having been censured for "unbecoming conduct" by Durán, and feeling cheated by de la Guerra in his business dealings.

171 Bancroft, *History of California*, 3:258; Robinson, *Life in California*, 109–10; William Hartnell to José de la Guerra, Monterey, June 12, 1834, DLG 492.

172 On Gómez-Farías's projects, see Rosaura Sánchez, *Telling Identities*, 108; Gómez-Quiñones, *Roots of Chicano Politics*, 115; Weber, *Mexican Frontier*, 185; and Hutchinson, *Frontier Settlement*, 161.

173 Reséndez, *Changing National Identities*, 68–69; and González, *This Small City*, 44.

174 Hutchinson, *Frontier Settlement*, 161–74; Bancroft, *History of California*, 3:336.

175 Padrés received his appointment July 12, 1833, and Híjar received his on July 15. Hutchinson, *Frontier Settlement*, 181–85.

176 Hutchinson, *Frontier Settlement*, 190–91; Rosaura Sánchez, *Telling Identities*, 128; Weber, *Mexican Frontier*, 185.

177 The diputación that assembled in mid-1834 consisted of Carlos Carrillo, Pío Pico, Francisco de Haro, Joaquín Ortega, José Antonio Carrillo, José Antonio Estudillo, and José Castro. Bancroft, *History of California*, 3:246.

178 Whether missionaries intentionally destroyed the mission herds at secularization is still a controversial topic. Antonio María Osio claimed that they did, although both he and the historian Hutchinson suggest that the motive was to ensure mission properties would in some form end up in Indian hands. Others note that the herds more likely ended up in private hands after secularization through expropriation or sale. Osio, *The History of Alta California*, 118–20;

Bancroft, *History of California,* 3:348–49; Hutchinson, *Frontier Settlement,* 249–50; Jackson and Castillo, *Indians, Franciscans, and Spanish Colonization,* 98–100.

179   Weber, *Mexican Frontier,* 64–66; Bancroft, *History of California,* 3:342–43.

180   For the full text, see Bancroft, *History of California,* 3:342–44.

181   Weber, *Mexican Frontier,* 66.

182   González, *This Small City,* 44.

183   The average age of the colonists, among them fifty-five women and seventy-nine children under age fifteen, was twenty years old. Weber, *Mexican Frontier,* 185. Hutchinson, *Frontier Settlement,* 419–22, lists the entire colony and their approximate ages and occupations. Figueroa received a letter dated December 7, 1833, from the Minister of War (at Santa Anna's request) directing him to remain comandante general of California instead of Padrés; on May 31, 1834, Santa Anna staged a coup and expelled Farías; and on July 25, 1834, Santa Anna revoked Híjar's appointment as civil governor. Hutchinson, *Frontier Settlement,* 195, 214; Bancroft, *History of California,* 3:270.

184   Francisco Lombardo, Minister of Relations, instructions, April 23, 1834, quoted in Hutchinson, *Frontier Settlement,* 210. See also Gómez-Quiñones, *Roots of Chicano Politics,* 116; Bancroft, *History of California,* 3:272–78; Hutchinson, *Frontier Settlement,* 197–206; and Robinson, *Life in California,* 110, 112–13.

185   Weber, *Mexican Frontier,* 186.

186   José Figueroa, *Manifesto to the Mexican Republic which Brigadier General José Figueroa, Commandant and Political Chief of Upper California, Presents on his Conduct and That of José María de Híjar and José María Padrés as Directors of Colonization in 1834 and 1835,* C. Alan Hutchinson, trans. and ed. (Berkeley: University of California Press, 1978).

187   Gómez-Quiñones, *Roots of Chicano Politics,* 116; Weber, *Mexican Frontier,* 186; Rosaura Sánchez, *Telling Identities,* 132–33.

188   Figueroa, quoted in Rosaura Sánchez, *Telling Identities,* 132–33.

189   Commissioners and administrators included Carlos, Joaquín, Domingo, and Anastasio Carrillo, Joaquín Ortega, Pío Pico, Ignacio del Valle, and Manuel Jimeno. Bancroft, *History of California,* 3:346, 353, 358–61.

190   See Hackel, *Children of Coyote,* 388–419; Hurtado, *Indian Survival,* 37, 46–47.

191   "[Y]a V. save muy vien lo que dice el reglamento que no pueden ser vendidas, no enajenadas las cosas que se les den, y que todo comprador perdera lo que huviere dado pr. lo que halla comprado." Domingo Carrillo to José de la Guerra, Los Berros, July 15, 1835, DLG 141. Los Berros ("The Springs") as a town no longer exists, but it is the name for the canyon where Mission La Purísima stood in 1834. Cathy Rudolph, former director of research for the Santa Barbara Trust for Historic Preservation, personal communication, February 16, 1999.

192   "[Y] yo nada tengo que ver con Cuchichito por ser hijo de familia, y estar bajo la patria potestad." Domingo Carrillo to José de la Guerra, Los Berros, July 20, 1835, DLG 141.

193   "Sino me lo huviera reclamado nada hubiera dicho." Domingo Carrillo to José de la Guerra, July 25, 1835, DLG 141.

194 *"Si el Reglamto. que rigue en este pueblo no se ha publicado en ese yo no tengo la culpa."* Domingo Carrillo to José de la Guerra, Los Berros, July 25, 1835, DLG 141. Less than a month later, in fact, Domingo Carrillo passed on responsibilities as mayordomo to his son Joaquín.

195 Rosaura Sánchez, *Telling Identities,* 99.

196 M. G. Vallejo, Juan Bautista Alvarado, et al., Monterey, October 16, 1834, DLG 118. It is unclear from the records whether José Antonio de la Guerra also began serving as a territorial deputy at this time. According to the election regulations, the diputación elected the national representative, but Bancroft's list of these deputies ["1st vocal, José Antonio Carrillo, absent as congressman; 2d, José María Estudillo, excused on account of sickness . . . 3d, José Castro; 4t Juan B. Alvarado . . . 5th, Manuel Jimeno Casarín; 6th, Antonio Buelna; 7th, absent and unknown (perhaps J. A. de la Guerra)"] and the list of electors in the records of the de la Guerra collection [M. G. Vallejo, Alvarado, José Antonio de la Guerra, José Antonio Carrillo, Manuel Domínguez, Juan María Marrondo] do not match. At one point, Bancroft claims that the territorial deputies elected in October 1834 did not meet until August 25, 1835, but at another, he recounts their correspondence with Híjar in October and November 1834. Bancroft, *History of California,* 3:275–78, 291.

197 Angustias married Jimeno on January 12, 1833, and they first lived with the Hartnells in Monterey. In addition, brothers Pablo and Joaquín de la Guerra arrived for tutoring in March 1834, and moved with Teresa and William Hartnell to the San José Seminary at Alisal in May 1835. Dakin, *The Lives of William Hartnell,* 169, 182.

CHAPTER FIVE

1 This statement comes from a preamble to resolutions passed in the session of October 10–14, 1835. On Alvarado's motion, the legislature called for the hanging of Figueroa's portrait in the legislative hall, and a monument to be built with the inscription, "To the Eternal Memory of General José Figueroa/Political and Military Chief of Alta California/Father of the Country." Bancroft, *History of California,* 3:296.

2 Alvarado's speech, in fact, contains a good summary of the ideal patriarch; in addition to the governor's efforts to improve the economy, Alvarado claimed, "he consoled the widow, shielded the orphan, succored the soldier, protected merit, and encouraged honor." Speech reprinted in Robinson, *Life in California,* 118.

3 The decree repealing secularization was dated November 7, 1835, though knowledge of it did not reach California until after the first of the year. The text read: "Until the curates mentioned in article 2 of the law of August 17, 1833, shall have taken possession, the government will suspend the execution of the other articles, and will maintain things in the state in which they were before the said law was made." Bancroft, *History of California,* 3:355. Between Figueroa and Chico, José Castro and Nicolás Gutiérrez served as interim jefe político and comandante general. Bancroft, *History of California,* 3:298.

4   For a discussion of political dissent and secessionist movements in New Mexico and Texas, see Reséndez, *Changing National Identities*, chaps. 5 and 6.

5   "*[T]odos ellos iban vestidos de negro y llevaban en el ojal de la levita una rosita encarnada (roja) que era el distintivo de los federalistas.*" Mariano Guadalupe Vallejo, "Recuerdos históricos," The Bancroft Library, BANC MSS C-D 19, pp. 80–81.

6   Alfred Robinson to William Gale, San Diego, December 5, 1836, reprinted in Ogden, "Business Letters," 326–27.

7   Alfred Robinson to Bryant, Sturgis and Co., San Diego, December 18, 1836, reprinted in Ogden, "Business Letters," 328.

8   Robinson to William Gale, San Diego, December 18, 1836, reprinted in Ogden, "Business Letters," 329.

9   Angustias de la Guerra, "Ocurrencias," The Bancroft Library, BANC MSS C-D 134; translation in Beebe and Senkewicz, *Testimonios*, 246.

10   Although the specific order to transform the government of California would not be passed until December 30, 1836, Chico himself used the new names on his arrival. Bancroft, *History of California*, 3:425. The only ayuntamientos that were allowed to function under the new regime were those that served as capitals of departments, such as Monterey, those that had populations over 4,000 at the coast or 8,000 inland (no California town was that large), or those that had existed prior to 1808. Los Angeles, San Jose, and Santa Cruz fit into the latter category. Weber, *Mexican Frontier*, 33–36; Reséndez, *Changing National Identities*, 175–76.

11   "*Chico nos promete honra, gloria, y grandezas si mansamente seguimos sus politicas; lo que equivale á decirnos que renunciemos á nuestros derechos de hombres libres y aceptemos de llano su plan de centralismo.*" Quoted in Mariano Guadalupe Vallejo, "Recuerdos históricos," The Bancroft Library, BANC MSS C-D 19, p. 109.

12   "*[S]e quitó la mascara y . . . trató de despotizar á la honorable Diputación.*" Mariano Guadalupe Vallejo, "Recuerdos históricos," The Bancroft Library, BANC MSS C-D 19, p. 104.

13   For a similar discussion of the connection between familial order and political authority in the French Revolution, see Lynn Hunt, *The Family Romance of the French Revolution* (Berkeley: University of California Press, 1992). For the American Revolution, see Fliegelman, *Prodigals & Pilgrims*.

14   "*Aunque separado de la vida publica en apariencia, 'sub rosa' tomaba parte activa en la politica . . . Nosotros estabamos al corriente del 'modus operandi.'*" Mariano Guadalupe Vallejo, "Recuerdos históricos," The Bancroft Library, BANC MSS C-D 19, p. 100.

15   Bancroft, *History of California*, 3:435; Angustias de la Guerra, "Ocurrencias," The Bancroft Library, BANC MSS C-D 134; translation in Beebe and Senkewicz, *Testimonios*, 243; Alvarado, "Historia de California," The Bancroft Library, BANC MSS C-D 3, p. 79; Mariano Guadalupe Vallejo, "Recuerdos históricos," The Bancroft Library, BANC MSS C-D 19, p. 121.

16   Angustias de la Guerra, "Ocurrencias," The Bancroft Library, BANC MSS C-D 134; translation in Beebe and Senkewicz, *Testimonios*, 243.

17   Ibid., 244.

18   Alvarado, who recounted this scheme, does not name the son but describes him as a "gamine of Paris" and a "good lad" who arranged outings in the country for his friends. The likeliest candidate is twelve-year-old Miguel. Alvarado, "Historia de California," The Bancroft Library, BANC MSS C-D 3, p. 80. See also Bancroft, *History of California*, 3:436.

19   "[L]e constaba que su hijo… no era capaz de guardar un secreto cinco minutos … el padre Duran á quien el gobernador Chico habia ordenado fuesen puestos pesados grillos (los grillos eran para invencion del "cadete") y conducido á bordo de un buque que debía conducirlo á la China para que se lo comiesen los salvages." Alvarado, "Historia de California," The Bancroft Library, BANC MSS C-D 3, pp. 80–82.

20   Angustias de la Guerra, "Ocurrencias," The Bancroft Library, BANC MSS C-D 134; translation in Beebe and Senkewicz, *Testimonios*, 244.

21   Steve Stern describes this as a "gendered etiquette of revolt." Stern, *The Secret History of Gender*, 205–9. For studies of the gendered nature of riot in Oaxaca and Morelos, see Guardino, *The Time of Liberty*, 62, 81.

22   Alvarado recalled that Durán was particularly loved in Santa Bárbara because "he imposed light penances, was very loving with children, and when the sun was very bright, he would always offer shade under his umbrella to the elderly." "[I]mponia penitencias livianas, que era muy cariñoso con los niños, y que cuando salia mucho sol, siempre ofrecia amparo bajo de su paragua á alguna anciana." Alvarado, "Historia de California," The Bancroft Library, BANC MSS C-D 3, p. 82.

23   Aguirre, born in Spain, became a U.S. citizen after being expelled from Mexico in the 1820s. He first arrived in California as a hide-and-tallow trader in 1833, with a ship registered in Mexico. Mary H. Haggland, "Don José Antonio Aguirre: Spanish Merchant and Ranchero," *Journal of San Diego History* 29, no. 1 (1983): 54–68.

24   Angustias de la Guerra, "Ocurrencias," The Bancroft Library, BANC MSS C-D 134; translation in Beebe and Senkewicz, *Testimonios*, 245. See also Alvarado, "Historia de California," The Bancroft Library, BANC MSS C-D 3, pp. 83–86.

25   "[L]os soldados californios… prefierren la muerte á pelear contra del pueblo de Santa Barbara que unanime defiende á su idolo." José de la Guerra, quoted in Mariano Guadalupe Vallejo, "Recuerdos históricos," The Bancroft Library, BANC MSS C-C 19, pp. 123–24.

26   Chico left Monterey on July 30, and when he arrived in Santa Bárbara, the townsfolk refused him permission to land. He eventually left the port of San Pedro for Mexico on August 10. Bancroft, *History of California*, 3:442. In Mexico, Chico was not given the troops he requested but instead was reprimanded for leaving his post without permission. Miller, *Juan Alvarado*, 43.

27   This resolution was made on motion of Castro and signed by him, Buelna, Alvarado, and José Antonio de la Guerra. Bancroft, *History of California*, 3:455.

28   Bancroft, *History of California*, 3:461; Osio, *The History of Alta California*, 155; Cassidy, "Life and Times," 54.

29   *Alta California Diputación Territorial.* "La Escelentisima Diputación de la Alta Calif. á sus habitantes." [broadside] Monterey, November 6, 1836. Huntington Library, MS 433152.

30   *"Constituidos en hijos obedientes de la Madre Patria y fieles defenzores de sus caras libertades, juraisteis solemnemente ante Dios y los hombres ser libres, ó morir antes que ser esclabos. En tal virtud adoptasteis para siempre, como el pacto sosial que os hubiera de regir, la constisucion[sic] federál del año de viente y cuatro: se organizaba vuestro Gobierno á costa de inmensos sacrificios que hijos desnaturalizados hoyaron, desconosiendolos para labrar sobre vuestras ruinas su fortuna y criminal ventura, y cuando parecia que érais ya seguro patrimonio del tirano ·ɐɹsᴉʇɔɔɹɐ̣ɐ, tremolasteis intrepidos el pabellon de los libres: FEDERACION O MEURTE es el del Californio la suerte... California es libre, y cortara todas sus relaciones con Mejico hasta que deje de ser oprimimido por la actual faccion dominante tituada gobierno central."* Territorial Diputación, "The Most Excellent Diputación of Alta California to Its Inhabitants," Monterey, November 6, 1836; broadside, Huntington Library, MS 433152.

31   Both José Castro and José Antonio de la Guerra made the pronouncement on November 7, 1836. Bancroft, *History of California*, 3:475.

32   Castillo Negrete's trip is narrated in Agustín Janssens, *The Life And Adventures in California of Don Agustín Janssens 1834–1856*, ed. William H. Ellison and Francis Price (San Marino, Calif.: Huntington Library, 1953), 56; and Bancroft, *History of California*, 3:463–66, 480–86.

33   Luis del Castillo Negrete, "Exposition Directed by the Judge of the District to the Ayuntamiento of Los Angeles on the Revolutionary Plan of Monterey," ca. December 5, 1836, quoted in Bancroft, *History of California*, 3:486.

34   Osio, *The History of Alta California*, 160, 162.

35   Chávez-García, *Negotiating Conquest*, 43–45.

36   Michael González describes the extent of Los Angeles liberalism and Mexican nationalism in *This Small City Will Be a Mexican Paradise*.

37   Gómez-Quiñones, *Roots of Chicano Politics*, 109; Rosaura Sánchez, *Telling Identities*, 233. Indeed, southerner Antonio María Osio remarked that during the 1836 uprising, native-born residents of Monterey "wanted to be called *californios* and not Mexicans. That is why," he explained, "the troops adopted the practice of answering the challenge 'Who goes there?' with the response 'California libre.' The individual who responded 'Mexico' would be punished with sentry duty." Osio, *The History of Alta California*, 185.

38   Gómez-Quiñones, *Roots of Chicano Politics*, 109, 164.

39   In his testimonio, Alvarado made sure to thank the people of Santa Bárbara, in particular, Father Narciso Durán, José de la Guerra, and "the widow Bernarda Ruiz who did so much to sway public opinion in favor of my party." "[L]a viuda

Bernarda Ruiz que *muchisimo habia contribuido á formar la opinion pública en favor de mi partido.*" Alvarado, "Historia de California," The Bancroft Library, BANC MSS C-D 4, p. 12. Ruiz and her husband, José de Jesús Rodríguez, had been the executors of a share of the Conejo ranch, backed in their claims to the property by José Antonio de la Guerra in 1833.

40   The terms of this agreement included a continued adherence to the Constitution of 1824 and a refusal to recognize new governors appointed from Mexico until this constitution was re-established. They also insisted that California's governor be native born. The election took place at the end of February, and the new deputies were holdovers José Castro, José Antonio de la Guerra, Juan Alvarado, and Antonio Buelna, plus Manuel Jimeno, José Estrada, Antonio María Osio, and Pío Pico. Bancroft, *History of California*, 3:506.

41   Angustias de la Guerra, "Ocurrencias," The Bancroft Library, BANC MSS C-D 134; translation in Beebe and Senkewicz, *Testimonios*, 250.

42   Teresa de la Guerra, "Narrativa," The Bancroft Library, BANC MSS C-E 67:2; translation in Beebe and Senkewicz, *Testimonios*, 62.

43   Yet Alvarado did not concede the underlying motive for the revolution to obtain local control: in his memoirs, he remembered Durán's efforts to obtain advantages for the missions and his own insistence on carrying forward the work of secularization. Bancroft, *History of California*, 3:492.

44   José de la Guerra to Editors, November 19, 1845, DLG 476 [translated by Nancy Appelbaum]. This letter was written in response to a narrative by Abel du Petit Thouars, reprinted in a Mexican newspaper, which claimed that de la Guerra had "continued through his speeches, and through his agitation to inspire and to maintain among the Californios the strongest feelings of hatred against the Mexicans, trying in every case to portray the latter as the oppressors." Quoted in Thompson, *El Gran Capitán*, 73. Replied de la Guerra, "No one alive could justly call me disobedient or presumptuous."

45   Alfred Robinson, "Statement of Recollections on Early Years in California," 1878, The Bancroft Library, BANC MSS C-D 147. This sentiment was seconded by William Streeter, an immigrant to California who claimed, "From old settlers I learned that he often acted as mediator and peacemaker between opposing factions, and his good offices frequently brought about a solution of difficulties that otherwise must have terminated in a revolution." Streeter, "Recollections," 170.

46   Alfred Robinson to Bryant and Sturgis, San Diego, December 18, 1836, reprinted in Ogden, "Business Letters," 328.

47   Robinson, in fact, had just married Anita de la Guerra that January, and they waited only until the birth of their first daughter, Elena, before they left for Boston on October 8, 1837, aboard the *California*. See the farewell letters of Alfred and Anita Robinson to José and Antonia María de la Guerra, October 8, 1837, The Bancroft Library, BANC MSS 74/116c; Alfred Robinson to José de la Guerra, Santa Bárbara, October 8, 1837, California Historical Society Library, quoted in Geiger, *The Letters of Alfred Robinson*, 5. An examination of de la Guerra's business correspondence does indeed show what appears to be a sig-

nificant fall off in trade during the years of civil unrest, from late 1836 to early 1839, and a settling up of accounts with Americans in particular. Accounts and business papers, 1830–39, DLG 1050.

48   Juan Alvarado to José de la Guerra, 1837, DLG 24; Bancroft, *History of California*, 3:510. The cattle were distributed on January 4, 1837, and the grant was officially confirmed by the diputación (José Antonio de la Guerra, Antonio Buelna, and Juan Alvarado) while Alvarado was still in Santa Bárbara, on April 19, 1837. Proceedings of California Land Cases, Southern District, Case 10 (San Julián). José de la Guerra, claimant. Huntington Library, MS Film 543:2, pp. 18–19.

49   Hartnell needed the job, as his school had folded in the summer of 1836 due to lack of funds and insufficient enrollment. Dakin, *The Lives of William Hartnell*, 186. He was sworn in as the recaudador, administering the treasury and customs departments, on December 25, 1836, and removed from office October 5, 1837. Bancroft, *History of California*, 3:474, 4:96; Dakin, *The Lives of William Hartnell*, 212; Francis, *An Economic and Social History*, 218.

50   This declaration, called the Plan of San Diego, was spearheaded by Juan Bandini, approved first by the town council of San Diego, then seconded by the ayuntamiento of Los Angeles. Bancroft, *History of California*, 3:507–28.

51   Bancroft, *History of California*, 3:529–30.

52   This news also arrived in a letter to José de la Guerra from his trading partner Antonio María Ercilla, but the date of delivery is unknown. Ercilla to de la Guerra, Tepic, July 21, 1837, DLG 262. Bancroft, *History of California*, 3:534–35.

53   Carlos Carrillo's motivations are unclear. He may have simply recognized the authority of the commission. Angustias de la Guerra, however, argued, "Everything he did to defend his rights as governor was because his brother José Antonio…and others had pushed him to do it." Angustias de la Guerra, "Ocurrencias," The Bancroft Library, BANC MSS C-D 134; translation in Beebe and Senkewicz, *Testimonios*, 251.

54   Ibid., 250.

55   According to Angustias de la Guerra, the commission for Carrillo was temporary, meant to meet the needs of an emergency, and for this reason did not bear the official rubric of the president nor the legalization of the minister of relations. For this reason, Alvarado refused to recognize it. Ibid., 249–50.

56   In particular, de la Guerra was instrumental at San Buenaventura, meeting with Carrillo's commander and negotiating for a withdrawal of his forces. Ibid., 250; Bancroft, *History of California*, 3:550.

57   The relationship was more complicated than that: Carrillo was a first cousin to Alvarado's aunt by marriage.

58   Bancroft, *History of California*, 3:561.

59   Alvarado, quoted in Ibid., 3:566.

60   Angustias de la Guerra, "Ocurrencias," The Bancroft Library, BANC MSS C-D 134; translation in Beebe and Senkewicz, *Testimonios*, 252.

61   Bancroft, *History of California*, 3:581–83.

62   *"[D]escomedidos é irrespetuosos."* Mariano Guadalupe Vallejo, "Recuerdos históricos," The Bancroft Library, BANC MSS C-D 19, p. 401.

63   *"[E]l arresto del venerable capitan retirado causaría una revolucion."* Ibid., p. 402.

64   *"[D]e ningun modo puede permitir que sus subalternos le den consejos."* Ibid., p. 404.

65   *"[C]uya joventud quizas no le permite conocer el torbellin que lo envolverá si no trata con mas cordura á un personaje que el pueblo ama y el clero respeta."* Ibid., p. 406.

66   *"Yo nunca pude rélegar al olbido ese atentado contra la ilustracion."* Ibid., p. 407.

67   *"[D]e ningun modo me hubiera prestado á dar libertad al señor De la Guerra y Noriega porque en esos momentos la mas pequeña muestra de debilidad me hubiese sido fatal."* Ibid.

68   *"[B]ien sabe Ud. hermano Guadalupe . . . Ud. ha tratado son dureza á mi esposo."* Ibid., pp. 411–12.

69   *"[M]e suplicó que relegase al olbido al pasado y estableciese buena armonia entre las dos familias."* Ibid., p. 412.

70   There may also have been promises to send supplies and salaries to the poverty-stricken soldiers of Santa Bárbara, whose numbers had dwindled to about fifteen by 1839. In April, de la Guerra demanded $12,000 in back pay, and in May, the presidio received $1,000. Bancroft, *History of California*, 3:584, 591. On January 31, 1839, Vallejo also named José Antonio de la Guerra Captain of the Port at $30 a year. Bancroft, *History of California*, 3:654, 4:98. It is somewhat unclear whether this post was held by the father or the son, but a clearance certificate of the English barque "Index" was signed by the elder José de la Guerra y Noriega, April 29–October 26, 1840, DLG 1051.

71   *"[A]lli en casa de esa apreciable matrona encontré reunidos á muchos de los que siempre habian hecho causa con los abaqueños pero todos yá habian aceptado la situacion y con muestras de cariño me vinieron á saludar."* Mariano Guadalupe Vallejo, "Recuerdos históricos," The Bancroft Library, BANC MSS C-D 19, p. 414.

72   Ibid., pp. 416–17.

73   *"Viva california libre—mete la mano [d]onde quiera."* Angustias de la Guerra, "Ocurrencias," The Bancroft Library, BANC MSS C-D 134, p. 102.

74   For more on Alvarado's program, see Rosaura Sánchez, *Telling Identities*, 135.

75   Robert Glass Cleland, *The Cattle on a Thousand Hills: Southern California, 1850–1880* (San Marino, Calif.: Huntington Library, 1941), 23; Hackel, *Children of Coyote*, 389; David Hornbeck, "The Ordinary Landscape of Hispanic California: Economic Differences Between Missions and Ranchos," in *Early California Reflections: A Series of Lectures Held at the San Juan Capistrano Branch of the Orange County Public Library*, ed. Nicholas M. Magalousis (Orange County, Calif.: County of Orange Library System, 1987), 9–10. Alvarado's regime, and those of his successors, did also permit land ownership by non-citizens,

and by 1845 about twenty percent to a quarter of the American and English population, naturalized or not, had secured some California land.

76   Angustias de la Guerra, in particular, took this view. "Because the government believed it owned the missions, it granted mission lands to others and loaned cattle to many government supporters so they could establish their own ranchos." Angustias de la Guerra, "Ocurrencias," The Bancroft Library, BANC MSS C-D 134; translation in Beebe and Senkewicz, *Testimonios*, 254.

77   Teresa de la Guerra, "Narrativa," The Bancroft Library, BANC MSS C-E 67:2; translation in Beebe and Senkewicz, *Testimonios*, 57.

78   At the time he issued the new rules, Alvarado was in Santa Bárbara, negotiating with Carlos Carrillo, who was still under house arrest for suspected conspiracy. Perhaps the appointment, then, was meant as another favor to the de la Guerras for their aid in reaching a settlement; in any case, Carrillo formally recognized Alvarado's authority two days later.

79   Dakin, *The Lives of William Hartnell*, 216.

80   Teresa de la Guerra, "Narrativa," The Bancroft Library, BANC MSS C-E 67:2 translation in Beebe and Senkewicz, *Testimonios*, 57.

81   Angustias de la Guerra, "Ocurrencias," The Bancroft Library, BANC MSS C-D 134; translation in Beebe and Senkewicz, *Testimonios*, 254.

82   Dakin, *The Lives of William Hartnell*, 235–41; Bancroft, *History of California*, 3:601. Manuel Jimeno informed his father-in-law of the Vallejo incident, commenting that the general was "deceiving himself, and becoming unworthy even of his interests, because he does not have the support of the Government." *"[T]odo esto es para mas desconseptuarse, y desmereser aun de sus intereses por que se encuentra sin apollo del Gobierno."* Manuel Jimeno to José de la Guerra, Monterey, May 26, 1840, DLG 556. Nonetheless, Alvarado was forced to accept Hartnell's resignation, and the post of visitador general was never again filled.

83   Angustias de la Guerra, "Ocurrencias," The Bancroft Library, BANC MSS C-D 134; translation in Beebe and Senkewicz, *Testimonios*, 254.

84   The diputación meeting in the early months of 1839 consisted of Alvarado, Buelna, de la Guerra, Jimeno, Estrada, and Osio—those elected originally in 1837. On May 3, a new diputación, renamed "junta departamental," was chosen, to meet on August 1, 1839. José Antonio de la Guerra was not elected, presumably because he preferred to oversee his new ranch. The new deputies were Manuel Jimeno as first vocal, Tiburcio Castro, Anastasio Carrillo, Rafael González, Pío Pico, Santiago Argüello, and Manuel Requena. This junta, however, did not actually meet until February 1840. Bancroft, *History of California*, 3:584–85, 590, 604.

85   Proceedings of California Land Cases, Southern District, Case 83, Los Alamos. Testimony of William Hartnell, 1853. Huntington Library, MS Film 543:10.

86   Father José Jimeno to José de la Guerra, Mission Santa Ynez, September 12, 1842, [Bowman, vol. 2, letter 613, pp. 504–5]. A year before, Jimeno commented on the situation, "Already you will have learned of the absurdities of Señor Don José Antonio," *"Y habra Y. sabido los despropositos del S. D. José Antonio."* Father José Jimeno to de la Guerra, Santa Ynez, October 7, 1841, DLG 548.

87   Proceedings of California Land Cases, Southern District, Case 83, Los Alamos. Testimony of José María Valenzuela, January 25, 1839. Huntington Library, MS Film 543:10.

88   Bancroft, *History of California*, 3:666.

89   "Sir, now that Father José has publically denounced me, I want at least for him to give me satisfaction by writing… it is not right that he who so shamelessly has taken my good name should not give it back to me in the same way." *"Sor. Ya que el P. José publicamente me ha desconseptuado yo quiero por lo menos que de una satisfaccion por escrite para de ese modo quede mi reputasion en bierta pues creo que ya todo esta en mi fabor segun los declarantes y no es justo que el que tandescaradamente me ha quitado el eredite se quede undebolviamelo en la mismo manera de melo quito."* José Antonio de la Guerra to his father José de la Guerra, Santa Elena, July 18, 1842, DLG 377.

90   When de la Guerra finally made the delivery in February 1842, the administrator of Santa Ynez claimed that everything had disappeared but *"unos cuantos muebles inservibles,"* and the livestock had been killed or scattered. As far as the documents reveal, de la Guerra was never convicted or punished.

91   Santa Paula y Saticoy was eventually granted in 1843, and the next year, Jimeno received eleven leagues in Cousa County, known simply as the "Jimeno Ranch." Bancroft, *History of California*, 4:643, 671.

92   *"El dicho terreno, esta solicitado por muchos y…por tener á mi entender un poco de mas meritos que otros, y que jamas molestaré á los indios que se allen establecidos en el terreno, antes bien los ausiliare y protejare en cuanto permita mis facultades."* Manuel Jimeno to José de la Guerra, Monterey, May 26, 1840, DLG 556.

93   *"Lo que si es necesario que V. me haga favor si puede, de que por alguna buena persona, ó de algun otro modo propio y combeniente de los haga saber á los indios que mas vale que me tengan por vecino, que no aquien los quiere ver quemados."* Ibid.

94   *"Creo que no tendra incombeniente para que mi hermano Cuchichito vea el modo de formar una casita de palo parad[o] aunque sea de por ahora, y un corral para el ganado."* Ibid.

95   *"[P]ienso que con un medio mayordomo hombre de bien, y un indio vaquero habra bastante, y se le podra señalar a uno y a otro el sueldo que V. conosiere suficiente."* Ibid.

96   Phillips, "Indians in Los Angeles," 436.

97   Camarillo, *Chicanos in a Changing Society,* 12.

98   Hackel, *Children of Coyote,* 388–419.

99   John Rockwell, "In Olden Times," *Santa Barbara Daily News,* June 27, 1896.

100   Edward Vischer, "Edward Vischer's First Visit to California [1842]," trans. and ed. Erwin Gustav Gudde, *California Historical Society Quarterly* 19, no. 3 (1940): 203.

101   Simpson, *Narrative of a Voyage,* 120.

102   Davis, *Seventy-Five Years in California,* 185.

103   *"Un sirviente mio llamadose Vidal, . . . deviendome 24p que lleva apuntados en su vale; . . . no se desentienda de mi reclamo, como se desentendio V. el año ppdo. con el que le reclame; el cual se estuvo en Tapo todo el tiempo que quiso."* José María Ramírez to José de la Guerra, [Mission] San Gabriel, December 10, 1842, DLG 815.

104   *"[P]or que no se hecha una mirada á las desventuradas misiones de S. Gabriel y S. Juan estas se han conbertido en lupanarez de los tres Mayordomos lo que tanto antes se criticaba, esto es aquellas numerosas familias la a ocupado aora la protutucion mas refinada."* Santiago Argüello to José de la Guerra, San Diego, January 1841, DLG 56.

105   See the baptismal record for April 30, 1843, BP01542, ECPP. Again in 1845, baptismal records list two children born to ex-neophytes and a man whose religious status was not recorded, all working as servants in the de la Guerra home. This time, the godparents were the youngest children of de la Guerra, still living at home. See the records for April 25, 1845, BP01672, and May 21, 1845, BP01678, ECPP.

106   Streeter, "Recollections," 68.

107   De la Guerra again took on the role of síndico, or treasurer, of the Franciscan missions after the former síndico, Martiarena, died in 1833. See Father José Moreno to "brother José" de la Guerra, Mission San Miguel, January 22, 1838, DLG 690; Father Blas Ordaz to Father Narciso Durán, San Buenaventura, March 7, 1837, DLG 773; Father Tomás Esténega to Father Narciso Durán, January 16, 1838, DLG 270; letters of Father Jimeno to José de la Guerra, Mission Santa Ynez, DLG 548; letters of Father José Moreno to José de la Guerra, Mission San Miguel, DLG 690; letters of Father Esténaga to José de la Guerra, Mission San Gabriel, DLG 271; letters of Father Abella to José de la Guerra, Mission San Luis Obispo, DLG 1.

108   Father Abella to José de la Guerra, Mission San Luis Obispo, June 17, 1838, [Bowman, vol. 2, letter 606, pp. 499–500].

109   José Aguirre to José de la Guerra, February 9, 1840 [Bowman, vol. 1, letter 460, pp. 310–11]; Father Fortuni to the Pious Fund, Mission San Buenaventura, March 14, 1840, DLG 305.

110   Father José Joaquín Jimeno to José de la Guerra, Mission Santa Ynez, June 4, 1836, note at bottom dated October 1836, DLG 732. Father Jimeno, in this letter, transfers an old mission claim of two hundred cattle against the estate of Romualdo Pacheco to de la Guerra.

111   See, for example, Weber, *Mexican Frontier*, 139.

112   Even in this relatively cash-poor era after secularization, de la Guerra continued to maintain large supplies of coin, generally selling for cash, not credit, and loaning money to rancheros and merchants at interest. One Boston merchant estimated in the early 1840s that de la Guerra had "at least $250,000" in cash. Davis, *Seventy-Five Years in California*, 186.

113   Ibid.

114   *"[P]ude lograr persuadirlo a que se asiniese a recibir 550 ps. . . . Aseguro a V que en el principio no crei sacar tan buen partido . . . Me es satisfactorio haberse*

concluido este asunto y opino que debe V quedar contento." Antonio José Cot to José de la Guerra, Los Angeles, January 18, 1838, DLG 203.

115   Sometimes the former missionaries and new administrators seem to have co-operated in buying and distributing goods. Father Moreno, for example, told de la Guerra in 1838 that the cotton cloth he had bought from de la Guerra "was bought by the administrator for the worship *(fue comprada por el Admin-istrador para el culto)."* Father Moreno to José de la Guerra, Mission San Miguel, July 27, 1838, DLG 690.

116   "[E]*l trato es que le fie yo por parte de este Pueblo 200 ps en los efectos que le dio la gana, á satisifacerlos en plata, . . . Quiere decir, que Cot es el ganansioso."* Domingo Carrillo to José de la Guerra, Pueblo de los Berros, July 20, 1835, DLG 141 [translated by Lillian Guerra].

117   Davis, *Seventy-Five Years in California,* 185; *"remitire a Vmd una pacotilla de mil a dos mil pesos."* Juan Machado to José de la Guerra, "Puerto," January 24, 1844, DLG 613.

118   My number excludes whaling ships, which did very minimal trading; if they are included, the percentage of American ships increases to forty-five percent. The rest of the ships were predominantly English and Russian vessels, but ships from at least twenty nations visited California in these years. According to David Igler, from 1786 to 1847, 45 percent of ships in total flew the American flag, 13 percent British, 12 percent Spanish, 12 percent Mexican, 7 percent Russian, and 11 percent some other flag. David Igler, "Diseased Goods: Global Ex-changes in the Eastern Pacific Basin, 1770–1850," *American Historical Review* 109 (June 2004): 693–719. See also Adele Ogden, "Trading Vessels on the Cal-ifornia Coast: 1786–1848," The Bancroft Library, BANC MSS 80/36 c. Bancroft himself also lists vessels by year; for 1836–40 see *History of California,* 4:100–106. A. B. Thompson estimated that an even higher 40 percent of the ships anchoring at Monterey came from Mexico and South America in the years 1838–41. Alpheus Thompson to John Sutter, San Francisco, April 13, 1841, quoted in Cassidy, "Life and Times," 59–60. See also Accounts and Business Papers 1830–39, DLG 1050; and Accounts and Business Papers 1840–49, DLG 1051. De la Guerra's major trading partners were Americans and English-men Alfred Robinson, William S. Hinckley, Captain Wilson, James McKinley, and Eli Southworth. His Latin American partners were Juan Bautista Mar-tiarena, Antonio María Ercilla, Antonio José Cot, Miguel Pedrorena, Juan Machado, and José Aguirre.

119   A series of letters deals with the wheat purchase. José de la Guerra to Mariano Guadalupe Vallejo, Santa Bárbara, November 11, 1844 [Bowman, vol. 1, let-ter 495, p. 328]; Salvador Vallejo to José de la Guerra, Sauzalito, December 18, 1844 [Bowman, vol. 1 496, p. 329]; Jacob Leese to José de la Guerra, Sauzalito, December 18, 1844 [Bowman, vol. 1, letter 497, p. 329]. At the other end, Cap-tain Phelps noted in his journal on September 24, 1840, that he "took the Car-penter & one Man on Shore & repaired and put in operation Don Noriega's grist mill, horse power." Phelps, *Alta California,* 73.

120   Ramón Valdez to Joaquín de la Guerra, San Buenaventura, August 1, 1844, DLG 992; Robinson, *Life in California,* 173.

121   De la Guerra traded with both Californios and Americans who had settled in California to run small shops. These included John Temple, Henry Fitch, Tomás Yorba, and Juan Bautista Leandry.

122   Tomás Antonio Yorba to José de la Guerra, July 30, 1836, DLG 1037.

123   According to Angustias, Jimeno left Santa Bárbara near the end of February, following Alvarado north to Monterey. Angustias de la Guerra, "Ocurrencias," The Bancroft Library, BANC MSS C-D 134; translation in Beebe and Senkewicz, *Testimonios*, 254. In May, a new junta was elected, and again Jimeno took the post of first vocal. Bancroft, *History of California*, 3:590, 4:584.

124   The junta departamental met in Monterey from February through March 1839, February through May 1840, and not at all in 1841.

125   Officially, Alvarado signed over the reins of government from July 4, 1839, to November 24, 1839, and from September 21, 1841, to December 31, 1841. José Castro to Justices of the Peace and Administrators, Pueblo of San Juan, July 4, 1839, Huntington Library, MR 78; Bancroft, *History of California*, 3:593–96, 5:193.

126   In March and April 1840, for example, Jimeno sent down a music box for José de la Guerra's name day, and Angustias de la Guerra sent down tablecloths and napkins for her mother and two tunics for her youngest sister. Manuel Jimeno to José de la Guerra, Monterey, March 26, 1840, DLG 543; Manuel Jimeno to José de la Guerra, Monterey, April 7, 1840, DLG 556.

127   The first sub-prefect appointed for Santa Bárbara was Raymundo Carrillo, the nephew of María Antonia Carrillo (de la Guerra's wife). Bancroft, *History of California*, 4:585. Municipal affairs in Santa Bárbara were handled by a series of alcaldes or *jueces de paz*: Fernando Tico (compadre with José Antonio, Teresa, Francisco, and Angustias de la Guerra); Joaquín Carrillo (José de la Guerra's nephew and godson); Juan Camarillo (Francisco de la Guerra's compadre); José Covarrubias (compadre to Francisco and María Antonia de la Guerra); and Nicolás Den (compadre of José de la Guerra and María Antonia de la Guerra).

128   On the new liberal value of hard work as a sign of masculine honor in Los Angeles, see González, *This Small City*, 42–43; for a similar dynamic in Peru, see Chambers, *From Subjects to Citizens*, 192–200.

129   Streeter, "'Recollections," 69.

130   "[I]nsustancial y quimerico," José de la Guerra to Juan Bautista Alvarado, [Santa Bárbara], ca. 1839, DLG 471.

131   Manuel Jimeno to José de la Guerra, Monterey, May 26, 1840, DLG 556. See also Bancroft, *History of California*, 3:654; and Raymundo Carrillo, Sub-Prefect, to the Prefect of the Second District, Santa Bárbara, July 10, 1840, Los Angeles Court Cases, vol. I, p. 446B, Huntington Library, MS 382.

132   Bancroft, *History of California*, 3:654. See also Manuel Jimeno to José de la Guerra, Monterey, November 23, 1939, DLG 556.

133   Captain José de la Guerra y Noriega to Raymundo Carrillo, Santa Bárbara, August 4, 1840; Raymundo Carrillo [Sub-prefect] to Santiago Argüello [Prefect], report, Santa Bárbara, August 5, 1840, Los Angeles Court Cases, Huntington Library, MS 382, 1:302, 415–16.

134   Los Angeles Court Cases, Huntington Library, MS 382, 1:489A. José de la Guerra to Manuel Jimeno, n.d., DLG 472. Manuel Jimeno to José de la Guerra, Monterey, January 26, 1841, DLG 556. In a similar case of 1843, José Pedro Ruiz, the grantee of Rancho Calleguas, complained that José de la Guerra was encroaching on his property from neighboring Rancho Simi. The judges and prefects of Los Angeles ruled in Ruiz's favor, but on de la Guerra's appeal to the governor, the ruling was overturned. See documents on this issue, May–July 1843, DLG 1055.

135   "[Q]ueremos ver buenos almasenes en tierra, y muchas otras cosas que dice veremos." Manuel Jimeno to José de la Guerra, Monterey, January 26, 1841, DLG 556.

136   Francis, *An Economic and Social History,* 171–81.

137   Osio, *The History of Alta California,* 196.

138   Ibid., 52, and Bancroft, *History of California,* 4:99.

139   Julio Carrillo, "Statement," The Bancroft Library, BANC MSS C-E 67:8, p. 133.

140   Bancroft, *History of California,* 4:374–78; Francis, *An Economic and Social History,* 276–89.

141   The organization and personnel of the customs house changed repeatedly in the 1830s and early 1840s. A plan drawn up in 1830 provided for an administrator/comisario to be paid 1,000 pesos a year, a contador, or accountant, at 800 pesos, and various guards and sailors. In December 1836, Alvarado as revolutionary governor named William Hartnell to the combined post of recaudador, or tax collector, for both the customs and treasury departments, but in October 1837, he was removed and a new regulation was put into place with an administrator at 3,000 pesos, contador at 2,000 pesos, first official at 1,500 pesos, second official at 1,000, clerk at 500, alcalde at 1,500, commandant at 2,000, and various wardens and sailors. In early 1838, the customs and treasury departments were officially separated, and Antonio María Osio was sworn in as *administrador* of the customs house. Pablo de la Guerra was his first official. Francis, *An Economic and Social History,* 221–29.

142   Juan Alvarado to Pablo de la Guerra, Santa Bárbara, January 2, 1839, DLG 25; Bancroft, *History of California,* 4:97. Pablo's salary was $1,500 a year.

143   When Governor Manuel Micheltorena took over from Alvarado in September 1842, Osio resigned his post, and the administratorship went to Manuel Castañares. Castañares did little more than collect his salary, and left the day-to-day running of the customs administration to Pablo de la Guerra. A year later, in December 1843, Castañares was named deputy to congress, and Pablo received a promotion to contador, or chief inspector. William Hartnell served as his first officer. Osio, *The History of Alta California,* 309; Bancroft, *History of California,* 4:357, 377, 431; Cassidy, "Life and Times," 65; Manuel Castañares to Pablo de la Guerra, Monterey, December 4, 1843, DLG 165.

144   Bancroft, *History of California,* 4:431–432; Pablo de la Guerra to José de la Guerra, Monterey, May 12, 1844, DLG 401; Governor Micheltorena to José de la Guerra, Monterey, August 30, 1844, DLG 676. This job, at 15 pesos per month (the same salary de la Guerra received as retired captain), did not pay well, but gave the merchant great influence at the port.

145   "*[A]unque van cosas que conozco no seran muy bien recibidas sin embargo me he visto en la precision de tomarlas fundado en el principio de mas vale algo que nada.*" Pablo de la Guerra to José de la Guerra, Monterey, July 26, 1839, DLG 397. For more examples of this sort of negotiation by proxy, see also Pablo de la Guerra to José de la Guerra, Monterey, November 8, 1839, November 22, 1839, and December 21, 1839, DLG 397; and Pablo de la Guerra to [his mother] María Antonia Carrillo de la Guerra, Monterey, February 4, 1840, and March 25, 1840, DLG 398.

146   Angustias de la Guerra, "Recuerdos," December 31, 1880, DLG 727, translation in Beebe and Senkewicz, *Testimonios*, 291–92. Carlota Koch, "Spanish Blood in Their Veins: Gaspar and María Antonia Oreña, Spanish-Californians," November 1936, p. 75, 79, available at the Research Center of the Santa Barbara Trust for Historic Preservation.

147   See the discussion of this in chapter four.

148   Haas, *Conquests and Historical Identities*, 83.

149   "*[M]i rancho del Pájaro.*" Angustias de la Guerra, "Ocurrencias," The Bancroft Library, BANC MSS C-D 134; translation in Beebe and Senkewicz, *Testimonios*, 230. On property and the economic independence of Californian women, see Chávez-García, *Negotiating Conquest*, 52–85.

150   Bayard Taylor, *Eldorado or Adventures in the Path of Empire*, (New York: George P. Putnam, 1850; reprint, Lincoln: University of Nebraska Press, Bison Books, 1988), 108.

151   Teresa de la Guerra, "Narrativa," The Bancroft Library, BANC MSS C-E 67:2; translation in Beebe and Senkewicz, *Testimonios*, 56–57.

152   Angustias de la Guerra, "Recuerdos," December 31, 1880, DLG 727, translation in Beebe and Senkewicz, *Testimonios*, 289.

153   Teresa de la Guerra, "Narrativa," The Bancroft Library, BANC MSS C-E 67:2; translation in Beebe and Senkewicz, *Testimonios*, 66.

154   These interactions will be covered more fully in the next chapter.

155   For the impact of liberalism on women's status in Latin America generally, see Arlene J. Díaz, *Female Citizens, Patriarchs, and the Law in Venezuela, 1786–1904* (Lincoln: University of Nebraska Press, 2004) 105–70; Lara Putnam, Sarah C. Chambers, and Sueann Caulfield, "Transformations in Honor, Status, and Law over the Long Nineteenth Century," in *Honor, Status, and Law in Modern Latin America*, ed. Sueann Caulfield, Sarah C. Chambers, and Lara Putnam (Durham, N.C.: Duke University Press, 2005), 1–24; Sarah Chambers, *From Subjects to Citizens*, 200–215; and Christine Hunefeldt, *Liberalism in the Bedroom: Quarreling Spouses in Nineteenth-Century Lima* (University Park: University of Pennsylvania Press, 2000).

156   "*[É]l todas las noches los leía con grande gusto.*" Mariano Guadalupe Vallejo, "Recuerdos históricos," The Bancroft Library, BANC MSS C-D 19, p. 113.

157   Osio, *The History of Alta California*, 160. Both Ramón Gutiérrez for New Mexico and María Raquél Casas for California note that a rise in romantic notions of love and companionate marriage challenged parental authority to arrange marriages in the early nineteenth century. Gutiérrez, *When Jesus Came*, 328–36; Casas, *Married to a Daughter of the Land*, 104–5.

158 Dakin, *The Lives of William Hartnell*, 121. The origin of this quotation is un-known, but it must date to before Hartnell's death in 1854. Over her married life, Teresa de la Guerra de Hartnell gave birth nineteen times and had occasional health problems, both during pregnancy and with breastfeeding. Ibid., 102–3. The large number of children that elite women bore typically put them at risk for complications more frequently than did the smaller number of pregnancies that non-elite women had.

159 Jean Franco, *Plotting Women: Gender and Representation in Mexico* (New York: Columbia University Press, 1989), 90.

160 González, *This Small City*, 174–75.

161 Jeanne-Marie le Prince de Beaumont, *Biblioteca Completa de Educacion o Instrucciones para las Señoras Jovenes en la Edad de Entrar ya en la Sociedad y Poderse Casar. Instruye una Sabia Directora á sus nobles discípulas en todas las obligaciones pertenecientes al estado del matrimonio y á la educacion de sus hijos*, trans. Joseph de la Fresna, 1780, vols. 1 and 3; inscribed "Angustias Jimeno," Santa Barbara Mission Archive-Library.

162 "Republican motherhood" emerged out of the immediate post-revolutionary periods of both France and the United States. In the United States, Benjamin Rush was a leading proponent of female education. French revolutionary Louis Prudhomme summed up the notion in 1791, "the liberty of a people is based on good morals and education, and you [women] are their guardians and their first dispensors," quoted in Hunt, *The Family Romance of the French Revolution*, 122. On republican motherhood in Mexico, see Arrom, *Women of Mexico City*, 14–15, 85; and Franco, *Plotting Women*, 81–92.

163 There are only two letters from Teresa in the de la Guerra papers, both from 1854, DLG 660.

164 Their daughter, Elena, was considered too young for the journey around the Horn, and was left with her grandparents in Santa Bárbara.

165 Elizabeth White Fairly to her daughter Agnes, Washington, D.C., July 2, 1908, The Bancroft Library, BANC MSS 74/116 c, folder 12.

166 Alfred Robinson to José de la Guerra, Boston, June 10, 1838, DLG 833, translation in Geiger, *The Letters of Alfred Robinson*, 5–7. See also Anita de la Guerra to José and María Antonia de la Guerra, Boston, June 11, 1838, translation in Geiger, *The Letters of Alfred Robinson*, 7.

167 Alfred and Anita Robinson to José and María Antonia de la Guerra, Boston, November 15, 1838, DLG 833, translation in Geiger, *The Letters of Alfred Robinson*, 7–9.

168 "[P]ues, para mi seria vergonzoso volverme otra ves sin haberme primeres adelantado algo en mis estudios . . . Tambien conozco para VV. seria gustoso de tener una hija educada como las muchachas que veo aqui todas los dias." Anita de la Guerra to her parents, New York, February 27, 1839, DLG 836.

169 "Mi niña algun dia tendra necesidad de los buenos ensayos de su madre, y ahora es el tiempo de lograr cuando se me ha presentado una ocasion tan buena." Anita de la Guerra to her parents, Bridgeport, Connecticut, January 10, 1840, DLG 836.

170   *"Como siento que la María Antonia no vino."* Alfred Robinson to María Antonia Carrillo de la Guerra, ca. February 26, 1839, DLG 831; Alfred Robinson to his "parents," New York, February 26, 1839, DLG 833, translation in Geiger, *The Letters of Alfred Robinson,* 9–11.

171   María del Rosario was the daughter of Jacinto Lorenzana, a foundling who had become a soldier in the Santa Bárbara presidial company, and María del Carmen Rodríguez. María del Rosario was baptized at the presidio chapel on May 14, 1816. See the record BP00493, ECPP. Francisco's mother, María Antonia Carrillo, had herself grown up with another expósito, Apolinaria Lorenzana, who was taken into Raymundo Carrillo's household in 1800. For more on the foundling home, see Beebe and Senkewicz, *Testimonios,* xiii–xvi.

172   Officially, according to a decree of 1794, foundlings were no longer to be assumed illegitimate, and were to be given the benefit of the doubt when it came to racial status, but in practice many continued to make that connection. Caulfield, Chambers, and Putnam, *Honor, Status, and Law,* 5. Twinam, *Public Lives, Private Secrets,* 19–20, 298–306.

173   Chávez-García, *Negotiating Conquest,* 159–60.

174   For a discussion of this common process of legitimation, see Twinam, *Public Lives, Private Secrets,* 26, 75, 128–36. Santiago is recorded twice in the Santa Bárbara Baptismal Registry, BP01202 and BP01247, ECPP. Clotilde was baptized in Santa Bárbara as well, BP01321. In both cases, Francisco came forward to claim his children although by the time Clotilde was born, he was no longer free to marry her mother. In 1858, after the deaths that year of both María del Rosario Lorenzana and José de la Guerra, Francisco had his first two children publicly recognized and brought into the family home. Santiago and Clotilde took the family name "de la Guerra," and according to family correspondence seem to have been treated as equal members of the family. Under American law, they could not be formally legitimated, but they may have had their legal status as heirs of their father changed through adoption.

175   Proceedings before Antonio Rodríguez, Juez de Paz ad interim, May 23, 1839, Proceedings of California Land Cases, Southern District Case 10, San Julián. José de la Guerra claimant. Huntington Library, MS Film 543:2, p. 20.

176   Proceedings of California Land Cases, Southern District Case 103, Simi. José de la Guerra claimant. Huntington Library, MS Film 543:13.

177   Francisco took up the culture of a ranchero as well. In 1841, for example, he and José Sepúlveda contracted to run a horse race in Santa Bárbara. "To the Honorable Judge of First Instance of Los Angeles," Los Angeles, July 13, 1841, Los Angeles Court Cases, Huntington Library, 1:537A.

178   The de la Guerras bought the ranch from José Gertrudis Carrillo, who had originally petitioned through his father, Carlos, in 1833. The price was fifty dollars in coin and six hundred cattle: "three hundred cows of two years old and upwards, two hundred and fifty steers of the same age, and fifty bulls of the same age." Witnesses later testified that the de la Guerras did not live at this ranch, but placed an overseer and servants in the house. Proceedings of California Land Cases, Southern District Case 117, Las Positas. Huntington Library, MS Film 543:15.

179 Ascención Sepúlveda was pregnant, and the vaccine had been tainted with syphilis. Streeter, "Recollections," 68.

180 Alfred Robinson to José de la Guerra, New York, January 20, 1845, DLG 833, translation in Geiger, *The Letters of Alfred Robinson*, 19. He comments on Ascención's death that they will all miss her "because of her ability in directing domestic affairs in the house… May God be pleased that María Antonia with her love and devotion to her father remain for many years."

181 Cesareo Lataillade to José de la Guerra, Yerba Buena, September 11, 1842, DLG 574.

182 María Antonia, however, was still well under the age of consent in even the most pro-individualist states. Arrom, *Women of Mexico City*, 92.

183 There is only one reference to Miguel's presence in Hawaii, based on family remembrance. Koch, "Spanish Blood," 38.

184 The earliest reference to Antonio María in Chile is in a letter from Robinson, referring to missing him at Valparaíso. Alfred Robinson to José de la Guerra, Monterey, June 20, 1840, DLG 833, translation in Geiger, *The Letters of Alfred Robinson*, 15.

185 Dakin, *The Lives of William Hartnell*, 190; Patrick Short to Antonio María de la Guerra, Valparaíso, August 3, 1843, DLG 917; José de la Guerra to Antonio María de la Guerra, February 1843, DLG 1104.

186 *"Le tengo cargados en Cuenta Pesos 889#6rs. por los ultimos gastos en Chile, pasage al Callao, y Acapulco, y avilitacion para embarcarse dicho Sr. hijo de V., lo que le servirá de govno."* Juan Bautista Valdeavellano to José de la Guerra, Lima, Peru, May 13, 1844, DLG 988. See also José de la Guerra to José Antonio Cot, Santa Bárbara, November 24, 1844, DLG 473, [translated by Nancy Appelbaum].

187 *"[B]a a seguir la carera de medicina y aora me a quebrado la cabeza conque quiere Marcharse para esa y seguir la carrera del comercio porlo que espero de la Bondad de V. lo mire como hijo."* Lorenzo de Oreña to José de la Guerra, Cádiz, April 8, 1841, DLG 739.

188 Ana de la Guerra y Noriega Robinson to Señor Don Gaspar de Oreña, Care of Frederick A. Gay, New York, ca. October 1841, The Alfred Robinson Papers, The Bancroft Library, BANC MSS 74/116 c, folder 21, letter 4.

189 Gaspar Oreña to José de la Guerra, San Pedro, December 4, 1842, DLG 734. Juan Machado to José de la Guerra, "Puerto," [Mazatlán], January 24, 1844, DLG 613.

190 Alfred Robinson to José de la Guerra, Mazatlán, February 6, 1843, DLG 833, translation in Geiger, *The Letters of Alfred Robinson*, 16–17.

191 José de la Guerra to Antonio José Cot, Santa Bárbara, November 28, 1844, DLG 473 [translated by Nancy Appelbaum].

192 Juan Bautista Valdeavellano to José de la Guerra, Lima, Peru, July 8, 1845, DLG 988.

CHAPTER   SIX

1   Bancroft, *History of California*, 5:109–21, 145–50; Neal Harlow, *California Con-*
     quered: The Annexation of a Mexican Province, 1846–1850 (Berkeley: Univer-
     sity of California Press, 1982), 97–105; Rosenus, *General M. G. Vallejo*, 108–19;
     Lisbeth Haas, "War in California, 1846–1848," in Gutiérrez and Orsi, *Contested*
     Eden, 331–55.

2   For example, Ken Burns used Vallejo for this purpose in his PBS documentary
     The West. See also Manuel Gonzáles, *The Hispanic Elite of the Southwest*,
     Southwestern Studies 86 (El Paso, Texas: Texas-Western Press, 1982), 6–9.

3   Julio Carrillo, "Statement," The Bancroft Library, BANC MSS C-E 67, p. 8. Juan
     Alvarado also referred to the Mexican government as the *madrastra*, or "step-
     mother" of California, echoing the earlier colonial critique of the viceroy as
     California's "stepfather." Alvarado, "Historia de California," The Bancroft Li-
     brary, BANC MSS C-D 5, p. 105.

4   Pitt, *Decline of the Californios*, 19–20; Weber, *Mexican Frontier*, 199–202.

5   Bancroft, *History of California*, 4:122–39.

6   In 1841, some two hundred foreigners arrived, including the first overland mi-
     grants from the Missouri, the Bidwell Party, who settled in the Central Valley
     with Dr. John Marsh. None arrived in 1842; a few more did in 1843, fifty in 1844,
     250 in 1845, and over 500 in 1846. Weber, *Mexican Frontier*, 202.

7   Weber, *Mexican Frontier*, 206. In the first decades of Mexican Independence,
     the annual rate of population increase in Mexico as a whole stood at about
     1.1 percent. In California, the rate was a healthy five percent, but in Texas, it was
     a staggering one hundred percent a year.

8   As noted previously, the central government of Mexico did attempt planned
     colonization to California, sending 150 convicts in 1829 and 1830, and 239 set-
     tlers with the Híjar-Padrés colony in 1834, but these were singular efforts.
     Weber, *Mexican Frontier*, 184–90.

9   Bancroft, *History of California*, 4:2–41.

10   Robinson, *Life in California*, 128.

11   Angustias de la Guerra, "Ocurrencias," The Bancroft Library, BANC MSS
     C-D 134; translation in Beebe and Senkewicz, *Testimonios*, 256.

12   *"Este declaró que en efecto tenian hecho un plan al modo de Tejas."* Manuel Ji-
     meno to José de la Guerra, Monterey, April 7, 1840, DLG 556.

13   *"[D]ejando aqui á los casados y á los de conosida honrrades &c."* Manuel Jimeno
     to José de la Guerra, Monterey, April 30, 1840, DLG 556.

14   José de la Guerra to Juan Alvarado, Santa Bárbara, April 13, 1840; cited in Ban-
     croft, *History of California*, 4:14.

15   Bancroft, *History of California*, 4:15, 29.

16   Pablo de la Guerra to Mariano Guadalupe Vallejo, Santa Bárbara, April 16, 1840,
     in Vallejo, "Documentos para la história de California, 1769–1850," The Ban-
     croft Library, BANC MSS C-B 1:30, quoted in Hansen, *Search for Authority in*
     California, 33.

17   Robinson, *Life in California*, 130.

18   In November 1840, the British obtained a judgment for $24,000 in compensation for the Graham Affair.

19   Bancroft, *History of California*, 4:298–329.

20   "[*P*]*ero no la entregué…Amenazó echar abajo la puerta de la Aduana, y le repondí que hiciera lo que gustase.*" Angustias de la Guerra, "Ocurrencias," The Bancroft Library, BANC MSS C-D 134; see also the translation in Beebe and Senkewicz, *Testimonios*, 258.

21   Robinson, *Life in California*, 146–47.

22   "The Capture of Monterey, To the Editors," ca. 1843, in the hand of Pablo de la Guerra, DLG 438.

23   Streeter, "Recollections," 26.

24   The president also smoothed ruffled feathers, however, by giving both native sons promotions in rank. Vallejo received promotion to lieutenant colonel, and Alvarado to colonel of the militia. Osio, *The History of Alta California*, 309n.

25   Angustias de la Guerra, "Ocurrencias," The Bancroft Library, BANC MSS C-D 134; translation in Beebe and Senkewicz, *Testimonios*, 258–59.

26   Manuel Micheltorena to José de la Guerra, Los Angeles, December 2, 1842, DLG 674.

27   Pablo's role as customs inspector within his family's economic empire is discussed in the previous chapter.

28   "[*J*]*oven de esmerada educacion de integridad…quien presta las garantias de ser de familia acomodada y remite las fiazas á satisfaccion para disfrutar el sueldo.*" Governor Micheltorena to the President of Mexico, Monterey, December 10, 1843, DLG 675.

29   Bancroft, *History of California*, 4:361.

30   Cassidy, "Life and Times," 66; Angustias de la Guerra, "Ocurrencias," The Bancroft Library, BANC MSS C-D 134; translation in Beebe and Senkewicz, *Testimonios*, 259; Osio, *The History of Alta California*, 309.

31   Angustias de la Guerra, "Ocurrencias," The Bancroft Library, BANC MSS C-D 134; translation in Beebe and Senkewicz, *Testimonios*, 259.

32   Ibid., 259–60.

33   Manuel Micheltorena to chief of staff, December 12, 1844, quoted in Bancroft, *History of California*, 4:467.

34   "*Los hijos de California nos haran justicia.*" Juan Alvarado and José Castro to Manuel Micheltorena, Alisal, January 6, 1845, DLG 785. José Castro was Alvarado's first cousin, and the two often worked closely together.

35   Bancroft, *History of California*, 4:455–517.

36   Although Francisco de la Guerra still officially served on the junta, he was not present for this emergency session. Bancroft, *History of California*, 4:495.

37   "[*E*]*l ardiente deseo…por el restablicimto. de la paz y evitar los malos que son consiguientes á la Guerra civil.*" Interestingly, conservative de la Guerra signs

these letters, "God and Liberty." José de la Guerra to Pío Pico, February 7, 9, and 14, 1844, Santa Bárbara, DLG 475.

38   Bancroft, *History of California*, 4:515.

39   The December 1 Treaty of Campo Santa Teresa is found in the de la Guerra collection, folder 785.

40   "*[A]migos recomendables*," Manuel Micheltorena to Pablo de la Guerra, February 25, 1845, DLG 675.

41   "*[N]o puede menos de sernos de suma sensibilidad, pues nos priva de la compañia de VE.*" Pablo de la Guerra to Manuel Micheltorena, May 25, 1845, DLG 400.

42   Pío Pico to Pablo de la Guerra, Monterey, March 17, 1845, DLG 786; Pablo de la Guerra to Pío Pico, Monterey, April 15, 1845, DLG 402. Pablo de la Guerra to Juan Alvarado, Monterey, April 29, 1845, DLG 403; Pío Pico to Pablo de la Guerra, Los Angeles, April 30, 1845, DLG 786.

43   Pío Pico to Pablo de la Guerra, Los Angeles, July 17, 1845, DLG 786; José María Covarrubias to José de la Guerra, Los Angeles, July 18, 1845, DLG 214.

44   "*[D]eseo que ser occupado por sujeto de capacidad y buenas circunstancias.*" Pío Pico to José de la Guerra, Los Angeles, July 12, 1845, DLG 785.

45   "*[C]omo es necesario que los hombres notables ocupan los desinos del gerarquia para ver si se puede conservar el orden.*" José María Covarrubias to José de la Guerra, Los Angeles, July 18, 1845, DLG 214.

46   Comandante José Abrego to José de la Guerra, Los Angeles, August 4, 1845 [Bowman, vol. 1, letter 516, p. 344]. Pío Pico to José de la Guerra, Los Angeles, June 3, 1845, DLG 785; Pío Pico to José de la Guerra, Los Angeles, July 11, 1845, DLG 785.

47   It is not clear if Jimeno did not, in fact, also bow out of politics because of ill health; this is the opinion of Bancroft, *History of California*, 4:692. The only mention of him in the de la Guerra documents in these years refers to him receiving an application of leeches, which confirms some sort of health problem. Cesareo Lataillade to José de la Guerra, Monterey, May 25, 1845, DLG 574.

48   Angustias de la Guerra, "Ocurrencias," The Bancroft Library, BANC MSS C-D 134; translation in Beebe and Senkewicz, *Testimonios*, 265.

49   John Coffin Jones to Thomas Oliver Larkin, March 21, 1845, quoted in Bancroft, *History of California*, 4:519.

50   "*[H]acer participe al E.S. Gobernador del Departamento de . . . el inmanente*[?] *peligro en que nos encontramos de una invasion por mar y tierra.*" José Castro to Pablo de la Guerra, Monterey, April 27, 1846, DLG 177.

51   Bancroft, *History of California*, 4:539–40.

52   Ibid., 5:37–53.

53   Ibid., 5:1–21; Haas, "War in California," 338–39.

54   Harlan Hague and David J. Langum, *Thomas O. Larkin: A Life of Patriotism and Profit in Old California* (Norman: University of Oklahoma Press, 1990), 114–16; Harlow, *California Conquered*, 78–80.

55 Larkin to Department of State, Monterey, April 20, 1846, in Thomas Oliver
    Larkin et al., *The Larkin Papers: Personal, Business and Official Correspon-
    dence of Thomas Oliver Larkin, Merchant and United States Consul in Cali-
    fornia*, ed. George P. Hammon, 10 vols. (Berkeley: University of California Press,
    1968), 4:314.

56 "[P]or cuenta de los de los derechos que ha de pager su Barca." José Castro,
    "Quartermaster General," to Pablo de la Guerra, Santa Clara, July 2, 1846,
    DLG 177. Aguirre was the merchant who had accounts with California's Pious
    Fund, played a role in the thwarted expulsion of Father Durán, helped arrange
    the education of Antonio María de la Guerra in Chile, hired Gaspar Oreña as
    a clerk, and took the expelled foreigners to Mexico after the Graham Affair.

57 Angustias de la Guerra, "Ocurrencias," The Bancroft Library, BANC MSS
    C-D 134; translation in Beebe and Senkewicz, *Testimonios*, 264–65.

58 Bancroft, *History of California*, 5:235.

59 "[S]atisfecho como estoy, de la buena reputacion de que con justicias son V. V.
    considerados entre estos habitantes, asi como su creeido entuciasmo en favor
    del bien estar de la patria." Pío Pico to Francisco de la Guerra and Antonio Ro-
    dríguez, Commissioners, Santa Bárbara, June 23, 1846, DLG 788. On his return
    from rounding up fighters, Francisco traveled to Los Angeles as Pico's repre-
    sentative to persuade the junta departamental to convene in Santa Bárbara and
    later served on a committee to draw up military regulations. Bancroft, *History
    of California*, 5:141–42, 264.

60 Pío Pico to Departmental Treasury, Santa Bárbara, June 30, 1846, DLG 785. A
    note appears at the bottom of the receipt in de la Guerra's handwriting: "paid
    by Don Pío."

61 For more on Anglo-American stereotypes of Mexicans in this era, see David J.
    Weber, "Scarce More than Apes," *New Spain's Far Northern Frontier: Essays on
    Spain in the American West, 1540–1821*, ed. David J. Weber (Albuquerque: Uni-
    versity of New Mexico Press, 1979), 293–307.

62 Stockton to President Polk, August 26, 1846, quoted in Harlow, *California Con-
    quered*, 152.

63 Bancroft, *History of California*, 5:267–75; Harlow, *California Conquered*, 147–49;
    Cassidy, "Life and Times," 84.

64 Cassidy, "Life and Times," 85.

65 Bancroft, *History of California*, 5:267.

66 José de la Guerra, Gregorio López, and Antonio Leiva before Antonio María
    Ortega, the Judge of the First Instance, Rancho San Julián, August 28, 1846
    [Bowman, vol. 1, letter 530, pp. 351–53].

67 H. Ford, Lt. William Maddox, and Capt. G. P. Swett to José de la Guerra, no date
    or place, [Bowman, vol. 1, letter 530, pp. 351–53].

68 Bancroft, *History of California*, 5:286–87.

69 Haas, "War in California," 342.

70 Bancroft, *History of California*, 5:316–22; José Flores to José de la Guerra, Los
    Angeles, November 25, 1846 [Bowman, vol. 1, letter 532, p. 354].

71   In 1851, Pablo attempted to receive compensation for this loan from the Mexican government. Pablo de la Guerra to unidentified Mexican, probably José María Castaños, June 1851, DLG 411.

72   José de la Guerra was not the only ranchero to suffer forced loans to the American army; northerners experienced this a great deal as well, including William Hartnell at Alisal, near Monterey. Miller, *Juan Alvarado*, 126–27.

73   Bancroft, *History of California*, 5:363; Angustias de la Guerra, "Ocurrencias," The Bancroft Library, BANC MSS C-D 134; translation in Beebe and Senkewicz, *Testimonios*, 268. Other sources claim that the other brother imprisoned was Joaquín.

74   Streeter, "Recollections," 169.

75   Ibid.

76   George Nidever, *The Life and Adventures of George Nidever*, ed. William Henry Ellison (Berkeley: University of California Press, 1937), 65.

77   Nidever, *Life and Adventures*, 65.

78   Edwin Bryant, *What I Saw in California* (New York: D. Appleton & Co., 1849; reprint, Palo Alto, Calif.: Lewis Osborne, 1967).

79   Nidever, *Life and Adventures*, 67–69.

80   John Charles Frémont, *The Expeditions of John Charles Frémont: Volume 2, The Bear Flag Revolt and the Court Martial* (Chicago: University of Illinois Press, 1973) 238.

81   Haas, "War in California," 343–45; Harlow, *California Conquered*, 232. See the text of the treaty in Bancroft, *History of California*, 5:404–5.

82   General William T. Sherman, *Recollections of California, 1846–1861* (Oakland, Calif.: Biobooks, 1945), 9.

83   Ibid., 11.

84   Quoted in Pitt, *Decline of the Californios*, 23.

85   Robinson, *Life in California*, 51.

86   Among the works that deal specifically with nineteenth-century images of Californianas, their racial and gender stereotypes, and the role such images played in the Mexican-American War are Castañeda, "Gender, Race, and Culture"; Castañeda, "The Political Economy of Nineteenth Century Stereotypes"; Harry Clark, "Their Pride, Their Manners, and Their Voices"; and Langum, "Californio Women and the Image of Virtue," 245–50.

87   Edward Otho Cresap Ord to William Minor, Monterey, August 19, 1847, Colville Jackson Minor Letters, The Bancroft Library, BANC MSS 87/25 c.

88   What remains of de la Guerra's journal is a copy made by Rebecca Ord, her only child by her second husband. All three sources are found in English translation in Beebe and Senkewicz, *Testimonios*, 193–296.

89   Angustias de la Guerra, "Ocurrencias," The Bancroft Library, BANC MSS C-D 134; translation in Beebe and Senkewicz, *Testimonios*, 268.

90   Ibid., 268–70.

91   Ibid., 265.

92   "[T]oda la culpa la tiene la distancia del centro de donde se manda todo, y la falta de poder llegar a Mejico pronto!... lo que llegue á suceder, atribuirlo todo al 'Destino'!" Angustias de la Guerra, Journal, September 17, 1846, DLG 725, see also the translation in Beebe and Senkewicz, *Testimonios*, 275.

93   "[L]a toma del país no nos gustó nada a los Californios, y menos a las mujeres," Angustias de la Guerra, "Ocurrencias," The Bancroft Library, BANC MSS C-D 134; see also the translation in Beebe and Senkewicz, *Testimonios*, 265.

94   Beebe and Senkewicz, *Testimonios*, 272; "Tiene razón Don Guillermo dije yo, porque yo estaba... oyendo todo." Angustias de la Guerra de Jimeno, Journal, May 14, 1846, DLG 725.

95   "Si han de venir los Americanos, que vengan pero que manden gente decente, gente que sepa tratarnos con mas acierto que lo hizo Fremont, vino queriendonos mandar." Angustias de la Guerra de Jimeno, Journal, July 1846, DLG 725, translation in Beebe and Senkewicz, *Testimonios*, 272.

96   "[S]i hemos de juzgar por los que han venido y se han casado con las hijas del pais [...]cuando uno piensa todo lo que han hecho los que vinieron aqui; quien sabe si con el tiempo sea esto la envidia del mundo." Angustias de la Guerra de Jimeno, Journal, July 20, 1846, DLG 725, translation in Beebe and Senkewicz, *Testimonios*, 273.

97   "Como se sentiran los que vienen de esas Grandes cuidades cuando no ven aqui desparramados y cada uno con leguas de tierra?" Angustias de la Guerra de Jimeno, Journal, September 3, 1846, DLG 725, translation in Beebe and Senkewicz, *Testimonios*, 274.

98   "[L]a tristeza que he tenido, tiene algo de trajico parece que es la agonia, con todos sus dolores, de una época que se acaba, que se muere!" Angustias de la Guerra de Jimeno, Journal, October 3, 1846, DLG 725, translation in Beebe and Senkewicz, *Testimonios*, 276.

99   "[C]on todo esto de riza y baile estamos todos anhelosos porque no sabemos en que quedarémos los dueños de todo esto!" Angustias de la Guerra de Jimeno, Journal, January 1847, DLG 725, see also the translation in Beebe and Senkewicz, *Testimonios*, 278.

100   Angustias de la Guerra, "Ocurrencias," The Bancroft Library, BANC MSS C-D 134; translation in Beebe and Senkewicz, *Testimonios*, 258.

101   Ibid., 263.

102   Ibid.

103   Gillespie was carrying orders for Larkin and Frémont from President Polk, and played a large role of his own in the impending conquest. It is likely that Castro did know who Gillespie was, but was attempting to exclude Californio women from the political arena by lying to Angustias. Gillespie himself, sensing the local suspicion, left town at midnight on the night of the ball. See Rosaura Sánchez, *Telling Identities*, 258.

104   "Pero no hay que quejarse porque no entraron los Americanos con cañonazos— nos conquistaron—primero a las mujeres—y por eso se quedaron tan bonitamente, hubo un monton de descontentos, y entre ellos muchos de mis parientes—pero ellos siempre han querido mandar, y les va mal." Angustias de

la Guerra de Jimeno, Journal, February 14, 1847, DLG 725, translation in Beebe and Senkewicz, *Testimonios*, 278.

105   "[C]asi ni se puede creér, que hay esta envidia y celo entre personas enjendradas en el mismo vientre de una madre." Angustias de la Guerra de Jimeno, Journal, August 21, 1847, DLG 725, translation in Beebe and Senkewicz, *Testimonios*, 280.

106   Angustias de la Guerra de Ord, "Recuerdos," December 31, 1880, DLG 727, translation in Beebe and Senkewicz, *Testimonios*, 293–95.

107   "[A]y! ay! que gusto!" Angustias de la Guerra de Jimeno, Journal, February 16, 1847, DLG 725, see also the translation in Beebe and Senkewicz, *Testimonios*, 279.

108   Angustias de la Guerra de Jimeno, Journal, January, 1847. This English-language quote comes from a translation of the full journal found in Father Joseph Thompson's unpublished manuscript "Casa de la Guerra," at the Santa Barbara Mission Archive-Library. Thompson appears to have had access to a page of the journal that is now missing.

109   Francis J. Lippitt, *Reminiscences of Francis J. Lippitt: Written for His Family, His Near Relatives and Intimate Friends* (Providence, R.I.: Preston & Rounds Co., 1902), 70.

110   The only other writing from Anita to survive from these critical years came in the form of a brief postscript to her parents, in which she made no comments on the war or politics. Anita de la Guerra to José de la Guerra, New York, November 24, 1846, DLG 833, translation in Geiger, *The Letters of Alfred Robinson*, 22.

111   Teresa de la Guerra, "Narrativa," The Bancroft Library, BANC MSS C-E 67:2; translation in Beebe and Senkewicz, *Testimonios*, 58.

112   Dakin, *The Lives of William Hartnell*, 255.

113   Alfred Robinson to José de la Guerra, New York, January 20, 1845, DLG 833, translation in Geiger, *The Letters of Alfred Robinson*, 18–19.

114   Alfred Robinson to Thomas Oliver Larkin, New York, May 29, 1845, Larkin Papers, vol. 1, p. 205. See also Alfred Robinson to Thomas Oliver Larkin, New York, September 28, 1844, Larkin Papers, vol. 2, p. 242.

115   Robinson, *Life in California*, 157.

116   Angustias de la Guerra de Jimeno, Journal, May 14, 1846, DLG 725, translation in Beebe and Senkewicz, *Testimonios*, 271.

117   [T]odos como buenos Yanquis no dicen a las calladitas que no nos vamos a arrepentir si pertenecemos al Gobierno de los EEUU." Angustias de la Guerra de Jimeno, Journal, July 1846, DLG 725, translation in Beebe and Senkewicz, *Testimonios*, 273.

118   Alfred Robinson to Pablo de la Guerra, New York, September 20, 1846, DLG 834, translation in Geiger, *The Letters of Alfred Robinson*, 25–26.

119   Ibid. Robinson made similar appeals to his father-in-law as the war progressed. See, for example, Alfred Robinson to José de la Guerra, New York, October 21, 1847, DLG 833, translation in Geiger, *The Letters of Alfred Robinson*, 22–25.

120   James Lynch, *With Stevenson to California* (San Luis Obispo, Calif.: Tierra Redonda, 1896), 24.

121   Ibid., 23.

122   Lippitt, *Reminiscences*, 70.

123   Pablo had been courting Josefa while customs administrator in Monterey, and when the war broke out, had only just succeeded in winning her father's approval. Fray José Anzar to Pablo de la Guerra, San Juan Bautista Mission, January 20, 1846, DLG 36.

124   *"Recordaba haber oido á su difunto hermano el senador Dn Pablo de la Guerra decir á sus amigos que, el señor Robinson en su narracion habia dado prueba de mucha parcialidad."* Teresa de la Guerra, "Narrativa," The Bancroft Library, BANC MSS C-E 67:2; translation in Beebe and Senkewicz, *Testimonios*, 59.

125   Bancroft, *History of California*, 5:631. Luis was the second son of Anastasio Carrillo, married to María de Refugio Ortega, herself a first cousin of José Antonio de la Guerra's wife, Concepción.

126   Harlow, *California Conquered*, 265–66.

127   Theodore Grivas, "Alcalde Rule: The Nature of Local Government in Spanish and Mexican California," *California Historical Society Quarterly* 40, no. 1 (March 1961): 20–23.

128   Ibid., 23.

129   At almost the same time, José de la Guerra went one step further, reactivating his Spanish citizenship through son-in-law Cesareo Lataillade on May 1, 1847. Thompson, *El Gran Capitán*, 176; Cesareo Lataillade to José de la Guerra, Santa Bárbara, July 13, 1847, DLG 576. From 1846, Lataillade served as the Spanish vice consul, although he lived in Santa Bárbara.

130   Bancroft, *History of California*, 5:631.

131   Richard Barnes Mason to Pablo de la Guerra, "Alcalde at Santa Bárbara," Monterey, June 14, 1847, DLG 658. Kearny served as governor from March 1 to May 31, 1847. In another test of wills, in July 1847, Pablo de la Guerra refused to respect the American military line and was stopped by a sentry for trespass. Captain Lippitt, however, hurried to send a profuse apology. Francis J. Lippitt to Pablo de la Guerra, Barracks at Santa Bárbara, July 24, 1847, DLG 587.

132   Pablo de la Guerra, May 17, 1847, First Court of Santa Bárbara, Los Angeles Court Cases, vol. 2, Huntington Library, MS 382:495.

133   August, 1847, Los Angeles Court Cases, vol. 2, Huntington Library, MS 382:495; Harlow, *California Conquered*, 286.

134   Grivas, "Alcalde Rule," 23–24.

135   Bancroft, *History of California*, 5:631. Anastasio Carrillo, "Proclamation," Santa Bárbara, January 8, 1848 [translation only, Bowman, vol. 1, letter 537, p. 357].

136   Pedro Carrillo was one of only four Spanish-surnamed alcaldes by 1848. Grivas, "Alcalde Rule," 24, 31n83.

137   Pedro Carrillo was the son of Carlos Carrillo, María Antonia's brother.

138   In July 1847, for example, he heard a rumor from "an old California woman, secretly friendly to the Americans," that General Piñeda was marching to attack his force of seventy with 500 men. Early the next year, Lippitt feared the return

of former military governor José Castro from Mexico. Lippitt, *Reminiscences*, 74–75.

139   Col. Stevenson, General Headquarters, Southern District, Los Angeles, April 3, 1848, DLG 125; and Andrés Pico to Francisco de la Guerra, San Fernando, April 4, 1848, DLG 125. See also Andrés Pico to Francisco de la Guerra, Los Angeles, March 11, 1848, DLG 125. Much of the Lost Cannon correspondence has been translated or summarized by Father Joseph Thompson for his unpublished manuscript "Casa de la Guerra," SBMAL.

140   William Tecumseh Sherman to Francisco de la Guerra, Monterey, April 12, 1848, DLG 125.

141   Francisco de la Guerra (draft, in the hand of Pablo de la Guerra) to Andrés Pico, Santa Bárbara, n.d., DLG 125 [translated by Thompson, "Casa de la Guerra," SBMAL, p. 62].

142   Francis J. Lippitt, Santa Bárbara, April 18, 1848, DLG 125.

143   Testimony of José Genaro Alvarez, Santa Bárbara, April 18, 1848, DLG 125.

144   Declaration of Pedro C. Carrillo, Santa Barbara, April 20, 1848, DLG 125. José and Pedro Carrillo were both grandsons of María Tomasa Lugo, Bernarda Ruiz's aunt.

145   Testimony of Juan Rodríguez, Santa Bárbara, April 18, 1848, DLG 125; and Testimony of Bernarda Ruiz, Santa Bárbara, April 18, 1848, DLG 125.

146   Testimony of José Carrillo, April 23, 1848, DLG 125 [translated by Dedra McDonald and Thompson, "Casa de la Guerra," SBMAL, pp. 68–69].

147   Declaration of Pedro C. Carrillo, Santa Bárbara, April 20, 1848, DLG 125.

148   Bernarda Ruiz, married to José de Jesús Rodríguez, was comadre with Joaquín de la Guerra once, and her first cousin María Antonia Carrillo de la Guerra twice. The de la Guerras also were the godparents of Juan Rodríguez. In the course of his investigations, Lippitt also called Indians from the nearby ranchería. Most of them also demurred, except for Andrés, who reported that he had heard from Felipe Peña, the Indian alcalde, that "the people had hidden the cannon from the beach… and that the people were very restless." Under oath, Peña denied telling him this. Testimony of Andrés, Alejo Chato, Bernabé, Bruno, and Felipe Peña, April 22, 1848, DLG 125, translated in Thompson, "Casa de la Guerra," SBMAL, pp. 76–79.

149   William Tecumseh Sherman to Francis J. Lippitt, Monterey, April 12, 1848, reprinted in Sherman, *Recollections*, 48.

150   William Tecumseh Sherman to Francisco de la Guerra, Monterey, April 12, 1848, DLG 125.

151   Francisco de la Guerra to William Tecumseh Sherman, Santa Bárbara, April 20, 1848, DLG 125, [translation in Thompson, "Casa de la Guerra," SBMAL, p. 73].

152   Ibid. Three days later, in a sworn statement, he denied knowledge of the lost cannon beyond what the American officers had told him. Testimony of Francisco de la Guerra, April 23, 1848, DLG 125.

153   Streeter, "Recollections," 165–66.

154   García had taken an active part in the southern armed resistance of 1846–47.

155   *"El proyecto de robar el cañon fue ideado por Dn. José Anto. De la Guerra, hijo del Capn. De la Guerra, y José Lugo... Estando allí nos mandó llama Dn. Franco. de la Guerra y llevandonos á un cuarto, nos dijo muy serio, que los Americanos estaban muy enojados por los del cañon y que tuviéramos mucho cuidado de no hablar á nadie sobre ello... en caso que se ofrecimos hacer revolucion contra los Americanos."* José E. García, "Episodios históricos de California," 1878, The Bancroft Library, BANC MSS C-D 85, pp. 1–5.

156   "A Fourth of July in Santa Bárbara in the Year 1848," copy in Thompson, "Casa de la Guerra," SBMAL, pp. 79–83.

157   Bancroft, *History of California,* 5:587, 631. Jonathan Drake Stevenson to José de la Guerra, receipt for $45, Santa Bárbara, July 4, 1848, DLG 125.

158   *"[P]arese que pertenicemos á nuestra amada Patrial Republica Mejicana."* Andrés Pico to Francisco de la Guerra, San Fernando, June 11, 1848, DLG 778.

159   Harlow, *California Conquered,* 303; Bancroft, *History of California,* 5:611. News of the proclamation reached Santa Bárbara immediately afterward. José Abrego to Pablo de la Guerra, Monterey, August 7, 1848, DLG 4.

160   Bancroft, *History of California,* 5:587, 631.

161   Dana, married to a daughter of Carlos Carrillo, was a former alcalde and grantee of the Nipomo Ranch, along the culprits' escape route.

162   Bancroft, *History of California,* 5:639–40; Juan Miguel Price, alcalde of San Luis Obispo to William Dana; Juan Miguel Price, descriptions of suspects, San Luis Obispo, December 7, 1848, DLG 821.

163   Cesareo E. Lataillade, "Fifty Years and More in Santa Bárbara," as told to Michael J. Phillips, *Santa Barbara News,* August 1, 1922, Hastings Scrapbook, pp. 33–35, Gledhill Library, Santa Barbara. The posse was made up of Cesareo Lataillade; Antonio, José, and Ramón Rodríguez; Tomás Valle; José Olivera; Juan Pablo Ayala; David Streeter; Juan Leyba; Francisco and Eugenio Lugo; Valentín Cota; Charles Hefferman; Frederick Schlotterbeck, and Antonio María Villa. Cesareo Lataillade, ca. April 1849, DLG 821.

164   For more on the Reed family murderers, see Wallace V. Ohles, *The Lands of Mission San Miguel* (Fresno, Calif.: Word Dancer Press, 1997); and William B. Secrest, *California Desperadoes: Stories of the Early California Outlaws in Their Own Words* (Clovis, Calif.: Word Dancer Press, 2000).

165   Cesareo Lataillade to José Antonio [Toño] de la Guerra, December 10, 1848, DLG 821.

166   "Acta," December 12, 1848, DLG 821. Italics in original document. The act was signed by: Anastasio Carrillo, Carlos Anto. Carrillo, Richard Ridley, Joaquín Carrillo, John J. Smith, Anto. Ma. de la Guerra, Juan Gómez, Gaspar Oreña, Francisco Badillo, Guillo. Carrillo, Raymdo. Carrillo, Carlos Rodríguez (X), Vicente García (X), Franco. Caballero (X), D. Pedro Avila (X), Gerónimo Ruiz (X), Juan Debis (X), Teodoro Arellanes (X), José Lorenzana (X), Francisco Cordero (X), Francisco Salgado (X), José Gabriel Hernandes (X), Manuel Goycoechea, Joaquín Cota (X), Franco. Areyanes (X), Cristóval Valencia (X), Juan Ygnacio Valencia (X), Pedro Ruiz (X), Franco. Villa (X), Tomás Juan Rodríguez, D. B. Streeter, Cesareo Lataillade, Charles Hefferman, Antonio Rodríguez,

Tomás Valle, José Olibero, Juan P. Ayala, Trifón García (X), Juan Leiba (X), Antonio Arellanes, Miguel García (X), Valentín Cota, Alejo Leiba (X), Luis Arellanes (X), Franco. Carrillo, Federico Schlotterbeck, Joqn. Marroquín, Antonio Palacio (X), and José de Jesús Carrillo.

167   The other members of the jury were equally prominent: Californios Francisco de la Guerra, Joaquín Carrillo, Anastasio Carrillo, Carlos Carrillo, and Gaspar Oreña (the nephew of José de la Guerra); Henry Carnes and Carlos Hefferman of Company F, and Daniel Hill, Richard Ridley, and Thomas Robbins, naturalized Americans married to Californianas. Ridley had been among those taken prisoner during the Bear Flag Revolt, and Robbins was married to a daughter of Carlos Carrillo. Jury records, Santa Bárbara, December 24 and 26, 1848, DLG 821.

168   Edward Ord to "My dear Sir," Santa Bárbara, December 29, 1848, DLG 821, and Edward Ord to "Sir," Santa Bárbara, January 11, 1849, DLG 821.

169   R. B. Mason to Cesareo Lataillade, Monterey, January 24, 1849, DLG 821; and R. B. Mason to E. O. C. Ord, Monterey, January 25, 1849, DLG 821.

170   E. O. C. Ord to R. B. Mason, Monterey, January 26, 1849, DLG 821.

171   R. B. Mason to E. O. C. Ord, Monterey, January 28, 1849, DLG 821.

172   In March 1849, Mason's replacement Gov. Riley appointed Joaquín Carrillo as the last alcalde of Santa Bárbara, and on March 20, 1849, Pablo de la Guerra and Henry Carnes presented him with the Reed family murder documents, "produced by the Pueblo of Santa Bárbara." Bancroft, *History of California*, 7:446; Pablo de la Guerra and Henry Carnes to Raymundo Carrillo, Santa Bárbara, March 20, 1849, DLG 821.

173   "[E]l Srio. del Gobierno . . . me encargó que indicara á V. y á Cuchichito [Francisco] que tomaran empeño por venir como delegados ó Diputados por el partido de Santa Bárbara por que ayudarian á la empresa, mejor que otros." Manuel Jimeno to Pablo de la Guerra, Monterey, June 30, 1849, DLG 557.

174   "*Tengo mucho gusto de recibir Vd. en la lista de ellos que llamen Yankees y como Vd. ha sido un buen Mexican seras un mejor Yankee.*" James L. Ord to Pablo de la Guerra, June 12, 1849, DLG 729.

175   Taylor, *Eldorado*, 109–10. The convention debates have been recorded in J. Ross Browne, *Report of the Debate in the Convention of California, on the Formation of the State Constitution, in September and October, 1849* (Washington, D.C.: John T. Powers, 1850).

176   The Californios included Pablo de la Guerra, Mariano Guadalupe Vallejo, José María Covarrubias, José Antonio Carrillo, and Antonio Pico. Gómez-Quiñones, *Roots of Chicano Politics*, 225; Harlow, *California Conquered*, 338.

177   Harlow, *California Conquered*, 339–41.

178   Pablo de la Guerra, quoted in Browne, *Report of the Debate*, 63.

179   Ibid.

180   Hastings, quoted in Browne, *Report of the Debate*, 64.

181   Pablo de la Guerra, quoted in Browne, *Report of the Debate*, 273.

182   Joaquín Carrillo, prefect of the District of Santa Bárbara, to Pablo de la Guerra, Santa Bárbara, November 24, 1849, DLG 148.

183   See DLG 1066 for Nicasio documents.

184   Tomás Almaguer, *Racial Fault Lines: The Historical Origins of White Supremacy in California* (Berkeley: University of California Press, 1994), 26, 70. In 1850, seventy-three percent of residents were between twenty and forty, and of those, ninety-two percent were men.

185   "[V]olaran aca cuanto pillo haya por alla ... ¿Que sera de nosotros en un Estado republicano cuya mayoria de habitantes sea canalla? Dues liberet nos." Pablo de la Guerra to Antonio María de la Guerra, Santa Bárbara, March 10, 1853, DLG 416.

E P I L O G U E

1   "[U]n immenso caballo con un hombre montado con chaparreras, etc, etc. Todo hecho de siruelas pasadas ... te diré que se ha lucido España en todo de California." Delfina de la Guerra to Francisca de la Guerra, Niagara Falls, June 22, 1893, DLG 360.

2   "¿Quiere Vd. entrar señorita? pasen Vds. con mucho gusto les permitimos a Vds. como españoles, ... cuando les hablabamos español era tanto el gusto, que se ponian colorados y se trastornaban de tal manera, que por unas momentos no sabian ni que decir, la verdad que se me llenaban de agua los ojos porque me ponia yo en el lugar de ellos." Ibid.

3   Delfina de la Guerra to Josefa Moreno de la Guerra, Mexico City, January 31, 1894, and Monterrey, Mexico, September 27, 1894, DLG 361.

4   See, for example, Camarillo, *Chicanos in a Changing Society*; Gómez-Quiñones, *Roots of Chicano Politics*, 1994, 234; and Pitt, *Decline of the Californios.*

5   Louise Pubols, "Fathers of the Pueblo: Patriarchy and Power in Mexican California, 1800–1880," in Samuel Truett and Elliott Young, eds., *Continental Crossroads: Remapping U.S.-Mexico Borderlands History* (Durham, N.C.: Duke University Press, 2004).

6   Joaquín and Miguel led more private lives, devoting themselves to the family lands and businesses.

7   Chávez-García, *Negotiating Conquest.*

8   Casas, *Married to a Daughter of the Land,* 63; Beebe and Senkewicz, *Testimonios,* 52–53.

9   Pablo de la Guerra to Henry W. Halleck, October 9, 1852, The Bancroft Library, Halleck, Peachy & Billings Papers, Box 1, folder 111, [MF 865, G86, 2]. BANC MSS C-B 421.

10   Angustias de la Guerra to Pablo de la Guerra, Mexico City, April 3, 1855, May 10, 1855, September 18, 1855, October 28, 1855, December 15, 1855, and January 3, 1856, DLG 726. Also Pablo de la Guerra to Antonio María de la Guerra, Mazatlán, December 9, 1854, and Mexico City, January 6, February 16, March 25, and March 29, 1854, DLG 416.

11 *"Los que suscribimos acabamos de imponernos del irrespetuoso, antifilial y denigrante lenguaje usado por ti, contra las venerandas cenizas de nuestro amado Padre en un escrito que acabamos de recibir. Esto, junto con las calumniosas imputaciones que en el viertes contra nuestro caracter, nos demandan el imperiosisimo deber de cortar toda relacion fraternal y cualquier otra con tigo para siempre."* Francisco, Pablo, Joaquín, and Antonío María de la Guerra to Angustias de la Guerra, Santa Barbara, July 8, 1858, DLG 369.

12 In the settlement, Angustias and her husband, James Ord, withdrew their case in consideration of one thousand head of cattle, one thousand head of sheep, twenty mares, twelve horses, a town lot in Santa Barbara, and the privilege of living in part of her father's house without paying rent. Beverly E. Bastian, "The Family and the Land," in "Casa de la Guerra: A Study of Time and Place, 1818–1924," Beverly E. Bastian, Grace Murakami, and Louise Pubols, for the Santa Barbara Trust for Historic Preservation, June 1990, p. 43.

13 *Angustias de la Guerra de Ord vs. James L. Ord*, January 8, 1875, District Court of the First Judicial District, Santa Barbara, Gledhill Library of the Santa Barbara Historical Society.

14 See deed books at the Santa Barbara County Courthouse, especially Book D, pp. 303 and 472; Book G, p. 791; Book H, p. 512; Book N, p. 382; Book O, p. 4; Book Q, p. 56; and Book V, p. 353.

15 Bastian, "The Family and the Land," 34–51.

16 The railroad did not arrive in Santa Barbara until 1887; travelers came by sea or stage from Los Angeles. On the post-war demographic changes, see Camarillo, *Chicanos in a Changing Society*, 41–46.

17 *Santa Barbara Daily News*, June 17, 1919, quoted in Stella Haverland Rouse, *Santa Barbara's Spanish Renaissance & Old Spanish Days Fiesta* (Santa Barbara, Calif.: Schauer Printing Studio, Inc., 1974), 38–39.

18 Rouse, *Santa Barbara*, 39, 58.

19 Preservation Planning Associates and Milford Wayne Donaldson, "Historic Structure Report on the Casa de la Guerra," prepared for the Santa Barbara Trust for Historic Preservation, 1991.

20 Preservation Planning Associates and Milford Wayne Donaldson, "Historic Structure Report"; and Rouse, *Santa Barbara*.

21 Rouse, *Santa Barbara*, 69.

22 Padilla, *My History, Not Yours*. Griswold del Castillo, "The del Valle Family."

23 Preservation Planning Associates and Milford Wayne Donaldson, "Historic Structure Report," 6.

Bibliography

Manuscript Sources

The Bancroft Library, University of California at Berkeley
    Alfred Robinson Papers
    Bancroft's "Pioneer Sketches," or "Testimonios"
    Colville Jackson Minor Letters
    Departmental State Papers
    Halleck, Peachy, and Billings Papers
    José de la Guerra y Noriega Papers, *Documentos Para la Historia de California*
        (Transcripts of de la Guerra papers; most originals found in the Santa
        Barbara Mission Archive-Library)
    Oreña Papers
    Vallejo Papers

City Clerk's Office, City of Santa Barbara
    Minutes of the Common Council and City Council of the City of Santa Barbara,
        1850–85
    Ordinances
    Petitions

County Clerk's Office, Santa Barbara County
    Book of Deeds, 1844–82
    Minutes of the Santa Barbara County Court of Sessions and Board of
        Supervisors, 1850–80

Gledhill Library, Santa Barbara Historical Society
    A. B. Thompson Papers
    California State Census, Santa Barbara County, 1852 (copy)
    De la Guerra Genealogy File
    Rancho San Julián Archive
    Santa Barbara County Tax Rolls, 1851–70
    Santa Barbara County (District Court, 2nd Judicial District) Court Cases,
        1850–80

Huntington Library, San Marino, California
  Abel Stearns Collection
  California File
  California Historical Documents Collections
  Early California Population Project Database, 2006
  Halleck, Peachy, and Billings Papers
  Land Claims Cases, Southern District (microfilm)
  Los Angeles County Court Cases, 1823–50 (microfilm)
  Mariano Guadalupe Vallejo Collection
  Monterey Collection
  Oreña Family Collection

Santa Barbara Mission Archive-Library
  Baptismal Records of Our Lady of Sorrows, vols. 1 and 2
  De la Guerra Papers, ca. 1790–1930
  Thompson Papers

Unpublished Secondary Sources

Bastian, Beverly E., Grace Murakami, and Louise Pubols. "Casa de la Guerra: A Study of Time and Place, 1818–1924." Santa Barbara, Calif.: Santa Barbara Trust for Historic Preservation, 1990.

Imwalle, Michael. "Comprehensive Archaeological and Architectural Investigation of the Casa de la Guerra," edited by Michael Imwalle and Louise Pubols. Santa Barbara, Calif.: Santa Barbara Trust for Historic Preservation, 1994.

Koch, Carlota. "Spanish Blood in Their Veins: Gaspar and Maria Antonia Oreña, Spanish-Californians." Santa Barbara Trust for Historic Preservation, 1936. Photocopy.

Preservation Planning Associates and Milford Wayne Donaldson. "Historic Structure Report on the Casa de la Guerra." Santa Barbara Trust for Historic Preservation, 1991.

Renga, Alan. "The Books of José de la Guerra." University of California at Santa Barbara, 1995. Santa Barbara Trust for Historic Preservation. Photocopy.

Published Primary Sources

Browne, J. Ross. *Report of the Debate in the Convention of California, on the Formation of the State Constitution, in September and October, 1849.* Washington, D.C.: John T. Powers, 1850.

Carrillo, Carlos Antonio. *Exposition Addressed to the Chamber of Deputies of the Congress of the Union by Señor Don Carlos Antonio Carrillo, Deputy for Alta California Concerning the Regulation and Administration of the Pious Fund,* edited and translated by Herbert Ingram Priestly. San Francisco: John Henry Nash, 1938.

Davis, William Heath. *Seventy-Five Years in California: Recollections and Remarks by One Who Visited These Shores in 1831, and Again in 1833, and Except When Absent on Business Was a Resident from 1838 until the End of His Long Life in 1909,* edited by Harold A. Small. San Francisco: John Howell Books, 1967.

Duhaut-Cilly, Auguste. "Duhaut-Cilly's Account of California in the Years 1827–28," translated by Charles Franklin Carter. *California Historical Society Quarterly* 8, no. 2 (June 1929): 131–65.

Figueroa, José. *Manifesto to the Mexican Republic which Brigadier General José Figueroa, Commandant and Political Chief of Upper California, Presents on his Conduct and That of José María de Híjar and José María Padrés as Directors of Colonization in 1834 and 1835,* translated and edited by C. Alan Hutchinson. Berkeley: University of California Press, 1978.

Janssens, Don Agustin. *The Life and Adventures in California of Don Agustin Janssens 1834–1856,* edited by William H. Ellison and Francis Price. San Marino, Calif.: Huntington Library, 1953.

Larkin, Tomas Oliver, et al. *The Larkin Papers: Personal, Business and Official Correspondence of Tomas Oliver Larkin, Merchant and United States Consul in California,* edited by George P. Hammon. 10 vols. Berkeley, Calif.: University of California Press, 1968.

Lippitt, Francis J. *Reminiscences of Francis J. Lippitt: Written for His Family, His Near Relatives and Intimate Friends.* Providence, R.I.: Preston and Rounds Co., 1902.

Lugo, José del Carmen. "Life of a Rancher." *Historical Society of Southern California Quarterly* 32, no. 3 (September 1950): 185–236.

Lynch, James. *With Stevenson to California.* San Luis Obispo, Calif.: Tierra Redonda, 1896.

Nidever, George. *The Life and Adventures of George Nidever,* edited by William Henry Ellison. Berkeley, Calif.: University of California Press, 1937.

Osio, Antonio María. *The History of Alta California: A Memoir of Mexican California,* translated and edited by Rose Marie Beebe and Robert M. Senkewicz. Madison: University of Wisconsin Press, 1996.

Phelps, William Dane. *Alta California 1840–1842: The Journal and Observances of William Dane Phelps, Master of the Ship "Alert,"* introduction and edited by Briton Cooper Busch. Glendale, Calif.: Arthur H. Clark Co., 1983.

Rockwell, John. "In Olden Times." *Santa Barbara Daily News,* May 30–July 3, 1896.

Sherman, William T. *Recollections of California, 1846–1861.* Oakland, Calif.: Biobooks, 1945.

Simpson, Sir George. *Narrative of a Voyage to California Ports in 1841–42.* San Francisco: T. C. Russell, 1930.

Streeter, William A. "'Recollections of Historical Events in California, 1843–1878' of William A. Streeter," edited by William H. Ellison. *California Historical Society Quarterly* 18, nos. 1–3 (March, June, and September 1939): 64–71, 157–79, 254–78.

Taylor, Bayard. *Eldorado, or Adventures in the Path of Empire.* 1850. Reprint, Lincoln: University of Nebraska Press, 1988.

Vischer, Edward. "Edward Vischer's First Visit to California [1842]," edited and translated by Erwin Gustav Gudde. *California Historical Society Quarterly* 19, no. 3 (1940): 193–216.

Published Secondary Sources

Acuña, Rodolfo. *Occupied America: A History of Chicanos.* New York: Longman, 1972.

Almaguer, Tomás. *Racial Fault Lines: The Historical Origins of White Supremacy in California.* Berkeley: University of California Press, 1994.

Alonso, Ana María. *Thread of Blood: Colonialism, Revolution, and Gender on Mexico's Northern Frontier.* Tucson: University of Arizona Press, 1995.

Anderson, Benedict. *Imagined Communities: Reflections on the Origin and Spread of Nationalism.* New York: Verso, 1983.

Anzaldúa, Gloria. *Borderlands/La Frontera: The New Mestiza.* San Francisco: Spinsters/Aunt Lute, 1987.

Archibald, Robert. "The Economy of the Alta California Missions, 1803–1821." *Southern California Quarterly* 58 (Summer 1976): 227–40.

Arrom, Silvia Marina. "Marriage Patterns in Mexico City, 1811." *Journal of Family History* 3, no. 4 (Winter 1978): 376–91.

———. *The Women of Mexico City, 1790–1857.* Stanford, Calif.: Stanford University Press, 1985.

Balmori, Diana, Stuart Voss, and Miles Wortman, eds. *Notable Family Networks in Latin America.* Chicago: University of Chicago Press, 1984.

Bancroft, Hubert Howe. *History of California.* 7 vols. San Francisco: The History Company, 1884–89.

———. *California Pioneer Register and Index 1542–1848: Including Inhabitants of California, 1769–1800 and List of Pioneers.* Extracted from *The History of California.* Baltimore: Regional Publishing Company, 1964.

Barr, Juliana. "A Diplomacy of Gender: Rituals of First Contact in the 'Land of the Tejas.'" *William and Mary Quarterly* 61 no. 3 (2004): 393–434.

———. *Peace Came in the Form of a Woman: Indians and Spaniards in the Texas Borderlands.* Chapel Hill: University of North Carolina Press, 2007.

Beebe, Rose Marie, and Robert M. Senkewicz, eds. *Lands of Promise and Despair: Chronicles of Early California, 1535–1846*. Berkeley, Calif.: Heyday Books, 2001.

———. *Testimonios: Early California through the Eyes of Women, 1815–1848*. Berkeley, Calif.: Heyday Books, 2006.

Blackhawk, Ned. *Violence over the Land: Indians and Empires in the Early American West*. Cambridge, Mass.: Harvard University Press, 2006.

Bolton, Herbert E. "The Iturbide Revolution in the Californias." *Hispanic American Historical Review* 2 (May 1919): 188–242.

———. "The Mission as a Frontier Institution in the Spanish American Colonies." *American Historical Review* 23, no. 1 (October 1917): 42–61.

Bouvier, Virginia. *Women and the Conquest of California: Codes of Silence*. Tucson: University of Arizona Press, 2001.

Boyer, Richard. *Lives of the Bigamists: Marriage, Family, and Community in Colonial Mexico*. Albuquerque: University of New Mexico Press, 1995.

Brading, David A. *Miners and Merchants in Bourbon Mexico, 1763–1810*. Cambridge: Cambridge University Press, 1971.

———. *The Origins of Mexican Nationalism*. Cambridge: The Centre of Latin American Studies, 1985.

Brooks, James F. *Captives and Cousins: Slavery, Kinship, and Community in the Southwest Borderlands*. Chapel Hill: University of North Carolina Press, 2002.

Brooks, James F., Christopher R. N. DeCorse, and John Walton, eds. *Small Worlds: Method, Meaning, and Narrative in Microhistory*. Santa Fe, N.M.: School for Advanced Research, 2008.

Brown, Kathy. *Good Wives, Nasty Wenches, and Anxious Patriarchs: Gender, Race, and Power in Colonial Virginia*. Chapel Hill: University of North Carolina Press, 1996.

Burkholder, Mark A., and Lyman L. Johnson. *Colonial Latin America*. 5th ed. New York: Oxford University Press, 2004.

Camarillo, Albert. *Chicanos in a Changing Society: From Mexican Pueblos to American Barrios in Santa Barbara and Southern California, 1848–1930*. Cambridge, Mass.: Harvard University Press, 1979.

Campbell, Leon G. "The First Californios: Presidial Society in Spanish California, 1769–1822." *Journal of the West* 11, no. 4 (October 1972): 582–95.

Casas, María Raquél. *Married to a Daughter of the Land: Spanish-Mexican Women and Interethnic Marriage in California, 1820–1880*. Reno: University of Nevada Press, 2007.

Cassidy, Joseph E. "Life and Times of Pablo de la Guerra." PhD diss., University of California at Santa Barbara, 1977.

Castañeda, Antonia. "Gender, Race, and Culture: Spanish-Mexican Women in the Historiography of Frontier California." *Frontiers: A Journal of Women's Studies* 11 (1990): 8–20.

———. "The Political Economy of Nineteenth Century Stereotypes of Californianas." In *Between Borders: Essays on Mexicana/Chicana History,* edited by Adelaida R. Del Castillo. Encino, Calif.: Floricanto Press, 1990.

———. "Presidarias y Pobladoras: Spanish-Mexican Women in Frontier Monterey, Alta California, 1770–1821." PhD diss., Stanford University, 1990.

———. "Engendering the History of Alta California, 1769–1848: Gender, Sexuality and the Family." In *Contested Eden: California Before the Gold Rush,* edited by Ramón A. Gutiérrez and Richard J. Orsi. Berkeley, Calif.: University of California Press, 1998.

Castro-Klarén, Sara, and John Charles Chasteen. *Beyond Imagined Communities: Reading and Writing the Nation in Nineteenth-Century Latin America.* Baltimore, Md.: Johns Hopkins Press, 2003.

Caulfield, Sueann, Sarah C. Chambers, and Lara Putnam, eds. *Honor, Status, and Law in Modern Latin America.* Durham, N.C.: Duke University Press, 2005.

Chambers, Sarah. *From Subjects to Citizens: Honor, Gender, and Politics in Arequipa, Peru, 1780–1854.* University Park: University of Pennsylvania Press, 1999.

Chandler, Alfred D. *The Visible Hand: The Managerial Revolution in American Business.* Cambridge, Mass.: Harvard University Press, 1977.

Chávez-García, Miroslava. *Negotiating Conquest: Gender and Power in California, 1770s to 1880s.* Tucson: University of Arizona Press, 2004.

Clark, Harry. "Their Pride, Their Manner, and Their Voice: Sources of the Traditional Portrait of the Early Californians." *California Historical Quarterly* 53, no. 1 (Spring 1974): 71–82.

Cleland, Robert Glass. *The Cattle on a Thousand Hills: Southern California, 1850–1880.* San Marino, Calif.: Huntington Library, 1941.

Costello, Julia, and Philip Walker. "Burials from the Santa Barbara Presidio Chapel." *Historical Archaeology* 21 (1987): 3–17.

Couturier, Edith. "Women in a Noble Family: The Mexican Counts of Regla, 1750–1830." In *Latin American Women: Historical Perspectives,* edited by Ascuncion Lavrin. Westport, Conn.: Greenwood Press, 1978.

Cowan, Robert G. *Ranchos of California: A List of Spanish Concessions, 1775–1822, and Mexican Grants 1822–1846.* Fresno, Calif.: Academy Library Guild, 1956.

Craver, Rebecca McDowell. *The Impact of Intimacy: Mexican-Anglo Intermarriage in New Mexico, 1821–1846.* Southwestern Studies 66. El Paso, Texas: Texas-Western Press, 1982.

Cronon, William. "A Place for Stories: Nature, History, and Narrative." *Journal of American History* 78, no. 4 (March 1992): 1347–76.

Cuello, José. "Beyond the 'Borderlands' Is the North of Colonial Mexico: A Latin-Americanist Perspective to the Study of the Mexican North and the United States Southwest." In *Proceedings of the Pacific Council on Latin American Studies* 9, edited by Kristyna P. Demaree. San Diego, Calif.: San Diego State Press, 1982.

Cutter, Donald, ed. *Writings of Mariano Payeras.* Santa Barbara, Calif.: Bellerophon Books, 1995.

Dakin, Susanna Bryant. *The Lives of William Hartnell.* Stanford, Calif.: Stanford University Press, 1949.

Dana, Richard Henry. *Two Years Before the Mast and Twenty-Four Years After.* Edited by Charles W. Eliot. Harvard Classics 23. New York: P. F. Collier and Son, 1909. Reprint, 1969.

Deeds, Susan M. "New Spain's Far North: A Changing Historiographical Frontier?" *Latin American Research Review* 25, no. 2 (1990): 226–35.

De la Teja, Jesús F., and Ross Frank. *Choice, Persuasion, and Coercion: Social Control on Spain's North American Frontiers.* Albuquerque: University of New Mexico Press, 2005.

Demélas, Marie-Danielle, and François-Xavier Guerra. "The Hispanic Revolutions." In *Elections Before Democracy.* New York: St. Martin's Press, 1996.

Deverell, William. *Whitewashed Adobe: The Rise of Los Angeles and the Remaking of Its Mexican Past.* Berkeley: University of California Press, 2004.

Díaz, Arlene J. *Female Citizens, Patriarchs, and the Law in Venezuela, 1786–1904.* Lincoln: University of Nebraska Press, 2004.

Eversole, Robert Wayne. "Towns in Mexican Alta California: A Social History of Monterey, San José, Santa Bárbara, and Los Angeles, 1822–1846." PhD diss., University of California at San Diego, 1986.

Fliegelman, Jay. *Prodigals and Pilgrims: The American Revolution against Patriarchal Authority, 1750–1800.* Cambridge: Cambridge University Press, 1982.

Forbes, Jack D. "Black Pioneers: The Spanish-Speaking Afroamericans of the Southwest." *Phylon* 27, no. 3 (Fall 1966): 233–46.

Francis, Jessie Davies. *An Economic and Social History of Mexican California.* PhD diss., University of California at Berkeley, 1935. Reprint, New York: Arno Press, 1976.

Franco, Jean. *Plotting Women: Gender and Representation in Mexico.* New York: Columbia University Press, 1989.

Geary, Gerald J. *Secularization of the California Missions (1810–1846).* Washington, D.C., Catholic University of America, 1934.

Geiger, Maynard, O. F. M., trans. and ed. *The Letters of Alfred Robinson to the De La Guerra Family of Santa Barbara: 1834–1873.* Los Angeles: Zamorano Club, 1972.

Ginzburg, Carlo. "Microhistory: Two or Three Things That I Know about It." *Critical Inquiry* 20, no. 1 (Autumn 1993): 10–35.

Gómez-Quiñones, Juan. *Roots of Chicano Politics, 1600–1940.* Albuquerque: University of New Mexico Press, 1994.

Gonzáles, Manuel. *The Hispanic Elite of the Southwest.* Southwestern Studies 86. El Paso, Texas: Texas-Western Press, 1982.

González, Deena. *Resisting the Favor: The Spanish-Mexican Women of Santa Fe, 1820–1880.* New York: Oxford University Press, 1999.

González, Michael J. "'The Child of the Wilderness Weeps for the Father of Our Country': The Indian and the Politics of Church and State in Provincial California." In *Contested Eden: California Before the Gold Rush,* edited by Ramón A. Gutiérrez and Richard J. Orsi. Berkeley: University of California Press, 1998.

———. *This Small City Will Be a Mexican Paradise: Exploring the Origins of Mexican Culture in Los Angeles, 1821–1846.* Albuquerque: University of New Mexico Press, 2005.

Griswold del Castillo, Richard. *The Los Angeles Barrio, 1850–1890: A Social History.* Berkeley: University of California Press, 1979.

———. "The del Valle Family and the Fantasy Heritage." *California History* 59, no. 1 (Spring 1980): 3–15.

———. "Neither Activists Nor Victims: Mexican Women's Historical Discourse: The Case of San Diego, 1820–1850." *California History* 74, no. 3 (Fall 1995): 230–43.

Grivas, Theodore. "Alcalde Rule: The Nature of Local Government in Spanish and Mexican California." *California Historical Society Quarterly* 40, no. 1 (March 1961): 11–19.

Guardino, Peter. *Peasants, Politics, and the Formation of Mexico's National State: Guerrero, 1800–1857.* Stanford, Calif.: Stanford University Press, 1996.

———. *The Time of Liberty: Popular Political Culture in Oaxaca, 1750–1850.* Durham, N.C.: Duke University Press, 2005.

Gudeman, Stephen. "The Compadrazgo as a Reflection of the Natural and Spiritual Person." *Proceedings of the Royal Anthropological Institute of Great Britain and Ireland for 1971* (1972): 45–71.

Guinn, J. M. *Historical and Biographical Record of Southern California: Containing a History of Southern California from Its Earliest Settlement to the Opening Year of the Twentieth Century.* Chicago: Chapman Publishing Co., 1902.

Gutiérrez, Ramón A. "Honor Ideology, Marriage Negotiation, and Class-Gender Domination in New Mexico, 1690–1846." *Latin American Perspectives* 44:12, no. 1 (Winter 1985): 81–104.

————. "Ethnic and Class Boundaries in America's Hispanic Past." In *Social and Gender Boundaries in the United States*, edited by Sucheng Chan. Lewiston, N.Y.: Edwin Mellon Press, 1989.

————. *When Jesus Came, the Corn Mothers Went Away: Marriage, Sexuality, and Power in New Mexico, 1500–1846.* Stanford, Calif.: Stanford University Press, 1991.

Gutiérrez, Ramón A., and Richard J. Orsi, eds. *Contested Eden: California Before the Gold Rush.* Berkeley: University of California Press, 1998.

Haas, Lisbeth. *Conquests and Historical Identities in California, 1769–1936.* Berkeley, Los Angeles, and London: University of California Press, 1995.

————. "War in California, 1846–1848." In *Contested Eden: California Before the Gold Rush,* edited by Ramón A. Gutiérrez and Richard J. Orsi. Berkeley: University of California Press, 1998.

Hackel, Steven W. *Children of Coyote, Missionaries of Saint Francis: Indian-Spanish Relations in Colonial California, 1769–1850.* Chapel Hill: University of North Carolina Press, 2005.

————. "Land, Labor, and Production: The Colonial Economy of Spanish and Mexican California." In *Contested Eden: California Before the Gold Rush,* edited by Ramón A. Gutiérrez and Richard J. Orsi. Berkeley: University of California Press, 1998.

Haggland, Mary H. "Don José Antonio Aguirre: Spanish Merchant and Ranchero." *Journal of San Diego History* 29, no. 1 (1983): 54–68.

Hale, Charles A. *Mexican Liberalism in the Age of Mora, 1821–1853.* New Haven, Conn.: Yale University Press, 1968.

Hall, Peter Dobkin. "Family Structure and Economic Organization: Massachusetts Merchants, 1700–1850." In *Family and Kin in Urban Communities, 1700–1930,* edited by Tamara K. Hareven. New York: New Viewpoints, 1977.

Hämäläinen, Pekka. *Comanche Empire.* New Haven, Conn.: Yale University Press, 2008.

Hansen, Woodrow J. *The Search for Authority in California.* Oakland, Calif.: Biobooks, 1960.

Harlow, Neal. *California Conquered: The Annexation of a Mexican Province, 1846–1850.* Berkeley: University of California Press, 1982.

Heizer, Robert F., and Alan F. Almquist. *The Other Californians: Prejudice and Discrimination under Spain, Mexico, and the United States to 1920.* Berkeley and Los Angeles: University of California Press, 1971.

Hernández, Salomé. "No Settlement Without Women: Three Spanish California Settlement Schemes, 1790–1800." *Southern California Quarterly* 72 (Fall 1990): 203–33.

Hornbeck, David. "Land Tenure and Rancho Expansion in Alta California, 1784–1846." *Journal of Historical Geography* 4 (1978): 371–90.

———. "The Ordinary Landscape of Hispanic California: Economic Differences Between Missions and Ranchos." In *Early California Reflections: A Series of Lectures Held at the San Juan Capistrano Branch of the Orange County Public Library,* edited by Nicholas M. Magalousis. Orange County, Calif.: County of Orange Library System, 1987.

Hunefeldt, Christine. *Liberalism in the Bedroom: Quarreling Spouses in Nineteenth-Century Lima.* University Park: University of Pennsylvania Press, 2000.

Hunt, Lynn. *The Family Romance of the French Revolution.* Berkeley: University of California Press, 1992.

Hurtado, Albert L. *Indian Survival on the California Frontier.* New Haven and London: Yale University Press, 1988.

———. *Intimate Frontiers: Sex, Gender, and Culture in Old California.* Albuquerque: University of New Mexico Press, 1999.

Hutchinson, C. Alan. *Frontier Settlement in Mexican California: The Híjar-Padres Colony and Its Origins 1769–1835.* New Haven, Conn.: Yale University Press, 1969.

Igler, David. "Diseased Goods: Global Exchanges in the Eastern Pacific Basin, 1770–1850." *American Historical Review* 109 (June 2004): 693–719.

Jackson, Robert H., and Edward Castillo. *Indians, Franciscans, and Spanish Colonization: The Impact of the Mission System on California Indians.* Albuquerque: University of New Mexico Press, 1995.

Kells, Robert E., Jr. "The Spanish Inheritance: The Mexican Forces of Alta California, 1822–1846." *Journal of the West* 20, no. 4 (1981): 12–19.

Kicza, John E. "The Great Families of Mexico: Elite Maintenance and Business Practices in Late Colonial Mexico City." *Hispanic American Historical Review* 62, no. 3 (1982): 429–57.

———. *Colonial Entrepreneurs: Families and Business in Bourbon Mexico City.* Albuquerque: University of New Mexico Press, 1983.

Kropp, Phoebe. *California Vieja: Culture and Memory in a Modern American Place.* Berkeley: University of California Press, 2006.

Langum, David J. "Californio Women and the Image of Virtue." *Southern California Quarterly* 59, no. 3 (Fall 1977): 245–50.

———. *Law and Community on the Mexican California Frontier: Anglo-American Expatriates and the Clash of Legal Traditions.* Norman and London: University of Oklahoma Press, 1987.

Langum, David J., and Harlan Hague. *Thomas O. Larkin: A Life of Patriotism and Profit in Old California.* Norman: University of Oklahoma Press, 1990.

Lavrin, Asuncion, ed. *Sexuality and Marriage in Colonial Latin America.* Lincoln: University of Nebraska Press, 1989.

Lepore, Jill. "Historians Who Love Too Much: Reflections on Microhistory and Biography." *Journal of American History* 88 (June 2001): 129–44.

Levi, Giovanni. "On Microhistory." In *New Perspectives on Historical Writing,* edited by Peter Burke. University Park: Pennsylvania State University Press, 1992.

Liss, Peggy. "Creoles, the North American Example, and the Spanish American Economy, 1760–1810." In *The North American Role in the Spanish Imperial Economy 1760–1819,* edited by Jacques A. Barbier and Allan J. Kuethe. Manchester: Manchester University Press, 1984.

Lothrup, Gloria Ricci. "Rancheras and the Land: Women and Property Rights in Hispanic California." *Southern California Quarterly* 86 (Spring 1994): 59–84.

Lynch, John. *The Spanish American Revolutions 1808–1826.* New York: W. W. Norton and Co., 1986.

Madison, Elizabeth Style. "Hacienda De La Guerra: Yesterday and Today in a Spanish *Casa* Built by Three Thousand Indians." *Sunset* 26 (January 1911): 34–47.

Mallon, Florencia. *Peasant and Nation: The Making of Postcolonial Mexico and Peru.* Berkeley: University of California Press, 1995.

Martin, Cheryl English. *Governance and Society in Colonial Mexico: Chihuahua in the Eighteenth Century.* Stanford, Calif.: Stanford University Press, 1996.

Martinez-Alier, Verena. *Marriage, Class, and Color in Nineteenth-Century Cuba: A Study of Racial Attitudes and Sexual Values in a Slave Society.* 2nd ed. Ann Arbor: University of Michigan Press, 1989.

Mason, William. *The Census of 1790: A Demographic History of Colonial California.* Ballena Press Anthropological Papers 45. Menlo Park, Calif.: Ballena Press, 1998.

———. *Los Angeles Under the Spanish Flag: Spain's New World.* Burbank, Calif.: Southern California Genealogical Society, 2004.

McAlister, Lyle N. "Social Structure and Social Change in New Spain." *Hispanic American Historical Review* 43, no. 3 (August 1963): 349–70.

McWilliams, Carey. *Southern California: An Island on the Land.* 1946. Reprint, Santa Barbara: Peregrine Smith, 1973.

———. *North from Mexico: The Spanish-Speaking People of the United States.* 1948. Reprint, New York: Greenwood Press, 1968.

Miller, Robert Ryal. *Juan Alvarado: Governor of California, 1836–1842.* Norman: University of Oklahoma Press, 1998.

Miranda, Gloria E. "Gente de Razón Marriage Patterns in Spanish and Mexican California: A Case Study of Santa Barbara and Los Angeles." *Southern California Quarterly* 63, no. 1 (Spring 1981): 1–21.

———. "Hispano-Mexican Childrearing Practices in Pre-American Santa Barbara." *Southern California Quarterly* 65, no. 4 (Winter 1983): 307–20.

———. "Racial and Cultural Dimensions of Gente de Razon Status in Mexican California." *Southern California Quarterly* 70 (Fall 1988): 265–78.

Monroy, Douglas. *Thrown Among Strangers: The Making of Mexican Culture in Frontier California.* Berkeley: University of California Press, 1990.

Moorhead, Max L. *The Presidio: Bastion of the Spanish Borderlands.* Norman: University of Oklahoma Press, 1975.

Mora-Torres, Gregorio, trans. and ed. *Californio Voices: The Oral Memoirs of José María Amador and Lorenzo Asisara.* Denton: University of North Texas Press, 2005.

Northrop, Marie E. *Spanish-Mexican Families of Early California: 1769–1850,* 2 vols. Burbank, Calif.: Southern California Genealogical Society, 1984.

Norling, Lisa. *Captain Ahab Had a Wife: New England Women and the Whalefishery, 1720–1870.* Chapel Hill: University of North Carolina Press, 2000.

O'Dowd, Patrick. "Pirates and Patriots." *La Campana*, Santa Barbara Trust for Historic Preservation (Winter 1997–98): 2–16.

Ogden, Adele. "Hides and Tallow: McCulloch, Hartnell and Company 1822–1828." *California Historical Society Quarterly* 6, no. 3 (1927): 254–64.

———. "Boston Hide Droughers Along California Shores." *California Historical Society Quarterly* 8, no. 4 (December 1929): 288–305.

———. *The California Sea Otter Trade, 1748–1848.* Berkeley: University of California Press, 1941.

———. "Alfred Robinson, New England Merchant in Mexican California." *California Historical Society Quarterly* 23, no. 3 (September 1944): 23–193.

Ogden, Adele, ed. "The Business Letters of Alfred Robinson." *California Historical Society Quarterly* 23, no. 4 (1944): 301–34.

Ohles, Wallace V. *The Lands of Mission San Miguel.* Fresno, Calif.: Word Dancer Press, 1997.

Padilla, Genaro M. *My History, Not Yours: The Formation of Mexican-American Autobiography.* Madison: University of Wisconsin Press, 1993.

Partner, Nancy. "Making Up Lost Time: Writing on the Writing of History." *Speculum* 61 (1986): 90–117.

Phillips, George Harwood. "Indians in Los Angeles, 1781–1875: Economic Integration, Social Disintegration." *Pacific Historical Review* 49, no. 3 (August 1980): 427–51.

Phillips, William Henry. "Don José Antonio Julián de la Guerra y Noriega, of California." Master's thesis, University of Southern California, 1950.

Pitt, Leonard. *The Decline of the Californios: A Social History of the Spanish-Speaking Californians, 1846–1890.* Berkeley and Los Angeles: University of California Press, 1966.

Premo, Biana. *Children of the Father King: Youth, Authority, and Legal Minority in Colonial Lima.* Chapel Hill: University of North Carolina Press, 2005.

Preston, William. "Serpent in the Garden: Environmental Change in Colonial California." In *Contested Eden: California Before the Gold Rush,* edited by Ramón A. Gutiérrez and Richard J. Orsi. Berkeley: University of California Press, 1998.

Reséndez, Andrés. *Changing National Identities at the Frontier: Texas and New Mexico, 1800–1850.* Cambridge: Cambridge University Press, 2005.

Ríos-Bustamante, Antonio. *Mexican Los Angeles: A Narrative and Pictorial History.* Encino, Calif.: Floricanto Press, 1992.

Ríos-Bustamante, Antonio, and Pedro Castillo. *An Illustrated History of Mexican Los Angeles: 1781–1985.* Los Angeles: Chicano Studies Research Center Publications, University of California, Los Angeles, 1986.

Robinson, Alfred. *Life in California: During a Residence of Several Years in That Territory, Including a Narrative of Events which have Transpired since that period when California was an Independent Government.* 1846 and 1891. Reprint with an introduction by Andrew Rolle, Santa Barbara and Salt Lake City: Peregrine Smith, 1970.

———. "José Antonio de la Guerra." In *Representative and Leading Men of the Pacific,* edited by Oscar T. Shuck. San Francisco: Bacon and Company, 1870.

Rodríguez, Jaime. *The Independence of Spanish America.* New York: Cambridge University Press, 1998.

Rosenus, Alan. *General M. G. Vallejo and the Advent of the Americans.* Albuquerque: University of New Mexico Press, 1995.

Rouse, Stella Haverland. *Santa Barbara: Spanish Renaissance and Old Spanish Days Fiesta.* Santa Barbara, Calif.: Schauer Printing Studio, 1974.

Sánchez, Nellie Van de Grift. *Spanish Arcadia.* 1929. Reprint, New York: Arno Press, 1976.

Sánchez, Rosaura. *Telling Identities: The Californio Testimonios.* Minneapolis and London: University of Minnesota Press, 1995.

Sandos, James. *Converting California: Indians and Franciscans in the Missions.* New Haven, Conn.: Yale University Press, 2004.

———. "Levantamiento!: The 1824 Chumash Uprising Reconsidered." *Southern California Quarterly* 67, no. 2 (1985): 109–33.

———. "From 'Boltonlands' to 'Weberlands.'" *American Quarterly* 46, no. 4 (1994): 595–604.

Secrest, William B. *California Desperadoes: Stories of the Early California Outlaws in Their Own Words.* Clovis, Calif.: Word Dancer Press, 2000.

Seed, Patricia. *To Love, Honour, Obey in Colonial Mexico: Conflicts over Marriage Choice 1574–1821.* Stanford, Calif.: Stanford University Press, 1988.

Socolow, Susan Migden. *The Merchants of Buenos Aires, 1778–1810.* Cambridge: Cambridge University Press, 1978.

———. *The Women of Colonial Latin America.* Cambridge: Cambridge University Press, 2000.

Stern, Steve J. *The Secret History of Gender: Women, Men, and Power in Late Colonial Mexico.* Chapel Hill: University of North Carolina Press, 1995.

Taylor, Quintard. *In Search of the Racial Frontier: African Americans in the American West, 1528–1990.* New York: W. W. Norton and Co., 1998.

Tays, George. "Revolutionary California: The Political History of California from 1820 to 1848." PhD diss., University of California at Berkeley, 1934.

Thompson, Joseph A. *El Gran Capitán: José de la Guerra.* Los Angeles: Cabrera and Sons, 1961.

Thompson, Father Joseph. "Casa De La Guerra—Santa Barbara." Edited by Maynard Geiger. *Noticias* 17, no. 1 (Spring 1972): 1–7.

Truett, Samuel, and Elliott Young, eds. *Continental Crossroads: Remapping U.S.-Mexico Borderlands History.* Durham, N.C.: Duke University Press, 2004.

Tutino, John. "Power, Class, and Family: Men and Women in the Mexican Elite 1750–1810." *The Americas* 39, no. 3 (January 1983): 359–81.

Twinam, Ann. *Public Lives, Private Secrets: Gender, Honor, Sexuality, and Illegitimacy in Colonial Spanish America.* Stanford, Calif.: Stanford University Press, 1999.

Van Young, Eric. *The Other Rebellion: Popular Violence, Ideology, and the Mexican Struggle for Independence, 1810–1821.* Stanford, Calif.: Stanford University Press, 2001.

Voss, Barbara L. *The Archaeology of Ethnogenesis: Race and Sexuality in Colonial San Francisco.* Berkeley: University of California Press, 2008.

Walker, David W. *Kinship, Business, and Politics: The Martínez del Rio Family in Mexico, 1824–1867*. Austin: University of Texas Press, 1986.

Weber, David J. *Bárbaros: Spaniards and Their Savages in the Age of Enlightenment*. New Haven, Conn.: Yale University Press, 2005.

———. *The Mexican Frontier, 1821–1846: The American Southwest Under Mexico*. Albuquerque: University of New Mexico Press, 1982.

———. "John Francis Bannon and the Historiography of the Spanish Borderlands: Retrospect and Prospect." *Journal of the Southwest* 29 (Winter 1987): 331–63.

———. *The Spanish Frontier in North America*. New Haven, Conn.: Yale University Press, 1992.

Weber, David J., ed. *New Spain's Far Northern Frontier: Essays on Spain in the American West, 1540–1821*. Albuquerque: University of New Mexico Press, 1979.

INDEX

A

Abella, Ramón, 222
Acapulco, 88, 125, 206, 238
agriculture, 81, 141
  labor force, 71, 153, 164, 215, 220
  products from California, 33, 102,
    108–9
aguardiente (brandy), 49, 82, 118–19, 132,
  241
  produced by de la Guerras, 128, 223
Aguirre, José Antonio, 246, 365n23,
  373n118
  dealings with José de la Guerra, 203,
    222, 238–39, 256
Alamán, Lucas, 186, 360n159
alcalde (magistrate), 99, 282, 375n141
  Francisco Javier Alvarado as, 101
  José Antonio de la Guerra as, 180–82
  José de la Guerra as, 42
  Luis Carrillo as, 273–74
  Manuel Gutiérrez as, 100
  Manuel Jimeno as, 195, 200
  Pablo de la Guerra as, 273–74, 276
  Pedro Carrillo as, 276–77, 280, 281
  role of, 98, 180, 225, 274, 282
alférez (2nd lieutenant or ensign), 17–18,
  63, 64, 78, 169
Alipás, Gervasio, 205
Alta California. *See* California
Altimira, José, 130–31
Alvarado, Francisco Javier, 91, 101
Alvarado, Juan Bautista, 184, 197, 253, 262
  altercation with Rodrigo del Pliego,
    161–62
  compromise with southerners, 209–10
  on convict soldiers, 252
  as customs inspector, 253

  on distribution of mission lands,
    216–17
  on expulsion of Father Durán, 202
  as governor, 204, 207–8, 213, 214,
    224–25
  on immigration, 243–44
  land grants made by, 226
  liberal education of, 153–56, 350n18
  Manuel Jimeno as secretary to, 224–25
  on Manuel Victoria, 171
  obligations to José de la Guerra, 228
  order to arrest illegal immigrants,
    245–46
  ousting of Nicolás Gutiérrez, 204, 214
  political rivalries of, 210–11, 244
  prohibition of foreign vessels, 227
  resignation, 250
  as secretary for *disputación*, 194
  support for secularization, 208, 214,
    355n90
  surrender to Commodore Jones, 248
  testimonio, 366n29
  on threat from United States, 250
  warned of American uprising, 245
Alvarado, Juana, 67
Alvarez, Bernardina, 91–92, 176
Alvarez, José Genaro, 278
Alvarez, Pedro Miguel, 62
Alvitre, Sebastián, 98
Amador, José María, 56, 178
America. *See* United States
Anderson, Stephen, 138
Andrade, José, 226
anti-American sentiment, 249–50, 257,
  260
anti-immigrant sentiment, 243, 245
anti-Mexican sentiment, 159–60, 162, 201,
  252

on intermarriage, 266
interviewed by Thomas Savage, 9,
    263–65
on José María Padrés, 156, 349n16
journal of U.S.-Mexico War, 9, 263,
    265–69, 271
land owned by, 218–19, 230–31, 292–93
life in Monterey, 141–42, 195, 200, 225,
    228–29
on Manuel Victoria, 125–26, 163, 171
marriage to James L. Ord, 263, 292–93
marriage to Manuel Jimeno, 96–97,
    123, 126, 142, 147
memoir, 9, 263, 265, 269
and Monterey politics, 230–31, 235
on mother's response to political
    rivalry, 211
on paternal authority, 177
on political graft, 254
portrait, 148
prank pulled on Richard Barnes
    Mason, 268–69, 274
reception of Americans by, 263–64
on resignation of Governor Alvarado,
    250
on response to U.S. occupation, 257,
    265, 271
on Rodrigo del Pliego, 162
separation from Manuel Jimeno, 292
on sexual behavior of gentiles, 74
on smuggling, 228–30, 239, 264
and sons' educations, 287
on support for U.S. takeover, 271
on surrender to Commodore Jones,
    248
on threat posed by change, 266
visits to sister María Antonia, 237
warned of American uprising, 245
on wedding celebrations, 87, 91, 93
as wife of political insider, 264, 285
willfulness, 228–29, 264
on Ysidro Molina, 71
Guerra y Carrillo, Anita de la, 119, 144,
    194, 198, 301
acquaintance with Francis Lippitt,
    270–72
birth, 30
death, 293
education in New England, 234–35,
    237, 238, 263, 269
family tree, 302
as godparent, 146

marriage to Alfred Robinson, 105–7,
    123, 146–47, 233–34
portrait, 104
Guerra y Carrillo, Antonio María de la,
    235, 238, 261, 283
on challenging of father's will, 292–93
death, 293
as elected official, 291
family tree, 302
Guerra y Carrillo, Francisco de la, 30, 133,
    219, 256, 258
accused of conspiracy, 277
affair with María del Rosario
    Lorenzana, 236, 378n174
anti-American sentiment, 260
arrest of Americans, 261
on challenging of father's will, 292–93
death, 293
education, 91, 176–77
family tree, 301
given Rancho San Julián, 236
as godparent, 85, 339n45
letter from Andrés Pico, 281
and Lost Cannon Affair, 278–79
marriage to Ascención Sepúlveda, 236
as miner, 287
political career, 251, 255, 259, 285, 291
purchase of horse from ex-neophyte,
    193
as ranch manager for father, 236
as resistance organizer, 257, 262, 267,
    276–77
as town father, 280, 288
as witness, 283
Guerra y Carrillo, Joaquín de la, 30, 141,
    147, 200, 253
on challenging of father's will, 292–93
death, 293
family tree, 302
Guerra y Carrillo, José Antonio de la, 39,
    119, 138, 224
as *alcalde*, 180–82
attempts to own land, 188, 218
birth, 30
as cadet in Santa Bárbara Company,
    106–7, 120, 158, 176
death, 293
defiance, 156, 158–59, 175, 179
education, 176, 179, 182
as elected official, 179, 291
as godparent, 85–86, 179, 331n122
on land ownership dispute, 180–82